Iran, Iraq, and the Arab Gulf States

# Iran, Iraq, and the Arab Gulf States

Edited by Joseph A. Kechichian

palgrave

IRAN, IRAQ, AND THE ARAB GULF STATES
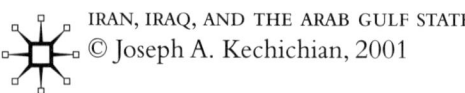
© Joseph A. Kechichian, 2001

All rights reserved. No part of this book may be used or reproduced in any manner whatsoever without written permission except in the case of brief quotations embodied in critical articles or reviews.

First published 2001 by PALGRAVE™, 175 Fifth Avenue, New York, N.Y. 10010 and Houndmills, Basingstoke, Hampshire RG21 6XS. Companies and representatives throughout the world.

PALGRAVE is the new global publishing imprint of St. Martin's Press LLC Scholarly and Reference Division and Palgrave Publishers Ltd (formerly Macmillan Press Ltd).

ISBN 0-312-29388-7 hardback

Library of Congress Cataloging-in-Publication Data

   Iran, Iraq, and the Arab Gulf States / edited by Joseph A. Kechichian.
      p. cm.
     Papers presented at an international conference coordinated and hosted by
       Gustave E. von Grunebaum Center for Near Eastern Studies, University
       of California, Los Angeles, 3-4 May, 2000.
     Includes bibliographical references and index.
     ISBN 0-312-29388-7
      1. Persian Gulf Region—Politics and government—Congresses. 2. Persian Gulf Region—Foreign relations—Congresses. I. Kechichian, Joseph A. II. Gustave E. von Grunebaum Center for Near Eastern Studies.

   DS326 .I68 2001
   953.05'3—dc21                                                       2001032756

A catalogue record for this book is available from the British Library.

Design by Westchester Book Composition.

First edition: December 2001
10 9 8 7 6 5 4 3 2 1

Printed in the United States of America

# CONTENTS

*Acknowledgments* vii
*A Note on Transliteration* ix
*List of Tables, Figures and Maps* x
*Contributors* xii
*Preface* xxi
*List of Abbreviations* xxiii

## PART I—INTERNAL CONCERNS

### THE ISLAMIC REPUBLIC OF IRAN

1. Tensions and Options among the Iranian Clerical Establishment, *Olivier Roy* — 3
2. Reformists, Conservatives and Iran's Parliamentary Elections, *Shaul Bakhash* — 13
3. Civil-Military Relations in the Islamic Republic of Iran, *Ahmed S. Hashim* — 31

### THE REPUBLIC OF IRAQ

4. The Position of the Iraqi Clergy, *Joyce N. Wiley* — 55
5. Domestic Politics in A Post-Saddam Iraq, *Laith Kubba* — 65
6. The Military in Iraqi Politics, *Andrew Parasiliti* — 83

### THE KINGDOM OF SAUDI ARABIA

7. Assessing Saudi Susceptibility to Revolution, *Mark N. Katz* — 95
8. Image, Imagination And Place: The Political Economy Of Tourism In Saudi Arabia, *Gwenn Okruhlik* — 111
9. Saudi Arabia: Measures Of Transition From A Rentier State, *Robert E. Looney* — 131

### THE ARAB GULF STATES

10. Domestic Politics in the United Arab Emirates: Social and Economic Policies, 1990-2000, *Fatma Al-Sayegh* — 161
11. Kuwait and Bahrain: The Appeal of Globalization and Internal Constraints, *May Seikaly* — 177
12. Kings And People: Information and Authority in Oman, Qatar, and the Persian Gulf, *Dale F. Eickelman* — 193

## PART II—REGIONAL CONCERNS

### BORDER DISPUTES

13. Down to the Usual Suspects: Border and Territorial Disputes in the Arabian Peninsula and Persian Gulf at the Millennium, *Richard Schofield* — 213
14. The Kuwait-Iraq Border Problem, *Hussein Hassouna* — 237
15. Yemeni-Saudi Relations Gone Awry, *Mohammed A. Zabarah* — 263

### RELATIONS BETWEEN GCC STATES

16. Unity on the Arabian Peninsula, *Joseph A. Kechichian* — 281
17. Forging Institutions in the Gulf Arab States, *R. Hrair Dekmejian* — 303
18. The GCC States: Internal Dynamics and Foreign Policies, *Muhammed Saleh Al-Musfir* — 313

### THE GULF STATES AND WESTERN POWERS

19. Constants and Variations in Gulf-British Relations, *Gerd Nonneman* — 325
20. The Impact of U.S. Policy on the Stability of the Gulf States: A Historian's View, *Rosemarie Said Zahlan* — 351
21. Gulf States' Links with Their Post-Soviet Northern Neighbors, *Theodore Karasik* — 367

## PART III—TRENDS FOR THE FUTURE

22. The UAE Vision for Gulf Security, *Sultan bin Zayed bin Sultan Al Nahyan* — 383
23. The Gulf Cooperation Council: Future Trends, *Saif bin Hashil Al-Maskery* — 393
24. The Arabian Gulf At The New Millennium: Security Challenges, *Hassan Hamdan Al-Alkim* — 407
25. Outlook for Iranian-Gulf Relations: Greater Cooperation or Renewed Risk of Conflict?, *Shireen T. Hunter* — 427
26. What Makes the Gulf States Endure?, *J.E. Peterson* — 451

*Bibliography* — 461

*Index* — 464

# ACKNOWLEDGMENTS

On 3–4 May 2000, the Gustav E. von Grunebaum Center for Near Eastern Studies at the University of California in Los Angeles hosted an international conference on "Iran, Iraq, and the Arab Gulf States," which formed the basis of this volume. The gathering assembled 25 Middle Eastern, European, and American analysts to provide appraisals of the situation in the Gulf region in early 2000 and identify trends for the next decade.

Both the conference and this book were made possible through the generous support of His Highness Shaykh Zayed bin Sultan Al Nahyan, the president of the United Arab Emirates. Much like his contribution on "Gulf Security: The View from Abu Dhabi," which was published in *A Century in Thirty Years: Shaykh Zayed and the United Arab Emirates,* (Washington, D.C.: Middle East Policy Council, 2000), that of his son, Shaykh Sultan bin Zayed Al Nahyan, the deputy prime minister of the UAE, adds value to it by contributing yet another comprehensive essay on the critical subject of Gulf security. To my knowledge, these two essays are the only ones written by high-ranking Gulf officials, to clarify evolving perspectives on regional security affairs. I thank His Highness for his sustained efforts and foresight.

His Excellency Shaykh Saif bin Hashil Al-Maskery, the former assistant secretary-general of the Gulf Cooperation Council, graciously agreed to travel from Muscat to Los Angeles to participate in the conference and write a paper that highlights the genuine search for peaceful resolution of conflicts within the region. By doing so, he joins several Gulf diplomats and scholars who seek to reverse the complacency trend by sharing their unique perspectives with a wider audience.

Several individuals at the Office of the Deputy Prime Minister in Abu Dhabi, including His Excellency Sultan bin Omeir Al Mashgouni and his assistant office director, Khalifah bin Sabha Al Qubaisi, were gracious with their time and hospitality. Mr. Muhammad Khalifah, the multitalented executive director of the Zayed Center for Coordination and Follow-Up, was equally cordial. To them, and many others, I owe a special debt of gratitude.

At UCLA, Professors Irene A. Bierman and Afaf Lutfi Al-Sayyid Marsot, respectively the director and the assistant director of the Center for Near Eastern Studies, welcomed and supported me at the university between the fall of 1998 and the spring of 2001. Both recognized the conference's value when I first discussed it with them in the fall of 1999. The Center team, including Jonathan Friedlander, Lisette Hurtado Mora, and Diane James, coordinated the conference and assisted in hosting 25 scholars from 14 countries. I thank all of them for their assistance in what was truly a gargantuan task.

To Angelica—my inspiration—I owe deep gratitude for accepting her father's many absences from home.

The Palgrave team performed in its usual professional practice. Editors Karen Wolny and Ella Pearce shepherded the manuscript through an excessively long "blind referee" process. Donna Cherry, Rick Delaney, Sabahat Chaudhary, Meredith Howard, Alan Bradshaw, and Sonia Wilson proved to be devoted to this project as they did their level best to make-up some of the lost time. Rodney Williams copy-edited our text—with its multi-cultural and multi-linguistic twists—with his usual skill. These are true professionals and it is a pleasure to work with such a team.

Last, but not least, I thank my colleagues who first accepted the invitation to participate in the conference, wrote superb original papers, answered my repeated queries, and considered many of my emendations. This collective book is testament that each and every one has added value.

# A NOTE ON TRANSLITERATION

A modified version of the Library of Congress transliteration system has been adopted throughout the book. In rendering Arabic words and names, however, and because several authors use various spellings, I relied on the style used by the International Journal of Middle East Studies. Thus a name that is commonly rendered in English, for example Mohammed, becomes Muhammad, and Mecca becomes Makkah. Whenever known, I used the common English spellings for proper names, as well as for names of countries. Thus Fahd rather than Fahad (although the latter is used if the individual writes his name with that spelling) and Oman rather than 'Uman. Although special care was devoted to standardize the spellings of as many transliterated words as possible, there are—inevitably—a few inconsistencies which, I trust, readers will understand. For practical purposes, all diacritical marks for long vowels and velarized consonants have been eliminated. Arabic and Persian speakers will know the correct reference for the transliterated words throughout the text.

# LIST OF TABLES, FIGURES AND MAPS

**TABLES**
- 9.1 Saudi Arabia: Rates of Growth, 1964–1998.
- 9.2 Saudi Arabia: Economic Structure, 1970–1998.
- 9.3 Saudi Arabia: Public Sector Budget, 1979–1998.
- 9.4 Saudi Arabia: Influence of Public Expenditure on the Private Sector Economy.
- 9.5 Saudi Arabia: Summary of Results.
- 19.1 UK Imports from the Gulf States, 1991–1999 (in £ Million).
- 19.2 UK Visible Non-Defense Exports to the Gulf States, 1991–1999, (in £ Million).
- 19.3 UK Visible Non-Arms Exports to the Gulf States, by Broad Commodity Group, 1998 (in £ Million).
- 19.4 Recent And Current Arms Contracts UK–GCC.
- 25.1 Persian Gulf: Size of Countries.
- 25.2 Persian Gulf: Population of Countries.
- 25.3 Persian Gulf: Ethnic Composition of Non-Nationals in Percentages.
- 25.4 Persian Gulf: Proven Oil Reserves.

**FIGURES**
- 9.1 Saudi Arabia: Evolution of the Non-Oil Economy, 1964–.
- 9.2 Development Model 1: Saudi Arabian Development during the Oil Boom Years.
- 9.3 Development during the Post–Oil Boom Years: Pessimistic Assessment.
- 9.4 Development during the Post–Oil Boom Years: Optimistic Assessment.
- 9.5 Saudi Arabia: Future Virtuous Cycle.
- 12.1 Faisal al-Kassim Broadcasting from Al-Jazeera.
- 12.2 Palestinian News Reporting.

## MAPS
13.1 Territorial and Maritime Boundaries in the Gulf Region.
13.2 Saudi-Yemeni Boundary.
13.3 Bahrain Boundary Issues.
14.1 Kuwait-Iraq Border.

# CONTRIBUTORS

**Dr. Hassan Hamdan AL-ALKIM** is professor of political science at the UAE University in Al-Ain, where he has taught since 1986. He spent 1991 as a visiting professor at the University of California at Los Angeles (on a Fulbright scholarship) and 1992–93 at the University of London. He earned his B.A. from Seattle University and an M.A. and Ph.D. in political science from the University of Exeter. Dr. Al-Alkim is a member of numerous editorial boards as well as academic associations such as the Royal Institute for International Affairs and the International Institute for Strategic Studies in London. His books in English include *The GCC States in an Unstable World: Foreign Policy Dilemmas of Small States,* (London: Saqi Books, 1994) and *The Foreign Policy of the United Arab Emirates* (London: Saqi Books, 1989).

**Dr. Shaul BAKHASH** is Clarence Robinson Professor of History at George Mason University, where he teaches Iranian and modern Middle Eastern history. Currently he is a Public Policy Scholar at the Woodrow Wilson Center in Washington D.C. He is the author of *Reign of the Ayatollahs: Iran and the Islamic Revolution, Iran: Monarchy, Bureaucracy and Reform under the Qajars, 1858–1896,* and other publications. He writes frequently for *The New York Review of Books* and has published numerous articles in scholarly books and journals, most recently in *Foreign Policy* and *The Journal of Democracy.* His op-ed pieces have appeared in *The New York Times, The Washington Post, The Los Angeles Times,* and other publications. Until 1979, he worked as a journalist in Iran writing for *Kayhan International* and reporting from Iran, at various times, for *The Economist, The Times,* and *The Financial Times.*

**Dr. R. Hrair DEKMEJIAN** teaches political science at the University of Southern California in Los Angeles. Earlier, he taught at the State University of New York at Binghamton; Columbia; and the University of Pennsylvania. He is the author of several books, most recently *Troubled Waters: Geopolitics of the Caspian Region* (co-authored with Hovann I. Simonian, I. B. Tauris, 2001), *Islam* in Revolution (Syracuse University Press, 1995), *Patterns of Political Leadership* (SUNY Press, 1975), and *Egypt Under Nasser: A Study in Political Dynamics* (SUNY Press, 1971).

**Dr. Dale F. EICKELMAN** is Ralph and Richard Lazarus Professor of Anthropology and Human Relations and chair of the Department of Anthropology at Dartmouth College. Since 1968 he has worked extensively in the Middle East, including long-term field research in Morocco and the Sultanate of Oman. His publications include *Moroccan Islam* (1976); *The Middle East and Central Asia: An Anthropological Approach* (1981; 3rd ed., 1998); *Knowledge and Power in Morocco* (1985); *Muslim Travellers: Pilgrimage, Migration and the Religious Imagination* (coedited with James Piscatori, 1990); *Russia's Muslim Frontiers: New Directions in Cross-Cultural Analysis* (edited, 1993); *Muslim Politics*, co-authored with James Piscatori (1996); *New Media in the Muslim World: The Emerging Public Sphere* (coedited with Jon Anderson, 1999); and numerous scholarly articles and contributions to edited books. He was a 1976–1977 member of the Institute for Advanced Study in Princeton, 1991 President of the Middle East Studies Association of North America, a 1992 Guggenheim Fellow, a 1996–1997 fellow at the Woodrow Wilson International Center for Scholars, and a 2000–2001 fellow at the Wissenschaftskolleg zu Berlin.

**Dr. Ahmed S. HASHIM** is a defense analyst at the Center for Naval Analyses in Washington, D.C. He earned a doctorate in political science from the Massachusetts Institute of Technology in 1991, and was a fellow at the Center for Strategic and International Studies, as well as a research analyst at the International Institute for Strategic Studies. In 1997, he co-authored (with Anthony Cordesman) *Iraq: Sanctions and Beyond,* and *Iran: Beyond Dual Containment,* both published by Westview Press. While at the IISS, he published, among others, *The Crisis of the Iranian State: Domestic, Foreign and Security Policies in Post-Khomeini Iran* (Adelphi Paper number 296, 1995).

**Ambassador Hussein HASSOUNA** is the permanent representative of the League of Arab States to the United Nations. Before assuming his current post in 1997, he was assistant minister of foreign affairs of Egypt for international legal affairs and treaties (1996–1997) and ambassador of Egypt to Morocco (1992–1996) and to Yugoslavia (1989–1992). Over the years, he filled a variety of diplomatic posts in Cairo, Paris, Washington, D.C., and New York. Ambassador Hassouna earned a doctorate in international law from Cambridge University in the United Kingdom, where he wrote a dissertation on the Iraq-Kuwait border dispute, and published, among others, *The League of Arab States and Regional Disputes: A Study of Middle East Conflicts* (Oceana, 1975).

**Dr. Shireen T. HUNTER** is the director of the Islamic Studies program at the Center for Strategic and International Studies (CSIS) in Washington, D.C. She previously served as director of the Mediterranean Studies program with the Centre for European Policy Studies in Brussels. Dr. Hunter is the author of several books, including *The Future of Islam and the West: Clash of Civilization or Peaceful Coexistence?* (CSIS/Praeger, 1998), *Central Asia Since Independence* (CSIS/Praeger, 1996), and *The Transcaucasus in Transition: Nation-Building and Conflict* (CSIS, 1994). Her articles have appeared in leading journals such as *Foreign Affairs, Foreign Policy, Current History,* the *Middle East Journal, Security Dialogue,* the *International Spectator, Relazioni Internazionali, Third World Quarterly,* and the *SAIS Review,* as well as prominent newspapers including the *Los Angeles Times* and the *Christian Science Monitor*. She holds a Ph.D. in political science from the Institut des Hautes Etudes Internationales in Geneva and an M.A. from the London School of Economics and Political Science.

**Dr. Mark N. KATZ** is professor of government and politics at George Mason University in Fairfax, Virginia. He received a Ph.D. in political science from the Massachusetts Institute of Technology in 1982. His books include *Russia and Arabia: Soviet Foreign Policy toward the Arabian Peninsula* (Johns Hopkins University Press, 1986), *Revolutions and Revolutionary Waves* (St. Martin's Press, 1997), and *Revolution: International Dimensions,* editor, (Palgrave, 2001). During 1999–2000, he was president of the National Capital Area Political Science Association.

**Dr. Theodore W. KARASIK** is a resident consultant at RAND in Santa Monica and is Editor, *Russia and Eurasia Armed Forces Review,* Gulf Breeze: Academic International Press. He received a doctorate in history from the University of California, Los Angeles. He is a frequent contributor to the *Central Asia-Caucasus Monitor,* Johns Hopkins University. Dr. Karasik has thirteen years work experience in Russian, Caucasian and Middle Eastern affairs for the RAND Corporation. His RAND publications include "Foreign and Security Policy Decision-making Under Yeltsin," RAND, MR-831-OSD, 1997 (co-authored with F. Stephen Larrabee). Dr. Karasik has also worked on Air Force and Army projects exploring air power and MOUT including "Organizing, Training and Equipping the Air Force for Crises and Lesser Conflicts," MR-626–AF, 1995 (co-authored with Carl H. Builder). Other publications include "Chechnya: A Glimpse of Future Conflict?," *Studies in Conflict & Terrorism,* with John Arquilla, "Putin and Shoigu: Reversing Russia's Decline, *Demokratizatsiia,* Summer 2000, and "The Crisis in Azerbaijan: How Clans Influence the Politics of an Emerging Republic," *Middle East Journal,* Summer 1995 (with Joseph Kechichian).

**Dr. Joseph A. KECHICHIAN** is a fellow at UCLA's Gustav E. von Grunebaum Center for Near Eastern Studies, and the CEO of Kechichian & Associates, LLC, a consulting partnership that provides analysis on the Arabian/Persian Gulf region, specializing in the domestic and regional concerns of Bahrain, Iran, Iraq, Kuwait, Oman, Qatar, Saudi Arabia, the United Arab Emirates, and Yemen. He received a doctorate in Foreign Affairs from the University of Virginia in 1985, where he also taught (1986–1988), and assumed the assistant deanship in international studies (1988–1989). In the summer of 1989, Dr. Kechichian was a Hoover Fellow at Stanford University (under the U.S. State Department Title VIII program). Between 1990 and 1996, he was an associate political scientist at the Santa Monica-based RAND Corporation and a lecturer at the University of California, Los Angeles. He published *Succession in Saudi Arabia* (New York: Palgrave, 2001) and *Oman and the World: The Emergence of an Independent Foreign Policy* (RAND, 1995), and edited *A Century in Thirty Years: Shaykh Zayed and the United Arab Emirates* (Middle East Policy Council, 2000). He is currently completing a study tentatively titled *The UAE and the World*. Dr. Kechichian received a RAND President's Award for Research Excellence in January 1995. A frequent traveler to the Gulf region, he is fluent in Arabic, Armenian, English, French, Italian, and Turkish, and is learning Persian.

**Dr. Laith KUBBA** was born and raised in Baghdad, Iraq. He had his bachelor's degree from the University of Baghdad (1976) and his Ph.D. from the University of Wales, in the United Kingdom (1982). Dr Kubba was an active participant in a number of Iraqi organizations. He served on the Iraqi Joint Action Committee, the first broad alliance of the Iraqi opposition. He coordinated the INC meeting in Vienna and was a spokesman for the organization in 1992. Following the Iraqi invasion of Kuwait, Dr. Kubba took a high public profile and participated in numerous debates and media shows on Iraq. Also, he was a columnist for two Arabic weekly magazines and served on the boards of regional institutions including the Iraq Foundation, the Arab Organization for Human Rights, and the International Forum for Islamic Dialogue. For the period 1993–1998, he worked for Al Khoei Foundation in London as their director of international relations. At present, he is the senior program officer for the Middle East at the National Endowment for Democracy, in Washington D.C.

**Dr. Robert E. LOONEY** is a professor of national security studies at the Naval Postgraduate School in Monterey, California. He is the author of several studies including, *The Economic Development of Iran: A Recent Survey With Predictions to 1981* (Praeger, 1973), *Iran at the End of the Century: An Hegelian Forecast* (Lexington Books, 1977), *A Development Strategy for Iran* (Praeger, 1977), *Saudi Arabia's Growth Potential* (Lexington Books, 1981), *Economic Origins of the Iranian Revolution* (Pergamon, 1982), *Third World Military Expenditures and Arms Production* (Macmillan, 1988), *Economic Development in Saudi Arabia: Consequences of the Oil Price Decline* (JAI Press, 1990), *The Economic Causes and Consequences of Defense Expenditures in the Middle East and South Asia* (with David Winterford, Westview Press, 1994), *Manpower Policies and Development in the Arab Gulf Region* (Praeger, 1994), *Industrialization in the Arabian Gulf* (JAI Press, 1994), *The Economics of Third World Defense Expenditures* (JAI Press, 1995), and *The Pakistani Economy: Economic Growth and Structural Reform* (Praeger, 1997).

**His Excellency Saif bin Hashil AL-MASKERY** is the head of the Oman Consultancy Group in Muscat, Sultanate of Oman. From 1987 to 1993, he was assistant secretary-general for political affairs of the Riyadh-based Gulf Cooperation Council (GCC), when the Persian Gulf region was mired in two major wars. Earlier, he served as ambassador and permanent representative of the Sultanate of Oman to the United Nations in Geneva, Switzerland.

**Dr. Muhammed Saleh AL-MUSFIR** is a senior associate at the ministry of foreign affairs in the State of Qatar. He started his diplomatic career as acting council general in Pakistan (1975–1976), and acting cultural attaché in London (1976–1978), before becoming chancellor (1978–1983) and deputy to the permanent representative (1984–1986), of the United Arab Emirates delegation at the United Nations in New York. Between 1999 and 2001, he was a visiting professor at Yarmouk University in Jordan and, from 1986 to 1999, professor of political science at the University of Qatar in Doha. In 1995, he assumed the editorship of the Doha daily *Al-Rayah*, for a period of two years. A frequent participant on television programs throughout the Arab world, Dr. Al-Musfir writes a regular political column in various Gulf and Arab newspapers, and has published *Regional Organizations: Backgrounds of origins and principles* (National Press, 1987), *United Nations Organization: origins and principles* (Ali Bin Ali Press, 1996), *The Arabs, the West and Globalization* (Ali Bin Ali Press, 1999 [all in Arabic]). He earned his doctorate in political science from the State University of New York at Binghamton in 1984.

**His Highness Shaykh Sultan Bin Zayed AL NAHYAN** is the deputy prime minister of the United Arab Emirates, a position he has held since November 1990. His primary responsibilities include the day-to-day operations of the federal government. In addition, as the third-highest-ranking member of the ruling family, His Highness conducts special assignments on behalf of the state—he represented the UAE at the fiftieth anniversary of the United Nations in New York in 1995. Shaykh Sultan graduated from Sandhurst Academy in the United Kingdom in 1972 and served in both the Abu Dhabi (1973–78) and UAE armed forces. After a distinguished career that spanned a decade, His Highness was appointed general commander of the armed forces (1978–82). In addition to his federal position, Shaykh Sultan is the chairman of the Abu Dhabi Public Works Department, responsible for the Emirate's infrastructure, as well as the vice-chairman of the Abu Dhabi Executive Council, the highest governing body in the Emirate. His Highness also serves on the Supreme Petroleum Council and is the chairman of the Executive Committee of the Abu Dhabi Fund for Arab Economic Development, of the Zayed Center for Coordination and Follow-Up, and of the UAE National Heritage Council. A frequent participant in various cultural festivities in the UAE, Shaykh Sultan is interested in world history and Arab civilization.

**Dr. Gerd NONNEMAN** is Reader in International Relations and Middle East Politics at Lancaster University. He is also the Executive Director of the British Society for Middle Eastern Studies (BRISMES). Born in Flanders and educated at Ghent University, Belgium, in oriental philology (Arabic) as well as development studies, he worked in Iraq for a number of years during the 1980s, before returning to academia teaching Middle East politics and political economy at Manchester and Exeter universities. After a spell as visiting professor at the International University of Japan, he joined the faculty at Lancaster in 1993. His publications include: *Political and Economic Liberalisation: Dynamics and Linkages in Comparative Perspective* (editor, Lynne Rienner, 1996), *Muslim Communities in the New Europe* (editor, Ithaca Press, 1997), *Development, Administration and Aid in the Middle East* (Routledge, 1988), *War and Peace in the Gulf: Domestic Politics and Regional Relations into the 1990s* (with A. Ehteshami, Ithaca Press, 1986), *Yemen: The Search for development, Stability and Unity, 1960s-1990s* (Hurst Publishers, 2000), and *The Political Economy of Iraqi-Kuwaiti Relations* (forthcoming).

**Dr. Gwenn OKRUHLIK** is an Assistant Professor of political science at the University of Arkansas. She earned a doctorate in government from the University of Texas at Austin in 1992 and was the first female political scientist to do fieldwork in the Kingdom of Saudi Arabia in 1989–1990 on a Fulbright doctoral grant. Her publications include "Rentier Wealth, Unruly Law and the Rise of Opposition: The Political Economy of Oil States" (*Comparative Politics*); "Excluded Essentials: Ethnicity, Oil and Citizenship in Saudi Arabia" (in *The Global Color Line: Racial and Ethnic Inequality and Struggle From a Global Perspective*), "The Politics of Border Disputes in the Arabian Peninsula" (*International Journal*), "National Autonomy, Labor Migration and Political Crisis: Yemen and Saudi Arabia (*Middle East Journal*) and "From Imagined Scholarship to Gendered Discourse: Bringing the Peninsula in from the Periphery" (*Middle East Report*). Her current research projects focus on gender and civic mythology; Islamist social movements; meanings of citizenship in Saudi Arabia, alternative historic narratives, and migrant labor in the Peninsula.

**Dr. Andrew PARASILITI** is director of the Middle East Initiative at the John F. Kennedy School of Government, Harvard University, and a specialist on Iraq and Gulf security issues. From 1996–1999, he was director of programs at the Middle East Institute in Washington, D.C., where he directed the institute's programs and research projects dealing with Gulf energy security, Iraq, and Iran. Dr. Parasiliti has conducted field research and interviews in Iraq, Iran, Syria, and Jordan, as well as other countries throughout the Middle East. He is a regular contributor to scholarly publications and the popular press about developments in Iraq. Recent publications include "US Policy on Iraq: A Dangerous Drift?" (with Jon B. Alterman), in *Middle East Economic Survey* (18 October 1999); and "Political Risk in Iraq," in *Middle East Economic Survey* (24 May 1999). He received a Ph.D. from the Paul H. Nitze School of Advanced International Studies, Johns Hopkins University.

**Dr. John E. PETERSON** is a historian and author based in Tucson, Arizona. After receiving his doctorate from Johns Hopkins SAIS, he was a research analyst at the Library of Congress and then taught at Bowdoin, William and Mary, the University of Pennsylvania, and Portland State before joining the Office of the Deputy Prime Minister for Security and Defense of the Sultanate of Oman. His principal publications include *Oman in the Twentieth Century,* 1978; *Yemen: The*

*Search for a Modern State*, 1982; *Defending Arabia*, 1986; *The Arab Gulf States: Steps Toward Political Participation*, 1988; *Historical Dictionary of Saudi Arabia*, 1993, and *Defending Oman: A History of the Sultan's Armed Forces* (forthcoming).

**Dr. Olivier ROY** studied philosophy and oriental languages (Persian), obtained an agrégation de philosophie as well as a Ph.D. in political science. He is presently a senior researcher at CNRS (French National Center for Scientific Research) and a consultant for the French Ministry of Foreign Affairs. Olivier Roy was also a consultant for UNOCA (United Nations Office of the Coordinator for Afghanistan) in 1988, and special envoy for the OSCE in Tajikistan (August-December 1993), then head of OSCE's Mission for Tajikistan (February-November 1994). He completed fieldwork throughout the Middle East and Central Asia. His main publications are *Islam and Resistance in Afghanistan* (Cambridge University Press, second ed., 1990 [translated from the French]), *The Failure of Political Islam* (Harvard University Press, 1994, [translation of *L'Echec de l'Islam politique*, Le Seuil, 1992]), *Généalogie de l'islamisme* (Hachette, 1995), *Iran: comment sortir d'une révolution religieuse* (with Farhad Khosrokhavar, Le Seuil, 1999), *Vers un islam européen* (Editions Esprit, 1999), and *The New Central Asia: The Fabrication of Nations* (I. B. Tauris, 2000).

**Dr. Fatma AL-SAYEGH** is an associate professor in the Department of History at the UAE University at Al-Ain, where she joined the faculty as an assistant professor in 1990. Her areas of specialization are the history of the UAE, the societies of the Gulf countries, and women's studies. She earned her bachelor's degree in modern history from Kuwait University, her M.A. from the University of Wisconsin at Milwaukee, and her Ph.D. from Essex University (1989). She was the recipient of a Fulbright research grant for the 1993–94 academic year. Dr. Al-Sayegh received the Shaykh Rashid bin Said Award for Educational and Scientific Achievement in 1991 and the al-Owais Award for the best book about the UAE in 1996: *The United Arab Emirates and the British Air Route to the East* [in Arabic]. She is also the author of *The United Arab Emirates from Tribalism to Statehood* (1997) [in Arabic].

**Dr. Richard SCHOFIELD** is convenor of the MA in International Boundary Studies and deputy director of the Geopolitics and International Boundaries Research Centre at the School of Oriental and African Studies (SOAS), University of London. He is also a senior officer of the British Society of Middle Eastern Studies and a founding editor of *Geopolitics* (formerly *Geopolitics and International Boundaries*), the triannual journal published by Frank Cass. He is the author of several publications, including *Evolution of the Shatt al-Arab Boundary Dispute*, 1986; *Kuwait and Iraq: Historical Claims and Territorial Disputes*, 1991 [2nd ed., 1993]; and *Unfinished Business: Abu Musa, the Tunbs, Iran and the UAE* (forthcoming). He was editor of *Territorial Foundations of the Gulf States*, 1994, as well as of numerous documentary collections on Arabian/Persian Gulf boundaries and associated territorial questions. In addition, he has penned numerous articles on these subjects in academic journals and edited collections. He is currently working on three major research projects: writing a commissioned work on the political economy of territory and resources in the Middle East, compiling an atlas of Arabian boundary disputes, and constructing a bibliographical database on Iran's northern borderlands with the Caucasus and Central Asia.

**Dr. May SEIKALY** is associate professor of history at Wayne State University in Detroit, Michigan. She earned a doctorate in modern Middle East socioeconomic history from Oxford University in 1983. Her publications include: *HAIFA: Transformation of an Arab Society: 1918–1939* (I. B. Tauris, 1995, 2000, [with an Arabic translation in 1997]), "Women and Socio-Political Change in Bahrain," *International Journal of Middle East Studies* (1994), "Women and Religion in Bahrain: An Emerging Identity," in John Esposito and Yvonne Haddad (eds.), *Islam, Gender and Social Change* (Oxford University Press, 1997), "Bahraini Women in Formal and Informal Groups: The Politics of Identification," in Dawn Chatty and Annika Rabo (eds.), *Organizing Women: Formal and Informal Women's Groups in the Middle East* (Berg, 1997), "Living with the Memory: Legitimacy, Justice and Nationhood," in Naim Ateek and Michael Prior (eds.), *Holy Land-Hallow Jubilee* (Fox Publishers, 1999), "Attachment and Identity: The Palestinian Community of Detroit," in Michael Suleiman (ed.), *Arabs in America: Building a New Future,* (Temple University Press, 1999), and "Haifa at the Crossroads: An outpost of the new World Order," in Leila Fawaz (ed.), *European Modernity and Cultural Difference From the Mediterranean Sea to the Indian Ocean 1890–1920* (Columbia University Press, 2001).

**Dr. Joyce N. WILEY** is an associate professor of government and international studies at the University of South Carolina, Spartanburg. She earned a doctorate in international studies from the University of South Carolina at Columbia in 1988. She has taught in Iraq and Saudi Arabia and traveled extensively throughout the Middle East. Her research interests are Islamic political movements and Iraqi politics. In 1992, she published *The Islamic Movement of Iraqi Shi'as* (Lynne Rienner Publishers) and contributed, among others, various essays to the *Oxford Encyclopedia of the Modern Islamic World* (on Ayatollah Hakim and Ayatollah Khoi in particular). Her chapter on the *'alima* Bint al-Huda was published in *The Most Learned of the Shi'a* (2001).

**Dr. Mohammed A. ZABARAH** is a professor of political science at the University of Yemen in Sanaa. He was the Dean of the Faculty of Commerce and Economics (1991–1993), and chairman of the political science department on two occasions. Before going to Sanaa University, he taught at King Abdul Aziz University in Jeddah, Saudi Arabia. He is the author of *Yemen: Traditionalism vs. Modernity* (Praeger, 1992).

**Dr. Rosemarie Said ZAHLAN** is a historian, author, and consultant. Her first publication on the Gulf was in 1970, examining the 1938 Reform Movement in Dubai. Her books include *The Origins of the United Arab Emirates: A Political and Social History of the Trucial States* (Macmillan and St. Martin's Press,

1978), *The Creation of Qatar* (Croom Helm and Barnes and Noble, 1979), and *The Making of the Modern Gulf States: Kuwait, Bahrain, Qatar, the United Arab Emirates and Oman* (Unwin Hyman, 1989, 1998). As an academic and consultant, she has also contributed to the *Financial Times,* the *Wall Street Journal, Oxford Analytica, Middle East Economic Digest, Middle East Review, South Magazine,* the BBC World Service, and others.

PREFACE

Two decades after the epoch-making 1979 Islamic Revolution in Iran and an eight-year-long (1980–1988) protracted war between Iran and Iraq, and a decade after the historic War for Kuwait (1991), the Persian Gulf region remains mired in conflict and uncertainty. Few doubt the importance of the area to its inhabitants as well as to the economic welfare of industrialized societies. Yet, despite momentous—even cataclysmic—events and unabated concerns, few can forecast that the area will be free of additional convulsions.

For decades, the entire region was pigeonholed in terms of how "vital" it was and, within the East-West contest for world hegemony, how critical to the survival of a certain "way of life." In the event, and despite the Christmas Eve 1979 invasion—and decade-long occupation—of Afghanistan, the Soviet Union failed to gain a foothold in the area. Moscow's lukewarm relations with Iraq and the People's Democratic Republic of Yemen (PDRY) did not get the Soviets what earlier tsarist intentions had long craved. Both Iraq and the PDRY fared poorly too. Western powers, led first by the United Kingdom and later by the United States, emerged as the dominant outside forces that shaped the course of events. Washington weathered the repercussions of the Iranian Revolution—especially the humiliating 444-day-long hostage crisis—strengthened its presence on the Arabian Peninsula, and fought a regional hegemon under a United Nations–sanctioned intervention. It deployed more than half a million troops and a unique armada to ensure, inter alia, the territorial integrity of Kuwait and the sovereignty of the conservative Arab Gulf monarchies. Although the United States neutralized putative Iranian and Iraqi capabilities, it failed to accelerate political changes—especially of the regime variety—in both countries and, in early 2001, was still confronted by political forces deemed too hostile for comfort.

To be sure, Iran and Iraq opposed the perceived American hegemony throughout the Persian Gulf region, even if Teheran longed for improved relations and Baghdad yearned for a speedy departure. Many Iranians remained apprehensive of American intentions notwithstanding limited but positive contacts. Many Arabs, including in the Gulf Cooperation Council states, harbored uneasiness as well. A majority rejected the strangulation of the Iraqi population but failed to persuade their Western allies to lift UN-imposed economic sanctions on Baghdad. Most aimed to find a balance among internal, regional, and international commitments, to ensure their survival. Both Iranians and Arabs aimed to regain the upper hand in determining their respective destinies even if more powerful forces shaped them. In the end, all feared the spillover effects of regional instability, a burgeoning arms race, and dramatic economic and social changes. Indeed, they were all confronted by new paradigms that challenged traditional interpretations and threatened to alter the body politic of each regime.

Against this background, what are the political, military, religious, and socioeconomic trends for Bahrain, Iran, Iraq, Kuwait, Oman, Qatar, Saudi Arabia, the United Arab Emirates, and Yemen? Will internal, regional, and international tensions threaten existing regimes, or will the latter survive growing pressure points? Will Gulf states' incredible endurance capabilities be altered? Will the next decade witness fundamental changes that could destabilize the Persian Gulf, or will new institutions equip each state with the wherewithal to function and grow more effectively?

These are the fundamental questions and issues that the following 26 contributions attempt to answer and analyze. They articulate American, European, and Middle Eastern perspectives to widen the ongoing debate among scholars and decision makers. Indeed, by discussing issues from several perspectives, these essays aim to elucidate rather than sermonize.

The integrated papers that follow are divided into three parts. Part One provides an overview of Gulf states' internal concerns—focusing on political, military, economic, religious, and social matters. While the focus of the first papers are on Iran, Iraq, Saudi Arabia, and the smaller Gulf states, these are not intended as country profiles. Rather, they purport to analyze currents and trends, to alert the reader to fundamental changes. Part Two offers detailed examinations of three of the most significant issues that presently affect the area. Despite recent progress on several fronts, including a significant accord between Bahrain and Qatar as well as intense negotiations between Saudi Arabia and Yemen, thorny border disputes are analyzed to identify significant trends for future political behavior. Regional issues, including institution-building measures, are also analyzed to identify groundbreaking sociopolitical changes throughout the region. Finally, key relations with Britain, the United States, and Russia are assessed, to weigh their repercussions both for indigenous leaders as well as for their Western counterparts. Part Three consists of overview essays of the Gulf region in terms of the changing foreign policy environment. They provide fresh appraisals of Gulf security and conflict resolution.

As the bulk of these essays were written almost a year before the book appeared in print, what follows may well have been overtaken by time. Nevertheless, it is fully expected that the underlying analyses and interpretations will continue to serve useful purposes, to encourage debate among scholars, and to provide policymakers with concrete reference points.

# LIST OF ABBREVIATIONS

| | |
|---|---|
| ACC | Arab Cooperation Council |
| ADIA | Abu Dhabi Investment Authority |
| AIPAC | American Israel Public Affairs Committee |
| AMU | Arab Maghreb Union |
| APC | Armored Personnel Carrier |
| APOC | Anglo-Persian Oil Company |
| ASEAN | Association of South East Asian Nations |
| BPD | Barrels Per Day |
| CDLR | Committee for the Defense of Legitimate Rights |
| DRY | Democratic Republic of Yemen |
| ECO | Economic Cooperation Organization |
| ESDI | European Security and Defense Identity |
| EU | European Union |
| FLOSY | Front for the Liberation of South Yemen |
| FNC | Federal National Council [UAE] |
| GCC | Gulf Cooperation Council |
| GDP | Gross Domestic Product |
| GNP | Gross National Product |
| GPC | General People's Congress [Yemen] |
| IAEA | International Atomic Energy Agency |
| ICJ | International Court of Justice |
| ICP | Iraqi Communist Party |
| ILSA | Iran-Libya Sanctions Act |
| IMF | International Monetary Fund |
| INC | Iraqi National Congress |
| IRGC | Islamic Revolutionary Guards Corps [Pasdaran-e Engelabe-e Islami] |
| IRNA | Islamic Republic News Agency [Iran] |
| ISA | Internal Security Agreement [of GCC] |
| LAS | League of Arab States |

| | |
|---|---|
| LNG | Liquefied Natural Gas |
| LSY | League of the Sons of Yemen |
| MBPD | Million Barrels Per Day |
| MBT | Main Battle Tanks |
| NATO | North Atlantic Treaty Organization |
| NDF | National Democratic Front [Yemen] |
| NIS | New Independent States [former Soviet Union] |
| NLF | National Liberation Front [Yemen] |
| NPT | Nuclear Non-Proliferation Treaty |
| OIC | Organization of Islamic Conference |
| OPEC | Organization of Petroleum Exporting Countries |
| PDRY | People's Democratic Republic of Yemen |
| PLO | Palestine Liberation Organization |
| RCC | Revolutionary Command Council [Iraq] |
| RUSI | Royal United Services Institute |
| SAVAK | National Organization of Information and Security [Sazeman-e Amniyat-e va Ettela`at Keshvar] |
| SCC | State Consultative Council [Oman] |
| SCIRI | Supreme Council of the Islamic Resistance in Iran |
| UAE | United Arab Emirates |
| UNDP | United Nations Development Program |
| UNIKBDC | United Nations Iraq-Kuwait Boundary Demarcation Commission |
| UNMOVIC | United Nations Monitoring, Verification and Inspection Commission |
| UNSCOM | United Nations Special Commission [for Iraq] |
| USSR | Union of Soviet Socialist Republics |
| WEU | Western European Union |
| WMD | Weapons of Mass Destruction |
| WTO | World Trade Organization |
| YAR | Yemen Arab Republic |
| YSP | Yemen Socialist Party |

# PART I

*Internal Concerns*

# THE ISLAMIC REPUBLIC OF IRAN

## CHAPTER 1

### Tensions and Options Among the Iranian Clerical Establishment

#### Olivier Roy

It may be argued that the Iranian revolution is the only "religious revolution" in the modern world. Whether a religious revolution is even possible, however, is an entirely different question. Still, it is clear that any transition in post-revolutionary Iran, as embodied by the spring 2000 elections, will have to deal with the religious legacy and legitimacy of the regime.[1] What to do with the clergy and how to interpret Islam in Iran are two of the most critical questions facing any analysis of the Islamic republic.

Given the country's recent history, it is clear that the two issues are intermingled, as any form of secularization has to find some support among clerical circles. And the clerics, whatever their political positions, have to express these positions in terms of Islam. Inasmuch as these questions are critical, it is equally important to ask why the debate among clerics is vital for the future of the Iranian Islamic republic. Without a doubt, it is not so much because the clergy rules. In fact, the Iranian revolution has been far less clerical than many assume. Rather, the real stake is the role played by the Guide, Ayatollah Ali Khamenei, based on the concept of *Velayat-e Faqih* (or "rule of the jurisconsult").[2] To be sure, this is not an abstract theological debate, but a key issue for the future of democracy in Iran. Any political evolution depends on the Guide, which in large part explains why the debaters are divided between those who would limit the principle of Velayat-e Faqih (liberals as well as some traditionalists) and those conservatives who see in the Velayat-e Faqih the last vestige of the Islamic regime.

### Defining the Issues

Instead of empowering the clergy, the Islamic Revolution has in fact limited the traditional autonomy of the high clergy, in favor of the state. During his tenure, Ayatollah Khomeini bypassed the traditional clerical institutions and eliminated or sidelined all of the Great Ayatollahs of his generation, including Ayatollahs Mohammed Qazem Shariat-Madari, Mohammed Reza Golpaygani, Mohammed Qomi, and Abol-Qazem Khoi, among others. Khomeini established his rule through a body of lay intellectuals, figures like Ali Akbar Velayati and Mir Hossein Musavi, and mid-level clerics like Hojjat-ol Islam Ali Akbar Hashemi Rafsanjani and Ali Hossein Khamenei. The real hierarchy was political, even for the clerics, which meant that religion was subordinated to politics. In fact, the clergy lost its financial autonomy, as religious taxes were collected through the state. Ayatollah Khomeini also balanced the clergy's academic freedom, as censorship on religious seminaries became common, while clerical courts were established to control dissident clerics.

Ironically, traditional rules of succession and the devolution of authority among Great Ayatollahs were ignored by the state when appointing the new Guide. Moreover, the "clericalization" of the state apparatus promoted middle-level clerics (Hojjat-ol Islam), to the detriment of the Great Ayatollahs. Today, the Guide holds a political and ideological position, more than a religious one, as it is explicitly stated in the constitution amended in 1989. Thus, the Guide is not necessarily the highest religious authority, although he should be "politically conscious" and "aware of his time" (*agah be zaman*). It must be noticed that this contradiction has been unraveling after the death of Ayatollah Khomeini, and particularly since the election of President Mohammed Khatami.[3] These emendations indicated that ideological considerations, and sheer political debate, were more relevant than the strict theological debate. Consequently, the crisis of religious legitimacy in the Islamic Republic led to a growing discrepancy between "religion" and "religious ideology." In turn, the crisis meant a reshuffling of political alignments, in which clerics were found on all sides.

## The Role of the Clergy

In the years since, it has become amply clear that the clergy does not control the state apparatus. To be sure, they dominate the Council of Guardians and the judiciary (whose current head, Mahmud Hashemi-Shahrudi is appointed by the Guide), and control family courts. Still, their position within the state apparatus is defined by the state itself. The Guide appoints clerics, who are not necessarily entrusted to their influential posts by their peers. Simply stated, there is no autonomy for the clergy in the political field, as most institutions that are strongholds of conservative elements are not headed by clerics, including the Guardians of the Revolution, the various foundations, and the political Motalefe coalition that supports conservative candidates. Interestingly, the number of clerics elected as members of parliament has regularly decreased since the first elections in the mid-1980s. Of course, state mollahs, who occupy key positions in the judiciary and the Council of Guardians, and who sit in parliament, or who are appointed by the state—as are most of the Friday preachers (*Imam-e Jome*)—are members of conservative factions. Yet, even if they defend the ideological nature of the regime, they act more as members of an interest group rather than as a clerical faction.

In addition to state mollahs, two other categories of clerics fall outside the state apparatus: first, the bulk of the clergy—many of whom are apolitical—and, second, all of the remaining Great Ayatollahs, who keep aloof of daily politics but are preoccupied with their religious duties. Usually very traditionalist on social issues, they are increasingly in favor of a full rehabilitation of the clergy's autonomy, some voicing their criticism of Ayatollah Khamenei's position as Guide. Many do not have a political movement of their own, and the more vocal among them are now under pressure from the state.

If senior clerics are mildly engaged, a new school of thought has emerged among younger clergymen, including Mohsen Kadivar, Hassan Yusuf Eshkevari, and Mohsen Said Zadeh, who advocate a rethinking of Islamic law and a revival of Islamic philosophy. Several younger clerics have publicly discussed secularism (Kadivar), but they do not hold institutional positions within the clerical hierarchy—by having a specific affiliation with a specific mosque, for example. Most are preoccupied with their writings and are closer to secular/liberal intellectuals than to the traditional clergy.

Under these circumstances, if the clergy is no longer as important as a corporate institution in Iranian politics, to what extent is the internal debate relevant? For some time now, any reform in Iran has necessitated a formulation in terms of fidelity to the legacy of Imam Khomeini. A reformist leader needs to find vocal support among clerical circles and cannot risk a confrontation with the clerical coalition. The alliance of traditional ayatollahs and liberal clerics with the reformist coalition is a prerequisite for a smooth transition toward a more democratic system. But such a transition would require—at the very least—the neutrality of the Guide to withstand a conservative backlash. The key for the transition is the attitude of the Guide, Ayatollah Khamenei, whose position embodies the prevalence of religious ideology over religion.

An important feature of Shia Islam—which clarifies the role of the clergy—requires attention. There is a well-known specificity of the Twelver-Imami Shia clergy that looks like a corporate institution, with unified aims and a hierarchy centered on a collegial leadership embodied by the Great Ayatollahs. But this corporatism in fact failed to translate itself into politics because the clergy was not instrumental in controlling the state. Moreover, and despite this structural cohesion, the Shia clergy is far from being homogeneous in terms of political alignments and philosophical conceptions. Thus, the conflict between liberals and conservatives—which divides the Iranian political establishment—does not translate into a conflict between laymen and clerics. On the contrary, the conflict is to be found within the clergy itself. This anxiety between the ideal of a corporate institution and existing tensions is anecdotally expressed in the names of various factions, as they all bear almost similar appellations. For example, the Jame-ye Ruhaniyyat-e Mobarez-e Teheran (Teheran Militant Clergy) gathered clerics who were pro-revolution. Yet, a leftist—and now liberal—breakaway adopted the name Majma-ye Ruhaniyyun-e Mobarez (Militant Clerics Association) in the late 1980s.

As this example illustrates, the situation is rather complex, because existing political alignments do not necessarily reflect religious and ideological ones. In support of President Mohammed Khatami, for example, one finds "liberal" clerics favoring a rethinking of Shariah (Mohsen Kadivar, Mohsen Mojtahed

Shabestari, Hassan Yusuf Eshkevari); "traditionalists," many of whom are unhappy about the extreme politicization of the clergy and the decline of the traditional spiritual leadership (Fazel Lankarani, for example, who refused to endorse the candidacy of the conservative Ayatollah Nateq Nouri against Mohammed Khatami in the 1997 presidential race); and, finally, "Islamic leftists," who, on the contrary, stress the social and anti-imperialist dimension of the revolution and its purely political message (Ali Akbar Mohtashemi, Mohammed Sadeq Khalkhali, Youssof Sana'y). These three groupings disagree on various issues, including the "fatwa" against Salman Rushdie, the role of Shariah, the meaning of democracy, the need for privatization or for support of a state-controlled economy, among others. Traditionalists, for example, maintain that Shariah should be implemented and are rather reluctant supporters of the concept of democracy. Leftists, on the other hand, favor elections, because the "people's will" is far more important than a strict interpretation of the Shariah. Liberals, for their part, have accepted the concept of secularization. Other complications exist as well, including the fact that several leading figures, after 20 years of militancy, have almost crossed the whole political spectrum, usually from radicalism to liberalism (Hossein Ali Montazeri, Mohammed Khoeiniha).

Thus, the division is both religious and political, as the role of the Guide, or more exactly the nature of the Velayat-e Faqih, is increasingly questioned. This unique institution embodies the complex relationships between religion and politics that, in the end, subordinates religion to politics through the ideologization of the former. As long as all the institutions of the Islamic Republic were held by individuals sharing similar views, that is, until the end of President Ali Akbar Hashemi Rafsanjani's term in 1997, the Velayat-e Faqih was not an issue as such. Since the 1997 election of President Mohammed Khatami, and the parliamentary election of 2000, liberal elements have come to power, which in turn have propelled conservatives to rally around the Velayat-e Faqih. Conservatives, then, perceived the Velayat-e Faqih as their last leverage to prevent a drastic evolution toward liberalization. Without a doubt, the importance of the conceptual debate on the Velayat-e Faqih is now directly linked to the political stakes of the day. The conservatives can oppose the democratic evolution of the republic only by calling for the predominance of a strong Velayat. What is even clearer is that the intellectual debate is linked to very concrete and short-term political issues. Simply stated, conservative elements cannot wage a coup—either military or constitutional—against President Khatami without the full approval of Ayatollah Khamenei. This fact leads to an ambiguous situation. The Guide can act as an arbiter and protect Mohammed Khatami against a coup. On the other hand, and because he heads the military and appoints senior members of the judiciary, Ayatollah Ali Khamenei can legally dismiss the president and dissolve parliament.

What this means is that the position of the Guide is the cornerstone of the institutions of the Islamic Republic. Yet, as the constitution of Iran explicitly mentions two sources of sovereignty, namely God's will, expressed by the Guide, and the people's will, any process of democratization will of course tend to assert the second. This would occur not necessarily against God's will, but by voiding the power of the Guide and relegating him to a more symbolic position. If the

Velayat-e Faqih is thus weakened, the present constitution could provide an institutional framework for full democracy, and a de facto secularization. Conservative forces cannot, naturally, manage a coup against President Khatami without the explicit approval of the Guide.

This centrality of the Guide explains why the debate in Iran today is centered on the concept of the Velayat-e Faqih. Paradoxically, it is rarely addressed as such, because that debate would be labeled an open assault against the Islamic Republic, and would be immediately treated as political rebellion if not treason. Therefore, many clerics avoid the issue of the Velayat-e Faqih either because they do not want to be branded as opponents of the regime or because they fear the consequences. One of the few to speak on the subject has been Ayatollah Hossein Ali Montazeri, the former heir to Imam Khomeini.

Although critics of the Velayat-e Faqih underlined most of the debate among clerics, two other issues are openly debated, that of the redefinition of the Shariah and that of secularization, understood not as separation of church and state, but as a separation between politics and religious activities.

## The Velayat-e Faqih

The concept of Velayat-e Faqih is not really new in Shia thought, even if it was never considered as being a very practical theory. Of course, it has been established as the cornerstone of the Iranian political system, immediately following the 1979 revolution. It took on a political and ideological position, as enunciated in the constitution, and was no longer a purely religious reference.[4] In the previous religious literature, the Faqih was no less than the hidden Imam, or His representative on earth, that is, the most learned alim. Yet, according to the 1980 constitution, the Faqih is not necessarily the highest religious authority, although he is above that learned scholar. Such a concept, by definition, has met from the very beginning a strong opposition among many high-level clerics, including those who favored the concept of an Islamic State. The reason for this opposition was the undeniable fact that it introduced a competing hierarchy to the clerical one. Traditionally, the Iranian clergy was led by a college of Great Ayatollahs, known as the *marja'e taqlid* (sources of imitation). Ayatollah Khomeini was both a marja' and the Guide, and his proclamation as Guide did not contradict the traditional hierarchy, even if it introduced another hierarchy among the marja'. At his death in June 1989, however, the question as to which was prevalent arose: the religious legitimacy or the political one? The appointment of the then Hojjat-ol Islam Ali Khamenei, who not only was not a marja' but not even an ayatollah, highlighted inherent contradictions. The discrepancy unraveled in 1993, at the death of the last marja' of the time, Ayatollah Araki. Of course, the only way to reconcile both would have been to declare Hojjat-ol Islam Khamenei a marja', but the majority of the ayatollahs reacted negatively to such a proposal discreetly advanced by Khamenei's allies. The proposal was quietly withdrawn. Today, and although the marja'iyya has not been abolished, and some Great Ayatollahs are said to be marja's, the institution itself does not seem to function as originally intended.

It must be recalled that several leading ayatollahs were reluctant, even at the time of the revolution, to endorse the Velayat-e Faqih. This list included such major learned clergymen as Ayatollahs Shariat-Madari, Mahmud Taleqani, Mohammed Tabatabai Qomi, and others. In addition, alims like Nasir Makarem Shirazi preferred to limit the power of the Vali.[5] This reluctance became more vocal after the appointment of Hojjat-ol Islam Khamenei and was shared both by liberal clerics, like Ayatollah Montazeri, and by some very conservative clerics, like Ayatollah Azeri-Qomi (d. 1998). In fact, the Velayat-e Faqih came under attack both from liberals, who pushed for more democracy, a greater role for parliament, and a rethinking of the Shariah, and by traditionalist clerics, who advocated the implementation of Shariah under clerical supervision, even if they preferred to see the restoration of the traditional marja'iyya system, that is, the appointments of the supreme religious authority by a college of equals with no meddling of politics and ideology. Fazel Lankarani and Makarem Shirazi regularly criticized Abdul-Karim Soroush, and leading liberal clerics, about their conception of *Fiqh* (jurisprudence) and Shariah, but at the same time, they opposed Ali Khamenei. Ayatollah Taqi Bahjat, another leading traditionalist, protested in 1997 to the closure of Ayatollah Montazeri's seminar.

The parallel evolution of Montazeri and Azeri-Qomi is interesting and must be discussed in detail to highlight the crisis within the marja'iyya. Both were staunch supporters of the revolution, Montazeri more "leftist" and Azeri-Qomi more "conservative." Azeri-Qomi, who published a very traditionalist newspaper, *Resalat,* approved the eviction of Montazeri in 1989, and supported the then Hojjat-ol Islam Ali Khamenei to succeed Ayatollah Khomeini, arguing that the leader need not be a Great Ayatollah, or even a marja'. At the time, he was the theoretician of the "absolute rule of the jurist," or Velayat-e Motlaq-e Faqih, which was inserted into the revised 1989 constitution. But, in the early 1990's, Ayatollah Azeri-Qomi distanced himself from Ali Khamenei. The gap that emerged between the two men's views grew so wide that Azeri-Qomi even questioned the concept of absolute Velayat-e Faqih in 1997, which promptly earned him house arrest. In 1994 he supported Ayatollah Mohammad Taqi Bahjat rather than Ali Khamenei for the marja'iyya. Three years later, Azeri-Qomi published an open letter in which he blamed Ayatollah Khamenei for accepting the position of Guide.

Ayatollah Montazeri, who was a supporter of the Velayat-e Faqih, changed his mind as well, not about the function of the institution, but about its role. He publicly opposed the concept of "absolute" Velayat-e Faqih and proposed, instead, a "supervisory" role for the Faqih (Nazarat).[6] This concept is also developed by the young Hojjat-ol Islam Mohsen Kadivar, recently jailed by a clerical court.[7] Under this interpretation, the role of the Faqih should only be to check the conformity of the laws with Islam. Kadivar even shows that Khomeini himself was in favor, before the revolution, of Nazarat and not Velayat, which was probably his worst crime in the eyes of conservatives. To buttress his claims, Kadivar provided critical inquiries about key references on the Velayat-e Faqih in Shia thought, and illustrated how none of them could establish the present definition.[8]

Thus, what emerges is a convergence of the critics, against the Velayat-e Faqih. Yet, to abolish it would trigger a political conflict and entail a severe backlash from the Guide and his supporters. Consequently, what seems to be developing is a gradual amalgamation of views between traditionalists and liberals, to slowly void the position of most of its power and confer upon the Guide a role of "moral consciousness." In other words, the Guide is evolving into the guarantor of the institutions that have limited his role, as the British and Scandinavian monarchies did some time ago. The result might be a kind of "constitutional theocracy." Opponents of the Velayat-e Faqih rely on the fact that the concept, as established by the constitution, stresses more than ever the political nature of the Islamic Revolution. They claim that if politics were to prevail, then democracy would be the best regime.

Faced with this growing criticism, the conservative faction has adopted a clear strategy to counter-attack. To concentrate the debate on the defense of the Velayat-e Faqih, and to establish its prevalence against all other institutions, namely the presidency and the parliament, conservative leaders have adopted new strategies. In short, their aim is to dissociate "God's sovereignty" from the people's sovereignty, whereas the constitution is based on the idea that there can be no real rift between the two. A call for the restoration of the absolute Velayat-e Faqih is a convenient way for them to dismiss or ignore the massive electoral support for liberal forces and to openly call the Guide to dismiss the president and dissolve parliament. Thus, defense of the Velayat-e Faqih is the only way to play on constitutional tools to defeat liberal arguments. Conservatives would favor a "constitutional coup d'etat," because the Guide—presumably accepting this strategy—has the constitutional right to dismiss both president and parliament. Indeed, Ayatollahs Emami Kashani and Misbahi Yazdi are leading a vocal campaign in support of the Velayat-e Faqih, precisely to achieve such an outcome. Ayatollah Ali Akbar Meshkhani went so far as to declare that the Guide had the same powers that the Prophet and the imams enjoyed,[9] whereas Ayatollah Javadi Amoli claimed that people needed a tutor (*qayyem*) and that democracy was not in Islam.[10]

## The Debate on Islam, Fiqh, and Secularization

Another issue of concern to the current debate is the one around various interpretations of Fiqh. Ayatollah Mojtahed Shabestari, Hojjat-ol Islam Mohsen Kadivar, Hassan Yusuf Eshkevari, and Mohsen Said Zadeh, in particular, have initiated a debate about the need to "modernize" Fiqh. To buttress their arguments, they rely on an already classical feature, namely the distinction between the "message" of Islam and the sociopolitical conditions of its expression. The present Fiqh, they argue, has largely been inherited from an Arab *Bedu* (tribal and patriarchal) society and should be rationalized through ijtihad, taking into account sociocultural changes. Said Zadeh, for example, has concentrated on laws pertaining to women, and insists on the absolute equality between the sexes.[11]

Interestingly, enough of these "new theologians" (*Kalam-e No*) are close to a fundamental principle of the Iranian revolution, namely the historicization of Islam. Still, the Guide, who should be conscious of his time (*agah be zaman*), and even Imam Khomeini—who stressed the prevalence of politics over the pillars of religion—seem to have been overtaken by the new theologians.[12] Importantly, the new theologians rely on the intellectual tools familiar to Shia religious thinking, namely reason, ijtihad, maslahah, to further strengthen their various interpretations.

But they also go further than advocating a mere reformation of Fiqh. Without a doubt, they argue that secularization is not contradictory to Islam, but good for it. By advancing such arguments, they clearly cut whatever ties they may have had with the Islamic Revolution. Mojtahed Shabestari claims the sacred should be spared from involvement in daily politics. For him, the mundane is the realm of imperfection, finitude, errors, and approximation, and since all prophets tried to disentangle the sacred from the customs and institutions of a given society, so must the Iranian. Moreover, the relation to God is a purely spiritual one, and it is a matter of faith—even of individual faith. It is based on a personal choice, and its values are solid because it is a personal choice, a self-conscious choice (*entekhab-e agahane*).[13] It is clear that this theological vision of religion, as a personal and free choice, is congruent with the political choice of democracy and elections. In this connection, President Mohammed Khatami's reference to "puritans" stresses what is common between democracy and religion: that a religious civil society, which agrees that politics and religion should be separated, but where everybody is supposed to a believer, is the preferred option.

Against this strong argument, conservative elements within Iranian society could not tolerate such a blatant attack, not only against the concept of an Islamic State, but also against the traditional perception of Fiqh. A clerical court quickly sentenced both Kadivar and Said Zadeh to jail terms after they publicized their "heretical" views—as was Abdollah Nouri, the former minister of the interior, in October 1999. The fact that Nouri was a cleric did not spare him from the wrath of religious puritans.

Nevertheless, the reliance on clerical courts has also drawn criticism from traditional circles, even if few endorse the ideas of the "new theologians." Ayatollahs Youssof Sana'y and Abdol Karim Musavi Ardebili, for example, condemned the sentencing of Abdollah Nouri. Perhaps this was due to the tradition of intellectual debates among Shia clergymen, but it was also a sign of the excesses many perceived. In this instance, as well, it is easy to identify a rapprochement between traditionalists and liberals, to resist conservative encroachments on civil liberties.

## Conclusion

As a consequence of the overlapping debate between the Velayat-e Faqih and Fiqh, conservatives appear effectively conservative in terms of religious thinking, although they themselves refer to a new concept, that of the Velayat-e Faqih. Without explicitly declaring it, conservative arguments differ from Ayatollah Khomeini's well-known views, with Shariah being subordinate to the political context. Hence the difficult position of the conservatives who tend to fall back on perennial arguments, or who stress the fidelity to a historical event, the Islamic Revolution, to buttress meager claims. What they engage in, however, is a pure oscillation between political ideology and mere neo-fundamentalism.

During the course of the past few years, the debate between so-called liberals and conservatives in Iran has been sharper because of the input that lay philosophers, like Abdul-Karim Soroush, have introduced. Today, religious thinking is encroaching on the clergy's monopoly of religious discourse. The "corporate" identity of the clergy is again at stake, given that the religious debate is no longer a monopoly of learned—and not so learned—clerics. The fact that some clerics express their views in the dozens of journals and magazines that flourish in Iran has also contributed to "de-specialization" of the religious debate. It has also opened it for public discussion. Even if liberal clerics are sometimes ambivalent about such a level of openness—Mohsen Kadivar rarely misses the opportunity to stress his religious credentials against the lay Abdul-Karim Soroush, for example, even when their views are not dissimilar—it is clear that the religious debate is linked to the political one, not only because of the conceptual issues involved, including the thorny Velayat-e Faqih, but also because it has now spread outside traditional religious schools. It must be emphasized that secularization and democracy have permanently changed the patterns of religious debates.

In this context, the conservatives, by definition, lack a popular and secular audience. Many tend to entrench themselves in their religious institutions. An ultra-conservative cleric, like Misbahi Yazdi in his "rah-e haqq" religious school, for example, advocates violence against the new enemies of Islam (*mahareb*). Importantly, Misbahi Yazdi has been challenged by the minister of culture—and was invited to face a televised public debate with him on the topic—which, in and of itself, is another break with the traditional pattern of dispute settlement among clerics.

Thus, and although the Iranian context is very different from currents in the rest of the Muslim world, it is clear that the debate among fundamentalists, traditionalists, and liberals in the Islamic Republic touches on the same issues: the evolving roles of the Shariah, women, individualization, the crisis of religious education, and self-proclamation of religious competence, among others. Nevertheless, the Iranian debate is not reflected in the rest of the Muslim world. While the revolutionary writings of Imam Khomeini and Ayatollah Morteza Mottahari, for example, have been largely translated and published (by the Iranian state itself, specifically in Arabic), nothing has actually happened—as far as the liberals are concerned—to encourage change. No translations of Mohsen Kadivar or Abdul-Karim Soroush seem to be available in Arabic as of today, thereby limiting the exposure of non-Persian-speaking Muslims to this lively debate. Still, the revolution in Iran is too embedded in the political discourses to appear as a reflection on Islam, but it is clear that the ongoing intellectual contentions have a more general meaning for the whole Muslim world.

## Notes

1. Scholars like Said Arjomand would probably refuse to call "revolutionary" what they see as a conservative movement. See Said Amir Arjomand, *The Turban and the Crown: The Islamic Revolution in Iran*, Oxford: Oxford University Press, 1988. But for others, and me, the Islamic Revolution is much more. It is the heir to Third World progressive movements of the mid-nineteenth century rather than a mere product of a clerical movement.
2. For a thorough discussion of the Velayat-e Faqih, as well as the bases for the present discussion, see Shahrough Akhavi, "Contending Discourses on Shi'i Law on the Doctrine of Velayat-e Faqih," *Iranian Studies* 29:3–4, summer-fall 1996, pp. 262–65.
3. Olivier Roy, "The Crisis of Religious Legitimacy in Iran," *The Middle East Journal* 53:2, spring 1999, pp. 201–16. See also Akhavi, *op. cit.*, pp. 262–65.
4. Roy, *op. cit.*, pp. 201–16.
5. On the published proceedings of the committee in charge of drafting the constitution and on its internal debates, see Asghar Shirazi, "The Constitution of Iran," *Politics and the State in the Islamic Republic*, London: I. B. Tauris, 1998, chapters 2 and 3. On Makarem Shirazi's views, see page 46 in ibid.
6. Hossein Ali Montazeri, *Derasat fi Velayat-e Faqih va Fiqh-ol Dowlat-ol Eslamiya* [Lectures on the Velayat-e Faqih and Islamic State Law], published in Qom, and summarized in "Nazarat-e Faqih" [Supervision of the Jurisconsult], *Rahe Now*, number 18, 31/5/1377 (1998).
7. Mohsen Kadivar, *Nazarieha-ye Dowlat Dar Fiqh-e Shie* [The Views on the State in Shia Law], Ney Publishers, 1376 (1996–97). See also Mohsen Kadivar, "Hokoumat-e Valai," *Rahe Now*, number 15, 10/5/1377 (1997–98).
8. Mohsen Kadivar, "Hokoumat-e Valai, Barrasi-e Maghbouley-e Omar Ibn-e Hanzale," *Rahe Now*, number 18, 31/5/1377 (July 1998).
9. *Resalat*, 16/10/1376 (January 1998).
10. *Keyhan*, 24/8/1376 (November 1997).
11. For a summary of his views, see Seyyed Mohsen Said-Zadeh, "Man-az Moddaiyane Eslam Vahame Daram" [I Am Afraid of Those Who Claim (to Know) Islam], *Jame-ye Salem*, 8/1376. See also "Be ja-ye Tamdid, Dar Qanoun-e (Diyeh) Tajdid-e Nazar Konid" [Do Not Extend but Reconsider the Law of Diyeh (blood-price)], *Zanan*, 5/1376 (1996).
12. A famous case is that of the prohibition of the pilgrimage in 1987, to protest the alleged killings of Iranian pilgrims by the Saudi police.
13. In this instance, *entekhab* means "election." See Mohammad Mojtahed Shabestari, "Shera Bayad Andishey-e Dini ra Naghd Kard?" [Why Should One Apply Critical Analysis to Religious Thinking?], *Kian*, number 18, 1–2/1373 (1994).

# THE ISLAMIC REPUBLIC OF IRAN

CHAPTER 2

*Reformists, Conservatives, and Iran's 2000 Parliamentary Elections*

Shaul Bakhash

In February 2000, a reformist coalition supporting President Mohammad Khatami won a sweeping victory in Iran's Majlis, or parliamentary, elections. The reformists in the incoming Majlis seemed strategically poised to carry out an ambitious agenda to expand political freedoms, strengthen oversight of governmental organizations, and break the monopoly exercised by a small faction in the ruling group over power and the economy. But within weeks of the election, and even before the new Majlis convened, the country experienced a powerful conservative backlash. Virtually the entire reformist press was closed down, reformist journalists were arrested, and institutions such as the judiciary, the Council of Guardians, and the authority of the Leader himself were brought into play to block the reformist agenda. The Majlis election thus proved to be a key moment in the contest between reformers and conservatives that had been triggered by Khatami's election as president in 1997. The election and its aftermath, in addition, proved a revealing moment in the history of the Islamic Republic. Political factions articulated their ideologies, programs, and visions for Iran's future. In voting, Iranians expressed their preferences among these competing visions. In both the election and the fierce political tug of war that followed it, political factions and the institutions of the state tested their relative strengths and political acumen. The post-election political struggle exposed the political and constitutional fault lines in the Islamic Republic.

## The Khatami Presidency

The issues at stake in the Majlis election are best understood against the background of developments during the first three years of Khatami's presidency. Khatami was elected president in 1997 with a substantial majority. He galvanized voters by stressing the rule of law, protection of the rights and privacy of Iranians, tolerance for a variety of views, and openness to the outside world. As president, he eased restrictions on the print media, while his minister of culture, Ataollah Mohajerani, issued dozens of licenses for new newspapers and magazines, giving rise to a flourishing and vibrant press in which major political issues were debated. Book publishing and cultural activity received a new lease on life. Greater freedom of association allowed older political and professional associations to renew activity and new ones to be established. In 1999, for the first time in the history of the Islamic Republic, elections were held for village, town, and city councils, creating thousands of representative bodies at the local level, although it remained to be seen how effective these councils would prove in practice. Khatami insisted on the removal of the notorious minister of intelligence (state security), Ali Fallahian, who had been implicated in the assassination of Iranian dissidents abroad and intellectuals and opposition figures at home.

Khatami also brought about significant change in foreign policy. He improved relations with the Arab states of the Persian Gulf. Saudi Arabia's Heir Apparent Abdallah became the highest Saudi official to visit Iran since the Islamic Revolution when he attended the Organization of Islamic Conference summit in Teheran in December 1997—an indication Khatami was able to generate much greater trust in Iran's intentions among the Gulf states. In September 1979, Khatami paved the way for improved relations with European countries by giving the EU written assurances that Iran had no intention of enforcing the death sentence that Iran's late leader, Ayatollah Khomeini, had pronounced in 1989 against the British writer Salman Rushdie. Rushdie's novel, *The Satanic Verses,* contained passages Khomeini had deemed insulting to Islam. The "death edict," which no previous Iranian leader had dared explain away, had bedeviled Iran-EU relations for nearly a decade. In a television interview with CNN in January 1998, Khatami invited Americans to join Iranians in a "thoughtful dialogue," clearly an attempt to begin the process of repairing an 18–year estrangement between the two countries.

Except for improvement of relations with Europe and the Persian Gulf states, these measures met with stiff resistance from the clerical conservatives and their allies. Khatami faced opposition in the Majlis, where conservatives could usually muster a majority. Although Khatami named the cabinet, the principal levers of power, including the judiciary, the intelligence agencies, national radio and television, and the military and security services—the ministry of intelligence, the police, the Revolutionary Guards, the army and the *Basij,* a paramilitary force used for crowd control and internal security—came under the purview of the supreme leader, Ayatollah Ali Khamenei. Khamenei tended to side with the conservatives.

Teheran's powerful and popular mayor, Gholam Hosain Karbaschi, who had helped engineer Khatami's electoral victory, was put on trial in 1998 on specious corruption charges, sentenced to five years in jail, and barred from holding public office for 20 years. In June 1998, the Majlis by a no-confidence vote secured the dismissal of Khatami's interior minister, Abdollah Nouri. The conservatives considered him too lenient in issuing permits for public meetings and the formation of political and professional associations. When Nuri went on to publish a new and outspoken newspaper, *Khordad,* he was tried and sentenced to five years imprisonment for violating Islamic sanctities. The Majlis also attempted but failed to oust Khatami's minister of culture, Mohajerani. The clerical thinker

Mohsen Kadivar was tried and sentenced to 18 months in jail for articles that questioned the extensive powers and prerogatives claimed for the Leader in the Islamic Republic.

The judiciary closed down several of the new reform-minded papers supportive of Khatami, although the clampdown initially proved ineffective due to Mohajerani's liberality in granting newspaper publishing licenses. For example, when the first of the popular reformist papers, *Jameeh,* was closed down in summer 1998, it reappeared in two days with an identical format, editorial staff, and reporters but under a different name, *Tus.* When *Tus* was shut down, it reappeared under yet a third name. (The newspaper was to undergo five name transformations before the judicial authorities shut it down for good in the year 2000.) The conservatives deployed a club- and chain-wielding vigilante group, the *Ansar-e Hezbollah,* or the Helpers of the Party of God, to break up reformist meetings and lectures. Nouri and Mohajerani were assaulted and insulted by Ansar operatives in September 1998, after leaving Friday prayers on the Teheran University campus.

In winter 1998 a number of intellectuals and opposition leaders were mysteriously killed, some in their own homes. However, the press persisted in pursuing the issue of the "serial killings," as they came to be called, and Khatami insisted on an investigation. The intelligence ministry was finally forced to admit its own agents were responsible for the murders, although it claimed these operatives were acting without authorization. The principal intelligence agent accused in the case, Said Emami, was in jail awaiting trial when the authorities announced he had committed suicide by drinking a bottle of hair removal preparation. The secret killings stopped, but in March 2000 there was a nearly successful assassination attempt against Said Hajjarian, a key adviser to Khatami and one of the leading thinkers of the reform movement. Earlier, in July 1999, when students protested the closure of another reformist newspaper, *Salaam,* police forces and Ansar club-wielders joined in an attack on Teheran University dormitories. The dormitories were trashed and several students injured. Meantime, Leader Khamenei largely aborted Khatami's initiative toward the U.S. by ruling out negotiations or relations with America.

The conservatives also used the pulpit, Friday sermons, and newspapers to denounce Khatami's policies, although the president was rarely mentioned by name. One leading cleric suggested that those defending freedom really wanted a passport for sexual license. "In legislation, Islam and democracy cannot in any way be reconciled," he asserted. Another cleric accused the supporters of the president of pursuing "Satanic" goals. In remarks made to a closed meeting of Revolutionary Guards officers and leaked to the press, the Guards commander, General Rahim Safavi, said liberals were in control of the universities, clerics had become agents of deceit, and the liberal press was undermining national security. "Our tongue is our sword," he said, and warned that the Guards would have to "cut the throats and tongues" of those who were undermining the regime.[1]

The country prepared for the election to the sixth Majlis against this background of intense rivalry between elements supporting and opposing Khatami and his reforms.

### The 2000 Majlis Election

The 2000 election was mainly a contest between two loose coalitions. Some 18 political parties and groups came together as the 2nd Khordad Front, taking their name from the date in May, 1997 when Khatami was elected president. Some 15 conservative organizations came together as the Followers of the Line of the Imam and the Leader, indicating by their choice of name their devotion to both the founder of the Islamic Republic, Imam Khomeini, and the current leader, Khamenei. The 2nd Khordad Front was led by the Islamic Iran Participation Front (IIPF), headed by Reza Khatami, the president's brother. It included the Executives of Construction, a centrist political group of high-level civil servants and technocrats with close ties to former president Rafsanjani.

The Executives of Construction had come together to contest the 1996 Majlis elections and supported Khatami's 1997 presidential bid. Although they joined hands with other Khatami supporters for the 2000 election, there were differences between the Khatami camp and the Rafsanjani "Executives." Unlike those closest to Khatami, the Executives of Construction emphasized economic rather than political reform. Rafsanjani and a number of other prominent figures supported by the Executives were not popular with the Khatami reformers. Khatami's Islamic Iran Participation Front and the Servants of Construction agreed to support common lists of candidates in the provinces; but they went their separate ways on candidate lists in Teheran. The 2nd Khordad Front also included the Society of Militant Clerics, one of the two principal clerical organizations in the country, and the Mujahedin of the Islamic Revolution. In the past, both these groups had been identified with the left, were hostile to the private sector, and favored strong state control of the economy and wealth-distribution measures in favor of the poor. But both groups claimed they had moved to center in their political and economic views.

The Followers of the Line of the Imam and the Leader were led by the country's principal clerical organization, the Association of Combatant Clerics of Teheran (not to be confused with the Society of Militant Clerics), which had dominated the Majlis and the principal offices of state for a decade and more and included various Islamic associations. The coalition also included other groups and organizations: the *Mo'talefah* group, the Moderation and Unity Party, *Chekad-e Azad-Anishan, Jamiyyat-e Isargaran-e Enqelab-e Islami.*

A third group, calling itself the "nationalist-religious union" and composed primarily of centrist intellectuals and professionals who were not at home (or not accepted in) either of these two large coalitions, also contested the election. The group included many prominent figures, including those associated with the Iran Liberation Movement. But its candidates did not make a strong showing in the subsequent balloting. A number of independents also ran for seats.

Each of the two large coalitions represented a spectrum of political views, and neither coalition issued a detailed platform. Nevertheless, for the voters, the choices were, in a general way, clear. The 2nd Khordad reformists ran as the agents of change, the conservatives as the defenders of the status quo. The reformists promised an expansion of press and political freedoms; the conservatives opposed such a policy. The reformists emphasized the primacy of the Majlis, political parties, and civic associations; the conservatives emphasized the authority of the Leader and institutions under conservative control, such as the Revolutionary Guards, the Council of Guardians, and the judiciary. The reformers wished to curb, the conservatives to maintain, the power of the Council of Guardians to bar "unqualified" candidates from running for elected office. The reformers appeared to desire an official dialogue with America; the conservatives opposed such talks.

On voting day, the voter turnout, at around 70 percent, was high; voters by a large majority supported the Khatami reformists.

### The Conservatives Feel Threatened

The conservatives had good reason to feel disquiet at the election results. They reflected an almost wholesale rejection of the conservatives and the status quo and an embrace of the idea of change and reform. Of 290 Majlis seats, 224 were decided in the first round. (Candidates need 25 percent of the vote to win in the first round; if there is no clear winner, the two top vote-getters for each seat go on to a second round.) The 2nd Khordad coalition and the centrist Executives secured a majority of seats and were expected to solidify this majority in second-round elections in the 66 constituencies where there was no clear winner.[2] The Islamic Iran Participation Front, the political group headed by Khatami's brother, and its allies secured the largest single bloc of votes in the new Majlis. In the all-important Teheran constituency, the reformist coalition won 29 of 30 seats. It made almost a clean sweep of other large cities, including Isfahan, Mashad, and Shiraz. The protest nature of the vote was unmistakable, at least in Teheran. The candidate with the highest number of votes in the capital, with over 60 percent of the total votes cast, was President Khatami's brother, a political unknown until the election campaign. The second highest number of votes in Teheran went to another political novice, Ali Reza Nouri, brother of former interior minister Abdollah Nouri, who had lost his ministerial post and subsequently went to prison for his liberal policies and views. Jamileh Kadivar, who secured the third highest number of votes, was the sister of the dissident cleric Mohsen Kadivar.

Even more striking was the rout of the conservatives and the rejection of the status quo. Only 70 incumbents were reelected. Fewer than 35 of those elected were clerics. Some of the most prominent conservatives, including Mohammad Reza Bahonar, Hasan Ruhani, and Mohammad Ali Movahedi-Kermani, all three- and four-term Majlis deputies, failed to be reelected. Bahonar was deputy Speaker and a majority leader in the fourth and the outgoing fifth Majlis. Ruhani was an influential member of parliament's foreign affairs committee and secretary-general of the powerful National Security Council. Generally respected, he too fell victim to the anti-establishment sentiments of the electorate. Movahedi-Kermani, the Leader's personal representative to the Revolutionary Guards, was defeated, as were several other multi-term deputies, singled out because they had led the opposition to Khatami's policies and ministers.

Former intelligence minister Fallahian and former Revolutionary Guards commander Mohsen Rezai culled few votes.

Particularly striking was the fate of Ali Akbar Hashemi-Rafsanjani. The two-term former president (1989–97) and former Speaker of the Majlis (1980–89) was until 1997 regarded as the second most powerful man in Iran. As president, he had nurtured a reputation as a pragmatist and a centrist; and in his first term as president, he liberalized economic policy and eased up on social (but not political) controls. He helped keep out of parliament and eventually neutralize the radicals on the left. But his policies were not always popular with the hardliners in the Majlis. Rafsanjani's lieutenants formed the Executives of Construction to contest the 1996 Majlis elections because the conservative and politically dominant Association of Combatant Clerics of Teheran refused to allow Rafsanjani to include a few of his own choices on a common list of candidates for Teheran. As already noted, the Executives, headed by Teheran mayor Karbaschi, had helped ensure Khatami's electoral victory in 1997.

However, Rafsanjani's standing among reformists and Iranians hungry for change deteriorated during his second term as president, when he failed to stand up to the conservatives as they tightened political and social controls. His family was believed to be involved in lucrative business enterprises. He had done nothing in 1994–96, when several prominent writers were found dead in mysterious circumstances. He grew critical of the reformers, and identified increasingly with the conservatives, as the reformist movement gained breadth and depth under Khatami and reformists began to talk of fundamental change in the political system. When he announced his candidacy for the 2000 parliament, he claimed to be above factional politics. But reformers saw him as the conservatives' secret weapon. They believed he would be elected Speaker of the new Majlis and rein in the reform movement. The identification with the conservatives badly hurt Rafsanjani. He barely squeaked into the Majlis, coming in 27th among Teheran's 30 deputies. Widespread rumors suggested that only tampering with the vote count allowed him to be elected at all. His daughter, Faezeh Hashemi, who in 1996 secured the second highest number of votes in Teheran, failed to get elected at all, finishing a humiliating 54th, primarily because during the campaign, she had supported her father and attacked her father's critics in the reformist camp.

### The Reformist Agenda

Two other sources of concern for the conservatives were the reformist agenda and the role of the reformist press. Members of the reformist majority in the incoming Majlis announced an agenda that threatened to consolidate the political opening made possible under Khatami and to challenge the centers of power still controlled by the conservatives, including the judiciary, the intelligence agencies, the Council of Guardians, the Revolutionary Guards, and the *bonyads,* the parastatal foundations that own hundreds of expropriated industries and enterprises. The bonyads played a significant role in the economy. Reluctant to give up their own lucrative holdings, they acted as a barrier to privatization. They were suspected of siphoning off funds to leading clerics, which were then used for patronage purposes. Yet they gave no public accounting of their operations.

Reports in the reformist press and statements by incoming reformist deputies suggested that the new Majlis would pass laws to guarantee greater freedom of the press, assembly, and association and to ease the formation of political parties; exercise Majlis oversight of the ministry of intelligence and national radio and television, whose news coverage was one-sided and favored the conservatives; look into the sources of wealth of high officials (many of whom were clerics); insist on transparency and accountability in the bonyads; and end involvement of the security agencies, the Revolutionary Guards, and other organizations in business and profitmaking operations. Deputies suggested the Majlis would conduct its own investigations into the "serial killings" of 1998, the attack on student dormitories in the summer of 1999, and the March 2000 attempt on the life of Said Hajjarian.

The new Majlis was also expected to attempt to de-politicize the judiciary and to reform or do away with the special press and clerical courts—institutions used by the conservatives to shut down newspapers, jail dissidents, and stifle criticism; to eliminate what they described as "multiple centers of power," a clear reference to the tendency of official and quasi-official organizations and individual clerics to pursue private agendas not approved by the cabinet; and to restrict the authority of the Council of Guardians to disqualify candidates running for public office.[3]

## Role of the Press

The reformist press had become a powerful instrument in the reformers' arsenal. True, several newspapers, including *Resalat, Jomhuri-ye Islami, Kayhan,* and *Abrar,* spoke for the conservative cause. But the new reformist papers dominated the political discourse and captured the readers' imagination. Despite bans and closures, the circulation enjoyed by a succession of reformist newspapers— *Jameeh, Neshat, Khordad, Bahar, Entekhab, Gunagun, Sobh-e Emruz, 'Asr-e Azadegan, Fath, Mosharekat,* and others—far exceeded the circulation of the conservative dailies. A group of articulate and talented commentators wrote for the reformist press. These commentators helped popularize ideas regarding civil society, individual rights, judicial reform, accountability of officials and state institutions, transparency of government operations, and a degree of separation of state and religion. They called for an end to the clerical monopoly of power. They played an important watchdog role, drawing attention to excesses of the security agencies or what they regarded as the politicized nature of the courts. For example, unlike the conservative newspapers, the reformist press gave wide publicity to Nouri's spirited defense during his trial, and they extensively reported the wreckage caused by security forces at Teheran University student dormitories during the summer 1999 attack. When the police commander and 17 officers charged and tried for the dormitory attack were acquitted, the reformist press expressed astonishment and outrage.

These newspapers served as quasi-official party organs (as did those on the right), publicizing the reformist cause and helping bring about the reformist victory. Broadly speaking, the reformist press, along with the reformist parties, offered an alternative to the ruling conservative clerics and their system of rule. Articles by the well-known commentator Akbar Ganji, in *Sobh-e Emruz* and *'Asr-e Azadegan,* appeared to have particularly grave implications for the regime and some of its most prominent figures. Ganji indirectly implicated shadowy elements in the ministry of intelligence, other security agencies, and the Revolutionary Guards, as well as unnamed senior officials and clerics, in the 1998 "serial killings," the attempt on Hajjarian's life, and earlier murders of intellectuals and political dissidents. Ganji hinted at clerics who issued *fatwa*s, or religious decrees, sanctioning killings and wrote of "grey eminences" and "shadowy figures" who met in dark rooms to agree on eliminating intellectuals and political figures. Ganji seemed specifically to target Rafsanjani, during whose presidency, unresolved killings had taken place.[4]

After the Majlis election, several other journalists took up this issue. The well-known columnist Emad ad-Din Baqi extensively echoed Ganji's charges in *Fath*. Hamid-Reza Jala'ipur, criticizing the judiciary for lack of objectivity in trials of journalists and dissidents, referred to attempts of a "secret government" and "a government within a government" to stifle reform.[5] Addressing Rafsanjani, Sadeq Zibakalam wrote in another article: "The nation wants to hear from you [as to] what happened to 70–80 [killed] writers and political opponents over the last ten years. On the command of which person or official were they murdered?"[6] Such charges found their way into the provincial press.[7] Even an adviser to President Khatami talked of "forces unknown to the president" who, he said, were carrying out actions that damaged the government at home and abroad.[8]

Finally, a freer press posed the danger that the extensive powers and prerogatives of the Leader himself would become a subject for discussion, giving rise to demands to circumscribe them. Early in the Khatami presidency, student leaders and columnists had spoken of the desirability of curtailing, or defining more clearly, the powers of the Leader, limiting his tenure (he is now selected for life), and subjecting his conduct in office to greater scrutiny. Although public discussions of this highly sensitive and explosive issue had practically ended by 1999, nevertheless the question of the Leader's virtually unlimited powers loomed in the background; and there was fear in the Leader's and the conservative camp that it would be raised again. In 1997, for example, *Rahe Now* published an essay by Ayatollah Qasem Khoi that seemed to question the need for a supreme religious guide. In 1998, the reformist press carried a statement by Ayatollah Hossein-Ali Montazeri, a cleric prominent in the first decade of the revolution but now out of favor and under house arrest, criticizing the extent to which the Leader interfered in state affairs. In February 2000, in an interview with an Arabic-language newspaper, *Sharq al-Awsat,* Montazeri condemned "dictatorship by a certain faction that has monopolized Islam and taken to describing its opponents as heretics and infidels," and said the people have a right to elect, depose, limit the term of, and restrict the power of the Leader.[9]

## The Conservative Response

Initially, the conservatives appeared to be licking their wounds, disoriented by the sheer size of their electoral defeat. The conservative parliamentary leader, Bahonar, said he and his colleagues needed to take stock of the election results, review the mistakes they had made, and prepare for the next elections. In a Friday sermon on March 3, Ayatollah Jannati, the secretary of the Council of Guardians, urged all Iranians to accept the election verdict: "Some will be satisfied . . . and some will be unhappy," he said, "but everybody should accept the results without 'ifs' and 'buts'." [10]

But hardliners in the conservative camp appear to have concluded that the threat posed by the reformist victory and its implications was too serious to be ignored and to have succeeded in shaping the conservative response. The sharp conservative backlash that began in the spring took several forms. The conservatives used the judiciary to close down reformist newspapers and to jail, harass, and silence reformist journalists, intellectuals, and lawyers. The outgoing Majlis put in place supportive legislation. The Council of Guardians attempted to alter the election results and weaken the reformist control of the new Majlis. Conservative clerics and newspapers launched a propaganda campaign designed to depict the most outspoken reformers as a threat to Islam, the revolution, and the security of the state. Finally, the Council of Guardians and the Leader came up with constitutional interpretations and claims designed severely to curtail parliament's authority.

Aware that Khatami and the reformers were very popular among the younger generation, the outgoing Majlis had already raised the voting age from 16 to 17 in the lead-up to the election. In its dying days, in early April, the Majlis approved a new and highly restrictive press law. The judiciary then used this law to move against the reformist press. On April 23, the judicial authorities closed down eight dailies, four weeklies, and one monthly, including *Sobh-e Emruz, Fath,* and *Iran-e Farda.* On April 27, they shut down *'Asr-e Azadegan* and *Mosharekat,* followed by *Bayan* in June and *Bahar* in August. A number of provincial papers were closed as well. In a period of ten weeks, over 20 publications, virtually the entire reformist press, were suppressed. On June 18, over 150 deputies, a majority, in the new Majlis, signed a letter to the chief of the judiciary asking him to end the newspaper closures, to reverse orders of closure, and to respect the right of journalists to freely express their opinion (by now several journalists had been arrested or faced charges). But the judiciary chief rejected their demands.

In addition to closing down publications, the judiciary tried and jailed several of the most outspoken journalists and editors, including Mashallah Shams ol-Va'ezain, editor of *'Asr-e Azadegan;* Latif-Safari, the editor of the banned newspaper *Neshat;* and Emad ad-Din Baqi of *Fath.* Shams ol-Va'ezain was sentenced to 30 months, Latif-Safari to 27 months, Baqi to five and a half years. Ganji was jailed in June, pending trial. These journalists generally faced a clutch of charges for writing or publishing articles that allegedly violated Islamic sanctities, undermined state security, incited readers against the institutions of the state, and "confused" public opinion. Often, a complaint by another (conservative) newspaper, or an institution like the Revolutionary Guards, claiming it had been misrepresented or defamed, was enough to trigger charges, arrest, and trial. Between March and August, several other editors and journalists were summoned by the judicial authorities to answer charges or questions in the preliminary stages of an investigation.[11] Although these preliminary interrogations did not necessarily lead to formal charges and trial, they were clearly intended to intimidate the journalists and warn off others.

In April, judicial officials also cracked down on ten or more Iranian intellectuals, lawyers, and journalists and one cleric who attended an academic conference on Iran at the Heinrich Böll Institute in Berlin. At the conference, several of the participants made remarks mildly critical of aspects of the Islamic Republic or conservative policies. For example, Mehrangiz Kar, a lawyer and women's rights activist, spoke of legal discrimination against women in Iran. Hassan Yusef Eshkevari, the cleric, argued for the possibility of an Islam compatible with pluralism, democracy, and religious tolerance. Ganji spoke of the agenda and prospects of the reform movement in Iran. All had expressed similar views, orally or in writing, in Iran. But the judiciary now found their views grounds for possible prosecution. In addition, Iranian exiles and dissident groups in Europe had crashed the conference, attempted to disrupt it with verbal interruptions and displays of nudity, and expressing strong opposition to the Islamic Republic. (They also condemned the Iranian participants as collaborators in a reprehensible regime.) Film footage of these activities was widely disseminated on Iranian television; and the participants were condemned by clerics and the conservative press for attending a conference featuring "immoral" activity and attacks on the Islamic Republic. All this served as grounds for additional charges. Almost all the participants were interrogated upon return. Several spent various periods in prison. Over ten of the participants were subsequently put on trial. Six were sentenced to prison terms of 4 to 10 years. Eshkevari was separately tried by the special clerics court and found guilty of "waging war against God" and insulting Islam, crimes that carry the death sentence. Ganji, tried separately by the press court, was sentenced to 10 years in prison and an additional 5 years in internal exile, although an appeals court reduced the prison term to 6 months and overturned the judgment on internal exile. Conservative clerics, politicians, and press used the conference for a broader attack on the whole reform movement.[12]

In June, two lawyers, Shirin Ebadi and Mohsen Rahami, were arrested on charges of taping and disseminating allegedly false allegations made by Farshad Ebrahimi, a self-confessed member of Ansar-e Hezbollah. In the long and rambling tape (whose contents subsequently received wide publicity), Ebrahimi described his own participation and that of other Ansar elements in breaking up student and reformist meetings. He alleged that in the early 1990s, the Ansar received encouragement and financial assistance, variously, from senior clerics, nationally prominent leaders of hardline conservative political groups, and senior interior ministry officials. He claimed presence at meetings, or personal knowledge of meetings, at which senior clerics and police and security officials had discussed means of causing unrest to undermine Khatami and the 2nd Khordad movement and where the killing of reformists and dissidents was described as religiously permissible.[13]

None of the allegations could be independently confirmed; but the tape or its transcript, clandestinely and widely disseminated, caused a sensation. Ebrahimi appeared to corroborate the allegations made by Ganji, Baqi, and others of clandestine groups in the security agencies and government, or close to the centers of conservative power, who were plotting against the reform movement. Ebadi had agreed to serve as Ebrahimi's lawyer. Rahami (who had served as Nouri's lawyer) was acting on behalf students injured by the police during the summer 1999 Teheran University dormitory attack. Both lawyers cited duty to clients to explain why they taped Ebrahimi's remarks. By their own account, they had in any case immediately turned over Ebrahimi's tape to the authorities. But Ebadi and Rahami were tried behind closed doors in July on charges of disseminating falsehoods and endangering the security of the state, and were each barred for 5 years from practicing law.

The Council of Guardians meantime nullified the election results in nine constituencies, all seats won by reformists. In three other constituencies, it cancelled a number of ballot boxes, throwing the election to the conservative rather than the previously announced reformist candidate. These decisions led to disturbances in Gachsaran, Arak, Firuzkuh, Khalkhal, and other towns. The Council of Guardians also alleged improprieties in the Teheran elections, where the interior ministry had given the reformist list 29 of the 30 Teheran seats. It began a time-consuming and indecisive recount of the ballots, which it proved unable to complete, and repeatedly delayed announcing the Teheran results. Finally, on May 18, three months after the election and only a week before the new Majlis was to open, the Council of Guardians wrote the Leader that it was unable to validate the Teheran ballot due to irregularities. Khamenei, however, citing time constraints and other considerations, instructed the Guardians to announce the Teheran results on the basis of their best information to date. The Teheran results, finally endorsed by the Council of Guardians and based on the Guardians' own partial recount and investigation, differed only in two respects from the results originally announced by the interior ministry: A candidate of the "nationalist-religious union" who had been previously confirmed was dropped in favor of a conservative candidate, and Rafsanjani was bumped up from 29th to 20th on the Teheran list. Rafsanjani, unpopular with the reformists and certain he would not be elected Speaker, resigned his seat before taking it up.

The interventions of the Council of Guardians reduced the reformist majority but did not materially affect the balance of forces in the new Majlis. In the runoffs, held in early May, the 2nd Khordad Front had won 47 of 66 seats, the conservatives 10, and independents 9, giving the reformers solidly in the Khatami camp a comfortable majority. Estimates differed as to the size of this majority. But when parliament convened at the end of May, with 248 deputies present, analysts generally agreed that the Islamic Iran Participation Front, the president's own party (and itself something of a coalition), had by itself won over 150 seats.[14] The reformers appeared in a position comfortably to shape the legislative agenda.

## The Ideological Counter-Offensive

In the months following the February election, conservative clerics and political figures also used the pulpit and the press to wage an extensive war of words against the reformers. This ideological counter-offensive preceded, then accompanied, the crackdown on the reformist press, journalists, and intellectuals and was designed in part to set the stage and provide the rationale for it. The themes of sermons, newspaper articles, and statements by official spokesmen—for example, of the judiciary or the Revolutionary Guards—were similar: Internal enemies posed a threat to Islam, the revolution, and the country's independence. The reformist press was intentionally or inadvertently undermining the people's faith in religion, the institutions of the state, and the revolution itself. The ultimate aim was to divorce religion from governance, to destroy the revolution, and to open the door to foreign domination of the country. "Reform," however attractive in principle, was often a cover for these dangerous ends.

A number of clerics, newspapers, and political figures led this campaign. But the campaign was shaped primarily by Khamenei himself. As Leader, he spoke with the most authoritative voice. In a series of major statements between March and August 2000, he set the tone for the campaign, articulated its major themes, and elaborated its rationale. He clearly feared that the momentum and demand for reform would get out of hand, lead to unrest, or threaten the very essence of the Islamic Republic. Over a period of several months, he gradually elaborated an extensive argument against the drive for a freer press and a more open political system. His speeches and sermons often set the stage for direct action by the judicial authorities. He set down the red lines beyond which criticism would not be tolerated. He said he welcomed competition and reasonable rivalry between the two parliamentary factions. But he took the lead in emphasizing the distinction (common in conservative discourse) between *khodi* and *ghayr-e khodi,* or "us and them," "insiders and outsiders," and "supporters and enemies" of the system. He endorsed the idea of freedom of the press and open debate, but he harshly condemned the reformist press and praised the judiciary that had crushed it. Khamenei initially appeared to support Khatami's call for economic and administrative reform, but by the summer he was labeling the call for reform a foreign plot to dominate Iran.

In a Friday sermon in April, Khamenei drew a distinction between "legitimate" and "illegitimate" violence. He condemned lawlessness and thuggery as illegitimate uses of violence. But he said the state is justified in using "legitimate violence," even in applying the death sentence, against lawbreakers and troublemakers.[15] The sentiments he expressed appeared on the surface unexceptionable—a routine justification of the legal use of force by the state and perhaps even a condemnation of the vigilantism of the right. But Khamenei was also responding to critics of alleged police and judiciary brutality (and perhaps to critics of capital punishment) and laying the ground for the arrest of journalists, lawyers, and intellectuals that followed.

Ten days later, Khamenei launched a sharp attack on the press. A dozen or 15 papers, he said, had become the "bases of the enemy" and were "directed from one headquarters." They were causing "discord and division, spreading disorder, and implanting confusion and pessimism among the people." They were undermining Islamic sanctities. They were promoting the cause of "enemy agents" and "attempting to discredit faithful, loyal and useful persons" in the Revolutionary Guards, the army, and the Basij forces.[16] The crackdown on the reformist press followed hard on the heels of these remarks. In May, in a sermon devoted largely to the theme of "insiders" and "outsiders," and in what appeared as an attempt to split the reformist ranks, Khamenei demanded that loyal political groups distance themselves from those he described as enemies of the Islamic Republic. "Dregs of the former regime," secularists who had joined the revolution but never believed in Islamic government, and Iranians supported by "spy networks," foreign radios, and foreign money, he said, were now "chanting reformist slogans" and talking about "freedom and the rule of the people and democracy." Their real aim was to change the Islamic nature of the regime and allow "the American masters to take control of our economy, our culture and our social affairs." Political factions loyal to the regime, he said, "must make their stance clear . . . define their borders."[17]

In other statements, Khamenei defended Council of Guardians' rulings invalidating elections in certain districts; and he defended the judiciary against critics who questioned its neutrality. These critics, he said, "intend to weaken the judiciary in order to ensure it will not have the power to act."[18]

In his various statements, Khamenei remained careful to appear supportive of the president, describing him as a pious Muslim, a disciple of Ayatollah Khomeini, and a cleric dedicated to the principles of the Islamic Republic. In the spring, he endorsed the principles of Khatami's reform program. Although he said nothing of expanding the political space, he underlined the need for administrative and economic rationalization and for dealing with red tape, the over-staffed bureaucracy, and official corruption. However, returning to the reform theme in July, his tone was far less supportive. He cast doubt on the purpose of reforms that, he alleged, were being enthusiastically supported by outside powers, including the United States and England. "What is the enemy's objective when he expresses support for Iranian reforms?" he asked. The answer: Foreign enemies sought to destabilize and destroy the Islamic Republic, just as they had helped destroy the Soviet Union through Gorbachev's reforms. Khatami and other officials, he noted, "have repeatedly said our reforms are Islamic and revolutionary. Very well, that is fine. But we need more precise explanations and a clearer picture."[19]

These themes were reiterated by conservative spokesmen. Rafsanjani defended the newspaper closures. "They are putting freedom before Islam, freedom before faith," he said. By belittling the regime's accomplishments, journalists "pave the way for those who want to come in and take over the country."[20] The Association of the Seminary Teachers of Qom described the reformist press as "mouthpieces and stooges of foreign powers." In a Friday sermon, Ayatollah Ebrahim Amini asserted, "these newspapers call the Islamic system into question. They call the guardianship of the supreme jurisconsult into question. They sometimes even call Islam into question."²¹ Another senior cleric invited believers to kill unnamed reformers.²² After Khamenei's remarks on "legitimate violence," the Revolutionary Guards issued an official statement calling for unity and warning unnamed "enemies" opposing the regime that they "will feel the reverberating impact of the hammer of the Islamic revolution in their skull . . . they will never [again] be able to engage in hatching plots."²³ The declaration caused considerable alarm. Rumors that the Guards intended to overthrow Khatami grew so widespread that the Guards had to issue a second statement denying they were planning a coup. Clerics and the conservative press took up the distinction Khamenei had made between "Islamic-style" reform which was right for the country, and "American-style" reform which they condemned.

## A New Constitutional Theory

The Council of Guardians and Khamenei also advanced novel interpretations of the constitution. These were designed to curtail the authority of the new Majlis in the crucial areas of legislative powers and oversight. In April, in response to a move by some members of the outgoing Majlis to exercise oversight of the judiciary, the Council of Guardians ruled that the legislature had no authority to look into the affairs of institutions that came under the purview of the Leader. This meant that, in addition to the judiciary, the Majlis was barred from investigating or scrutinizing the operations of the armed forces and Revolutionary Guards, the broadcast media and the bonyads. The chief officers of all these organizations are appointed by the Leader. When members of the Majlis demurred, the Expediency Council, a body that adjudicates differences between the Council of Guardians and the Majlis, upheld the Council of Guardians in its novel interpretation of the constitution.

On August 6, Khamenei himself intervened to bar the new Majlis from overturning or revising the repressive press law that the judiciary had used in its press crackdown. Revision of the press law was the first order of business on the agenda of the Majlis when it opened for formal business. In asking the Majlis to drop the matter in a letter he addressed to the Majlis Speaker, Khamenei cited a danger that the print media would fall under foreign influence or control and the threat this posed to Islam and to national security.²⁴ Khamenei did not cite any constitutional grounds for this almost unprecedented attempt at extension of the Leader's authority. Nor did he explicitly instruct the Majlis to drop the press law. But his language pointed in that direction and was so interpreted by Karrubi and Khamenei's other clerical supporters. By citing a threat to Islam and state, Khamenei was implicitly invoking his duty to protect both. Moreover, the Speaker made the constitutional argument for Khamenei that Khamenei did not explicitly make for himself. He described Khamenei's letter as a *hukm-e hukumati*, a term applied to rulings by the Leader involving matters of high state interest. Karrubi also reiterated a claim advanced, but also challenged, in the past, that the Leader has absolute power and is owed absolute obedience. He admonished deputies unhappy with Khamenei's directive that they owed the Leader such obedience.

These two rulings were fraught with implications for the Majlis and the constitutional order. The idea that the Majlis lacked authority to scrutinize organizations that came under the Leader's purview was entirely novel and bound to prove problematic. In the 1990s, the Majlis had in fact investigated the largest of the bonyads, the Foundation for the Disinherited, and the operations of national radio and television. The report resulting from the latter inquiry led to the dismissal of the broadcast media chief. The Majlis enacted the laws that governed each of these organizations. The bonyads aside, each year it voted the budgets of the institutions coming under the Leader's purview. Even the bonyads received various forms of assistance by the acts of the Majlis. Article 76 of the constitution empowers the Majlis "to investigate and examine all the affairs of the country." To place a group of state institutions beyond the scrutiny of the Majlis was bound to raise practical and constitutional issues.

The expanded claim implicitly made for the Leader's prerogatives in the press law case was likely to prove equally controversial. The constitution empowers the Leader to set the broad policies of the Islamic Republic. But the authority of the Leader to dictate to the Majlis even on major legislation was by no means an established principle. The constitution lays down a procedure for dealing with "problematic" legislation. The Council of Guardians can veto legislation it considers in violation of the constitution or Islam; and if the Majlis disagrees with the ruling, the Expediency Council has authority to adjudicate differences between the Guardians and the deputies. It remained unclear why Khamenei chose to bypass this process. Khamenei's intervention left the Majlis with two unpalatable choices. The majority could pursue the press law and invite a confrontation with the Leader or cause the Leader to lose face; or the Majlis could abandon the press law and implicitly concede that the Leader had the power to dictate to the Majlis the issues it could discuss and the bills it could enact into law. Such a concession could gravely diminish, if not emasculate, the Majlis's powers.

In February 2000, the reformist coalition, riding the wave of an impressive electoral victory, seemed poised to change in significant ways the political landscape in Iran. At the very least, the reformers and their supporters expected greatly to expand the political space that Khatami's election three years earlier had made possible. By August, a bare six months later, the balance of forces seemed dramatically altered. The reformist press was shut down, reformist journalists and intellectuals were in jail, Khamenei had sided decisively with the anti-reform forces, and new interpretations of the constitution, if allowed to stand, threatened greatly to diminish the role and authority of the Majlis.

The reform movement itself was at a critical crossroads and faced difficult choices. In addition, the confrontation between reformers and conservatives had raised fundamental constitutional issues regarding the extent and limits of the authority of the Leader, the Majlis, the Council of Guardians, and other state institutions. To whom, Iranians were bound to ask themselves, was the government ultimately accountable? If not in the immediate future, then in the longer term, these unresolved issues threatened to plunge the country into a serious constitutional crisis.

## Notes

1. For these citations and further details, see Shaul Bakhash, "Iran's Unlikely President," *The New York Review of Books,* 5 November 1998, p. 50.
2. Estimates of the exact breakdown of seats among the reformists, conservatives, and independents differed, depending on whether the Executives of Construction and smaller groups believed sympathetic to but not directly affiliated with the 2nd Khordad Front are included in the reformist totals. However, there was general agreement that the reformers had a comfortable majority in the first round, although this was no guarantee they would vote as a bloc on every issue. For a more detailed breakdown of final figures, see further in the contribution and note 14.
3. The agenda of the reformists can be culled partly from statements made during the election campaign, numerous scattered statements made by reformist leaders and individual deputies after the election, and commentary by newspaper editors and columnists associated with the reformist cause. For a reference to some of the issues on the reformist agenda, see "Ideology is Dead: Now the Rule of Law Will Prevail," an interview with Hamid Reza Jala'ipur, editor of *'Asr-e Azadegan,* in *La Republica,* 22 February 2000, cited in Foreign Broadcast Information Service, Near East and South Asia (hereafter *FBIS/NESA*), 22 February 2000. Also interview with Majlis deputy Karbalai, "We Will Definitely Not Vote for Hashemi-Rafsanjani as Majlis Speaker," *'Asr-e Azadegan,* 4 March 2000, cited in *FBIS/NESA,* 4 June 2000; and Howard Schneider, "New Parliament Readies Changes in Iran," *Washington Post,* 8 July 2000.
4. See, for example, Ganji's interview, "Serial Murders, Elections and Threats," with *Sobh-e Emruz,* 21 February 2000; "Akbar Ganji: Assassination Attempts Cannot Be Prevented as Long as Naqdi Is Head of the Intelligence and Security Branch," *Sobh-e Emruz,* 2 April 2000, as cited in *FBIS/NESA,* 2 April 2000. In addition to his articles, Ganji published a collection of his essays in a book, *Tarik-khaneh-ye Ashbah* [The Dark House of Ghosts] (Teheran: Tarh-e Now, 1378/1999), elaborating on these charges. For a summary and an interview with Ganji, see Robert Fisk, "The Untold Story of President Rafsanjani of Iran and the Killing of Intellectuals" and "Revealed: Role of a President in the Murder of His People," *The Independent,* 8 March 2000. In addition to Ganji, at least two other journalists wrote books in a similar vein. See Shahram Rafi'zadeh, *Shilik be Eslahat* [Firing (a Bullet) at Reform], (Teheran: Aknun Publications, 1379/2000), and Hamid Reza Kaviani, *Dar Jostehju-ye Mahfel-e Jenayat-karan: Baz-khani-ye Parvandeh-ye Qatl-ha* [In Search of the Society of Criminals: A Review of the File of Political Murders] (Teheran: Negah-e Emruz, 1378/1990).
5. Baqi was arrested and tried for these allegations. For Jala'ipur, see his article, "A Secret Government," in *Gunagun,* 13 July 2000, cited in *FBIS/NESA,* 21 July 2000.
6. Sadeq Zibakalam, "Hashemi Rafsanjani and Another Look at 29 Bahman," *'Asr-e Azadegan,* 28 February 2000, cited in *FBIS/NESA,* 6 April 2000.
7. For the provincial press, see, for example, "'Final Curtain' for 'Gray Cardinals'," *Omid-e Zanjan,* 10 May 2000, cited in *FBIS/NESA,* 20 June 2000.
8. Susan Sachs, "As Ballots are Counted, Iran's Moderates Fear Backlash," an interview with presidential adviser Hosain Valeh, *New York Times,* 22 February 2000.
9. Cited in *FBIS/NESA,* 25 May 2000.
10. *FBIS/NESA,* 3 March, 2000
11. These included the president's brother, Mohammad Reza Khatami, of *Mosharekat;* the Leader's brother, Hadi Khamenei, of *Hayat-e Now;* Jala'ipur of *'Asr-e Azadegan;* Ali-Akbar Mohtashami of *Bayan;* Morteza Alviri of *Hamshahri;* and Fereydun Valinejad, the managing director of the Islamic Republic News Agency (IRNA). Unlike the state-controlled broadcast media, IRNA did not slant its reporting in favor of the conservatives. At least two provincial journalists were also jailed, but reporting on provincial newspaper closures and arrests were not always comprehensive.
12. In addition to Mehrangiz Kar, Eshkevari, and Ganji, the Iranian participants who subsequently got into trouble with the authorities (as far as could be determined from published reports) included Shahla Lahiji, a publisher; Ali Afshari, a student leader; Ezzatollah Sahabi, publisher of the subsequently banned *Iran-e Farda* and a member of the Iran Liberation Movement, a centrist political movement barely tolerated by the authorities; journalist Jala'ipur; writer Ali-Reza Alavi-Tabar; and Changiz Pahlavan, an academic, sociologist, and writer. Kar, Eshkevari, Ganji, Lahiji, Afshari, and Sahabi all spent various periods in jail. At the time of writing, Alavi-Tabar and Jala'ipur had both been summoned for questioning. Pahlavan did not immediately return to Iran.

13. Two versions of the transcript of the tape appeared to be in circulation, although differences between them were not major. One version, translated from *Al-Sharq al-Awsat*, 4 June 2000, appeared in *FBIS/NESA*, 6 July 2000.
14. Behzad Nabavi, a leader of the Mujahedin of the Islamic Revolution and one of the architects of the 2nd Khordad Front, calculated after the runoffs in May that the 2nd Khordad coalition, its affiliates, and supporters held 200 seats, the conservatives 58, and independents 18. (The religious minorities accounted for 5 seats, while 9 additional seats, in constituencies where the vote had been invalidated by the Council of Guardians, remained to be filled.) See *FBIS/NESA* 7 May 2000, quoting Nabavi's remarks published in *Iran,* and *FBIS/NESA*, 8 May 2000, citing the same Nabavi interview as reported by IRNA. According to other reports, seats in 11 constituencies had been invalidated and remained to be filled in runoffs. Nabavi suggested that some 150 deputies were members of the Islamic Iran Participation Front (IIPF), the party run by Khatami's brother, which constitutes the core Khatami group in parliament. I have added the results of the Teheran vote (not finalized when Nabavi spoke) to Nabavi's figures to get the above totals.

    But Nabavi's figures appear inflated. The votes cast in the House in elections for the officers of the new Majlis seemed to provide a better gauge of the distribution of forces in the new parliament. Mehdi Karrubi of the Militant Clerics Society, a compromise and supposedly centrist candidate that the Khatami camp was persuaded to accept even though he was not their first choice, became Speaker, with 186 out of 249 votes cast. Karrubi could count on conservative votes but probably lost some reformist ones. Behzad Nabavi and Mohammad Reza Khatami were elected first and second deputy Speakers, with, respectively, 155 and 135 votes, which suggests that, the conservatives aside, the substantial bloc of some 50–60 votes of deputies affiliated with the Militant Clerics Society, the small bloc of about 15 deputies belonging to the Executives of Construction, and some independents would not always vote with the Khatami people. The usually reliable *Payam-e Emruz* (Tir/Mordad 1379, p. 40) reported that 150 of the deputies were fully committed to the 2nd Khordad agenda. This is very close to the number that Nabavi, in the remarks cited above, described as members of Khatami's own party, the IIPF. In a May 31 despatch to Agence France-Presse, Kianouche Dorrani also gave the IIPF 150 seats in the new Majlis. Even 150 votes would give the pro-Khatami faction a solid majority, with likely additional votes coming from affiliates and supporters.
15. Voice of the Islamic Republic of Iran, cited in *FBIS/NESA*, 14 April 2000.
16. Voice of the Islamic Republic of Iran, cited in *FBIS/NESA*, 20 April 2000.
17. "Khamenei Sermon Stresses Islam, Unity," *FBIS/NESA*, 12 May 2000.
18. "Khamenei Addresses Judicial Officials," *FBIS/NESA*, 27 June 2000. I have slightly corrected the translation.
19. "Khamene'i's 9 July Address to Scholars, Senior Officials," *FBIS/NESA*, 11 July 2000.
20. Susan Sachs, "Top Iranian Cleric Defends Closing of Reformist Publications," *New York Times*, 29 April, 2000.
21. Seminary teachers, in *'Asr-e Azadegan*, 8 April 2000, cited in *FBIS/NESA*, 13 April 2000. Ayatollah Amini, in *FBIS/NESA*, 8 May 2000.
22. See reference in Susan Sachs, "Iran Reformers Feeling Pressed by Hardliners," *New York Times*, 25 April 2000.
23. "IRGC Issues Statement Supporting Khamenei," *FBIS/NESA*, 16 April 2000.
24. The text of the letter appears in both *Hamshahri* and *Jomhuri-ye Islami* of 7 August 2000.

# THE ISLAMIC REPUBLIC OF IRAN

CHAPTER 3

## *Civil-Military Relations in the Islamic Republic of Iran*
### Ahmed S. Hashim

The role of the military in Iranian politics seems essentially unexplored when examined against the backdrop of the enormous output of literature on civil-military relations generated in the past four decades on societies as disparate as Argentina and Zimbabwe. Studies of Iran have consumed a great deal of scholarly energies. Historians, sociologists, and political scientists have applied their diverse skills to reach some sort of reasonable understanding concerning the origins and consequences of the Pahlavi dynasty for Iran; the 1979 Iranian revolution; and the evolution of the Islamic Republic since then. Over the past decade and a half, there has been a proliferation of works dealing with the performance of the Iranian military during the Iran-Iraq War, the post-war modernization programs of the Iranian armed forces, and Iran's attempts to acquire weapons of mass destruction.

However, the actual link between politics and the military appears to have been generally neglected in the literature. Iran has never of course enjoyed the dubious distinction of constant military intervention or rule along the lines of so many post-WWII "developing" states. Indeed, it stands in stark contrast to its immediate neighbors, such as Pakistan, Iraq, and Turkey, where military establishments have repeatedly intervened in the political process over the course of the past several decades.

Few scholars in the field of comparative politics or of Iranian studies saw the necessity of studying the sociopolitical role of the Iranian military when they examined the monumental 1979 revolution.[1] The lack of attention given to the military dimensions of revolutions arises out of the tendency among most scholars to believe that once the underlying socioeconomic and political causes of revolution are in place, revolution is practically inevitable.[2] This is ahistorical. No one disputes that short-, medium-, and long-term causes of revolution are key to an understanding of why a revolution occurs. Indeed, revolutions have been one of the most fruitful areas of study in comparative politics. Scholars have constructed elaborate theories and then applied them to case studies.[3] Still, students of revolutions should pay closer attention to the fears of revolutionaries—often available in their writings after they have seized power—who have to deal with the potential backlash of military power as they set out on their endeavor. It was Lenin, the archetypal revolutionary, who stated: "No revolution of the masses can triumph without the help of a portion of the armed forces that sustained the old regime."[4] This help can range from actively siding with the revolutionaries to merely standing by and watching the *ancien regime* succumb to the revolutionary tide.

There is little that represents a consistent and analytical attempt to look at the Iranian military in its own political and social right. More broadly, there is little that attempts to link the Iranian military experience to the universal literature on military sociology and politics, with its emphasis on how and why soldiers are drawn into the political process and the way they act on this involvement. Finally, what little that exists on Iranian civil-military relations fails to compare or contrast the Iranian military experience with that of other Middle Eastern states and other developing countries.

There are, of course, many societies in which civil-military relations remain unexplored. In some societies, where the potential for serious domestic conflict is all too real, the neglected link between the military and politics is especially surprising. The Islamic Republic of Iran is currently in the midst of domestic turmoil; if the legitimacy of the state and its ideology were to witness a catastrophic collapse, much of politics would then be reduced to the exercise of coercion. All social structures are dependent to some degree on the use of force, but there is a difference between putative and applied force, and the distinction is eroded where the state faces a crisis of legitimacy. In these circumstances, individuals and institutions with access to the instruments and technologies of violence—the military being in the forefront—can, and often do, play a decisive role in the political process. As Alfred Stepan notes in his study of the Brazilian military, the response of soldiers to conflict in divided societies provides "a large part of the answer to the question of who wins and who loses, who has power and who has not." He adds further:

> When the armed forces prevent the winner of a presidential election from taking office, when they remove a government whose economic policies favor one class at the expense of another, or when they stage a coup to preserve the dominance of a racial, religious, tribal or linguistic group in a communally divided society, their actions clearly help determine which social groups will gain or lose some of their most important values. Even those coups that are unrelated to group conflicts, primarily involving the defense of corporate interests, are likely to affect political and economic outcomes.[5]

This chapter is an analytical history of civil-military relations in the Islamic Republic of Iran. However, the country's past history of civil-military relations is critical to an understanding of the more recent evolution of civil-military relations. In this context, the Iranian military has been key in the process by which power has been seized in the past (Reza Shah in 1921), and by which power has been retained (again, Reza Shah between 1921 and 1941, and Mohammed Reza Shah between 1941 and 1979). Its inability, or failure, to support the Shah in 1978–1979 proved to be a critical factor in the fall of the Pahlavi dynasty. If the Islamic Republic of Iran does not succeed in resolving its domestic problems, the military is likely to play an increasingly critical role in the political life of the country.

While space will prevent a lengthy theoretical analysis of civil-military relations, the most salient aspects of the voluminous literature need to be addressed to provide a framework for our analysis of civil-military relations in the Islamic Republic.[6] Civil-military relations represent an enduring problem in politics. Over the course of human history, states created military forces to protect them and their people, from both external and internal enemies. Yet, states have also grown to fear that very instrument of violence that they created, and on which they often spent vast resources.

The military does not have to intervene overtly in the political process (i.e. taking over power by means of a coup d'état) for it to have an important behind-the-scenes role. For example, the mere expression of opinions by the senior officer corps on any topic of national import constitutes intervention in the political process. On the other hand, there may be situations in which the civilian authorities do their utmost to prevent the military from intervening in the political process. Yet, these very same civilian authorities may ultimately rely on the military for much of their legitimacy or power. Shah Mohammed Reza, for example, totally muzzled his senior officer corps and forbade the officers from playing a role in the political process. Yet, the Imperial Iranian military was a key *institution of the state*, because the Shah relied on it so much.

Thus the Imperial Iranian military was always a *political* force. In this context, this chapter will posit that the military has played an important political role in Iran ever since the 1920s.[7] Moreover, the fact that the Iranian military has not yet mounted a coup attempt—at least in recent years—does not mean that it has not tried to do so in the past or that it may not try to do so in the near future. Furthermore, non-intervention in the political process, particularly during times of crisis—including revolution—is as meaningful a statement as actually taking direct political action either against or for the revolutionary forces. On the other hand, inaction on the part of the military during a revolutionary situation almost always by default favors revolutionary forces.

## Historical Background

Iran is an ancient state with a respectable and sophisticated military tradition that goes back many centuries.[8] In ancient times the military was under the control of a high-ranking official, the *Iran-sepahbadh,* who was the minister of war, the highest-ranking officer of the army, and a senior diplomat who could also negotiate peace treaties. He reported directly to the emperor and was part of the small circle of royal councilors.

Unlike several of its neighbors, however, neither ancient nor early modern Iran developed a unified military establishment under national control. The lack of a national army was particularly evident as Iran entered the early modern era. From the seventeenth century onward, Iranian rulers, particularly those of the Qajar dynasty, relied on tribal levies or small and ineffective quasi-regular forces that were haphazardly trained by European officers on loan. Both the tribes and the European officers intervened in the Iranian political process with depressing regularity. In the mid-nineteenth century, defeats at the hands of Ottoman and Russian forces persuaded the rulers of the Qajar dynasty that they needed to create a modern military institution that would not be dependent on the tribes or European powers.[9]

While the Qajari rulers managed to break their link with and dependence upon the tribes for military power, they were largely unsuccessful in their endeavors to create a single unified and modern national military force. Moreover, the attempts to create a modern military establishment merely increased the roles of foreign powers. By the late nineteenth and early twentieth centuries, Iran witnessed the emergence of several quasi-national military forces that were trained, led, and influenced by different European countries. Among the most important were the Cossack Brigade, whose senior officers were Russian; the Gendarmerie, led by Swedes and Germans; and the South Persia Rifles, under the command of British officers.[10] These forces played significant roles in the political process, including the Constitutional Revolution, but always with mixed results. More often than not, these European-trained and officered forces placed the interests of their own respective countries above those of the Iranian monarch whom they ostensibly served.

By the end of the second decade of the twentieth century, many Iranian nationalists had become affronted by the precipitous decline in the political fortunes of their country. In particular they resented the influence of so many powers in the court at Teheran, an influence that was often exercised by means of their control of the quasi-independent military forces. Indeed, some of these forces were used by the Iranian monarch with the connivance of foreign powers to put down progressive forces seeking to do away with tyrannical and arbitrary government and establish some semblance of constitutional order in the country.[11] One such individual was a senior Iranian officer in the Cossack Brigade, Colonel Reza Khan, who ultimately rose to the rank of commander of the brigade.

Reza Khan used that position to stage the first modern coup in Iranian history, on 21 February 1921. This move was undertaken against the corrupt politicians in the capital, Teheran, and was not aimed at overthrowing the Shah. Reza Khan helped a reformist civilian, Sayyid Zia Tabatabai, come to power as prime minister. In turn, Sayyid Zia promised many reforms, but managed to alienate key people in the process, including the man who had brought him to power, Reza Khan himself. Following the elimination of Sayyid Zia in May 1921, Reza Khan was elevated to the position of minister of war. He used this position to cement his control over the various security forces in the country—by merging them into one force and removing foreign officers—and to put down various dissident and separatist movements throughout the country.

Over the years, Reza Khan steadily accumulated power, as he set about creating a unified national army out of the disparate military forces in the country. In the process, he quashed a serious threat from the Gendarmerie, whose officers resented the rise of Reza Khan.[12] Five years after his first coup, Reza Khan undertook the second coup in Iran's history when he overthrew the moribund Qajar dynasty and had himself crowned Reza Shah of the Pahlavi dynasty in late 1926. Without a doubt, the army constituted the key institution in the new Pahlavi dynasty, and the new ruler relied on it to maintain his power and enhance his legitimacy.[13] Yet, at the same time, Reza Shah tried to keep the army officers as far away from the political process as possible. This, of course, stands in marked contrast to the period when he merely headed the army and used it to promote his political agenda. By late 1926, he was the civilian authority, and the undue influence of the army in the political process was clearly unwelcome.[14]

In this context, to keep the army loyal and satisfied that its corporate interests were being taken care of, Reza Shah devoted considerable attention and resources to the army. He continued to enlarge and modernize it, so that, over time, it became quite professional. He paid particular attention to the senior officer corps, whom he kept loyal by means of promotions and lavish benefits. However, Reza Shah purged, dismissed, or rotated those who he thought were too independent or who constituted a potential threat to the dynasty. Last but not least, he kept the army preoccupied with putting down domestic threats to internal security.[15]

Despite its early successes, the new unified national army failed one key test: defense of the homeland against foreign invaders. During World War II, Iran adopted a pro-German neutrality that was opposed by both Britain and the Soviet Union. Furthermore, Iran was an important producer of oil and a supply route to the Soviet Union. In the event, Teheran's haphazard policies during the war placed the country on a collision course with the Allies. This was ultimately resolved by a joint Anglo-Soviet invasion in 1941. Following the defeat and utter collapse of his army, Reza Shah abdicated in favor of his shy and reserved son, Mohammed Reza, on 16 September 1941. The new Shah had to rebuild the legitimacy of the Pahlavi dynasty if he was to survive. To succeed, he needed to rebuild the armed forces and establish his and the monarchy's political ascendancy and control over them.

To his credit, Mohammed Reza Shah managed to persuade the Americans, not without some reluctance on their part, to rebuild and modernize the Iranian armed forces. However, as far as the issue of civilian or, more accurately, monarchical control over the armed forces, Mohammed Reza Shah was to face considerable difficulties for a long period of time. In this context, in the early 1950s, a "recalcitrant" nationalist prime minister, Mohammed Mossadeq, challenged the monarch for control over the armed forces, among other things. Mossadegh made plenty of promises to the armed forces, but he was never able to swing the officer corps to his side. Lacking an institutional power base, Mossadegh was removed from power by the Shah and his Western allies. Nonetheless, over the course of a decade, that is to say, between 1953 and 1963, the Shah's authority over the armed forces was challenged on three separate occasions, each time with serious implications for the stability of civil-military relations.[16]

These crises underscored to the Shah the centrality of the armed forces in Iranian political life. The Shah concluded that the military must remain under tight monarchical control, that it must not interfere in political life, and that it must be carefully monitored for unlawful political activities. Toward that end, he took his title of supreme military commander very seriously and, as he once put it: "In this country, if the king is not the commander-in-chief of the armed forces, anything can happen."[17] By the late 1960s, the Shah had succeeded in establishing full control over the armed forces. The process actually began with the creation of an internal security organization to monitor the military. In the event, an elaborate state security and intelligence organization (*Sazeman-e-Amniyat-e-va Ettela'at Keshvar*, or SAVAK) was developed. Other organizations, such as military intelligence and the Special Bureau of Intelligence, also kept close watch over the armed forces.

Nevertheless, the Shah did not merely rely on security organs to control and maintain the loyalty of the armed forces, he also tightly involved himself in the most routine of military administrative matters, such as vetting the promotion of officers above the rank of major. He encouraged rivalry among senior officers and prevented the emergence of a cohesive officer corps. Officers from different branches of the armed forces rarely met one another except in the presence of the Shah. The monarch satisfied the corporate interests of the armed forces. No elite group in the political establishment was more favored than the officer corps. They were provided with special privileges that included augmented pay, subsidized housing, free education for offspring, and heavily subsidized military stores. Finally, the Shah engaged in a furious military build-up from the early 1970s onward that gave Iran one of the most impressive military forces in the developing world by 1979.

None of this mattered much when the Iranian revolution destroyed the Pahlavi dynasty in 1979. Many analysts have convincingly argued, on the basis of historical evidence, that if a beleaguered government manages to maintain the loyalty of the armed forces and uses it decisively, no revolution can succeed.[18] The Shah neither retained the loyalty of the armed forces—the senior officer corps remained immobile, proving to be incapable of action, and the rank and file fraternized with the revolutionaries—nor was himself able to act decisively to stem the tide of revolution. Furthermore, the revolutionaries, particularly the clerical establishment under the charismatic leadership of Ayatollah Khomeini, targeted the armed forces, imploring them not to support the tyrannical rule of the Pahlavis by shooting their fellow countrymen. Soldiers were also encouraged to desert and go home. They were even provided with cash and civilian clothes to do so. Finally, by the late 1970s the military had little experience in dealing with domestic discontent. This is ironic in light of the fact that the military had been an instrument of domestic control from 1945 to the early 1960s.

The Shah left Iran in January 1979 as his army collapsed around him. A caretaker government under Prime Minister Shahpour Bakhtiar was unable to retain the loyalty of the senior officers, many of whom followed the Shah into exile or began negotiating with the revolutionaries. On 1 February 1979 Ayatollah Khomeini returned to Iran to a tumultuous welcome. For a while the army remained precariously balanced between the revolutionaries and the disintegrating government of Shahpour Bakhtiar. On 11 February, the Supreme Council of the Armed Forces met one final time. After heated discussions between moderates (those who favored a deal with the revolutionary forces) and hawks (those who favored supporting Bakhtiar), leading senior officers decided to declare the military neutral in the struggle between the Shah's last government and the revolutionaries. Perhaps realizing the futility of the struggle, Prime Minister Bakhtiar fled, and the revolution triumphed.

*Civil-Military Relations after 1979*
The Islamic Republic has gone through three phases. The "first republic" (1979–1989) was a period characterized by extreme revolutionary turmoil, internal opposition, threats, and war. The military had ample opportunity to try and intervene in the political process, but it either could not or chose not to—notwithstanding a number of amateurish and poorly planned coup attempts. Nor did it choose to intervene in the political process at the height of the bloody war with neighboring Iraq. The "second republic" (1990–1997) under President Rafsanjani, was a more stable period in Iranian political history, but was characterized by some serious tensions in civil-military relations. Under the "third republic" (1997–present), Iran has been trying to move toward a post-revolutionary era of constitutionalism and normalcy with President Mohammed Khatami. These attempts have, however, met with strenuous opposition on the part of entrenched conservative forces who fear that liberalization could lead to the unraveling of the Islamic Republic. Conservative forces rely on a number of civilian institutions, and legal means, to stymie further efforts to bring about progressive change in the country. Ultimately, they may try to rely on sympathetic forces within the military establishment to eliminate any "breakdown in law and order."

*Civil-Military Relations: The First Republic, 1979–1988*
Once the victory against the Shah had been consummated, the various revolutionary parties fell out among themselves. They had very different agendas from one another. It was the clerics who emerged as the ultimate victors of the revolution. One of the reasons they succeeded in "hijacking" the revolution was because of better organizational skills, but also because they managed to gain control over the remnants of the armed forces. If there is one thing that Iran's clerics do not suffer from, it is naiveté, or idealism. Iran's revolutionary clerics recognized the importance of military power in Islamic history. Indeed, to a large extent Islamic history is military history, and no other religion has been so intricately tied with military endeavor. From the very outset of the revolution, the clerics understood the role of the military as a key instrument of the Pahlavi state. Not surprisingly, during the course of the revolution, they devoted considerable effort to detaching that instrument of state power from its moorings. Following their revolutionary victory, the task was to

ensure control of the armed forces so that it would not succumb to "counterrevolutionary" tendencies (i.e., try to bring the Shah back) or become an instrument in the hands of other revolutionary parties with whom the clerics had differences.

In this context, the clerics set out to purge the armed forces. This has been extensively analyzed in various studies. Suffice it to state that the purges had three specific goals: (a) punish the military for its "sins" against the people during the course of the revolution; (b) remove all vestiges of Pahlavism and imperial culture; and (c) "Islamize" the military (i.e., create an ideological force). To consolidate their ideological control over the armed forces, the clerics also set up the Ideological-Political Directorate of the Armed Forces (IPD), or *Modiriyat-e-Aghidat-e-va Siyasi Artesh*. The IPD infiltrated its clerics and agents from the Joint Staff down to the platoon level. One of the more effective tactics of the IPD clerics was to promote officers from religious families or from those with familial ties to clerical families. The clerics also ensured that a wide variety of security and intelligence services maintained close watch on the armed forces.

Last but not least, the clerics created their own military force, the *Pasdaran-e-Engelab-e-Islami*, or the Islamic Revolutionary Guards Corps (IRGC), in early May 1979. The missions of the IRGC were to protect the revolution, maintain domestic law and order, fight dissident movements, and balance/watch the regular armed forces, of whom the clerics maintained a healthy suspicion. Recruits tended to be ethnic Persians or Azeris between the ages of 17 and 28 and generally hailed from poorer or religious families. Applicants had to undergo a rigorous test of their religious and spiritual credentials. Once an applicant was approved for membership in the IRGC, he was sent to a military installation for training in basic fieldcraft and small unit tactics.[19] To put down separatist movements in the various peripheral regions of the country, the revolutionary government used both the regular army and the IRGC extensively. Much like the Pahlavis before them, the clerics were a nationalistic elite that believed in a centralized government, and frowned extensively on the autonomist aspirations of the country's ethnic minorities. Consequently, both the regular army and the Revolutionary Guards were dominated by Persians and Azeris, the two dominant ethnic groups in the country, and thus did not object to their use as forces for centralization. Both groups cooperated to put down a Kurdish insurgency in Iranian Kurdistan.

Still, both regular army–Revolutionary Guards cooperation and civil-military relations were put to the test during the sanguinary Iran-Iraq War (1980–1988). Early in the war, Iran's response to the Iraqi invasion was haphazard and uncoordinated, which in turn added to the mistrust already existing between the military and the Pasdaran. Furthermore, attempts by revolutionary Iran's first president, Abol Hasan Bani-Sadr, to promote the regular military as the premier force in the struggle against Iraq roused the ire and suspicions of the clerical establishment and of Revolutionary Guards officers. Senior government officials concluded that Bani Sadr suffered from Bonapartist tendencies and was hoping to march back to Teheran at the head of a military column to claim political power for himself, after claiming success on the battlefield. For its part, the IRGC accused Bani Sadr of trying to make the regular army "a tool in his own hands, so that he could wield it as a powerful weapon against the Imam's Line."[20]

The demise of Bani Sadr in 1981 was followed by the creation of a unique military structure that was able to appeal to and mobilize different segments of the population in the struggle against Iraq. This three-tiered military structure was divided into the regular army, the Revolutionary Guards, and the Mobilization of the Oppressed, or *Basij*. Middle-class nationalists found their place in the technologically developed regular army. For this group, the war was a national struggle to defend Iran's territorial integrity and honor against a despised enemy, the Arab. Islamic revolutionaries and religiously oriented youth from more humble backgrounds flocked to the Revolutionary Guards. Young and old from rural areas volunteered for the Basij. For members of these two latter organizations, the struggle against Iraq was a "holy war" in defense of Islam against the atheists of the Iraqi Baath Party.[21]

This three-tiered military structure represented the high point in the emergence of harmonious civil-military relations during wartime, and it was responsible for the Iranian victories in Khuzistan in the spring and summer of 1982. Once Iran sought to move into Iraq in its own counter-invasion, the three-tiered military structure began to unravel and problems reappeared in civil-military relations. The regular army was not too enthusiastic about invading Iraq in 1982. However, it chose not to oppose the wishes of Ayatollah Khomeini. The Revolutionary Guards showed more enthusiasm for the crusade, but as Iranian offensives into Iraq failed in the teeth of Iraqi defenses, the Guards' leadership complained about lack of support from the regular army. The Basij proved unequal to the task of supporting an endeavor as complicated as the invasion of Iraq. Indeed, it ended up being a burden on the Revolutionary Guards, which was responsible for its training and logistical needs. As Iran's war effort faltered in 1987, the Revolutionary Guards Corps not only lost large numbers of well-trained soldiers but also its enthusiasm for the war. The complete unraveling of the three-tiered military structure into three uncoordinated forces fighting their own separate wars aggravated matters. Iran was decisively defeated on the battlefield in the summer of 1988 by superior Iraqi forces. Last-ditch efforts to create better and more effective coordination between Iran's forces failed to stem the tide of defeat. In early June 1988, Ayatollah Khomeini appointed Majlis Speaker Ali Akbar Hashemi-Rafsanjani—a man heavily involved in Iran's war effort—acting commander-in-chief of the armed forces. His mission was to ensure full coordination among the various forces and to eliminate waste and inefficiency in the conduct of the war.[22]

Although armies returning home in defeat almost invariably pose a threat to the stability of civil-military relations, the Iranian case illustrated fundamental changes in this outlook. To their credit, the clerics managed to quickly and effectively thwart any threat to their power in the aftermath of defeat, by rapidly addressing and rectifying its causes.

## Civil-Military Relations: The Second Republic, 1989–1996

Ali Akbar Hashemi-Rafsanjani was elected president of the Islamic Republic twice. His first term ran from 1989 to 1993, and the second from 1994 to 1997. Both terms were characterized by some very tense periods in civil-military relations. At one point the tension in civil-military relations stemmed from Revolutionary Guards fears that its corporate interests—embedded in its sense of identity as a separate entity from the regular army—were in the process of being threatened by civilian authorities. In the mid-1990s the tension in civil-military relations resulted from the state's request that the military establishment put down growing urban disturbances.

### Revolutionary Guards' Corporate Interests

The Iran-Iraq War ended in a catastrophe for the country's armed forces. In the aftermath of the war, Teheran had to allay the suspicions of the Islamic Revolutionary Guards Corps (IRGC) that they would bear the brunt of the blame for operational failures at the front, particularly those during 1988. While the regular army had always counseled caution, and had adopted a conservative and methodical approach to operations, the IRGC was always more confident of victory in the face of Iraq's growing technological superiority. Needless to say, this confidence proved misplaced in the wake of humiliating defeats suffered at the front between April and July 1988. Not surprisingly, much of the blame for Iran's precipitous collapse at the front in the final months of the war lay with the Revolutionary Guards. Indeed, at one stage, Revolutionary Guards commander Mohsen Rezai was publicly humiliated when he was forced to admit to certain mistakes at the front. Even the regular army was not spared the purging of some of its senior officers. Nonetheless, to their credit, the ruling clerics admitted that the government made mistakes over the course of the war as well. In this context, the ruling clerics did not go out of their way to blame the armed forces for the defeat.

In a speech to IRGC commanders in October 1988, then–President Rafsanjani tackled the issue—of the post-war Revolutionary Guards Corps—head on, as IRGC commanders were seriously worried that their prospects were in jeopardy. Rafsanjani sought to allay such fears, assuming they existed, and praised the IRGC. He stressed that they were, indeed, an integral element in Iran's conception of national defense. He also emphasized their role in the defense of Iran's territories when the Iraqis invaded Iran in 1980. Rafsanjani went so far as to clarify that the IRGC excelled in its defensive activities against the invader, stating:

> There is a time when the enemy comes to fight against us; when he brings about conditions like those in Afghanistan; when someone comes and occupies your land; occupies your homes; or like Palestine; or like in parts of Lebanon; or like ourselves at the beginning of the war when they attacked our homes and brought the war deep into our country. Under those conditions one may say that one should fight with Molotov cocktails or with stones or by strapping bombs around our waist and going under the tanks, as some people say. This is one kind of situation . . . [23]

Still, Rafsanjani added—somewhat cautiously—that the IRGC has to change with the times. In the early stages of the Iran-Iraq War, the IRGC was characterized by a loose and informal structure, but developed into a more structured and better-disciplined force over the course of the years. The end result, Iranian leaders anticipated, would be the emergence of a formal military institution that was more disciplined, better trained, and able to handle heavy weapons. In Rafsanjani's own words:

> The IRGC now is not as it was in the early days. Now it has organization; its units and departments are also organized. However, these organizations should be completely military organizations.... This is one of the responsibilities of the IRGC commanders, to think and to change their organization into a military one, a completely military organization. Training should be taken very seriously. I spoke earlier about the time when we were attacked. Well, with only a few hours preparation the least one could do was to equip oneself with G-3s or Kalashnikovs and to fire them. However, that is not sufficient for us now. We have gradually come to realize—the IRGC commanders have realized—that matters such as rank and hierarchy, salary—a just level of pay—and so on constitute the necessities for an armed force ... if we are to rely on the IRGC as an armed force, if the regime is to serve God, the IRGC must not think that when it is attacked it can fight with Molotov cocktails.[24]

Following Rafsanjani's election to the presidency, Teheran prudently decided that it would drop the idea of merging Iran's wartime forces into a single, large operation. Yet, it also became clear that Iran could never have efficient and organized forces if the three-tiered structure was maintained intact, without changes. As it stood, the structure fostered massive waste and unhealthy competition between regular troops and IRGC units, and brought about duplication of efforts in the defense industries.[25] Rafsanjani was determined to bring about greater efficiency to Iran's military forces, even if they were to remain divided into three separate organizations. The IRGC would become more efficient by becoming a professional force with ranks and a hierarchical structure similar to that of the regular armed forces. Most of the new IRGC ranks were equivalent to those of the regular army, a fact that may have generated some unease among both forces. Ayatollah Khomeini's designated successor, Ayatollah Khamenei, echoed and supported Rafsanjani's view that the Revolutionary Guards Corps must professionalize itself and pay attention to training and modern and scientific methods of warfare.[26] However, to allay putative fears of the Revolutionary Guards Corps concerning its future, Ayatollah Khamenei declared that the IRGC would remain in existence to "carry out its crucial responsibility of militarily defending the Revolution."[27]

Finally, in order to maintain the loyalty of the armed forces as well as to ensure the country's national security, the ruling clerics moved with surprising alacrity following the end of the war with Iraq to cater to the military's corporate interests, emphasizing benefits and modern weaponry. As the 1990s progressed, and the country suffered economic crises and isolation, it became clear that the Islamic Republic would have serious problems in meeting these rekindled corporate interests. Given the fact that a major cause of dissatisfaction on the part of senior officers in any army is the lack of an adequate supply of weapons and resources, this could constitute a problem for the civilian authorities in Iran. Yet, it is not clear that the armed forces have blamed the civilian authorities for Iran's inability to arm itself properly, with sufficient sophisticated conventional weapons, over the past decade. Indeed, the civilian authorities have successfully managed to argue that too much reliance on foreign weapons is contrary to the national interest, and that such weapons do not add much to national security. Noticeably, and while one should be aware of propagandistic claims, Iran has made tremendous strides in the development of its own domestic arms industries. This has been a source of considerable pride for Iranian officers, many of whom extol the virtues of domestically produced weapons quite openly.

### *The Armed Forces and Law and Order*
By the mid-1990s President Rafsanjani's position in the structure of the ruling elite had been weakened as a result of manifest failures in many areas. First, his socioeconomic programs that had managed to cause considerable distress to the lower classes—but did not manage to set Iran on the road to economic recovery—proved problematic. Moreover, many within the ruling hierarchy opposed the president and his technocratic, "Western-oriented" advisers. Second, Rafsanjani failed to significantly improve Iran's relations with the outside world. Third, he became embroiled in political infighting with conservative elements, at the expense of implementing his programs. The clearest symbol of his decline came in the June 1993 presidential elections when he was re-elected for his second and final term. Whereas Rafsanjani had received 95 percent of the votes in 1989, he managed a mere 63 percent in 1993.

To make matters worse, riots and demonstrations in shantytowns that crowded the major urban centers became regular occurrences during the course of 1994. To be sure, the worsening economic and social conditions during Rafsanjani's second term presented a situation that was fraught with potential dilemmas between the civilian authorities and the armed forces. A decline in law and order, especially in the volatile urban areas, constituted a dangerous situation for civilian authorities precisely because the armed forces could have stepped in. As military leaders frown on the task of putting down domestic grievances, the threat of a coup looms large.

In this context, both the IRGC and the regular army played critical roles during the August 1994 uprising in Qazvin, which alarmed the government. The refusal of the Qazvin garrison's IRGC commander to put down rioting by the city's population was endorsed by senior officers from both the regular army and the IRGC. Teheran airlifted a special internal rapid deployment security force to quell these disturbances, which they did rather brutally. Not long afterwards, a letter written by four senior officers representing the ground forces, the IRGC, the air force, and the paratroop/special Forces was sent to the political leadership. It called upon the leadership not to rely on or use the armed forces to quell popular manifestations of discontent.[28] The letter expressed the officers' deep concern over the "growing political, economic and social chaos in Iran."[29] Almost a month later, a respected former police-general, Azizollah Amir Rahimi warned the clerics that the continuation of their rule would lead to the "total annihilation of Iran and Islam." Furthermore, he called upon the Rafsanjani government to step down and organize free elections.[30]

While Teheran may have been alarmed by the reluctance of the armed forces to crush domestic discontent, it did not show it. Instead, it moved swiftly to ensure that the Basij would don the mantle of internal security force. In terms of size and commitment to the revolution, the Basij constitutes a formidable force. There are 300,000 full-time members, and in times of crisis, the government may be able to call upon another 1 million part-timers. The organization's budget was reportedly increased dramatically over the course of the mid-1990s.[31] Its members were provided with greater benefits and privileges to ensure their continued loyalty to the Islamic Republic.

In spite of severe socioeconomic and political problems that beset the country in the first half of the 1990s, the armed forces never directly intervened in the political process in the country, no doubt to the considerable relief of the ruling clerics. Under the circumstances, it was highly unlikely that the military ever thought of intervening to overthrow the political system. Senior officers probably sensed that any hasty actions would add to the country's political difficulties. Moreover, most probably realized that they had neither the political nor the administrative expertise—not to mention technical skills ranging from economic expertise to political savvy—to put Iran on the road to recovery and stability. Indeed, it was left to the existing civilian political system to find a way out of the impasse starting in the mid-1990s.

### Civil-Military Relations: The Third Republic, 1997–2000

In May 1997, Iranians elected a little-known cleric, Mohammed Khatami, to the presidency of the Islamic Republic. When Iranians went to the polls, citizens and foreign observers alike expected the conservative candidate, Majlis Speaker Ali Akbar Nateq Nouri, to win the election hands down. Instead, the underdog, Khatami, overwhelmingly defeated his opponent, winning 70 percent of the 29 million votes cast. Khatami's victory was facilitated by the desire for change on the part of millions of Iranians. They were encouraged by Khatami's promises to change Iran peacefully, and by his calls for limiting the influences of various power centers throughout the country, institutionalizing the rule of law, and ending Iran's regional and international isolation.[32]

On a superficial level, the military played no role in this election, as the overall reaction was supportive of the assumptions made earlier, that military intervention in the political process need not be measured solely by displays of military might in the streets or, *in extremis,* by undertaking a coup. Nevertheless, disturbing signs of politicization within the armed forces, particularly in the Revolutionary Guards, were apparent during the presidential elections. Against a ban on the involvement of the armed forces in politics, Pasdaran chief Mohsen

Rezai, along with other senior Guards officers, sided with the conservative candidate. Inasmuch as the radical right or conservatives viewed the rise of reform-oriented moderates as paving the way for the revolution to deviate from its true path, this frightened senior Revolutionary Guards leaders, because of their extensive socioeconomic stake in the system. This political partisanship on the part of the Revolutionary Guards leadership led to criticism of the force in the pro-Khatami press. Moreover, it roused the fear of the ruling clerical establishment that any political partisanship on the part of the armed forces during the elections could open the floodgates to further armed forces politicization. What aggravated the situation further was that the Revolutionary Guards had developed, over the years, a strong tendency toward politicization. Ayatollah Khomeini and other senior members of the clerical regime from the early days of the creation of the Revolutionary Guards had noticed this tendency.[33] As the political situation in Iran took a direction that was less and less to its liking, the IRGC began to exhibit greater signs of involvement in the process.

In an effort ostensibly designed to soothe people's fears, Mohsen Rezai stated that the Revolutionary Guards should refrain from involvement in politics and from taking sides between political groups. Nonetheless, he felt compelled to issue a warning: "(But) if domestic political issues end up as threats against the Islamic Revolution, in that case the Basij and revolutionary forces will also carry out their task within the framework of the law."[34] It is not quite clear what Rezai meant by his statement. Did he mean that if the political situation between the reformers and the hardliners worsened, the Revolutionary Guards would step into the political arena? Under such circumstances, and if they were to be that involved, would that not constitute a partisan involvement on the side of conservative elements? Or, did he mean that the Revolutionary Guards would move to re-establish law and order, if there were a danger of political violence erupting in the urban centers? Finally, could he have meant that the Revolutionary Guards would step into the political arena if there were a threat to the corporate interests of the Revolutionary Guards?

### *Khatami and the IRGC*
President Khatami's political, socioeconomic, cultural, and foreign policy agenda, briefly discussed above, represented a threat to both the ideological and corporate interests of the Revolutionary Guards. It also endangered the Guards' conception of Iranian national security and its global orientation. To be sure, Khatami used the Guards' expressions of hostility to criticize what he perceived as a dangerous process of politicization. On 15 September 1997, for example, he exhorted the country's armed forces to stay out of politics, adding that the armed forces should abstain from factional politics. A few days later, Mohsen Rezai stepped down from his post, as a result of pressure exerted by the Supreme Leader, who—presumably—wished to avoid a potentially disruptive tug of war between hardliners and reformers.

Yet, on two separate occasions, the new commander of the Guards, General Rahim Safavi, issued some strongly worded comments against the policies of President Mohammed Khatami. In April 1998, at a meeting of IRGC navy commanders held in the holy city of Qom, Safavi was quoted as saying that the Islamic Republic should "cut off the heads" or "tongues" of its opponents. The meeting was supposed to be confidential and off the record. However, a journalist from the state-owned Islamic Republic News Agency (IRNA) leaked its contents. In turn, this generated a storm of controversy in various political circles throughout the country. Some even feared that Safavi's confidential statements were not just merely symbolic of the IRGC's deep politicization, but indicated that hardliners in the organization were considering active intervention in the political process to reverse the reform tide.[35]

Safavi countered that his confidential statements concerning the threat to Iranian national security posed by Khatami's policies were taken out of context and distorted by enemies and counterrevolutionaries. To clarify his position, Safavi gave a lengthy interview to the IRGC's magazine, *Payam-e-Enqelab* (Message of Revolution), in which he emphatically stated that it was the business of the Guards to pay particular attention to all threats to the national security of Iran and to the security of the Islamic Republic, no matter where they may come from. As Safavi pointed out, the IRGC focused its attention on "ensuring and safeguarding the security and confronting the counter-revolution and internal threats."[36]

Importantly, Safavi implicitly criticized the cultural aspects of Khatami's policies, drawing—once again—sharp differences between the two agendas. Safavi believed that threats to Iran's Islamic culture would come from opening up to the West in an indiscriminate manner as envisioned by Khatami supporters. This, he argued, would constitute a serious threat to "our national security"[37] because many Westerners—and he quoted several—believed that the Islamic Republic could be overthrown only by changing the cultural mores of the population.

As the interview illustrated, Safavi was not one to shy away from controversy. In early June 1998 he made additional inflammatory remarks in front of 2,000 Basij students, when he issued venomous statements against the pragmatists and reformers:

> The nation must be vigilant. A third current [*jaryan-e-svvom*] is lying in wait and is trying to pit forces loyal to the revolution against each other. This third current, which is sponsored by foreigners, intends to destroy the foundations of religion in this country.... The IRGC is keeping this third current under observation and will not allow soiled hands to steal the Islamic revolution from the Iranian nation.[38]

Not surprisingly, these comments created a stir in Iran, and not only among the pragmatists/moderates who were the intended target, but also among leftists and the ruling circles. The pragmatists called upon the government to dismiss General Safavi. Leftist commentators suggested that the general change his military uniform for civilian attire, arguing that this would enable him to enter the political arena. The Supreme Leader, Ayatollah Khamenei, was profoundly disturbed by Safavi's verbal onslaught, not only because he supported the reformist policies of Khatami and his circle, but because of his deep fear of overt politicization of the armed forces. Khamenei called upon Safavi to desist from making any more political statements. The IRGC leadership issued its own warning that attacks on its commander should be halted.

Not only was the IRGC wary of Khatami's ideological platform, his calls for administrative and bureaucratic reforms to eliminate corruption and nepotism in the system of governance and from various government organizations could not have been viewed with anything but alarm by organizations like the IRGC. By the time Khatami had been elected to the presidency, the IRGC had added economic enterprise to its impressive credentials as a military and law enforcement force, as well as a civic organization that constructed railways and roads. The appointment of Mohsen Rafiqdoust, a former minister for the Revolutionary Guards Corps as head of the *Bonyad-e-Mosta'azafin,* or Foundation of the Oppressed—a charitable organization that looked after the needs of the poor but also managed a large economic corporation—fostered close links between the two organizations. This enabled the IRGC to expand its economic activities beyond the defense industry and into shipping, commerce, agriculture, industrial manufacturing, banking, and cross-border trade.

### *Khatami and the Regular Armed Forces*
Very little data exists on the views of the regular armed forces toward the Khatami "phenomenon." To be sure, President Khatami does not have control over the armed forces, whereas Ayatollah Khamenei, as Supreme Leader, does. It is interesting to note, in this context, that Major General Hasan Firuzabadi, until recently the Iranian Armed Forces chief of staff, expressed sympathy for Safavi's position, but *only in the sense of saying that he believed that Safavi's remarks in Qom were distorted by the media.* Irrespective of who controls what institutions, Khatami has shown that he is very much worried by the politicization prospects of the armed forces. Clearly, an overt military involvement in the political process would make a mockery of Khatami's plans for the establishment of the rule of law. In the president's own words:

> Our armed forces should refrain from political tendencies and preferences, and instead, engage in the daily improvement of their scientific, organizational, and operational capabilities. This has been the case up to now and will remain so, with the blessings of God, in the future.[39]

In the final analysis, however, it is unlikely that the senior echelons of the armed forces perceived Khatami as a threat to their corporate interests or as a threat to Iran's national security. There were a number of reasons for this.

First, Khatami is unlikely to reduce the budget or fringe benefits of the armed forces, despite his many calls for economic reforms. In fact, members of the regular armed forces receive pitiful salaries. Interestingly, the regular army is so over-staffed and underpaid that it welcomes the $16,000 from those who choose to avoid the draft. Thus, Khatami does not control the purse strings of the armed forces—that means that he is not capable of treading on the army's corporate interests in any major way.

Second, Khatami is a nationalist, and has come out in favor of enhancing Iran's defensive capabilities on numerous occasions. This position is similar to that of Ayatollah Khamenei, the Supreme Leader and the man who commands Iran's armed forces.

Third, notwithstanding the scare of war with the *Taleban* in Afghanistan, Khatami's foreign and security policies have actually led to some enhancement of Iran's security. Ironically, if Khatami were to succeed in ending the country's isolation, such a result may not be perceived with a degree of equanimity by different sectors of the armed forces. We may, indeed, see a revival of the differences between a technically oriented regular army and a less technically oriented Revolutionary Guards Corps. Inasmuch as the regular armed forces are more likely to welcome the end of Iran's isolation, they would most likely support a regime that would provide new access to high-tech conventional weapons. The situation may be further complicated by the existence of proponents of non-conventional weapons, who might see the reversal of the country's quest for "weapons of mass destruction" as a condition for the re-integration of the country into the international arena.

## Future Scenarios

In February 1999 the Islamic Republic entered the third decade of its existence. A year has gone by since the thirtieth anniversary of the Islamic Republic. This is a critical period in the history of the Republic and, indeed, of Iran itself. Still, it remains an open question as to whether the Islamic Republic under Mohammed Khatami has the ability to draw up and implement domestic and foreign policies that would lead to the emergence of a flourishing and vibrant open society, worthy of emulation by the rest of the Islamic world.

A number of scenarios are offered in which the armed forces are likely to play an important role.

### *Continuation of the Status Quo*
Under this current scenario, Iran lurches from one political and socioeconomic "mini-crisis" to the next without either the pragmatists or the conservatives being able to consolidate power. Street violence and riots remain at a low and stable level that does not threaten public law and order or the security of the Islamic Republic. Furthermore, and as long as there is no further political polarization, there may be very little room for the armed forces—or Guards—to intervene politically in any meaningful way. If the Guards' leadership were to weigh in on the side of the conservative faction, they could set off a chain of events that would be far worse than if they were to refrain from open political intervention. Any overt Guards intervention in the political process could invite warnings from the regular armed forces to heed the leadership's calls for political neutrality on the part of all armed forces. Similarly, overt Guards intervention in

the political process could ratchet up the level of political violence in the country, particularly in major urban centers. Simply stated, and in the *long term*, this scenario is simply unrealistic and it implies that Iran is going to continue indefinitely in a state of *unresolved* political and socioeconomic turmoil.

### *Pragmatist Consolidation versus Conservative Backlash*

Khatami and the reformers could slowly but surely consolidate their power and ultimately supplant the conservatives as the dominant political group. In this context, Iran would move further along toward the desired end-state of pragmatists. Several events seem to confirm the view that the pragmatists are entrenching themselves. Khatami and his supporters made significant advances with their victory in the local council elections of 26 February 1999. These elections proved to be a key stage in the realization of Khatami's presidential aspirations to liberalize the political climate. These local elections gave reformers a strategic advantage for the 2000 parliamentary balloting. The pragmatists and reformist camp gained control of the Majlis in the parliamentary elections of February 2000.

Yet, this runaway success for the reformers is not necessarily a healthy sign, because political parties are non-existent and the climate is heavily polarized. In the past, the conservative faction was able to effectively use state judicial and revolutionary institutions to thwart any pragmatists' consolidation. If the pragmatists deprive them of those non-violent methods, there is the possibility of a dangerous right-wing backlash that could be initiated by the Hizbullahi youth. To restore law and order, conservative elements might then call upon the IRGC to intervene in the political process. To date, notwithstanding the overwhelming victory of the reformist camp in the parliamentary elections, the conservatives still have considerable resources at their beck and call. They have used these resources to intimidate prominent liberals, to shut down reformist newspapers. Furthermore, they have the resources to put obstacles in the way of the reformist Majlis. Ultimately, the conservatives have a long way to go before they openly call upon segments of the armed forces to step in and restore "law and order." They also realize that political intervention by the military, or at least elements sympathetic to the conservative agenda, should be the last resort.

### *From Spontaneous Urban Uprisings to Revolutionary Outbreak: "It's the Economy, Stupid!"*

The intense struggles between pragmatists and conservatives are struggles between elites and the politically aware segments of the population over the future direction of the country, indeed, over the heart and soul of the Iranian "nation." Both sides attempt to mobilize various socioeconomic strata within society. Increasingly, what motivates the lower classes into political action most is the status of their short-term economic position, not esoteric debates over the direction of the country. If the economic situation were to worsen and begin to look anything like the situation in the early 1990s, chances of a resurgence of spontaneous urban riots, demonstrations, and even small-scale uprisings cannot be ruled out. These have often been complemented by numerous assassination attempts against public officials and seemingly random acts of terror bombings. Ever since the emergence of the Islamic Republic in 1979, Iran has had its fair share of these acts.

Still, the 1990s witnessed the outbreak of serious disturbances in a number of urban areas that had the potential of spreading. These began in Shiraz in April 1992 when war veterans rioted against government corruption. A month later, citizens of Arak, protesting the treatment of destitute citizens, attacked various symbols of government power. These attacks were replicated in various other cities throughout Iran, including Teheran and Mashad. The year 1994 was a particularly troublesome one for Teheran, as serious riots and assaults on state property occurred in Zahedan, Mashad, Qazvin, Islamshahr, and Akbarabad.

Such incidents by themselves are spontaneous and cannot lead to the overthrow of the system. Outbreaks of urban violence, however, have potentially serious repercussions for any government. If regular police forces are unable to put urban disturbances down, the government is often forced to call upon the military establishment. In some of the incidents in 1994, rioters managed to disarm the police, thus forcing authorities to deploy Revolutionary Guards and regular army units. It is an undeniable fact, as noted earlier, that military establishments do not like to take on the role of policing domestic opposition. In the case of Iran, even the Revolutionary Guards—one of whose tasks is maintenance of domestic security—have questioned their use as a police force against the people.

If Iran succumbs to another series of urban outbreaks, the implications for the government could be more serious than in the past. It is unlikely that any future disturbances will be limited to the expression of pent-up social frustration and rage on the part of the lower classes over economic deprivation. More ominously, there has been considerable erosion in the scale and scope of social support for the regime among lower-class elements, whose expectations have not been met.[40] But as Leon Trotsky once observed: "The mere existence of privations is not enough to cause an insurrection; if it were, the masses would always be in revolt."[41] One could be less charitable and quote Lenin's famous statement that, left to themselves, the masses are capable of no more than "trade union consciousness," that is to say, that they are incapable of concerted and sustained revolutionary action. In other words, the masses need to coordinate their actions with other social forces. These other social forces—the middle classes and the intellectuals—often provide the ideological justification for opposition to the existing state of affairs. Significant elements of Iran's politically aware and literate population are increasingly expressing their discontent as the Islamic Republic struggles through its third decade. The debates over Iran's future direction are no longer esoteric ones confined to a narrow group of the political elite, especially the ruling clergy. The legitimacy of the system that Ayatollah Khomeini left in place is increasingly under threat. Indeed, if the declining political and religious legitimacy of the system is paralleled by the coordinated social action of opponents, then opposition may start expressing itself in seemingly spontaneous urban uprisings. Teheran may then be forced to deploy its armed forces to quell the threat to "law and order." Initially, the armed forces may acquiesce in this role, but if the "disturbances" are not quelled in a timely manner, even the senior officer corps may begin to sense that something is wrong, particularly if civilian authorities have become increasingly dependent on the military for advice and formulation of crisis policies. This moment of recognition by senior officer leaders, that the situation is more serious than a law and order problem, also constitutes the recognition that their country is in an acute revolutionary phase. What the armed forces choose to do next will have a critical bearing on the continued existence of the political system and hence the success or failure of a revolution.

## Unraveling of the State and Re-emergence of Centrifugal Forces

Just as war expands the powers of the state over society, revolutions, as Alexis de Tocqueville put it, end up "augmenting the power and rights of the public authority." In this context, the Islamic revolution was very much a centralizing phenomenon, just as was the Pahlavi dynasty in the 1920s. Indeed, one of the major reasons that Reza Khan marched on Teheran was due to his fear that Iran was about to disintegrate as a unitary state. From the early days of the Islamic Revolution, it rapidly became clear that the ultimate victors of the revolution, the clerical establishment, had no intention of presiding over the devolution or decentralization of the state. Rather, the 1979 constitution adopted the nationalist creed of the 1906–7 Basic Law, declaring Iran a united state. In fact, the 1979 Iranian constitution was more uniformly centralizing than its older model. In retrospect, it can be seen that the Iranian clerical establishment was as nationalistic as the dynasty that it replaced. Toward that end, maintaining intact the central state was fully endorsed and supported by the armed forces, from the earliest days of the revolution. Neither the regular army nor the Revolutionary Guards showed any compunction in putting down the various outbreaks of ethnic dissidence in peripheral provinces. Under the circumstances, and given this legacy, if the armed forces were to perceive that civilian authorities were incapable of maintaining intact the state, then a takeover by a military strongman in the mold of Nader Shah or Reza Khan would not be as remote a possibility as may be believed. In fact, one of the main reasons given by Reza Shah for his seizure of power with the help of a unit of the army, the Cossack Brigade, was to prevent the physical and moral collapse of Iran. Reportedly, Reza Shah opined:

> There are two sorts of misfortunes either one of which, if not remedied, is able to destroy the national identity of any deteriorating race of people. These are domestic disorder and insecurity, and chaos of thoughts, ideas and morals.[42]

## Conclusion

Iran stands at a very critical stage in its political history. The Islamic Republic is undergoing considerable domestic turmoil. There is every indication that the vast Iranian military establishment may play a growing role in the future of the country. Yet, observers of the dynamic Iranian political scene will not be especially well positioned to provide analyses or interpretations of civil-military relations in that critical country. The reason is not difficult to fathom: There is little available literature on civil-military relations in Iran. While some excellent studies have been written about aspects or important periods in Iranian civil-military relations, very little has been written on the evolution of civil-military relations in Iran that can provide a guide to an understanding of possible changes in, or breakdowns within, stable civil-military relations as the country stumbles politically from crisis to crisis. This is not surprising given the fact that the Iranian military has not often or successfully intervened in the political process of the country.

This stands in stark contrast to its neighbors, where the overt intervention of the militaries in the political process by means of the classical instrument of the coup d'etat has generated a considerable body of work on each country. Consequently, a number of primary sources have been made available during the past two decades to undertake full studies of the nature of civil-military relations in Iran. This brief essay was never intended to be one of those studies. Rather, this chapter merely sought to present some of the highlights of a lengthier analysis. The major theme of this chapter is that there is a distinction between a politicized and a political military. While politicized militaries can enter the political arena by means of voicing opinions or preferences, their hallmark is to engage in overt interventions in the political process of their respective countries. In short, they engage in coups that replace a civilian government with a military one, or even an existing civilian one with another, more to their liking. Not surprisingly, the phenomenon of the coup has generated a large body of literature that has been applied to numerous case studies. Still, the Iranian military has been a political military for almost all of its modern existence, and has been one of the bulwarks—if not the main bulwark—of the political system. However, it has been effectively prevented from emerging as a political force that can play an independent role in the political system.

Mohammed Reza Shah's system was not a military dictatorship, since the Shah ultimately relied on the military, even if he utterly controlled it. It is difficult to study the nature of civil-military relations in the so-called developing world, where the military is a political but not a politicized force. The question that now arises and that needs to be answered in any study of the evolution of civil-military relations in the Islamic Republic is whether the military will continue to be a governmental institution or will emerge as a politicized force.

## Notes

1. A number of well-known scholars who have addressed the Iranian Revolution have written small sections on civil-military relations in their studies, e.g., Said Amir Arjomand, *The Turban for the Crown: The Islamic Revolution in Iran,* New York: Oxford University Press, 1988, pp. 119–128.
2. Mark Hagopian, *The Phenomenon of Revolution,* New York: Dodd, Mead, 1974, especially chapter 4.
3. For an introduction to revolutions, see Chalmers Johnson, *Revolutionary Change,* 2nd edition, Stanford: Stanford University Press, 1982.

4. Quoted in Anthony Joes, *From the Barrel of a Gun: Armies and Revolutions*, McLean, Virginia: Pergamon-Brassey's, 1986, p. xi.
5. Alfred Stepan, *The Military in Politics: Changing Patterns in Brazil*, Princeton: Princeton University Press, 1971, p. 7.
6. I have relied in particular on the following works: Eric Nordlinger, *Soldiers in Politics*, New Jersey: Prentice-Hall, 1977; Amos Perlmutter, *The Military and Politics in Modern Times*, New Haven: Yale University Press, 1977; and Samuel Finer, *The Man on Horseback: The Role of the Military in Politics*, Harmondsworth: Peregrine, 1976.
7. Mark Roberts, *Khomeini's Incorporation of the Iranian Military*, McNair Paper number 48, Washington, D.C.: National Defense University, 1996, p. 5.
8. Arthur Christensen, *L'Iran sous les Sassanides*, Copenhagen: Ejnar Munksgaard, 1944, pp. 130–32.
9. For more details, see Robert McDaniel, *The Shuster Mission and the Persian Constitutional Revolution*, Minneapolis: Bibliotheca Islamica, 1974, p. 22.
10. The South Persia Rifles played the least important role in the political process in Iran. In fact, it was raised, trained, and officered by the British to protect their investment in the lawless but oil-rich semi-autonomous region of Arabistan (Khuzistan). The Gendarmerie and the Cossack Brigade competed with one another in their attempts to influence the political process at the center in Teheran.
11. For more on the Constitutional Revolution of 1906 and on the role of military forces, see, *inter alia*, Djafar Shafiei-Nasab, *Les Mouvements Revolutionnaires et la Constitution de 1906 en Iran*, Berlin: Klaus Schwarz Verlag, 1991, pp. 497–520.
12. On 6 December 1921 Reza Khan issued Army Decree Number One, which called for the merger of the Cossack Brigade and the Gendarmerie, as the first step toward the creation of a unified national army.
13. The following studies are important sources on the development of Reza Shah's military: Richard Stewart, *Sunrise at Abadan: The British and Soviet Invasion of Iran, 1941*, Praeger: New York, 1988; and General Hasan Arfa, *Under Five Shahs*, London: John Murray, 1964.
14. For more details on the military under Reza Shah, see, *inter alia*, Ahmad Mahrad, *Iran unter der Herrschaft Reza Schahs*, Frankfurt: Campus Verlag, 1977, pp. 91–133.
15. See Alvin Cottrell, "Iran's Armed Forces under the Pahlavi Dynasty," in George Lenczowski (ed.), *Iran under the Pahlavis*, Stanford: Hoover Institution Press, 1978.
16. In 1954 the government discovered that the Iranian Communist Party, the *Tudeh*, had infiltrated the armed forces since 1942. It had created a formidable network of 600 officers. In 1960 the Shah was faced with opposition from a variety of secular political forces as a result of widespread economic discontent. In 1963 it was the turn of the religious right to voice its opposition to far-reaching changes proposed by the Shah. Each time, the Shah relied on his military for support.
17. Quoted in Anselmo Avenido, *The Role of the Iranian Armed Forces in the Fall of the Shah*, Master of Military Art and Sciences, U.S. Army Command and General Staff College, 1984, p. 82.
18. Hannah Arendt, *On Revolution*, New York: Viking, 1963; Katherine Chorley, *Armies and the Art of Revolution*, Boston: Beacon Press, 1973, p. 16.
19. For more details on the IRGC, see James Dingeman and Richard Juppa, "Iranian Elite: The Islamic Revolutionary Guards Corps," *Marine Corps Gazette*, March 1988, p. 74.
20. *A Glance at Two Years of War*, Political Office, Islamic Revolutionary Guards Corps, Teheran, n.d., p. 33.
21. For more details on the development of this military structure, see Arnold Hottinger, "Der Iranische Feldzug in Khusistan" [The Iranian Victory in Khuzistan], *Neue Zurcher Zeitung*, June 20–21, 1982, p. 6.
22. "Rafsanjani Kundigt Neordnung des Militars im Iran an," *Nahost Monitor Dienst*, June 6, 1988, pp. 1–4.
23. "Hashemi-Rafsanjani Speaks on Future of IRGC," *Foreign Broadcast Information Service–Near East/South Asia* (henceforth *FBIS-NES*), October 7, 1988, p. 50.
24. Ibid., pp. 52–53.
25. Andrew Gowers and Sheherazade Daneshku, "A war machine split into two camps," *Financial Times*, June 28, 1988, p. 4.
26. For Ayatollah Khamenei's statements, see *FBIS-NES*, May 13, 1991, p. 57.
27. "Revolutionary Guard accepts new role," *Iran Focus*, November 1991, p. 8.
28. Rainer Hermann, "Von der Wirtschafts-zur Legitimationskrise: Die Ara Khamenei/Rafsanjani in der Islamischen Republik Iran," *Orient* 35:4, 1994, p. 545.

29. Ibid.
30. Safa Haeri, "Iranian general calls for end of rule by clerics," *The Independent*, September 28, 1994, p. 11.
31. Andrew Rathmell, "Khamenei Strengthens His Grip," *Jane's Intelligence Review,* October 1995, p. 450.
32. For more details, see Michel Naufal, "Iran: Khatami joue a quitte ou double," *Arabies,* November 1997, pp. 20–24; Nairi Nahapetian, "Iran: Nouvelles Constantes Politiques en Gestation," *Arabies,* March 1998, pp. 20–26.
33. For more details, see the definitive work on the Pasdaran by Kenneth Katzman, *The Warriors of Islam: Iran's Revolutionary Guards,* Boulder: WestviewPress, 1993.
34. *Kar-o-kargar,* 30 April 1997.
35. "Military Offensive in the Political Arena," *Mobin,* 2 May 1998, p. 5.
36. "General Safavi Chooses Dialogue," *Akhbar,* June 1, 1998.
37. Ibid.
38. "IRGC's Safavi Urges Vigilance against 'Third Current,'" Islamic Republic News Agency, June 2, 1998.
39. "Iran's Khatami on Military Issues, Missiles," speech by President Khatami, *Tehran IRIB Television First Program Network in Persian 1709 Greenwich Meantime,* August 1, 1998, in Foreign Broadcast Information Service–Near East/South Asia, on-line.
40. Ahmed Ghoreishi and Dariush Zahedi, "Prospects for Regime Change in Iran," *Middle East Policy* 5:1, January 1997, p. 86.
41. Leon Trotsky, *The History of the Russian Revolution,* translated by Max Eastman, New York: Monad Press, 1961, p. 249.
42. Quoted in Donald Wilber, *Reza Shah Pahlavi: The Resurrection and Reconstruction of Iran,* New York: Exposition Press, 1970, p. 73.

# THE REPUBLIC OF IRAQ

## CHAPTER 4

### The Position of the Iraqi Clergy
#### Joyce N. Wiley

The Iraqi Muslim clergy, or *ulama*, minister to a population that is about 60 percent Shia and 35 percent Sunni. Both Sunni and Shia clergy are in weakened positions, the Sunnis because of extreme government control, the Shias because of severe government oppression. Neither is able to exercise *shura*, i.e., to advise the government on what is permitted and what is forbidden in Islam, which has traditionally been a major function of the Muslim clergy. Neither any longer controls pious endowments, which have traditionally provided financing for clerical disbursements to seminarians and the needy. There are no more Shariah courts, where the clergy have traditionally adjudicated family law. Neither can preach at will because Friday prayers, being public gatherings, are monitored by government agents to ensure clerical compliance with government policies.

The Sunni clergy take their salaries and their assignments from the government. As state employees, they follow government guidelines in their sermons and choose their sermon topics from a book of Friday speech themes issued by their non-clerical supervisors in the Ministry of Endowments and Religious Affairs. The Shia clergy still take their salaries and their assignments from the *marja'iyya*, the Shia religious authority in Najaf[1]—although at least since 1979 when Saddam Hussein assumed the presidency, Iraq's Baath regime has been trying to get the same control over the Shia clergy that it has over the Sunni clergy. In the process it has killed an enormous number of them.

In response to the Shia clergy's resistance to government control, the government has moved to curb contact between them and the public. Some mosques have been closed; publication of Shia books has been banned; processions to commemorate Shia holy days have often been prohibited. Attendance at mosques has been deterred through harassment and arrest of worshipers. Financial sponsors of mosques have been persecuted. The highest-ranking Shia clergyman in Iraq, Ayatollah Ali Sistani, is under house arrest in Najaf.

## Traditional Role of the Clergy in Iraq

The present circumstances of the Iraqi ulama are far removed from their traditional role in Iraqi society. Iraq has historically been governed by Sunnis, and a small number of Sunni clerical families were part of the ruling elite. The Shias were not part of the ruling class, but senior Shia clerics functioned as liaisons between the Shia community and successive Sunni-dominated governments. Religious elites in both communities maintained their positions through intermarriage and, when appropriate, by directing their sons into religious studies.

Starting in the late nineteenth century, the attraction of religious studies for elite Sunni families eroded as the Ottoman Turks enacted reforms aimed at modernizing their empire and increasing the power of the central government at the expense of regional elites.[2] With their authority and privileges being reduced, families in the Sunni religious elite began, with Ottoman cooperation, to send their most promising sons into the upper levels of the bureaucracy and the professions, in essence moving their families into the modern middle class.

In the subsequent period under Iraq's Hashemite monarchy (1921–1958), the government paid the salaries of Sunni ulama and supported religion. The ulama advised the government on what was permitted and forbidden in Islamic law and exercised authority in Shariah courts. In the 1950s there was some religion-based political opposition in Iraq's Sunni Arab community, but it was from the Muslim Brotherhood, a primarily lay organization, not from the clerical establishment.

The Shia clergy, under both the Ottomans and the Hashemite monarchy, were an important part of the political leadership of the Shia community. Their financial support came from the Shia community, and an individual clergyman's means of rising to prominence depended upon the number of his followers and the amount of religious taxes paid to him. This system gave Shia clerics a large degree of autonomy from the government and injected responsiveness into their relationship with influential members of the Shia community.

The relationship between the Shia ulama and the country's political authorities was one of mutual sufferance. Religious studies continued to attract capable young Shia, both Iraqi and non-Iraqi. A decade before the Baathists came to power in 1968, there were nearly 2,000 students in Najaf's seminaries.[3] In contrast, at the beginning of the year 2000, there were only about 300 Shia clerics, including non-Iraqi seminarians, in all Iraq, a number grossly inadequate to minister to the 12 million Iraqi Shia.[4]

## Political Activism by the Shia Clergy

Excluded from governmental power for most of their history, the Shias for centuries maintained a millenarian attitude toward government, waiting patiently for God to return the Hidden Imam to establish justice and ideal government for them. In the 1950s, however, the attitude of many Iraqi clerics toward non-involvement in politics changed, a consequence of their struggle to counter the appeal of secularism and Western ideologies to their flocks. Ayatollah Muhammad Baqir al-Sadr (d. 1980) and other prominent clerics in Najaf came to believe that Muslims had an obligation to establish legitimate government themselves. The ideal form of government for the clerical activists became public knowledge in the late 1970s when Ayatollah al-Sadr issued his conception of a modern Islamic government.[5] The plan called for a government of three branches, with the executive and legislative branches elected via a system of universal suffrage. The judicial branch was to be appointed. The highest court was to consist of clerics, presumably including both Shias and Sunnis in Iraq, where the Muslim community consists of both sects. The court was to be charged with making sure that laws enacted by the legislature did not contravene Islam. This proposal was a much thought about attempt to create a modern system of *Shura* in which the governors consult with the governed via elections.

Two Quranic verses (Sura 3, verse 159, and Sura 42, verse 38) directed the Prophet Muhammad to *Shura*. In the past, Muslim governments were considered to have met this requirement by consulting with high-ranking clerics or other notable citizens. Ayatollah al-Sadr posited that such limited consultation with the people was no longer adequate, given the high level of education in the modern world and people's expectation of self-government. He believed that to be accepted, modern governments had to consult with their citizens through elections; hence the system of Islamized democracy that he proposed.

The political system outlined by Ayatollah al-Sadr was not inspired by Arab nationalism, an ideology that had the obeisance of many Iraqi Arabs but had no appeal, for obvious reasons, to Iraq's large Kurdish population. The Islamic activists expected a representative system of government to accommodate a variety of religious and political beliefs and to resonate favorably with the Muslim Kurds. Citing the Quran's warning against compulsion in religion, Ayatollah al-Sadr stressed that government should not attempt to impose religion on individuals. Non-Muslims were to be free to practice their religion and to take part in political activities, rights guaranteed to them by Quranic injunctions. They were to be afforded the protection and services received by Muslims.[6]

Along with their plan for representative government, the activist ulama and their supporters formulated a strategy for achieving it, a way of moving the Iraqi people from the minority-dominated, authoritarian government that they had, to this modern system of *Shura*. The plan required political assertiveness on the part of the Shia laity, and the creation of an alliance with those Sunnis willing to work for a modern Islamic government. To this end, Shia Islamists formed several clandestine political groups, the largest and best known of which was Hizb al-Da'wa (Party of the Call to Islam). They also joined forces with Iraq's Sunni Islamists, namely the Muslim Brotherhood, whose original leader, Muhammad Mahmud al-Sawaf, strongly supported cooperation between Sunnis and Shias.[7] The most important Shia supporter of the Shia-Sunni alliance was the Shia *marja' al-taqlid* (supreme authority or source of imitation), Ayatollah Muhsin al-Hakim. One manifestation of the alliance was the recruitment of Shias to membership in the Brotherhood. Likewise, an estimated 10 percent of the members of Hizb al-Da'wa were/are Sunni.[8] There was a geographical dimension to recruitment for most Islamic groups. Shia Islamists in Sunni areas would join the Brotherhood; Sunni Islamists in Shia areas would join Hizb al-Da'wa.

Iraq's Sunnis and Shias have never fought each other on religious grounds, and this political cooperation between the two communities had precedents; for example, in opposition to British colonial domination, Sunni and Shia clerics and laymen from both communities allied in the 1920 revolt. To be sure, some Sunni tribes and leaders did not join that effort, a fact that greatly helped the British to prevail. Indeed, a similar division in the Sunni community manifested itself regarding the Islamist alliance of the 1950s. After Shaykh al-Sawaf left Iraq in 1959, the Iraqi Muslim Brotherhood stopped accepting Shia members.[9]

It should also be noted that there was division in the Shia community, although it was not over cooperation with the Sunnis. The Shia division was over whether or not they should be politically active at all. Quietist clergy, both in the 1920s and later, interpreted their clerical responsibility narrowly, believing that their obligation was only to say what was right, not to take action to try to achieve it. The foremost of the quietist clerics in the 1970s and thereafter was Ayatollah Abol-Qazem Khoi. Ayatollah Khoi, who became the *marja' al-taqlid* after the death of Ayatollah Muhsin al-Hakim in 1970, upheld Shia political quiescence, which in Iraq meant leaving government to the Sunni Arab minority.

## Baath Policies toward the Clergy

The relationship of both Sunni and Shia clergy to the government changed substantially when the Baathists came to power in 1968. Within a year, Shaykh Abdul Aziz al-Badri, the Sunni *alim* (cleric) most associated with the Islamic movement, was arrested and killed in prison. Sunni mosques that had been independent of the government were closed. This early show of ruthlessness against the Muslim Brotherhood essentially eliminated religion-based opposition in the Arab Sunni community. The Sunni clergy confined themselves to carrying out their strictly religious duties of advising individual believers on Islamic law and comforting them with hope for life in the next world. The regime discouraged regular prayers by both Sunnis and Shias, but Sunnis fared better because they had family connections in the upper echelons of government.

The government targeted activist Shia ulama, but also endeavored to bring the entire clerical establishment to heel. In 1969 the government arrested and tortured two Shia clerics, Sayyid Mahdi al-Hakim and Sayyid Hassan Shirazi, who, like Shaykh al-Badri, were politically active Islamists.[10] At the same time, the Iranian seminarians in Najaf were arrested, and Shia endowment funds were confiscated. In the 1970s there were more arrests of Islamists. In 1980, the government arrested, tortured, and executed Ayatollah Muhammad Baqir al-Sadr and his sister, the *'alima* (cleric [feminine]) Bint al-Huda. In 1983 over 100 members of the clerical al-Hakim family were arrested by the government. Six of them were executed immediately, and the fate of most of the rest remained unknown.

During the eight-year Iran-Iraq War (1980–1988), Kurdish Islamists, who were Sunni and associated with the Muslim Brotherhood, participated in the armed opposition to the Baathist government. One of the prominent Kurdish Islamists, Mullah Uthman Abdul Aziz, fled to Iran with some 5,000 of his supporters, then returned to confront government forces shortly before the government's gassing of the Kurdish town of Halabja in March 1988.

The Shias were severely targeted again after the March 1991 *intifada* that occurred at the end of the Gulf War. Among the clergy arrested at that time were 16 members of the clerical Bahr al-'Ulum family, including Ayatollah 'Ala' al-Din, Ayatollah Izz al-Din, Ayatollah Jaafar, Hujja[11] Hassan, Hujja Muhammad Hussein, Hujja Muhammad Rida, and a number of their sons.[12] No account of their fate after arrest was given.

The 93–year-old *marja'*, Ayatollah Khoi, despite his abjuration of politics, was also arrested at that time, along with 108 of his followers, most of whom were not heard of afterwards.[13] The ayatollah may have aroused government wrath through his commitment to maintaining clerical autonomy and advising believers on Islamic law. After Iraq's 1991 invasion of Kuwait, Ayatollah Khoi declared it a sin for believers to buy goods brought back from Kuwait, a ruling based on his determination that the goods were stolen. Ayatollah Khoi died under house arrest in 1992, and his eldest son died in highly suspicious circumstances in 1994. The ayatollah's youngest son, Abdul Majid, escaped Iraq and now directs the Khoi Foundation, a large and active benevolent organization headquartered in London.

The most recent government campaign against the Shia clergy began in 1998 with the assassinations of Shaykh Mirza Ali al-Gharawi and Shaykh Murtada al-Borujerdi. In January 1999 a grenade attack against Shaykh Bashir Hussein al-Najafi and his seminary wounded the ayatollah and killed three others. In February, Ayatollah Sadiq al-Sadr and two of his sons were assassinated as they left Friday prayers, which the government had ordered the ayatollah not to lead. Ayatollah al-Sadr expected to be killed and was wearing a death shroud as he led his last prayers and at the time of his assassination. Another of the ayatollah's sons, along with a large number of seminarians who studied under the ayatollah, were arrested later in the year.

In the weeks preceding Ayatollah Sadiq al-Sadr's assassination, many of his aides were arrested and their houses demolished. The whereabouts and fate of most of the arrestees remained unknown.[14] In January, Shaykh Awas, imam of the Nasriyah city mosque, was arrested. When an unarmed crowd of his supporters demonstrated to demand his release, security forces killed 5 and arrested 300.[15] The imam of al-Thawrah mosque in Baghdad was reportedly killed in demonstrations protesting the death of Ayatollah al-Sadr, as was Shaykh Ali al-Sahlani, imam of the main mosque in Amara. The chief Shia clerics in Basra and Nasriyah were arrested, apparently to prevent their leading religious gatherings.

When some pious Shias started attending prayers at Sunni mosques after their own mosques were closed, the government began checking food ration cards at mosque entrances and meting out severe penalties to people who attempted to pray at unauthorized locations.[16] Toward the end of 1999, 19 of Ayatollah Sadiq al-Sadr's followers were executed, including Shaykh Muhammad al-Numani and Shaykh Abdul-Razzaq al-Rabi'i.[17]

As of 2000, there were almost no Shia ulama from the venerable clerical families left in Iraq. Some members of the prestigious Shia clerical families have survived by leaving Iraq. The Sunni clerical institution is not faring much better. Because religious studies are under government control, pious young Sunnis are avoiding religious careers.

Religious studies continue to attract Shia Arab students to the seminaries in Qom, Iran, and the small centers in Lebanon, but clearly the loss of senior clerics is problematic. Arab Shias have always sought to have at least one Arab among the Grand Ayatollahs in order to make sure their distinct interests are not overlooked by a totally Iranian leadership. To have an Arab among the Grand Ayatollahs, Arab Shias have had to give overwhelming support to one candidate—which has become very hard to achieve given the present paucity of Iraqi clerics and the circumstances in Iraq, where the majority of Arab Shias live. Shaykh Muhammad Hussein Fadlallah in Lebanon has considerable support, but only Iraq has an Arab Shia population large enough to provide the base for a *marja'*. Arab Shia clerics and Iraqi merchants have a strong interest in maintaining Najaf as the site of the *marja'iyya*, given that most of the shrines that attract Shia pilgrims and therefore generate revenues are in Iraq.

### Surviving Religious Leaders

Although there is a ranking cleric inside Iraq for each religious community, neither man has any freedom of action. The ranking Shia, Ayatollah Ali Sistani, was born in Mashad, Iran, in 1930 and took his early studies there. He then enrolled in Qom for advanced jurisprudence courses. From Qom, he moved to Najaf to study in the seminaries there. At the age of 31 he received his *ijaza* (certification as a mujtahid) from both Ayatollah Khoi and Shaykh Hussein al-Hilli. Sistani began teaching Islamic jurisprudence in Najaf and continued to do so until placed under house arrest by the Baathist government. Although Ayatollah Sistani is forbidden to lead prayers and is severely circumscribed in his activities, his liaison office in London undertakes religious and educational projects in his name.[18]

The ranking Sunni cleric inside Iraq is Abdul Karim al-Mudarris, the *qadi* (religious judge) of Baghdad. One expects a qadi to enforce Islamic law, but Shaykh Mudarris's authority is confined to pedestrian decisions such as declaring when Ramadan begins.

Outside Iraq, several Iraqi religious authorities are active and influential. One of them is Sayyid Muhammad Baqir al-Hakim, who was born in Najaf in 1939 into a prominent Iraqi clerical family, his father Ayatollah Muhsin al-Hakim being the leading mujtahid from 1955 to 1970. Sayyid Muhammad Baqir was educated in the *hawza* (center of religious studies) at Najaf and became a leader in Iraq's Islamic movement, writing books and articles for the call to Islam. He was imprisoned and tortured by the Baath government in 1972 and 1977. When public pressure effected his release in 1979, he fled to Iran. He has been chairman of the Supreme Council of the Islamic Resistance in Iraq (SCIRI) since its establishment in 1982. During the Iran-Iraq War, he supervised the 15 Iraqi refugee camps in Iran and SCIRI's military forces.[19] Importantly, Sayyid al-Hakim has cooperated with Sunni Arab and Kurdish groups and has supported the election of a consultative assembly to write a new constitution for Iraq.

A second prominent Shia cleric is Dr. Muhammad Bahr al-'Ulum, who was born in Najaf in 1927 into a prominent Iraqi clerical family. His ancestor Ayatollah Mahdi Bahr al-'Ulum was the leading Shia mujtahid of the late eighteenth century. Dr. Bahr al-'Ulum was educated in the hawza at Najaf and was among the first to graduate from Iraq's College of Theology after it was established in the early 1960s. As one of Ayatollah Muhsin al-Hakim's staff, he was obliged to flee Iraq in 1969 after the Baath government accused the ayatollah's staff of conspiracy. Sayyid Bahr al-'Ulum proceeded to obtain a master's degree from the University of Teheran and a Ph.D. from the College of Sciences at Cairo University.[20] Today he directs Ahl al-Bayt, a London-based organization ministering to Iraqi refugees.

Among Iraqi Sunni clerics outside Iraq, Dr. Taha Jaber al-Alwani, president of the Graduate School of Islamic and Social Sciences in Leesburg, Virginia, is highly respected. He is from Ramadi and took his early education in Iraq in the classical Islamic disciplines. His master's and doctoral degrees are from al-Azhar in Cairo, the foremost school for Sunni clerics. He is an authority on Shafi'i law, and in his many books and articles, he addresses such varied subjects as the rights of the accused in Islam and the social implications of Islamic law.[21] Dr. al-Alwani has support from prominent Saudis and Jordanians and is not very involved with specifically Iraqi affairs.

Dr. Usama al-Tikriti, age 60, is another respected Sunni religious leader. He is not a clergyman but is president of the Iraqi Islamic Party, that is to say, of the Iraqi Muslim Brotherhood. He is a radiologist, practicing in Leeds, England. Dr. al-Tikriti completed secondary school in the town of Tikrit and medical school at the University of Baghdad. He joined the Muslim Brotherhood in the 1950s and was the leader of the Brotherhood in the United Kingdom from 1972 to 1978. From 1978 to 1991 he worked in the United Arab Emirates. On his return to England in 1991, he became president of a center for political studies and research and initiated publication of the Islamic Party's monthly magazine, *Dar al-Salaam* (House of Peace).[22]

Finally, it is important to note that the Kurdish population has its own clergy and two Islamic parties. The Islamic Unity Movement, *Harakat al-Wahda*, is a union of several smaller parties and is headed by Salah al-Din Baha al-Din. The other party, the Revival Movement, *Harakat al-Nahda,* is headed by Mullah Ali Abdul Aziz. Both parties maintain a working relationship with the Arab Muslim Brotherhood.

## Conclusion

The activist Shia clergy have written and spoken fairly often about their vision for a future government in Iraq. They are committed to a democratic system with an Islamic *sifa* (flavor), to use their word. They stress that in the long term any non-democratic government in Iraq would have to stay in power through coercion, and that Iraq has had enough government by coercion. They contend that minority government is not feasible in the modern world with its educated masses and modern telecommunications. As for Sunni Islamists, some of Iraq's Muslim Brotherhood also advocate a democratic government for Iraq. They say that the religiosity of the Iraqi people will add the Islamic "flavor" they too hope to see in a future political system. Because of the Baath regime's brutal suppressions, the Brotherhood has no organization left in the Arab part of Iraq, although some individual members remain.

Iraq's quietist Shia clergy continue to acquiesce to minority Sunni government, but reject the totalitarian government they have had under Saddam Hussein and his clan. This also seems to be the position of Iraq's Sunni ulama. Recent visitors to Iraq report Sunnis want Saddam's government replaced by that of a Sunni military officer who is able to control the street and prevent retribution against Sunnis.

Inasmuch as some Sunnis may fear the Shias would dominate a democratic system, it is important to ask whether the Shia community is politically homogeneous. In fact, it is quite unlikely that the Shias would vote as a bloc. More likely they would divide in the way that Iranians are dividing. In the 20–odd years of elections in Iran's Islamic Republic, generational differences and other interests have created a nascent multi-party system. Since Iraqi Shias run the gamut from left to right, from urban sophisticate to rural traditionalist and from affluent to poor, it is very likely they would divide into parties with both Sunni and Shia members—as they actually did between the time the British set up a constitutional monarchy in Iraq and the Baathists took over the Iraqi government, ending Iraqis' right to join parties other than the Baath Party.

The position of the clergy will remain important because both Sunni and Shia clergy are valued by observant Muslims for their knowledge of Islamic law and their ability to interpret the Shariah. The Iraqi people are going through a time of severe trial, a time when human beings tend to turn to religion. As might be expected, visitors to Iraq report increasing religiosity, as well as fear and depression, in both the Sunni and Shia communities. In the first months of 2001, the numbers of Iraqis visiting the mosque/shrine in Karbala far exceeded previous numbers.

Because Islam has deep, validated roots in Iraq, the regime of Saddam Hussein has gone to great lengths to muzzle the clergy and to eliminate clerics it cannot manipulate. At tremendous cost to themselves, the Shia clergy have resisted being brought under government control. Through their sacrifices, they have retained their leadership function and their credibility with believers. The fact that democracy is the aspiration of many educated Iraqis and of activist Shia clerics means a democratic government would have major support in the Shia community. It would probably have some Sunni support as well.

Whatever form of replacement government Iraq gets, many of its exiled clergy will return to rejoin the clerics who have survived the brutality of the last few decades within the country. Although sorely reduced in numbers, the Iraqi ulama can be expected to serve a positive, reconciliatory role in their ravaged country.

## Notes

1. Najaf is the southern Iraqi city that has, since the eleventh century, often been the preeminent locus for Shia jurisprudence and theology.
2. The clergy became subject to certain taxes and lost their control over education. In many cases, their landed estates became government property. For a detailed account of the late-nineteenth-century losses to Iraq's clergy, see Hanna Batatu, *The Old Social Classes and Revolutionary Movements of Iraq,* Princeton, New Jersey: Princeton University Press, 1978, chapter 7.
3. Fadil Jamali, "The Theological Colleges of Najaf," *The Muslim World* 50:3, 1960, p. 15.
4. Written communication from Muhammad Sadiq Bahr al-'Ulum, February 2000.
5. Muhammad Baqir al-Sadr, *Islamic Political System,* translated by M. A. Ansari, Karachi, Pakistan: Islamic Seminary, 1982.
6. Murtada Mottahari, *Jihad,* translated by Muhammad Salman Tawhidi, Teheran, Iran: Islamic Propagation Organization, 1985, p. 65. Although Iranian, Ayatollah Mottahari was closely associated with the activist Iraqi Shias.
7. Tarik Hamdi al-Azami, "The Emergence of the Contemporary Islamic Revival in Iraq," *Middle East Affairs Journal,* volume 3, number 1–2, winter/spring 1997, p. 132.
8. For an account of the Islamic movement of Iraqi Shi'as, see Joyce N. Wiley, *The Islamic Movement of Iraqi Shi'as,* Boulder: Lynne Rienner Publishers, 1992.
9. Al-Azami, *op. cit.*, p. 140n.
10. Sayyid is the honorific for a descendant of the Prophet Muhammad.
11. Hujja is the reduced form of *Hujjat al-Islam,* Proof of Islam, the title of a mujtahid, i.e., a cleric authorized to issue authoritative opinions on Islamic law.
12. Mohammad Sadiq Bahr al-'Ulum, "The Tragedy of the Bahr al-'Ulum Family," Iraqi Islamic Association of America, 1998, pp. 5–13.
13. "U.S. Department of State Annual Report on International Religious Freedom for 1999: Iraq," p. 4. On the World Wide Web at http://www.state.gov/www/global/human rights.
14. U.S. Department of State, "Human Rights Reports for 1999," pp. 12–13. At http://www.state.gov/www/global/human rights/1999 hrp report/iraq.html.
15. Ibid., p. 16.
16. Ibid., p. 25.
17. Ibid., p. 5.
18. "Ayatollah al-Sistani," http://www.najaf.org. See also "Ayatollah Sayyid Ali Sistani," http://playandlearn.org.
19. Ayatollah Sayyed Mohammad Baqir al-Hakim," http://playandlearn.org.
20. Bahr al-'Ulum, *op. cit.,* p. 4.
21. Written communication from Dr. al-Alwani's office.
22. Written communication from Dr. al-Tikriti.

CHAPTER 5

## Domestic Politics in a Post-Saddam Iraq
### Laith Kubba

Trends amongst Iraq's diverse ethnic and religious communities are critical factors for power projections and political predictions. The two devastating Gulf Wars, the March 1991 uprising, as well as the prolonged sanctions, have polarized Iraq's communities and weakened the prospect for democracy in a post-Saddam Iraq. Consequently, and for the foreseeable future, Iraq's stability may well require an authoritarian government, even if structural reforms are essential. In fact, the provisions for a modern, secular, and national framework are not sufficient to accommodate cultural and national aspirations of Iraq's diverse communities. Inasmuch as the failure of consecutive governments—to meet the aspiration of Iraq's vibrant communities—is rooted in the constitution and state institutions, the legacy of the past few decades necessitates fundamental reforms. A strong state and effective institutions are crucial to Iraq's stability.

### Introduction

Up until 1958, Iraq posed little threat to its neighbors, and was of little interest to policymakers and international institutions. The 1973 oil boom, and the two Gulf Wars, projected Iraq as a regional power. Still, research on contemporary Iraq is hindered by two factors. First, the Iraqi government carefully guards the flow of information and forbids independent research on its domestic affairs. The state's annual budget, for example, has been classified information since the early 1970s, and state employees who communicate general information to outsiders—without prior permission—are charged with treason. Foreign researchers who were permitted to move freely within the country faced a cautious and self-censored populace. Second, the numerous articles, papers, and books that have been published on Iraq since 1990 continue to be driven by the ongoing conflict between Iraq and the United Nations. Such material focuses mainly on the regime, its organizations and behavior, the mechanics of repression, and the impact of sanctions on the economy and social fabric. Little attention has been paid to the political impact of three decades of Baath Party rule, the two Gulf wars, and their associated sanctions on the inner dynamics of Iraq's various communities. In an attempt to develop an insight into the future dynamics of Iraq's domestic politics, and by relying on ongoing contacts and close association with Iraqis within the Diaspora, this chapter identifies and explores key trends for the future.

### The State and its Citizens

Iraq is predominantly Arab, with the exception of three provinces in the north (out of a national total of eighteen) that are predominantly Kurdish. Both Arabs and Kurds have strong tribal and religious loyalties that often override ethnic identities. Within these Arab and Kurdish provinces, there are cities with predominant ethnic communities that are bonded to Iraq through culture and religious beliefs. Iraqis differ amongst themselves in their many claims and counter-claims of the real percentages of the ethnic and religious composition of Iraq's population, as well as their share of its history and cultural identity. Iraq is truly mosaic in its composition, and it is not feasible to restructure a political system based exclusively on ethnic lines, or even along lines of religious belief.

Consecutive Iraqi governments sought to nurture a national identity through social development under the auspices of strong centralized state institutions. Post-Ottoman Iraq was multiethnic and tribal and lacked national identity. Nevertheless, Iraq was constituted as a unitary modern state with centralized executive, legislative, and judicial bodies. Moreover, British colonial leaders envisaged Iraq as an Arab state, headed by a constitutional monarchy, run by an elected government, and protected by a national army. In the event, Sunni elites in Baghdad, and tribal Arab Sunni leaders throughout the country, were better positioned to benefit from the new state structure. Some of Iraq's communities initially challenged consecutive governments to demand a special status and better services from the state. Prior to Iraq's independence, the Kurds, for example, pressed for a separate nation-state and later modified their demands to an autonomous region within Iraq. The Shia clergy, for their part, led the Arab tribes in challenging the British influence over the country and boycotted the government, thereby weakening their overall participation in state institutions. Initially, the state prevailed over Kurdish national aspirations and Shia demands, but the pressures of these communities for participation remained driving forces behind domestic political developments.

Iraq's stability hinged on the ability of the state to accommodate the aspirations of its overwhelming majority, the Arab and Kurdish tribes. Under the monarchy, there was an imbalance of power, in favor of the elites in Baghdad. Later, this imbalance tilted in favor of tribal Arab Sunnis. To be sure, the monarchy struggled to accommodate the political forces of its three main communities, and the rights and aspirations of other minority groups. There were minor conflicts and periodic tensions between Baghdad and many such entities, as state institutions were too weak to remain neutral. Few leaders could withstand the conflicting demands of Iraq's communities for political recognition and participation. The modern secular state provided key services and offered opportunities to all citizens but was not neutral in addressing communal aspirations. Eventually, the state caved to tribal Arab Sunni pressures, whose influence became dominant in the army and security organizations.

Not surprisingly, a popular military coup ended the monarchy in 1958, replacing its fragile democratic institutions with a military dictatorship. The state became the vehicle for senior army officers, mainly Arab Sunnis, to consolidate and expand their respective power bases. A decade of instability ended in 1968 with a coup that converged the Baath Party, the Iraqi army, and the tribal Arab Sunni leadership into a strong central government under the leadership of the Tikriti clan. The 1970s oil boom multiplied Iraq's income by several fold, and the state became central to the lives of most Iraqis. In turn, the regime developed full control over the state, by transferring its power structure from that of a traditional army rule into an intertwined trilateral combination of the army, the Baath Party, and a minority of Arab Sunni tribes. Within a relatively short period of time, and through complex security networks, the family of Saddam Hussein then led the regime.

The state of Iraq, as a constitutional monarchy and later as a republic, provided a national framework for the integration of Iraq's communities: Shia, Sunni Arab, and Kurdish tribes, and its other significant minorities of Assyrians, Turkomans, Caldeans, Sabians, Armenians, and Yazidis. Importantly, the state's main institutions, such as the army, judiciary, bureaucracy, parliament, and political parties, had the potential to provide full political integration, social development, and the emergence of a national identity without threatening sub-national identities. In fact, the development of an Iraqi national identity took place through the evolution of the economy, the growth of the middle class, and the development of a welfare state. State education and the integration of Iraq's communities in national politics further provided some of the most important elements of the emerging Iraqi national identity.

Despite these institutional changes, the main fault line of the Iraqi state remained in the disproportionate participation of its two largest communities, the Shias and the Kurds, in the leadership of its institutions. Since the early 1970s, it may be accurate to posit that the leadership of the army, state bureaucracy, security, and other state institutions developed in an uneven manner. Worse still, the state took sides in accommodating conflicting communal interests. Consequently, a majority of Iraqis today identify the state and government with Arab Sunnis. This perception has reinforced the reality and polarized Iraqi communities even further. In the case of a future inter-communal conflict, it is likely that the military as well as most security services—the state's main institutions—will identify themselves as the defenders of Arab Sunnis. Instead of attempting to include Iraq's two largest communities into the system, Baghdad camouflaged its narrowly based Sunni tribal power structure with national rhetoric, which played down communal sub-identities. Moreover, the totalitarian government of Saddam Hussein forced Iraqis to compromise their sub-identities in favor of an Iraqi national identity. Thus, the Iraqi state reached its peak rhetoric as a nation-state on the eve of Saddam Hussein's claim to the presidency in 1979, when Iraq had a strong welfare state and a booming oil-based economy that broadened its middle classes and enhanced its national identity. Although the system was open to all Iraqis, power remained unquestionably in the hands of a few. The government bought their loyalty through jobs, free education, health care, and other benefits.

Under normal circumstances, there should be legal and political distinctions between the state, the government, and the president of Iraq, but in reality, all have been reduced to the entity of the president. Today, Saddam Hussein and his family run a "security regime" that, in turn, manages the Baath Party, the military, and the bureaucracy. Although these power bases vary in their responsibility for initiating or implementing Saddam Hussein's policies, Baghdad is perceived by a majority of Iraqis as an extension of Saddam Hussein's regime. The ills of the policies of Saddam Hussein became the ills of the state itself. Irrespective of academic arguments about such distinctions, the end result of three decades of Baath rule brought to question not only the future of Saddam Hussein's regime but the future of the Iraqi state itself. Kurds tend to blame the state and Sunni Arabs for the emergence of the ultimate dictatorship of Saddam Hussein, while Shias tend to blame Sunni tribes for their support of the regime. So far, the problematic relationship of the Iraqi government with its communities has not led to inter-communal conflicts, but it certainly has undermined the credibility of the government in developing a national identity.

## State Relationships with Ethnic Communities

It is difficult to assess in detail the impact of the past three decades on the attitudes and dynamics of Iraq's ethnic communities without an assessment based on field research. To some extent, it is evident that Iraq's three main communities now diverge in their political perspectives, interests, and attitudes on a number of key issues and have developed different political agendas.

Shia Arab tribes, who are concentrated in relatively deprived areas of Baghdad and most southern cities, are perceived as a threat to the government. Sunni Arab tribes form the power base of the regime and, consequently, enjoy unique privileges. Still, Shia and Sunni Arab tribes are divided more by their contrasting realities than by their confessional beliefs. Indeed, the two Gulf Wars and their aftermath have divided and polarized the Arab tribes along Shia-Sunni lines. Up until 1990, the Shias, who form the majority of Arabs in Iraq, had no specific political demands beyond broad national reforms. Despite their religious bonds with Iranian Shias, for example, they fought a national war against Iran. However, a serious fault line between Shias and Baghdad emerged in the aftermath of the March 1991 uprising against the regime. To quell this opposition, the regime targeted Shias through indiscriminate attacks on their religious institutions. As a result, some Shias have now joined Kurdish leaders in demanding a decentralized state structure for a future Iraq.

The Kurds have an older and a more complex relationship with the state. Kurdish national aspirations were not met after the First World War, and since then, it may be accurate to posit that the Kurds have been struggling for national recognition. They were the first to be at odds with the newly established state and demanded autonomous rule. Their demands for self-rule resulted in a March 1970 agreement, but despite the progress reached then, they fought several wars with Baghdad for the realization of an autonomous region. Given this background, Kurdish successes in maintaining a de facto self-rule in northern Iraq since 1991 have far-reaching consequences on Iraq and its neighbors. In fact, it is difficult to reconcile the autonomous Kurdish region with an authoritarian centralized unitary state with an Arab national identity. Iraqi Kurds have opened a Pandora's box on future alternatives in Iraq that will have far-reaching effects on both Iran and Turkey.

In addition to the failure of the state, Iraq's national unity has been weakened due to the effects of the UN sanctions. To be sure, sanctions increased Iraqi dependence on the state, in securing food allocations through the miserly coupon distribution system known as the oil-for-food program. On the other hand, such dependency neither compensates for the diminishing role of the state as a framework for national integration nor contributes to the development or maintenance of a national identity. Moreover, sanctions have undermined the urbanized middle classes—especially in Baghdad—who are the real product of an Iraqi national identity. The destruction of the urbanized middle classes, the lack of state services in key sectors, such as health, education, and employment, and the inability of Iraqi polity to provide national alternatives have all contributed to the fragmentation of Iraq's national identity—with dire consequences.

## The Fragmentation of National Politics

Up until recently, the Iraqi polity was neither ethnic nor confessional. The political discourse was national and reflected the main political trends in the region, which are liberal, leftist, nationalist, and/or Islamist. These diverse political trends spread throughout Iraq and among its main communities, Shias, Sunnis, and Kurds. Some ethnic and marginalized communities leaned more toward national and secular political trends that held broad appeal, while others sought radical reforms to improve intrinsic conditions. Indeed, these variations in political tendencies were complex, and could not be reduced to mere ethnicity or religious confessions. For example, the Shia Maadan in the south, and Shias in the poorer Baghdad districts, were attracted to radical leftists, as well as Islamic movements. Kurds were attracted to nationalist, tribal, communist, and Islamic movements. Although Islamic and Kurdish movements seemed to be confessional and ethnic, respectively, they were better understood in the ideological and national context. For many decades, Iraqi politics had remained national and provided a framework for the emergence of a national identity and the integration of its communities.

Recently, however, Iraqi politics was reshaped by the emergence of ethnic and religious sub-identities and tribal loyalties, which overrode the traditional national discourse. Despite claims to the contrary, the most recent meeting of these groups in New York under the umbrella of the Iraqi National Congress (INC) amply illustrated the lack of this national discourse. The various groups expressed general aspirations for peace and respect for human and community rights, but did not opt to develop a genuine national agenda. More importantly, the politics of the exiled groups indicated that there has been a clear surge in ethnic sentiments, communal loyalties, and regional agendas. To some extent, the assertion of ethnic and communal identities may be understood as a backlash against three decades of a state policy that sought to promote a uniform identity and enforce a state version of sub-identities. Expressions of strong ethnic sentiments may also be understood in view of the fear of communities being left out, if and when the state is restructured and reformed. It may also be argued that the trends amongst the ethnic exile groups are not indicative of the real communal aspirations inside the country. Nevertheless, the narrow sectarian agendas of these self-proclaimed and exiled political groups cannot be dismissed. Their failure to provide an alternative national framework, as well as their active participation in the promotion of ethnic-confessional political options, will surely undermine further Iraq's national identity. Nowhere was this trend clearer than within the military.

## The Military

Under the monarchy, consecutive Iraqi governments used the army to quash community rebellion of Kurds, Assyrians, and Shias. The role of the military increased with its frequent interventions in politics as an instrument used to end chaos and restore order. The bloodless 1968 military coup was followed by a violent systematic campaign against dissidents. Since then, the Iraqi army has fallen under the tight control of emerging security agencies, which have become the key institutions buttressing the regime. Over the past three decades, the military's officer corps has been selected from Sunni tribes loyal to Saddam Hussein. Although the military ceased to intervene in politics, it retained its loyalty to the regime, thus becoming its ultimate line of defense.

## Prospects for Political Violence

The biggest threat to Iraq's long-term stability is its potential for communal and political violence. Over the years, Iraq's security agencies and the military have repressed Iraqis on a wide scale and increased their capacity for brutality, which can only lead to more injustice. Ironically, although overwhelming force succeeded in undermining armed resistance and deterred dissent, it has increased and developed the capacity for violence amongst Iraqis.

Yet, despite this tendency, there has been no inter-communal violence amongst Iraqis over the past few decades, with the exception of a few, low-key, inter-tribal confrontations in rural areas. These non-political incidents, which lasted a few days at the most, were resolved within tribal norms and did not develop into lasting disputes. In the years 1958–1963, Iraq's main cities witnessed serious political violence, the most evident of which were the infamous massacres in Mosul, Kirkuk, and Baghdad. Indeed, Iraq's short-lived episodes of political and tribal clashes drop to insignificant levels in comparison to its serious episodes of state–community violence. Although communal and political disturbances seem to be negligible—especially when compared to other countries, such as Lebanon, Somalia, and Afghanistan—the level of violence initiated and orchestrated by the state against its own citizens is one of the worst throughout the region.

In the early 1970s, the Baath government contained a major Kurdish rebellion in the north, as well as a small-scale communist guerrilla movement in the marsh areas in the south. Both operations were successful. In 1979, Iraq witnessed an upsurge of political violence triggered by the Islamic Revolution in Iran, the rise of Saddam Hussein to power, and the beginning of the Iran-Iraq War. Shia demonstrations in Baghdad were followed by an attempt on the life of Iraq's deputy prime minister, Tariq Aziz, that threatened the stability of the entire regime. These events led to a government-sponsored terror campaign that specifically targeted two political parties, the Islamic Dawah Party and the Iraqi Communist Party. In the event, two Shia communities were singled out as fifth columns: the Faili Kurds, and Shias of Iranian origin. Later, Baghdad targeted the Kurdish Democratic Party, led by the Barazani clan, and then targeted the second largest Kurdish party, the Patriotic Union of Kurdistan. Before long, the leading revolutionary council passed a capital punishment decree on all members of the Islamic Dawah Party, and public executions of opponents were ordered by special committees. Importantly, summary sentences were administrated by low-level Baath Party members, further drawing them into the regime's nest. Extra-judicial killings and executions did not spare religious men, tribal chiefs, army officers, or academics. A vicious cycle of violence, which was led by the state and followed by the opposition, was concluded in 1989 in favor of the state. During the eight-year-long Iran-Iraq War, Baghdad carried out thousands of public executions of dissidents and army deserters. As the high toll of war casualties synthesized violence and made death a normal part of life, the invasion of Kuwait—the intensity and ferocity of the second Gulf War and its widespread destruction—further diminished the value of life.

### *Rating the Survivability of the Regime*

If anything, Saddam Hussein has been consistent in his use of excessive and decisive force against his opponents. To date, his regime has been successful in using force and terror to secure stability, but whether it can survive for another decade through terror alone remains to be determined. Moreover, and in the event of the collapse of the regime, is it likely that violence will spread throughout Iraq and escalate through revenge, reprisals, foreign involvement, and easy access to weapons? Can the Iraqi state survive the downfall of the regime without breaking apart? In case Iraq survives the initial chaos, can this generation of Iraqis develop alternative structures based on democracy and the rule of law, or are they doomed to fail because of the many years of terror and repression that have deeply impoverished their political culture?

To be sure, Iraq's future is clouded with more uncertainties than that of any other nation of the Middle East. Speculation on Iraq's future ranges from the continuation of Saddam Hussein's dynasty for the foreseeable future to a prolonged civil war and an eventual fragmentation of the country.

In the short term, observers can only speculate on a wide range of possible scenarios such as a regional misadventure by Saddam Hussein, an escalation of violence between Iraq and the United States, the assassination of President Saddam Hussein, the crowning of one of his sons, a coup from within, an uprising, and so on. Yet, despite the regime's firm grip on power, Saddam Hussein's astonishing survivability, the firmness of the United Nations sanctions, and the Iraq–U.S. policy deadlock, Baghdad's siege cannot be maintained over the long term. Either Baghdad or Washington will agree to a more flexible position and move beyond the current deadlock. It is also possible to envisage another future in view of two likely scenarios. Indeed, a departure from the current deadlock would lead either to the revival of the regime or to its breakdown.

The first scenario could occur if and when there is change from within the regime, and it assumes that the country would remain intact through the use of force. It further assumes both the continuity of the regime and its ability, under present or a different leadership, to meet American and United Nations requirements for lifting sanctions. Finally, it also presupposes that the regime has the capacity to administer change and reforms, which would—eventually—rehabilitate it back into the world community.

A more realistic scenario is that of a defiant Saddam Hussein who would hold on to power until the country breaks down into chaos. Under this view, a new regime would emerge, perhaps out of the remains of surviving state institutions, with the ultimate result of communal conflicts. The collapse of the regime could unleash complex dynamics of change in which both state and social institutions become the determinants of Iraq's future. Of course, it is highly speculative as to whether or not Iraq's neighbors would be directly involved in its domestic affairs, but it is fairly certain that they will be indirectly involved through proxy militias and political groups.

## Prospects for Self-Reform and Rehabilitation

Whether Saddam Hussein's regime can in fact reform itself, and whether it would survive such reforms, are key questions as well. There have always been pragmatists within the current regime who argued for reforms, as is evident in numerous public statements by some of the top officials in 1989, 1991, and 1999. To be sure, such statements may be part of a sinister ploy to engage the international community in dialogue, with the false hope of achieving modest reforms. Tariq Aziz, for example, declared that Baghdad—under the present siege—would not proceed with plans for political pluralism, out of fear that such reforms may well undermine internal stability. Members of various exiled Iraqi groups reported that indirect mediation with Qusay Hussein, the president's powerful son and probable heir, aimed to open a dialogue, but most judged these as sham and insincere. Ultimately, it is Saddam Hussein who decides the extent to which such risky policies may be pursued, and, so far at least, he seems to reject genuine reforms. Openly and defiantly, the Iraqi strongman defies the Security Council in its numerous disarmament programs for Iraq, mistrusting even his closest "reformist" allies.

A good case in point is the lack of a response to Iraq's repeated "gestures" for a rapprochement with Washington. If there were to be a favorable change in the American political climate toward Iraq, then the regime would presumably posture more on reforms, engage itself with reform rhetoric, and push for normalization and a speedy suspension of sanctions. This would be a short-lived affair because the United States, even if it is under pressure to relax sanctions, is unlikely to change course, depart from its staunch anti–Saddam Hussein position, or engage itself in any dialogue with the current regime in Baghdad.

Moreover, as a time-tested leader, Saddam Hussein seems to have more faith in the effectiveness of his Stalinist-style rule, which has kept him in power—against all odds—for over 30 years. Under the circumstances, risky reforms may not be favored, especially since the ethos of the regime is based on fear and terror. For Saddam Hussein, the lessons of the Eastern Bloc clearly demonstrated that reforms weakened authoritarian regimes, and led to their meteoric collapse. Therefore, and unless reforms may be introduced at low risk—and high returns—Saddam Hussein will not allow any consideration. At present, the regime perceives the "reforms option" as a threat rather than an opportunity, and even if its benefits were to outweigh costs, Saddam Hussein will simply not permit it.

The reforms option is possible but it requires a change in the leadership. Over the past 30 years, Saddam Hussein has outmaneuvered his rivals, and hence a change from within is remote even if it cannot be ruled out. Conspirators against Saddam Hussein must not only have the capacity to physically remove him from office, but should also have certain assurances that they would be able to survive him, and retain power. Under such an outcome, the new leaders of Iraq would need Western—especially American—support to buttress their regime and allow the introduction of long-term reform programs. Moreover, the regime-reform agenda of a post–Saddam Hussein leadership would primarily focus on issues of mutual concern to Iraq and the United States, including attention to the Kurdish question, relations with Iran, the Palestinian refugee issue, regional security, oil policy, various military programs, and the rights of religious and ethnic minorities. Given this critical list of concerns, any regime in Baghdad would be reluctant to accommodate all of the American concerns, including the undefined role of the military—as the guarantor of internal stability—the power share of tribal Arab Sunnis, and the restraints on political and religious freedoms. Given the history of the country, such a leadership would surely be a softer version of Saddam Hussein's regime, willing to fulfill some of the aspirations of the Kurdish community, but refusing to honor Shia longings.

### *The Chaos Scenario*
There are many scenarios of how this regime might end, but none of them would be without chaos and bloodshed. Indeed, developments immediately following the March 1991 war shed considerable light on the patterns of revolt, and their likely targets. The uprising started in Basra by retreating soldiers who shot at Saddam Hussein's statues in anger. That symbolic act triggered groups of daring youth to take to the streets with light machine guns. In response, senior members of the Baath Party and security men, Shias and Sunnis alike, were

handpicked by angry mobs before being killed in summary executions. Then local offices of the Baath Party and other security organs were destroyed. Hundreds of officers, soldiers, junior members of the Baath Party, government employees, Shias and Sunnis alike, who were fortunate to escape the onslaught of the war, joined rebel factions, assuming leadership roles when necessary. The news of the rebellion spread and triggered similar defiance in most southern cities, with identical patterns.

Over time, and as rebellious Iraqis started to believe that the regime would collapse, many more joined the armed groups, formed their own checkpoints, and searched for state targets to vent their anger. Outrage was necessary to maintain the momentum of the rebellion. Local dignitaries and tribal leaders assumed leadership roles, but by the end of the first week, ordinary Iraqis—who were dazzled by decades of harsh authoritarianism—were in search of broader-based and collective leadership. Most Shias, for example, gravitated toward known religious figures and rallied behind Ayatollah Khoi, the 90-year-old spiritual leader in Najaf. Others called for Ayatollah Al Hakim, the exiled religious leader in Iran, to assume his rightful place. Neither of them was in a position to fill the emerging leadership vacuum or lead the country on a national level. Given such uncertainties, the uprising withered at the vine and, after a few days, ended in a bloodbath.

Within a very short period of time, Republican Guard units crushed the rebellion with merciless and indiscriminate force, as the uprising in the south was crushed. Southern Shias were frightened, a phenomenon that shaped their political outlook. Since 1991, the south has not witnessed any signs of popular unrest. When Mohammed Al Sadr, a senior clergyman, was assassinated in Najaf in 1991, it was not the Shias of the south but those in the poor districts of Baghdad who rebelled. So-called emergency forces in Baghdad moved swiftly to crush the unrest, and were kept at full display for several weeks as a deterrent.

The March 1991 uprising in the predominantly Kurdish north and Shia south targeted the regime's party and security institutions and made its men scapegoats. To be sure, the dynamics of the rebellion at the micro level were similar in both regions, although the eventual outcome in the north was drastically different from that in the south. It was days after the relatively successful uprising in the south that the Kurds mobilized against the state. This uprising, ironically, was initiated and led by Kurdish tribal leaders known as the Johoosh, who had been, until that day, collaborators of the Iraqi regime. On balance, the Johoosh decided to switch allegiances and declared their support for the exiled Kurdish leaders, Barazani and Talabani. What followed was nothing short of dramatic, as over a million Kurds drove across the borders to Iran and Turkey. Under international pressure, the Iraqi military withdrew from the three Kurdish provinces, where Kurds have been running an autonomous region ever since.

Whether a similar breakdown scenario is likely to occur again is difficult to anticipate. Neither Operation Desert Fox in 1998 nor the assassination of a Shia leader in 1999 was sufficient to trigger a mini-uprising. But if Shias perceive a breakdown in the authority of the regime, then an uprising could occur, with a slower pace but with a pattern similar to the March 1991 uprising—spontaneous, local, and unorganized. Yet, and to secure the loyalty of its troops, Baghdad eliminated their options to switch sides by implicating them in widespread war crimes and human rights violations. Active members of the Baath Party, special elite units within the military, and the security forces know that they will not be safe if they abandon the regime, or switch loyalties at the last hour. This knowledge substantially limits the various chaos scenarios one may fathom.

### The Kurds
Inasmuch as the March 1991 events clarified certain points, Kurdish attitudes would—presumably—be very different in the event of a new breakdown. Throughout the 1990s, the Kurds lived without Baghdad's day-to-day supervision, going so far as to declare a federal state within Iraq. Today, Kurds enjoy some international recognition, are sufficiently armed, and administer their own affairs. As a result, the prospect for another uprising in the north is not a salient issue, although it could affect politics in Baghdad. Simply stated, the Kurds could play Arab communal and political disputes to their advantage. The two Kurdish groups, led by Barazani in the provinces of Irbil and Dahuk, and Talabani in the province of Sulaymaniah, differ in their perspectives on how best to serve their long-term interests. They also differ in their immediate needs as well as narrowly defined tribal interests. In the past, they disagreed in their positions toward Iran and Turkey, the opposition and Baghdad, American covert operations, and so on. Barazani has been consistent in avoiding a confrontation with Baghdad and preserving the de facto autonomous state acknowledged by both Washington and Baghdad. Talabani, a close ally of Iran, is a risk taker who would seek more say in Baghdad, to buttress his limited influence in "Kurdistan."

### The Northeast
In addition to the Shias and the Kurds, tribal Arab Sunni groups in three provinces northeast of Baghdad—who did not rise against the regime in March 1991—deserve attention. It may be possible to impute that no uprising occurred there out of fear that a regime breakdown would result in a takeover by Shias and Kurds, presumably not in their best interests. In return for their loyalty, Saddam Hussein shielded them from the impact of sanctions. Today, tribal Arab Sunnis enjoy a standard of living better than that found in the capital and, not surprisingly, most do not wish to alter the existing balance of power. They contribute to elite military units, lead the state bureaucracy, manage various security organs, control portions of the economy, and identify their interests with that of the state. Importantly, and although several Arab Sunni mavericks attempted to assassinate Saddam Hussein, they have not joined others to undermine the regime. Most endured the cruel reprisals after each failed attempt, but continued to be loyal to preserve intrinsic interests. They see a national agenda led and defined by the military as their best vehicle for the future. It may be worth repeating that most tribal Arab Sunni elements maintain a high degree of cohesion, form a well-defined interest bloc, are properly armed, display some experience in governance, and may be ready to defend basic interests at all costs. In the case of another Shia uprising in the south or even in

Baghdad, for example, Arab Sunnis may be expected to close ranks. In the case of a breakdown of the regime, they may be expected to defend the integrity of the military and the state against all others.

## *The Capital*

Baghdadis, Shias and Sunnis alike, feared the impact of a breakdown in law and order and did not rise in March 1991. In the event, middle-class residents in and around the capital rejected a putative mob takeover. The most volatile district of Baghdad, Al Thawrah, which is carefully watched by the government and feared by Baghdadis (inhabited by an estimated two million deprived Shias), was relatively subdued in March 1991, sparing itself a brutal slaughter at the hands of Saddam Hussein's so-called emergency forces. Since then, conditions in Baghdad have gotten worse because of the sanctions and the overall lack of services. Importantly, middle-class elements are the worst hit by sanctions, and many seem to have little or no choice but to emigrate or wither silently.

If another uprising were to occur, Shia districts in Baghdad such as Al Thawrah could conceivably be optimal venues. Yet, the military and security forces would also fight hard to keep control over Baghdad, with or without Saddam Hussein in power. Without the leadership of Saddam Hussein, the military would find support among Baghdadis at grassroots level, but it would—conceivably—be a nightmare to imagine Baghdad without a forceful authority.

## From Chaos To Order

The demise of Saddam Hussein and the collapse of the regime would push Iraq into a new era. It would introduce a new set of dynamics and force most Iraqis to address issues other than Saddam Hussein. In fact, the new dynamics in a post–Saddam Hussein era are unpredictable, and its ultimate outcome is highly speculative. An authoritarian government supported by Iraq's main communities, or a prolonged civil war, and/or a possible fragmentation of Iraq define the upper and lower bounds of these speculations. These bounds exclude the emergence of a liberal democratic system in the short term.

Events that might follow the breakdown of the regime could be envisaged in two phases. The first phase assumes inevitable anarchy, with bloodshed, cycles of vengeance, and violent quests for power. Worse still, there is a danger that the military would disintegrate as a national institution and emerge as the spearhead of tribal Arab Sunni elements. Soldiers, who could access sophisticated weapons, including the country's chemical and biological arsenals, may well use them in their communal wars. Iraq's estimated one million men under arms might well be sucked into the cycle of violence and vengeance. It would not be surprising that violence would lead to additional conflict that would result in an orgy of inter-communal bloodshed. Extremists and provocateurs would be out of control and would lead their communities into anarchy. Tribal leaders, political groups, army officers, and foreign-backed groups would all compete to fill the void and expand their power bases. Under such circumstances, the period of bloodletting and the extent of violence are thus unpredictable, as the brutality would lead to an ongoing anarchy, especially in Baghdad. The Iraqi military, which has the capacity to "settle" military battles, would not be able to end political and communal violence without support from community leaders and political figures.

A second phase would emerge if and when Iraqis could put an end to lawlessness, control communal violence, and acknowledge the need for consensus and compromise. Outside the capital, where there are predominant and homogenous communities, there would be a quick end to anarchy. Moreover, community leaders would reach consensus on local issues but would differ on how to proceed further and address national issues. It must be clearly stated that today Iraq has no national organization, or known leaders, that could assume a leadership role on a national level, beyond existing ethnic and religious loyalties. Truth be told, the new-generation leaders lack mutual trust and political experience to conclude lasting compromises. Their exposure to regional influence would prolong the period of instability and muddy its ultimate outcome. Without a doubt, operatives from the communist, Islamic, and Baathist groups could all prove to be effective in serving others, but they would not be capable of leading the country. The least effective would be the American-backed exiled Iraqi opposition, who, ironically, may well be despised by most factions.

Nevertheless, and if all goes well, Iraqis would eventually come to terms with their collective needs, accept compromises, and develop aggregate measures to restore order. Although Iraqis could build confidence in reaching agreements on the future role of the state and acquiesce to various methods to develop the constitution, it is unlikely that they would proceed beyond law and order concerns into long-term national issues.

## An Agenda for the Future

There are no signs as of yet of meaningful dialogue or of setting a working agenda for political discourse in Iraq. Efforts to develop consensus, define an agenda, or agree on a new constitution are at their infancy. Iraq's various communities have not yet had the chance to exchange views and compromise their differences on the future.

Given that the majority of Iraqis are of tribal origins, with authoritarian leaders who acknowledge the need for consultation and consensus building but not democratic traditions of elections, accountability or participation is not impossible to fathom. Consecutive military rulers and political parties alike cashed in on Iraq's tribal authoritarian culture and discouraged the emergence of democratic traditions. Leaders often use the pretext of necessity, stability, and unity to justify the need for excess authority. A post–Saddam Hussein regime would be in real need of such stability and unity, and consequently a fresh agenda would be dominated by short-term concerns for security. Under the circumstances, few should anticipate a long-term agenda that aspires to democracy and an open society.

Still, Iraqis would attempt to reconstruct the country under a new constitution and restructure its many institutions. Naturally, Iraqis share aspirations and ideals for a peaceful country, but they lack the mechanisms to proceed on a number of key issues. So far, the debates amongst exile groups—which took place under the auspices of foreign powers and lacked credibility—clarified the need to develop consensus on a number of critical issues.

First, Kurdish demands for a federal state. Although Arabs endorse the need for self-rule and an autonomous status in "Kurdistan," they do not share with the Kurds an agenda for a federal state.

Second, the role of the army. Shias and Kurds alike will seek to limit the role of the military and broaden its base. The Iraqi army is supposed to be a national institution meant for the defense of the country, but the bulk of its officers are compromised tribal Arab Sunnis.

Third, the state structures. A decentralized structure appeals to Kurds, but some Arabs may reject it in defense of a strong central Iraq. The administration of the country from a central government in Baghdad has led to the marginalization of the regions and to fierce competition by Iraq's main communities.

Fourth, numerous foreign influences. Iraq's communities feel the need for foreign support, including demands for foreign assurances of rights and agreements. Moreover, many communities have been exposed to a high degree of foreign influence, which is perceived by leading Iraqis as undermining the country's national interest. Kurds, in particular, will insist on conducting their own foreign affairs and will seek foreign underwriting of their deals with other Iraqis.

Fifth, political participation. The main communities need to agree on an agenda concerning the principles of participation, governance, and accountability at local, regional, and central level. Although these may be agreed upon on a regional level, there are profound differences on how to proceed with respect to the central administration.

Sixth, developing the economy. The main communities need to agree on Iraq's central and regional economy, the allocation of resources, and the role of the state in providing welfare services.

Finally, civil liberties. The main communities need to agree on human and civil rights, minority status, freedom of expression and association, and other related issues and the extent to which these rights should be secured by international laws and agreements.

## *The Shia Political Agenda*

The 12 million Shias make up over 60 percent of Iraq's population and over 80 percent of its Arab population. Assuming that Iraq resolves the Kurdish demand for an autonomous federal region, it would be left with a minority of Arab Sunnis in government and an increased majority of Shias who will certainly demand wider participation in the decision-making process. Consequently, the Shia political agenda is crucial to Iraq's stability.

## *Who Are the Shias?*

The Shias of Iraq form neither a homogenous religious community nor a mass-based society. The majority are tribal Arabs, mainly concentrated in southern Iraq. Baghdad has influential Shia families and a highly urbanized Shia population, and more than half of its inhabitants are of tribal Shia origin. They constitute the poorest and most deprived citizens. Non-Arab Shias are better understood as ethnic communities in clearly defined districts; the Kurdish Failis in northeastern provinces, Turkomans in Kirkuk and Mosul, and Iraqis of Persian origin in the holy cities of Najaf, Karbala, and Khadmiya. Most of the latter are concentrated in specific districts, and their attitudes and interests differ from the majority tribal Arab Shias. Still, the three most influential Shia communities are those in Baghdad, the Arab tribes in southern Iraq, and the religious communities in the holy cities of Najaf, Karbala, and Khadmiya.

Shias are sub-divided on class, ethnic, and tribal lines, but they are bonded through shared beliefs, initiation rituals during the month of Muharam, and leadership by the ulama and the marja'. Shia's adhesion to religious institutions is deeply rooted in their communal traditions. These bonds, however, are not sufficient to make them a distinctive bloc like tribal Sunnis, Assyrians, or other minorities. Their religious affiliation plays little role in defining their daily interests but becomes of great significance during national crises.

The impact of Saddam Hussein's era on Iraqi Shias varied across the communities. In the 1980s, Faili Kurds and Iraqis of Persian origins, for example, were prime victims of the regime. Following the March 1991 uprising, the main victims were the Arab tribes in southern Iraq and those in the holy cities of Najaf and Karbala. Shias in Baghdad have suffered too, because of state neglect of their neighborhoods, but have not been targeted by the government. Baghdadi Shias suffered from a serious breakdown in their social fabric, unlike those in southern Iraq, because most lost their religious linkages with the south. The March 1991 uprising further illustrated that the Shias rallied around the traditional marja'iyya and other ulama in Najaf. They formed local communities to reflect parochial interests but could not lead or perform on a national level, because their capacity to organize and form effective structures was weak.

In this respect, it is critical to note that there are two important factors in defining the role of the clergy in Iraqi politics. First is the ethnic origin defined by the Arab-Persian element of the leadership. The religious hierarchy in Najaf has taken on a serious theological leadership role vis-à-vis Qom. However, Najaf has increased its Iraqi identity and enhanced its leadership amongst Iraqi Shias. Sayyed Sistani, for example, a non-Arab marja', commands influence amongst Shias outside, rather than inside, Iraq. The late Sayyed Sadr was a rising leader, and his assassination in 1999 left a political vacuum. In case of a future communal crisis, Iraqi Shias may well be galvanized toward an Arab Shia marja' from one of the known religious families, such as members of the Al Hakim family in Najaf.

The second factor is the political outlook of the marja'. As the highest religious authority in Najaf, the marja' stays out of politics, unless there is a national or religious crisis. In such times, Shias throughout Iraq tend to bypass their political and local leaders and abide by the direction of the marja'. This trend is neither religious nor political but cultural, and it is likely to continue. It is unlikely that the marja' of the Najaf school of thought will push for a political role, and if he did, Shia Iraqis would not necessarily accept his extended political leadership. Other clergymen are likely to seek a political role in conjunction with parties and alliances, and this too bodes ill for the future.

## Shia Politics

Political trends amongst the Shias reflect the national spectrum. These variations reflect class, communal, and educational pressures, as well as exposure to outside influences, the capacity of various players to accommodate regional demands, and the overall conditions within the region. For example, the Iraqi Communist Party and its members remain active and rooted in Shia communities. Fundamentalist Islamic (Shia) groups, such as the Islamic Dawah Party, are also active in secular communities throughout Baghdad. Even the Baath Party has a large Shia membership. These three parties are rooted in Shia communities and have the capacity to re-organize and re-enter the political fray as serious contenders for power. Their weaknesses, however, have led to the emergence of new leaders and alliances amongst the non-politicized sectors. New groups have emerged with local leaders, smaller groups, and social dignitaries. The clergy, tribal leaders, businessmen, and community leaders now provide a second tier of political players who can seek to aspire to national politics through broader alliances.

## Shia Sentiments

There are as many political views amongst the Shias as there are political groupings, and it is difficult to simplify the attitudes of Iraqi Shias on these matters. In a rare 1993 meeting hosted by the Al Khoi Foundation in London, more than 150 Shia intellectuals of different political affiliations met and expressed their views on a number of issues. The proceedings of these meetings have not been published as of yet, but a number of key issues were debated: the political crisis in Iraq, communal trends among the clergy, attitudes toward other communities, and those toward the state, Iran, and various Arab countries.

First, Shias—especially in the holy cities—resented the war with Iran on religious grounds. Some clergy and Islamic groups opposed the war, expressed sympathy to Ayatollah Khomeini, and sided with Iran. SCIRI continues to represent and lead that trend. Today most of the clergy and many of the Islamic groups in exile see Iran as a state that allows Iraqi Shias to advance their own interests. Shia members of the Baath Party and the ICP tend to be more hostile to Iran and cynical of its concerns about religious affairs. Iraqi Shias who took refugee in or were deported to Iran still perceive themselves as Iraqis and remain bitter over being in Iran.

Second, Shias have no religious or confessional problem with their Sunni brethren. This, they argue, is a cultural issue with Arab Sunnis. Shias feel bitter against those who held and abused power, and see their problem as being with the government, and not with Sunnis as such. They wish to foster good relations with Sunnis and seek assurances against power abuse.

Third, Shia political groups differ in their political programs, but they all agree on the need for broad political participation and call for the protection of civil rights. Islamic groups in particular call for an elected government based on Islamic referendum and seek an alliance with Sunnis and Kurds to accomplish such an objective. Liberal, secular, and leftist groups advocate a temporal democratic system with a decentralized government. Arab nationalists and Baathists see the need for a reformed centralized government backed with national reconciliation.

Fourth, Islamists do not have clear-cut views on the future of the Kurds. During the INC meetings, ten different views were expressed from amongst Islamist delegates. Shia liberals and nationalists, and even some leftist elements, saw the need for an autonomous Kurdish region and did not object to its creation.

Fifth, all Shia constituents look to Iraq's affiliation with Arab causes and concerns, but differ to the extent that such affiliations may compromise the country's intrinsic interests. Nationalists pursue Arab unity, Islamists pursue Muslim unity and closer ties to Iran, and liberal and leftist groups focus on a purely Iraqi identity.

Finally, there is also a strong cynicism of, and resentment toward, American policy vis-à-vis Iraq. In particular, many Shias resent the sanctions, Washington's obduracy toward the Iraqi population, and its inconclusive measures against Saddam Hussein. Shias do not object to the American regional policy even if the majority favors positive relations with the United States. Undoubtedly, Iran will continue to influence some of the Islamic groups, which might seek power by radicalizing public opinion against U.S. policies on Arab and Iraqi issues.

## *The Political Future of the Shias*
Shia communities are thus vulnerable and exposed to a wide range of influences. They face tough choices with serious consequences and have neither developed a political agenda nor identified a new political leadership. The most likely outcome is that they would go through a leadership crisis, which would be fulfilled by traditional clergymen in the short term. The marja' would be in a position to lead the community and restore a sense of direction. Nevertheless, it should come as no surprise if and when extreme and radical politics would flourish amongst Shias, during the transition period in Baghdad. The ICP and the IDP, for their part, would not be in a position to lead but they could be disruptive. Tribal leaders may well fill the power vacuum during any transition period in the south, and they would have the capacity to build bridges with Sunni elements, but in the long term, Shias would find—out of necessity—that it is in their best interests to reform the state and work within it.

## Conclusion

The two Gulf Wars, the United Nations sanctions, and the ruthlessness of Saddam Hussein's regime have all polarized Iraq's main communities—the Shias, the tribal Arab Sunnis, and the Kurds—along ethnic and confessional lines. The effects of this polarization are deep and irreversible, and will probably reshape both the roles of the state vis-à-vis Iraq's main communities and the country's inter-community relationships. Saddam Hussein's domestic policies, coupled with the decade-old sanctions regime, have weakened Iraq's national unity and identity, revived ethnic and religious sentiments, raised communal tensions, and undermined the role of the state.

What is truly undeniable is that relying on state institutions to benefit a minority of tribal Arab Sunnis, at the cost of Iraq's main communities—the Shias and the Kurds—has resulted in dire consequences. Saddam Hussein may survive sanctions or be survived by a relative in power, but ultimately the regime will face violent confrontations with the Shias and will make serious concessions and compromises. Irrespective of what eventually transpires in Baghdad, the Kurds will continue to maximize their returns, push for less central government, and seek constitutional concessions to and guarantees for their de facto autonomous region. The majority of Iraqis, including Shias, will settle for a broader political system and a centralized government. And tribal Arab Sunnis will most probably retain power through the military after they resist a larger share for Shias and Kurds in state affairs.

Today, Iraqi politics have been transformed, from those of competing ideologies to those that emphasize ethnic-tribal expediency. An entire generation of Iraqis no longer relates to traditional political parties and is influenced by foreign forces, communal rather than national interests, and even narrow perspectives.

The current deadlock in Iraq will surely end by either the revival of the regime or its breakdown. Either way, the prospects are bleak. Iraq's concerns may well be limited to its immediate needs for security and stability—rather than its long-term aspirations for democracy, development, or prosperity—but much of what will occur depends on existing institutions. The military and other state institutions are critical in ensuring stability, even if they cannot lead by force alone, or implement lasting reforms without the consent and cooperation of Shias and Kurds. If the regime can survive a change in its leadership, then it can carry out only reforms that would fall short of demands made by a majority of Iraqis. If Baghdad survives the bloody aftermath of the regime's removal, then it would either accommodate far-reaching reforms or risk fragmentation. Its chances for survival would then depend on the ability of Iraqi community leaders to reconcile existing differences. Can Iraqi Shia leaders, tribal Arab Sunni officials, and Kurdish chieftains agree on constitutional, state, and economic reforms? The prospects are indeed bleak, but many may well be prodded by their constituents to compromise and chart a new direction for the country.

# THE REPUBLIC OF IRAQ

CHAPTER 6

## The Military in Iraqi Politics

Andrew Parasiliti

Iraq's military has been and remains the final arbiter of political power, the key to a regime's survival or its demise. A legacy of military intervention underscores the lack of democratic institutions and processes in modern Iraqi politics and complicates the prospects for a democratic transition after Saddam Hussein. In order to draw the appropriate lessons from the past, political-military relations in modern Iraq should be understood in a broader historical context that takes into account the effects of ideology, colonialism, and dictatorship on Iraq's political development.

This chapter examines the role that the military has played in modern Iraqi politics; the influence of ideology in shaping that role; civil-military relations under the Baath, including both Gulf Wars; and some concluding thoughts about what this might mean for Iraq's military in the future.[1]

### Ideology and the Military in Modern Iraqi Politics

Arab nationalism has played an instrumental role in shaping the interventionist bent to Iraq's military. The problem in civil-military relations in Iraq can be understood, in part, as a result of the influence of a powerful anti-colonial and pan-Arab ideology on a developing state with weak political institutions.[2]

The first decade of independence gave the Iraqi monarchy and the traditional ruling classes no quarter from the revolutionary ideologies and movements of the day. A close association with Britain, the mandatory power until Iraqi independence in 1932, diminished the Iraqi monarchy's credibility among many Iraqi and Arab nationalists. Furthermore, the radical and nationalist ideologies that swept both Europe and the Arab world during the inter-war period contained a strong element of militarism. Iraq's education system, the Military College, and associated institutions propagated these ideas among Iraq's youth. In turn, many young Iraqi nationalists proved receptive to a way of thinking that stressed both pan-Arab identity and animosity toward a "colonial" Britain.

A central figure in introducing these ideas into Iraq's national education program was Sami Shawkat, who served as director-general of education (1931–33; 1939; 1940) and minister of education (1940). Shawkat is well known for, among other things, his 1933 speech "The Manufacture of Death," in which he argued that the ability to cause and accept death in pursuit of pan-Arab ideals was the highest calling. He was a prominent member of the Muthanna Club, which sponsored many talks and lectures on pan-Arabism. Under Shawkat's guidance, the Iraqi education curriculum introduced military-style instruction, including uniforms for both teachers and students. In 1939, he instituted *Al-Futuwwa*, a paramilitary youth organization named after a social organization of the Abbasid caliph al-Nasir al-din Allah. Shawkat's promotion of a nationalist education system and vanguard youth organization foreshadowed the Popular Army and youth organizations of the Baath Party four decades later.[3]

The curriculum at Iraq's Military College, which opened its doors in 1924, reinforced the nationalist, and anti-British, pedagogical approach of Sami Shawkat and his associates. Although British and Iraqi officers taught the classes, and used British manuals translated into Arabic, young cadets became exposed to the radical and revolutionary Arab ideologies of the time. Tawfiq Husain, a lecturer in military history, indoctrinated young Iraqi military officers into the ways of Arab nationalism, Iraqi-style. Husain, who was educated in the Ottoman military system and had served in the Turkish army, encouraged an activist role for the military in Iraqi political affairs. He soon gathered a coterie of military officers around him weaned on nationalist doctrine. He influenced, among others, officers who supported both Bakr Sidqi and the "Four Colonels" who backed Rashid Ali in 1941.[4]

Over time, the pan-Arabism of Iraq's educational and military systems encouraged an activist worldview centered on Arab unity, anti-imperialism (read anti-British), and the Palestinian issue. Young military officers and students of the period became indoctrinated in an ideology that challenged the pro-British inclination of the Iraqi monarchy and the pre-revolutionary era's most formidable politician, General Nouri Al-Said. The nationalist, ideological bent of Iraq's new officer classes eventually influenced both the Free Officer movement that overthrew the monarchy in 1958 and the Baath officers who took power in 1963 and 1968.

## The Assyrian Affair and Its Repercussions

The embryonic nature of Iraq's political institutions, the increasing restlessness of its officers and students, and the weakness of the Iraqi monarchy ushered in the era of military interventions. King Faysal I's death in September 1933 and the succession of Ghazi bin Faysal, his only son, to the throne signaled this new period in Iraqi politics. Ghazi had attended Iraq's Military College and identified with the nationalist spirit there. He also laid Iraq's first public and official claim to Kuwait.[5]

Ghazi had foreshadowed his nationalist inclinations during the "Assyrian affair" in the months prior to his ascension to the throne. Despite his general indifference to his responsibilities of governance, Crown Prince Ghazi had made known his disregard for Britain's role in Iraqi politics and thereby earned himself a following among those officers and students advocating a more independent line in Iraq's political affairs. Ghazi was a vocal advocate of the Assyrian campaign. The Assyrians were easy targets for nationalist provocateurs in both the government and the military. The architect of the eventual massacre was General Bakr Sidqi, who, though of Kurdish origin, espoused the demagogic nationalist rhetoric of the day.[6]

The Assyrian affair is noteworthy for three precedents that it set with regard to the role of the military in Iraq's politics.

First, it provided both the precedent and the raw material for the interventionist role that the army would eventually play in Iraqi politics. The government sought to capitalize on popular support for the Assyrian pogrom to expand the size and influence of the military, in the guise of containing possible threats in both the north and the south of the country. In fact, the Iraqi parliament passed the first mandatory conscription bill in 1934, against opposition from both tribal leaders and the British government. Soon thereafter the military became a career path for a generation of young men from all classes and regions of Iraq, who, concurrently, became exposed to the nationalist ideologies of the day. The advent of conscription broke down traditional bonds of loyalty based upon tribe and religion, replacing them with secular notions of national and, especially, pan-Arab identities. The ideological indoctrination of Iraq's officer class undermined the state-building role that militaries have traditionally played in developing some societies.

With conscription, "the military" could no longer be viewed as a "unitary actor" in Iraqi politics, as the armed forces became a favored institution for those of various ideological stripes committed to an independent and nationalist path for Iraq. Nationalists within the military included both the Iraq-first and pan-Arab currents, a tension and schism that has colored Iraqi nationalist movements ever since. In addition to the nationalist parties, the Iraqi Communist Party also had its followers among Iraq's new officers.[7]

These developments allowed Bakr Sidqi to parlay his hero status and undertake the first military coup in Iraq in 1936, beginning a period of coups and counter-coups that ended in 1941, when British forces intervened to overtake the Rashid Ali government. Not surprisingly, General Sidqi soon faced challenges of his own from competing nationalist quarters in Iraq's military, as well as from Nouri Al-Said, who waged his campaign against Bakr Sidqi from exile in Egypt. Bakr met an assassin's bullet less than a year after seizing power.

The second lesson from the Assyrian affair was that the popular support for the campaign displayed the depth of anti-British sentiment in Iraq, as well as the centrality of anti-imperialism in Iraq's Arab nationalist parties and movements. Fifteen years later, in 1948, Nouri Al-Said's re-negotiation of the 1930 treaty with Britain, known as the Portsmouth Treaty, provoked the largest anti-regime demonstrations to date, the so-called *watbah*, or uprising, of 1948, which brought down the new cabinet.[8]

Third, the Assyrian affair set a precedent for the military's role as guardian of Iraqi unity from domestic enemies, rather than neighboring powers. For here is where the army would have its most notable "successes," such as the subsequent campaigns against the tribes of southern Iraq and the Kurds of the north. In a similar vein, another tragedy of the Assyrian affair is that it foreshadowed the tactics of a later era, portraying an act of political violence under the guise of nationalism as an anti-imperialist crusade. The precedent of "foreign enemies" necessitating extreme actions at home became an unfortunate and regular feature of Iraqi, and especially Baath, politics.[9]

The role played by ideology in the pre-revolutionary era cannot be emphasized enough. Political developments regarding the formation of the state of Israel and the question of Palestine further shaped the Iraqi outlook, and offered politicians several opportunities to thwart rivals, under the guise of adherence to a pan-Arab idea or cause. The defeat of Arab forces in the 1948 War intensified calls in certain ideological circles for greater Arab unity. Nationalist sentiments grew, particularly among young Iraqi and Arab officers, who blamed the Arab governments for the defeat in the war. The situation of Iraqi Jews also became increasingly untenable, in part because they became scapegoats for the economic duress caused by the conflict, and their exodus from Iraq began. The economic and political challenges of 1948–49 forced the imposition of martial law and the return of General Nouri, who took the opportunity to move against the Iraqi Communist Party, which he blamed for ongoing strikes and demonstrations.

## Civil-Military Relations under the Baath

The relationship between the Iraqi military and the Baath Party is complex and related in ways that are often overlooked. Despite well-documented conflicts, purges, and regular coup attempts, the Baath and the military draw from an interconnected nationalist background and experience. Indeed, the Baath Party could not have pulled off two coups and two wars without the cooperation and complicity of its members in Iraq's armed forces. Hanna Batatu suggests that the rise of Baath Party members in the military hailing from Tikrit (the hometown of Saddam Hussein and Ahmed Hassan al-Bakr, among others) has to do with the positioning of Tikriti men in the Royal Military Academy, and their ability, through their Party and family connections, to outlive rival parties and clans.[10]

Foreshadowing the events of five years hence, the Baath Party allied itself in 1963 with nationalist military figures to bring about the removal of Abdul-Karim Qassem from power. Although Staff Marshal Abdul Salam Aref ruled in title if not deed as president of the republic after the Baath coup, real power rested in the hands of Baath Party figures, especially Ali Saleh Al-Sadi and his colleagues from the civilian wing of the Party. Al-Sadi sought to curtail the Aref-military power base to give more weight to the National Guard. As many officers betrayed Nasserite leanings, a popularly based paramilitary force placed under the command of Colonel Munir al-Wandawi, a trusted officer-Baathist, was rapidly created and beefed up to act as a balancer. The Guard, which grew from a force of 5,000 in February to 34,000 by August 1963, challenged military officers and their authority, and its actions and abuses earned it a nefarious reputation. When political rivalries spilled into open conflict in November 1963,

Aref, who had for a time stood a middle ground, finally called out his troops and put an end to the excesses of the Baath Party and its paramilitary wing. This swift action ended the short, brutal history of the first Baath regime.[11]

In reviewing the lessons learned from 1963, the Party articulated its troubled relationship with the military by blaming the demise of the first Baath regime on "a dominant rightist military aristocracy, cut off from the army, the people and the national movement."[12] Baathist ideology gave "urgent" priority to consolidating its leadership in the Iraqi military, purging "suspect elements," and integrating the "armed forces with the people's movement, directed by the Party, and [ensuring] its effective contribution to the revolutionary enterprise."[13] Toward this end, the Party "managed . . . to install its own, very substantial and effective organization in the armed forces. Supervised by the Party leadership, it has played its part as an avant-garde."[14] The Baath regime also established the General Intelligence Directorate, composed of Party members and apparatchiks, to consolidate its power over internal police and security operations.

Once in power again in 1968, the Baath Party sought to subordinate the Iraqi military to the government, and keep it out of domestic politics. Toward that end, Iraqi leaders, led by then–vice president Saddam Hussein, sought to reduce the influence of military officers in Iraqi politics. What followed was a re-ordering of the Baath Party hierarchy, including the elimination of rivals and perceived rivals, including many of the old-guard Baathist officers who had been the backbone of the Party and the 1968 coup d'état. The new regime stressed civilian leadership of the government and the Party, and looked to strategic tribal affiliations and patronage networks when staffing senior leadership posts. Immediately after the July 1968 coup, the Revolutionary Command Council (RCC) consisted entirely of military officers. By 1986, career officers played no significant role on the RCC, replaced by civilian party officials who owed their allegiance to Saddam Hussein.[15]

In 1970, the Baath Party transformed the National Guard into the Popular Army, which operated as a militia independently of the regular armed forces.[16] Four years later, Deputy Prime Minister and RCC member Taha Yassin Ramadan took over as its commander-in-chief. The Popular Army (also known as the People's Army or Party Militia) assumed responsibility for internal security, propagation of Baathist ideology, and protection of the regime from subversion by the regular armed forces. It included the Youth Vanguard, a paramilitary organization for secondary school students founded in 1975. By 1982, the Popular Army reportedly had 450,000 "active participants," both men and women, located in towns and villages throughout Iraq.[17]

The "Baathization" of Iraq's officer corps undermined morale and professionalism. Party apparatchiks in the armed services challenged traditional military lines of authority. In the late 1970s, the regime also set about purging Communist cells in the military as part of its brutal crackdown on the Iraqi Communist Party.

The Baath Party had thus recognized and implemented a strategy to deal with the dual roles of the armed forces: as a partner in achieving and holding onto power, and as an element of potential subversion against those in power.

Batatu argues that although the civilian wing of the Party sought and achieved primacy over the officer corps by the mid-1970s, it would be a mistake to view this as a zero-sum contest. Instead, despite the clear tensions in these competing wings of the Party, he perceives the civilian wing of the second Baathi regime as more, not less, reliant on the officer corps for maintaining power. He concludes that "so long as the Baath continues to be characterized by the insubstantiality of its ideological links and the volatility of its mass support, its ultimate reliance on the army is inescapable."[18]

### Saddam Hussein and the Expansion of Iraqi Military Power

Saddam Hussein utilized Iraq's oil wealth to fund an expansion of the Iraqi military's size and capabilities, seeking to make the armed forces an instrument of his strategic ambitions. Iraqi governments had historically talked a good fight regarding pan-Arab ideals and interests, but performance hardly matched rhetoric in 1948, 1967, and 1973. The second Baath regime articulated a more elaborate and refined ideological position toward Iraq's international and pan-Arab roles and responsibilities, but this time around, with expanded oil revenues after 1973, the regime set on a course to develop the economic and military capability to undertake a regional bid for dominance.

The ideological stance of the Baath emphasized what Ofra Bengio has labeled "three cycles of hostility," all rooted in the revisionist pan-Arab politics that have come to define Iraqi regimes since the time of the monarchy. The first cycle focused on the Arab struggle against "imperialism," both British and American. *The Central Education Program (al-Minhaj al-Thaqafi al-Markazi)*, published by the government in 1977, included a chapter on "The Arabs and Imperialism." This official document stressed the need for Arab strategies to thwart Anglo-American bids to frustrate Arab unity and control the region's oil resources.[19] The second cycle dealt with the Arab struggle against Israel and "Zionism," which is of course linked to the struggle against imperialism; and the third on the threat from Iran, including Teheran's alleged coordination with Israel in its presumed aggressive designs against Baghdad and the Arab world.[20]

The more elaborate and externally-focused worldview of the Baath coincided with an expansive economy. By 1980, Iraq had become OPEC's second largest oil producer, its income from oil exports exceeding $26 billion. The Iraqi economy grew apace with the rise in oil export revenues. GNP per capita increased in real terms, from $729 in 1973 to $5,639 in 1979, before dipping to $4,465 in 1980.[21] Buoyed by positive economic developments, Saddam Hussein—who believed that a strong military was essential for Iraq to play a leading role in international relations—accelerated his ambitious programs. In a June 1975 speech, he stressed both "the decisive weight of . . . a solid economic base and an effective military capability" in Iraq's regional role.[22] Between 1973 and 1980, Iraq's annual military expenditures averaged 18.4 percent of GNP. The size of the armed forces in terms of military personnel increased from 105,000 in 1971 (1 percent of the total population) to an estimated 430,000 in 1980 (3.3 percent of the total population).[23]

Iraq also expanded and diversified its arms procurement policies at this time, as Saddam Hussein orchestrated the Treaty of Friendship and Cooperation between Iraq and the Soviet Union in 1972. The treaty provided Baghdad with a valuable patron for arms supplies, military advice, and training. At the same time, Iraq cultivated France, Argentina, and several other countries to diversify sources of military technology and weaponry.

Iraq's economic and military ties with the Soviet Union, France, and other Western powers played a vital role in another military priority—the development of nuclear, chemical, and biological weapons. In 1976, Iraq purchased the Tammuz 1 (Osiraq) nuclear reactor from France, in its quest for a leading role in regional affairs. Saddam Hussein determined that a regional role required a strategic capability to challenge Israel and Iran.

Given this strategic objective, Saddam Hussein sought to complement his expansion of the Iraqi military with major political initiatives within the region and, to a lesser extent, at home. In 1975, the then–vice president of Iraq negotiated the Algiers Agreement with Iran, to end Iranian—and by extension American and Israeli—support for a Kurdish insurrection in Iraq that had been consuming the military's time and resources. While the Iraqi leader described the decision as "bitter and grave," because of the perceived injustice of Iraq's territorial concessions to Iran, he also defended the treaty as vital, at the time, to Iraq's development and reconstruction.[24]

## Saddam Hussein and the Iranian Revolution

The Iranian revolution presented Saddam Hussein with a challenge to his regime's security and an opportunity to expand Iraq's power, with implications for the course of civil-military relations in Iraq.

The overthrow of the Shah and the coming to power of Iran's revolutionary government in 1979 ended the relative peace and stability that had existed between the two neighbors since the Algiers Agreement. Iran's revolutionary leader Ayatollah Ruhollah Khomeini supported and encouraged Islamist opposition to Saddam Hussein's regime inside Iraq. Ayatollah Muhammad Bakr Al-Sadr, a distinguished and charismatic Iraqi cleric and jurist, galvanized Shia-based opposition to Saddam Hussein in the late 1970s. Not surprisingly, the Iraqi regime responded with customary brutality, arresting, executing, and expelling thousands of Iraqi Shias. In April 1980, Saddam Hussein ordered the execution of Bakr Al-Sadr and the ayatollah's sister, the Islamic feminist Bint al-Huda, as part of a severe crackdown on regime opponents. Simultaneously, Teheran's military and revolutionary units engaged in border skirmishes with Iraqi forces, and re-established ties with various Kurdish opposition groups in northern Iraq.

Against this background, Saddam Hussein sensed opportunity, while perceiving a threat emanating from Islamic Iran to his regime's security. He came to believe that the revolutionary government in Iran was fragile, and that a decisive military blow would end the revolutionary challenge once and for all. By attacking and defeating Iran, the Iraqi president could establish full Iraqi sovereignty over the Shatt al-Arab waterway dividing the two countries, reversing what was agreed to in Algiers. Finally, a victory over Iran would secure Iraq's place atop the Arab order, and leave it the preeminent power in the Persian Gulf. To peddle its design, the Baath regime cast its conflict with Iran as a pan-Arab obligation, claiming that Baghdad was the eastern flank of the Arab frontline against combined "Persian" and Israeli efforts to thwart pan-Arab ambitions.[25] Offering yet another justification for this ill-fated decision for war, Tariq Aziz posited that Iraq's experience in the war with Iran "provide[d] the Iraqi Army with the qualitative experience needed for the next battle against the Zionist enemy."[26]

The war with Iran dramatically influenced the course of civil-military relations in Iraq. The Baath Party credited the war for the emergence of a "deep, strong and creative Iraqi nationalism . . . for the first time linked to the Arab nationalist bond."[27] That war plays a vital role in the development of nationalism is a common theme in the international relations literature dealing with state development and evolution. Raymond Aron wrote that "nations have rarely achieved an expression of their will as states without the intercession of force."[28] In observing the situation in Iraq, Frederick W. Axelgard hypothesized that the war with Iran might have indeed contributed to a "potential transformation of political-military relations" in Baghdad because it forced the military into a newfound role: to defend the country against a foreign enemy, rather than to meddle in domestic politics.[29] Not surprisingly, the increase in the military's size and capabilities that began in the 1970s continued and expanded during the eight-year conflict. Furthermore, that Iraq's Shia community stood and fought, and did not cut and run, signaled to Axelgard and other observers that "the war has probably exerted a decisive, consolidating influence on Iraqi politics by cementing the national loyalty of Iraq's Shi'is."[30]

While the experience of war with Iran led to greater civilian control of the Iraqi military, the tension between Saddam Hussein and the Iraqi professional officer class worsened, rather than improved, as a result of the war with Iran. The Iraqi president regularly dominated the decision-making process regarding the conduct of battlefield operations, with less than glorious results, while purging and executing those senior officers deemed incompetent or disloyal. The resulting fear of retribution from above hindered the performance of the military, especially early on in the war. Reports of attempted coups and assassinations originating from the military against Saddam Hussein surfaced during and after the war, as did the subsequent purges and executions that would follow. Setbacks on the battlefield encouraged Saddam Hussein to give his generals more decision-making authority in the final years of the war, leading to some improvements in performance and adaptability in Iraq's military campaigns against Iran.[31] When celebrating Iraq's successful military campaigns against Iran, however, Saddam Hussein made sure that the final credit was his alone, reminding one of Edward Gibbon's observation that the first Caesars were not "disposed to suffer that those triumphs which *their* indolence neglected should be usurped by the conduct and valor of their lieutenants. The military fame of a subject was considered as an insolent invasion of the Imperial prerogative."[32]

That Iraq won the Iran-Iraq War also requires qualification. The eight-year war, started by Iraq, set back, rather than enhanced, Iraq's economic power and regional standing. The economic and human cost of the war signaled a decline in Iraq's power relative to its Gulf neighbors and rivals. This awareness of relative decline influenced Saddam Hussein's decision to invade Kuwait in 1990. After the war, Iraqi military officers and servicemen returned home to a broken economy with high unemployment. There appeared no "peace dividend" for Iraq's sacrifices. The Arab Gulf states, for example, were loath to recognize Iraq as pre-eminent Gulf power based upon Iraq's military sacrifices.

On another score, Saddam Hussein sought to use military power to solve the Kurdish problem in Iraq once and for all. Here, as in the Assyrian affair and the Kurdish insurgency of 1974–75, the army played its role as guardian of Iraqi unity against enemies from within the state. That both leading Kurdish opposition groups—the Patriotic Union of Kurdistan and the Kurdistan Democratic Party—had sided with Iran by 1986 allowed the regime to raise questions about the overall loyalty of Iraqi Kurds to the Iraqi state. In February 1988, the Baath government launched a brutal counter-insurgency military campaign, the Anfal (or "spoils"), against the Kurds, replete with village destruction, use of chemical weapons, and forced resettlement of Kurdish citizens.[33] Human Rights Watch/Middle East estimated that Iraqi forces destroyed 2,000 Kurdish villages and caused the disappearance of as many as 200,000 Kurds, most of them civilians. When asked about the regime's complicity in the Kurdish disappearances, Ali Hassan Al-Majid, secretary-general of the Northern Bureau of the Iraqi Baath Socialist Party and paternal cousin of Saddam Hussein, replied: "It couldn't have been more than 100,000."[34]

In the context of the complicated experience of prosecuting the war with Iran, including the developments and setbacks in civil-military relations and the qualified nature of the Iraqi victory, the Iraqi military had again turned its attention to the matter of defending the state from enemies within, prosecuting the anti-insurgency campaign against the Kurds with infamous ferocity.

## Saddam Hussein and the War for Kuwait

The second Gulf War raises further questions about the position of the Iraqi military in a post-Saddam transition. First, Iraq's professional military leaders appear to have played marginal roles in the decisions that led to the invasion of Kuwait and the subsequent confrontation with United Nations coalition forces. After the Iran-Iraq War, Saddam Hussein's decision-making circle had narrowed even further, granting pride of place to those trusted insiders, such as Husayn Kamil Al-Majid and Ali Hassan Al-Majid, whose loyalty was reinforced by family ties and tribal networks. Professional military officers, for the most part, were on the outside looking in, although the Republican Guard, the most elite and formidable branch of Iraq's armed forces, assumed greater prominence and, correspondingly, increased responsibility for regime security. Prior to and during the war, Iraqi generals had little opportunity for honest consultation and advice; Saddam Hussein countenanced no dissenting view. They prosecuted the war against the U.S.-led international coalition as best they could, given both the failings of Iraq's political leadership and the overwhelming superiority of American and coalition technology and military power.[35]

Second, the actions of Iraq's armed forces after the war both reinforces and complicates the military's legacy. The anti-regime rebellions in 14 of 18 Iraqi provinces following the Gulf War included many bitter and aggrieved soldiers returning from the front lines. But it was the Republican Guard, the best trained and most loyal of Iraq's military, which ruthlessly crushed the rebellions in both northern and southern Iraq. The actions of both rebellious soldiers and loyalist troops reflect the paradox of the military as both enemy and guardian of the Baath regime.

Third, whatever role Iraq's commanders may have played in the decisions that led to war, the military suffered a devastating blow to Iraq's sovereignty that included the loss of control over most of Iraqi Kurdistan, the establishment of no-fly zones in the north and south of the country, and the introduction of United Nations Special Commission (UNSCOM) weapons inspectors, who, from 1992 to 1998, documented and destroyed the major share of Iraq's proscribed non-conventional weapons systems.

As has been documented elsewhere, the cycle of mistrust between Saddam Hussein and the military continues, with reported coups and assassination attempts coming from within the armed forces, followed by the predictable purges and executions. In 1996, Saddam Hussein foiled a U.S.-backed coup attempt by Iraqi military officers that included members of the elite Special Republican Guard, the General Security Service, and the Republican Guard. In response, and since the 1991 Gulf War, Saddam Hussein has undertaken a series of measures to make his regime as secure as possible from military coups.[36]

## Conclusion

The Iraqi military continues to be the key to Saddam Hussein's survival and the best hope for his departure. This seemingly contradictory yet self-evident observation means that after Saddam Hussein, the Iraqi military remains the primary arbiter of Iraq's political future, as it has been throughout the country's modern history. Saddam Hussein's policies of intrigue, reward, and punishment have not resolved the dilemma of all modern Iraqi governments regarding the military's role in Iraq's domestic politics.

That said, the Baath Party's relationship with the military has been interrelated in ways that are often overlooked, a kind of "can't live with them, can't live without them" approach to politics. The Baath could not have engineered two coups and prosecuted two wars in the absence of an alliance with partners in the military. At the same time, the experience of both Gulf Wars deepened the hostility and mistrust between the Baath Party and the armed forces, while increasing the degree of civilian control over the military.

The challenges of a democratic transition in Iraq are greater because of the legacy of Baath rule and the complicated role of the military in modern Iraqi politics. In thinking about any post-Saddam scenario, the Iraqi military appears as the most likely agent of political change. While it may be difficult to foresee the political dispositions of future military figures, it is not hard to imagine a post-Saddam scenario that involves a military leader, a contender for power, who portrays himself and his followers as the guardians of Iraqi sovereignty and unity. The resolution to the problem of civil-military relations in Iraqi politics will therefore come only in the context of an eventual democratic transition and with the establishment of institutions and mechanisms that allow for both popular participation in Iraqi politics and the peaceful transfer of power. The transition in Iraq from dictatorship to democracy will not take place overnight. However, once these institutions and mechanisms are in place, the military may assume its proper role as defender of the country's borders, rather than as a power broker or partner in the intrigues of regime-minded politicians.

## Notes

1. An earlier version of this chapter appeared as Andrew Parasiliti and Sinan Antoon, "Friends in Need, Foes to Heed: The Iraqi Military in Politics," *Middle East Policy* 7:4, October 2000, pp. 130–140. Some of the material in this chapter is also adapted from Andrew T. Parasiliti, *Iraq's War Decisions*, Ph.D. dissertation, Baltimore, Maryland: Johns Hopkins University, 1998.
2. On the role of the military in developing countries, see Samuel P. Huntington, *Political Order in Changing Societies*, New Haven, Connecticut: Yale University Press, 1968), pp. 192–263.
3. Samir al-Khalil, *Republic of Fear: The Politics of Modern Iraq*, Berkeley and Los Angeles: University of California Press, 1989, pp. 177–79.
4. See Reeva S. Simon, *Iraq Between the Two World Wars: The Creation and Implementation of a Nationalist Ideology*, New York: Columbia University Press, 1986, pp. 127–30.
5. See David Finnie, *Shifting Lines in the Sand: Iraq's Elusive Frontier with Kuwait*, Cambridge, Massachusetts: Harvard University Press, 1992, especially pp. 106–13.
6. Stephen Hemsley Longrigg, *Iraq, 1900 to 1950: A Political, Social, and Economic History*, London: Oxford University Press, 1956, pp. 229–37; and R. S. Stafford, *The Tragedy of the Assyrians*, London: George Allen & Unwin Ltd., 1935, especially pp. 159–81.
7. See the relevant sections of Hanna Batatu, *The Old Social Classes and the Revolutionary Movements of Iraq: A Study of Iraq's Old Landed and Commercial Classes and of its Communists, Baathists, and Free Officers*, Princeton: Princeton University Press, 1978.
8. The events surrounding the Portsmouth Treaty and the uprising of 1948 are discussed in Phebe Marr, *The Modern History of Iraq*, Boulder: Westview Press, 1985, pp. 101–6; and Batatu, *op. cit.*, pp. 545–66.
9. Al-Khalil, *op. cit.*, pp. 166–76.
10. Batatu, *op. cit.*, pp. 1088–93.
11. On the first Baath regime, see ibid., pp. 1003–26.
12. *The 1968 Revolution in Iraq: Experience and Prospects: The Political Report of the Eighth Congress of the Arab Baath Socialist Party in Iraq, January 1974*, London: Ithaca Press, 1979, p. 103.
13. Ibid., p. 103.
14. Ibid., p. 105.
15. Isam al-Khafaji, "War as a Vehicle for the Rise and Demise of a State-Controlled Society: The Case of Ba'thist Iraq," in Steven Heydemann, ed., *War, Institutions and Social Change in the Middle East*, Berkeley and Los Angeles: University of California Press, 2000, pp. 267–8; and Amatzia Baram, "The Ruling Political Elite in Baathi Iraq, 1968–1986: The Changing Features of a Collective Profile," *International Journal of Middle East Studies* 21:4, 1989, pp. 447–93.
16. Arab Baath Socialist Party, Iraq, *The Central Report of the Ninth Regional Congress*, June 1982, Baghdad: January 1983, pp. 204–9 (translated by SARTREC, Lausanne, Switzerland).
17. The estimates of active members are from Christine Helms, *Iraq: Eastern Flank of the Arab World*, Washington, D.C.: The Brookings Institution, 1984, pp. 99–100, based upon her interview with Taha Yassin Ramadan. *The Central Report of the Ninth Regional Congress, June 1982*, cites a figure

of "120,000 fighters" involved in the battle with Iran; see *op. cit.*, p. 207; see also al-Khalil, *op. cit.*, pp. 29–33.
18. Batatu, *op. cit.*, p. 1079.
19. Ofra Bengio, *Saddam's Word: Political Discourse in Iraq*, New York: Oxford University Press, 1998, pp. 127–34.
20. Ibid., pp. 134–45.
21. U.S. Arms Control and Disarmament Agency, *World Military Expenditures and Arms Transfers*, various issues.
22. Saddam Hussein, "The National Potential and International Politics," *On Iraq and International Politics*, Baghdad: Translation and Foreign Languages Publishing House, 1981, p. 17.
23. U.S. Arms Control and Disarmament Agency, *World Military Expenditures and Arms Transfers*, various issues.
24. See Saddam Hussein's speech on the eve of Iraq's invasion of Iran in Baghdad Domestic Service, translated in Foreign Broadcast Information Service, *Daily Report: Middle East and North Africa*, 18 September 1980, p. E4.
25. For an official Iraqi articulation of this idea, see Saad al-Bazzaz, *Gulf War: The Israeli Connection* (translated by Namir Abbas Mudhaffer), Baghdad: Dar Al-Ma'mun, 1989.
26. Tariq Aziz, *Iraq-Iran Conflict: Questions and Discussion*, London: Third World Center, 1981, p. 44.
27. The Central Report of the Ninth Regional Congress, *op. cit.*, p. 40.
28. Raymond Aron, *Peace and War: A Theory of International Relations*, Malabar, Florida: Robert E. Krieger Publishing Co., 1981, p. 355.
29. Frederick W. Axelgard, *A New Iraq? The Gulf War and Implications for U.S. Policy*, New York and Washington, D.C.: Praeger and the Center for Strategic and International Studies, 1988, pp. 48–55.
30. Ibid., p. 29.
31. See Anthony H. Cordesman and Abraham R. Wagner, *The Lessons of Modern War, Volume II: The Iran-Iraq War*, Boulder: Westview Press, 1990, pp. 412–13.
32. Edward R. Gibbon, *The Decline and Fall of the Roman Empire*, London: Penguin, 1980, p. 29.
33. The best account of the Anfal is in Human Rights Watch/Middle East, *Iraq's Crime of Genocide: The Anfal Campaign Against the Kurds*, New Haven, Connecticut, and London: Yale University Press, 1995.
34. Cited in ibid., p. 230.
35. For an account of the role of the military in Iraqi politics prior to and during the Gulf War, see Saad al-Bazzaz, *The Generals are the Last to Know*, 2d Arabic ed., London: Dar Al-Hikma, 1996.
36. See Andrew Cockburn and Patrick Cockburn, *Out of the Ashes: The Resurrection of Saddam Hussein*, New York: HarperCollins, 1999, pp. 218–30; and Amatzia Baram, *Building Toward Crisis: Saddam Husayn's Strategy for Survival*, Washington, D.C.: The Washington Institute for Near East Policy, 1998, pp. 47–9.

# THE KINGDOM OF SAUDI ARABIA

CHAPTER 7

*Assessing Saudi Susceptibility to Revolution*

Mark N. Katz

An anti-Western revolution in Saudi Arabia would have severe negative consequences for the West, as the Kingdom possesses more proven petroleum reserves than any other country in the world. Indeed, the Saudi government has closely cooperated with the West in economic, political, and military affairs, and the United States has greatly benefited from its close partnership with the Kingdom ever since the discovery of oil there in the first part of the twentieth century. In fact, the strength and duration of Saudi-American cooperation has been remarkable, considering the many anti-American political movements and governments that have risen up during this period in the Middle East.

Should the Saudi monarchy ever be overthrown and replaced by an anti-Western revolutionary regime, several negative consequences might quickly arise. First and foremost, the price of oil could rise dramatically. Second, the vulnerability of pro-Western governments in the smaller Gulf Cooperation Council (GCC) states—Kuwait, Bahrain, Qatar, the United Arab Emirates (UAE), and Oman—would increase immediately, further driving up the price of oil if they too were overthrown. Third, a prolonged dramatic oil price increase would cause a worldwide economic crisis that could give rise to instability in many countries, which an economically weakened West would be hard-pressed to deal with.

Revolution in Saudi Arabia, then, is something that Western governments—along with the Saudi monarchy itself—understandably wish to prevent. But how susceptible to revolution is Saudi Arabia? On the one hand, Saudi Arabia seems more stable now than it was during the heyday of Arab nationalism in the 1950s and 1960s, or in the wake of either the 1979 Islamic fundamentalist revolution in Iran or the 1990–91 conflict with Iraq. If the Saudi monarchy could survive all these traumatic events, why shouldn't it continue to survive, especially in calmer circumstances?

Perhaps it can. However, the history of the twentieth century showed that non-democratic regimes are inherently unstable, displaying a marked tendency to fall sooner or later. Although the Saudi monarchy has avoided this fate to date, can it reasonably be expected to continue doing so? The question appears to be especially relevant to the Kingdom considering that absolute monarchy—the type of government in Saudi Arabia—has almost disappeared over the past two and a quarter centuries, a seemingly inexorable trend if ever there was one!

Although it would be a difficult task even under the best of circumstances, assessing the Kingdom's vulnerability is an assignment made all the more difficult by the opaqueness and secretiveness of Saudi politics. One possible means to compensate for this difficulty is to apply some of the theoretical literature on revolution to what is known about Saudi Arabia.

There are, of course, many contending theories of revolution, which focus on different factors as either the most important cause or determinant of it.[1] The purpose of this chapter is not to engage in the ongoing debate among proponents of these theories about which of them should take precedence, but to examine, instead, the implications of several theories with regard to Saudi Arabia.

Among the different theories of revolution that will be looked at here are those that focus on state breakdown, the nature of the opposition, the mobilization potential of the opposition, external intervention, democratization and revolution, and the internal military factor. It is, of course, impossible to predict whether revolution will actually occur in Saudi Arabia. Still, the analysis presented here may provide some indication of the extent to which the Kingdom appears to be (or not to be) susceptible to revolution.

### State Breakdown

The most influential perspective on revolution over the past two decades has been theorization focusing on the process of "state breakdown." According to this perspective, examining why opposition movements become strong is less important than analyzing why the power of the state declines. According to Theda Skocpol (one of the pioneers of the state breakdown theory of revolution), potential revolutionaries are always present. They are not able to achieve much, though, when the state they seek to overthrow is strong. It is only when the state becomes gravely weakened that it becomes vulnerable to overthrow by revolutionary movements. Skocpol further emphasizes that it is not the activity of revolutionary movements that leads to the weakening of the state; they are not sufficiently strong on their own to accomplish this. State breakdown results, instead, because of problems that are far more difficult for a regime to deal with effectively than the suppression of opposition movements. The breakdown of the state, then, is something revolutionaries do not cause themselves but take advantage of when it occurs.[2]

What is it that causes state breakdown? In Skocpol's case studies, the *ancien regime* was drawn primarily from an elite social class. Although Marxist analysis claims that the state is the instrument of the predominant class, Skocpol observed that while individuals running the states she examined were drawn from a predominant social class, the state itself had interests separate from that class. It is when the interests of the state and the elite diverge sufficiently sharply, Skocpol argued, that state breakdown can occur.[3] Skocpol herself saw this process occurring in predominantly traditional, agrarian societies, and thus not as something likely to occur in more modern, urban ones.[4] Other scholars analyzed how this process occurred in more urban settings.[5]

What could cause a sharp divergence between the state and the social class it was drawn from? Skocpol saw international military "pressures and opportunities" as an important cause of this phenomenon for two reasons. First, the state may engage in foreign conflict to the extent that this drains away domestic resources, thus undermining the strength of the hitherto dominant social class. Second, a state may respond to threats from abroad by attempting socioeconomic reforms, which strengthen it but weaken the dominant social class.[6] Resenting the ruler already, the elite resists increased taxes to the extent they fall on it (which they necessarily must if less privileged sectors of society are already "taxed to the max"). As the situation deteriorates, disaffected elites might attempt to thwart the ruler or seize power themselves through exploiting the long-standing grievances of non-elite segments of society, which, once aroused, may be impossible for disaffected elites to control.

An alternative, and in many ways more precise, state breakdown theory of revolution was articulated by Jack Goldstone. According to Goldstone, revolution is most likely to occur in countries experiencing rapid population growth that are unable to adequately respond to the challenges this poses due to decline in state capacity, elite conflicts, and mass mobilization potential.[7] According to Goldstone, it was this combination of circumstances that led to revolution in early modern Europe and in many countries of the contemporary developing world.[8] To be sure, the rapid growth of the non-elite population has negative consequences in Goldstone's model, but the rapid growth of the elite population has even more serious ones. In a country where it is primarily the state that employs and provides transfer payments to the elite, a crisis is inevitable when the ranks of the elite are growing but the discretionary resources available to the state are either stagnant or shrinking. If conflict erupts among the elite and order breaks down, a revolutionary situation will then emerge.[9]

Are any of the elements that the theories of Skocpol or Goldstone see as leading to state breakdown present now in Saudi Arabia?[10] Some, indeed, either appear to be present or may be in the process of developing.

Since the dramatic 1973 rise in oil prices, the Kingdom has maintained an ambitious spending program, which has included outsized expenditures on military hardware, expensive development projects, an extensive social welfare system, and massive transfer payments to the large ruling family. Riyadh has relied primarily on oil revenues to fund its expenditures, but these revenues have experienced downward pressure, due to the sustained decline in the price of oil occurring in the 1980s and throughout much of the 1990s. Although it has cut expenditures, the Kingdom's outlays have been greater than its revenues for several years. Some of these stubbornly high expenditures stemmed from the heavy cost of expelling Iraqi forces from Kuwait in 1991 as well as subsequent military expenditures aimed at deterring another Iraqi attack. While cutbacks have been made, Saudi Arabia has maintained high levels of social welfare expenditure on its rapidly expanding population—a price that the monarchy appears to see as necessary for maintaining social peace.[11] Accurate figures are not available on how much of Saudi income goes to the ever-growing ruling family. Whatever amount—undoubtedly substantial—goes to the Al Saud, nevertheless, is obviously unavailable to be spent on the non-royal population, whose standard of living appears to have stagnated or even declined in recent years.[12]

As a result of its expenditures being chronically greater than its revenues for the past two decades, the Kingdom has run up a massive budget deficit.[13] Although oil prices rose dramatically in 2000, it is doubtful that these can be sustained for long because the discovery of large quantities of oil in areas previously inaccessible to the West, such as the Caspian basin, is adding pressure on traditional oil exporters. Saudi Arabia's long-term financial situation, then, appears unlikely to improve.[14] Moreover, pumping significantly more oil for export is counterproductive in a glutted market where other producers can do the same, resulting in lower oil prices. Nor does the Kingdom appear willing to risk altering the tacit "no taxation, no representation" compact it has with its citizens, for fear that demands for the former will lead to demands for the latter.[15]

As far as conflict among the elite is concerned, there does appear to be a growing lack of "suitable positions," especially ones with real authority, for the ever-increasing number of princes. One of the reigning norms among Saudi princes is that "those with and without jobs are entitled to equal respect."[16] As the number of royal aspirants per position increases, whichever branch of the family holds the kingship may come to have increasing significance, due to the king's ability to favor his own branch. Up to now, succession to the throne has generally passed to the "eldest able" sons of Saudi Arabia's founder, King Abdul Aziz bin Abdul Rahman Al Saud. Determining who this is, of course, could easily become contentious. And as Abdul Aziz's remaining sons age, succession will, at some point, have to pass outside this group—most likely to one of the founder's grandsons. There are many of these, however. The choice of any one could leave competing branches highly dissatisfied, especially if they fear their permanent exclusion from the succession process.[17] This is the sort of conflict among the elite that, if allowed to get out of hand, could lead to state breakdown.

This is not to say, however, that Saudi Arabia is at present anywhere near experiencing the sort of state breakdown that could lead to revolution. What is being argued here instead is that some of the factors Goldstone identified as leading to state breakdown, including rapid population growth and the inability of the state to match revenues with the mounting expenditures it has led to, are currently present in Saudi Arabia. Moreover, the conflict within the elite that Skocpol and Goldstone both see as part of this process also appears increasingly likely. The factors Skocpol and Goldstone identified as leading to state breakdown appear to be getting stronger, not weaker, in Saudi Arabia.

## The Nature of the Opposition

Some theories of revolution see opposition activity as playing a far more important role in bringing about revolution than state breakdown theories of revolution suggest.[18] Yet, even assuming that the state breakdown approach is valid, studying the role of the opposition is important, since it is the opposition—or, more accurately, some part of it—that will shape the new regime if revolution successfully topples the old one. And while the opposition to the Saudi monarchy may be weaker now than in the aftermath of the 1991 Gulf War—as a front-page article in the *Washington Post* enthusiastically reported in January 2000—this perspective suggests that if state breakdown occurs, a much stronger revolutionary opposition will arise.[19]

Under the circumstances, what is the nature of the opposition that might arise in Saudi Arabia, if conditions were ripe? The question is important, since it is not so much any attachment to the Saudi monarchy—whose undemocratic government is repugnant to Western values, if not Western interests—as it is fear of what might replace it that makes revolution in the Kingdom such a frightening prospect. The reason this is so, of course, is due to Western fear that, unlike several countries where a strong pro-Western democratic opposition came to power through revolution in the past two decades, revolution in Saudi Arabia would result in the rise to power of anti-Western undemocratic forces.

Indeed, this fear appears to be well founded. From what is known about the Saudi opposition, it overwhelmingly consists of anti-democratic Islamic "fundamentalists," angry with the West for propping up the Saudi monarchy and similar pro-Western Arab regimes (which they believe the West controls), as well as for supporting Israel. This is amply documented in Mamoun Fandy's thorough study on the ideology of leading Saudi opposition figures.[20]

It may be worth noting that while democracy may have replaced its non-democratic rivals as the political system that most of the rest of the world regards as ideal, this does not appear to be true in the Arab world. There, authoritarian political ideologies, particularly "Islamic fundamentalism," appear to be genuinely popular. Still, as Nazih Ayubi has argued, "the more Irans and Sudans you get, the less impressive and appealing the Islamists' call will become."[21] Like their developing-world "Marxist" counterparts—fighting against colonial or right-wing regimes during the Cold War era—who ignored all evidence of the political and economic failure of Marxism-Leninism where it was in power, "Islamic fundamentalist" opponents of pro-Western (or secular anti-Western) dictatorships in the Middle East are either oblivious to, blame the West for, or otherwise explain away the glaring failures of existing "fundamentalist" regimes.[22] Whether or not one regards state breakdown theories of revolution as valid, it appears that the most active opposition movements at present in Saudi Arabia are anti-Western, "Islamic fundamentalist" ones. Nor does this appear likely to change in the foreseeable future.

## Mobilization Potential of the Opposition

Even more important than the existence of revolutionary opposition movements is, as Charles Tilly has argued, their mobilization potential.[23] It is first of all necessary to say something about the circumstances under which individuals support revolutionary opposition movements. Those who engage in revolutionary activity incur enormous risks, including imprisonment, severe injury, and death. While there may be a few risk-tolerant zealots willing to engage in revolutionary activity at any time, most people are risk averse and will not do so except under two extraordinary circumstances. The first arises when people are being oppressed so severely—that is, when they are being imprisoned, injured, or killed anyway—that engaging in revolutionary activity is either no more or actually less risky than not engaging in it. This, for example, is the circumstance that the Kosovar Albanians were placed in by the Serbs, and the Chechens by the Russians. The second such circumstance arises when the risks normally involved in engaging in revolutionary activity decline due to a reduction in the *ancien regime*'s ability or willingness to impose these risks on its opponents. The failure of the state to use force against its opponents, of course, is one of the most important stages in state breakdown (how it can occur will be discussed below). As the success of the revolution appears increasingly likely, the potential benefits of "joining the winning side" held out by the revolutionary opposition may appear increasingly attractive to large segments of the population with grievances against the *ancien regime*.[24]

Neither of these two circumstances is now present in Saudi Arabia. But if either or, perhaps, a combination of both ever are, then the possibility of mass mobilization would arise. Several scholars have noted that revolutionary opposition groups frequently attempt to mobilize support by promising to improve the status of hitherto deprived groups.[25] Saudi opposition groups, of course, could seek to mobilize support in this manner too. The question, then, is: Are there dissatisfied groups in the Kingdom that opposition movements could draw upon for support?

There appear to be four such possible groups: 1) non-royal Saudis; 2) non-Saudi Arabs; 3) non-Saudi Muslims; 4) non-Muslim non-Saudis. Each of these groups has reason to resent the Saudi monarchy. Non-royal Saudis (Hejazis, Asiris, Shias) have virtually no say in their government and, undoubtedly, resent the diversion of so much of its oil income to the large—and largely unproductive—ruling family.[26] Gwenn Okruhlik has vividly described the harsh conditions endured by the non-Western foreign workforce in Saudi Arabia.[27] Furthermore, there appears to be a strong sense among many non-Saudi Arabs that this country, including the two holy cities as well as its vast oil wealth, is the common property of all Arabs and not just the Saudi ruling family.[28] Thus, elements of each of these might well see rebellion against the monarchy as both desirable and advantageous, under conditions of state breakdown.

Given the "Islamic fundamentalist" political ideology of Saudi opposition groups, the fourth group—non-Muslim non-Saudis—is not one they are likely to even try to mobilize. Indeed, the expulsion of this group may well be a goal that helps to mobilize and unite the others. "Islamic fundamentalism," nevertheless, is an ideology that could help overcome divisions among Muslims, forging an alliance among non-royal Saudis, non-Saudi Arabs, and non-Saudi Muslims—an alliance that could potentially be quite powerful.

It must be emphasized, though, that disaffection among the deprived by itself is not a sufficient condition for revolution. Although they suffered mightily because of it, the over 750,000 Yemenis ordered out of the Kingdom in 1990 had no choice but to comply. Nor were there any other groups—Saudi or non-Saudi—that were willing to defend or champion them. Opposition mobilization is extremely difficult if disaffection among the elite and/or state breakdown has not occurred.

*External Intervention*
Just because powerful revolutionary opposition movements come into being, of course, does not mean that they are destined to succeed. They can be thwarted. One possible means of doing so is through external military intervention, which could probably be undertaken in this case only by the United States, either alone or in conjunction with other Western powers.

As is well known, externally mounted counter-insurgency efforts to suppress revolutionary opposition forces have proven to be costly failures in several instances, including the French interventions in Indochina and Algeria, the American one in Indochina, the Soviet one in Afghanistan, and the first post–Soviet Russian intervention in Chechnya.[29] On the other hand, externally mounted counter-insurgency efforts have succeeded in several instances, such as the British interventions in Greece, Malaya, and Oman.[30] Furthermore, the U.S.-led military operations resulting in the expulsion of Iraqi forces from Kuwait in 1991 and Serbian forces from Kosovo in 1999 hold out the prospect of rapid successful intervention elsewhere.[31]

Despite this history, what are the prospects for a successful American-led military intervention to suppress revolution in Saudi Arabia? There are many imponderables and at least one huge assumption—namely, that revolution in Saudi Arabia will break out—that make addressing this question extremely difficult. Should revolution break out in the Kingdom, however, this is a question that policymakers will have to address despite several imponderables, and so it is worth attempting to address it here.

Besides specific circumstances that cannot be foreseen under which revolutionary activity may grow serious enough to raise the question of whether external intervention should be undertaken to suppress it, there are two related factors affecting the probable success of any U.S.-led military intervention in Saudi Arabia to prevent revolution there. These are: first, the willingness of the American public to support such an intervention and, second, the effect of such an intervention on the political dynamics of the country it would occur in.

To be sure, the U.S. experience in Indochina as well as the belief in the existence of a "Vietnam syndrome" arising from it suggests that the American public would not be willing to support a long-term, costly intervention that does not succeed. On the other hand, the U.S. experience in both Kuwait and Kosovo illustrates that the American public would support, or at least tolerate, a short-term albeit costly military intervention that succeeds rapidly. As Bruce Jentleson put it, the American public is "pretty prudent"; it supports interventions that appear to have a reasonable prospect of rapid success (especially where it sees the stakes involved as significant) and opposes those that do not (especially where it sees the stakes involved as marginal). The type of military intervention that the American public appears least willing to undertake is an open-ended commitment aimed at propping up an unpopular dictatorial regime against its internal opponents.[32] What this implies for the willingness of the American public to support U.S. military intervention against revolutionary forces in Saudi Arabia is ambiguous. The public undoubtedly recognizes that Saudi Arabia is important to the global economy. On the other hand, the public may be less than enthusiastic about the prospect of losing American lives to protect the Saudi ruling family against its own people. And as occurred vis-à-vis Indochina,[33] initial public support for intervention can erode if the intervention is not seen to be successful.

This leads us to a consideration of the effect of external intervention on the country in which it occurs—a factor that has an important impact on whether external intervention succeeds or fails. In his comparative study of several revolutionary struggles waged by guerrilla forces, Timothy Lomperis concluded that the most important factor determining whether external intervention against them succeeds or fails is the effect of the external intervention on the legitimacy of both the regime it seeks to defend and the revolutionary forces opposed to it. Both the French and American interventions in Vietnam, for example, served to undermine the legitimacy of the regimes they sought to defend and to burnish the nationalist credentials of the Vietnamese communists. In Malaya, by contrast, the fact that the revolutionary opposition was drawn from an ethnic minority (the Chinese), combined with the promise of independence, served to legitimize British military intervention with the Muslim Malay majority.[34]

Importantly, assessing the potential impact of a U.S.-led military intervention to protect the Saudi monarchy is made somewhat easier by the fact that one has already occurred, in 1991. What was amazing about this experience was the extremely negative reaction by significant elements within Saudi Arabia to the presence of Western troops, even though they were there to defend the Saudi monarchy, whatever its faults, from being overthrown by what was widely known to be the far, far worse regime of Iraq's brutal dictator, Saddam Hussein.[35] Moreover, this experience also suggests that a U.S.-led intervention to protect the Saudi monarchy against its internal opponents would probably lead to an even more negative reaction than the one that occurred in 1990–91 against an external threat. Indeed, a strong U.S. role in defending the monarchy against "Islamic fundamentalist" revolutionaries could be expected to severely de-legitimize the former as well as legitimize the latter. Either anticipating or realizing this state of affairs, the American public is unlikely to support the initiation or continuation of U.S. military intervention in defense of a regime that the people living under it overwhelmingly appear to regard as illegitimate—unless the intervention can succeed rapidly and/or the regime can somehow be legitimized. As far as rapid military intervention is concerned, and while the U.S. and its allies have succeeded stunningly at this in Kuwait and Kosovo, in both cases this was done to remove occupying forces that the local populace clearly did not want there—a task far more amenable to rapid accomplishment than defending a government whose citizens either actively oppose or are unwilling to defend it. This is exactly the sort of military task that the American public—and Congress—appear most unwilling to undertake.

It is possible, of course, that a country other than the United States might intervene militarily to protect the Saudi monarchy. It is difficult, however, to imagine any other Western government being willing to do so except in conjunction with Washington. Military intervention by any other Western—or, for that matter, non-Muslim—state is unlikely to be considered any more legitimate than U.S. intervention by the Saudi population anyway. This also suggests that intervention undertaken by a Muslim country might be considered more legitimate, and hence have greater prospects for success. In the event, there are two problems with this potential. First, it is highly doubtful that any other Muslim government would be either willing or able to undertake this task—even with U.S. and Western support. Second, while troops from Western or other non-Muslim countries are unlikely to find "Islamic fundamentalism" appealing, troops from Muslim countries could well be susceptible to it, clearly reducing their reliability as defenders of the Saudi monarchy.[36]

In sum, external intervention to protect the Saudi monarchy against a revolutionary opposition would be fraught with difficulty.

There also exists, of course, the possibility that external powers could support Riyadh's internal opponents. While this is something that the Saudi as well as Western governments fear, several studies suggest that attempts by external powers to foment revolution in another country usually fail. It is when conditions are ripe for revolution internally that external support for a regime's revolutionary opponents can play an important role—though not always.[37] Since there are currently no strong internal opposition movements in Saudi Arabia, the subject of what external powers might support them and how effectively will not be addressed here.

### *The Democratic Bypass*

It was noted at the beginning of this chapter that the twentieth century showed that non-democratic regimes are inherently unstable, displaying a marked tendency to fall, sooner or later. Still, violent revolution is not the only means by which dictatorships have fallen. Some have been transformed via a fairly orderly democratization process, while others have succumbed to non-violent democratic revolution.[38] Could this happen in Saudi Arabia?

Up to now, of course, the Saudi ruling family has displayed precious little willingness to allow any meaningful democratization to occur. The appointed Consultative Council, possessing no authority to legislate and only a limited range of issues on which it may even offer advice (that the government may simply ignore), can in no sense be considered a representative, democratic body.[39] Nor does the Saudi monarchy appear willing to countenance anything like one, under current conditions. Under the circumstances, what are the prospects for democratization in Saudi Arabia if serious revolutionary activity breaks out there?

Jeane Kirkpatrick asserted over two decades ago that democratization could not occur when a regime is fighting for survival against "totalitarian" opponents.[40] Robert Pastor, though, has shown that the democratic transformation of an unpopular dictatorship can occur even when non-democratic revolutionary forces seeking to overthrow it have grown quite powerful. He has also shown, however, that democratization efforts under these circumstances can fail.[41] What, then, accounts for whether they succeed or fail? The crucial factor, according to Pastor, is not American foreign policy. American administrations, whether Democratic or Republican, all encourage democratization when anti-American revolutionary opposition forces seriously threaten pro-American dictatorships. What *is* the crucial factor, according to Pastor, is the reaction of the middle classes to these democratization efforts. If the middle classes embrace them, then non-democratic revolution can be averted, as occurred in the Philippines in 1986 and Chile in 1988–89. If, however, the middle classes reject such efforts, and choose to ally with an anti-Western, non-democratic revolutionary opposition instead, then the prospects for democratization are poor and those for non-democratic revolution, good—as in Cuba in 1958–59 and Iran and Nicaragua in 1978–79.[42]

Naturally it bears asking, why would the middle classes embrace the non-democratic opposition, seemingly in contrast to both their interests as well as the expectations that outside observers might have? Pastor cites the presence of a number of factors that could allow this to occur: regime resistance to democratization, middle-class mistrust of American support for democratization after years of U.S. support for dictatorship, and perhaps most important, a naïve faith on the part of the middle class that if it allies with the revolutionary opposition to get rid of the *ancien regime,* it will be able to co-opt the opposition and dominate the new regime afterwards.[43]

There is no way, of course, to accurately forecast how middle-class elements in Saudi Arabia would behave in the event of a revolutionary situation arising. There are, however, several reasons to suspect that they might not embrace democratization but side with the non-democratic opposition instead. To begin with, Pastor notes that the middle-class is more likely to embrace democratization in countries that have had previous experience with it, and less likely to do so in those that have not.[44] Saudi Arabia, of course, falls into the latter category. In addition, while Marxism-Leninism was a revolutionary ideology that privileged the interests of the "workers" and "peasants" above those of the middle-class, several scholars have argued that "Islamic fundamentalism" is a middle-class ideology.[45] It is well known that the Teheran merchant class—the *bazaaris*—were among the most important supporters of the Ayatollah Khomeini. Ervand Abrahamian has argued that Khomeini saw himself as the defender of the Iranian middle-class, of which the Shia clergy was very much an integral part.[46]

The Islamic opposition in Saudi Arabia is also a middle-class movement. As Joseph Kostiner observed, "the new fundamentalist opposition's most important characteristic has been its educational and socio-economic base. Its members were neither lower class nor tribally identified. Instead the common denominator was membership in the new middle class: graduates . . . working as professionals or administrators."⁴⁷ It must not be forgotten that Usama bin Laden, the alleged Saudi mastermind behind various attacks against American targets, himself hails from this background.⁴⁸

Because of Saudi Arabia's lack of experience with democracy, the improbability of the Saudi monarchy ever allowing meaningful progress toward it under any circumstances, the resentment that non-royal Saudis undoubtedly harbor toward the U.S. for supporting the anti-democratic Saudi monarchy so firmly, and the demonstrated appeal of Islamic fundamentalism to middle-class audiences in the Middle East, there is strong reason to doubt that the Saudi middle-class would embrace whatever belated efforts to encourage democratization Washington would probably make if a revolutionary situation arose in the Kingdom.

## *The Internal Military Factor*

A country's military may not be able to prevent revolutionary activity breaking out. However, its actions—or lack thereof—play a crucial role in determining whether or not revolutionary activity succeeds. In his classic book, *The Anatomy of Revolution,* Crane Brinton argued this point forcefully. "No government has ever fallen before attackers," concluded Brinton, "until it has lost control over its armed forces or lost the ability to use them effectively—or, of course, lost such control of force because of interference by a more powerful foreign force . . . and conversely . . . no revolutions have ever succeeded until they have got a predominance of effective armed force on their side."⁴⁹ Timothy Wickham-Crowley advanced a similar argument in his study of Latin American insurgencies. He pointed out that established militaries are almost always stronger than guerrillas fighting against them in terms of manpower, weaponry, and overall resources. This superiority, however, will not prevent revolution unless the military is loyal: "Loyalty to the government is the most critical qualitative characteristic of armed forces, for the outcomes of rebellions and revolutionary wars hinge on that loyalty."⁵⁰ Wickham-Crowley went on to describe how foreign assistance to a regime's military does not enhance its ability to prevent revolution if the military (or key elements of it) is disloyal. Foreign arms transfers intended to strengthen the government side, for example, can be either diverted to the revolutionaries or used by the army against the government. Wickham-Crowley also cites instances of Latin American officers who had received U.S. military training later defecting to rebel forces and putting their training to effective use for them.⁵¹

It should also be noted that an army does not have to (even partially) defect to the opposition in order for revolution to succeed. Just the refusal of the armed forces—for whatever reason—to fire upon the opposition may assure its victory. There have also been instances, such as in the period just before the Shah of Iran was driven out of power, when the *ancien regime* refused to allow the use of force against its revolutionary opponents for fear of its own armed forces using the occasion to seize power.⁵²

It is, therefore, important to ask: Would the Saudi armed forces remain loyal to the monarchy if revolutionary activity broke out in the Kingdom? We cannot really know the answer to this question unless and until such activity occurs. There is no conclusive indication that they would be disloyal. On the other hand, there is no guarantee that they would be completely loyal either. Indeed, there is at least some reason to question whether everyone in the Saudi armed forces would be so under these circumstances. There is also reason to doubt the effectiveness of Saudi forces against a strong opposition. Toward that end, it is worth recalling that soon after Arab nationalist revolution broke out in neighboring North Yemen in 1962, nine Saudi air force pilots defected, with their aircraft, to Nasser's Egypt (which was then Riyadh's rival).[53] In 1979, some Saudi troops reportedly refused to fire on the rebels who had seized the Grand Mosque in Makkah.[54] Since then, several observers have also claimed that the Saudi army exhibited an aversion to engaging in conflict with Iraqi forces during the 1990–91 crisis over Kuwait.[55] This certainly raises the question of how willing Saudi forces would be to fire upon fellow citizens.

Besides these indications from the past—which may, or may not, have relevance for the future—there is a more important reason to question the continued loyalty of the Saudi armed forces to the Al Saud. As is well known, many of the most important positions in the Saudi armed forces are reserved for Saudi princes. Indeed, there are Saudi princes at various levels throughout the officer corps.[56] Human nature being what it is, there can be little doubt that non-royal Saudi officers must resent the fact that their own promotion prospects are limited due to the policy of favoring princes for top positions. This resentment is only likely to increase if the Saudi ruling family sees the armed forces as a convenient means of employing even a portion of the ever-growing number of young princes it is producing.[57]

Assuming the existence of resentment against the princes on the part of Saudi non-royals in the armed forces, it is not too difficult to imagine how they might actually be attracted to the ranks of a revolutionary opposition—especially if they could cut a deal with it whereby they obtain from the new regime those positions now held by members of the ruling family. Such a deal is conceivable. A revolutionary regime would, after all, need trained officers far more than revolutionary militants for managing its armed forces. And even if the revolutionary opposition had no intention of honoring such a deal once in power, making it might prove very effective in helping them seize it.

Like many other Arab armed forces, Saudi Arabia's appear to be designed less for use against external enemies than internal ones, including from within the armed forces themselves.[58] One of the principal missions of the Saudi National Guard, for example, appears to be to prevent the regular armed forces from seizing power.[59] This may serve as one more factor demoralizing the non-royal officer corps. Under the circumstances, if a leadership struggle arose in the Kingdom resulting in the army and National Guard being controlled by rival princes, this could contribute to state breakdown and the rise of revolution. On the other hand, if the non-royal officer corps feared that a revolutionary opposition force would eliminate their positions (or even their lives) once in power, it may well remain loyal to the monarchy despite whatever grievances it felt.

One possibility for the non-royal officer corps is to attempt to solve both problems by overthrowing the monarchy and seizing power itself. Still, as Michael Herb has pointed out, Saudi princes already permeate the officer corps so extensively that it would be extremely difficult for non-royal officers to organize sufficiently to mount a coup without being detected.[60] But while the Al Saud may be able to prevent disgruntled non-royal officers from mounting a coup, they may not be able to make them fight effectively against, or not defect to, internal opposition forces, should any rise up. Again, it cannot be foretold with any degree of confidence how the Saudi armed forces would react to the emergence of a revolutionary situation in the Kingdom. If a significant portion defected, this could provide a tremendous windfall in weaponry and trained military manpower to the opposition as well as serve as a catalyst for further such defections. Likewise, if the Saudi armed forces cannot or will not defend the monarchy against a revolutionary opposition, it is highly doubtful that the monarchy could survive.

## Conclusion

The above analysis suggests that several factors that various theories have identified as being strongly associated with the occurrence of revolution are either already present or could arise in Saudi Arabia. This does not mean, however, that revolution is destined to occur there—even in theory.

David Kowalewski's macro-analysis of revolutions in the nineteenth and twentieth centuries demonstrated that while the outbreak of revolutionary activity has occurred frequently, "successes are rare and show no 'megatrend' corresponding to activity."[61] Goldstone has also argued that "state resource failures, elite alienation and divisions, and popular mass mobilization potential" are the three key factors that lead to revolution. The presence of just one or even two of these factors would cause problems for any government, but would not necessarily lead to its overthrow: "Only when all these conditions *come together* do they have sufficient force to shatter existing institutions and create a revolution."[62] For his part, John Foran has argued that revolution is most likely to occur when five factors are present: (1) dependent development; (2) "a repressive, exclusionary, personalist state"; (3) a powerful culture of resistance; (4) an economic downturn; and (5) "a world-systemic opening."[63] According to Foran, the absence of any two of these factors is highly likely to prevent revolution from succeeding. Indeed, even the absence of one of them may be enough to do so.[64]

To the extent that the factors leading toward revolution—assuming they have been accurately identified in the theories examined above—are now present in Saudi Arabia, they do not appear to be so in sufficient magnitude to bring about the conjuncture of factors that both Goldstone and Foran see as necessary. On the other hand, the analysis presented here indicates that if things do start to go wrong in Saudi Arabia, the monarchy and its external supporters may not be able to repair them. Revolution in Saudi Arabia is hardly inevitable but neither is its absence.

## Notes

1. This literature is far too voluminous to cite in its entirety. Essays discussing contending theories of revolution can be found in Theda Skocpol, *Social Revolutions in the Modern World*, Cambridge: Cambridge University Press, 1994; Nikki R. Keddie (ed.), *Debating Revolutions*, New York: New York University Press, 1995; John Foran (ed.), *Theorizing Revolutions*, London: Routledge, 1997; and Mark N. Katz, *Reflections on Revolutions*, New York: St. Martin's Press, 1999.
2. Theda Skocpol, *States and Social Revolutions: A Comparative Analysis of France, Russia, and China*, Cambridge: Cambridge University Press, 1979, pp. 14–18.
3. Ibid., pp. 24–33.
4. Skocpol, *Social Revolutions in the Modern World*, chapter 9. Skocpol acknowledged, nevertheless, that the urban-based Iranian revolution of 1979 was an exception; ibid., chapter 10.
5. Eqbal Ahmad, "Comments on Skocpol," *Theory and Society* 11:3, 1982, pp. 293–300; Jeffrey D. Simon, *Revolution without Guerrillas*, R-3683-RC, Santa Monica: RAND, 1989; and Farideh Farhi, *States and Urban-Based Revolutions: Iran and Nicaragua*, Urbana: University of Illinois Press, 1990.
6. Skocpol, *States and Social Revolutions*, p. 31.
7. Jack A. Goldstone, "Population Growth and Revolutionary Crises," in Foran, *Theorizing Revolutions*, pp. 102–20.
8. Ibid. See also Jack A. Goldstone, *Revolution and Rebellion in the Early Modern World*, Berkeley and Los Angeles: University of California Press, 1991.
9. Goldstone, *Revolution and Rebellion*, pp. 24, 117–19, 228–32, 395–6.
10. It must be emphasized that there are other such theories, but they are essentially variations on the same theme; see Jeff Goodwin, "State-Centered Approaches to Social Revolutions: Strengths and Limitations of a Theoretical Tradition," in Foran, *Theorizing Revolutions*, pp. 11–37.
11. Rayed Krimly, "The Political Economy of Adjusted Priorities: Declining Oil Revenues and Saudi Fiscal Policies," *The Middle East Journal* 53:2, spring 1999, pp. 254–67. See also Nawaf Obaid and Patrick Clawson, "The 1999 Saudi Budget: Reform in the Face of Acute Problems," Washington Institute for Near East Policy, *Policywatch*, number 359, January 5, 1999.
12. For just one of many recent articles on declining standards of living in Saudi Arabia, see Douglas Jehl, "Life in Saudi Arabia Is Transformed by Hard Times," *The New York Times*, 20 March 1999.
13. "Analysis: Saudi Seen Keeping Most Debts at Home," Reuters, 2 September 1999.
14. Heir Apparent Abdallah was quoted as saying, "The years of the boom are over and will not return," see Obaid and Clawson, *op. cit.* The recent rise in oil prices has only enabled the Kingdom to reduce its current budget deficit. See "Saudi Arabia's Deficit to Drop 66%," Agence France-Presse, 13 September 1999.
15. While Qatar and Oman introduced income taxes in 1994, and the Kuwaiti parliament is reportedly considering them, this is not a step that the Saudi government has yet been willing to take. See Krimly, "The Political Economy of Adjusted Priorities," *op. cit.*, p. 267.
16. Michael Herb, *All in the Family: Absolutism, Revolution, and Democracy in the Middle Eastern Monarchies*, Albany: State University of New York Press, 1999, p. 32.
17. On how the Saudi ruling family has so far dealt with the succession issue, see ibid., pp. 87–108. Although Herb argues that the Al Saud are unlikely to allow succession disputes to become crises, he does note the existence of rivalry between King Fahd and his full brothers on the one hand and their half brothers, including Heir Apparent Abdallah, on the other (pp. 105–106).
18. See Charles Tilly, *From Mobilization to Revolution*, Reading, Massachusetts: Addison-Wesley, 1978. See also Jack A. Goldstone, "The Comparative and Historical Study of Revolutions," *Annual Review of Sociology*, 1982, pp. 192–194.
19. Howard Schneider, "Saudi Arabia Finds Calm after Storm," *The Washington Post*, January 9, 2000, pp. A1, A23.
20. Mamoun Fanny, *Saudi Arabia and the Politics of Dissent*, New York: St. Martin's Press, 1999.
21. Nazih N. Ayubi, *Political Islam: Religion and Politics in the Arab World*, London: Routledge, 1991, p. 238. For a similar argument, see Found Ajami, "The Summoning," *Foreign Affairs* 72:4, September/October 1993, pp. 2–9.
22. Mark N. Katz, *Revolutions and Revolutionary Waves*, New York: St. Martin's Press, 1997, p. 113.
23. Tilly, *From Mobilization to Revolution*.
24. On the changing risk-reward structure individuals face with regard to supporting a revolutionary opposition movement as the latter's influence increases, see Timothy J. Lomperis, *From People's*

*War to People's Rule: Insurgency, Intervention, and the Lessons of Vietnam*, Chapel Hill: University of North Carolina Press, 1996, pp. 74–82.
25. On the promises that were made to such groups in the Western Hemisphere's revolutions, see Lester D. Langley, *The Americas in the Age of Revolution, 1750–1850*, New Haven: Yale University Press, 1996, passim; see also Christopher McAuley, "Race and the Process of the American Revolutions," in John Foran (ed.), *Theorizing Revolutions*, pp. 168–202. On the promises made to non-Russian groups by the Bolsheviks during the Russian Revolution, see Bohdan Nahaylo and Victor Swoboda, *Soviet Disunion: A History of the Nationalities Problem in the USSR*, New York: The Free Press, 1990, chapters 2–5. Needless to say, the revolutionary movements that made these promises did not necessarily keep them.
26. Fandy, *Saudi Arabia and the Politics of Dissent*. See also Herb, *All in the Family, op. cit.*, pp. 168–73; and Graham E. Fuller and Rend Rahim Francke, *The Arab Shi'a: The Forgotten Muslims*, New York: St. Martin's Press, 1999, chapter 8.
27. Gwenn Okruhlik, "Excluded Essentials: The Politics of Ethnicity, Oil, and Citizenship in Saudi Arabia," in Pinar Batur-Vanderlippe and Joe Feagin (eds.), *The Global Color Line: Racial and Ethnic Inequality and Struggle from a Global Perspective (Research in Politics and Society*, volume 6), Stamford, Connecticut: JAI Press, 1999, pp. 215–35.
28. I have heard this viewpoint expressed repeatedly and vehemently by Arabs from relatively poor countries.
29. Lomperis, *From People's War to People's Rule*, chapters 4–5, 10. See also Andrew Bennet, *Condemned to Repetition? The Rise, Fall, and Reprise of Soviet-Russian Military Interventionism, 1973–1996*, Cambridge, Massachusetts: MIT Press, 1999.
30. Lomperis, *From People's War to People's Rule*, chapters 7, 9. See also John Akehurst, *We Won a War: The Campaign in Oman, 1965–1975*, Wilton, United Kingdom: Michael Russell, 1982.
31. William J. Taylor Jr. and James Blackwell, "The Ground War in the Gulf," *Survival* 33:3 May/June 1991, pp. 230–45; and Adam Roberts, "NATO's 'Humanitarian War' over Kosovo," *Survival* 41:3, autumn 1999, pp. 102–23.
32. Bruce W. Jentleson, "The Pretty Prudent Public: Post Post-Vietnam American Opinion on the Use of Military Force," *International Studies Quarterly* 36:1, March 1992, pp. 49–74.
33. For an analysis of the evolution of American public opinion on the war in Vietnam, see Guenter Lewy, *America in Vietnam*, New York: Oxford University Press, 1978, pp. 432–7.
34. Lomperis, *From People's War to People's Rule*, pp. 265–87.
35. Herb, *All in the Family*, p. 171; Fandy, *Saudi Arabia and the Politics of Dissent*, passim; and Schneider, "Saudi Arabia Finds Calm after Storm."
36. Nor is it clear how effective Arab armies would be at undertaking this mission. As Risa Brooks put it, the means employed by Arab regimes to maintain control over them "often undermine the combat potential of the armed forces." See Risa Brooks, *Political-Military Relations and the Stability of Arab Regimes*, London: International Institute for Strategic Studies, 1998, p. 10.
37. Timothy P. Wickham-Crowley, *Guerrillas and Revolution in Latin America: A Comparative Study of Insurgents and Regimes since 1956*, Princeton: Princeton University Press, 1992, pp. 85–91; Stephen M. Walt, *Revolution and War*, Ithaca: Cornell University Press, 1996, pp. 18–43; Mark N. Katz, *Revolutions and Revolutionary Waves*, New York: St. Martin's Press, 1997, pp. 25–54; and Fred Halliday, *Revolution and World Politics: The Rise and Fall of the Sixth Great Power*, Durham: Duke University Press, 1999, pp. 94–132.
38. On the different ways in which democratization occurred in late-twentieth-century authoritarian regimes, see Samuel P. Huntington, *The Third Wave: Democratization in the Late Twentieth Century*, Norman: University of Oklahoma Press, 1991, chapter 3.
39. R. Hrair Dekmejian, "Saudi Arabia's Consultative Council," *The Middle East Journal* 52:2, spring 1998, pp. 204–18; and Herb, *All in the Family*, pp. 169–70.
40. Jeane Kirkpatrick, "Dictatorships and Double Standards," *Commentary*, November 1979, p. 44.
41. Robert A. Pastor, "Preempting Revolutions: The Boundaries of U.S. Influence," *International Security* 15:4, spring 1991, pp. 54–86.
42. Ibid.
43. Ibid., pp. 77–9.
44. Ibid.
45. See, for example, Nazih Ayubi, *Political Islam: Religion and Politics in the Arab World*, London: Routledge, 1991, chapter 7; and Olivier Roy, *The Failure of Political Islam*, Cambridge, Massachusetts: Harvard University Press, 1994, chapter 3.

46. Ervand Abrahamian, *Khomeinism: Essays on the Islamic Republic,* Berkeley and Los Angeles: University of California Press, 1993, chapter 2.
47. Joseph Kostiner, "State, Islam and Opposition in Saudi Arabia: The Post Desert-Storm Phase," *The Middle East Review of International Affairs,* June 19, 1997, p. 4.
48. Fandy, *Saudi Arabia and the Politics of Dissent,* p. 180.
49. Crane Brinton, *The Anatomy of Revolution,* 3rd ed., New York: Vintage Books, 1965, p. 89.
50. Wickham-Crowley, *Guerrillas and Revolution in Latin America,* p. 64.
51. Ibid., pp. 68–75, 77–80.
52. Gary Sick, *All Fall Down: America's Tragic Encounter with Iran,* New York: Penguin Books, 1986, pp. 165, 198–201.
53. Fred Halliday, *Arabia without Sultans,* Harmondsworth: Penguin Books, 1974, p. 67. Halliday also reported that opposition movements were discovered within the Saudi armed forces in 1968 and 1969; Ibid., p. 68.
54. Herb, *All in the Family,* p. 171.
55. *U.S. News & World Report* noted the following in regard to the late January 1991 battle over Khafji (a Saudi border town): "When the Iraqis surrendered . . . the victorious Saudis swaggered through the streets shouting and waving their national flag. It was the first land battle that Saudis had fought in the modern history of their kingdom. Some observers, though, said the tough fighting was led by the Qataris (whose ground forces were largely Pakistani mercenaries)." U.S. News & World Report, *Triumph without Victory: The Unreported History of the Persian Gulf War,* New York: Times Books/Random House, 1992, p. 270. Anthony Cordesman assessed Saudi military performance more positively, but in a back-handed manner: "[T]he Saudi Army did well during Operation Desert Storm—very well if its low pre-war readiness is considered." But even after the experience of the Gulf War, Cordesman noted that the Saudi army takes "a minimum of 7–10 days to redeploy a brigade to a new front or city," questioned the effectiveness of its organization, training, and equipment, and concluded that "the Saudi Army is still too static and defensive in character and lacks strategic focus." See Anthony H. Cordesman, *Saudi Arabia: Guarding the Desert Kingdom,* Boulder: Westview Press, 1997, p. 135.
56. Herb, *All in the Family,* pp. 34–5.
57. According to Cordesman, "senior Saudi officers unrelated to the royal family have been denied promotion because of a wide range of internal political disputes." See Anthony H. Cordesman, *After the Storm: The Changing Military Balance in the Middle East,* Boulder: Westview Press, 1993, p. 565.
58. Ibid., and Brooks, *Political-Military Relations and the Stability of Arab Regimes.*
59. F. Gregory Gause III, *Oil Monarchies: Domestic and Security Challenges in the Arab Gulf States,* New York: Council on Foreign Relations Press, 1994, p. 68.
60. Herb, *All in the Family,* pp. 34–5.
61. David Kowalewski, "Periphery Revolutions in World-System Perspective, 1821–1985," *Comparative Political Studies* 24:1, April 1991, p. 92.
62. Jack A. Goldstone, "An Analytical Framework," in Jack A. Goldstone, Ted Robert Gurr, and Farrokh Moshiri (eds.), *Revolutions of the Late Twentieth Century,* Boulder: Westview Press, 1991, p. 40.
63. John Foran, "The Comparative-Historical Sociology of Third World Social Revolutions: Why a Few Succeed, Why Most Fail," in John Foran (ed.), *Theorizing Revolutions,* p. 228.
64. Ibid., pp. 259–61.

# THE KINGDOM OF SAUDI ARABIA

CHAPTER 8

*Image, Imagination, and Place:*
*The Political Economy of Tourism in Saudi Arabia*

Gwenn Okruhlik

Sandwiched in the travel brochure between advertisements for trips to the Himalayan Kingdoms of Nepal and Bhutan, a Kenyan Christmas Family Safari, and a Summer in Tuscany, the alluring teaser reads: *Saudi Arabia's recent decision to welcome select groups of travelers to the Kingdom affords a thrilling opportunity to those seeking a truly unique travel adventure.* In an age of eco-tourism, adventure travel, and culturally sensitive travel, Saudi Arabia is truly one of the last frontiers in international tourism. As a latecomer, Saudi Arabia offers an especially interesting vantage point from which to observe how politics and tourism intersect. The consumption of tourist services (including the choice of sites) cannot be extracted from the social and political relations in which they are embedded.[1]

Tourism is at the nexus of global capitalism and national identity. Global capitalism, as articulated by the World Trade Organization (WTO), mandates a freer flow of information, capital, and people. A national identity is one that transcends family and region, and gives content to the idea of self. Identity, and particularly a national identity, is not simply inherent or primordial. Indeed, it can be strategic and positional.[2] Thus, what becomes important are the facets of identity that one chooses to emphasize, or de-emphasize, in the construction of a nation's image. Most interesting is understanding the variability in what is included and what is excluded from this representation.[3]

Tourism, as a dynamic of capital accumulation, is about creating and marketing experiences, in which place is commodified and reduced to an image for consumption.[4] Tourism suggests an invitation to come in and view yourself, so it prompts various questions: What image of self is offered for viewing? What representation of self is projected? These are important questions because the production of a national image has internal and external components[5] that can be negotiated and revised, even as the producers of the dominant image promote its authentic essence.

The focus of this chapter is to inquire how tourism exposes contested voices over identity issues within Saudi Arabia, where the state pursues two objectives simultaneously—it seeks, on the one hand, to accommodate global capitalism (by joining the WTO) as it attempts, on the other hand, to forge a national identity that responds to domestic struggles and voices (such as Islamism, class, gender, and region). Clearly, the pursuit of the former exposes tender spots in the pursuit of the latter. Saudi Arabia is simultaneously defining a national identity while opening itself to foreign investors, international institutions, and tourists. A particular representation of "what it means to be a Saudi" has been shaped and is being marketed to foreign audiences even before it is fully accepted (or experienced) by Saudi Arabian citizens.

Indeed, tourism in Saudi Arabia reveals much about the articulation of a truly national identity at a time of global imperatives, because it exposes "muddy edges." These reflect the tensions that emerge from competing preferences of the state and of the tourist. In Saudi Arabia, it is the state that defines tourism (through representatives of the ruling family working with private Saudi operators), rather than independent, individual private entrepreneurial citizens. Several members of the Al Saud family spearhead the effort to promote tourism. For now, tourism is tightly controlled and the state is constructing the image to be marketed abroad, to private tourists. Thus, the itinerary is highly structured, and it is impossible to deviate from it. It is not quite containment tourism or enclave tourism, but it is very much controlled tourism. Still, there are inevitable encounters between tourist and inhabitant—encounters that can (re)shape "image." And it is these encounters, or "muddy edges," experienced by people paying for the privilege of observation and participation, that make it hard for the state to completely control a discourse on identity and development. The muddy edges exemplify the maneuvering and contestation over such things as photography, dress, and mobility that go on between international tourists and national voices that seek to define and protect an identity. The way in which the muddy edges play out, and the skill with which they are handled, will affect the future of tourism in Saudi Arabia; and from those edges, one may indeed learn something about the emergent national identity by examining the outcomes of such encounters.[6]

The politics of tourism are evident throughout the world; in the Middle East it is certainly so in Egypt, Israel, Jordan, and Morocco. What makes Saudi Arabia especially interesting is timing. Saudi Arabians are only now struggling to (re)construct the content of national identity (including citizenship and belonging) quite independently of tourism or the WTO. The coincidence of the two processes provides a fertile field for examining relations between the definition of self and other.

Throughout this chapter, an effort is made to analyze the politics and power of the touring experience in Saudi Arabia. How and why Saudi Arabia recently opened its gates to tourism; who participates in the experience as producers or consumers; and how Saudi Arabia is officially represented through the itinerary are together revealing of national image and international imagination.[7] An analysis of these important variables, along with a discussion of the "muddy edges" of tourism, highlights how tourism contributes to a loss of the state's monopoly on discourse. Such an analysis is situated in the literatures of both politics and cultural anthropology.[8]

## The Politics of Place: Image and Imagination

Tourism has been formally introduced into a country that was previously off-limits to travelers. The only way to access Saudi Arabia was through Hajj (pilgrimage), visitation of relatives, or employment. In 1991, while still prohibiting tourism, Saudi Arabia sent abroad a fabulous exhibit of itself, entitled "Saudi Arabia: Yesterday and Today." For some observers, it conveyed the statement "You can't come to Saudi Arabia, so we will come to you."[9]

To appreciate the power and significance of the tourism opening, one must comprehend the long-standing regulations against mobility and travel in Saudi Arabia. Every foreigner (approximately 6.2 million, about one-third of the estimated total population) is required to be "sponsored" by a Saudi Arabian citizen, who in turn holds legal, financial, and social responsibility for the behavior of the expatriate. This means that sponsorship is extraordinarily difficult to attain, except in the case of simple employment or to conduct the religious rituals of the Hajj in Makkah and Madinah. Expatriate workers have restricted mobility; they are not allowed to travel more than 50 kilometers from their place of residence without the written, signed, and dated permission of their sponsors. This extensive system of regulation and oversight ensures appropriate conduct while in country, and has acted in many ways as an extension of the authoritarian state. Until very recently, tourist visas did not even exist.

There has been no transition period in which individual travelers or small independent groups negotiated their way through Saudi Arabia. In Egypt, for example, individual travelers choose among their activities. They decide where to stay, what to eat, which sites are worthy of their time, what souvenirs to purchase, and how to negotiate the costs of their experience. In contrast, in Saudi Arabia, several government entities have been established to manage such dilemmas about sites, representation, costs, accommodations, and interaction between locals and tourists. There is less individual experimentation in encountering Saudi Arabia. This means that questions regarding authenticity are not going to be answered slowly and over time in a give-and-take process between tourist and local culture; rather, choices must be made up front because of the formal, structured nature of tourism in Saudi Arabia.[10]

## The Politics of Place: Conflict Avoidance

The tourist opening is purposefully slow, cautious, and targeted for social and political reasons. According to a Saudia Airlines tourism manager, "the Saudis have received religious traffic and Gulf visitors for hundreds of years. It's not a new thing. But Saudi tourism will not be for the masses. It will be well targeted."[11] A travel marketer in Jeddah was more explicit: "We want to be more open, but not like Dubai." That city, in addition to serving alcohol and allowing freedom in dress and mobility, also has a significant trade in prostitution. A marketing director for a resort hotel was also cautious, "[T]his will happen in small doses in a very controlled way. It should be a gradual transition as we don't want to shock anyone."[12] Prince Bandar bin Khaled, who works with tourism in the Asir region, was straightforward about the political implications of tourism: "Hundreds of thousands of people from different cultures could offend the local population without even knowing it." A public backlash "could delay (foreign) tourism for years."[13]

For those advocates of tourism, the challenge is to gently promote tourism (and the hoped-for accompanying opening of society) while avoiding a crackdown from socially conservative forces. It is a delicate balancing act because in other Middle Eastern countries, the tourist sector has become a rallying point for opposition forces, most notably in Egypt, with serious consequences.

Saudi Arabian officials refer to their approach as "clean tourism," travel without negative environments such as gambling, casinos, alcohol, or prostitution. There are, of course, no public entertainment venues, clubs, cinemas, or discotheques in Saudi Arabia. Rather, tour groups will visit archeological sites, historic locations, lakes, festivals, and museums. To be sure, there are plans for eco-tourism, snorkeling in the coral beds of the Red Sea, and treks in the Empty Quarter desert. In fact, bedouins are apparently "gearing up to take tourists to desert encampments." A new hotel and golf course are planned on the sea with a private beach where Westerners can swim.[14] The latter is relevant because it expands the distinction between behavior in the private and in the public space to encompass the tourist trade. Foreign women could wear bathing suits on such a private beach that was designed and maintained strictly for tourists. Such a resort is similar to enclave tourism; but unlike enclave tourist development in much of the developing world, where separation is required by the increasing disparity between the wealth of tourists and the poverty of the countries they visit,[15] such separation in Saudi Arabia would be prompted by normative differences.

## Why Now, Why Tourism?

In a region of majestic pyramids, winding suqs, Islamic architecture, and pre-Islamic ruins, the Saudi Arabian decision to finally encourage tourism was a response to domestic needs.[16] The context of the 1990s was difficult for Saudi Arabia, both politically and economically. Begun with the turmoil of the Gulf War, the decade was a time of Islamist opposition forces on the ascendancy, King Fahd's illnesses, succession struggles in the Al Saud family, and new social problems. Guns, drugs, and crime were increasingly reported in Saudi Arabia. The population continued to grow at an astounding rate of about 3.5 percent per year. Unemployment figures among Saudi citizens spiraled. Among recent college graduates, the unemployment rate was about 30 percent. Yet there was a continuing dependence on an imported foreign labor force, which constituted between 95 percent of the private sector force. The once-fabulous infrastructure was deteriorating; this was especially true of schools and hospitals. Oil prices hit a ten-year low in 1998. Per capita income had tumbled from $16,650 in 1981 to $6,526 in 1998. The ratio of public sector debt to GDP was more than 120 percent in late 1999, the seventeenth straight year of deficit. Clearly, Saudi Arabia needed a new source of revenues that could buffer the economy from the volatility of oil prices. It also needed a new source of employment.

By the end of the decade, Heir Apparent Abdallah bin Abdul Aziz Al Saud had introduced a series of reform measures designed to build confidence in his leadership and foresight. He continued King Fahd's program of deporting illegal expatriate workers, doubled visa fees on foreign labor, slashed subsidies on electricity and petrol, and instituted limits on princely prerogatives (use of phone, planes, and electricity). Abdallah established a Supreme Economic Council to regulate the shares market, revamp the tax code, and amend property and employment laws in order to gain membership in the WTO, for which Saudi Arabia had applied in 1993. Its membership application had been adversely affected because, as representatives of the WTO argued, the Saudi economy was too heavily subsidized and the market too protected. Troublesome issues included the lack of transparency in public procurement, intellectual property rights, investment rules, and tariff rates.

In response to these problems, Saudi Arabia announced in 2000 a series of sweeping economic changes intended to facilitate its membership in the WTO.[17] For the first time, 100 percent foreign ownership of companies is allowed; foreign companies will have access to favorable loans from the Saudi Industrial Development Fund, and foreign investors can now invest in the local bourse. To further assist the business community, the General Investment Authority (GIA) was established as a one-stop shop to issue licenses and to incorporate foreign and joint ventures, and importantly, it appears that the old requirement that all foreigners have a Saudi sponsor will be altered. There is discussion that foreigners will be allowed to own property in Saudi Arabia, that judicial protection will be strengthened, and greater public disclosure for investments will be fostered. It is into this ferment and "opening" that busloads of tourists are arriving for the first time ever in Saudi Arabia.

The state seeks to achieve several objectives through the new promotion of tourism. As a demonstration of openness, it will facilitate application to the WTO. The development of the tourist infrastructure in Saudi Arabia will also increase investment opportunities, attract select groups of foreign visitors, and encourage Saudi citizens to remain in country for their holidays. Unofficial estimates are that Saudi citizens spend more than $16 billion on vacations abroad annually.[18] Furthermore, this economic activity will not only create jobs in this growing service sector, but importantly, the jobs that are created will be acceptable positions for many unemployed Saudis. In addition to formal training, two of the primary attributes required of Saudi Arabians who are employed in the tourism trade are a) generosity of hospitality and b) a proud self-image. That is to suggest that the newly created positions will be compatible with social norms. This matters because the effort to "Saudiize" the economy has long been hindered by the fact that many positions held by foreign laborers are unattractive to citizens due to social norms and incentive structures.

A challenge for Saudi Arabia will be to keep profits from tourism in the country, and to circulate that capital throughout the various regions and economic sectors. The state and private business communities must build backward and forward linkages throughout the economy (in construction, services, agriculture, and transportation) so that Saudi citizens benefit from the new activity. In short, tourism must stimulate the local economy, develop capital-producing activity that is independent of oil cycles, and provide acceptable jobs. Unfortunately, experience elsewhere suggests that increasing international integration of the tourist industry decreases the amount of expenditure that remains in the host country. The broad-based relaxation of foreign investment regulations in Saudi Arabia, which has accompanied its application to the WTO, will further weaken local control over capital. Indeed, four of the six hotels that were utilized in a recent tour included an Intercontinental, a Meridien, a Sheraton, and a Marriott. It may well be that the economic imperatives of joining the WTO mitigate against the diversification, privatization, and Saudiization of the economy, all long sought after goals in the country.

Aware of the sector's potential benefits, many Saudis want tourism to work, and tremendous resources are being expended. Since 1995, Saudi Arabia has invested an estimated $6.66 billion on tourism projects, mostly geared toward internal tourism (Saudis and citizens from neighboring states of the Gulf Cooperation Council, who do not require visas).[19] The tourist infrastructure is most developed in the southwestern province of Asir: in the resort town of Taif and in Yanbu on the Red Sea, both favored spots for holidays. It remains to be seen whether the needs of tourists from the Arabian Peninsula are similar to those of tourists from farther-flung origins. In the event, Saudi Arabia forecasts 3 million visitors in the next five years and, once the infrastructure is complete, expects 1 million tourists per year. A new Prince Sultan School for Tourism and Hotel Sciences opened in Abha to train Saudi citizens for roles in the tourism sector. At the helm of all of this is Sultan bin Salman—a former air force pilot who flew on the Space Shuttle Discovery in 1985—newly appointed secretary-general of the Higher Organization for Tourism (HOT). Salman al Sudairy assists him. In his capacity as minister for civil aviation, Defense Minister Sultan bin Abdul Aziz supports this venture as well, especially as Saudia Airlines serves as sponsor of tour groups. The HOT is responsible for tourism policy in the country and will evaluate infrastructure, "remove whatever obstacles might hamper tourist activity," and survey and protect tourist sites and folklore items such as handicrafts, markets, and cottage industries.[20]

### *Cultural Markers That Entice*

A primary lure to tour Saudi Arabia is the sense that it is somehow shrouded, off-limits, and secretive. Pre-trip literature clearly states that all female tourists must wear an *abaya* and cover their hair with a scarf for the duration of the trip. Furthermore, all participants are required to sign a document that details extreme political restrictions in Saudi Arabia to which they must abide, or be held liable. To my knowledge, no tourist on the January 2000 tour expressed concerns about waiving the right to expression. Though many of the tourists complained often about the constraints that were placed on them in the country (regarding dress, photography, mobility), the restrictive quality might also have been the same reason they paid for the experience. The slightly taboo nature of Saudi Arabia is a primary attractant to tourism. Image and imagination fertilize each other here, and trips continue to fill at this time. It is not yet clear how long this can be sustained; as more tourists experience Saudi Arabia, the country will indeed be less "shrouded in secrecy."

The "off-limits" character of Saudi Arabia is utilized as a selling point for the tour. The advertisement letter notes that, even now, no tourist visa exists for entry to the country; each visitor must be sponsored by an influential Saudi and approved by the ruling family. Saudi Arabia is introduced as "mysterious and exotic," a "blank spot on the map for most travelers." The pioneering opportunity to be among the first in the door of the country is heralded. In fact, the tour "offers a rare chance to explore a country before the imprint of tourism changes it forever." Clearly, the primary draw is to be first, a pioneer traveler to a previously closed Kingdom, which has long resisted outside influence. The image of a pristine country, blessed by oil and urban centers but grounded in the desert and tradition, is articulated. The day-by-day itinerary, with a description of each day's activities, follows the letter of introduction.

### *Producers and Consumers of Place*

The introduction of tourism in Saudi Arabia necessitated a major change in the long-standing system of sponsorship and oversight of foreigners in the country. In an early concession to tourism in September 1999, the state approved a plan that allowed Muslims coming to Saudi Arabia to perform *umrah* (minor pilgrimage) to travel around the country instead of being confined to the holy cities of Makkah and Madinah.[21] In April 2000, the state announced it would issue tourist visas that allow foreigners access to the country for reasons other than Hajj or employment.[22] While this is a major step in "opening up," it is not as though the Kingdom will be overrun by legions of backpacking college students anytime soon. The new visa will apparently require tourists to travel in the country through a local company that will take charge of the trip in its entirety and will ensure that all tourists leave the country after their visit. The visa will be valid for one month and will be issued only for group entry rather than for individual travel. The visas are so new that during a January 2000 tour, there was still no "tourist visa" box to check off on the airline form. Yet in the first four months of formal availability, between April and July 2000, 6,546 tourist visas had been issued, mainly to tourists from Europe, Japan, and the United States.[23]

It is important to note that participation in tourism is quite selective in Saudi Arabia, and the "producers of knowledge" include a wide range of professionals. Each tour group is led by a foreign tour operator (thus far, American, German, Italian, or Japanese) who manages all logistics and organization. That foreign operator works in conjunction with local tour guides, who are critical to the success of the venture. The Saudi Arabian guides bear responsibility for negotiating, representing, and interpreting their country. They, in turn, work closely with key princes who oversee tourism. The tour I accompanied also benefited from the participation of a representative of the United States museum that sponsored the trip and two study leaders, there to provide expertise.

Participants in the tour were fairly homogenous in demographic traits, and this makes intuitive sense, given that such tourism requires two things: time and money. By and large, the 30 consumers were white, elderly, well-to-do and retired (or able to turn their business affairs over to someone else for two weeks). As a group, they were extraordinarily well traveled. The participants had walked on the Great Wall of China, wandered around Red Square in Moscow, hunted on African safaris, and relaxed on Caribbean beaches. Touring Saudi Arabia was one of many travel adventures in their lives. The price of access was $7,200 for 13 days in the country, inclusive of all travel, food, accommodations, and tips. No monetary transactions were necessary once in the country (except for personal shopping). A Saudi Arabian newspaper has already reported that tourists are complaining about the high price of trips, writing that "a large number of tourists believe that tour operators are charging exorbitant prices to arrange trips to the kingdom. Tour operators will have to bring down prices to attract more tourists."[24]

In the event, the schedule for the January 2000 tour was highly structured, and demanding. One could not deviate from the pre-planned schedule or strike off on one's own to explore different sites. The only exception to this was within the Aramco compound in Dhahran, where ex-Aracoms, as they refer to themselves, were allowed to search out their old homes from years past. Even there, several Aracoms had a run-in with security guards patrolling the compound. Participants were always free to stay behind in the hotel if they chose (but that too was difficult, as there are not yet swimming pools or gyms available to women travelers).

As guides always serve an important role in the success of the touring experience, the experience of this tour was no exception. They are "vilified and praised, lampooned and treated with respect and generally emerge as critical figures in the minds of tourists."[25] Tour guides are simultaneously pathfinders, mentors, brokers, educators, and interpreters.[26] In countries like Saudi Arabia, where basic information is at a premium, the role can feel overwhelming in its power. Tour guides serve as mediators between foreign consumers and the local environment. All information is processed. The Saudi Arabian tour operators were crucial in their ability to relay explanations of behavior in a way that was often humorous and non-threatening to the tourists. Both local guides were superb in their skills; their personalities were engaging. Interestingly, one guide spoke exquisite English, but did so with an accent. He was perceived by some tourists to be not as skilled as the other guide, whom they embraced more openly.

In my role as study leader, and as an educator by profession, I sought to explain the nuance and complexity of dress, social norms, and behavior. Most of the tourists had little patience for meaningful discussion and preferred instead clear, and vastly over-simplified, answers. The risk is that cultural markers and symbols are de-contextualized. Their meaning and place become secondary to the visual image absorbed through the tourist gaze.[27] Of course, scholars always influence the construction of knowledge by the questions they choose to pursue or exclude. I was cognizant, and wary, of my own role as mediator and interpreter of knowledge about a place in which I, too, was the other.[28]

*Representation and the Itinerary*
The representation being sold to these pioneering tourists actually covers a wide swath of Saudi Arabia (see Appendix for sites). It will be important over time to observe which sites are added, or deleted, as the touring process is refined. Saudi Arabia must find the places and experiences that will, in MacCannell's words, animate a "simultaneous caring and concern for another person and for an object that is honored and shared but never fully possessed."[29] Toward that end, it is important to briefly discuss both the inclusions and the exclusions from the itinerary, the latter obviously being as important as the former.

The tour focused on six primary regions, each typified through the compacted lens of tourism. Riyadh, a huge, bustling city, is the foreign affairs center, the national archive, and the center of history and the origins of the state. The portrait of Dhahran in the Eastern Province was high technology, petrochemical industry, Aramco, expatriate faces, oil, and consumerism. The days up north in al Jouf, by the border with Jordan, left an impression of the importance of extended family, new central pivot agricultural lands, and the transitions that settled Bedouins make. The experience in the marvelous Red Sea city of Jeddah is difficult to typify, but likely was perceived as cosmopolitan and commercial. The image of the Asir was of traditional dance, unique architecture, and ruins. The tour group was actually exposed to a fairly broad spectrum of Saudi Arabia; they certainly experienced much more than some may have appreciated.

Among the landmarks worthy of attention was the National Museum in Riyadh—spectacular by any stretch of the imagination-which opened in 1999. Given that particular chapters of Saudi Arabian history have long been taught in the school curriculum,[30] it was important to see how history had been assembled methodically and displayed in a way that conveys a message through visual, tactile, and aural mediums. The history of Arabia has been distilled into a national narrative.[31] The exhibit carefully combines religious development, economic activities, technological advancement, climate, and peoples to weave a fabric in which the threads of continuity and traditions of the past are stitched together to produce a spiritual, industrial, and educated place of the future. That is, it offers a construction of identity derived from an exemplary past, which will bring the state into the age of "modernity with meaning." The museum constructs and institutionalizes a particular telling of history, as has been common in national museums.[32] The Saudi National Museum conveys a story about the founding of the Kingdom and its development over the decades, which emphasizes the power of Islam, the wisdom of King Abdul Aziz bin Abdul Rahman, and the unity of peoples under the Al Saud family. The official narrative presents the historical past, from which it can selectively appropriate, and an optimistic vision of the future.

This official representation of self and history is not always congruent with what one hears in private conversations. The museum does not reconstruct the many alternative tellings of history that exist throughout the country. It does not recount episodes that were painful for many people during the formative years of the country, such as the massacres in the south, or the walls of bodies at Taif. It does not speak about the negative impacts of the oil boom of the 1970s that reverberated throughout the country, or about obsequious consumption.

Importantly, the museum does acknowledge a pre-Islamic history. Only a decade ago, this was not openly discussed; now a large section of the museum is devoted to it. The architecture and ambience of the museum are remarkable. An observer moves *literally* from the age of ignorance and darkness via escalator into the brightness and illumination of the age of Islam. To foreign tourists, this museum accomplished a great task; as I had been asked repeatedly about the impending clash between religion and science—and how a faith like Islam could possibly survive in the age of computers—the museum answered many of these questions indirectly. Indeed, the entire complex constitutes a high-technology exhibit of Islam, and Saudi Arabia. Sultan bin Salman, the new secretary-general of tourism, stresses that cultural heritage is preserved while not impeding the path of progress. He recently underscored that Saudi Arabia "believes in change for the sake of progress, and not for the sake of change."[33]

This remarkable exhibit notwithstanding, the representation of Saudi Arabia portrayed by the itinerary excluded two important parts of the population. First, tourists did not see the underbelly of Saudi Arabia. This would be expected in any tour of any country[34]; it is just that in Saudi Arabia the underbelly is really quite large, even if hidden from view. There was no discussion of the 7.2 million foreign laborers on whom Saudi Arabia depends to staff the economy. The tourists were not exposed to the self-contained housing compounds, designed to group workers together by nationality and to prevent mobility. They did not see the sub-standard living conditions of millions. Saudi Arabian guides did, however, explain that because of the change in oil markets, the country does have different economic classes for the first time. In fact, Saudi Arabia has always been home to different economic classes; it is just that structurally the underclass has always been composed primarily of foreigners.

Second, except for pre-planned excursions, the tour group did not encounter any Saudi Arabian women, fully half of the population. Although the group visited a school for girls, and had dinner in two Saudi homes at which women were present, the absence of women on the streets, in the markets, or in the hotels, troubled several. When I lectured on the ways in which women work within and around the norm of gender segregation in order to achieve their ends, several individuals were genuinely troubled, some were offended. To others, the physical absence of women in the public realm was equated with total and complete oppression and servility. Rather than examine the ways in which women creatively negotiate their lives and empower themselves to survive and, perhaps, prosper in constrained circumstances, some participants sought reinforcement of pre-existing images.

Finally, were it not for my lectures, members of the group would not have been exposed to the myriad ways in which oil affects society, politics, and economics. The official sites trumpeted the technological glories of oil production; I discussed the ways in which oil affected urbanization, social change, and norms.

## The Muddy Edges of Controlled Tourism: Globalism and Identity

To be sure, international group tourism is highly structured, with every minute of every day accounted for by planners. There is lacking spontaneity, flexibility, and indigenous interaction. The most revealing moments of tourism occur, then, when the pre-planned itinerary does not proceed as scheduled, or when participants refuse to abide by the rules of the game. These "muddy edges" provide rich soil for analysis of the interplay between globalism and identity, or between the needs of tourists and the protection of domestic jurisdiction.

There are three such intersections in Saudi Arabia, at which there is some tension, but where national identity clearly has the edge—that is, globalism will accommodate identity and tourists will abide by local rules and norms. These concern prayer times, religious separation in the holy cities, and the death penalty waiver.

First, within the constructs of a tour, regular prayer time plays havoc with tour itineraries. In my role as study leader, I sought to explain the power and simplicity of community prayer, and to suggest that the call to prayer was part of the fabric of daily business. The tour operator, however, as I was cognizant of, had to time to the minute every route and every stop to work around prayer times. Two minutes late and the group would miss entering a museum on time; they would have to cool their heels inside a parked bus in a lot. Or, should a suq be closed for prayer, the delayed shopping excursion would have repercussions for the remainder of the day, since it would then be too dark to see, for example, the world's largest oasis. Therefore, tour operators will have to learn to build exciting and feasible tour schedules around prayer times; prayer will not, and of course should not, accommodate tourism.

Second, non-Muslims are not allowed into the holy cities of Makkah and Madinah. The tour group utilized a nice hotel on the outskirts of Madinah as a departure point for a long bus ride north to the magnificent ruins of Madain Saleh. The architecture of the hotel where the group was confined was interesting, designed so that most windows faced inward toward a courtyard. Tourists could barely catch a glimpse of Madinah from their hotel room windows. The hotel, while comfortable, was silent and solitary. Again, tourism will accommodate identity. Perhaps as more international tour groups go to Saudi Arabia, the atmosphere of the hotel will become more lively and interactive—a way station for non-Muslim tourists.

Third, the state requires that all tourists sign a waiver before a visa is issued. Being asked to sign a document that you will abide by all laws of a state while you are there is acceptable. This particular document, however, stipulates as well that tourists "shall respect the morals, customs, values and feelings of Saudi society." It further stipulates that the signatory is "aware that alcohol, drug narcotics, pornographic materials, and all types of religious, political or cultural leaflets, pamphlets, magazines, books, audio tapes, video tapes, films, or other references of all sorts, contradictory to Islam are prohibited from entering the Kingdom of Saudi Arabia, whether for personal use or otherwise. Any types of illegal drugs and narcotics smuggling in, and distribution inside, the Kingdom of Saudi Arabia is punishable by DEATH." Although the language of this document may be revised, tourists will still be required to sign something before entering Saudi Arabia.

## "Muddy Edges"

In addition to the three clean intersections of globalism and identity, there are four "muddy edges" in Saudi Arabia that are the sites of maneuvering and contestation between international tourists and national identities. These concern photography, security, social norms/dress, and foreign labor. The way in which these issues play out and the skill with which they are handled will affect the future of tourism in Saudi Arabia. The individuals who champion a very gradual opening are cognizant of the possibility of a "backlash" from socially conservative forces, which could be precipitated by such incidents.

### *The Photography Muddy Edge*

As stated above, the participants in the tour were exceedingly well traveled, and all were experienced at hosting travel slide shows for their friends. All had beautiful photo albums of their international adventures. It became very difficult (and taxing) to explain repeatedly, and often to no avail, why an expenditure of $7,200 for this experience did not entitle them to snap pictures freely. The trip was perceived as a transaction in which the admission price entitled them to the privilege of contravening local norms. The truth is that opening the country to tourism is one thing; reproducing images freely is quite another. Although an effort was made to carefully explain the source of constraints on photography in Saudi Arabia—which stem from considerations of religion (only God can produce a human), social norms (to protect the privacy of women and family), and security (broadly construed)—several tourists could not comprehend them. Others simply thought it was silly and chose to disregard the constraints. No matter how many cautions, prohibitions, and explanations were articulated, many tourists continued to snap photos, often with telephoto lenses. It was a constant bone of contention, and became a serious issue at a museum stop in a small town on the way to Madain Saleh. One woman, having just been told that photographs were prohibited in this town, walked to the far side of the bus and began to snap away. The *mutawwa* (loosely translated as "morals security") approached her. She simply turned and walked away, making the situation even worse. It appeared that she not only violated the agreements, but then added insult to injury by rebuking local authorities. The Saudi tour operators were placed in a very uncomfortable position of having to negotiate themselves out of this situation. In the event, the process was long and difficult, and required the intervention of the local museum director.

In Dhahran, the men and women tourists split into groups so that each could observe a private primary school in operation, the men attending the boys' side, the women going to the girls' section. Not surprisingly, a male participant asked a female cohort to slip a camera under her *abaya*, to take a picture of unveiled females. This apparently happened on another tour as well, as recorded in a recent photo-essay.[35] Neither of the two was, apparently, successful.

On another occasion, when an older woman consented to have her photo taken by tourists, she kept her face covered as she posed by a fire in a tent. But after countless poses and photos, her scarf would fall from her face and participants would try to sneak a peek of a Saudi Arabian woman. It is not clear to me how long this kind of cat-and-mouse game can continue. Will the family put its collective foot down and forbid photos of women while still graciously hosting tour groups? Or, alternatively, was this acceptable and perhaps indicative of the beginning of photos of women outside of the family unit?

In Dhahran, the group stopped with some fanfare to see the first well in Saudi Arabia from which oil flowed in the 1930s. Well #7 is a symbol of the fabulous boom of Saudi Arabia—it captures a mythology about the transformation of a country from tribal desert beginnings to bustling urban centers, from a nomadic people to a state at the heart of the global economy. Everyone disembarked to snap this fabled place, only to be told—in no uncertain terms—that photos of the well were not permitted. Clearly, one is able to explain constraints on taking pictures of women, the human form in general, and military installations, but frankly, this was difficult to spell out. A capped hole in the ground behind a fence does not appear to constitute a security installation, but, as this case illustrated, security is broadly defined in Saudi Arabia.

Yet, the real concern is less over the private memories of individual tourists and more over potential reproductions on the Internet. What if a tourist surreptitiously photographs a beheading—will tour group itineraries affect executions? What if a tourist posts on his Web site travel photo gallery pictures that were secretly snapped of unveiled Saudi women? It is not clear how long Saudi Arabia can invite foreign tourists to visit and yet restrict their memory banks. With tourism at the intersection of globalism and national identity, how long can restrictions be placed on paying tourists? Lest one conclude that these are mere academic concerns, a debate on the issue is under way in Saudi Arabia, as evidenced in an editorial in which the author searches for an explanation of the many restrictions on photography.[36] The observer argues that forbidding photography serves no real purpose, and in some cases actually creates ill will, bad publicity, and misunderstanding. He makes repeated references to incidents involving foreign tourists.

### *The Security Muddy Edge*

The second, and closely related, muddy edge is that of security and permissions. During the January 2000 tour, the bus arrived at the Jeddah airport Hajj Terminal—a structure that has won many awards and is striking in its open, stark beauty, with rows of white "tent peaks" arrayed against a brilliant blue sky—and tourists walked freely about the open-air facility, taking pictures even after the local guide asked them to refrain. The discussion went back and forth; tourists simply disregarded his words. Finally, exasperated and uncomfortable, he pleaded with me, "This is serious. We do not have permission. Make them stop." Protracted negotiations took place between the local tour operators and terminal security guards. There was a good deal of running between offices and there was much permission to seek. Curiously, the tourists and the U.S. operator were blissfully unconcerned with the delicate position in which the local guides were placed. The U.S. operator assured me, "We are OK. We have permission." Ironically, the difficulty might well be a difference in nuance, as few recognize that in Saudi Arabia, not all permissions are equal. And sometimes, one needs several permissions. This incident reinforced an earlier observation that it is neither the tourists nor the foreign operators who pay the price for such incidents. It is the local tour guides who are put in precarious positions that require social skills and negotiating abilities.

### The Social Norms Muddy Edge

The third muddy edge concerns social norms and proper covering of women. Not surprisingly, female tourists chafed constantly about having to wear an *abaya* and headscarf. Rather than simply assume that it must be worn (as they had agreed prior to the trip), many constantly asked, "Do we *have* to wear this thing?" The endeavors to explain how different styles and degrees of covering reflect differences in ideology, class, and region were not enough. Most participants never did appreciate the significant variations that exist within the general norm of covering; it was just all black and it was all hot. One foreign tour company put what they believe is a positive spin on the dress requirement in their press coverage. They suggest that rather than taking away from the experience of traveling to an exotic place, such rules on covering reinforce the exoticism. "There aren't that many places in the world where you have to mesh yourself into the country to see it. It adds an interesting perspective."[37]

Most women grudgingly wore the *abaya*; however, one woman was particularly troublesome. At the old suq in al Hofuf, where group tourism really is a new thing, she paraded through the narrow rows of stalls with her *abaya* unsnapped, so that it flowed open toward the back as she walked. She wore a bright white, tight T-shirt and strolled with her hands in her pockets, calling attention to herself. As if to provide a double insult, she purchased a bedouin *burqa*, a particular style of face veil. When she wore the *burqa*, her face was fully covered in black, yet her hair was uncovered and her *abaya* flapped open as she walked through the rows of merchandise.

Another encounter with different social norms became evident after a dinner in a private home. Interestingly, as the group boarded the bus to return to the hotel, one of the tourists was wearing something new. She had apparently walked out of the home with the personal coat belonging to a family member. One can only assume that she complimented the coat, and in turn the host insisted that she keep it. Saudi Arabians take the social norms of hospitality to new heights. When guests compliment an item, hosts may feel obligated to give the item to the admirer, even if the family is not wealthy. The tourist wore this coat proudly for the duration of the trip, in place of her *abaya*. But one wonders how long families can play hosts to tourists if they lose their private possessions. There is a steep learning curve involved for all participants.

### *The Expatriate Muddy Edge*

The fourth muddy edge is one that is hidden from the tourist gaze; i.e., living conditions of the foreign labor force. At a road security stop in the Hejaz, it became clear in watching the animated discussion between security and the local guides that the bus driver lacked a proper *ikama* (residency/work permit). Had the local operator not been so skilled at negotiation, the group would have had to turn around and scrap the days' itinerary. On another day, a Filipino bus driver accidentally caught the bus on a large boulder that had tumbled onto the edge of the street during construction. As he could not maneuver the bus, we were stuck, and while he followed the instructions of the Saudis to disengage from the rock, the side mirror then caught on a tree branch. It was hot and humid. The all-important closely timed itinerary was in jeopardy. Tempers flared in a quietly contained manner. The bus would not budge; the group sat inside the bus as the men tried to remedy the situation. Several tourists inquired, with genuine sincerity, "What will happen to the driver now? What will they do to him?" There was some unease that he would be deported, refused salary, or worse. When these concerns were relayed to the Saudi guide, he explained into the microphone that the firm had to fill out insurance forms in triplicate to submit their claims to get the repairs done. Hearing this, the tourists sighed with relief. This muddy edge was just barely and accidentally exposed. It cannot be hidden forever.

### Tourism and Sociopolitical Discourse: Losing the Monopoly

Nevertheless, even with such nuanced characteristics, Saudi Arabia hopes to promote old-fashioned, private, for-profit tourism. This is an important distinction to understand because it fundamentally affects control of the discourse. Saudi Arabia has long hosted visiting delegations of specialized groups, e.g., non-specialist scholars.[38] These delegations have traveled under the auspices of cultural and educational exchange; the trips are significantly subsidized, so those travelers are essentially guests of the country. In exchange for the trip, participants are normally expected to contribute different kinds of community outreach upon their return, including talks or newspaper articles on the country. Private tourism is quite different; anyone with time and money can sign up for the excursion. Since they paid a hefty price for the tour, no expectations are incumbent upon participants. They may write or evaluate the experience in whatever ways they choose. There is no pretense of scholarly or cultural exchange; these are simply tourists seeing the world. Consequently, the phenomenon fundamentally changes the dynamics of travel because the state can no longer control the discourse about its development.

Already, within this first year of tourism, the impact is clear. Two full pages of a newspaper were devoted to Saudi Arabia after a writer joined a tour and wrote an account of his experience.³⁹ Interestingly, these articles are not in the travel section, but comprise the cover story of the "Perspective" (editorial) section, and are headed "Foreign Affairs." The essay opens with this rather strong sentence, "Stand the U.S. Constitution on its head, and you have Saudi Arabia," and it continues, "Absent the oil equation, it's a fair surmise that U.S. policy toward this desert kingdom would manifest—at least to some degree—the abhorrence aimed at such repressive regimes as communist North Korea and the Taleban fundamentalists of Afghanistan. Saudi Arabia has ample trappings of a police state." The writer goes on to detail the absence of press freedom, constraints on women, the absence of any free expression, the absence of basic political rights, as well as the lack of movies and concerts.

The first major coverage of tourism in Saudi Arabia appeared in *Travel & Leisure*, a glossy monthly magazine that caters to the industry and to well-heeled tourists. The magazine sent a writer and photographer to accompany one of the first U.S. tour groups. In this instance, the table of contents reads, "Shifting Sands: One of the most secretive of the OPEC members, Saudi Arabia has finally decided to open its doors to Westerners. Hitch a ride with the first American tour group to visit a kingdom that still isn't sure that tourists are a good idea."⁴⁰ In reference to a brief stay on the outskirts of Madinah, the writer asks, "Since the fall of the Soviet Union, how many places are left on earth where you can be restricted to your hotel?" *Newsweek,* too, carried a very brief blurb on "Touring Muslim Style," in which the author suggested rules of the road for visits to Islamic countries. The only mention of Saudi Arabia was that all female tourists would be issued a black *abaya,* the voluminous cloak Saudi Arabian women wear.⁴¹

It is apparent from these reports that the state will lose its monopoly on the discourse; permitting tourism and the construction of tourist memories, then, is actually a rather bold and risky move on the part of its sponsors.

### Identity and Tourism: On Being and Belonging In Saudi Arabia

The complexity of the political economy of tourism in Saudi Arabia is demonstrated in its muddy edges. It is also illustrated in the loss of the state monopoly of discourse, the inclusions and exclusions in representation, and the motivations of tourists to travel there. The tourist experience demonstrates how quickly things are changing in Saudi Arabia. Sites that were pristine ten years ago are now ringed in tourist villas and amusement parks. Ruins that were poignant in their worn majesty have been restored to gleaming newness. Suqs that were off the beaten track are now on international itineraries.

Yet, it is also evident that new spaces for public discourse are cautiously opening in Saudi Arabia. There simply is more discussion about more subjects in public than previously. Saudi Arabian society is opening faster than state structures. For the first time in recent memory, there is acknowledgment of differences among Saudi Arabians. That is, different regions, costumes, and customs are acknowledged and even celebrated in museums and shows. Together with a dominant narrative of Islam and Abdul Aziz, there also exists acknowledgment of diversity. In addition, there is for the first time a new comfort level in acknowledging the pre-Islamic past. Rather than denying it, it is analyzed in museums.

It must be underscored that there is a tremendous upside to the fact that Saudi Arabia is such a latecomer to international tourism and to archeology. Rich ruins that lay beneath the desert are so late in being discovered—archeology is just unfolding—that the sites are protected. Shards and monuments will certainly be documented by a new generation of Saudi archeologists. They will not be looted and taken to capital cities on other continents. The sense of self and domestic jurisdiction (vis-à-vis foreigners) is embedded strongly enough to protect national resources. Furthermore, tourism was only initiated in the year 1999, long after the jargon of "sustainable development" became a part of our lexicon.[42] Indeed, the late-late incorporation into the global tourism economy may prove to be a benefit and allow Saudi Arabia to avoid pitfalls that marred tourist development in the years prior to cognizance of sustainability.

In a tangential but parallel vein, the massive recently published encyclopedia of Saudi Arabian folklore is described as "a truly nationalist project." Its contributors claimed that such an endeavor could not be undertaken until the last decade because tribal and regional divisions continued to plague the country. One of its contributors recognized that "until Saudis spoke the same Arabic dialect and tribal and regional cultural differences diminished, a project examining the country's heritage would have been too contentious to be approved by the censors."[43] Again, the country was late in preserving its heritage, but the long delay also made preservation feasible.

"Being a Saudi" has been defined in recent years vis-à-vis the other—the other being the millions of foreign laborers who staff the economy. Identity and citizenship were about belonging to a community that was distinguished from expatriates by particular social norms and by economic privilege. Over time, the rights and obligations of citizenship have been defined in social and economic ways to encompass Islamic values, loyalty to the ruling family, conformist social behavior, and the centrality of the family unit. This construction of citizenship is being challenged as more people seek representation. Tourism, situated at the nexus of global capitalism and identity, is very much about this evolving national narrative on being and belonging. As discussed above, the muddy edges of cultural representation reflect contested voices within Saudi Arabia, about gender, religion, ethnicity, and social norms.

## Appendix: Description of Tour Itinerary

In Riyadh, located in the Central Province, participants visited the stunning new National Museum, the fortress-like Diplomatic Quarter, Qasr al Tuwaiq, al Dir'iyah (the ancestral home of the Al Saud family), Mismak Fort (where Abdul Aziz and his band of 40 men captured the Najd back from the Rashids), and a camel market. In Dhahran, in the Eastern Province, participants visited the high-tech exhibit at Aramco, Well #7 (where oil was discovered in 1938), the infrastructural wonder of the causeway that links Saudi Arabia to the island state of Bahrain, and a private school. An excursion to the old suq in al Hofuf was also on the itinerary, as was a stop at a date market. The wonderful stay in al Jouf was shaped by our experiences with the family of the Saudi Arabian tour guide. Also there, tourists saw many ruins, including Domat al Jandal, Sakaka, Qasr Zabel, Qasr Marid, the mosque of Omar, and Rajajil, a small Stonehenge-like monument of standing rocks. The group then used a hotel on the outskirts of Madinah proper as a point of departure for a trip up north to see the remnants of the Hejaz Railway and the tombs cut into rock in the dramatic landscape of Madain Saleh. In the beautiful port city of Jeddah, tourists visited the Abdul Raouf Khalil Museum (a private collection of artwork of varied quality and origin), the Greek Island Restaurant (to which Saudis would never go), the Hajj Terminal, the historic home of the Naseef family, and the old Jeddah suq. The highlight of the city was a dinner in the backyard of a private villa, complete with laser and sound show as well as a fashion show. Finally, the days in the Asir included stops at the National Park, Habala Village, Rigal al Ma, and the market of Khamis Mushayt.

## Notes

1. J. Urry, "The 'Consumption' of Tourism," *Sociology* 24:1, 1990, pp. 23–35.
2. Stuart Hall, "Introduction: Who Needs Identity?" in S. Hall and P. DuGay (eds.) *Questions of Cultural Identity*, California: Sage, 1996.
3. For discussion of identity and tourism, see Simone Abram, Jaqueline Waldren, and Donald McCleod, *Tourists and Tourism: Identifying with People and Places*, Oxford: Berg, 1997.
4. Colin Michael Hall, *Tourism and Politics: Policy, Power and Place*, Chichester: John Wiley and Sons, 1994, p. 194.
5. Susan Ossman, "Boom Box in Ouarzazate: The Search for the Similarly Strange," *Middle East Report* 25:5, September-October 1995, pp. 12–14.
6. I do not suggest that tourism has shaped identity or prompted social change; rather, that it exposes ongoing internal debates.
7. The empirical part of this analysis is based on my participation in one of the first study tours of Saudi Arabia in January 2000. I served as the study leader for a private tour group from the United States that traveled under the auspices of a national museum. This analysis is in no way associated with the tour operators, nor does it reflect upon their performance, which was outstanding in every respect. Rather, it is an attempt to grapple with new and complex sociopolitical issues that emanate from tourism. The author is solely responsible for the views expressed herein.
8. In the former state socialist countries of eastern Europe, Hall has suggested, tourism acted, among other things, as "a catalyst for social change, by permitting greater and closer interaction between host populations and those from the outside world, particularly as constraints on tourist accommodations and itineraries [we]re eased." See Hall, *op. cit.*, p. 109.
9. Susan Slyomovics, "Tourist Containment," *Middle East Report* 25:5, September-October 1995, p. 6.
10. On authenticity, which I think will be an important question in Saudi Arabia, see Donald Getz, "Event Tourism and the Authenticity Dilemma," in *Global Tourism: The Next Decade*, William Theobald (ed.) Oxford: Butterworth-Heinemann, 1996; see also S. Lash and J. Urry, *Economies of Sign and Space*, London: Sage Publications, 1994; Erik Cohen, "Contemporary Tourism-Trends and Challenges: Sustainable Authenticity or Contrived Post-Modernity," in Richard Butler and Douglas Pearce (eds.), *Change in Tourism: People, Places, Processes*, London: Routledge, 1995; John Hutnyk, "Magical Mystery Tourism," in Raminder Kaur and John Hutnyk (eds.), *Travel Worlds: Journeys in Contemporary Cultural Politics*, London: Zed Books, 1999; and Hazel Tucker, "Tourism and the Ideal Village," in Abram, *op. cit.*
11. "Saudis Seeking Tourists, Preferably the Well-Off," Agence France-Presse, Dubai, 11 May 2000.
12. "Hotel Operators Eye Opportunities in Saudi Arabia," Reuters, Dubai, 16 May 2000.

13. Eileen Alt Powell, "Saudi Tourism: Conservative kingdom is finally opening its door to foreign visitors," Associated Press, Abha, in the *Northwest Arkansas Times*, 16 May 1999.
14. Ibid.
15. Tim Mitchell, "Worlds Apart: An Egyptian Village and the International Tourism Industry," *Middle East Report* 25:5, September-October 1995, pp. 8–11.
16. For a critical analysis of tourism in the Middle East, see "Tourism and the Business of Pleasure," *Middle East Report* 25:5, September-October 1995.
17. "James Gavin, "Saudi Arabia: All Change," *Middle East Economic Digest* 44:26, 30 June 2000, pp. 19–20.
18. Abdullah al Shihri, "Saudis Establish Tourism Body," Associated Press, Riyadh, 17 April 2000. Such figures suggest that Saudi Arabia is not simply a receptor destination, as is the case for much of the developing world; rather, Saudi Arabians themselves are active travelers elsewhere.
19. "New Challenge for Riyadh," *Gulf News* (editorial), 8 April 2000.
20. "New Council to Promote Tourism," *Saudi Arabian Embassy Newsletter* 17:5, May 2000.
21. "Hotel Operators Eye Opportunities in Saudi Arabia," Reuters, Dubai, 16 May 2000.
22. "Saudi Tourism Will Have Slow Start," *Gulf News*, 6 April 2000; see also "Saudi Minister Says Sponsorship to be Scrapped," Reuters, 27 April 2000.
23. "6,500 Tourists Get Saudi Visas," Agence France-Presse, 31 July 2000.
24. *Arab News*, 30 July 2000.
25. Philip L. Pearce, *The Social Psychology of Tourist Behavior*, Oxford: Pergamon Press, 1982, p. 137.
26. Ghana Gurung, David Simmons, and Patrick Devlin, "The Evolving Role of Tourist Guides: The Nepali Experience," in Thomas Hinch and Richard Butler (eds.), *Tourism and Indigenous Peoples*, London: International Thomson Business Press, 1996, pp. 107–28.
27. The phrase was coined by John Urry, *The Tourist Gaze: Leisure and Travel in Contemporary Societies*, London: Sage, 1990.
28. Saudi Arabian colleagues, who have long criticized my scholarship as being too harsh, might be interested to learn that some tourists perceived me as "seeing Saudi Arabia through rose-colored glasses."
29. Dean MacCannell, *The Tourist: A New Theory of the Leisure Class*, Berkeley and Los Angeles: University of California Press, 1999, p. 203.
30. Madawi Al Rasheed, "Political Legitimacy and the Production of History: The Case of Saudi Arabia," in L. Martin (ed.), *New Frontiers in Middle East Security*, New York: St. Martin's Press, 1999, pp. 25–46.
31. As well as a 12–volume Arabic-language *Encyclopedia of Folklore of the Kingdom of Saudi Arabia* that was published in 1999. See Judith Miller, "Encyclopedia Raises Veil on Ancient Saudi Culture," *New York Times*, 20 June 2000.
32. On museums, see Michael Hitchcock, Nick Stanley, and Siu King Chung, "The South-east Asian 'Living Museum' and Its Antecedents," in Abram, *op. cit.*
33. "Tourism Secretary General Praises Riyadh in London Speech," Saudi Arabian Embassy, Washington, D.C., press release, 10 May 2000.
34. Though there now appears to be a new mode of international voyeur tourism, in which the itineraries of foreign tourists are purposely designed to bring busloads into the ghettos and shantytowns of the developing world.
35. Ted Conover and Brown W. Cannon III, "Shifting Sands," *Travel & Leisure*, March 2000, p. 228.
36. Khalid al Maeena, "Clicking Off the Curbs of Out-dated Practices," *Gulf News*, 24 May 2000.
37. Powell, *op. cit.*
38. Gwenn Okruhlik, "Bringing the Peninsula in from the Periphery: From Imagined Scholarship to Gendered Discourse," *Middle East Report* 27:3, July-September 1997, pp. 36–37.
39. Jack Schnedler, "Saudi Arabia: Our Strange Bedfellow," *Arkansas Democrat Gazette*, 16 April 2000, Section J, pp. 1, 8.
40. Conover and Cannon III, *op. cit.*, p. 154.
41. Carla Power, "Touring Muslim Style," *Newsweek*, 10 July 2000, p. 70.
42. Peter E. Murphy, "Tourism and Sustainable Development," in Theobald, *op. cit.*, pp. 274–90.
43. Sa'ad al Sowayan, in Judith Miller, *op. cit.*

# THE KINGDOM OF SAUDI ARABIA

CHAPTER 9

*Saudi Arabia: Measures of Transition from a Rentier State*

Robert E. Looney

The purpose of this chapter is to assess the extent to which Saudi Arabia's long-term economic development strategy is meeting its objectives. Early on after the 1973–74 oil boom, the government decided that a high proportion of the country's oil revenues should be spent in a manner that would encourage private sector investment and production.[1] Part of a larger political/military strategy,[2] the economic component was to diversify the economy away from oil to the extent that self-sustaining growth could occur in the major non-oil sectors of the economy. Clearly, the goal is the creation of an economy capable of functioning independently of developments in the oil sector. This strategy was intended to provide more stability to the country's pattern of economic growth and development, and while several oil-producing countries express this desire, the Kingdom's planners put together a coherent investment strategy, focused on achieving this result.[3] At least publicly, the strategy has remained in place since the early 1970s.

While goals of this strategy seem straightforward, arriving at an objective assessment of progress made to date is extremely difficult. Examining the patterns of private sector growth does not necessarily come to grips with the issue. Output can expand simply through a continuation of government expenditures or momentum from past public allocations. If one could show that, over time, a linkage from private expenditures to private output was growing stronger than that of public expenditures to private output, then one might argue that the economy had evolved a bit, but that private expenditures themselves could not be sustained without a steady infusion of government funds. Conceptually, therefore, the methods by which one defines and measures oil independence are at the crux of assessing the success of the country's development accomplishments.

The chapter is divided into several parts. The first sections provide a brief overview of the macro-economy. Trends in output and expenditure are examined, and the more relevant patterns identified. Several linkages are made to earlier studies of the country's growth mechanisms.[4] The second part of the study develops an operational test for measuring the extent to which the private sector is replacing government expenditures as the prime mover of the non-oil sector. Relatively new statistical techniques are introduced, including co-integration and error correction, to shed light on various issues. Based on this discussion, particular statistical tests are devised to measure changes over time in the Kingdom's economic mechanisms. Ultimately, these tools are used to ascertain whether the public sector is becoming less dominant and in what sense, and whether the private sector is showing that it is now primarily responsible for large segments of non-oil sector growth. Once these questions are properly assessed, and based on the results of this analysis, the final section discusses several policy implications.

## Patterns of Growth and Expenditure, 1964–1998

Saudi Arabia has experienced periods of remarkable growth and other periods of relative stability and even decline. For the 1964–98 period as a whole, gross domestic product (GDP) at constant prices increased at an average annual rate of 5.7 percent, but with private sector GDP and non-oil GDP increasing at an even faster 6.8 and 6.7 percent, respectively (Table 9.1). Public expenditures experienced a sharp deceleration, increasing by double digits in the 1964–80 period, but with negative rates associated in investment and non-defense disbursements during the subsequent period. Private expenditures were a bit more stable, but these too experienced a general downtrend in the latter time periods.

Several other patterns emerge out of these data. First, after an initial surge following the 1973–74 oil price increases, public sector investment/infrastructure expansion was flat, actually experiencing a fairly large (-6.4 percent per annum) contraction over the 1980–98 period. Second, public consumption was the only major category of governmental expenditures to indicate a positive rate of growth in the post-1980 period. Third, of major government expenditure categories, defense was the fastest-growing sector during the last decade (1989–98). Fourth, and in contrast, private sector investment generally expanded more rapidly than consumption over the 1980–98 time frame. Fifth, the general pattern of private sector expenditures was considerably more stable than those of the public sector. Sixth, construction was by far the most volatile sector, growing at an average annual rate of 42.3 percent during the 1964–80 period, but at a -0.3 percent rate during the 1980–98 period. Finally, and ironically, one of the fastest-growing sectors, agriculture, was the one in which the country enjoyed the least natural advantages.

Despite Riyadh's persistent efforts to diversify the economy away from oil, the hydrocarbon industry is still dominant in several important regards. Oil production still accounts for roughly 30 percent of GDP, 90 percent of exports, and 70 percent of budget revenues. Therefore, the economy remains highly vulnerable to fluctuations in international oil markets. This is readily apparent, as in 1998, when nominal GDP contracted by 12 percent, mainly due to a 25-year low price of Arabian Light, the benchmark Saudi crude, averaging below $12 a

Table 9.1  Saudi Arabia: Rates of Growth, 1964–1998 (average annual %)

| Sector | 1964-1998 | 1964-1980 | 1964-1989 | 1974-1998 | 1980-1998 | 1989-1998 |
|---|---|---|---|---|---|---|
| **SECTOR OUTPUT** | | | | | | |
| Agriculture | 5.3 | 3.4 | 6.7 | 6.9 | 6.9 | 1.5 |
| Mining | 6.7 | 12.9 | 8.8 | 3.9 | 1.6 | 1.2 |
| Manufacturing | 9.4 | 14.8 | 12.0 | 7.4 | 4.9 | 2.6 |
| Electricity, Gas, Water | 6.3 | 13.6 | 7.8 | 7.0 | 0.3 | 3.2 |
| Construction | 14.8 | 42.3 | 18.4 | 7.9 | −0.3 | 4.3 |
| Wholesale, Retail Trade | 7.6 | 14.6 | 10.1 | 6.5 | 1.7 | 1.1 |
| Transport, Communications | 11.8 | 23.9 | 15.9 | 5.7 | 7.8 | 1.3 |
| Ownership of Dwellings | 5.5 | 13.1 | 7.1 | 2.3 | −0.8 | 1.2 |
| Finance, Insurance | 5.6 | 9.6 | 7.8 | 4.5 | 1.0 | 0.7 |
| Services | 5.3 | 7.2 | 7.2 | 4.7 | 2.9 | 1.2 |
| **TOTAL OUTPUT** | | | | | | |
| GDP | 5.7 | 11.0 | 6.7 | 3.1 | 1.2 | 3.0 |
| Oil GDP | 4.3 | 10.0 | 3.8 | 0.7 | −0.5 | 5.8 |
| Non-Oil GDP | 6.7 | 11.7 | 8.5 | 5.2 | 2.3 | 1.8 |
| Private Sector GDP | 6.8 | 11.4 | 8.7 | 5.6 | 2.9 | 1.5 |
| Public Sector GDP | 6.4 | 12.5 | 7.8 | 4.4 | 1.2 | 2.6 |
| **PUBLIC EXPENDITURES** | | | | | | |
| Investment | 5.8 | 21.4 | 8.9 | 0.4 | −6.4 | −2.3 |
| Infrastructure | 5.7 | 19.2 | 7.6 | 2.2 | −5.0 | 0.6 |
| Consumption | 7.8 | 15.0 | 10.6 | 4.3 | 1.8 | 0.5 |
| Defense | 8.7 | 21.0 | 11.1 | 4.7 | −1.1 | 2.5 |
| Non-Defense | 5.1 | 15.7 | 8.5 | 3.2 | −3.5 | −3.7 |
| Total National Account | 6.3 | 14.6 | 8.6 | 3.9 | −0.5 | 0.1 |
| **PRIVATE EXPENDITURES** | | | | | | |
| Investment | 7.2 | 5.9 | 8.4 | 4.1 | 2.3 | 1.2 |
| Consumption | 6.4 | 12.5 | 8.6 | 5.0 | 1.3 | 0.5 |
| Total Private | 6.6 | 12.6 | 8.6 | 4.8 | 1.5 | 1.2 |

Source: Saudi Arabian Monetary Agency, Annual Report, various issues.

barrel. After the early 1999 market rally, the whole atmosphere of the country has dramatically changed, from one of frustration and despair to that of confidence and optimism.[5]

On the other hand, the differential growth rates noted above have created major structural shifts in the Saudi economy during the last several decades. In particular, the share of agriculture in (non-oil) GDP increased, from 8.1 percent in 1975 to 13.4 percent in 1998. This stands as a clear difference, with similar trends in most developing countries. Similarly, manufacturing showed a steady expansion, from 5.5 percent of non-oil GDP in 1975 to 9.5 by 1998. Non-oil GDP also experienced a steady expansion, increasing from 36.5 percent of GDP before the 1970 oil boom to nearly 70 percent by 1998. With regard to public expenditures, investment showed the most dramatic change, falling from 12.9 percent of GDP in 1980 to 5.9 percent in 1998. In contrast, public investment was only 5.3 percent of GDP before 1970, and public consumption increased from 16.8 percent of GDP in 1970 to 33.1 percent in 1998. As noted above, defense expenditures remained relatively high, at 12.6 percent of GDP. This was up from 7.4 in 1970 but down from 16.0 in 1990. Non-oil revenues were still quite low, accounting for only around 8.7 percent of GDP, although this was up from 0.9 in 1970. Private investment showed good progress, increasing from 5.1 percent of GDP in 1970 to 12.6 percent in 1998. Still, compared with countries in the same income range, Saudi Arabia has a higher share of GDP allocated to consumption and a lower share to investment when private and public expenditures are combined (Table 9.2).

The public sector budget has also undergone considerable structural change, with detailed and consistent budgetary data available starting in 1979 (Table 9.3).

The most dramatic gains in budgetary share were in the area of human resource development. This expenditure category increased its budgetary share from around 8.5 to over 23 percent by 1998. Health and social development expanded faster than the overall increase in budgetary allocations as well, increasing their share from 4.6 in 1997 to 8.4 in 1998. Interestingly enough, these two categories were the only ones averaging a positive growth rate (2.8 for human resource development and 0.6 per annum for health). The biggest budgetary declines were in transport and communications (–7.3 percent per annum), economic resource development (–6.8), and infrastructure (–7.7). Other major contractions were in government lending institutions (–20.2 percent) and public administration (–4.3 percent). Defense, although growing at an average annual rate of –0.3, still increased its share from 26 percent in 1979 to nearly 40 percent by 1998. Given these patterns, and together with the fact that the total budget contracted at an average annual rate of 2.5 percent, several sectors were clearly more "protected" than others. According to reliable studies, the manner in which countries protect selected components of the budget during periods of austerity indicates that defense and civil service sectors are far more vulnerable.[6]

In fact, the average decline in the growth of real government expenditures was 13 percent.[7] Associated with this decline was a contraction of only 5 percent in the social sectors (producing a vulnerability index of 0.4). By contrast, the index was 0.6 for the administrative and defense sectors, and over 1 percent for production and infrastructure. In short, the various social sectors were less vulnerable to cuts than defense and administration, which, in turn, were considerably less vulnerable than production and infrastructure, contrary to the generally accepted view.

The fact that social sectors and defense were both relatively protected suggests that there were high political costs associated with reducing them. On the other hand, several countries in various case studies appeared to have been more willing to cut spending on infrastructure and production, which, of course, is likely to have adverse implications for longer-term growth, but few early direct and immediate costs.

Saudi Arabia appears to fit this pattern fairly well, although some of the King-

Table 9.2  Saudi Arabia: Economic Structure, 1970 – 1998 (average annual %)

| Sector | 1970 | 1975 | 1980 | 1990 | 1995 | 1998 |
|---|---|---|---|---|---|---|
| **SECTOR OUTPUT (% NON-OIL GDP)** | | | | | | |
| Agriculture | 12.7 | 8.1 | 6.1 | 13.9 | 13.6 | 13.4 |
| Manufacturing | 6.0 | 5.5 | 6.0 | 8.6 | 8.8 | 9.4 |
| Mining | 0.6 | 0.7 | 0.5 | 0.5 | 0.5 | 0.5 |
| Refining | 16.9 | 9.0 | 6.2 | 9.1 | 12.9 | 13.0 |
| Electricity, Gas, Water | 3.7 | 2.3 | 3.9 | 3.3 | 3.7 | 3.8 |
| Construction | 11.9 | 21.9 | 20.0 | 9.1 | 8.8 | 9.0 |
| Wholesale, Retail Trade | 13.1 | 15.4 | 22.4 | 20.5 | 20.2 | 20.1 |
| Transport, Communications | 18.3 | 10.4 | 11.9 | 11.6 | 11.5 | 11.3 |
| Ownership of Dwellings | 8.6 | 12.8 | 11.5 | 6.6 | 6.6 | 6.6 |
| Finance, Insurance | 4.5 | 4.5 | 5.0 | 4.2 | 4.0 | 3.9 |
| Services | 3.1 | 2.4 | 2.1 | 2.3 | 2.2 | 2.2 |
| **TOTAL OUTPUT (% GDP)** | | | | | | |
| Oil GDP | 63.5 | 71.1 | 69.6 | 38.0 | 37.2 | 30.2 |
| Non-Oil GDP | 36.5 | 28.9 | 30.4 | 62.0 | 62.8 | 69.8 |
| Private Sector GDP | 25.9 | 17.3 | 17.1 | 36.1 | 36.5 | 40.6 |
| Public Sector GDP | 10.7 | 11.6 | 13.3 | 25.9 | 26.1 | 29.2 |
| **Public/Private Output (% non-oil GDP)** | | | | | | |
| Private Sector GDP | 70.2 | 59.8 | 56.3 | 58.3 | 58.1 | 58.2 |
| Public Sector GDP | 29.8 | 40.2 | 43.7 | 41.7 | 41.6 | 41.8 |
| **PUBLIC FISCAL (% GDP)** | | | | | | |
| Investment | 5.3 | 10.7 | 12.9 | 11.0 | 5.3 | 5.9 |
| Consumption | 16.8 | 17.6 | 15.8 | 31.2 | 26.1 | 33.1 |
| Defense | 7.4 | 9.1 | 13.3 | 16.0 | 10.5 | 12.6 |
| National Account Expenditures | 22.2 | 28.3 | 28.7 | 42.2 | 31.4 | 39.1 |
| Budgetary Expenditure | 26.9 | 19.5 | 36.4 | 46.7 | 31.8 | 34.9 |
| Oil Revenues | 24.2 | 57.5 | 36.5 | 28.7 | 21.5 | 28.9 |
| Non-Oil Revenues | 0.9 | 3.6 | 4.2 | 12.4 | 7.1 | 8.7 |
| **PRIVATE EXPENDITURES (% GDP)** | | | | | | |
| Investment | 5.1 | 6.5 | 5.5 | 7.0 | 11.4 | 12.6 |
| Consumption | 28.4 | 14.6 | 22.2 | 40.5 | 41.1 | 42.2 |
| Total Private | 33.5 | 21.1 | 27.7 | 47.5 | 52.5 | 54.8 |

Source: Saudi Arabian Monetary Agency, Annual Report, various issues.

dom's budgetary categories do not overlap with the standardized International Monetary Fund (IMF) categories used by Hicks and Kubisch. In the Saudi case, three groups of budgetary items emerge, starting with highly favored categories, including those in the bottom part of Table 9.3 (in brackets), which actually expanded in real terms while the budget contracted; second, sectors that contracted at a slower rate than the overall budget and had an elasticity of less than 1; and finally, sectors that contracted at a rate more rapid than the overall budget (having an elasticity of greater than 1).

Table 9.3  Saudi Arabia: Public Sector Budget, 1979–1998 (average annual %)

| Sector | 1979 | 1985 | 1990 | 1995 | 1998 |
|---|---|---|---|---|---|
| **BUDGETARY SHARES (% TOTAL BUDGET)** | | | | | |
| Human Resource Development | 8.46 | 12.27 | 15.58 | 17.94 | 23.21 |
| Transport & Communications | 11.31 | 7.25 | 4.70 | 4.13 | 4.35 |
| Economic Resource Development | 6.89 | 4.54 | 2.56 | 2.57 | 2.97 |
| Health and Social Development | 4.55 | 6.45 | 6.82 | 6.77 | 8.36 |
| Infrastructure Development | 3.13 | 3.46 | 1.37 | 0.93 | 1.1 |
| Municipal Services | 5.88 | 5.95 | 3.31 | 3.25 | 3.34 |
| Defense and Security | 26.12 | 31.98 | 34.32 | 33.00 | 39.91 |
| Public Administration | 18.04 | 19.29 | 27.96 | 26.47 | 12.79 |
| Government Lending Institutions | 11.46 | 4.65 | 0.59 | 0.32 | 0.26 |
| Local Subsidies | 4.16 | 4.17 | 2.8 | 4.61 | 3.71 |
| **BUDGETARY GROWTH (% AVERAGE ANNUAL RATE)** | | | | | |
| Human Resource Development | 2.8 | 2.6 | 3.1 | −4.1 | 3.3 |
| Transport & Communications | −7.3 | −10.5 | −9.0 | −9.2 | −2.7 |
| Economic Resource Development | −6.8 | −10.0 | −13.2 | −6.7 | 0.1 |
| Health and Social Development | 0.6 | 2.2 | −1.5 | −6.9 | 0.8 |
| Infrastructure Development | −7.7 | −1.9 | −19.1 | −13.7 | −4.3 |
| Municipal Services | −5.4 | −3.4 | −13.4 | −7.1 | −1.6 |
| Defense and Security | −0.3 | −0.3 | −1.2 | −7.5 | 0.2 |
| Public Administration | −4.3 | −2.5 | 4.9 | −7.8 | −10.9 |
| Government Lending Institutions | −20.2 | −17.0 | −35.5 | −17.7 | 0.0 |
| Local Subsidies | −3.1 | −3.5 | −10.1 | 3.0 | 1.8 |
| Total Budget | −2.5 | −3.6 | −2.6 | −6.8 | −1.7 |
| **BUDGETARY GROWTH (ELASTICITIES)** | | | | | |
| Human Resource Development | [0.51] | [0.72] | [1.19] | 0.60 | [1.94] |
| Transport & Communications | 2.92 | 2.92 | 3.46 | 1.35 | 1.59 |
| Economic Resource Development | 2.72 | 2.78 | 5.08 | 0.11 | [0.06] |
| Health and Social Development | [0.24] | [0.61] | 0.58 | 1.01 | [0.47] |
| Infrastructure Development | 3.08 | 0.53 | 7.34 | 2.01 | 2.53 |
| Municipal Services | 2.16 | 0.94 | 5.15 | 1.04 | 0.94 |
| Defense and Security | 0.12 | 0.08 | 0.46 | 1.10 | [0.12] |
| Public Administration | 1.72 | 0.69 | [1.88] | 1.15 | [6.41] |
| Government Lending Institutions | 8.08 | 4.72 | 13.65 | 2.60 | 0.00 |
| Local Subsidies | 1.24 | 0.90 | 3.88 | [0.44] | [1.06] |

Source: Saudi Arabian Monetary Agency, Annual Report, various issues.

For the period as a whole, and for most of the sub-periods, human resource development, health, and social development fall in the highly favored category. Defense is usually favored, and in the 1990s it, along with public administration, was highly favored. Most of the economic sectors were not favored, with contradictory budgetary shares.

The patterns reported above are consistent with an earlier study of Saudi Arabian budgetary allocations using regression analysis.[8] That study concluded that only several sectors were able to increase their budgetary shares during periods of unintended budgetary deficits. These were: human resource development, health, and social development. They were also the only sectors to have their budgetary shares increase during periods of increased actual (realized) budgetary deficits. Moreover, human resource development and health did not have their shares expanded with increases in expected revenue. This finding is consistent with the notion that their funding levels were assured just because of high priority. Thus, marginal increases in revenue could be safely used by the authorities to fund lower-priority projects.

Equally important, the deficit-related expansion in human capital seems to have come in part at the expense of longer-term investment in economic capacity. Specifically, transportation and communications, economic services, and infrastructure all had their budgetary shares contract during periods of unexpected and actual deficits. In general, the main findings of this study confirm the high priority granted human resource development by Saudi authorities. Resources allocated to this sector have been preserved, relative to competing sectors, during periods of austerity. To be sure, budgetary cuts have occurred in Saudi Arabia, but education has been spared. The long-term nature of this commitment is further evident by the fact that it appears relatively safe from budgetary cuts when overall disbursements cause deficits. The same could be said for health and social expenditures. Finally, while defense has regained its leading share of the budget during the recent period of relative fiscal austerity, Riyadh does not appear to have fallen into the guns versus education syndrome. In fact, both types of expenditures appear to complement each other in the minds of Saudi budgetary authorities.

Because of its importance to the economy, budgetary dynamics and tradeoffs associated with defense expenditures have received special attention. In particular, the impact of defense expenditures on the economy revealed that budgetary tradeoffs were often more complex than those associated with other categories.[9] In part, this simply reflects differences in budgetary priorities across countries. However, this complexity also stems from the fact that increased levels of government deficits can offset or reinforce the impacts that expanded defense expenditures have on other budgetary shares. Further analyses indicate that defense/socioeconomic tradeoffs varied considerably depending on whether the country had an environment characterized by high or low levels of military expenditures. This usually occurs in both the central government budget and in relation to the overall size of the economy. During the 1980s, for example, defense expenditures in these two environments had a differential impact on economic growth as well. In high defense expenditure countries, increase in the share of resources allocated to that sector did not provide any appreciable stimulus to the economy. For those countries, defense increases in central government budgets actually tended to reduce the overall rate of growth. In low defense countries, however, defense increases did provide a positive stimulus to economic growth. Furthermore, increases in the share of defense did not retard that growth.

There are several explanations for these patterns. In the Middle East at least, high defense countries appear to cut economic expenditures, to free up resources for further expansion of the military. This may occur because of the political costs in cutting non-defense expenditures, particularly over long periods of time. Again, with several exceptions, low defense countries seem to have more flexibility in accommodating increased levels of military expenditure. As a result, economic programs may not be as susceptible to cuts in these instances. Long-run costs, associated with the manner in which Middle Eastern countries alter budgetary shares—to accommodate increased military expenditures—may also be a key factor. For high defense countries as a whole, increased budgetary shares throughout the 1970s had a positive impact on growth in the 1980s. Yet, increased shares to defense in the 1980s impacted negatively. Given the observed lagged nature of many negative impacts in these countries, this may indicate the neglect of economic services, infrastructure, and the like. If that is the case, countries like Saudi Arabia may be finding that high defense burdens are starting to take a heavy toll on economic growth. If these lagged impacts are stable, one can expect non-oil GDP growth to expand at rates somewhat below its long-run growth path. Indeed, for the Kingdom, a reorientation of budgetary priorities may not provide an immediate stimulus to the economy.

Although a leading Saudi political economist has painted a slightly brighter picture than the one summarized above, our findings are consistent with each other.[10] In the Saudi analyst's own words,

> What was surprising in Saudi Arabia's response to the challenges of the past decade is not merely the relative effectiveness of the state's responses but the minimum political costs they entailed. This suggested a degree of resiliency by the Saudi state that was much greater than could be expected for rentier states.

The author also noted that three areas in particular required further attention, including,

> (1) The domestic extraction capabilities of the state, [which] are still insufficient [and] almost entirely dependent on indirect taxation. Other Gulf states have already taken the important step of introducing personal income taxes to much demands; (2) the legal system and the official statistical base need[ed] urgent reforms if official plans to invite external investments [we]re to be realized; and (3) there [wa]s a need for the privatization program to proceed at a quicker rate and with greater transparency."[11]

Clearly the Saudi budget has changed considerably over the years. While the fall in expenditures is the most dramatic manifestation of this phenomenon, the more subtle and less publicized shift in the composition of expenditures is perhaps just as significant in our understanding of the country's growth dynamics. If, for example, a decline in the ability of governmental expenditures—to stimulate the non-oil sector—was recorded, it would be logical to ask whether this occurred because of some sort of diminishing returns to public expenditures. Equally important, was the cause of such a decline the result of changes in the composition of specific expenditures?

## Criteria and Tests of Non-Oil Development

To examine the possible linkages between public and private sector expenditures on non-oil production in Saudi Arabia, a co-integration error-correction analysis was undertaken. While mathematically technical, this method has a straightforward intuitive appeal.[12] Co-integration/error-correction formulae are attempts to determine whether two series (such as private expenditures and sector output) move together over long periods of time.[13]

The analysis accepts the fact that short-run shocks can occur, whereby rapid increases (i.e., public sector investment) in one variable cause movement in the other (i.e., construction). However, if the two variables have developed a long-run linkage, whereby an ongoing stable set of links have been established, then equilibrium will be restored, with the speed of adjustment affected by the deviation from that long-run pattern. Specifically, the speed of the longer-term adjustment will be dependent on the magnitude of the deviation from the long-run equilibrium pattern, as well as the strength of the linkage between the two variables. In short, the year-to-year growth of a sector such as non-oil manufacturing can be divided into two parts: the first associated with a short-run shock (increased public-sector consumption), and the second drawing on the longer-term linkages established with the causal variable (here public sector consumption).

The technique has been used successfully to assess several other facets of Gulf economies. For example, Al-Yousif's study of exports and economic growth in the region found that in the case of Saudi Arabia, Kuwait, the UAE, and Oman, there are no long-run relationships between exports and economic growth.[14] On the other hand, the study found that exports have had a positive and significant shorter-run impact on growth in all four countries. No doubt, one reason the long-run relationship did not hold up is because the significant relationship is not between exports per se, but how receipts are spent (invested) by respective governments. Moreover, and while highly dependent on oil, these Arab Gulf countries have been engaged in efforts to diversify their domestic economies and the structure of their trade. Apparently, these efforts have been successful in the sense that the economies are now capable of some measure of growth, independent of developments in the oil sector.

In another study of Saudi imports, the duration of import volume adjustments to changes in the explanatory variable was determined to be approximately two years.[15] This interval seems to be longer than that obtained by others. In one leading analysis, the long-run money demand function of GCC countries, using Johansen's co-integration methodology, was determined to have a nominal effect.[16] However, this occurred only in the Saudi case. In contrast, the results indicate the presence of a long-run demand function for broad money for Saudi Arabia and the UAE, when real GDP, interest rates, price levels, and nominal effective exchange rates are included in the system. Thus, the modeling of money demand in Saudi Arabia and Bahrain, should be done in real terms. In other words, the additional international interest rate variable plays an important role in determining the demand for money in Saudi Arabia, the UAE, and Bahrain.

In general, these studies demonstrate that the technique is capable of yielding insights not often captured by the more conventional regression methods. A common theme is that economic development in the Gulf is becoming a more complex process as the economies mature and begin to diversify away from a complete reliance on oil revenues and associated public sector expenditures. For the purposes of this study, the technique appears capable of developing a new, operational way to assess the extent of diversification from a rentier state.

In the early phases of economic development in oil-based countries, the expansion of many types of sectoral growth is highly dependent on government expenditures. One sign of achieving a diversified, self-sustaining economy should therefore be the severing, or at least the weakening, of the longer-term linkage with public expenditures. Ideally, these would be replaced by a similar linkage to the expansion of private sector production. Specifically, when and if the Saudi non-oil economy develops to the point at which its growth can occur independently of government expenditures, then one may conclude that it has graduated from a pure oil economy. Conventional regression analysis would not be able to make these distinctions, because short-run growth spurts associated with government expenditure shocks often mask the possible weakening of its longer-term links to the non-oil economy.

Accordingly, a proposed development classification scheme for non-oil sectors in Saudi Arabia may include four specific constants: first, beginning stages, when weak or non-existent long-term links with public and private expenditures affect non-oil output (short-term links may be present in this constant); second, a partial integration stage, when development of longer-term links with public expenditures, and possibly short-term links with private expenditures, further affect non-oil output; third, an integrated stage, when strong links are established with private expenditures (in this instance, possible government involvement with strong links to one or more major expenditure categories may be present. The result would be a possible weakening of short-term links); finally, a mature stage, which weakens long-term government linkages and maintains long-term linkages with private sector production.

To these we might add a final self-sustaining stage in which all long-term links to the public sector have been broken, while at the same time strong long-run links have been forged with private sector demand and/or output. As with all stage theories of economic development, a major area of controversy might center on how one moves from one stage to another. Is economic reform a key element? Is the composition of private sector investment critical, and if so, in what way? While these questions are largely beyond the scope of this study, the results below do shed some light on the subject.

## Results

The first step in the analysis was to examine the impact that various types of public expenditure, including investment, consumption, defense, and total budgetary allocations, have had on private sector GDP (Table 9.4).[17] The main findings revealed that:

- patterns have varied over time, with a general weakening of links to public expenditures;
- in particular, and with the exception of public investment, no type of public sector expenditure was statistically significant (at the 95 percent level) in the most recent (1974–98) time period;
- in contrast, public investment, defense, and total public expenditure's short-term link with private GDP had been statistically significant at the 95 percent level in the earlier (1964–1989) period;
- the long-term impacts also show a weakening. This is evidenced by the declining size of the coefficient on the error-correction term (the size of the coefficient indicates the strength of adjustments to the long-term pattern). For total public expenditures, the 1974–1998 coefficient was over half (0.33 vs. 0.15) of its 1964–1989 value. Moreover, long-term private investment gross domestic product was barely significant at the 95 percent level, while it had been highly significant in the earlier period;
- coinciding with the weakening of longer-term public sector links (a major source of private sector demand), private consumption was strengthened, increasing the statistical significance of its long-term adjustment with that variable from 90 percent in the first period to over 95 percent in the second.

Table 9.4 Saudi Arabia: Influence of Public Expenditure on the Private Sector Economy

| Variable | Short-Run Impact | | Error-Correction Term | | |
|---|---|---|---|---|---|
| | 1964–1989 | 1974–1998 | 1964–1998 | 1964–1989 | 1974–1998 |
| **Private Sector GDP** | | | | | |
| Public Investment | † | † | −0.03 (−4.74)† | −0.04 (−4.10)† | −0.03 (−2.12)† |
| Public Consumption | ★ | ins | −0.10 (−3.59)† | −0.24 (−6.93)† | −0.10 (−3.03)† |
| Defense | † | ★ | −0.04 (−2.61)† | −0.11 (−7.28)† | −0.07 (−5.12)† |
| Total Public Expenditures | † | ★ | −0.14 (−2.50)† | −0.33 (−7.26)† | −0.15 (−2.37)† |
| Private Consumption | ★ | ★ | −0.11 (−2.10)† | −0.15 (−1.95)★ | −0.15 (−2.50)† |

Notes: Data from Saudi Arabian Monetary Authority, Annual Report, various issues. All variables in constant 1969 prices. Error-correction estimations equilibration performed using Pesaran, M. H., and B. Pesaran. Microfit 4.0: Interactive Econometric Analysis. Cambridge: Camfit Data Ltd, 1997.

( ) = t–statistic; ins = statistically insignificant; ★ significant at the 90% level; † = significant at the 95% level.

To assess the extent to which this general pattern held up across various non-oil sectors of the economy, a similar analysis was undertaken for the various sectoral components of GDP, including agriculture, mining, construction, manufacturing (non-refining), transport, power, finance, services, and the like. For purposes of classification, our examination also focused on whether or not public expenditures were losing their stimulating effects on output, as well as whether these expenditures were being replaced by private expenditures. In the latter case, which type of private expenditure proved most effective was also deciphered. Of course, if private sector expenditures themselves remain highly linked to government disbursements, then the economy is not really becoming all that self-sufficient. Hence, a final set of error-correction tests were performed on the links between public and private expenditures, to assess the extent to which private sector expenditures have become less dependent on public expenditure allocations.

## Agriculture

For the agricultural sector, the analysis suggests a general weakening of public sector expenditures with time. This is evidenced by the statistically significant short-term impacts of non-defense expenditures and total budgetary expenditures in the 1964–89 period, giving way to statistically insignificant impacts in the 1974–98 period. In fact, in no case did any of the major categories of public sector expenditures have a statistically significant impact on short-run output during the 1974–98 period.

The longer-term pattern was even weaker. While consumption and defense appear to have a stable long-term pattern for the period as a whole, their links with the pattern of long-term agricultural growth during the 1974–98 period is only marginally (90 percent level) significant.

Anyone remotely familiar with Saudi Arabia knows the extent to which government subsidies and other supports have helped expand the Kingdom's agricultural sector. As noted in Table 9.3, there is a good chance that many of the government's initial programs have been scaled back. It is safe to conclude, therefore, that public expenditures are currently playing only a tangential role in stimulating further agricultural output. This may have been the case for some time.

A very different picture emerges for private expenditures. Here, all of the major categories—investment and consumption as well as total expenditures—increase their statistical significance with time. This is particularly true for short-term impacts in which all three categories had a statistically insignificant jolt on agricultural production in the earlier period. This changed to a positive and highly significant impact in the latter period. In addition, the long-term coefficients of adjustment did not decline with time, indicating that output in this sector has maintained a fairly constant expansion in line with private expenditures.

It is not clear whether this is a success story for the government. One interpretation might be that the declining government short-run (subsidy) impact is no longer necessary, after accomplishing its original objectives. These programs have hence been cut back and are no longer necessary to assure that sector's continued expansion. Looking at expanded non-oil output as a source of stimulus for the agricultural sector, it appears that none of the major categories—non-oil GDP and its components, private GDP and public GDP—have had a short-run impact on agricultural output. Yet, all three have established a long-term relationship with the sector. The coefficients on the error adjustment term suggest however that the links with private sector GDP are much stronger than those associated with increases in public sector GDP. In addition, the private sector coefficients have strengthened over time (increasing from 0.10 in 1964–89 to 0.15 in 1974–98), while public sector links have remained rather constant (at 0.03 to 0.04).

### *Non-Oil Manufacturing*

A fairly clear picture unfolds for the critical non-oil manufacturing sector. Here, a general weakening of links between public expenditures and output was observed. The pattern has developed in both the short and the longer term. For the short term, only defense remained statistically significant (95 percent level) in the latter period. For the longer-term patterns, consumption, defense, non-defense, and total budgetary expenditures formed a statistically significant long-term relationship with non-oil manufacturing in the 1964–89 period. By 1974–95 these patterns had broken down, with no statistically significant (95 percent level) links remaining.

The role of defense is hard to explain. Links may be associated with the Kingdom's defense procurement offset program and might account for the short-run impact, but with little carry-over to a stable long-term connection.

A totally different picture emerges for the private sector. Not only were the three main expenditure categories—investment, consumption, and total expenditures—statistically significant in both short-term periods, they were also statistically significant in the long term as well. Here, however, it should be noted that there was a general weakening of the longer-term links with time, supported by the decline in the value of the error-correction coefficient. Again speculating, the very limited impact of public sector investment in affecting growth of the non-oil manufacturing sector may, in turn, be a reflection of the limited role of this type of expenditure in increasing the productivity of private sector investments. This being the case, the productivity of private sector investments in this sector may be declining. For the major components of GDP, another picture emerges, with increases in private sector GDP providing a short-run stimulus to non-oil manufacturing output. Yet, private sector GDP has failed to establish any long-term stable pattern of expansion with non-oil manufacturing. Given manufacturing's stable long-term relationship with the private sector, one must conclude that the Saudi Arabian non-oil manufacturing sector largely caters to final demand, with little output entering into intermediate stages of private sector production. This pattern is fairly common at early stages of industrialization. No doubt the true test of the success of the country's industrialization program will be whether or not activity spreads into the intermediate and capital stages of production. There is little evidence of this occurring to date.

### Minerals and Mining

Saudi Arabia's mineral and mining sector is still a negligible segment of the non-oil economy. However, it does have the potential for rapid growth, as new mineral and ore discoveries are beginning to attract considerable attention. Historically, the public sector has had strong ties to this area, although there are signs that these may be weakening. Public investments, for example, which had statistically significant links to the sector in the 1964–89 period, found these disappearing in the more recent 1974–98 period. There were also fairly considerable declines in the size of the error-correction coefficient over time for both public consumption and defense expenditures. Private expenditures, on the other hand, appear to have strengthened their ties to the mineral and mining sector. Both private consumption and total private expenditures evolved from no short-run statistical links in the early period to highly significant ties in the latter. In contrast to the general pattern experienced by public expenditures, the size of the error-correction coefficient increased considerably in the case of private consumption and total private expenditures.

### Construction

No other sector epitomizes oil-fueled expenditures more than construction. Few can forget the images of 24-hour crash building programs in the years immediately following the 1973–74 oil boom. There is no doubt that in these initial years, output was driven almost exclusively by government infrastructure expenditures. This is clearly confirmed by the error-correction analysis indicating a strong link between public sector investment and construction activity. Still, contrary to what one might imagine, this association appears to be strengthening with time, as indicated by the fact that the size of the coefficient—on the error-correction term—nearly doubled during the latter 1974–98 period. Moreover, government consumption formed an extensive, albeit weak, long-term link in the latter period, where one was not present earlier.

An even more interesting situation arises with private sector expenditures. Here, it appears that for the first time, construction activity was not just fueled by government expenditures. Private investment, consumption, and total expenditures shifted from a strong long-run statistical link with the construction sector in 1974–98, where none had existed previously. Construction's links with real output also appear to have strengthened over time. Both public and private GDP formed no strong long-term links with the sector during the 1964–89 period. Nevertheless, both developed these patterns in the subsequent period. Based on the size of the error-correction coefficient, the link with private sector GDP was considerably stronger than that associated with public sector output. In addition, both public and private sector GDPs maintained strong short-term links to construction activity during both time periods.

Summing up, construction is not dominated by public sector activity, as in the past. Yet, it is apparent that in many ways the sector is still quite closely tied to the fates of government expenditures. On the other hand, there are clear indications that important links are being forged with the private sector. In the future, greater diversification of sources of stimulus should provide the sector with more stability than it has had in the past. While the boom-or-bust days are not completely over, it is apparent that the private sector is now able to pick up some of the slack when government expenditures contract sharply.

### *Wholesale and Retail Trade*

The trade sector also shows the declining influence of government expenditures. During the 1964–89 period, public investment, consumption, defense, and (at the 90 percent level) total budgetary expenditures all formed long-term relationships with the sector. By 1974–98, however, only consumption retained its links, and, based on a decline in the error-correction coefficient from 0.25 to 0.10, at a considerably weakened amount. Still, several public sector expenditures, including investment, defense, and total budgetary expenditures, were able to affect output in the sector over the short run.

Surprisingly, private sector patterns did not strengthen with time. This is an area in which one might anticipate that increased incomes and spending patterns throughout the Kingdom would be reflected in a rapidly expanding demand for retail goods and services. While it is true that the private sector did create ties to this sector early on, there is little evidence that they have strengthened with time. In fact, the long-term links between private sector investment consumption and total expenditures actually weakened during the latter 1974–98 period, though not quite to the extent of those expenditures associated with the public sector. Similar patterns occurred with real output. Both private and public GDP formed short- and long-term links with the sector, but there was a decline in the strength of the long-term relationship with the passage of time.

### *Electricity, Gas, and Water*

This sector is currently experiencing great changes with privatization, together with plans for increased investment and output. A complicating factor is that investment in the sector has lagged in recent years. Indeed, Riyadh now estimates that this industry alone will require an investment of $80 billion over the next 20 years, to cater to the country's rapidly growing population,[18] meaning that demand factors per se have been modified by capacity constraints.

As with several of the other sectors, public expenditure appears to be having less and less of a long-term effect on the sector's fortunes. Early on, the sector had formed statistically significant long-term bonds with government investment, consumption, defense, non-defense, and total budgetary expenditures. By 1974–98, only consumption maintained this link at a 95 percent level of confidence (and then at greatly diminished strength).

Private expenditures also formed early links with the sector. While these declined slightly in the second time period, they are currently much stronger than those derived from public expenditures. In recent years, private consumption has also forged a strong short-term bond with the sector. As for production links to the sector, the pattern is clearly one of strengthening longer-term ties with time, for both the non-oil economy as well as public GDP. Non-oil GDP lost its short-term link with the sector, even if this was clearly offset by the dramatic increase in the sector's long-term coefficient (0.22 to 0.73). The power sector stood out as the most promising for private investments. While public expenditures still play a role in stimulating output, private sector demand, along with non-oil GDP, appears to provide a capacity to rapidly control the pace of expansion.

### *Transport and Communications*
The patterns of expenditures/output on the transport/communications sector resemble those characterizing the power sector. Both public and private expenditures have played and continue to play an important role in affecting their expansion. There are several subtle differences, however. The short-term links associated with public sector expenditures have been consistently strong and are present more or less across the board. With the exception of defense expenditures in the earlier period, every type of public expenditure has had a strong short-term link to the sector's output. The long-term impact of public expenditures has somewhat weakened with time, in the sense that fewer categories have retained their statistical association with the sector's output. By 1974–98, public investment was no longer statistically linked with the sector's long-run movements. Also, in the latter period, non-defense expenditures declined in statistical significance. Offsetting these developments has been the slight increase in public consumption's long-term impact on the sector's growth.

Private sector links to the transport/communications area have, in general, strengthened over time. While the long-term link to private investment has weakened in recent years, both private consumption and total private expenditures have strengthened their long-term links to the sector's output. The latter two expenditure categories have also maintained their strong short-term links to the sector. Output links also appear to be strengthening. Non-oil GDP, public GDP, and private GDP have all experienced increases in the size of their long-run coefficient. At the same time, public GDP no longer has a short-term impact on the sector's output. The transport and communications field is another sector that appears to be undergoing a gradual shift from public sector demand-led growth to that associated with developments in the private sector. This development is occurring both in terms of expenditures as well as in terms of the strong links being forged with private-sector GDP.

### *Financial Sector*
Since the end of the 1991 Gulf War, the consolidated balance sheet of Saudi Arabia's banks has grown steadily, at an average annual rate of around 6.2 percent. Balance sheets grew by about 6.6 percent in 1997, and a further 2.9 percent to mid-year 1998, in line with the long-term trend. Leading this growth was the expansion of capital accounts, which increased at an average annual rate of more than 14 percent. The Bank for International Settlements (BIS) estimates that the capital adequacy ratios of Saudi banks as a group are upward of 16 percent, more than twice the BIS minimums.

The Saudi Arabia stock market is by far the largest in the Middle East, with a capitalization exceeding $50 billion. The World Bank has given the Saudi market high marks for its efficiency, transparency, and quality of regulation. Except for investment by GCC nationals in selected shares, and a single closed-ended fund, the Saudi market is largely closed to foreign investors. New measures to open the market are under review. Clearly, even small steps in that direction would buoy investor confidence. An even more aggressive opening could bring about the re-rating of the market, where investors come to evaluate share prices in terms of their relationship to earnings growth expectations, as opposed to the prevailing approach that focuses on dividend yields.[19]

This is an interesting sector in that expenditures associated with both the public and private sectors are highly significant in the longer term. Furthermore, and based on the expanded size of the long-term coefficient, there is clear evidence that these links are increasing with time. The short-run effects of public and private expenditures are also generally quite strong, especially the aggregate figures of total budgetary expenditures for the public sector and total private-sector expenditures for the private sector. Several of these patterns carry over into the sector's link with non-oil output. In particular, private-sector GDP has achieved strong links to the sector, in both the short and the long term. These links also appear to be strengthening with the size of the long-term coefficient, more than doubling (0.18 to 0.38) between 1964–89 and 1974–98. Still, there is evidence that links with public-sector GDP, while strong, are weakening a bit. Although public-sector GDP had a statistically significant short-run impact in the earlier period, the latter period showed no such link. Moreover, the long-run impact of the sector on public-sector GDP declined, with the size of this coefficient falling from 0.38 to 0.21.

Summing up, the sector as a whole appears to be gradually more dependent on private-sector activity, in terms of both direct demand and output. While the public sector still plays a major role, there is no reason to expect a reversal of these patterns in coming years.

### *The Service Sector—Community, Social, and Personal*

This is a diverse sector that has experienced relatively rapid growth in recent years. Like the finance sector, it has established a number of links with the public and private areas. The public sector's immediate expenditure stimulus appears to be weakening a bit. In recent years, public consumption, investment, total non-defense allocations, and, possibly, total budgetary allocations have all lost their respective abilities to provide a short-run stimulus to the sector. Yet, defense expenditures have maintained their strong short-run ties to the sector, while longer-term linkages are strengthening. Specifically, there has been an increase in the statistical importance of the long-run coefficient associated with public consumption, non-defense expenditures, and total budgetary allocations. At the same time, there has not been a significant change in the value of the long-run coefficients relative to the earlier (1964–98) period.

In contrast to the public sector, private sector consumption and total expenditures have maintained their strong short-run links to the sector. In addition, they have experienced the same stability over time in their long-run coefficients. It should be noted that the size of these coefficients are considerably larger, expenditure category by expenditure category, than those associated with public sector expenditures. This suggests, of course, that "riyal-for-riyal" private sector expenditures have a considerably greater long-run impact than those associated with public sector activity. This same pattern carried over to the links between the various categories of non-oil output and the service sector. As with private expenditures, all major categories of non-oil output experienced strong and continuous short-run links with service output. Output's longer-term impacts also showed considerable stability, with the size of the public sector's coefficient increasing significantly (0.13 to 0.23). It should be noted, however, that as with expenditures, the private sector appears to be considerably more efficient in stimulating longer-run output.

Summing up, the various components of non-oil GDP have shown considerable change over time. Each sector has moved up the scale of integration (Table 9.5). These patterns confirm the hypothesis that the government's development strategy to date has been successful in creating an environment conducive to sustained growth in the non-oil portions of the economy (Figure 9.1).

## Factors Affecting Private Sector Expenditures

While the previous sections have documented the increasingly important role of private sector expenditures in stimulating sectoral output, it is not completely clear, as noted earlier, that the private sector itself is all that independent of a steady infusion of funds originating from various government budgetary categories. Clearly, if the source of private expenditures is largely from public rather than private output, the ability of the private sector to provide adequate purchasing power independently of developments in the oil sector would be greatly reduced.

### *Total Private Expenditures*

Combining private consumption and investment provides a summary figure for private sector activity. Without a doubt, public sector expenditures have had a great influence on the pattern of private sector expenditures. Yet, it is quite apparent that that linkage is weakening.

Between 1960 and 1989, the main categories of public expenditure included investment, defense, non-defense, and total budgetary expenditures, which provided a strong short-run stimulus to the private sector. Over time, however, several of these short-run linkages (defense/non-defense and investment) have weakened to the point (1980–98) where they have ceased to operate. More importantly, the longer-run linkages between public and private expenditures are weakening. In 1960–89, public investment, defense, and total public expenditures had formed long-term linkages with private expenditures, and in turn these weakened considerably in the 1975–98 period. By 1980–98, none were statistically significant at the 95 percent level. Surprisingly, changes in oil's contribution to total GDP has not had a significant short-run impact on total private expenditures, even if oil has formed a stable long-term link with private expenditures. Based on the increasing size of this long-run coefficient, this link may well be increasing in importance. Nevertheless, private-production GDP

**Table 9.5   Summary of Results**

| Sector | Time [Classification] Period | Public/Private Linkages |
|---|---|---|
| <u>Agriculture</u> | | |
| 1964–89 | Slight public sector short-run impact, no long-run impact<br>Weak private sector long-run expenditure links, no short-run link<br>No non-oil short-run production link, established long-run production link | [Beginning Stages] |
| 1974–98 | No public-sector expenditure impact<br>Creation of strong short- and long-term private expenditure links<br>Strengthening of long-run non-oil production link | [Partial Integration Stage] |
| <u>Non-Oil Manufacturing</u> | | |
| 1964–89 | Strong public sector short- and long-term links<br>Strong private expenditure, short- and long-term links<br>Strong non-oil output, short- and long-term links | [Integrated] |
| 1974–98 | Significant weakening of public short- and long-term links<br>Slight weakening of private sector demand links<br>Slight weakening of long-run non-oil production links | [Mature] |
| <u>Mineral/Mining</u> | | |
| 1964–89 | Several long- and short-run public sector links<br>No short- or long-run private sector links<br>Weak short- and long-run non-oil production links | [Initial Integration Stage] |
| 1974–98 | Slight weakening of public short- and long-term links<br>Development of private short- and long-term links<br>Strengthening of production short- and long-term links | [Integrated Stage] |
| <u>Construction</u> | | |
| 1964–89 | Strong long- and short-run links to public investment<br>Short-run link to private investment, no long-run links<br>Strong short- and long-run links to non-oil output | [Initial Integration Stage] |

**Table 9.5  Summary of Results** (*continued*)

| Sector | Time [Classification] Period | Public/Private Linkages |
|---|---|---|
| Construction (continued) | | |
| 1974–98 | Strengthening of public investment linkages, weakening public non-investment links<br>Development of private long-term links, weakening of short-term links<br>Strengthening of non-oil short- and long-term production links | [Integrated Stage] |
| Trade Sector | | |
| 1964–89 | Strong long- and short-run links to public expenditures<br>Strong long- and short-run links to private expenditures<br>Strong short-run link to non-oil production | [Integrated Stage] |
| 1974–98 | Weakening of public sector's short- and long-term links<br>Slight weakening of private sector long-run expenditure links<br>Development of non-oil production links | [Mature Stage] |
| Power Sector | | |
| 1964–89 | Moderate short-term, strong long-term public expenditure links<br>Strong long-term, moderate short-term private expenditure links<br>Strong short-term non-oil production links no long-term links | [Integrated Stage] |
| 1974–98 | Weakening short- and long-term public expenditure links<br>Slight weakening of private long-term/short-term links<br>Development of long-term non-oil production links, loss of short-run link | [Mature Stage] |
| Transport/Communications | | |
| 1964–98 | Strong short- and long-run public expenditure links<br>Strong short- and long-run private expenditure links<br>Strong short- and long-run non-oil production links | [Integrated Stage] |

**Table 9.5  Summary of Results** (*continued*)

| Sector | Time [Classification] Period | Public/Private Linkages |
|---|---|---|
| Transport/Communications (continued) | | |
| 1974 – 98 | Weakening of long-run public expenditure links<br>Strengthening of private expenditure long-run links<br>Strengthening of non-oil long-run production links | [Mature Stage] |
| Finance/RealEstate | | |
| 1964–89 | Strong short- and long-run public expenditure links<br>Strong short-, no long-run private expenditure links<br>Strong short- and long-run non-oil production links | [Integrated Stage] |
| 1974–98 | Strengthening of public long-term expenditure links<br>Strengthening of long-run private expenditure links<br>Maintenance of short- and long-term production links | [Mature Stage] |
| Service Sector | | |
| 1964–89 | Strong short-run public expenditure links, Weak long-run links<br>Strong short- and long-run private expenditure links<br>Strong short- and long-run non-oil output links | [Integrated Stage] |
| 1974–98 | Weakening short-run public expenditure links, strengthening long-run links<br>Maintenance of long-run private expenditure links<br>Maintenance of short-, slight strengthening of long-run non-oil output links | [Mature Stage] |

has maintained strong short-run links to expenditure, and in addition, the longer-run links are highly significant and are strengthening with time.

It should be noted that the relative size of the private sector output coefficient dwarfs that associated with the oil sector. This suggests that while developments in the oil sector continue to have an important impact on private sector expenditures, they may account for a fairly low percentage of the year-to-year movement in this series.

**Figure 9.1** Saudi Arabia: Evolution of the Non-Oil Economy, 1964–

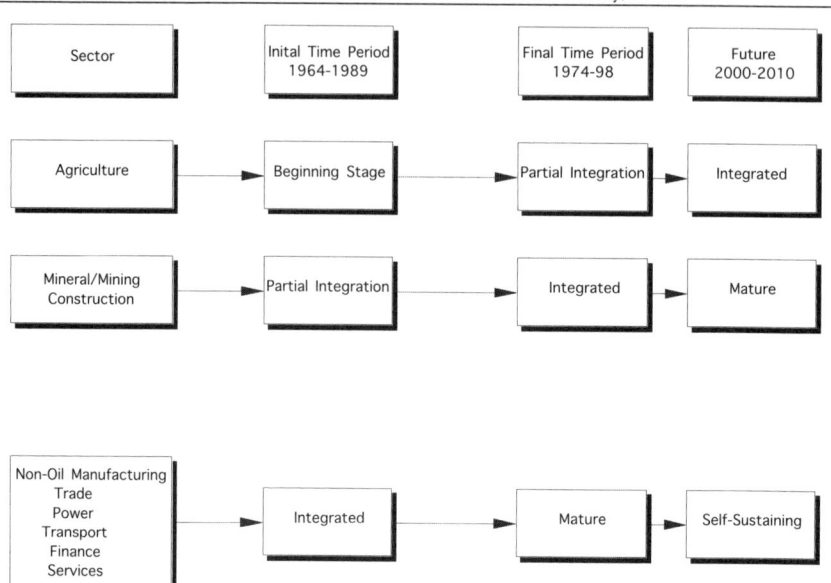

### Private Investment

Following Hirschman's unbalanced growth strategy,[20] the Kingdom's planners have attempted to stimulate private sector activity through developing and extending major infrastructure projects.

Between 1960 and 1989, this strategy appeared to be paying high dividends, with a strong short- and long-term link to private capital formation. Over time, however, this link has been severed to the extent that by 1980–98 no statistically significant links existed between the two forms of investment. This weakening is not really related to the sharp decline in public investment in recent decades. Rather, it simply signifies that public investment has become much less effective in stimulating follow-on private sector activity. A somewhat similar pattern has occurred with defense, non-defense, and total public expenditures. These began (1960–89) with strong linkages and finished (1980–98) with little influence on private capital formation decisions. The links between output (oil GDP and private sector GDP) and private investment are interesting in that oil GDP has not had much of an effect on the private sector's pattern of short-run investment. Again, and over time, private investment has adjusted to developments in the oil sector. In contrast to its links to the oil sector, private investment has been stimulated by short-run movements in private GDP, as well as adjusting to the expansion over time in that series.

As noted earlier, it should be clear that based on the size of the long-run coefficient, private investment responds much more dramatically to changes in private sector GDP than to changes in oil GDP.

*Private Consumption*

Since private consumption is the major component of private expenditures, the observed patterns are similar to those described above. Initially, public-sector expenditures across the board provided a strong short- and long-run impetus to this expenditure category. With time, these links have weakened to the point that, with the possible exception of short-run shocks associated with total budget allocations, private consumption patterns are affected by developments outside those controlled by the public sector. Therefore, private sector GDP appears to be a major factor determining the extent to which private sector consumption evolves over time. Yet, it is apparent that these lines are not nearly as strong as those associated with total private sector expenditures.

## Conclusions

The findings of this study have a number of implications for Saudi Arabia's future growth. In a sense, the results suggest that the Kingdom's development strategy of diversification has been a success. The private sector appears to be playing a more productive role with time in that many of the non-oil sectors appear capable of sustained growth without a steady infusion of government expenditures. More importantly, it is clear that the private sector is not just filling a vacuum left by the contraction in government expenditures.

However, there are several negative sides to these findings. First, if the private sector stumbles, it is not clear that the public sector will have the ability (even with increased funding) to jump-start the economy and sustain growth until private activity recovers. That growth will have to rely more and more on private sector activity and less on fiscal stimulus provided by the various types of government allocations. While effective in the past, these expenditures, with several exceptions, appear to no longer have a major impact on many of the key non-oil sectors of the economy. The underlying causes of the shifts in relative economic power are difficult to pinpoint, at least within the scope of the present study. Several plausible explanations exist for this development. As noted above, Middle Eastern countries with high (and sustained) levels of defense expenditures are beginning to pay the price for cutting back on economic expenditures to fund their military burdens. One might speculate that the defense-driven shift of Saudi expenditures away from economic to non-economic allocations has weakened the direct economic strength of public expenditures.

Another possibility is that the changing domestic and world environment requires a different composition of policies/expenditures and that perhaps many of the ongoing programs have simply hit diminishing returns. For example, it is clear that recent technological revolutions and the importance of rapid exchanges of massive amounts of information are incompatible with a state-led economy. In addition, the diversification of the economy has reached a point where Riyadh must consult with private sector leaders on the breadth and depth of any policy or—as was the case with the failed 1988 attempt to tax foreign businesses—suffer public embarrassment as well as the potential loss of valuable investment/technology.

A variant of this explanation is that while there has been a shift away from direct subsidies, in favor of an attempt to rely more on market-driven solutions, it is not apparent that Riyadh has fundamentally altered the manner in which it designs and carries out its economic programs. Ideally, as the private sector evolves from one stage to another (beginning stages, partial integration stage, integrated stage, mature stage), government policies would also shift in a manner designed to capitalize on their capability to tap private sector resources.

The second negative aspect of these results is that once the mature stage is reached, there is no assurance that the private sector, on either the expenditure or the production side, will be able to maintain established links. Weakening of private links has apparently occurred in the non-oil manufacturing, trade, and power sectors. Again, the co-integration/error-correction analysis cannot pinpoint the exact cause of this phenomenon. Still, there is no doubt that government regulations may have stifled investment and limited the ability of firms to adapt to changing circumstances. Over time, restrictive government programs might well weaken ties between private sector demand and non-oil sector output.

In particular it is safe to say that with a freer flow of international investment and market access, non-oil output might have performed even better than it did. An encouraging sign are a series of economic reforms initiated in 1998.[21] First, telecommunications was corporatized in spring 1998 as a prelude to a sell-off; a decision to merge all electricity companies as the first step in a similar process was approved in November of the same year. The electricity reforms included tariff increases that will reduce consumer subsidies and help limit the huge losses run up by the electricity companies. Operations at the ports and some local services were turned over to the private sector as well. A revised, less restrictive foreign investment code has been enacted.

Clearly, the key to the country's economic future is the manner in which economic reforms proceed. One observer has noted that the "dance" of Saudi economic reform often resembled a waltz—slow, slow, quick, quick, slow.[22] Yet, the numerous announcements made since mid-October 1999 suggest that reforms, such as the foreign investment initiatives noted above, are now well into the implementation phase. The mutual fund market has been opened to foreign investors, and non-Saudis will be allowed to own real estate and take unpenalized majority stakes in local joint ventures. The sixth round of negotiations for membership in the World Trade Organization (WTO) is moving forward, privatization is seen as a strategic choice, and, most importantly, the tax regime is under review for radical change.[23]

Expanded inflows of foreign investment are critical. Levels of foreign investment in the Kingdom have been very low in recent years. In 1996 and 1997, there were net foreign capital outflows of $1,877 million and $1,129 million respectively. Cumulative inflows in 1984–87 totaled a mere $4,317 million, compared to $36,020 million in Malaysia or $51,412 million in Singapore—both countries with smaller GDPs than Saudi Arabia's. Analysts who point to the punitive Saudi tax system and a restrictive regulatory environment as the main factors responsible for this poor performance agree that recently promised reforms could do much to reverse the trend and attract capital to the country.[24]

The empirical results presented above show that the private sector is capable of forging strong links to the non-oil economy. However, the results also indicate that in the mature phase into which some sectors (manufacturing, trade, power, for example) are moving, these links may also be weakening. What Saudi Arabia needs to do is draw on the progress made to date through developing a virtuous cycle. Specifically, the Saudi share market is already well managed, but it currently lacks the necessary depth or liquidity. A virtuous circle needs to be developed in which open capital markets, with a strong regulatory framework, can support the rapid growth of private sector investments. Higher levels of foreign direct investment (FDI) will be facilitated and will encourage further growth, of markets as well. It is through mechanisms like this that the process of increased private sector integration can be strengthened and extended to the next stages of self-sustained development.

Perhaps most importantly, the error-correction results noted above, together with the distinct possibility of developing a virtuous cycle, allow one to be much more optimistic about the Kingdom's economic prospects. Several years ago, the conventional wisdom was that the oil boom years produced an economic expansion that was not sustainable. The key components of this line of argument are laid out in Figure 9.2, which shows the close links between government expenditures and private investment, with non-oil output strongly linked to government consumption. The key element here is the declining effectiveness of government expenditures in stimulating output. Still, with high levels of government expenditure, the economy was able to expand during this period, with many of its structural weaknesses masked behind expanding budgetary allocations. Falling profitability of private investment and an apparent increase in capital outflows were ominous signs of what was to follow the end of the boom.

As noted, the conventional interpretation (Figure 9.3) of the economy during the post–oil boom years was quite pessimistic. Here, the focus has been on budgetary cutbacks, the seeming inability of the government to push through economic reforms, increased public sector debt, the drying up of credit to the private sector, capital outflow, and declining rates of private sector capital formation.[25] The conventional wisdom usually concluded that nothing positive was occurring in the non-oil economy. Furthermore, the non-oil economy would not be able to overcome mounting obstacles and constraints impeding its growth. The end result of this process were few accomplishments in terms of economic diversification and self-sufficiency. Instead, the economy was said to face years of increased unemployment, declining incomes, and eventual political and social instability.

The error-correction results noted above paint a somewhat different picture. Despite the decline in government expenditures, and the relatively slow pace of economic reforms, the private sector was still able to evolve in a positive manner, forging a complex set of links to key non-oil economic segments. At the same

**Figure 9.2** Development Model 1: Saudi Arabian Development during the Oil Boom Years

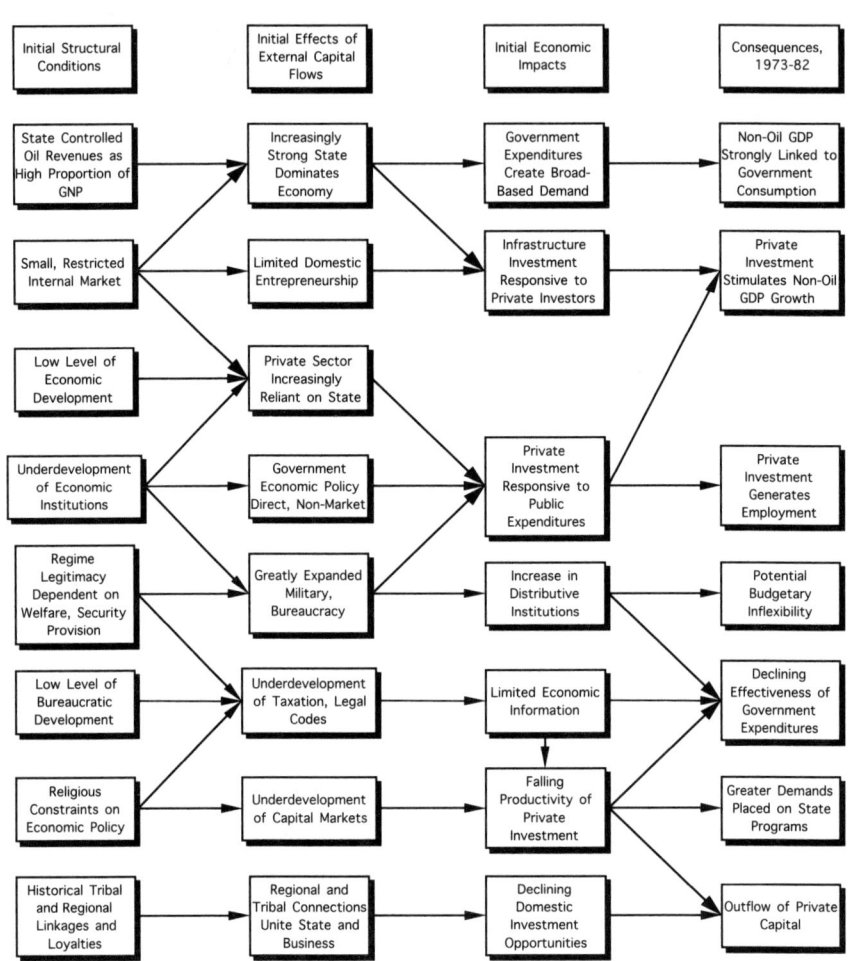

Source: Looney (1997, p. 49)

time, the private sector appears to have reduced its extreme dependency on governmental expenditures and direct subsidies. These developments and their possible causes are summarized in Figure 9.4. As for the future, a possible virtuous cycle model (Figure 9.5) may well allow the Kingdom to take advantage of rapid growth patterns.

**Figure 9.3** Development during the Post–Oil Boom Years: Pessimistic Assessment

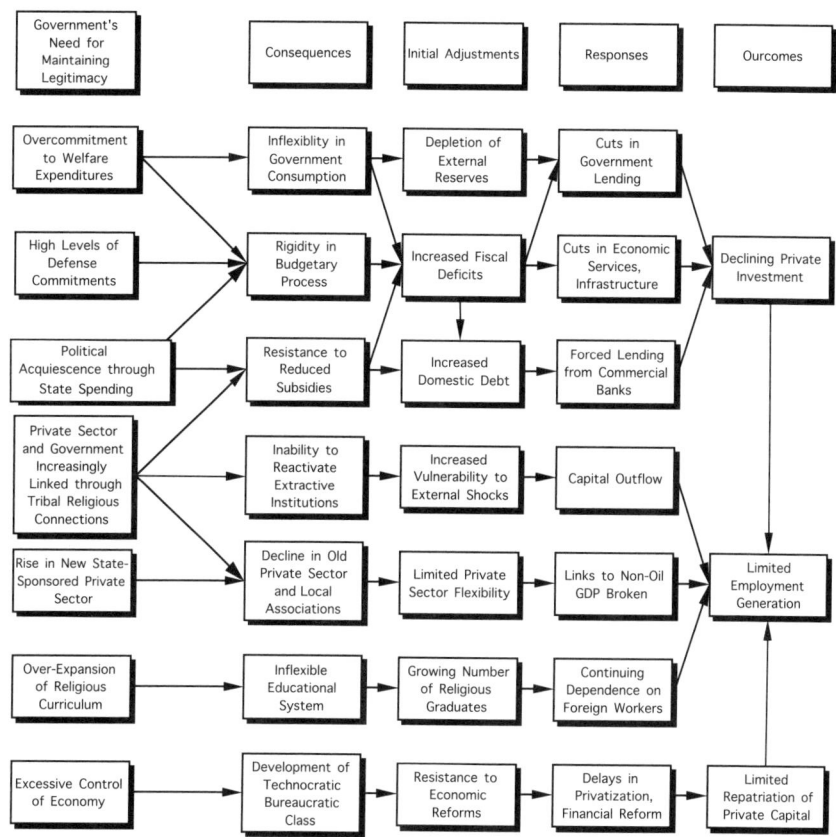

Source: Looney (1997, p. 50)

**Figure 9.4** Development during the Post–Oil Boom Years: Optimistic Assessment

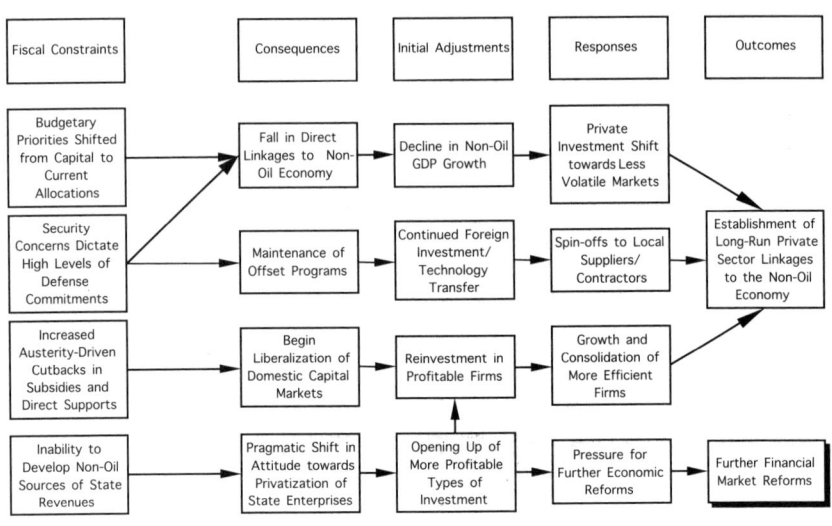

**Figure 9.5** Saudi Arabia: Future Virtuous Cycle

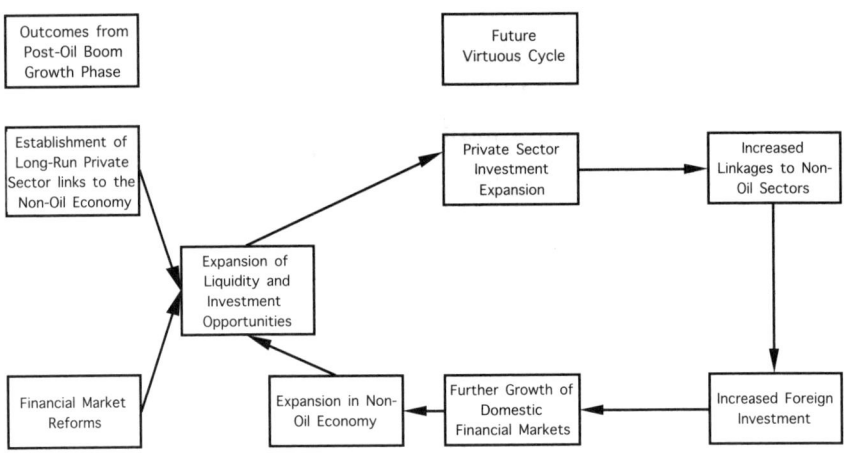

## Notes

1. Robert E. Looney and P. C. Frederiksen, "The Evolution and Evaluation of Saudi Arabian Economic Planning," *Journal of South Asian and Middle Eastern Studies* 9:2, winter 1985, pp. 3–19.
2. Joseph A. Kechichian, "Saudi Arabia's Will to Power," *Middle East Policy* 7:2, February 2000, pp. 47–60.

3. Robert E. Looney, "Saudi Arabia's Development Strategy: Comparative Advantage versus Sustainable Growth," *Orient* 30:1, March 1989, pp. 75–96.
4. Robert E. Looney, "Real or Illusionary Growth in an Oil-Based Economy: Government Expenditures and Private Sector Investment In Saudi Arabia," *World Development* 20:9, September 1992, pp. 1367–76. See also, idem, "The Budgetary Impact of Defense Expenditures in the Middle East," *The Middle East Business and Economic Review* 5:2, July 1993, pp. 39–49; idem, "A Post-Keynesian Assessment of Alternative Saudi Arabian Austerity Strategies," *Kuwait University Journal of the Social Sciences* 23:3, autumn 1995, pp. 251–73; idem, "Saudi Arabia's Economic Challenge," *JIME Review,* autumn 1996, pp. 37–56; and idem, "Diminishing returns and Policy Options in a Rentier State: Economic Reform and Regime Legitimacy in Saudi Arabia," *Political Crossroads* 5:1–2, January 1997, pp. 31–50.
5. Moin A. Siddiqi, "Saudi Arabia: Financial Report," *The Middle East Magazine,* number 294, October 1999, pp. 23–26.
6. N. L. Hicks and A. Kubisch, "Recent Experience in Cutting Government Expenditures," *Finance and Development* 21:3, September 1984, pp. 37–39. See also N. L. Hicks, "Expenditure Reductions in Developing Countries Revisited," *Journal of International Development* 3:1, January 1991, pp. 29–38.
7. Hicks and Kubisch, ibid.
8. Robert E. Looney, "Budgetary Priorities in Saudi Arabia: The Impact of Relative Austerity Measures on Human Capital Development," *OPEC Review* 15:2, summer 1991, pp. 133–152.
9. Looney, "The Budgetary Impact of Defense Expenditures in the Middle East," p. 48.
10. Rayed Krimly, "The Political Economy of Adjusted Priorities: Declining Oil Revenues and Saudi Fiscal Policies," *The Middle East Journal* 53:2, spring 1999, pp. 254–67.
11. Ibid., p, 256.
12. Robert E. Looney, "Defense Expenditures and Macroeconomic Stabilization in Pakistan: A Test of the Military Keynesianism Hypothesis," *Rivista Internazionale di Scienze Economiche e Commerciali* 95:3, September 1998, 599–614.
13. Ibid., p. 612.
14. Yousif Khalifa Al-Yousif, "Exports and Economic Growth: Some Empirical Evidence from the Arab Gulf Countries," *Applied Economics* 29:6, June 1997, pp. 1356–68.
15. K. Doroodian, Rajindar Koshal, and Saleh Al-Muhanna, "An Examination of the Traditional Aggregate Import Demand Function for Saudi Arabia," *Applied Economics* 26:9, September 1994, pp. 1357–69.
16. Nelson Perera, "The Demand for Money in the Members of the Gulf Cooperation Council: Evidence from Cointegration Tests," *The Middle East Business and Economic Review* 6:2, July 1994, pp. 10–26.
17. Detailed statistical data for all sectors, including agriculture, non-oil manufacturing, minerals and mining, construction, wholesale and retail trade, electricity, gas and water, transport and communications, the financial sector, and the service sector (community, social, and personal) are all available from the author (relooney@nps.navy.mil).
18. "Saudi Arabia on the Dole," *Economist,* 22 April 2000, pp. 47–48.
19. Kevin Taecker, "Saudi Arabia and the GCC: Exploring for Growth in a Troubled Global Economy," *Middle East Policy* 6:2, October 1998, pp. 29–35.
20. A. O. Hirschman, *The Strategy of Economic Development,* New Haven: Yale University Press, 1958.
21. Kemp, Peter, "Hard Times: No Easy Way Out," *Middle East Economic Digest* 43:2, 8 January 1999, p. 2.
22. Tom Everett-Heath, "The Saudi Quickstep," *Middle East Economic Digest* 43:46, 26 November 1999, p. 4.
23. Ibid.
24. Ibid.
25. F. Gregory Gause III, "Saudi Arabia Over a Barrel," *Foreign Affairs* 79:3, May/June 2000, pp. 80–94.

CHAPTER 10

## Domestic Politics in the United Arab Emirates: Social and Economic Policies, 1990–2000

Fatma al-Sayegh

The United Arab Emirates (UAE) is at an exciting crossroads in its short development. Thirty years since its establishment as a federation, its leaders have spent considerable energy to foster a unified and stable political system, support traditional yet modernizing social and economic structures—capable of adapting to dramatic and fast changes—and fund a diversified economy that is less dependent on fluctuating oil prices. Since 2 December 1971, two significant steps have marked the development of this country—first, a political union of the former Trucial States against some odds, and second, the genuine development of the less fortunate Northern Emirates.[1]

This chapter traces the UAE's domestic policies, as well as its tribal, social, and economic development paths, and identifies the transformation of the Emirates from a purely tribal system into a modernizing venture. Having constructed a remarkable infrastructure and shaped an impressive economy, the UAE is reassessing its experiences to ensure that its citizens are adequately prepared for the new millennium. The chapter further explores internal forces that might hinder unity. Factors such as domestic cohesion, proper planning, and economic integrity are of major concern to policymakers. Although the UAE is still a fairly new experiment in federation, the circumstances of its emergence, its economic prosperity, and its social structures define its unique environment. To be sure, UAE leaders relied on much of their traditions to forge union, but they also contributed much to its current success. It is through a historical perspective that current achievements are best appraised.

### Historical Background

The seven Emirates, prior to their independence and federation, had undergone a long history of British occupation dating back to 1820.[2] Though fundamentally of imperial nature, the British control in the lower Gulf differed in many respects from that exercised in Africa or India.[3] Britain, for the duration of its protective status in the area, showed no interest in the internal and tribal structures of the Emirates, except in cases where British interests were directly threatened. Although this policy resulted in a great measure of autonomy for the individual Emirates, it isolated the area from any form of internal progress and non-British external influences. Britain assumed full responsibility for foreign affairs, even if it promised not to intervene in the internal affairs of the Emirates.

Economically, the vast majority of the population of the Trucial States (a mere 180,000 in 1971) lived at subsistence level, virtually indistinguishable from that which they had reached centuries earlier. Pearling was important to the economies of the Trucial States before oil was discovered. Whereas pearl diving allowed most to survive on meager subsistence levels, living very modestly with few "luxuries," the direct benefits from oil income—distributed rather well and fairly rapidly—made a substantial difference. Overnight, the subsistence economy, based principally on pearl diving, the cultivation of dates and a few other locally consumed vegetables, as well as the raising of livestock, was literally transformed into an Eldorado.

The development of the pearl trade created a group of merchant entrepreneurs, some of whom utilized their innate skills in other businesses when the market for pearls collapsed.[4] This was especially true in Dubai, which built an entrepôt trade at the end of the nineteenth century, diverting traffic from the Persian port of Lingah after high customs duties were imposed there. Dubai, thus, became a major Gulf port, enjoying a rather considerable pre-oil prosperity from exports and re-exports. The contrast with its neighbors, whose economic eclipse was reversed only with the advent of oil income, was noticeable.

When the pearl industry fell on hard times during the early 1930s, as a result of the worldwide economic depression and the Japanese cultured pearl innovation, the Trucial States slid backwards in their progress. Reduced demand for pearls from key markets in Europe and the United States translated into substantial losses. The fatal blow came in 1946, when India, until then a large market for pearls, imposed heavy taxes that crippled the Gulf pearling industry. As a result of this overall decline, the number of boats proceeding to the pearling banks gradually decreased. The Trucial States' contacts with the rest of the world began to shrink at an ever-increasing rate, as the industry faltered and World War II entered its crucial phases.

It is important to emphasize that Britain played a key role in this respect. As British commitments—at least prior to World War II—were limited to the enforcement of a "maritime truce and peace at sea," London was not concerned with the implications of this decreasing source of income at the local level. To be sure, Britain avoided interference in the area's social and economic development, but, equally important, it demonstrated a lack of interest that bordered on negligence. It was almost a century after they first occupied the Lower Gulf, in 1939 to be precise, that British officials favored the opening of the first medical dispensary in Dubai. Wretched living conditions would then improve, at least for a few, as the rate of development progressively improved.

Abu Dhabi was the largest and strongest of the seven Emirates. Tribal and somewhat less cosmopolitan than Dubai, the Emirate had a smaller population, and experienced slower development. Ruled by the Al Nahyan family, Abu

Dhabi harbored the ambition to unify and rule the entire Trucial Coast for decades. These aspirations never developed, in part because British authorities were adamantly opposed to the idea.[5] Economically, life in Abu Dhabi at the turn of the twentieth century was virtually the same as it had been a hundred years earlier. Shipping, trading, and seafaring capabilities had been gravely crippled by the world economic depression, and by the absence of a major economic resource. With trading prospects severely curtailed, people were forced to rely upon meager earnings derived from the pearl industry.

Essentially a commercial city-state, Dubai was less affected by this economic depression. With its harbor facilities and its sophisticated merchant community, the Emirate quickly developed its entrepôt facilities and earned a key position in the overall Middle East transit trade. Less tribal and, perhaps, more urbane than the others, Dubai largely depended on trade and re-export of goods to Persia and the Indian subcontinent. In fact, the majority of its merchants were of non-Arab origin, coming largely from Iran or the Indian subcontinent, though most had been longtime residents.[6] These merchants played critical roles in helping the Al Makhtoum shape the Emirate's political and economic judgments. Guided by their consideration for the state's trade links with the outside world, many of these merchants added value to the emerging vision in Dubai and, if most benefited from their associations with the Al Makhtoum, the rewards were evenly divided. Sharjah, on the other hand, enjoyed a high level of intellectual and cultural life guided by the legacy of the Al Qawasim. Its inhabitants were—and remain—very proud of their history, especially their opposition to British military incursions. Still, although Sharjah was once the seat of the British political and military authority in the area, its modern development occurred well after independence.

The other Emirates, including Ras al-Khaimah, Fujairah, Ajman, and Umm al-Qiwain, were once part of the Qasimi empire. Most of the ruling families, as well as their populations, exhibit a delicate balance within the various Qasimi branches. Their infrastructures reflect poorer conditions that have dictated smaller, even simpler, governments and administrations. In these instances as well, federation benefited many, creating vital links with the larger Emirates of Abu Dhabi and Dubai.

### The Birth of the UAE

On 2 December 1971, the UAE was declared independent following three years of extensive negotiations among the nine Emirates of the Gulf: the seven Trucial shaykhdoms, along with Qatar and Bahrain. As the latter two opted for separate independence, a federation of the remaining seven was declared after considerable discussions.[7] A historic first meeting of the Supreme Council of the Federation of the UAE was then convened. During the meeting, Shaykh Zayed bin Sultan Al Nahyan, ruler of Abu Dhabi, was elected president. It was also announced that Shaykh Rashid bin Said Al Makhtoum, the ruler of Dubai, would be the country's first prime minister. Equally important, the Supreme Council declared that a provisional constitution would be drafted without delay.[8] Abu Dhabi was ostensibly identified as the capital of the state, although that decision would not be finalized for several years.

Since its establishment as a federation, the UAE has forged a distinct national identity through consolidation of its federal status, and now enjoys an enviable level of political stability. The UAE's political system, which is a unique combination of both traditional and modern laws, has underpinned this remarkable political success, enabling the country to develop a fresh administrative structure while at the same time ensuring that the best of its traditions are maintained, adapted, and preserved.

Given that the seven members of the federation vary in size and in economic resources—while Abu Dhabi, Dubai, and, to lesser extent, Sharjah have oil, the other four Emirates live virtually on subsistence economies—unification required certain adjustments. It was enough that the Emirates shared historical, sociopolitical, and cultural ties, as what was needed was a fairer distribution of wealth, development, and political power. Since 1971, and notwithstanding inevitable political skirmishes, Emirati leaders have amply demonstrated that their development and modernization paces were, indeed, fair and comprehensive. The first five-year plan, like the initial development schemes, was deemed a success. That the UAE has grown and prospered as a federation in the face of internal rivalries, external threats, and antipathies is clearly due to Shaykh Zayed's commitment to the concept of federal union, and his generous dispensing of Abu Dhabi's financial support to those less fortunate. On 20 May 1995, the Supreme Council of the Federation, at its historic meeting under the presidency of Shaykh Zayed, approved an amendment to the provisional constitution that deleted the term "provisional" from its clauses. The amendment also identified Abu Dhabi as the permanent capital of the state. During the meeting, Shaykh Zayed declared that "since the income of the UAE's citizens was among the highest in the world, no one in the Emirates should be in need."[9] Even in its simplest meaning, this statement identified the core of the UAE's domestic policy, namely that the country's resources would be shared across the board throughout the land. Few found fault in its premise. Even fewer could offer alternatives. Zayed's bold initiatives ensured that the legacy of the UAE would be rooted in economic fairness and justice for all UAE citizens.

Yet, despite this unique legacy, the UAE is undergoing rapid socioeconomic changes, with various strains and stresses that such phenomena entail. This process, along with the non-plurality of the social structure, as well as the low level of political participation, gives the UAE a special status.

## Economic Development

Until a decade ago, the structure of the Emirates' income, which mainly depends on oil, made it one of the least economically diversified states in the world. Unlike other developing countries, the UAE relies on a single resource, oil, whose value is determined by international markets. In other words, Abu Dhabi, along with its fellow oil-producing states, cannot control all three aspects that make a cartel, namely, production, prices, and markets. To be sure, the UAE's proven crude resources are estimated at around 98 billion barrels, representing 9.5 percent of world reserves and placing it in third position in terms of reserves—not an enviable spot. Capacity is currently estimated at around 2.5 million barrels per day (bpd), which will rise to 3 million by the end of 2000.[10] However, building a healthy and stable economic base requires the diversification of economic resources. Therefore, over the past decade, much has been made of the UAE's need to reduce its economic dependency on oil. In fact, officials drew sharp lessons from the mid-to-late 1980s period, when oil prices crashed to as low as $8 per barrel. Rates of growth domestic product (GDP) since 1988 confirm that the UAE's diversification plans are now paying dividends. Since 1988, there has been a steady increase in contributions from the non-oil sector to the GDP, estimated at around 64 percent in 1996, which is a far cry from the 1972 rate of 36 percent.[11]

The nature and structure of the economy suggests that the UAE's economic integration largely depends on federal rather than local policies. While Abu Dhabi, Dubai, and Sharjah are oil-producing Emirates, their smaller partners have no major economic resources. Still, the latter have benefited from federal development initiatives. For example, in the field of education, the Northern Emirates have hired federally funded and trained personnel to satisfy local requirements. Another area in which federal assistance was concretely displayed was tourism. Yet, much of these initiatives were the result of Abu Dhabi's financial largesse, which in turn dragged the Northern Emirates out of their pre-independence levels. In exchange for this largesse, Abu Dhabi secured substantial political power. Indeed, it might not be an overstatement to assert that Abu Dhabi has paid in the past—and is paying today—to stabilize the federation. By subsidizing the federation, Abu Dhabi helps the socioeconomic and political settings of the Emirates and asserts for itself a powerful role as a leader of the federation. From a purely financial perspective, nevertheless, the sensitive question of financing the union has only recently been settled, when each Emirate agreed to contribute a specific percentage of its national income to the federal budget. In 1995, the Federal National Council (FNC) endorsed a proposed 1996 expenditures bill, in which individual Emirate allocations were specified. The FNC advised that each party's share be based on estimated annual incomes and, in accordance with past provisions, that federal authorities make up deficits.[12]

In line with this general trend, development projects were designed to serve several Emirates, to further consolidate the nascent federation. Etisalat, the Emirates Telecommunications Company, for example, is a good illustration of this phenomenon. Over the years, Etisalat has become one of the strongest service companies in the UAE. A similar endeavor is the Water and Electricity Company, which has earned various accolades across the country. In 1997, it was announced that work would commence on the construction of the electric power grid that will connect various cities throughout the country, to prevent power shortages.[13] Meanwhile, privatization in public services is well under way. Greater involvement by the private sector in all aspects of the UAE's continued development remains a key plank of government policy. In fact, the move toward privatization of state-owned utilities forms an important element in this strategy. Privatization could enhance the quality of service to consumers, give a tremendous boost to domestic and foreign investors, and unburden the state from routine responsibilities. Having ensured viable institutions, the state is eagerly looking forward to distributing responsibilities on as many of its citizens as possible. The strategy is nothing short of gradual empowerment.

Local governments have also taken a number of key steps aimed at stimulating the economy. In Abu Dhabi, the development of the Saadiyat Free Zone, envisaging investments in excess of $21 billion over a ten-year period, was an imaginative step that is expected to play a significant role in business development in the future.[14] To be sure, Abu Dhabi's own expenditures exceed those of the federal budget, but that was primarily the result of how the Emirate's substantial revenues were dispersed. Abu Dhabi financed massive public service projects such as water resources, electrical power plants, and petrochemicals, which literally transformed the barren desert into a developing economy. Dubai, for its part, was equally clairvoyant, and invested in ambitious projects. Even if its methods differed, often securing necessary funds by borrowing from international and domestic sources, the end results were clearly illustrated in the massive expansion of several sectors, ranging from industry (Jabal Ali Free Zone) to tourism (luxury hotels and annual festivals).[15] Two of Dubai's projects, well under way in 1999, are Project Millennium and the expansion of the airport, vital to further attract international investors. But by far the most ambitious project in Dubai, which is hoping to transform the small Emirate into a regional technology hub, is the Dubai Internet City initiative that began in October 1999. This project aims at making Dubai the technological center of the entire Middle East. It is hoped that technology will provide a unique platform for the UAE, to further diversify its economy away from heavy dependence on hydrocarbon exports, and provide employment for nationals. Dubai already plays a powerful role in the information technology field, having been selected by almost all major international companies as their Middle East headquarters. To fulfill these ambitious initiatives, local authorities created the Dubai Technology, Electronic Commerce and Media Free Zone Authority, to draw up strategies and polices and encourage the business community to implement all projects in a timely fashion. Clearly, the purpose is to promote Dubai as a center for technology, electronic commerce, and media.[16] Diversifying into such ventures is further testament to the urgent needs—especially in the Northern Emirates—that local economies may face, especially after 2010, when both Dubai and Sharjah will receive very limited oil income.

Meanwhile, the smaller Emirates of Ras al-Khaimah and Ajman, with even fewer resources at their disposal, have drawn up equally ambitious domestic plans, even if more suited to their needs. Ras al-Khaimah authorized the construction of a cement factory to produce an estimated 200,000 tons per year. Ajman, famous for its fine marble, plans to enlarge its marble manufacturing plant. More modest activities are under consideration in both Emirates. Importantly, a new federal law has been proposed that would require every new industrial scheme of any type or size to obtain a federal license before it can be implemented. The main objective of this law is to ensure that new schemes serve the interests of the federation as a whole rather than those of an individual Emirate. The law would also prevent unnecessary duplication of industrial projects within the federation, as was the case in the 1970s.[17]

In the event, government intervention in connection with business development has been directed toward diversification, making the economy less dependent on oil. Toward that end, attracting international investors is high on the agendas of the rulers, who must approve most transactions.[18] The market in the Emirates has bent toward modernization in which keen competition has evolved, a mixture of traditional mercantilism and rapid adjustment to vastly widened business horizons.[19] Toward that end, free trade zones provide a significant impetus to further accelerate the process. Jabal Ali, for example, opened for business in the mid-1980s, and was an immediate success. Since then, free zones have been created at ports across the UAE: in Sharjah, Fujairah, Ajman, Ras al-Khaimah, and Umm al-Qiwain.[20] A similar effort was made to promote the tourism industry. If the idea of a tourism industry in the UAE seemed far-fetched in the 1980s—more of an aspiration than a real possibility—much has changed since then. In less than a decade, tourism has taken center stage in the country's economic development. In fact, in the case of Dubai, where greater efforts have been applied to this sector, revenues from tourism will overtake those from oil within a few years. Tourism's contribution to the UAE's GNP was expected to reach 10 percent by the end of 2000.[21]

This strategy of economic diversification, coupled with an upturn in oil prices in the latter half of 1999, has pushed the UAE GDP by 10 percent to 190.4 billion dirhams (Dhs) in 1999 (it stood at 173 billion Dhs in 1998).[22] The economy's strong performance led to a jump in reserves to 13.4 billion in 1999 against 3.5 billion in 1998. National savings reached 34.4 billion Dhs in 1999, up from 26 billion Dhs in 1998. The rate of inflation remained flat at 2 percent. However, inflation was projected to rise to 2.5 percent in the year 2000.[23]

These figures do not begin to decipher the complexities of the UAE economy. For example, while the majority of developing countries are confronted with a shortage of skilled manpower, in the UAE the problem assumes quantitative as well as qualitative dimensions. In an attempt to redress the imbalance in the workforce, the government adopted an "Emiratization" of certain professions, to encourage citizens to assume key posts. In line with government policy on increased participation of UAE nationals in the labor force, the Abu Dhabi Investment Authority (ADIA) endorsed the recommendations of the human resources development committee on the proposed phased increases in national banking personnel. It was agreed that from 1998, national participation in the banking sector would be increased to 4 percent annually, with the objective that in ten years, nationals would constitute 40 percent of the banking sector labor force. A number of well-planned training programs have been put in place to achieve Emiratization of almost half of the workforce by the year 2020. To date, however, these efforts have not produced the desired results, although special emphasis is placed on reducing the overall percentage of expatriates (from an all-time high of over 85 percent of the population).

To be sure, the active promotion of capital-intensive industries may somewhat ameliorate the quantitative shortages of unskilled labor but will certainly exacerbate the shortage of skilled workers so necessary to the efficient operation of such industries. Clearly, the encouragement of skilled or capital-intensive enterprises will rectify the labor imbalance, but only in the long run. In the short term, the adoption of a liberal immigration policy is a feasible, even if partial, solution to the labor shortage. In fact, various Emirates have chosen such a policy and are prepared to confront the risks it entails to the small indigenous population. This influx of foreign workers has and probably will continue to encounter political as well as social constraints, which will eventually place limits on immigration and diminish its effectiveness in this regard.[24] New regulations were necessary if for no other reason than to limit substantial state expenditures.

During 1998, the UAE economy benefited from continued government spending, which supported domestic economic activities. Meanwhile, the country's economic policy, which aims at diversifying sources of revenues and increasing growth rates for non-oil sectors, resulted in noticeable fluctuation. Inasmuch as improved oil revenues helped increase income and reduce deficits, the UAE could raise liquidity and support credit expansions. In doing so, Abu Dhabi matched the ongoing expansion within the non-oil sectors with significant GDP growth rates, which resulted in reducing local prices for goods and services.

Finally, it is also important to briefly discuss the UAE's agriculture policy, given remarkable achievements for a country that is physically inhospitable. Despite unfavorable soil and extremely difficult climatic conditions, the UAE has made major strides in developing a thriving agricultural industry, which defies all fallacious preconceptions. By using modern technology, the agriculture sector has made considerable progress in the past two decades, producing 2.64 billion Dhs worth of goods in 1995. Compared to an output of a mere 116 million Dhs in 1972, this reflects a growth rate of almost 15 percent per annum. Significant achievements in the field of agriculture continue to play a key role in securing the UAE's declared objective of full self-sufficiency in food production. In attempting a greater balance through economic diversification, the state is obviously encouraging the sector, not only for financial reasons but also for national security purposes. During the past three decades, the UAE's citizens have displayed a deep interest in agriculture, especially in Abu Dhabi. This has been reinforced by the personal attention that Shaykh Zayed showed to this field. Plots of land were distributed to citizens of Abu Dhabi, in addition to satisfactory loans to help farmers irrigate and manage their farms. In Liwa and Buraimi, plots of land were distributed freely, for both economic as well as political reasons.[25] Shaykh Zayed was greatly aware that UAE citizens needed to place "markers" throughout the country, to foster a sense of belonging and of strengthening existing roots. As a bonus to these initiatives, the progress that was achieved, according to various estimates, not only met basic local consumption needs but those of neighboring countries as well. From a situation of subsistence in the early 1970s, the agriculture sector has grown rapidly to become one of the most sophisticated in the region, in the process transforming the country into a fruit and vegetable exporter. In 1995, the UAE produced almost 720,000 tons of vegetables, worth 1.14 billion Dhs, which was indeed a significant accomplishment.[26]

## Social Development

Although social changes in the UAE are less visible than economic changes, the country is considered one of the key Arab Gulf crucibles for social change. Less than half a century ago, the area that comprises the UAE was one of the least developed areas in the whole region. Tribalism had been a feature of this land since time immemorial. Of the many different tribes that made up the country's population, very few were ever wholly nomadic, as the bulk were settled. The tribe has traditionally served as a cultural and ethnic frame of reference for the individual and often provided him with identity and social security. This was true then and it is true today.

Still, the country has one of the world's fastest growing populations and, even if most of the increase is due to foreign immigration, the land is now home to over 2.5 million people (1996 estimate) hailing from over 100 countries. The UAE, like most of the Arab Gulf, has a youthful population, of which almost 40 percent are under 25 years old. Those in the older age groups, who often require more health care, are the UAE nationals, given that labor permits restrict residence in the Emirates only while employed. As with most Arab Gulf countries, the UAE relies heavily on foreign manpower, and as discussed above, the government is making a concerted effort to reduce the imbalance. In addition to financial considerations, the purpose of boosting the national percentage and improving citizen participation in the workforce is to address the country's various social needs. A committee formed to address demographic issues, such as loopholes in the immigration laws, recommended a number of legislative changes to achieve these ends.[27]

Since independence, government investments in social development projects took on a semi-sacred role. UAE leaders emphasized various social issues that required rapid attention, including education, social security, health, and housing. Over the years, these sectors received the lion's share of the total federal budget, thus rivaling all other Gulf states in this field.[28]

To be sure, rapid improvement of human capital is a crucial element in the development process. The long-held notion that capital is the engine of growth has given way to the idea that investment in education and training—both formal and informal—is also a precondition for successful development. Indeed, many Emiratis consider that education is their best investment, for themselves and the community at large. Importantly, until independence, Kuwait had provided funding for educational facilities to several Emirates. Indeed, lack of resources had prevented the "dependent" shaykhdoms from establishing formal educational systems. The idea was virtually inconceivable. Indeed, not until 1953 was there a modern school in the area again, it may be worth repeating, despite over a century of British presence in the Lower Gulf. The marginal status of education in the former Trucial States was accurately reflected in the illiteracy rate, which exceeded 90 percent in 1968 among men and almost 99 percent among women.

However, since independence, education has been made a key priority. At first, only a tiny number enjoyed access to formal schooling, and of those the majority were boys. The great importance placed by the UAE government on building a system that would provide education for all is amply reflected in the fact that education allocations within the budget have increased 23–fold since 1973. In 1997, education consumed 3.19 billion Dhs, constituting more than 16 percent of the federal budget. The number of public schools in the UAE rose from 132 in 1972 to some 668 in 1997–1998, and the number of students increased from 40,115 in 1972 to 312,000 in 1997–1998.[29] The process of bringing the modern educational system in line with the requirements of the new millennium is supervised by the Ministry of Education, which is preparing a "2020 plan," to re-evaluate the existing educational system and introduce changes suitable for the requirements of the economic market and whatever challenges may arise in the twenty-first century. Indeed, it may be safe to conclude that education has become a far more important commodity in the Emirates, reflected in annual capital outlays—to remedy physical shortages for appropriate facilities and to fully eradicate illiteracy—that, without a doubt, reflect UAE leaders' vision for the future.

Following the successful establishment of the UAE University in 1977, the Higher Colleges of Technology in 1988, and Zayed University a decade later, the UAE government is now re-evaluating their curricula to ensure that they meet with the country's requirements. With female students numbering almost 75 percent of these institutions, certain social and economic changes are on the horizon. Until 1997, the UAE University awarded more than 17,267 diplomas to both genders, but only 800 graduates of the Higher Colleges of Technology joined the workforce.[30] Meanwhile, a number of private universities opened their doors in 1997–1998, among which the American University in Sharjah, Sharjah University, and the American University of Dubai stand out. These universities are considered as significant additions to existing educational facilities, but, unlike state universities, private institutions have open-door policies toward non-nationals. Consequently, they can attract certain students who, in turn, may contribute in different ways to the Emirati labor pool.

Housing is another area of social services in which the federal government is visibly active. Housing for UAE citizens has been a major concern of the government, believing as it does that it is one of the essential requirements for a stable family life and for society as a whole. Toward that end, and to meet various housing needs, federal and local departments as well as individuals and private firms jointly implemented an ambitious plan.[31] The plan extended to rural and urban areas in a bid to help Emiratis remain in their localities and to create balanced social and economic links between the regions.

For example, in Dubai, and aside from long-term no-interest loans provided by local authorities, the federal government initiated a new housing project to provide complimentary housing. The establishment of the Shaykh Zayed Housing Program in June 1998 was intended to address significant difficulties in the housing market—further complicated by premium rates on local facilities—to help UAE citizens improve their living standards. Besides low-income housing, the program provides no-interest loans for nationals for the purpose of building their own homes, repayable over a 20-year period. Meanwhile, the government of Abu Dhabi has launched a program of its own called the Social Services and Commercial Buildings Office, whose purpose is to build and manage the commercial buildings granted to citizens of the Emirate. In 1995, this program funded 230 commercial buildings, at a cost of 202 billion Dhs.[32]

If several generations ago there was an overwhelmingly rural population in the Lower Gulf, the UAE population has been mostly urbanized by the qualitative changes that have occurred since 1971. By 1995, almost 90 percent of the population were urban. In the span of a few short decades, the greater part of the population has been displaced from traditional rural modes of existence, to artificial urban settings. In like fashion there has been an equal acceleration in the everyday movement of people. Easy access to technology has made those distant places and foreign ideas familiar to Emiratis whose parents never ventured more than a few miles from their place of birth. Universal education, the availability of domestic and foreign goods with relative ease, and the constant exposure to foreign media outlets have all provided a constant barrage of new ideas, images, and tastes.

Although the basic elements of UAE society remain intact, several signs of the disruptive forces of accelerated modernization are visible. One index is the noticeable change in social habits, behavior, and values, with serious implications for the future, that is affecting the young and the old. It has been necessary in recent years to establish homes for the elderly and rehabilitation centers for juvenile delinquents, two phenomena that are necessary but alien to the culture. These developments are, thus far, modest in scope, but they represent, in a society as profoundly family-centered as the UAE, a disturbing sign.

While tribal values are fading fast in Dubai, they still play a strong role in Abu Dhabi and some of the Northern Emirates. Meanwhile, changing attitudes among the UAE's youth should provide one of the obvious indexes to anticipate variations in social behavior patterns. Many young Emiratis who studied in Western countries are returning with a palpable appreciation for Western values and culture. In addition, the opening up of UAE society—in which, it may be worth repeating, most cultures are well represented and interaction is inevitable—has created a taste for such forms of social behavior. Others vociferously object to such behavior and call on UAE officials to curtail available freedoms. Why some Emiratis are drawn to the teachings of militant Islam while others partake in more tolerant social behavior is certainly a key development for the country's future stability. In fact, such potential social confrontations cannot be ruled out, further illustrating current dilemmas.

To be sure, most Emiratis value and respect traditional forms of authority, familial and governmental. Yet, it seems certain that deference to the past paternalistic ways is slowly becoming less pervasive.[33] In any event, what has perhaps been most surprising in the course of the UAE's greatly accelerated development is the capacity of traditional society to absorb massive change. Social institutions and cultural patterns have preserved their essential vitality. Perhaps more important is the role of Islam, which continues to serve as the stable foundation of society. Islam both provides the essential explanation of the meaning of individual and collective existence, and serves as a safety valve.

It cannot be doubted, nevertheless, that significant social changes are occurring that will greatly alter the basic values of UAE society. Unlike developed and relatively wealthy countries, there is little connection between wealth and work in the UAE. The message is clear: "Without efforts of self-denial, one can expect nothing in return." To remedy this lacuna, Dubai authorities initiated a scheme to help young people start their own businesses and taste the rewards of incrementalism. Designed to help young nationals stand on their feet, the program— which is called "Tamouh," or "enterprise"—has helped hundreds of young Emiratis. Any young national with experience but lacking capital can indeed benefit from the program. As a result, many small businesses have sprung up in Dubai during the past few years. This vital project helped to ease pressure on the public sector by channeling the growing pool of talent to the private sector. In addition, training courses for nationals are being offered to educate young Emiratis in their new responsibilities.

Parallel to the education, housing, and labor initiatives adopted by the UAE within its Emiratization program, Abu Dhabi introduced a unique new agenda in 1993 to encourage citizen matrimony. The Marriage Fund Program provides national men with a grant to enable them to meet the high cost of marriage to national women. It is also designed to limit UAE males' marrying foreign women. Between 1993 and 1995, the fund benefited over 3,084 citizens, with a 20 percent increase in 1995 over 1994. The 3,084 "grants" amounted to a total of 220 million Dhs, certainly a significant investment in the citizen population, and yet another illustration of the state's plan.[34]

One of the most noticeable changes in the UAE is the position and status of women. This is amply evidenced by the United Nations Development Program's Human Resources Development Report for 1997, which pointed out that women in the UAE have achieved the highest rate of development in all Arab countries. Indeed, the expanding role of women within UAE society over the past 30 years is largely due to a fundamental commitment made by senior government officials to promote women in all fields.

In the past, while some women were active outside of the home, most were primarily homemakers. Their contributions had never been considered as "organized employment." Since independence, the UAE constitution has granted women equal employment opportunities and equal wages, and those with marketable skills were encouraged to participate in the public sector. Government national policies helped bring women out of their seclusion and into the modern market. Once women attained the right to equal educational opportunities, they became further aware of the importance of their social roles and their contribution to the economy. As a result, women's participation in the UAE workforce has risen from 29,548, or a mere 5 percent of the total labor force of 577,521 in 1980, to 79,971, or 8 percent in 1994 (out of 994,844). By

1995, the figure stood at 119,290, or 12 percent of the UAE's total labor force.[35] As the country enters the twenty-first century, many UAE women are employed in the government sector, particularly in traditional areas such as education and health, although they are now spreading across the federal civil service. Nevertheless, schoolteachers still account for around 40 percent of the total women's workforce.

It is important to note that within the civil service, women have reached the rank of ministerial undersecretary and assistant undersecretary. Women are also breaking new ground in the police forces, with a growing number of officers performing various functions, from criminal investigations to customs control. In addition, hundreds of women are working side by side with their male compatriots in the armed forces, filling all types of posts except those involving front-line combat. If substantial progress has been accomplished in this area, credit must be given to the UAE First Lady, Shaykha Fatima bin Mubarak, wife of Shaykh Zayed, and chairwoman of the UAE women's association. Although women's societies have played a major part in galvanizing society at large, the role and influence of the First Lady proved critical. To their credit, dozens of specialized associations throughout the country helped reduce illiteracy among women, which dropped to just 11.3 percent in 1995 from a high of 77.6 percent in 1980. In particular, the Abu Dhabi Women's Federation, chaired by Shaykha Fatima, has led a strong campaign to help women fight illiteracy, and along with appropriate state resources, it aimed to achieve total literacy among women by the end of 2000.

Naturally, a near-future political role for women would be the obvious reflection of this increasing position within society. Following calls by Shaykha Fatima that local women be encouraged to join the Federal National Council (FNC), women began to prepare themselves for parliamentary life. As equal opportunities are safeguarded within the constitution and there are no articles that prevent women from parliament, or discriminate against them in their duty for political participation, it will not be long before the UAE adopts ventures similar to the ones under development in Oman, Qatar, and Kuwait.

## Conclusion

Three decades after independence, what are the UAE's prospects for political survival, and hopes for stability and prosperity?

In 2000, the seven Emirates and their rulers were more committed to the success of the federation than when the "experiment" first began. Steps to preserve the unity of the country have been taken in a multitude of ways. Wealth distribution, social security, and economic prosperity, all vital factors for political stability, are ensured. UAE citizens have seen progress in all aspects of development, from the burgeoning economic sector, through social and cultural initiatives, to international ties. In fact, the country's functioning development programs have provided UAE citizens with all the benefits of modern society. At the same time, both the government and Emiratis in general are determined that their political experience should be preserved. There is a widespread belief throughout the country that by holding on to their unity, they will be able to survive in a world that does not encourage small entities.

There are, without a doubt, formidable challenges ahead, including external threats to the UAE in particular and to Gulf security in general. The issue of unbalanced social structures is also perceived as major threats to the UAE. Nonetheless, the UAE is still holding on to its "experiment." Internally, the degree of mutual suspicion and distrust has diminished considerably, and the perceived benefits of federal union far outweigh fears. Emiratis are keenly aware of their "interests" that can best be preserved through union. What is a problem, however, is the difficulty in overcoming individual Emirates' prerogatives and preferences. As discussed above, immigration is one such concern, with each UAE federation member adopting a separate policy to satisfy local labor needs.[36] Surely the day will come when immigration rules will be regulated across the board.

In the end, the UAE has an international stature far greater than its physical size, population, and breadth of resources would seem to indicate. Like many other traditional states, it is facing the dilemma of combining its rich cultural heritage with elements of modernization, and despite evidences of success, only time will tell whether the "experiment" will evolve. Much like the country's first provisional constitution, which eventually became a permanent political document, the Union may yet surprise many by growing in stride.

## Notes

1. Although the development of the country was planned in Abu Dhabi, and because the largest Emirate was the wealthiest, many assumed that the poorer Northern Emirates would be neglected. To be sure, Abu Dhabi stood to gain more, but, to their credit, its leaders shouldered federal responsibilities with aplomb. Even if the standards were uneven, the Northern Emirates benefited from Abu Dhabi's largesse, a record that compared well within similar federal set-ups.
2. Ali Mohammed Khalifa, *The United Arab Emirates: Unity in Fragmentation*, London: Croom Helm, 1979, p. 9.
3. Ibid., p. 9.
4. Both town dwellers along the coast and Bedus from the interior manned the hundreds of ships that put out to sea to harvest the pearl banks. Expeditions were harsh and lasted almost six months, starting in May and ending in October each year. This was a significant resource and literally defined the area's economic life. Pearl diving benefited few, even though a large number of locals were thus "employed." See Hassan M. Al-Naboodah, "From a Traditional Society to a Modern State," in Joseph A. Kechichian (ed.), *A Century in Thirty Years: Shaykh Zayed and the United Arab Emirates*, Washington, D.C.: Middle East Policy Council, 2000, pp. 9–30.
5. Mohammed Al-Fahim, *From Rags To Riches: A Story of Abu Dhabi*, London: The London Centre of Arab Studies, 1995, p. 34.
6. Malcolm Peck, *The United Arab Emirates: A Venture in Unity*, London: Croom Helm, 1986, p. 127.
7. Ras al-Khaimah did not join the union until 10 February 1972. There were several reasons for Ras al-Khaimah's early decision, including Iran's occupation of the Tunb islands, the question of representation within the Federal National Council, as well as the role played by Saudi Arabia. A few months after the UAE was created, Shaykh Saqr Al Qasimi was persuaded by his own subjects to join the nascent federal entity. See Frauke Heard-Bey, *From Trucial States to United Arab Emirates: A Society in Transition*, 2nd edition, London: Longman, 1996; and Fatma Al-Sayegh, *Al-Imarat al-Arabiyyat al-Muttahidat: Min al-Qabilat ila-dawlat* [The United Arab Emirates: From Tribalism to Statehood], Dubai: Markaz al-Khalij lil-Kutub, 1997.
8. Ibrahim Al Abed, Paula Vine, and Abdullah Al Jabali (eds.), *Chronicle of Progress, 25 Years of Development in the United Arab Emirates*, London: Trident Press for the Ministry of Information, 1996, p. 14.

9. Al-Abed, *op. cit.*, p. 412.
10. Ibrahim Al Abed, Peter Hellyer, and Paula Vine, *United Arab Emirates, Yearbook 1998*, London: Trident Press for the Ministry of Information, 1998, p. 72 (hereafter Yearbook 1998).
11. It is also important to note that the gap between the UAE's oil production and exports, as in most Arab Gulf states, is extremely narrow. This is an indication of how little oil was consumed locally. While total UAE oil exports in 1976 were 710 million barrels, the figure for 1996 reached 2.23 million bpd. Moreover, oil exports reached 54 billion Dhs in 1996 against 44.6 in 1995. Oil provides for approximately 75 percent of the UAE's public revenues. Meanwhile, UAE national economic policy, which took shape roughly in 1973, has endeavored to introduce some sense of balance between the oil-producing Emirates and the less fortunate ones. In addition, the UAE operates a very open trade policy and is committed to trade liberalization as a means of encouraging industrial growth. See Ibrahim Al Abed, Peter Hellyer, and Paula Vine, *United Arab Emirates, Yearbook 1997*, London: Trident Press for the Ministry of Information, 1997, pp. 66, 78 (hereafter Yearbook 1997).
12. Al-Abed, *op. cit.*, p. 411.
13. Al-Abed, *op. cit.*, p. 410.
14. Yearbook 1997, p. 97.
15. Khalifa, *op. cit.*, p. 70.
16. *Gulf News*, 6 February 2000.
17. Ragaei El Mallakh, *The Economic Development of the United Arab Emirates*, New York: St. Martin's Press, 1981, pp. 58–9.
18. While it is not a requirement to choose a local agent (*kafil*) in every transaction, the practice is widely followed, to limit foreign exposure to a minimum.
19. El Mallakh, ibid., p. 160.
20. Yearbook 1997, p. 103.
21. Yearbook 1997, p. 108.
22. *Gulf News*, 30 January 2000.
23. *Gulf News*, 31 January 2000.
24. El Mallakh, *op. cit.*, p. 60.
25. This step has political implications, since Saudi Arabia claims this land.
26. Yearbook 1997, p. 117.
27. The perceived political and security threats from the huge numbers of migrant workers in the UAE (around 1.13 million in 1997 and predicted to increase by 2 percent annually) is a widely discussed subject. For example, a fairly typical editorial in *Al-Khaleej*, a leading UAE daily, described the issue as a serious threat to external and internal security, and called on the government to take major steps to solve it. In a country where foreigners outnumber natives by more than one to five, such fears are natural. See *Al-Khaleej*, 17 April 1999.
28. Khalifa, *op. cit.*, p. 75.
29. Yearbook 1997, p. 178.
30. Ibid., p. 179.
31. Every UAE male national is entitled to a free house. However, only females in need are given free housing. See Yearbook 1998, p. 124.
32. Al-Abed, *op. cit.*, p. 404.
33. Peck, *op. cit.*, p. 73.
34. Al-Abed, *op. cit.*, p. 405.
35. Yearbook 1997, p. 194.
36. Peck, *op. cit.*, p. 132.

# THE ARAB GULF STATES

## CHAPTER 11

### Kuwait and Bahrain:
### The Appeal of Globalization and Internal Constraints

May Seikaly

Political observers and economic analysts on the Gulf are agreed that the whole Arabian Gulf region is undergoing a crisis demanding basic changes that should impact the basic fabric of Gulf society. Although such voices, and often the same ones, have been giving these premonitions of impending disasters and the urgent need to remedy them for a long time, their quest seems more desperate and their fears substantiated at this stage. Economic but also political and social indicators of this condition are clear and spell serious repercussions for the near future. The most recent literature on the subject, internationally and from the Gulf region, clearly emphasizes the theme that this condition, spawned by the nature of the regimes in the region and now sparked by regional and international events, has accelerated its pace, reaching irreversible proportions. The threat to the stability of the region and its societies has become serious. This "crisis in slow motion," as Gary Sick calls it, has reached full bloom.[1]

One Kuwaiti writer portrayed the region as a fragile oasis of relative tranquility that has become the eye of the storm, surrounded by a turbulent sea of demographic explosion and mobility. In this he was referring to the economically poor human masses encircling the region. He estimates that in one decade, population in the Indian subcontinent will reach a billion; at the same time, that of Iran will swell to 120 million, in Egypt to 100 million, and in Yemen to 50 million. Yemen alone would have a population exceeding that of all the GCC countries put together.[2] Today the estimated total number of Gulf nationals is below 18 million, and even with the very high demographic growth of 3.5 percent per year, the region will need much more than a decade to catch up with its neighbors. Such statements express deep-seated vulnerability and insecurity about what the future holds for the Gulf nations, but also significantly telling is the awareness and sense by people in the region that their nations are demographically small, perceived as wealthy, and targeted by the waves of globalization.

Today the region finds itself part of a world that is growing smaller, where resources are fewer, where inequities are contested, and where human rights are internationally approved and proclaimed. Taking into consideration the phenomenal social and material achievements that societies of the Gulf states have accumulated during the last 50 years, this feeling of claustrophobia, threat, and impending disaster is understandable; especially when these nations are pressed to change and to open their societies and economies to the waves of global change.

Since the 1991 War for Kuwait, the Gulf states as a whole, including Kuwait and Bahrain, the subjects of this chapter, have survived under an umbrella of two conflicting pulls: externally the hegemonic Western impact toward globalization, and internally the increase of ripples and roars within these societies calling for economic and social rationalization, cautious liberalization, and even introversion. These internal pulls have triggered a process often ambiguously expressed by domestic religious, traditional, tribal, familial, and economic reactions.

The military advent of Western powers into the region, particularly that of the U.S., in 1991 brought home the reality of the new world order. While CNN introduced every home to "American-style and slanted" media information on the war, it also informed about U.S. culture and lifestyle. The people in the Gulf were not immune to the technological revolution and all its implications; however, at that time it reached all and affected all aspects of their lives. The dramatic impact of the war, its expense, and their entanglement in it became a reality. In addition to the trauma of war, Gulf governments and societies had to squarely face the possibilities of economic loss and indebtedness, and the need to reassess resources, achievements, and challenges. Khaldoun al-Naqeeb in his latest article entitled "The Gulf . . . where to?" does exactly that in his usual trenchant style, however with clear tones of exasperation and desperation.[3] He repeats and endorses the opinions and concerns of a growing number of Gulf writers and intellectuals, now a second generation of Gulf nationals calling for change.

While the war and its legacy shook the basic pillars of the state systems in Kuwait and Bahrain, it also awakened and gave life to historically present but muted and diverted popular demands. Today the voices coming from these two countries reflect the exact nature their two regimes have evolved into, the freedom they accord their citizens, and their response to the situation. While Kuwaiti analysts boldly criticize and demand fundamental changes, Bahraini voices, on the other hand, are ambivalent and use riddles and allegories to propose the same changes. However, there is a consensual view on the roots of the crisis and the overall outline for its remedy.[4] The foremost demand is for accountability of national economic management. Demands are for rationalizing development by balancing projections for future growth with diversified investment, balancing military expenditures with realistic strategic and security needs, and balancing national wealth distribution with a gradual phasing out of the pervasive welfare system. Under discussion are employment policies to take into account the demographic balance between Gulf nationals and foreign workers, thus involving labor legislation and enforcement. Another concern has been with education and the need to promote a modern generation with social and political consciousness, ready to assume an active role as responsible citizens.

All these needs, while recognized on the official level as expressed through government promises and statements, have been impossible to implement; although some half-hearted, partial attempts have been noted. Such demands challenge the fundamentals on which these family states are based and the type of relationships they have forged with their subjects. It is clear that the problem rests in the structural foundation of these states, within which their societies have been nurtured for the last 50 years. The Gulf state formation depended on two basic structural pillars: first and foremost, a wealthy rentier economy leading to a rentier societal "ethos" (if we could use the term in this way), and second, the gradual evolution of the regimes into authoritarian, mostly militarist/police-state apparatuses that fully controlled all resources, their distribution, and channels of power. These two pillars complement each other and feed upon each other.[5] Furthermore, this type of economy has been instrumental in altering the value system of Gulf societies, creating a mentality and attitude of dependency that explain the reaction to the crisis today. Resistance to facing the realities of this crisis is not only by the regimes who are reluctant to apply obviously unpopular economic policies as solutions, but also by the people, who have come to expect welfare benefits as their birthright.

This is the situation that both Kuwait and Bahrain find themselves in. The oil sector dominates revenue of both countries in the form of royalties or rents to cover the major part of their national income. For Kuwait, over 97 percent of revenue comes from oil sales and investment of oil money. Bahrain, the poorest of the oil-producing countries, depends on oil for 50 percent of its immediate national income. Other revenues come from domestic investment in industries and in services and from Saudi subsidies, again all indirectly dependent on the same commodity. Oil prices fluctuated from over $40 to less than $10 a barrel from the 1970s to 2000, and with them the economies and fortunes of these countries swayed. Oil prices hit record lows in the mid-to-late 1980s and in the late 1990s.[6] There are no indications that the present low prices can attain the boom levels of the 1970s or will change in any drastic fashion for the foreseeable future. Furthermore, both countries have been operating at a deficit since the 1991 war and have depleted their reserves as well as taken out loans. Albeit, it should be noted that due to some improvement in oil prices in 1999, this budget deficit has been reduced from $5.5 billion to $3 billion as specified by official government reporting.

Kuwait bore the heaviest load of the war drama and its repercussions, such as the violence of occupation, of flight, and of human and economic loss. It is estimated that the GCC countries paid heavily to cover the expenses of liberating Kuwait, at least $65 billion in 1990 and $70 billion in 1991.[7] The Kuwaiti share in the war was approximately $65 billion. This, along with various expenses as a result of war ramifications, has sliced Kuwait's national reserves by over 60 percent. Out of $100 billion in reserves in 1980, the value has dwindled to $35 billion in 1995, with $30 billion in outstanding foreign debt.[8] Furthermore, the immediate economic consequence of the war has held the Kuwaiti economy hostage to increasing demands for arms and security and protection expenses, as well as the burdens of innumerable expenses for the sake of recovery. The social and political developments in Kuwait during the last decade have been colored by these consequences and explain the complex accommodations, adjustments, and achievements that Kuwaiti society is undergoing.

Bahrain too, similar to the whole region, experienced many immediate realities and results of the war—in the form of Kuwaiti refugees and U.S. forces and maneuvers as well as Iraqi Scud missiles. Along with other Gulf governments, Bahrain's had to tighten its belt, which meant constricting the welfare benefits of society while at the same time pursuing a race to purchase arms and tighten security. But the long-range economic effects were tremendous on Bahrain, the worst hit of the Gulf states; it took the form of unemployment, social and political unrest, and a serious environment of malaise.[9]

Thus in Bahrain, the poorest and least endowed of the Gulf states and the one that suffers most from economic distress, this malaise has been most vocally illustrated. It has translated into a violent sustained uprising that has claimed lives and property and pitted a population demanding economic fairness against a political system projected as withholding equality and justice.[10] Within the Gulf system, Bahrain's condition is the most intense case, but there are signs that opposition demanding economic fairness, equitable sharing in the wealth of the country, and a say in its fate has emerged in other areas too.

### Historical Background

While it is beyond the purview of this paper to detail the development of political society in these two states, it is pertinent to briefly review the historical precedents for sociopolitical development in both. It should be noted that in both Bahrain and Kuwait a movement of nationalist consciousness started earlier than in any other region of the Gulf, and their societies have been strongly impacted by that. The political discourse in Kuwait and Bahrain still reflects a legacy of nationalist activism, experience of some democratic life, and undercurrents of opposition to the ruling regime.[11]

We can distinguish two developmental stages in the two states where economic and social structures were directly affected by the oil industry: The first started in the 1950s and culminated in the late 1970s, and the second unfolded in the 1990s. While the first stage was the founding period for the economic basis of society and molded its sociopolitical character and direction; the second stage has been and still is the period in which these societies search for an identity and grounding within a regional and a global setting.[12]

Particularly in the 1970s, the tremendous growth in oil wealth successfully built up the infrastructure and other manifestations of the state along modern lines and provided citizens with a wide range of services such as education, health, social services, even entertainment. These were centralized projects by the state, the supreme employer and provider of benefits to this welfare system. Therefore the ruling institution played the major role in creating and withholding opportunities. It also rationalized its legitimacy through these achievements and by building a network of alliances based on tribal, sometimes religious, and/or economic interests.[13] Economic favors in the form of money or land donations or control of power-generating posts have been some of the means by which these alliances were and are cemented. During this period, the state evolved into a powerful apparatus with the technology and measures of control and coercion.

This process created modern-looking societies without solving the dilemmas of rapid Western modernization and the persistence of traditional cultural values with political tribal/sectarian relations. All modernization techniques introduced into Kuwait and Bahrain since the inception of the state have been tailored to endorse this relationship and confirm these roles. Modernization also meant the creation of departments and an apparatus to ensure control and order, such as the Central Statistics Department. This system successfully kept taps on every citizen and resident in the state through a sophisticated computerized network linked to police surveillance. The police/internal-control and security system became closely identified with the ruling institution and its apparatus.

On the social and political levels, the 1960s and 1970s were decades of nationalism, liberation, and enthusiastic development. They were the boom years in the oil economies, affecting the whole region: both producers and benefactors of oil economic growth. This put in motion many societal developments that were to affect all sectors of society: mass education, employment, protective legislation and organized lobbying for labor representational rights. Most achievements were state sponsored and were considered essential when the state was forming its power bases. This period also witnessed urbanization/sedentarization, high fertility, and mobility.

By the 1980s the economies of the Gulf as a whole, including those of Bahrain and Kuwait, had become incorporated into the global capitalist structure and were affected by the general drop in real prices of primary commodities, including oil. When oil prices fell in 1986 (from $28 to $7), the whole region was adversely affected, and this was reflected in economic and political difficulties. The region had become indebted to international lenders. Austerity measures were instituted and social upheavals became common; also, repression intensified.[14] The governments of both states found themselves in the position of balancing and accommodating their survival on the basis of the demands of the various sociopolitical forces that these societies had produced in the decades of oil wealth.

During the late 1960s and the 1970s—a period of sharp economic prosperity—a large middle class, mainly urban, concentrated in the metropole, and Sunni, emerged. The late 1980s saw these developments, in varying degrees, reach the rural and tribal sectors of society, both Sunni and Shia as well as those of some of the ethnic minorities (the Beduns, the Balushis, and the Persians). Educational, health, and other services to both rural and urban areas were built, along with high-rise office buildings and other modern outlets. The local economic market expanded, as various corporations (monopolies by certain families of established status and wealth) were set up and employment in the service sector increased. It was a period of major material expansion that raised the economic and social expectations of people; however it also happened at a time when signs of economic contraction as well as class and sectarian differences were felt.

Gradually in the 1980s and 1990s, the social structure in both states began coalescing into two economically homogenous classes with a growing gap between them. This was more pronounced in Bahrain than in Kuwait due to higher resource wealth in the latter and a historical legacy that permitted a somewhat more equitable wealth distribution in Kuwait than in Bahrain. Nevertheless, a stratum of glaringly wealthy merchant and technocrat families and high government officials, mostly from traditional merchant families and a few newly elevated families, particularly Shias of Arab or Persian origins, grew. These made up the upper middle class. Also, a conglomerate of various ethnic groups coalesced into a professional salaried and broker merchant stratum whose power was dependent on income from government-sponsored services or economic opportunities.

The lower middle class developed from another very large combination of mostly ethnic/religious groups with minimal education whose standard of living had been forcibly raised and who found themselves constantly in search of more income while anxiously protecting what they had already acquired. This class was more closely aligned to the lowest economic stratum, with little substantial difference in their economic or conservative structure. This poorest stratum, having benefited from the enlarged education and health services of the state, acquired more political awareness and expectations for development, with no corresponding opportunities.

Similar to what occurred in other Arab and Gulf states, the oil revolution of the 1970s in Kuwait and Bahrain left a very conservative social order characterized by a laissez-faire capitalist, open-door economic policy; a policy that did not democratize opportunity and had no contingencies for the period of reversed fortunes. While the business community, the upper classes, and the upper middle class merchant strata experienced a boom with proliferation of visible accumulated wealth—palatial houses, residential compounds, spectacular business centers, and a wealthy lifestyle—as well as the mushrooming of Western enterprises (Kentucky Fried Chicken, McDonald's, Woolworth's, etc.), by the 1980s the lower middle class was experiencing a contraction in its purchasing power, and vulnerability in its employment. It was worst among the lower classes, whose expectations had been whetted through education and through the obvious signs of prosperity at its doorstep,[15] a prosperity denied to it by the contracted resources, growth in population, heightened expectations, and demand for employment. This situation was more pronounced in Bahrain than Kuwait. However, by that date, the political order in both states, with its paternalism, welfare policy, and limitation of popular participation, had become the norm and only sporadically contested.

Nevertheless, the reversal in the fortunes of the oil-producing nations and the Gulf War brought contractions in the economic strength of Kuwait and Bahrain and the available funds for state-sponsored projects. By this phase, state budgets had to heed the danger signs and limitations imposed by their global financial liabilities while at the same time temper demands and sensibilities of the citizens. For the last decade, the economic crisis, detailed at the outset of this paper, has intensified and reluctantly pushed the regimes and their citizens into new forms of relationships and accommodations. While economic constraints are being defined by the incorporation of local economies into the wider global financial networks, their application on the ground has to accommodate sociopolitical realities on the national, i.e., local, level.[16]

It should be noted that Western influence and the infiltration of Western social behavior and economic presence, as well as the unfolding of a lesser Arab nationalist discourse and an implied acceptance of the American sponsorship for normalization with Israel, all promoted socially and morally laden controversies and elicited the anger of the conservative and religious sensibilities in both countries. The quiet endorsement by officials of Western projects, their presence, and influence deepened popular anti-Western and anti-government feelings.[17] All this had been festering and circulating even before the war in 1991 and the peace initiatives (the Oslo Accords) that followed. Such moods hit a basic chord particularly within the economically depressed strata and those who felt the impact of official restriction and monitoring.

It was in these conditions and through the feelings of frustration and discontent they generated that the Islamist movements found adherents and support. The Islamist discourse provided the opposition with refuge and response to its outcry against conceived injustices as well as the unresolved dilemma of reconciling tradition to the flood of Westernization. Furthermore, with the complete absence of legal political channels for expressing grievances, revitalized popular Islam filled the vacuum. All through the 1980s the Islamic idiom was inching in on all levels of life and most particularly among the lower middle classes and the lower strata of society. The religio-political thrust of these movements stimulated a discourse of hope and redemption induced by the modern crisis on the moral, economic, and political levels.[18] In view of the previously mentioned transformations in society, the social implications of revived Islam gradually became pervasive and it acclimatized itself to the particular grievances of the moment and the dilemmas of identity that these societies were undergoing.

It was the 1991 Gulf War, with its dramatic impact of occupation, flight, fragmentation of Kuwaiti society, and Kuwaitis' sense of extreme dislocation, vulnerability, and disarray, that finally initiated a new stage in the process of introspection, analysis, and reaction among Gulf societies. The war and its aftermath brought to the fore pre-existing societal controversies, intensified and compounded economic hardships, and provided an outlet for popular reaction. Kuwait and Bahrain became the platforms for the most intense reactions, one as the scene of the war and the second as the scene of an ongoing popular uprising. In both, the legitimacy, sovereignty, and legislative power of the tribal/familial government has been challenged by the growing calls for accountability and economic rights, and the demands by Islamists for power sharing. In both states, the movement for women's empowerment as well as the move toward freedom of expression, democratization, and human rights have become the stage in which society faces its history, its traditions, its social evolution, and its relationship to the political establishment and ultimately to the new economic forces impacting its future.

## The Unfolding of the Current Crisis in Kuwait and Bahrain

Economic and political indicators make it clear that Kuwait and Bahrain are in the front line of all the Gulf states facing economic problems, but more clearly both are facing the inevitability of political change and possible explosions. National revenue has reached a ceiling and both governments have already dipped into their reserves. The welfare bill is growing and is weighed down by demographic increase and a new generation of graduates ready for employment. At the same time, these countries are continuously urged by international monetary commitments to streamline their budgets and expenditure and to balance their finances by involving their citizens in both revenue generation and decision making. Although these are the obvious necessary steps in the process to fall in line with global economic systems, such a formula of action would entail drastic revision of the basis and the status quo on which these societies have been remodeled since the discovery of oil. In other words, a change in the economic relationship between the ruling institution and the citizens means a fundamental reassessment on the part of the ruling families and the people of these Gulf states; a reassessment of the power system that governs their lives, its permanence and continuity. This is the crux of the dilemma that both the society and the regimes are facing, a situation that is hard to accept and harder to apply.

While the regimes are hard-pressed to lower the welfare bill, they are very reluctant to give up their prerogatives of absolute control over the sources of wealth and power. Citizens of these states, for their part, seem to expect a more open political system, with authoritative and institutionalized legislature as a basic right for their involvement in the economic burdens of the state. While voices of criticism and demands are loud and more persistent from within these societies, there has been no consensus on issues of fundamental significance to their future, whether that concerns the future and nature of the welfare system or the ideological identification of society. The issue of identity, the pull between tradition and modernity and the obsession with authenticity are of particular concern, in view of Western economic hegemony and influence. In both Kuwait and Bahrain these issues are the focus of debate that is shadowed by the controversy of state economic dependency on the global/Western economic system.

What will the future character of these states and these nations be? Is it Islam or secularism? The debate is particularly intense between the Islamists and the secular liberals. These are concerns that are debated in the Kuwaiti parliament, in the professional clubs, in the streets, diwaniyas, and mat'ams of Kuwait and Bahrain as well as among the opposition camps abroad. Nevertheless it is important to reinforce the point that these debates, whether Islamist or liberal, do not demand the drastic change of the political system, or the overthrow of the ruling families; at least that is what they officially declare; nor are they agreed on the principle for changing the welfare system or the form it should take.

## The Shaykhdom of Kuwait

In Kuwait these debates have acquired serious tones in recent months, indicating a more intense stage in the socioeconomic crisis. Since the war, Kuwaiti society has been consumed by recovery from the trauma and making good on the opportunity to institutionalize democratic politics. Armed with previous parliamentary experience and a relatively open political atmosphere, Kuwaitis valued that right and established it as the most precious national recompense after the war. Thus a return to the constitution was universally demanded during the hottest period of the conflict, making the return of the ruling family contingent upon it. As promised by the ruler, though reluctantly, at his meeting with Kuwaiti citizens in Jeddah, which has been held to be the new covenant between the government and the people for the post-war era, the constitution and free elections were re-established.

The first elected parliament brought representation of all political currents, with a strong deputation of Islamist groups. Although the numerical strength of the elected Islamists in the parliament of 1992 was large, there was no coordination among the various groupings representing Islamic ideological currents then. During the sessions of that parliament, energies were devoted to the many problems and vendettas left over from the occupation, with pitched battles against the ruling family, particularly over their financial role and accountability during and after the war. On the whole, achievements of the parliaments since 1992 have not been very significant, and their efforts have been taken up with petty squabbles among members and no substantial results.[19]

As for the latest parliament, elected in July 1999 with 80 percent turnout, and coming after six years of inertia, it promised a lively political life with more serious debates and actions.[20] This was at a time when the economic and political crisis had intensified and its ramifications had become more commonly discussed. Unlike its predecessor, in this parliament three Islamist groupings were able to form a coalition with the tribal blocs, thus controlling one-third of the Majlis al-Umma (the parliament). Soon after that and through a deliberate policy of muscle flexing, the Islamists were able to plunge the country into a state of political excitement by challenging public secular liberties.

By the end of the year 2000, infringements on publically accepted social norms attributed to the Islamists had accumulated and reached explosive dimensions. These had come in the wake of various incidents of physical attacks, supposedly by Islamists, on video shops considered to be upholders of loose morals and non-Islamic propaganda, as well as legal attacks on women writers and publishers accused of immoral and irreligious views. Up to February 2001, the Islamists vigorously pushed their moral-laden agenda by demanding control of socioeconomic activities, as in the banning of entertainment activities associated with the traditional trade festivals mounted during the month of February. Such ideological platforms were and are meant to convey to the public the new image the Islamic currents in Kuwait wish to project; that is, their role as custodians of moral and social behavior, whether on public dress, comportment, lifestyle, or thought. In this challenge, the Islamists have opened wide the door of debates on identity, authority, and democracy within the framework of the economic situation and its constraints.

This situation has raised the fear of a powerful Islamist bloc using its position in the new parliament, and the democratic process, to impose its own social and cultural definition of society on all citizens. Since liberation, Islamists have attracted popular support; however, these more recent activities have incited fears among the secular liberals and others. These events have shown that the Islamists have become the strongest political bloc in the parliament and are capable of imposing their definitions and solutions to the ills of society. It was within this challenge that the Islamic bloc took a stand to defeat the Amiri decree of October 1999 that gave women the right to vote and run for office. On one hand, the blocking of that law was meant to prove the application of constitutional power over that of the ruler—in other words, that the ruler's decree could no longer be held above the constitution—and, on the other hand, its defeat was to confirm the ideological line of the Islamic current. In fact this exhibited their capacity to impose their religio-cultural interpretation upon social development and women's rights.[21]

In view of the very feeble and lukewarm reaction from the ruling family, it is clear that that partner in the political process took a backstage position, that of an observer more than that of a participant. Again, this role has evolved gradually since the end of the war and the family's less than courageous stance then. Furthermore, rumor has it that the Al Sabahs are, similar to other Gulf ruling families, undergoing dynastic competition and the emergence of younger members with ambition and more modern projects. The ruler himself, Shaykh Jaber, has been absent from the scene for a long time; the crown prince–prime minister is reportedly seriously ill; and Sabah al-Ahmad Al Sabah, who has been running the affairs of governing, has also kept a low profile. The family is facing a growing popular demand to separate the role of the prime minister from that of the heir apparent, clearly with the intention of having the future prime minister come from the nationals and not from the ruling Al-Sabahs, thus gradually confining them to a more nominal political role.

Since June 2000 the situation has galvanized political life in Kuwait in reaction to the growing Islamist influence and control of the democratic process. *Al-Quds* newspaper of 1 May 2000 reported, from the Kuwaiti newspaper *Al-Ra'y al Amm,* that a group of intellectuals, writers, and politicians (30 of them) representing Kuwaiti liberals and old politicians, among whom were Jasim al-Saqr, Yacoub Jani, Awad Al-Humoud, Khalifa Loujian, and Muhammad al-Rumaihi, met and declared their pessimism, despair, and opposition to the growing atmosphere of political regression and religious fanaticism within the parliament (Majlis). These views have also been transferred to the newspapers, where they have expressed the public loss of confidence in its elected body—the parliament—as well as fears for the future. This group of 30 called for a popular committee to represent all national elements opposing what they consider the coercive trend in the parliament.

Within the folds of this struggle, however, is the matter of power that all currents of the political society covet. It is the power to define the direction of social and economic development at this stage when economic strains and reduced resources have become a threat to all. Although liberal politicians started fighting back against the growing Islamist influence and power, this will probably trap society into a protracted struggle that will only detract from facing the serious economic crisis and its social repercussions. Furthermore, these latest events of confrontations with the Islamists are bound to trigger negative results for the constitutional movement as a whole, and undermine efforts within that work toward transforming the economy and hopefully society. Nevertheless, there are new voices from within the Islamist currents expressing more moderate views concerning gender issues and women's voting rights.[22]

In the latest events unfolding since the New Year, Kuwaiti political life has been slightly shaken out of its inertia and paralysis. While the absence of royal family leadership has become an accepted reality, the popular voice has coalesced between moderate Islamists and some of the traditional liberal symbols to form an active opposition front. The demand for change by this front resulted in the dissolution of the government in late January 2001 and has now raised the hopes that the new government will embody serious and essential changes, such as distancing the royal family from executive power and giving credence to democratic demands.[23] However, only time will tell how such a front, made up of discordant ideological elements, will fare when and if reforms for socioeconomic transformations are finally put on the table.

## *The Shaykhdom of Bahrain*

As for Bahrain, where a grassroots anti-government protest uprising (an *intifada*) has been going on since the summer of 1994, the economic crisis has been translated into this explosive situation. The socioeconomic history of Bahrain is testimony to the role that economic property, distribution of wealth, and the emergence of sharp economic differences have played in creating an opposition. The basic motivation for this movement is economic, and the common solution demanded by the protestors is a return to the constitution, to the democratic process scrapped by the ruling family in 1975.[24] A constitutional rule is seen as the panacea that would heal the evils of an absolutist, self-interested regime. Thus the implications of these demands are that in times of economic depredations, the political contract with a paternalistic, authoritarian rule becomes null and void.[25] Although the articulation of these demands has come from various currents, elements, groups, and strata of the Bahraini society—Shias and Sunnis, liberals, leftists and Islamists, workers, professionals and intellectuals, men and women—it is the Islamic currents that have given cover to the largest and strongest thrust of this opposition movement.

Today there are some signs of innovative measures to alleviate the tense atmosphere in the country resulting from the crisis it has been enduring for the past decade. While the outward impression has been that of a state of political paralysis where nothing seems to be happening, more recently there have been feeble indications of shifts and alternative propositions. Nevertheless, as is usual in countries where the police machinery is overly oppressive, one has to observe the unimportant and the trivial in order to get at the underlying currents and signs of political and social stirrings; furthermore, official proclamations and proposals should be seriously but very critically analyzed.[26]

Information from the opposition still claims continued brutal police treatment, arrests, imprisonment, and infringement of basic human rights. These happenings are rarely commented upon officially, especially concerning the claims from the Shia rural opposition. Although a good number of political prisoners have been released and some who had been exiled have been pardoned, the opposition still claims continued police supervision and re-internment of some of those released. Every now and then, Sunnis renew their voices of opposition, complaining of economic and social deprivations. These have come from the pulpit of the mosques in Muharaq, a traditional stronghold of the ruling Al Khalifah family. Clerics are taking exception to the life of luxury and entertainment that some sectors of the society live by and have access to, such as car and horse races, golfing and surfing, art and trade exhibits; while, as they claim, people go hungry and economic conditions are worsening. Furthermore, secular professional unions, such as the General Union of Bahraini Workers, in the hope of a more open political environment under the new ruler, Hamad bin Isa, attempted to reorganize, but opposition reports indicate that they were immediately threatened and silenced.[27]

On another level, many of the younger members of the Al Khalifah family are actively sponsoring and hosting cultural and trade programs, all part of an obvious campaign to drive home their role and staying power. Succession has been confirmed in the Amir's son, a graduate of American schooling but fully steeped in the political culture of the family. Other sons, cousins, nephews, and even nieces are promoted as carriers of the banner for the ruling family and its role in the country. The younger generation of educated family members are awarded the most prestigious positions: women as ambassadors, all the key ministerial roles, as well as the sensitive military posts. Most of the deputy ministerial positions, the second in line commanding the executive power of these ministries, have been assigned to young Al Khalifahs. Since his accession a year ago, the ruler has also increased the monthly stipends doled to each family member, approximately 3,000 of them. Such a clear policy of "Khalifahization" of jobs is meant, on one hand, to consolidate the new Amir's position vis-à-vis his family, the main supporters of the regime, to score internal political victories against his uncle, the prime minister, but even more significantly in order to confirm and entrench the position of Al Khalifahs as the ruling institution in Bahrain.

A few measures of appeasement have been introduced by the new Amir, such as bestowing Bahraini passports upon and giving naturalized status to some 850 Beduns, people who had been living in Bahrain for generations with no legal documentation. This had been long due and its implementation now does not threaten the state or the demographic balance between Sunni and Shia, and therefore is politically acceptable. Other signs of opening up, and what the government considers liberalizing measures, included the promise by the ruler, during the National Day celebrations, to initiate municipal elections giving even women the right to vote, but not to run for office, as was the case in Qatar; this, when Bahraini women had been among the earliest and most active in the nationalist and constitutional movements of the 1960s and 1970s. In this latest uprising, women have also been active in petition writing and demanding constitutional rights. However, in order to placate an insistent demand by women for participation, it is ironic that a few of them were appointed to the latest Consultative/Shura Council.

In an attempt to appease and divert the demands for reinstating the constitution, in line with other Gulf states and following the war in 1992, the government has appointed this Shura/Consultative Council. However, this council as well as the proposed municipal elections did not measure up to the demands for real democratic political rights, and opposition remained adamant in its demands for a constitutional parliament similar to that of Kuwait. While there have been a few official announcements in the international media promising the return to constitutional life and a more democratic political atmosphere, this has not been translated into reality yet.

The final and most recent stage in the proposed reforms by the Amir was the call for a referendum to be held on February 14–15, 2001, on a national charter (*mithaq*) meant to change the suspended constitution. In this charter, a bicameral assembly is proposed that is made up of two bodies: an appointed upper house and an elected house, both with equal legislative powers. Also an independent judiciary is accounted for as well as full suffrage for all citizens, including women. As for the ruler, his powers remain above all authorities, the legislative, executive, and judiciary. Furthermore, the "Charter describes Bahrain as a hereditary monarchy," implying transforming Bahrain into a monarchy[28] presumably on the model of Jordan, which the Amir is known to admire. Such measures, and at this time, fall in with the general trend adopted by most Gulf ruling powers, which are grappling with the dilemmas posed by global demands for democratization, human rights, and recognition of women's rights but looking on these demands through the prism of their dynastic rule.[29]

The opposition has expressed its serious misgivings over the proposed charter and its generalities and ambiguities, especially concerning the powers assigned to the ruler and the Shura Council. Such a proposal imposed from above is seen as circumventing the sovereignty of the people as the base of authority specified in the original Bahraini constitution. Furthermore the lack of transparency attributed to the government in the initiation, elaboration, and plans for execution of this proposal exacerbates the situation and adds to the list of grievances against the government. These overtures seem to be measures to buy time and procrastinate a democratic resolution of the crisis.

## Conclusion

It is clear from all this that both the regimes and the public in Kuwait and Bahrain are aware of a developing economic crisis and that the solutions have to be both economic and political. The public outcry for change has taken many forms, mostly sharp and forceful because of the intense effect of conditions in both countries, one still reeling from the war and the other from strongly felt poverty. It is also clear that while the problems are recognized, there is no consensus on solutions, and whatever these are, they are acknowledged to be difficult, painful, and therefore easier to be ignored for a little while longer. Demands for remedy, however, have been colored and tempered by conservative as well as liberal views and concerns. In the competition that these two discourses generate, the public is confused and a solution is delayed. In the last decade the public reaction to the crisis has been reflected sometimes in indecisiveness and domestic squabbles, as was the case in Kuwait for a few years after the 1991 war, and in Bahrain in a violent reaction bordering on revolution.

The nature of the crisis demands a revision of the structural base on which power and society rest. Because this crisis ultimately threatens all components of these societies, the ruling institutions and the people, solutions have to be comprehensive. All changes of political and social norms are difficult, especially if the process endangers the status of the power that needs to carry it out. But also the uncertainties involved in its application play on the fear and concern of all. An essential part of the process is to bring about change in the meaning of citizenship, which needs to be reinvested with rights and responsibilities: a new definition to belonging and identification.[30] In spite of a growing awareness by the regimes that resolving the malaise in their societies has become urgent, they still look for solutions that perpetuate their dynasties and power bases. At the same time, the new generation of young Gulf nationals who aspire to a modern meaning of citizenship have become more forceful in demanding change. Political and social analysts continue to press for recognition of the enormous, slow crisis that is unfolding and the need to meet its challenges. Maybe it will need much more drastic shocks than just the war to bring about the realization that to survive it will be necessary for both the people and the regimes in the region to cooperate in transforming the economic and political structures of society.

## Notes

1. Gary G. Sick, "The Coming Crisis in the Persian Gulf," in Gary G. Sick and Lawrence G. Potter, eds., *The Persian Gulf at the Millennium: Essays in Politics, Economy, Security, and Religion,* New York: St. Martin's Press, 1997, pp. 12–13. See also the latest literature coming from Gulf intellectuals published mainly in Arabic periodicals and publications, such as *Al-Arabi, Al-Mustaqbal al-Arabi, Majalat al-Dirasat al-Ijtima'ya*. In particular see: Abdul-Khaliq Abdulla, ed., *Al-Khaleej al-Arabi wa-Furas wa-Tahadiyat al-Qarn al-Wahid wal-Ushrun* [The Arabian Gulf and the Challenges of the Twenty-first Century], annual meeting of the Muntada al-Tanmiya, Abu Dhabi, 1999.
2. Muhammad al-Rumaihi, *Al-Khaleej al-Arabi wal-Furas, wal-Tahadiyat al-Hadariya wal-Ma'rifiya lil-Qarn al-Wahid wal-Ushrun* [The Arabian Gulf: Opportunities and Cultural and Informational Challenges for the Twenty-first Century], in Abdulla, ed., Muntada Al-Tanmiya 1999, *op. cit.,* pp. 112–113.
3. Khaldoun Hasan al-Naqeeb, "Al-Khaleej . . . ila-Ayn?" [The Gulf . . . where to?], *Al-Mustaqbal al-Arabi* 22:253, March 2000, pp. 4–22.
4. Abdul-Khaliq Abdulla, ed., *Al-Khaleej al-Arabi wa-Furas wa-Tahadiyat al-Qarn al-Wahid wal-Ushrun*. This book published the deliberations of the twentieth annual meeting of the Muntada al-Tanmiya, in 1999, in Abu Dhabi, and was dedicated to the study and analysis of the crisis facing the Gulf states and proposals for its solution. The Muntada is a forum of Gulf thinkers who have been meeting yearly for the last two decades, in different cities of the Gulf states, in order to discuss and share their concerns and proposals for the future of their region. Five prominent Gulf scholars—Abdul-Khaliq Abdulla, Adnan Shihab al-Deen, Hasan Hamdan Alkim, Muhammad Al-

Rumaihi, and Abdulla Ibrahim al-Quwaiz—contributed to this publication. Each scholar dealt with one angle of the challenge facing the Gulf states and suggested solutions for its remedy. See also Khaldoun al-Naqeeb, *Al-Mujtama' wal-Dawla fil-Khaleej wal-Jazira al-Arabiya* [Society and State in the Arabian Gulf and Peninsula], Beirut: Centre for Arab Unity Studies, 1987; Baqer al-Najjar, *Sociologia al-Mujtama' fil-Khaleej al-Arabi* [Sociology of Arabian Gulf Societies], Beirut: Dar al-Kunouz al-Adabiya, 1998.

5. For a thorough and interesting discussion of this relationship and its significance to the development of the Gulf societies see Khaldoun al-Naqeeb, "Al-Khaleej . . . ila-Ayn?," *op. cit.*, pp. 4, 9–11; see also: F. Gregory Gause III, *Oil Monarchies: Domestic and Security Challenges in the Arab Gulf States*, New York: Council on Foreign Relations, 1994, pp. 42–44; al-Rumaihi, in Muntada al-Tanmiya, *op. cit.*, pp. 106–109.
6. Gause, *op. cit.*, pp. 44–58. See also *The Economist*, 14 March 1998, and 6 June 1998.
7. See graph showing military expenditures for the GCC countries for the period 1990–1998 at http://www.defenselink.mil/pubs/allied_contrib2000/allied2000-chp3.pdf Saudi Arabia alone has paid an estimated $70 billion as contribution to the coalition allies and $10 billion for the oil spill. See John Thomas Haldane, *Washington Report on Middle East Affairs*, December/January 1991–1992, p. 89.
8. Sick, "The Coming Crisis," in Sick and Potter, *op. cit.*, p. 14; and Gause, "The Political Economy of National Security in the GCC States," in Sick and Potter, *op. cit.*, p. 68.
9. The discussion in the two articles referred to in the previous note (Sick and Potter) on belt tightening in the whole Gulf region applies to Bahrain too. See May Seikaly, "The Economy of Political Opposition in Bahrain: The Post–Gulf War Period," unpublished lecture presented to the MESA Conference in Providence, Rhode Island, 22 November 1996. Reports on the negative economic conditions in Bahrain come from various sources, from international scholarship and organizations as well as from local opposition groups.
10. Munira A. Fakhro, "The Uprising in Bahrain: An Assessment," in Sick and Potter, *op. cit.*, pp. 167–88.
11. For the history of this development, see Fuad Khoury, *Tribe and State in Bahrain*, Chicago: University of Chicago Press, 1985; see also Muhammad al-Rumaihi, *Al-Betrol wal Taghayur al-Ijtima'i fi al-Khaleej al-Arabi* [Oil and Social Change in the Arabian Gulf], Kuwait, 1984; Abdulhadi Khalaf, "The New Amir of Bahrain: Marching Sideways," in *Civil Society* 9:100, April 2000, and Fakhro, *op. cit.*
12. The Gulf states produce a tremendous amount of materials to stress the issue of identity, loyalty, and belonging to the region. This takes the form of literature, educational materials, films, propaganda, and floods of television programs. More recently *Al-Jazeera*, the Qatari-based satellite channel, has also televised some talk shows in which inter-Gulf relations and contentions are debated.
13. Baqer al-Najjar, "Ma'uqat al-istikhdam al-amthal lil-Qiwa al-'Amila al-wataniyya fi al-khaleej al-Arabi wa-imkaniyat al-Hall [Drawbacks to the Proper Utilization of National Manpower in the Arabian Gulf and Possible Solutions], in *Conference of Experts on Policies for Arab Labor Mobility and Utilization*, Kuwait: Economic and Social Commission for West Asia (ESCWA) and Kuwait Institute of Planning, 1985; Muhammad al-Rumaihi, "Athar al-naft 'ala wad' al-mar'a al-'Arabiyyah fi al-Khalij" [The Effect of Oil on the Condition of Arab Women in the Gulf], in *al-Mar'a wa-Dawruha fi Harakat al-Wehda al-Arabiyya* [Woman and Her Role in the Arab Unity Movement], Beirut: Centre for Arab Unity Studies, 1982; May Seikaly, "Women and Socio-Political Change in Bahrain," *International Journal of Middle East Studies* 26:3, August 1994, pp. 415–26.
14. Under the subtitle "The Myth of Wealth," Gary Sick details the unsubstantiated mirage of wealth that the Gulf states find themselves in today. See Sick, "The Coming Crisis," pp. 15–22.
15. Particularly in Bahrain, what exacerbated conditions for the lower classes and rural communities was the encroachment of "garden residential compounds" onto the heart of the villages. In those ultra-luxurious living compounds, mostly foreign communities resided, oblivious to the squalor and poverty surrounding them and insensitive to the conservative traditional lifestyle of the villagers. The current intifada was ignited by an incident in these villages when some foreign residents were taking part in a running marathon and crossed these villages wearing what was perceived as indecent sports clothes.
16. Sick, "The Coming Crisis," pp. 16–21; see also Gause, *op. cit.*, pp. 42–118.
17. The anti-Western feeling is quite pervasive among the poorer strata and the more conservative strata of the middle classes. It is also a clear political stand of the intellectual circles, mainly the progressive currents among them. This is endorsed by overt expressions as well as attitudes of

these elements vis-à-vis the wealthier and more powerful strata of society and the policies of their governments. Very recently a new association has been set up by groups of progressive thinkers in the Gulf to oppose the policies of normalization with Israel. The religious currents in both states, as well, see the signs of Western economic and educational influence as a threat to religion, culture, and the future identity of their societies. Furthermore, in places where Western presence is directly associated with the government's repressive machinery, such as in Bahrain, this adds to popular complaints against the West. The fact that Ian Henderson is a British subject but was also the commander of the police in Bahrain did not sit well; he is still seen as the person responsible for building and training the system of brutal investigation of internees. There has been direct references to his role in the protest petitions sent to the Amir during this uprising.

18. Eqbal Ahmad, "Islam and Politics," in Haddad, Haines, and Findly, eds., *The Islamic Impact*, Syracuse: Syracuse University Press, 1984, p. 25; Al-Naqeeb, "Al-Khaleej . . . ila Ayn," p. 15; Gause, *op. cit.*, pp. 31–41.
19. Roy P. Mottahedeh and Mamoun Fandy, "The Islamic Movement: The Case for Democratic Inclusion," in Sick and Potter, *op. cit.*, pp. 34–35; see also *The Economist*, 6 June 1998.
20. For the development of Islamist groups in Kuwait, see Falah al-Mudairis, *Jama't al-Ikhwan al-Muslimeen fil-Kuwait* [The Muslim Brotherhood in Kuwait], Kuwait: Dar Kurtas, 1999; and Falah al-Mudairis, *Al-Jama'a al-Salafiya fil-Kuwait* [The Salafiya Muslim Group in Kuwait], Kuwait: Dar Kurtas, 1999. See also *The Economist*, 10 July 1999.
21. *The Economist*, 22 May 1999, 27 November 1999; see also Al-Naqeeb, "Al-Khaleej . . . ila Ayn," p. 15.
22. A special report from Kuwait aired by CNN news on 5 August 2000 reported that women will be given their democratic rights to vote and run for office. It was also reported that this move was heralded by Islamist women as a right within the precepts of Islam.
23. See *Al-Quds*, January 30, 2001; Hasan Omar reporting from Kuwait.
24. Khalaf, "The New Amir," in *Civil Society*; Ahmad al-Shamlan, ed., *Al-Haraka al-Dusturiya: Nidal Sha'ab al-Bahrain min ajl al-Dimokratiya* [The Constitutional Movement: The Struggle of the People of Bahrain for Democracy], Beirut: Dar al-Wihda al-Wataniya, 1997; Seikaly, "The Economy of Political Opposition" (unpublished).
25. Since the beginning of this uprising, it has been widely reported in the press, regionally and internationally. See *Rose al-Yusif*, 16 January 1995; *Crescent International*, 16–31 January 1995; *Le Monde Diplomatique*, March 1995; *Al-Sharq al-Awsat*, last week of April 1995 (series of five articles by Fouad Matar); *The Wall Street Journal*, 12 June 1995; *The Washington Post*, 13 June 1995; *The Economist*, 6 April 1996, 12 April 1997, 23 January 1999; to name a few only. In all the articles reporting on this crisis, the economic factor is attributed to be the major cause, as well as the worsening condition of the poorer strata of society. The Shia population, especially the village dwellers representing the more economically depressed elements with particular grievances against the government, became associated with the most vocal and, gradually, the violent aspects of the protest. Sunnis have also taken part in this protest movement since its inception, although haltingly at different stages of its development.
26. One of the methods used by the opposition to publicize its case and propagate its grievances has been through fax and audio recording. In fact this has informed supporters and sympathizers abroad of events as they were happening.
27. Human rights abuses have been reported by international human rights organizations such as Human Rights Watch and Amnesty International and reported in their annual reports and in the press. Furthermore, the Voice of Bahrain, the mostly Shia voice of the opposition based in London, has been active in disseminating information on what they consider as infringements on the democratic and basic human rights of the Bahraini people, both Shia and Sunni.
28. Amy Hawthorn, "Bahrain's National Charter and Political Reform in the Gulf," in *PolicyWatch*, number 514, 25 January 2001.
29. Khalaf, *op. cit.*; accounts of these happenings in Bahrain are also circulated orally among people in Bahrain and abroad. For a fresh analysis of the role of monarchical rule in the Gulf states, see Michael Herb, *All in the Family*, New York, SUNY Press, 2000.
30. For insightful discussions and analyses of this necessity, see Sick, "The Coming Crisis," pp. 24–25; and al-Naqeeb, "Al-Khaleej . . . ila Ayn," p. 11.

# THE ARAB GULF STATES

CHAPTER 12

## Kings and People: Information and Authority in Oman, Qatar, and the Persian Gulf

Dale F. Eickelman

For the Arabian Peninsula, the substantial growth in mass education over the last three decades, the proliferation and accessibility of new media and communications, and the increasing ease of travel make it increasingly difficult for state and religious authorities to monopolize the tools of literary culture. The ideas, images, and practices of alternative social and political worlds have become a daily occurrence. They enter domestic space through satellite and cable television, and are better understood than in the past. Rapidly rising levels of literacy and familiarity with an educated Arabic formerly restricted to an elite facilitate this better comprehension. They also rehearse viewers to respond to those in authority in the common language of the Arabic of the classroom and the media.

Mass education was important in the development of nationalism in an earlier era.[1] In recent years, the proliferation of media and means of communication have multiplied the possibilities for creating communities and networks among them, fragmenting religious and political authority, dissolving prior barriers of space and distance, and opening new grounds for interaction and mutual recognition.

To be sure, the power of new media to challenge and fragment claims to religious and political authority had become evident at the time of the 1978–1979 Iranian revolution. Audiocassettes—easy to smuggle and duplicate—were then the subversive media of choice. Since then, the accessible nature of newer media and rising levels of education have increasingly blurred the boundaries between producers and consumers. Fax machines, desktop publishing, photocopying machines, the Internet, and new uses of older media make communications more participatory and create new audiences. The greater ease of travel—for education, pilgrimage, tourism, labor migration, and emigration—also accelerates the flow of ideas and practices.

More important, some new media seen as innovative in the early 1980s are now almost taken for granted. In countries such as Saudi Arabia, the same fax machines that rapidly disseminate criticisms of the regime from opposition groups abroad are also essential to the conduct of business. The state is powerless to limit their use without disrupting the economy, and attempts to counter "faxed criticisms" in other media—such as the press—by warning readers against disseminating them further, merely draws subsequent attention to their existence.[2]

Since Iran's May 1997 presidential elections, some Iranian intellectuals and Western observers have gone so far as to speak of a new era of "post-Islamism," in the Islamic Republic in particular and the rest of the Muslim world in general.[3] Clearly, this post-Islamism is defined by the widespread awareness of alternatives to existing dominant ideologies and institutional arrangements. Fariba Adelkhah, for example, argues that this transformation is as significant as the original revolution. It is fueled by the combination of rising levels of education and the coming of age of a new generation of Iranians—now the majority of the population—not even born at the time of the 1978–1979 revolution. This new generation, she argues, is creating an Iranian "religious public sphere" (*espace public confessionel*). In spite of resistance from conservatives, many in this generation employ the public use of reasoned argument, which, even if developed primarily in private or semi-private settings, "also has repercussions on the political scene."[4]

In most of the Arabian Peninsula Gulf states, discussions concerning the nature of just and appropriate governance and the role of religion in politics is not as foregrounded and public as in Iran. Kuwait is a partial exception, although the legitimacy of royal authority in Kuwait is not a subject for public debate. Other matters, even legislative initiatives by Kuwait's ruler, have been hotly contested, including women's right to vote in parliamentary elections.[5]

Nevertheless, the rapidly expanding range of public discourse about politics and religion within the Arabian Peninsula is rapidly outstripping the pace of change in formal institutions. A public sphere is emerging throughout the region in which messages and images in face-to-face conversations, newspapers, books, magazines, anonymous leaflets, video and audiocassettes, and satellite and regular television criss-cross, overlap, and build on one another. When censored or suppressed in one medium, such messages recur in another. Images of alternative institutions and practices, once on the periphery of the social imagination of much of the public, are now concrete and foregrounded. Even silence contributes to the public sphere, when some topics are avoided because of real or imagined penalties for direct public expression. Authoritarian limitations on participation in discussions and debate over public issues are resented and increasingly easy to evade. These discussions are not confined to immediate locality but increasingly include attention to wider, regional, and transnational issues.

Not surprisingly, some critics downplay the emergence of the public sphere in the Arabian Peninsula, as well as elsewhere in the Arab world. Seymour Martin Lipset, for example, asserts that Muslim, "particularly Arab," notions of political authority are especially hostile to democracy because Islamic political doctrines are "alien" to political freedom.[6] The result is to assume that Muslims, more than the followers of other religions, are guided by religious doctrines that inhibit a shift to democratic rule. Others argue that expectations of authority throughout the region are pervaded by "cultural schemas" that have hardly changed over centuries. These schemas supposedly privilege hierarchical master-disciple relations in the religious and political spheres, severely limiting alternative political and institutional styles.[7]

This chapter challenges such bleak assumptions. It compares the changing context in which "information"—political and religious—is managed in two contrasting Gulf states, Qatar and the Sultanate of Oman. The emphasis is less on formal political institutions than the commonly shared, often implicit, ideas of what is right, just, or religiously ordained—those taken-for-granted ideas upon which any community or group of individuals form cooperative relations.

Qatar and Oman show marked dissimilarities in state attitudes toward information, the media, and control over public expression. Qatar abolished censorship in 1995 and its Ministry of Information in 1996, although a high degree of self-censorship continues in Doha. Qatar's Al-Jazeera satellite television has emerged as the flagship for uncensored news and discussion throughout the Arab world. Media market forces oblige other satellite media, sometimes with reluctance, to emulate Al-Jazeera's lead.

Oman has no such unfettered media. Its 1996 Basic Charter allows freedom of opinion expressed in words and writing, but in the circumspect 1999 State Department report on Human Rights Practices, "these provisions have yet to be implemented."[8] No fewer than three government agencies censor books and magazines in the Sultan Qaboos University library. Nothing controversial or critical of the government or religiously controversial appears in the local print or broadcast media. Unabashedly, Muscat practices an older form of control and supervision over what is said in public. Yet, even if formal Omani information practices change at a glacial pace, Omanis, like the citizens of other Gulf states, have ready access to alternative sources of information. As elsewhere, anonymous faxed messages and photocopied leaflets have emerged to contest the ruling elite and state decision making. Such developments point to basic transformations in the collective imagination of religion and politics that permeate the entire region, regardless of specific government policies.

### Mass Higher Education, Language, and Community

Mass education is a more recent development in the Arabian Peninsula. Elsewhere in the Middle East, it began only in the 1950s—1952 for Egypt and 1956 for Morocco, for example. In Kuwait, the commitment to universal education began shortly after 1961, and in Oman only in the early 1970s. In all cases, it was only 15 to 20 years after the introduction of mass primary education that large numbers of students began to complete the advanced cycles of secondary and post-secondary education. It was only at this point that the consequences of widespread education could be clearly discerned.[9]

Omani figures offer a sense of the compressed period in which the rise of mass education occurred. In 1975–76, a mere 22 students attended secondary school. Little more than a decade later, in 1987–88, 13,500 did. In 1997, there were 77,000, and there were more than 8,000 students in post-secondary institutions, including the national university, which opened in 1986.[10]

A major distinction between the Arabian Peninsula Gulf states, blessed with oil wealth, and the rest of the Arab world is that educational expansion has kept up with population growth in quantity if not always in quality. As a consequence, large numbers of citizens, especially those born in the last three decades, speak the common language of formal Arabic, the language of schoolrooms, newscasts, political and religious discussions, and other public speech. There often is a great divide in Arabic between the colloquial speech of everyday use and the formal, standard language of newspapers, radio, and educated public speech. Education, especially higher education, in the language of formal, literary Arabic, allows people to "talk back" to religious and political authorities in this public language.

Education, like mass communications, also makes citizens more conscious of their political and religious beliefs and practices and encourages thinking of them as a system, allowing for comparison with other ideas and practices. Education and the greater ease of communication also erode intellectual and physical boundaries and enable connections to be made across formerly impenetrable boundaries of class, locality, language, and ethnic group.

### Satellite Television: Qatar

Even if political institutions in the Arabian Gulf are slow to change, Qatar's ruler, Shaykh Hamad bin Khalifah Al Thani, takes almost the attitude of Prussia's Frederick the Great (1712–1786) in fostering open information and debate and offering a model for what might become prevalent in regional and local contexts. Thus, as a leading television commentator in the Arab Gulf recently observed, "Satellite TV has become as important a symbol of sovereignty as having a flag or a national airline."[11]

Indeed, satellite television has contributed to creating new public spaces in the Arab Middle East, especially when unimpeded live televised debates are combined with call-in questions and comments. Today, such uses of the media bring speakers and listeners closer together, allowing authorities to be questioned. Uncensored satellite television in Arabic creates ready and open alternatives to the "official story" promulgated by state-controlled broadcast and print media, challenging other media, obliging them to respond with editorials or rebuttals, and entering many different domains of discussion.

In short, satellite television is playing an increasing role in redefining public space in the Gulf and elsewhere, contributing to the emergence of a "network" society.[12] Only 10–15 percent of Middle Eastern Arabs regularly watch satellite broadcasts,[13] although the issues and commentaries on uncensored satellite television increasingly shape regional discussions and debate, linking these discussions to those held among Arab professionals in Europe and North America.

It must be emphasized, nevertheless, that distinguishing between ideas of the *public sphere* and *civil society* facilitates the understanding of the rapidly changing "background" significance of politics and religion in Arabian Peninsula societies.

The idea of the *public sphere* implies a space separate from the formal structures of religious and political authority and the space of households and kin. Ideally, in this space, ideas are presented on their own merits, rather than as emanating from such authoritative intermediaries as preachers, judges, and rulers. Although this notion can be traced back to Immanuel Kant, it currently is closely associated with the work of Jürgen Habermas. His development of the idea of the public sphere is largely based on the historical emergence in Europe of "rational-critical" discourse within bourgeois society.[14]

Habermas, like others who have developed the notion of the public sphere, downplays the role of religion in its development and expansion. Yet, one of the most important developments in the contemporary Arab world and other Muslim-majority states has been the increasingly open contest over the authoritative use of the symbolic language of Islam and its implications for religious and political authority.[15]

The term *civil society* is used in a narrower contemporary sense. In fact, it has rich connotations dating back to the sixteenth century in Europe, when it was

**Figure 12.1.** Egyptian religious conservative Safinez Kazim (standing, right) accuses Toujan Faisal (left), the first woman member of Jordan's parliament, of blasphemy during a live broadcast of *The Opposite Direction* on Al-Jazeera satellite television in 1997. Moderator Faisal al-Kassim (center), thrives on open, uncensored debate, which has made *The Opposite Direction* one of the most successful television formats in the Arab world.

contrasted to "fanaticism."[16] As used by political scientists and policymakers since the 1980s, however, the term refers to the creation of organizations subject to the state's "rule of law" and recognized by the state but otherwise independent of state initiative and control. By most measures, the status of civil society in most of the Arab world, including the Arabian Peninsula, remains precarious. Nonetheless, the public sphere is rapidly expanding.

As a contributor to the expanding public sphere, Qatar's Al-Jazeera satellite channel remains almost unique in the Middle East. The announced April 2000 move of some of its operations to Egypt's "free media" zone indicates the volatility of contemporary communications, and also suggests how "market forces" place significant pressure on existing government restrictions.[17] There are numerous Arab satellite channels, but most stick to entertainment because of political constraints. Al-Jazeera began broadcasting in November 1996. The core

**Figure 12.2.** In recent years, reliable public opinion polling has become possible in some Middle Eastern contexts, as with this survey of Palestinian views of the most "independent" television news reporting.

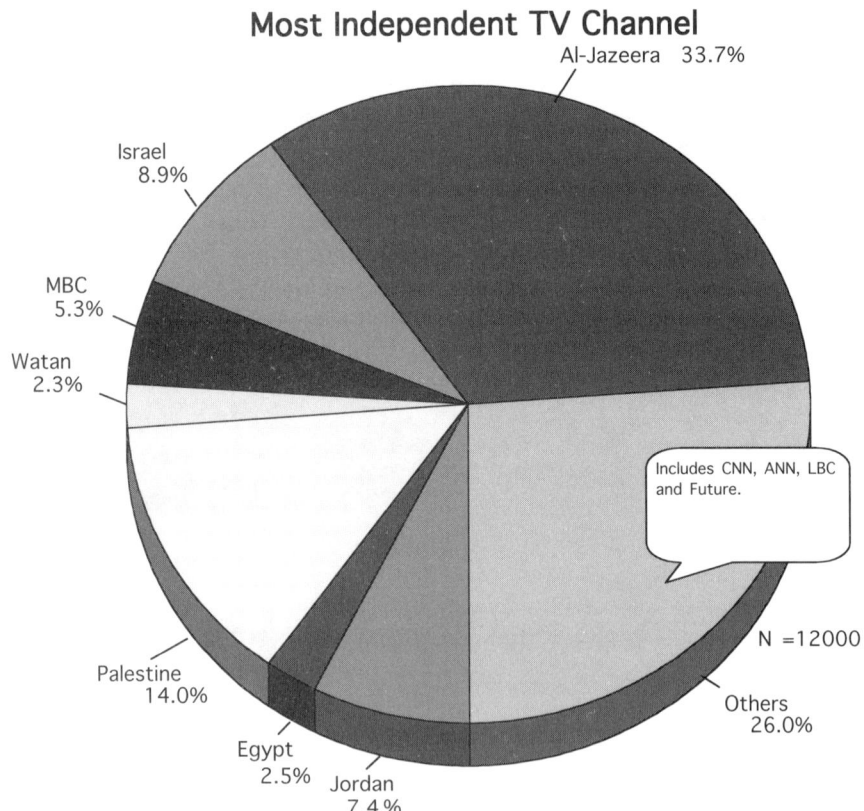

Source: Jerusalem Media and Communication Center, *Palestinian Opinion Pulse* 1, no. 33 (November 1999), p. 9.

of its personnel were imported from a failed BBC effort, backed by a Saudi company, Orbit Communications, to expand into satellite broadcasting. The BBC effort failed in part because the satellite dishes and decoders needed to receive its signals were prohibitively expensive, thus limiting its potential audience.[18] Additionally, the BBC's Saudi backers objected to its unflattering news coverage of Saudi Arabia and wanted content control. Not surprisingly, the BBC refused, so Orbit cancelled its annual $35 million payment, and BBC Arabic programming stopped after 20 months of broadcasting. Twenty of the BBC's Arab editors, reporters, and technicians were quickly hired by Qatar and formed the core of Al-Jazeera's team.[19]

The Al-Jazeera formula resembles the one pioneered by CNN, although its discussion programs are more vigorous and controversial. One example is the weekly program *Al-Ittijah al-Mu'akis* [The Opposite Direction], moderated by Dr. Faisal al-Kassim. A Syrian by origin, al-Kassim graduated top of his class in English from the University of Damascus in 1983, and won a scholarship for graduate studies in Britain. His doctoral thesis at the University of Hull was on political iconoclasm in modern British drama. He began working part-time for the BBC in 1988 and made the shift from BBC radio to television in 1994, a position that lasted until the collapse of the BBC's Arabic satellite transmissions in May 1996.

In *The Opposite Direction,* two guests with contrary views square off in the studio in Qatar, although occasionally the program broadcasts from elsewhere in the Arab world. With al-Kassim moderating, the guests talk to one another for about an hour, followed by telephone call-ins. The program is live, including the telephone calls, which are not pre-screened or subject to the "time delay" technology common in American broadcasting. The topics and the broadcasts join the central debates of the Arab world—the Arab-Israeli crisis, the state of the economy, Iran and the Gulf, Kuwait-Iraq animosity, polygamy, Turkey-Israel relations, human rights and Islam, Syria's negotiations with Israel over the Golan Heights, and democratization. At least one program dealt with Qatar's municipal elections.

As an example of Al-Jazeera's style, an early program on Islam and secularism featured a heated discussion between Yusuf al-Qaradawi, a leading religious conservative, and Syria's Sadeq al-'Azm, a committed secularist. For many in the audience, al-'Azm's presentation was the first time they heard a spirited "secularist" argument. Another program featured a debate on polygamy between Toujan Faysal, the first woman in Jordan's parliament and a secularist, and Safinaz Kazim, a religiously conservative Egyptian. When Faysal said at one point that Qur'anic doctrine was out of date, the Egyptian accused her of blasphemy, ripped off her microphone, and got up to leave. Al-Kassim reminded her that she was on live television. She shot back:" I don't care if we're on Mars. I'm not tolerating this blasphemy," and left the studio. The incident also suggests how satellite television is allowing women to join public religious discussions, albeit cautiously, as *The Opposite Direction* never pairs women with men. In October 1999, a former Algerian prime minister, Reda Malek, unhappy with a particularly sharp telephone question, asked al-Kassim to stop the tape. Al-Kassim replied, "I can't. We broadcast live. You're not in Algeria." Furious, the Algerian cursed on air and stormed out of the studio.[20]

Al-Jazeera programs also focus on regional issues. Thus Sudan's Hasan al-Turabi, paired with Saudi Arabia's Turki Suhaili, the editor of a Riyadh newspaper and a member of the ruling family, described the Saudi political system as a "plague" (*bilwa*). Abdallah Nafisi, in a program discussing economics, blurted out an attack against the then head of Saudi Arabia's Supreme Council of Ulama, Shaykh bin Baz (1912–1999), when he declared:

> I defy bin Baz to say something about royal corruption in Saudi Arabia. His country is infested with corruption. He can do fatwas on Viagra, but not mention [regime opponents like] Safar al-Hawali, people languishing in prison. We cannot separate politics from money in the Arab Gulf. The rulers [he used the insulting phrase "the shopkeeper rulers" (*al-hukkam al-tujjar*)] only care about opening bank accounts in the West.[21]

Such comments sometimes draw strong reactions from official circles outside of Qatar, and Al-Jazeera has been denied membership in the Union of Arab Broadcasters because it violates the "brotherly" code of conduct in which political opponents are never allowed to criticize incumbent rulers. Although accused of bias against the Saudis, a Saudi specialist in media studies recently published a program-by-program analysis of *The Opposite Direction,* concluding that it showed no political or religious bias.[22] The publication of such a book in Saudi Arabia itself suggests the rapidly evolving public sphere, as the "craft" of censorship becomes increasingly public.

Undoubtedly, the contribution of Al-Jazeera to the public sphere is manifested in the speed with which videotapes of its programs circulate freely in the shops and private homes in Damascus, Casablanca, Muscat, Amman, Riyadh, and elsewhere, among those without direct access to satellite television. For many viewers, its Arabic news broadcasts have become the standard against which other broadcasters are judged. Given that reliable surveys of viewing habits and trust in the televised media are lacking for the Arab Gulf states, the evidence is largely anecdotal. Yet, dependable figures for Gaza and the West Bank place Qatar's Al-Jazeera TV as the most reliable source for information (33.7 percent), followed by other satellite channels (26.0 percent), with local television from the Palestinian National Authority (14.0 percent) and Israeli television (8.9 percent) lagging far behind, but still ahead of MBC, Egyptian, and Jordanian broadcasts.[23]

Moreover, satellite television tilts the balance of public argument in favor of ideas and practices that can be explained, defended, and foregrounded.[24] The speed and intensity with which it facilitates the circulation of ideas, images, and practices also distinguishes contemporary public spaces from those of the past. Likewise, journalists and newspaper editors can comment almost simultaneously on events because they can read any of the 34 Arabic-newspaper Websites for reactions to current events. Uncensored satellite television enables a wider public to participate in such discussions.

Arabic-language satellite channels, like the other "new" media, have had profound consequences for the political and religious imagination. First, they create and sustain a new public. Modern mass education not only means more widely spread skills than prior patterns of elite education, but also offers wider, competing repertoires of intellectual techniques and authorities and the erosion of exclusivities that previously defined communities of discourse, extending them also to women and minorities.

Second, viewers can now watch religious and political authorities and commentators explain their views and answer questions more as equals than as distant orators who cannot directly be challenged. Moreover, it is not just religious specialists who debate religion, but other educated persons and public figures. The distance between authorities and their audiences is diminished, and claims to the mantle of authority become more open. Finally, satellite television introduces audiences to new ways of thinking, in favoring effective and reasoned presentations.

Satellite television thus plays a major role in creating and sustaining a new public sphere. It expands the space of public dealings beyond one's face-to-face consociates to those whom Alfred Schutz called contemporaries.[25] Satellite television and other new media contribute to turning anonymous or unknown contemporaries into consociates that share common assumptions of civility and morality. Not everyone can telephone guests on politically and religiously sensitive talk shows, and the number of callers from outside the Arab world still outnumbers regional callers. But even this fact reminds people of the limits to expression in their immediate locality. The viewing public, however, is no longer mass and anonymous, but defined by mutual participation—indeed, by performance. In this sense, which Benedict Anderson refers to as a growing sense of reading together, the public sphere emerges less from associations, more strictly the domain of civil society, than from ways of dealing confidently with others in an expanding social universe of shared communication.[26]

## Religious and Political Expression in Oman

Oman, after virtually no publicly expressed political dissent since the early 1970s, began in 1996 to witness public expressions of discontent in the form of occasional student demonstrations, anonymous leaflets, and other rather creative forms of public communication. Only in Oman has the occasional donkey, as in coastal al-Suwayq in spring 1998, been used as a mobile billboard to express anti-regime sentiments. There is no way in which police can maintain dignity in seizing and destroying a donkey on whose flank a political message has been inscribed.[27] Oman is in no imminent danger of being swept away on a tide of radical Islam. Nonetheless, Oman has an elaborate state apparatus that attempts to control religious expression. A review of Omani efforts suggest how states have lost the ability to control the public sphere, even if they have retained control of the formal communications media.

The rapid rise of mass education over a short time span in Oman has already been noted. Nearly 80 per cent of the population has basic literacy skills, with near-universal literacy for the younger generation.[28] The exposure of large numbers of young Omanis to a written, formal, "modern standard" Arabic through schooling and the mass media has altered the style and content of authoritative religious discourse and the role this discourse plays in shaping and constraining domestic and regional politics. One sign of this shift has been the re-emergence of sectarian discourse.

In Oman, like most other countries of the Arabian Peninsula, explicit controversy over political and religious issues does not form part of the standard fare of local newspapers or the broadcast media. The ruler's National Day speeches, the major annual occasion on which he addresses the Omani people, scrupulously avoid religious issues except to invoke "our heritage" (*turathuna*) and to pray to God "to guide us for the glory and prosperity of our dear countrymen."[29] Likewise, Islam forms part of the school curriculum at all levels, but the mention of sectarian differences is carefully avoided, as is also the case for the model Friday sermons that have been distributed for the guidance of preachers in Oman since 1983.[30] Reticence in articulating sectarian matters would at first appear to be prudent in Oman. Roughly 50–55 percent of its citizen population is Sunni, 40–45 per cent is Ibadhi, and less than 2 percent is Shia.

Direct, state-sanctioned discussion of sectarian issues occurs only rarely. A pivotal instance was a two-hour television "lesson" (*dars*) by Oman's Grand Mufti, Shaykh Ahmad bin Hamad al-Khalili, on 2 February 1987.[31]

To emphasize the event's significance, it was broadcast live from Sultan Qaboos University at "prime time," nine in the evening. The mufti's appearance on weekday television—his Friday sermons are broadcast regularly—was an unusual event, signaling approval at the highest levels of the state. The subsequent distribution of videotapes of the mufti's "lesson" to Omani student communities throughout the Arab world, Europe, and the United States further suggests the significance attributed to it. The content, context, and style of his lesson offer an exemplar of contemporary authoritative religious discourse and its role in domestic and regional politics. It also indicates the limits of state-authorized discourse.

Basically, al-Khalili was responding to a Saudi religious opinion (*fatwa*) issued 12 December 1986 (8 Rabia II 1407) by a senior Saudi religious scholar and member of the Saudi Supreme Council of Ulama, Abdulaziz bin Abdallah bin Baz. The issue at hand is obscure to secular modernists—whether or not the faithful would see God on Judgment Day. In essence, bin Baz argued that those who say that God will not be seen on Judgment Day—the Ibadhi perspective—deserve to be put to the sword.[32] Bin Baz wrote that the "mufti of the Ibadhis [a derogatory way of referring to the mufti of Oman] told me personally that the Ibadhis do not believe that God will be seen on Judgment Day. I tried to advise the Ibadhis to abandon this belief." In his televised lesson, al-Khalili read bin Baz's virulently anti-Ibadhi decree in full, even though it doubled as a personal attack on his scholarly integrity. The result was an unprecedented act of religious drama on Omani television that has not been repeated since.

Throughout his lesson—broadcast 13 years ago—Shaykh al-Khalili shifted between two levels of Arabic: a classical Arabic, full of citations from theological treatises, which even members of his audience educated in modern, secular Arabic admitted that they could not readily follow, and an Omanized but correct modern standard Arabic. Unusual for an Omani public appearance, the mufti used gestures, and his voice registered anger as he recounted his visit with a delegation of other Omanis to the office of Shaykh bin Baz on 13 January 1986 (2 Jumada I 1406), their second day in Saudi Arabia:

> We were anxious to benefit from [Shaykh al-Baz] and to listen to his advice and to learn from his words, but we were taken by surprise. . . . Immediately upon entering his office he took us to a narrow place and began . . .to shout [about] what he had heard [of my *fatwa*s]. . . . He referred to Ibadhism as astray and far from the truth that was brought by the prophet from God. I replied first by thanking him for his advice and then said:
> "Truth is claimed by everybody, and everyone who opposes his opponent claims that he is right and his opponent is wrong. But truth is not arrived at through presumptions but through correct proof. It is therefore our duty to reveal the truth through quite objective discussion to be transmitted to the people through the voice of the Quran in Makkah, and through the Saudi Television. Also other radio stations and television stations. . . ."
> The Shaykh strongly refused this suggestion. I asked him what he wanted and he said he wanted us to abandon our [beliefs] . . . and to adopt their [beliefs]. . . .I told him that if a Christian or a Jew or a Magian came to you and criticised Islam, would you refuse to discuss with him before listeners and viewers? He replied that Islam obliges such discussions only with non-Muslims.[33]

As one Shia Omani commented: "All Omanis stood with the mufti after his televised address. Before it, we heard rumors of what happened between him and bin Baz. The attack on him had nothing to do with sects in Islam. He was attacked as an Omani, and that is how we understood bin Baz's words. It was a national issue."[34]

The mufti repeated this dramatic confrontation many times in public appearances over the next two years, until the Iraqi invasion of Kuwait silenced virtually all public religious expression.[35] One such repetition of his controversy with bin Baz was an audiocassette subsequently translated into English and published in booklet form as *Who Are the Ibadhis?* Like the televised address, the booklet demonstrates a strong sense of an oppositional Ibadhism, elaborated in the explicit context of beliefs challenged by other Muslims. For the first time in modern Oman, the booklet offered a comprehensive account of contemporary Ibadhi belief, practice, and history.

The cassette/booklet responded to a letter from an Omani student in the United States. He wrote the mufti that some "Sunni brothers" in America warned against allowing Ibadhis to lead prayers or participate "in the administration of our mosques and Islamic Centers in this place on the claim that they are a section of the Khawarij."[36] The student asked for guidance in responding to such claims and "the reason for not circulating [Ibadhi] books and references in the libraries and in the Muslim Universities."

The mufti's televised address, like the pamphlet in English, is part of a more widespread movement throughout the Muslim world compelling the objectification of religious thought and practice. It is no longer sufficient to practice Islam; one must now be able to explain beliefs. Hence the utility of catechism-like documents such as *Who Are the Ibadhis?*

Clearly, mass education has had a major impact upon the style of religiosity of younger Omanis, even as state authorities seek to use education to preserve "traditional" values and to distance education from the political sphere. An unintended consequence of making Islam a part of the curriculum is implicitly to make it a subject alongside others that must be "explained" and "understood." However, treating Islam as a system of belief and practice implicitly highlights differences within the Muslim community. Before 1982, students from many of Oman's provinces had to complete the final years of secondary education in dormitories in the capital area. Moreover, outside of the classroom, students who were engaged in long discussions and debates on sectarian differences—however generic the formal curriculum may have been—were under pressure "not to convince the others to change their sect (*madhhab*), but to maintain our side (*tarafina*)."[37] Such discussion requires participants to emphasize the distinctive features of their respective beliefs. As the student's letter to Shaykh Ahmad indicates, the awareness of sectarian differences is accentuated even more when Ibadhi Muslims are juxtaposed with their counterparts from other Muslim groups, sometimes perceived as hostile or misinformed outside of Oman.

Participation in Muslim societies and study groups, and exposure to video and audiocassettes and the books and literature of various groups, shifts shared perceptions of Islamic thought and the context in which it is shaped. Although a seemingly obvious point, it should be kept in mind that ready access to the printed word, or to expositions of Islamic doctrine in a modern standard Arabic, again largely derived from modern education and radio and television, is a recent development for most Omanis.

## The Limits of State Guidance

In Oman, a significant shift in religious and political sensibilities began in the early 1980s, when young Omanis throughout the country began to ask for such seemingly apolitical amenities as libraries in the youth clubs associated with every major town and village, and for provisions to be made for Friday sermons. The move to open libraries was often met with suspicion, as those most interested were university students active in various Islamic community organizations outside of Oman. Permission was often denied under various pretexts.

The movement to institute Friday sermons at mosques throughout the Sultanate constituted a more subtle challenge to state authority. The reasons given for the movement are impeccably Islamic. As one of Oman's first generation of village schoolteachers observed of the northern Oman interior in the mid-1980s, "People here do not know Islam; they pray and sacrifice, but they do not know why."[38] Before the mid-1970s, such a statement would have been almost incomprehensible in most of the towns and villages of the Omani interior and coast. By the late 1980s, however, such statements had become common.

When the movement to institute Friday sermons began, persons with a sufficient command of formal Arabic to engage in public speaking sought access to the pulpits in some communities. Such uses of the *minbar* (pulpit) aroused considerable concern in official circles. As one official explained, if access to the minbar is not controlled, then the "uneducated," who are not aware of what is and is not appropriate to sermons, will take anything said in the sermon to be authoritative. Because a good preacher can sway emotions, it is all the more important to ensure that what he says is based upon "sound" religious knowledge: "The preacher (*khatib*) can draw upon his own experience for his sermons, but he must elaborate only the ideas of Islam, not other ideas, so no mention of television programs, of AIDS, or of political issues."[39]

Friday sermons now fall under state supervision, albeit usually through the adroit use of local kinship and community ties so that this supervision does not appear entirely alien or intrusive. In the process, state authorities are becoming aware that their actions can shape religious discourse but not control it. In many regions, the consequence of state intervention has been to shift more radical religious discourse away from mosques and into informal discussion groups among trusted peers. In this respect, the proliferation of teachers' training schools and other forms of education have played an important role in creating cross-regional ties of village teachers and others who influence events in their respective communities and share information on implicit government policies and personalities.

Formal political authority in Oman remains as it was before the coup: an absolute monarchy—the Omani state encourages modernization, renewal, and transformation in all other spheres except that of selection for rule at the top. Even in this sphere, the rhetoric of modern legitimacy requires a commitment to change. The Sultanate's slow progress through State Consultative Councils, initiated in the early 1980s and gradually expanded, gives a semblance of transparency to governmental actions.[40] Since 1997, limited protests have taken place in Oman, the first since the early 1970s. These serve as a reminder that even when the state controls expression in the formal media, the movement of ideas and people means that state authorities are losing their hold over people's imaginations. Indeed, even if consultative councils such as Oman's are regarded by some of the newly educated as "talking shops" with no real decision-making authority, their very presence suggests an awareness on the part of the government of the need for greater transparency.[41] Televised questions to ministers are never spontaneous, and most members of the audience are aware of this limitation. These broadcasts, contrasted with what is known of comparable bodies elsewhere, remind viewers of the differences between their consultative council and similar bodies in the region.

As Oman's ruler has said, "It will be a very happy day for me when more people will take responsibilities from my shoulders. But we have to take into consideration the situation of our culture, our religious heritage and guidance, our traditions."[42] At another level, there is blunt and open criticism of the state and its key personnel, in the form of anonymous pamphlets and leaflets circulated by fax and left throughout the capital area.[43] Such documents show the raw edges of the "new era" of unfettered information.

Another less sensational but equally significant indicator of change beneath the surface is exemplified in such documents as a modest booklet by an Omani municipal judge, *What Knowledge of the Law Means to You*.[44] In a catechism-like question-and-answer format, the first of its kind for Oman, the booklet sets out a citizen's basic rights, and the limits of police authority. Such a document requires judges who can write accessible prose and assumes a readership. Such initiatives are becoming more common throughout the Gulf, and presage a change in ideas of rule and authority both profound and far-reaching, implying the growth not only of the public sphere but also of civil society.

## Conclusion

In the end, these shifts in background understandings of religion and politics may not always appear dramatic, but they suggest sea changes in understandings of legitimate authority. Until the eighteenth century, most of the world's population was subject to royal authority. Since then, the number of ruling monarchs has steadily declined, with their replacements claiming authority directly from "the people."[45] However, with the exception of the Yemen Arab Republic, the states of the Arabian Peninsula remain monarchies. Unlike earlier times, however, both rulers and their subjects are profoundly aware of competing principles for justifying authority, and the shifting contexts in which royal authority is asserted, thus creating new and significant challenges.

Ruling monarchs have not become an endangered species on the Arabian Peninsula. Yet, in sharp contrast with past epochs, their subjects are profoundly aware of alternatives to dynastic rule. Even if some monarchs privately assert a divine mandate, publicly they stress their unique vocation to guide the nation's destiny. The late Shah of Iran went so far as to assert that Persian kingship was based on the will of the people, and that Iran would never be devoid of a monarch because of his people's "customs, habits, history [and] religion."[46] Slogans such as the late Shah's "Revolution of the Shah and the People" and Hassan II's (Morocco) "Revolution of the King and the People" may have been considered banal by some subjects and hypocritical by others. Still, the existence of these slogans a quarter century ago implicitly acknowledged that claims to legitimacy increasingly intimate the ability of monarchs and ruling families to self-transform and widen the base of participation in government.

Consultative councils and national assemblies, both appointive and elected, have proliferated throughout the Arabian Peninsula as a result of changing domestic attitudes and the need to persuade Western supporters of local regimes that they are capable of self-transformation. Nevertheless, the pace of institutional change may not match that of the background understandings of civil society and democracy now current in the public sphere of the Gulf states, but both rulers and subjects are increasingly aware of the disparity between the public sphere and the current prospects for civil society.

## Notes

1. Ernest Gellner, *Nations and Nationalism,* Ithaca: Cornell University Press, 1983, pp. 28–29.
2. "Shaykh Muhammad al-Utayman, "A Discussion of Incendiary Publications: Whoever Publishes These Leaflets and Pamphlets, Copies Them, or Distributes Them Commits a Major Sin and Bears Responsibility for His Own Crime and for the Crime of All Those Influenced by Them," (in Arabic), *Al-Sharq al-Awsat,* 20 November 1994.
3. Olivier Roy, "Le Post-Islamisme," *Revue des Mondes Musulmans et de la Méditerranée,* numbers 85/86 (1999), pp. 11–30.
4. Fariba Adelkhah, *Being Modern in Iran,* New York: Columbia University Press, 2000, p. 177.
5. Mary Ann Tetreault, "Just Say No: Women's Rights in Kuwait," *Current History* 99: 699, January 2000, pp. 27–32.
6. Seymour Martin Lipset, "The Social Requisites of Democracy Revisited," *American Sociological Review* 59: 1, February 1994, p. 6.
7. For example, Abdallah Hammoudi, *Master and Disciple: The Cultural Foundations of Moroccan Authoritarianism,* Chicago and London: University of Chicago Press, 1997, p. 8; see also Hisham Sharabi, *Neopatriarchy: A Theory of Distorted Change in Arab Society,* New York: Oxford University Press, 1988.
8. U.S. Department of State, "1999 Country Reports on Human Rights Practices: Oman," at <http://www.state.gov/www/global/human_rights/1999_hrp_report/oman.html>
9. Dale F. Eickelman, "Mass Higher Education and the Religious Imagination in Contemporary Arab Societies," *American Ethnologist* 19: 4, November 1992, pp. 643–55.
10. Sultanate of Oman, Ministry of Development, *Statistical Year Book, 1996,* Muscat: Ministry of Development, 1997, p. 541, and prior editions.
11. Interview with Dr. Faisal al-Kassim, Doha, 20 March 1999.
12. Manuel Castells, *The Rise of the Network Society,* Malden, Massachusetts: Blackwell, 1996.
13. John B. Alterman, *New Media, New Politics? From Satellite Television to the Internet in the Arab World,* Washington, D.C.: The Washington Institute for Near East Policy, 1998, p. 15.
14. Craig Calhoun, "Introduction," in *Habermas and the Public Sphere,* Cambridge, Massachusetts: MIT Press, 1991, p. 7.
15. Dale F. Eickelman and Jon W. Anderson, "Redefining Muslim Publics," in *New Media in the Muslim World: The Emerging Public Sphere,* Dale F. Eickelman and Jon W. Anderson (eds.), Bloomington: Indiana University Press, 1999, pp. 1–28.
16. Dominique Colas, *Civil Society and Fanaticism: Conjoined Histories,* Stanford, California: Stanford University Press, 1997.
17. Andrew Hammond, "Al-Jazeera to Set Up in Egypt," Reuters, 17 April 2000.
18. Alterman, *New Media,* pp. 26–29.
19. John F. Burns, "Arab TV Gets a New Slant: Newscasts without Censorship," *New York Times,* 4 July 1999, pp. A1, A6.
20. DFE interview with Faisal al-Kassim, 30 October 1999.
21. DFE interview with Faisal al-Kassim, 20 March 1999.
22. Sulayman bin Jazi' al-Shamri, *Barnamij al-Ittijah al-Mu'akis: Dirasa 'Ilmiyya Akadamiya* [The "Opposite Direction" Program: An Academic Study], Riyadh: Department of Information, King Saud University, 1998.
23. Jerusalem Media and Communication Center, *Palestinian Opinion Pulse* 1: 33, November 1999, p. 9, based on JMCC polls carried out on 21 and 22 October 1999.
24. Charles Taylor, "Modernity and the Rise of the Public Sphere," in *The Tanner Lectures on Human Values,* volume 14, 1993, p. 213.

25. Alfred Schutz, *Collected Papers I: The Problem of Social Reality*, edited by Maurice Natanson, The Hague: Martinus Nijhoff, 1967, pp. 15–19.
26. Benedict Anderson, *Imagined Communities: Reflections on the Origin and Spread of Nationalism*, London: Verso, 1991, pp. 37–46.
27. An incident reported to have happened in al-Suwayq, an oasis in the Batinah region, March 1998.Interview, Muscat, 19 June 1998.As economic conditions improved in Oman, donkeys became redundant to the local agricultural economy, and increasingly were set free to forage on garbage and other "found" sustenance. Hence their availability for displaying political messages inscribed on their flanks. An Iraqi colleague challenges the uniqueness of this Omani initiative, saying that the same vehicle was earlier used in southern Iraq, following the Iraqi defeat in Kuwait in 1991.
28. U.S. Central Intelligence Agency, *World Factbook 1999*, "Oman," at <http://www.cia.gov/cia/publications/factbook/mu.html>.
29. Text of the seventeenth annual National Day speech, 15 November 1987, as reported in the *Times of Oman*, 19 November 1987, p. 2.
30. For textbooks, see, for example, Sultanate of Oman, Ministry of Education, *Al-Tarbiyya al-Islamiyya* [Islamic Education], 1st intermediate level, 4th ed., Muscat: Ministry of Information, 1985.The 1983 sermons have been collected in a book, *Al-Muwahab al-Sunniyya fil-Khutab al-Jam'iyya* [The Sanctioned Traditional Gift of Friday Sermons], part 1, edited by Ahmad bin Hamad al-Khalili, Muscat: Ministry of Justice, Awqaf and Islamic Affairs, 1983.Later sermons have been issued in monthly booklets.
31. Videotape supplied by the Embassy of the Sultanate of Oman, Washington. For a detailed analysis of this talk and its significance, see Dale F. Eickelman, "Identité nationale et discours religieux en Oman," in Gilles Kepel and Yann Richard (eds.), *Intellectuels et militants de l'Islam contemporain*, Paris: Seuil, 1990, pp. 103–28.Part of this account is a revised version of this earlier analysis.
32. Shaykh Ahmad identified bin Baz's fatwa as number 772, dated 8/3/1407.
33. Ahmed bin Hamed al-Khalili, *Who Are the Ibadhis?* translated by Ahmed Hamoud al-Maamiry, Zanzibar: Al-Khayira Press, n.d. [1988?]), pp. 23–24.This pamphlet repeats the passages of the videotape almost verbatim.
34. Interview, London, 16 June 1987.
35. Harith al-Ghassany, "Kitman and Renaissance: Domination and the Limits of Development," doctoral dissertation presented to the Departments of Middle Eastern Studies and Anthropology, Harvard University, 1995, p. 2.
36. The letter is reproduced on p. 1 of the pamphlet. The charge that the Ibadhis are part of the Khariji movement originating in the first Islamic century is standard in sectarian polemic. Actually, the Ibadhis originated as a breakaway sect from the Khariji movement and rejected the Khariji tenet that all non-Kharijis were infidels who merited death. Except for strict Ibadhi adherence to the early traditions of the Muslim community and the Sunna, and Ibadhi views on religious and political leadership, Ibadhi and Sunni doctrine coincide in most major respects. Other minor differences include the required movements during the obligatory prayers, the lack until recently of minarets in Ibadhi mosques, and the absence, again until recently, of Friday sermons (*khutbas*). See Dale F. Eickelman, "Ibadhism and the Sectarian Perspective," in B. R. Pridham (ed.), *Oman: Economic, Social and Strategic Developments*, London: Croom Helm, 1987, pp. 31–50.
37. Interview with an Omani student, New York, 20 May 1985.
38. Interview, Nizwa region, 9 March 1988.
39. Interview, Ministry of Justice official, 22 March 1988.Many younger officials have studied in Europe and the United States and are fully aware of competing Muslim discourses.
40. Dale F. Eickelman, "Kings and People: Oman's State Consultative Council," *The Middle East Journal* 38: 1, winter 1984, pp. 51–71.Initially appointive only, the Council was later relaunched, with limited suffrage, which continues to expand.See "Oman Widens Council Ballot, More Women Get Vote," Reuters, 15 April 2000.
41. Interview, 21 June 1998.
42. "How the Sultan Sees the Tasks Ahead," *The Financial Times*, Oman Survey, 13 January 1983.These comments are identical to ones published earlier in Arabic in "Sultan Qaboos to *al-Majalla*," *Al-Majalla* (London), 1 May 1982, p. 17.
43. Undated, anonymous leaflet beginning (in Arabic) with "The fury is unleashed, O Qaboos, and the time has come for the people to rise up . . ."

44. Khalifah bin Muhammad bin Abdallah al-Hadhrami, *Ma Yuhimmak Ma'rifatihi Min al-Qanun* [What Knowledge of the Law Means to You], Muscat: privately printed, 1999.
45. Reinhard Bendix, *Kings or People: Power and the Mandate to Rule,* Berkeley and Los Angeles: University of California Press, 1978.
46. Cited in E. A. Bayne, *Persian Kingship in Transition: Conversations with a Monarch,* New York: American Universities Field Staff, Inc., 1968, p. 61.

# PART II

*Regional Concerns*

# BORDER DISPUTES

CHAPTER 13

## *Down to the Usual Suspects:*
## *Border and Territorial Disputes in the Arabian Peninsula and Persian Gulf at the Millennium**

Richard Schofield

Many of the contemporary headlines dealing with Arabian land boundary issues (with the exception, perhaps, of the Saudi-Yemen boundary question) should be seen in a regional context in which states are striding actively to finalize the political map. It should be remembered that the majority of Arabian states have experienced full independence only very recently and that, in most cases, territorial limits have had to be negotiated and finalized. Indeed, the relevance of the postmodern discourse on territory and boundaries to this area seems spurious at best. Never mind de-territorialization (as some would argue is occurring within the European context) or re-territorialization (as has clearly occurred with the collapse of empire and the rise of ethno-nationalism in the Caucasus and the former Yugoslav federation); the prerequisite process of territorialization has not yet been completed among the states of the region. While four GCC states have fully implemented that regional organization's customs union agreement—in a sense, a step toward de-territorialization—the eastern three-quarters of the boundary between Saudi Arabia and Yemen has only just been established, and the Oman–United Arab Emirates land border remains to be absolutely finalized.

In many ways, another set of considerations applies to the seemingly intractable set of disputes surrounding or lying across Gulf waters. Arab-Iranian rivalry has often found expression in territorial disputes, and in this respect, it is probably little coincidence that the Shatt al-Arab dispute between Iraq and Iran and the Lower Gulf islands dispute between Iran and the United Arab Emirates (UAE) remain alive to varying degrees. Cynics in the region and elsewhere tiring of a half-decade of stalemate in the latter dispute might ultimately question

---

*This paper was written in the spring of 2000. Since that time, there have been important developments, such as the conclusion of a Saudi-Yemeni boundary treaty in June 2000 and, more recently still, the issue by the International Court of Justice of an award for the Bahrain-Qatar maritime boundary in March 2001. These developments are covered in the conclusion to this chapter.

the desire of each party to see it settled. After all, there is an element of safety and convenience in channeling regional rivalries through island sovereignty disputes and therefore, some might argue, a possible value in keeping them less than fully settled. As Victor Prescott commented in 1987, an international boundary always represents the potential for both conflict and cooperation,[1] though its utility will normally be greatest in this respect if it is not subject to a binding agreement that has been signed, sealed, and delivered.[2]

When considering Arab-Iranian boundary and territorial disputes, it is well to recall Jacques Ancel's perennially applicable observation that "there are no problems of boundaries, only problems of nations."[3] In other words, disputes over boundaries and territory are frequently little more than the physical manifestation of wider but perhaps less tangible differences and rivalries between states. While this view might be accurate when looking at these disputes in isolation, it does little to explain Iraq's long-established dissatisfaction with its narrow shoreline and its lack of access to Gulf waters, a geostrategic predicament that has clearly been a factor in recent decades of conflict in the northern Gulf. Here, the positioning of its international boundaries with both Iran and Kuwait has given rise to a negative Iraqi mentality concerning access and communications, even if most of the problems historically may have been more perceived than real. Stephen Jones's rather gory imagery of 1945 helps shed more light on this perspective, whereby "a boundary, like the human skin, may have diseases of its own or reflect the illnesses of the body."[4] Boundaries can therefore be both the source and the symbol of disputes.

## Behind the Headlines in 2000

A brief tour d'horizon is necessary to establish the contemporary importance of territorial questions in the Gulf (Map 13.1).

### *The Saudi Arabia–Yemen Border*

Serious incidents continued recently to occur along the Saudi-Yemeni borderlands, most notably and recently the military clash of January 2000 in the mountains of Asir, which resulted in two Yemeni fatalities.[5]

Before June 2000, one could make a strong case for arguing that, of all Arabian territorial issues excepting the Iraq-Kuwait boundary, the Saudi-Yemeni boundary question presented potentially the greatest challenge to regional stability. It may still (see conclusion). Bilateral negotiations have been ongoing (if intermittently) since the summer of 1992 toward finalizing Arabia's last indeterminate territorial limit. Although progress toward nominating the last missing fence in the desert has been painfully slow, there have been some notable developments, especially in the half-decade since the 1994 Yemeni civil war. First, the February 1995 memorandum of understanding (MoU) recommitted the two sides to the existing 1934 Treaty of Taif line in the west, while establishing a procedural framework for addressing the remainder of the border to the east. In the summer of 1996, during a session of the joint committees introduced by the 1995 MoU, Yemen forwarded a traditional boundary claim, the first occasion

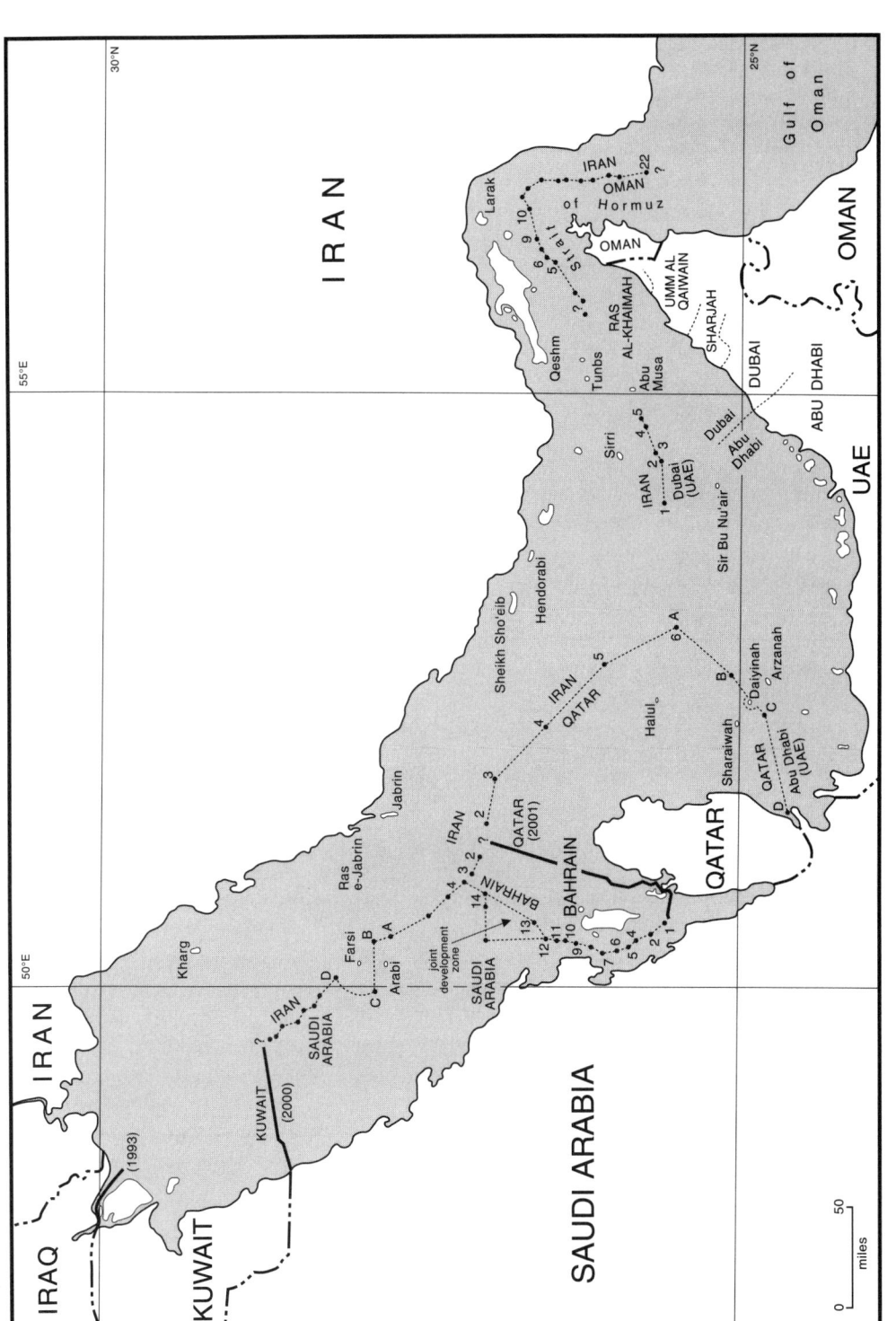

upon which a Sanaa government had ever issued a cartographically depictable claim to the indeterminate borderlands. The result was a considerable overlap in Saudi and Yemeni territorial claims (Map 13.2). There were reports that the basis of an agreement had been reached on the shores of Lake Como in late 1997, which would apparently have seen a line introduced to effectively bisect the area of overlapping claims. This would have been a delimitation that would have run in a straight line westward from the Saudi-Yemeni-Omani tripoint in the east to a point to the northeast of Jabal al-Thar (the eastern terminus of the 1934 Taif line) in the west.

Yet, with time, it seems clear that the Como agreement was not the breakthrough that it portended to be. Serious incidents continue to occur along the length and breadth of the borderlands on land and sea. Furthermore, these incidents have been violent, with significant losses of life—best illustrated by the Duwaima island episode in the summer of 1998, and the renewed hostilities along the Taif line in January 2000. Though all the right diplomatic signals are issued about progress having been made in sessions of the boundary delimitation committees, the reality confirms that a negotiated settlement of the boundary is still some way off. Hence the surprise generated by the June 2000 agreement (see conclusion). Noticeably, in the half-decade since the 1995 MoU, a pattern has emerged of impasse, incident, and high-level patch-up. Impasse will be reached in the routine sessions of the boundary committees. This will typically be broken by a violent flare-up somewhere along the borderlands, after which senior political figures from Riyadh and Sanaa will convene to address the immediate negative political fall-out and to re-inject some momentum into the border negotiations. It is to be hoped that this largely negative and unproductive cycle can be broken in the future.

## *The Iran-UAE Islands Dispute*

There continue to be occasional reports of possible initiatives to free the Iran-UAE dispute over the Lower Gulf islands of Abu Musa and the Tunbs from its current stalemated status. Just as often, the war of words associated with this dispute periodically becomes heated, though this is hardly a new phenomenon.

Soon after its resurrection following Iranian heavy-handedness on Abu Musa island in 1992, the Iran-UAE dispute over the sovereignty of the Lower Gulf islands crystallized into a stalemated war of words. Support lent to any peaceful efforts the UAE might undertake to restore its sovereignty over the three islands (typically by the GCC at year-end summits) would ordinarily be greeted in Teheran by trophic blasts of defiance. The assertion that the UAE would have to "cross a sea of blood" to recover the features has been an almost standard Iranian counter-statement, albeit a particularly graphic and symbolic one designed predominantly for domestic consumption.

In the mid-1990s the UAE enjoyed real success in internationalizing the Lower Gulf islands dispute, but, ironically, its chances of regaining full control over the islands probably diminished. For the UAE's very success would engender a defensive posture in Iran, and the adoption of the islands question as a national issue, one inextricably linked to regime legitimacy. Indeed, for much of the

**Map 13.2** Saudi-Yemeni Boundary

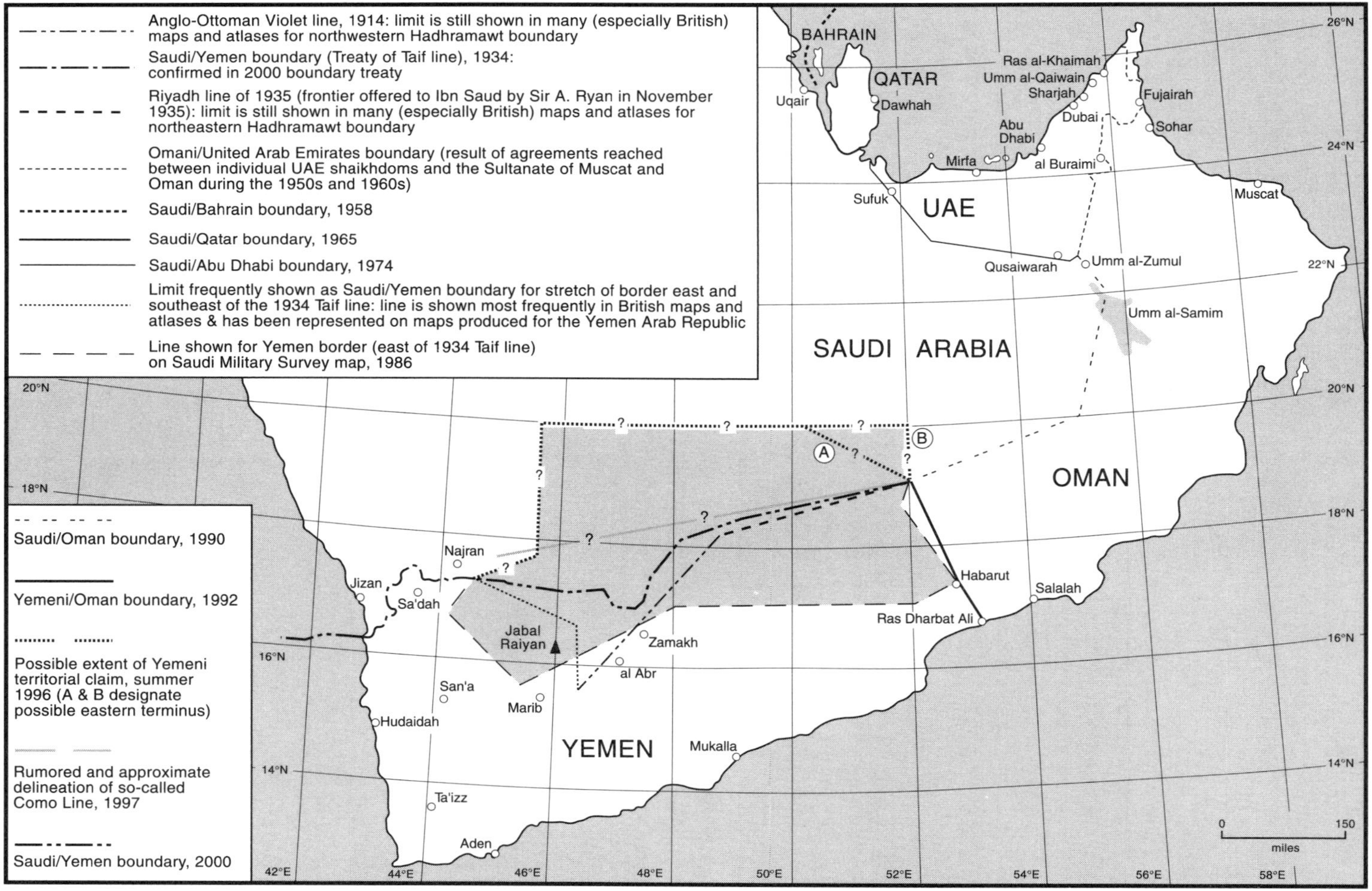

1990s, the Lower Gulf islands dispute would play a symbolic role as the focus of Arab-Iranian rivalries across Gulf waters. This was a position traditionally experienced by the Iran-Iraq dispute over the Shatt al-Arab river boundary, but with Iraq's regional and international isolation since 1990, the gaze moved southward.

To be sure, there has always been a strong "window of opportunity" aspect to the resurrected Lower Gulf islands dispute. In the medium term, presuming Iraq's eventual re-integration within the Arab fold, it seems likely that the Shatt al-Arab dispute (currently dormant rather than resolved) will resume its traditional symbolic role as a barometer of Arab-Iranian relations, and the current concentration on the islands dispute will dilute. The focus on the islands dispute is already blurring, however, as a consequence of a tentative but tangible shift in the power dynamics of the region—best illustrated by the emerging Saudi/Iranian entente of the last two years. It is within this bigger regional picture that the UAE has charged Riyadh with failing to fully support its claims to the islands. Notwithstanding the creation of a special GCC subcommittee (that includes Qatar and Oman), whose task is to promote a peaceful settlement of the dispute, there is a feeling amongst some UAE officials that the window of opportunity is narrowing and that, after eight years in the limelight, the islands question is not the regional issue it once was.

### The Bahrain-Qatar Row

In December 1999 Bahrain and Qatar pledged to conduct full diplomatic relations for the first time and, since that time, have made encouraging noises about trying to reach an "out of court" settlement of their dispute over the sovereignty of the Hawar islands, the Dibal and Jaradeh shoals, and the locality of Zubarah.

Since December 1999, at least on the formal level, relations between Manama and Doha seem to have improved dramatically. While this has led some to speculate that the long-established and intransigent dispute over the Hawar islands might be settled bilaterally, it is probably more accurate to assert that these are moves typical of states whose disputes are about to be decided upon by international courts. Though many verdicts passed down over the years by the International Court of Justice (ICJ) have been characterized by a degree of fudging, every case—to a lesser or greater extent—has a winner and a loser. The recent "breakthrough" in Bahraini-Qatari relations should be seen, therefore, as an acknowledgment that each side realizes that it may lose, and that it is prepared for such an outcome. Court hearings in The Hague were scheduled for late May 2000 and ran for five weeks. The ICJ verdict would ultimately be issued on 16 March 2001 (see conclusion).

Importantly, the dynamics seemed to have changed in this boundary dispute as well. For the three years before the ICJ ruled—in July 1994—that it did, after all, possess jurisdiction to try this dispute (and for at least a year thereafter), Bahrain stalled. As the court was about to rule on ownership of the features—while the Hawar islands (save for Zubarah) were occupied by Manama—which Britain had previously recognized as belonging to the island state, Bahrain had everything to lose and Qatar everything to gain. Indeed, Bahraini perceptions were clarified when, in February 1995, a senior government official commented that the features in question would be relinquished to Qatar (should the ICJ have ruled in its favor) "over our dead bodies." Yet, recent developments have given Bahrain a greater appetite for the fray, notably Qatar's request that the ICJ "disregard" 82 pieces of documentary evidence contained within its memorial and counter-memorial, after their provenance had been questioned by Manama. Never before has the authenticity of evidence played such a prominent role in the history of boundary cases before the ICJ.

## *The Oman-UAE Border Accord*
In the last week of March 2000, Oman and the UAE announced the ratification of the May 1999 Oman-UAE (Abu Dhabi) boundary agreement and added that the territorial limit would be demarcated in the near future.[6]

This development should be seen in the context of the great strides made to finalize the Arabian territorial framework during the last decade. It represents part of the process of rounding off sharp edges that has continued since the mid-1990s, following the large-scale material progress achieved through the conclusion of international boundary agreements in the first half of the decade. There are other recent developments that can be placed in this "icing on the cake" category. For instance, there were relatively lavish celebrations during 1994 and 1995 to greet the completion of the demarcation of the Oman-Yemen land boundary and the production of a detailed series of maps by a joint Omani-Saudi survey team of the delimitation agreed back in 1990. Further north, it would not be until June 1999 that the demarcation of the Qatar–Saudi Arabia delimitation would be completed, despite this measure having been agreed upon seven years earlier (December 1992), in the context of Egyptian mediation of the Khafus incident in September of that year.

As for the Oman-UAE boundary, it must be stated that while there are no major issues in dispute between the two states, the delimitation has not yet been wholly finalized. It has evolved in a piecemeal fashion since the late 1950s, with agreement having been reached at various stages on various parts of the boundary, especially during the period before the proclamation of the UAE in December 1971. The May 1999 agreement concerning the Abu Dhabi–Oman border was in itself a delayed implementation of the announcement, made some six years earlier by the Omani government, that this delimitation had been settled as the result of "a lasting agreement" between the two states. A final agreement has apparently still to be reached on delimitation between Oman and the Qasimi emirates of Sharjah and Ras al-Khaimah, after which time one might expect to see a further and final Oman-UAE agreement, ratifying all the earlier agreements and understandings reached since the late 1950s.

## *The Iraq-Kuwait Boundary*
In recent months, there have also been a number of comments in the Gulf media recognizing that the question of Iraqi access to the Gulf may well resurface, notwithstanding the May 1993 United Nations award for the Iraq-Kuwait boundary.

Understandably, given its hugely traumatic experience at Iraqi hands, Kuwait adopted—at least officially—something of an ostrich mentality with respect to its northern neighbor for much of the 1990s. Yet if Baghdad considers itself a geographically disadvantaged state with its meager shoreline in the northern Gulf, Kuwait, too, can claim to be locationally challenged, surrounded as it is by the dominant regional powers of Iran, Iraq, and Saudi Arabia.

Exceptionally, the Iraq-Kuwait boundary is guaranteed against physical infraction by the United Nations, as Baghdad accepted—without equivocation—the UN ruling in November 1994. In terms of international law, this territorial limit is finalized, but the degree to which it can therefore be considered as a "solved" regional problem is open to question, especially since Iraqi claims on Kuwaiti territory had such a vexed history before they culminated in the disastrous 2 August 1990 move.

Moreover, and despite a history of dispute and conflict, Iraqi-Kuwaiti relations have also been characterized by limited functional cooperation in the economic sphere. Consequently, a much greater measure of regional economic integration in the northern Gulf than has hitherto been achieved seems the best means to ensure against future conflict. This is the emerging consensus among Gulf intellectuals addressing the question of Iraqi access to the Gulf.

## Finalizing the 1990s Arabian Political Map

Having undertaken this regional review, it is important to underline the degree and nature of progress made toward finalizing the Arabian political map during the 1990s.[7]

### *Bilateral Boundary Agreements*

Through the conclusion of bilateral boundary agreements, especially within southeastern Arabia—Saudi Arabia–Oman (1990), Oman-Yemen (1992), and Oman–United Arab Emirates (1999)—Muscat, Riyadh, and Abu Dhabi have gone a long way to finalizing their boundary delimitation. Oman's recent boundary agreements have also rightly been lauded for their sophistication in providing for free trans-boundary movements for the nomadic populations of southeastern Arabia. Likewise, the Iraq-Kuwait boundary has been settled in international law, while the ICJ will probably deliver its verdict in the Bahrain-Qatar case by the end of 2000. Meanwhile, Saudi Arabia and Yemen continue to negotiate their respective territorial limits astride the Rub al-Khali. As discussed above, the progress of the late 1990s consisted of tidying up loose ends following the conclusion of bilateral treaties earlier in the decade, or rounding off key sharp edges created by boundary incidents (e.g., Khafus in September 1992) that had occurred during the process of finalizing limits to state territory.

Compared to this momentum toward finalizing Arabian land boundaries, there has been nowhere near as much progress in completing the maritime political geography of the Gulf. Excluding the 1993 United Nations Iraq-Kuwait Boundary Demarcation Commission award of a median line along the

Khor Abdallah (which, for some reason, was not extended fully to the mouth of that water inlet proper), there have been no continental shelf boundary agreements concluded since 1974 (Map 13.2). Although there are a number of reasons for this state of affairs, the existence of territorial disputes over three groups of islands (Umm al-Maradim and Qaru in the northern Gulf between Kuwait and Saudi Arabia, the Hawar islands and shoals dispute between Bahrain and Qatar, and the Lower Gulf islands dispute between Iran and the UAE) is clearly preventing the conclusion of maritime boundary delimitation between these states. Indeed, after their eight-year long war, Iran and Iraq have failed to conclude a maritime boundary agreement of their own.

Still, there is (and has been for some time) the promise of progress. The International Court of Justice would not only adjudicate on the ownership of various insular formations lying between Bahrain and Qatar, but would also announce a maritime boundary delimitation between the two states, later in 2000. For their part, Saudi Arabia and Kuwait have repeatedly stated that the announcement of a maritime boundary delimitation is imminent. It was back in October 1995, in point of fact, that delegations from Kuwait and Saudi Arabia began the latest round of discussions toward this end, though it would seem that the two sides have so far failed to reach agreement upon how the sovereignty of Umm al-Maradim and Qaru should be broached in advance of the drawing of any maritime delimitation. Importantly, in May 1995, the Iranian ambassador to Kuwait also announced Teheran's preparedness to tackle the problem of finalizing maritime boundaries in the northern Gulf. In the fall of 1995, the Kuwaiti government confirmed that an agreement had been reached in principle to commence negotiations toward this end. The onset of these agreements is dependent upon a successful conclusion of the ongoing (and seemingly stalled) negotiations between Kuwait and Saudi Arabia on national maritime limits.[8]

When discussing existing maritime boundaries within Gulf waters, the point also needs to be made that the agreements that introduced them are dated by modern standards. There is no single agreement in which a geodetic datum set is specified. Datums in all cases are spheroidal/ellipsoidal, reflecting Britain's long influence and continuing presence in the region. In fact, the crudity and paucity of the information that comprises the datums used to draw charts upon which maritime boundary delimitation have been drawn indicate that there is, in practice, a huge error factor in physically locating exactly where these limits lie in Gulf waters.[9] This is a problem that is distracting oil companies when identifying seismic lines or drilling for oil. Where exactly is the boundary? In short, it is currently impossible to determine. Since the conclusion of maritime boundary agreements in the Gulf, the advent of global positioning systems has made possible the realistic relation of national datums to an appropriate global reference within acceptable limits of accuracy. Thus, the margin for error in trying to physically locate a maritime delimitation has potentially been reduced from hundreds of meters (as is now the case with the region's agreements) to a matter of centimeters. There is a strong case, therefore, for suggesting that all existing maritime boundary agreements be modified in light of these technological advances.

### Norms of International Law

The texts of agreements reached in the early 1990s (and some agreed at a much earlier stage, e.g., Saudi Arabia–Qatar [1965]) have increasingly been registered at what the international legal community regards as the appropriate international institutions—typically the United Nations Secretariat in New York. This is, indeed, a recent phenomenon. One observer commented as early as 1991 that the Saudis, for example, had been "reluctant to finalize their agreements according to those international rules which would entitle them to consider that their arrangements constituted a permanent feature of the international map."[10] The position has now changed to the degree that Riyadh can now point to the fact that it has renegotiated or modified all of the territorial understandings concluded between Ibn Saud and the British (or frequently imposed by the latter) during the early part of the century. This is doubtless of importance to the Kingdom. The growing evidence that the territorial framework has evolved to a point of no return should also reassure Saudi Arabia's small but historically mindful neighbors along the western/southern Gulf littoral. Iraq has not been the only territorially acquisitive state within the region!

### Regional and Institutional Considerations

GCC states have been preoccupied, since 1991, with the further entrenchment, institutionalization, and, where appropriate, finalization of the Arabian territorial framework. GCC policy toward the resolution of Arabian disputes, and the finalization of the political map of the region, has not been proactive but reactive. In fact, it has been, and will probably continue to be, a response to regional instability. Moreover, GCC states have focused on the need for the tidy appropriation of natural resources.

Against this background, the March 1991 Damascus Declaration (concluded among the six GCC states, Egypt, and Syria) remains an important statement of policy, principle, and intent, as far as the regulation of state territory in the region is concerned. To further strengthen their rapidly evolving positions, the following measures were explicitly promoted: greater regulation of existing borders; the peaceful resolution of disputes; respect for international law, mutual non-interference and good-neighborliness. In the aftermath of the "resurrection" of the Lower Gulf islands dispute in 1992, a further principle was added to these: the "inadmissibility of the acquisition of land by force."[11] Noticeably, the fifteenth Manama GCC summit meeting (December 1994) was not so clear on the enunciation of any new principles regulating limits to state territory, reiterating the apparent keenness of the Supreme Council to see territorial disputes between member states and neighbors settled peacefully. Yet, and significantly in relation to the ICJ's recent treatment of the Bahrain-Qatar territorial dispute, the GCC appeared to favor bilateral negotiations, as opposed, for instance, to arbitration or judicial settlement. With time, however, these developments would prove to be less significant than they had initially appeared. This had everything to do with the discernible tendency for statements of GCC territorial policy to reflect the immediate and foreign policy concerns of the states hosting annual summit meetings. Thus Bahrain's "interest" in keeping the

Hawar dispute from being treated in The Hague had been instrumental in late 1994.

It should also be stressed that pragmatic considerations have been fueling much of the progress toward finalizing the political map during the last decade. Beginning in the early 1990s, several Arabian states embarked upon exploration drives for hydrocarbons in border regions, many of which were still indeterminate. Because of their politically sensitive location and general remoteness, these fields had generally been ignored prior to this point, but the economic imperatives of maximizing production in a flat oil market and of compensating for the maturing of older fields were now to outweigh such considerations. In such circumstances, the need for precise and unambiguous boundary definitions was clear, so that states could safely prospect and develop resources right up to the limits of their territories. This process has also produced boundary incidents (e.g., the 1992 Khafus border post incident between Saudi Arabia and Qatar) and disputes over how existing treaties cater to trans-boundary resources—best illustrated by the UAE's boycott of the opening of the trans-boundary Shaybah (Saudi Arabia) oil field in 1999. Only four-fifths of this field lies within Saudi territory, but the 1974 boundary treaty between the two states specifies that the Kingdom has the rights to all of its resources.

## Down to the Usual Suspects

The disputes that confront the region in 2000 are generally the ones that have lingered, which Britain recognized to be problems during its rule over the region, yet ones for which it could apparently find or broker no effective and lasting solution. Thus, the usual suspects under discussion here are Iraq's boundaries at the head of the Gulf, and the Lower Gulf islands dispute, while some might add the Bahrain-Qatar island and shoal disputes to such a category. While no one can downplay the continuing violence of repeated Saudi-Yemeni border incidents, it is difficult to characterize this dispute as a "usual suspect," since bilateral negotiations toward establishing a boundary in the desert wastes of the Rub al-Khali have been ongoing, and then intermittently, only since 1992.

Moreover, to classify the Iraq-Kuwait boundary as a "usual suspect," in a category of ultimately unresolved disputes, is also contentious and technically wrong. Given that the United Nations Security Council unanimously approved the secretary-general's demarcation team's award for this territorial limit in May 1993—while the governments of Iraq and Kuwait had effectively lent their approval two years earlier to any arrangement that would ultimately be arrived at—it must clearly be placed in a unique category. The fact that Iraq formally and fully accepted the UN award without equivocation in November 1994 and that the integrity of this demarcation is physically guaranteed against infraction by the Security Council reinforces the notion that this boundary has been finalized and is here to stay. Certainly it has now fully evolved in international law. Yet, to assume that a historically explosive regional problem has thereby been removed is dangerous. How many experienced observers of northern Gulf affairs could confidently predict that the last has been heard of a plea by successive Baghdad governments for greater access to Gulf waters at the expense of Kuwait?

Historically, therefore, what has made this persistent group of usual suspects so resistant to permanent and final settlement has been their cyclical nature. Until very recently, it has often seemed that however these boundaries or territorial questions were regulated in international law at various points in their history, and whether or not the territorial limits introduced have been delimited and/or demarcated, they have tended to move from long periods of dormancy to much shorter and intense periods of activity. Often, the principal determinant or trigger that activates these disputes from dormancy has been intrinsic or perceived shifts in the regional balance of power. Where the history of the Lower Gulf islands is concerned, as well, this would also seem to have been proven right, as illustrated by:

1. The 1887 assertion of more direct control by the Persian Qajar government over the eastern Gulf littoral, and the banishment of the northern flank of the Qawasim (the ruling families of Sharjah and Ras al-Khaimah) from their semi-autonomous base in southern Persia at the port of Lingah and the nearby Sirri island;
2. The British government's advice to the Qawasim in 1903 to emplace flags on Abu Musa and Greater Tunb. The Belgian-run Persian customs police, who hoisted the Persian flag instead on the features, then removed these. When it finally realized what had happened—some months later—Britain used the threat of force to get Persia to climb down, with the result that in 1904 the Al Qasimi flags were re-hoisted on the islands;
3. Iran's move on the islands on the last day of November 1971, the day before Britain departed Gulf waters as protecting power. Prior accommodation had been reached with Sharjah (reluctantly but voluntarily on behalf of its ruler) for the shared administration of Abu Musa, though the Tunb islands were taken forcibly from Ras al-Khaimah;
4. The period from 1992 to the present, which has witnessed the reactivation and internationalization of the Abu Musa/Tunbs dispute. Iran's clumsy reactivation was almost certainly attributable to its frustration at its regional isolation and its exclusion from post–Gulf War plans for regional security.

### Long-established and appreciated nature of disputes

The crux of each dispute within this "usual suspect" category has long been recognized by those who have been involved in efforts to try and resolve them. As far as the protecting power, Britain, was concerned, certain of these disputes presented different problems, ranging from territorial questions that genuinely posed a potential threat to regional stability, to those that were regarded as, above all, tedious spats between neighboring ruling dynasties. Several quotations from British government records illustrate this point.

In 1939 the Foreign Office commented in the following manner upon Iraq's desire for greater access to Gulf waters, placing this dispute firmly into the former, more serious category:

> It is understandable that the state which controls the Mesopotamian plain should desire to have undivided control of at least one good means of access to the sea and [British foreign secretary] Lord Halifax thinks that on a long view, it is likely that, if Iraq were given this access, it would make for steadier conditions in that part of the world for years to come.[12]

The irritant caused by the persistence of other disputes, however, is the most distinctive feature of the following comments:

> Having been involved at various levels in efforts to resolve the Lower Gulf islands dispute while serving as a diplomat along the Western and Southern Gulf littoral, Sir Glen Balfour-Paul would comment in his book of 1991 that the dispute had, by the turn of the 1970s, assumed a scale in Anglo-Iranian relations "grossly disproportionate" to the islands' size and importance.[13]

Likewise, former British resident Sir William Luce, having been brought back at around the same time specifically to broker a settlement of outstanding issues with Iran in the face of Britain's imminent departure from the Gulf, allegedly uttered, in a moment of obvious exasperation:

> The Persians took Sirri while we weren't looking in 1887. I sometimes wish they had taken the Tunbs and Abu Musa as well.[14]

In his heavily anecdotal account of his years as "Adviser to the Ruler of Bahrain," Sir Charles Dalrymple Belgrave would recall the enduring symbolic significance attached by the ruling Al Khalifah family to the locality of Zubarah, little more than a set of ruins lying on the northwestern coastline of the Qatari peninsula. Claims were maintained with a conviction and intensity that completely baffled him:

> When Shaykh Hamad died in 1942, I remembered the words which were attributed to Queen Mary Tudor: "When I am dead ... you shall find Calais lying on my heart," but in this case the word would have been Zubarah.[15]

A candid, recently declassified Foreign and Commonwealth Office memorandum by Donal McCarthy was equally revealing. The 1969 memorandum reviewed the status of various unresolved boundary questions that Britain would bequeath to the region when it left in December 1971. Following in similar vein to many of the above observations was the remark that:

[t]he mentality of these rulers is such that they are prepared to dispute a barren sand dune till judgement day, while tribal views on e.g., access to wells are pressed with an urgency which does not comprehend Western ideas on rigid frontiers.[16]

In a sense, of course, this last quote was a bit rich. Having introduced a Western-style consciousness of territoriality to Arabia (or at least to its rulers), it ought not really have been a cause for complaint when the ownership of specific localities became the subject of fierce contention, albeit usually for reasons best explained as personal or dynastic rather than national rivalries. All of this is interesting and informative, but in the end, however Britain and others since have characterized the conflict potential of these cyclical disputes, it does not necessarily make any of them easier to settle.

### *Limitations of International Law*
Observers of the Gulf region were jolted when a prominent American international lawyer asserted in New York that, owing to the deliberations of the UN demarcation team and the Iraqi government's unequivocal acceptance of its findings, the Iraq-Kuwait boundary had been "settled for all time."[17] While it is to be hoped that peace and stability will characterize these borderlands in decades to come, there is clearly a danger of creating hostages to fortune for the future. A few miles to the northeast, the Shatt al-Arab dispute has proven resistant to its own supposedly final settlement in international law.

Nowhere were the limitations of international law more accurately illustrated than with the fate of the 1975 Algiers Accord and follow-up bilateral treaties between Iran and Iraq of the same year. The package of agreements that defined and regulated the Shatt al-Arab river boundary was, by common consent, the most sophisticated ever to be concluded for a divided river boundary in international law, containing every conceivable safeguard against future disputes over the alignment and status of the territorial limit. Yet it demonstrably failed to prevent conflict, when Iraqi president Saddam Hussein graphically tore to pieces—before an Iraqi television audience—the original he had signed as vice-president. That was the prelude to the invasion of Iran in September 1980. Within a few weeks of the onset of the Iran-Iraq War, the wreckage of abandoned or burnt-out vessels blocked the Shatt al-Arab, and Iraq was effectively landlocked. It seems likely that the Iraqi president had calculated (wrongly as it turned out) that circumstances were favorable for the restoration of the Shatt al-Arab to its "rightful owner." This served to demonstrate that no comprehensive territorial settlement is a panacea if one of the signatories remains unconvinced of what it has committed itself to, and is ultimately prepared to use force to change the geographical facts that the legal instrument has introduced. The whole episode provides an important and painful lesson of which Kuwait must be only too aware.

Thus, a reflection upon the convoluted history of the Iraq-Kuwait boundary and sovereignty disputes in the period before 1990 identifies a number of critical factors and constants. Indeed, the future treatment and management of the dispute may well determine whether or not territorial stability will characterize the borderlands of the northwestern Gulf, notwithstanding the recent accomplishment of the UN demarcation team. What do these critical factors and constants mean?[18]

First, that the Iraqi access to the Gulf is limited. Iraq is classifiable as a geographically disadvantaged state. Its meager coastline is largely undevelopable, and the state was effectively landlocked during the recent wars of its own making in the northern Gulf. It has consistently sought territorial concessions from Kuwait that might improve this access, typically involving requests for Kuwait's cession or lease of the islands of Warbah and Bubiyan and a strip of land territory south of Iraq's second dry-cargo port, Umm Qasr.

Yet the politics of access have been equally important, engendering from Iraq a certain historical restlessness, or negative consciousness. Baghdad has always believed itself to be squeezed out of the Gulf. History affords partial if indirect support for such a viewpoint inasmuch as it was the genesis of Britain's treaty relationship with Kuwait at the turn of the century, and its urgency not to allow imperial rivals a foothold upon what it regarded as a British lake at this time, that would result in a fairly explicit policy of minimizing the Ottoman shoreline in the northern Gulf.[19] Britain's success in squeezing out the Ottomans from the Gulf has certainly contributed to Iraq feeling squeezed out ever since.

Historically, too, there has been some sympathy for Iraq's arguments for greater access to Gulf waters. This extended at various stages to the British government itself, while it was responsible for the conduct of Kuwait's foreign affairs. Lacy Baggallay's important 1939 quote has already been presented, but a Foreign Office telegram wired to Bahrain in 1957 would make much the same point:

> In my view it would be in Kuwait's interest to make an earlier frontier settlement at the cost of ceding the territory necessary to provide Iraq with a deep water channel to Umm Qasr under Iraqi sovereignty.[20]

Amazingly, international sympathy did not totally disappear, even with Iraq's disastrous move on Kuwait on 2 August 1990. Leaving aside whatever Ambassador April Glaspie did or did not say in the immediately preceding weeks, Thomas Pickering, the then U.S. Ambassador to the United Nations, apparently relayed the following message on 6 August 1990 for delivery to the Iraqi government via the U.S. Ambassador to Jordan:

> We acknowledge your need for an opening to the Gulf, and the issue of access to the islands is one we could look upon favorably.[21]

Ironically, international sympathy for Iraq's arguments for greater access would certainly disappear once the Baghdad government announced the annexation of Kuwait a week into its occupation. For this Iraq obviously had only itself to blame.

Second, the Iraq-Kuwait territorial disputes are inter-related with the Shatt al-Arab question. There is a proven historical pattern, with the triangular relationship usually expressing itself during those periods in which Iran has held the upper hand in the Shatt al-Arab dispute. Inasmuch as Iraq has looked south to Kuwait to compensate itself for its geostrategic misfortune, four historical phases are particularly noteworthy to establish the linkage.[22] In 1938, Iraq requested port facilities outside the Shatt al-Arab for the first time, and Britain decided that its gaze should be focused upon the Khor Zubair rather then Kuwait Bay. Iraq argued several reasons for the request, including that the Shatt al-Arab was becoming unreliable, because of its status as a disputed international river boundary; that the waterway was becoming congested, because of river traffic levels (a debatable charge at this point); and that Iraq wanted to extend its railway beyond Basra to the coast. Moreover, Iraqi troops advanced a few miles into Kuwaiti territory south of Umm Qasr in 1969 (and would remain there until the thaw in Iraqi-Kuwaiti relations of 1977) following the Shah's abrogation of the 1937 Teheran treaty. During the 1980–1988 Iran-Iraq War, with the Shatt al-Arab blocked and the planned large-scale expansion of Umm Qasr postponed, Iraq twice requested the use of Warbah and Bubiyan islands even if Kuwait did much to bolster its own presence on the features during this time. Two weeks into its occupation of Kuwait, Iraq surprised many observers by apparently abandoning territorial claims to the whole of the Shatt al-Arab river when accepting Iranian terms for a final settlement of the Iran-Iraq War. This understandably raised questions as to how, if at all, the two events were related.[23]

Third, the Iraqi government had abrogated supposedly final international boundary agreements, as discussed above.

Fourth, the Iraqi state and population have developed a sense of "territorial consciousness." That Kuwait "rightfully" belongs to Iraq is almost certainly a prevailing view on the streets of Baghdad and elsewhere within Iraq. Ironically, it was probably much easier for Saddam Hussein to recognize the UN verdict on the boundary than it would have been for Iraqi opposition groups ultimately desirous (but obviously incapable) of replacing the current Iraqi regime. The UN decision on the course of the Iraq-Kuwait land boundary, when first announced in April 1992 (albeit not in its final detail), was denounced not only by the current regime but also by these exiled opposition groupings.

Fifth, the (in)ability of Iraq, Kuwait, and Iran to cooperate in the management of the borderlands of the northwestern Gulf has created certain undeniable conditions. Occasionally, Iran and Iraq have agreed to boundary delimitation along the Shatt al-Arab river, but never have the two sides managed to agree upon a sustainable joint program for the conservancy of the waterway. Earlier, Britain and the Basra Port Authority had found such a goal elusive as well.

While effective cooperation in the management of the Shatt al-Arab has always eluded Iran and Iraq, the treaties, protocols, and annexes of 1975 ironically provided elaborate guidelines in this direction. With some irony, Iran and Iraq had also agreed upon a scheme for clearing and cleansing the Shatt al-Arab just a few weeks before the Iraqi invasion of Kuwait. Clearly, if one accepts that in the medium term, the thalweg has to be regarded as the definitive boundary, Iran and Iraq will have to cooperate in the conservancy of this shared river.

To make matters worse, the United Nations Iraq-Kuwait Boundary Demarcation Commission (UNIKBDC) award of 1993 for the Iraq-Kuwait boundary has left the navigation channels along the Khor Abdallah dredged, cut, and deepened by Iraq since the early 1960s, entirely within the Kuwaiti territorial sea.[24] Despite statutory rights of passage for Iraqi vessels, the need for cooperation in the future management of this stretch of the borderlands would seem all too clear. As things stand, for instance, Iraq cannot maintain its navigation channels along the Khor Abdallah.

Importantly, a history of sporadic though significant functional cooperation has been highlighted between Iraq and Kuwait.[25] In the twelve-month period before the 1990 Iraqi invasion, the two states had agreed to integrate their electricity grids, while the go-ahead was given for a limited supply of Iraqi freshwater from the Shatt al-Arab to be supplied to Kuwait via a pipeline traversing the Faw peninsula. This admittedly small-scale level of limited functional cooperation had paralleled the two traditional Iraqi claims on Kuwait and its territory before 1990. Since there is a certain logic to it, it should come as no surprise if and when it is resurrected in the future.

### *Legal Dilemmas and Political Realities*

States of the Arabian Peninsula/Persian Gulf region have displayed a particular penchant and determination in recent years for concluding boundary agreements that affect precise divisions of sovereign territory. Yet, with the apparent intractability of the "usual suspects," as identified above, it might be worth considering whether there is no greater scope for looking at arrangements that might fall short of a full sovereign solution of the territorial dispute in these cases. Furthermore, in the 1971 Iran-UAE and the 1934 Saudi-Yemeni cases, arrangements along these lines were already in place. The 23 November 1971 Iran-Sharjah memorandum of understanding regarding Abu Musa was an imaginative agreement that reflected the regional realities pertaining at the time of its conclusion but which, while introducing the shared administration of the small island, deliberately ducked the question of its sovereignty. The May 1934 Taif treaty (or the Saudi-Yemeni "Treaty of Islamic Friendship and Brotherhood") remains in force, largely because it is an agreement that provides sufficient grey areas for each party to maintain divergent interpretations about the status of the boundary it introduced.

### *The 1971 Iran-Sharjah MoU*

The essentially pragmatic Iran-Sharjah MoU was most notable for the manner in which it accommodated the full sovereign claims of both Iran and Sharjah to the island. Its preamble stated that "neither Iran nor Sharjah will give up its claim to Abu Musa nor recognize the other state's claim."[26] In other words, the question of sovereignty was completely fudged in the agreement—it merely provided for the divided administration of the island. The MoU, nevertheless, provided for the positioning of Iranian forces in key strategic areas—basically, around the hill called Mount Halvah in the northern reaches of the island—defined on a map attached to the text of the agreement. Within this designated area, the Iranian flag flew and Iran possessed full jurisdiction, but outside, the

Sharqawi flag remained hoisted and jurisdiction fell to Sharjah as before. Iran and Sharjah each recognized a territorial sea for the island with a breadth of 12 nautical miles in which nationals of both parties would enjoy equal fishing rights. The Buttes Oil Company (which succeeded Occidental as holder of the Sharjah offshore oil concession) would continue to exploit hydrocarbon reserves from the nearby Mubarak oil field (now operated by Crescent of Sharjah) under the conditions specified in its existing concession agreement with the ruler of Sharjah—for as long as these were acceptable to Iran. Lastly, Iran was to give Sharjah £1.5 million annually in aid until such time as its oil revenue reached £3 million annually, which in practice would take about three years. Given the previous impasse in this dispute, an arrangement that allowed for the flying of each party's flag on the island seemed, on the surface, a fairly logical and sustainable compromise.

### *The 1934 Saudi-Yemeni Taif Treaty*

The 20 May 1934 Saudi-Yemeni "Taif" accord was a peace treaty following the Saudi-Imamate war earlier that year. It introduced boundary delimitation from the Red Sea margins in the west to Jabal al-Thar in the Asir Mountains in the east. The "grey area" provided in this treaty is the rather bizarre obligation contained within its text to renew it every 20 lunar years. Operative again since 1995, this provision allows the Yemeni government to argue to this day before its own domestic constituency that no boundary line can be considered "permanent and final" if the treaty that introduced and governs the said territorial limit itself requires renewal. Despite this, Saudi Arabia can argue that the agreement to physically brick up and re-demarcate the Taif line contained within the February 1995 Saudi-Yemeni memorandum of understanding will, when it is finally implemented, give the said line a physical permanence on the ground.[27]

To be sure, neither of these agreements is particularly meritorious, and they are certainly not models for the governance of international boundaries or territorial disputes. Rather, the premise that lies behind them is worth noting, however. These agreements are obviously deficient in terms of international law, but they do, in sum, seek to govern or manage disputes rather than resolve them, while both were clearly the product of the regional realities pertaining at the time of their conclusion.

### *Shared Political and Economic Space*

Thus, not only is the precedent of existing boundary/territorial agreements that are short on law clearly established, but these are more geared to regional realities than many of their more legally sophisticated counterparts. Shared political and economic space has a proven utility in Arabia and the Persian Gulf.[28] Two such cases are the Kuwait–Saudi Arabia and Iraq–Saudi Arabia neutral zones that were introduced by the Uqair Protocol late in 1922 and that survived as unique features of the Arabian political map until new bilateral agreements were drawn up to partition them in 1969 and 1981 respectively. However, the area of the former Kuwait–Saudi Arabia neutral zone is still subject to the joint economic regime that dates from the era of the neutral zones.[29] A small neutral zone continues to exist between individual emirates of the UAE (Abu Dhabi–Dubai since 1961), while a shared zone existed for at least the late 1950s between Fujairah and Sharjah. Similar features existed between Oman and Ajman and Sharjah respectively during the 1960s, while the bizarre arrangements for the shared administration of Abu Musa with the MoU of 1971 have already been discussed. Given the recent predilection of Arabian states for arriving at fully sovereign settlements of territorial questions and the genuine progress made toward this end, the further appearance of shared political space in Arabia seems unlikely. The eastern three-quarters of the Saudi-Yemeni border remains, as already established, the last missing fence in the desert. It is known to this author, however, that the possible institution of such a feature in the area east of the Yemeni Mashreq—an area for which there are few historical precedents in terms of claims or evidence of effective occupation—has at least been discussed during the last eight years of negotiations between the two states.

If little progress was reached on shared political space in the one and a half decades before Britain vacated the Gulf as protecting power, a great deal of progress was made in drawing up national zones of maritime jurisdiction in or underlying that water body itself. Some of the arrangements drawn up for continental shelf boundary delimitation were innovative and influential, such as the 1968 Iranian-Saudi agreement with its treatment of the islands of Farsi and Arabi. Importantly, however, the Persian Gulf would also be the major testing ground for the institution of joint economic space. The first continental shelf boundary agreement to be concluded in this region was between Bahrain and Saudi Arabia on 22 February 1958. The boundary agreement recognized a simple median line delimitation that in effect disregarded all interlying (and previously disputed) high- and low-tide elevations. This had been one of several possible boundaries mooted in Anglo-Saudi negotiations convened in August 1951 to discuss the seabed question. The main problem to be sorted out in the years following these negotiations was the northern terminus of the Saudi Arabia–Bahrain maritime boundary in the vicinity of the Bu Saafah shoal, the disputed status of which was accentuated by the presence of an underlying oil field. Instead of opting to share ownership of the feature by instituting a neutral zone, the 1958 agreement provided that Bu Saafah be ceded to Saudi Arabia but specified that in future Bahrain would receive half of the revenue accruing from the exploration of the associated oil field.[30]

The March 1969 Abu Dhabi–Qatar maritime boundary agreement resolved the dispute over ownership of the offshore Bunduq oil field in a similarly imaginative manner. Terminal point B on the maritime boundary was offset slightly from the true equidistant lines between the adjacent coastlines to coincide directly with the location of the oil field. For practical reasons it was specified that only one concessionaire (representing Abu Dhabi) be allowed to develop the field, though, importantly, all revenue from Bunduq was to be shared in perpetuity.[31]

The joint sharing arrangements agreed in 1971 for the Mubarak oil field between Sharjah and Iran have been detailed above, but, given that Abu Musa has been and remains a symbol of Arab-Iranian rivalry, it is important to repeat that some cooperative measures are in place across Gulf waters. Officially, this seems to have been the only example of Arab-Iranian joint development of disputed mineral resources at sea. However, during the course of legal proceedings before the Iran–United States Claims Tribunal in The Hague, a copy of a continental shelf delimitation agreement negotiated between Abu Dhabi (UAE) and Iran was produced. Although there is nothing officially on the record to suggest the existence of this maritime boundary, it seems certain that the text (concluded in the mid-1970s) formed the basis of a working arrangement at least. The agreement/arrangement is interesting for the manner in which it deals with the trans-boundary offshore Salman (previously referred to as Sassan) oil field. With respect to the joint management of the Salman field, the agreement did not set any production limits or quotas on either party. Still, before the onset of the Iran-Iraq War in 1980, there were a number of meetings convened to exchange technical information on the field between the parties.[32]

Clearly, not only has there been a history of cooperation in dealing with territorial and resource issues in Gulf waters, but also a history of Arab-Iranian cooperation in these issues. There is no reason whatsoever why these precedents cannot be expanded upon in future years and decades as the offshore political map of the Gulf is finalized.

## Conclusion

Article 10 of the GCC charter, signed on 25 May 1981, defined the responsibilities of that organization's "Commission for the Settlement of Disputes." To date, there is no evidence that it has ever met, to treat territorial disputes between member states. Ironically, it seems conceivable that the commission could finally be activated to deal with boundaries at some future point (following the likely deliverance of the ICJ's judicial award in the Hawar case later in 2000) when there are no disputes remaining between member states. In March 1997, it was suggested to this author that the commission might yet play a monitoring role in this regard, a promising idea that deserves to be developed. After all, the Gulf Cooperation Council is likely to play an important role in promoting regional territorial stability. It is worth recalling that there is no equivalent region/continent-wide convention aiming for the preservation of the prevailing framework of state territory, as there is in Latin America with the institutionalized acceptance of the principle of *uti possidetis,* and as there is in Africa following the Organization of African Unity's "sacrosanctity" declaration, delivered in Cairo in 1964.

Yet, if the GCC states themselves have done much to get their own house in order in the last decade or so, real territorial challenges surround this regional grouping of states. Although progress towards finalizing the political map on land and sea in the region continues to gather pace in the early spring of 2001, problems linger.

In June 2000, Saudi Arabia and Yemen finally (yet rather suddenly) agreed

**Map 13.3** Bahrain Boundary Issues

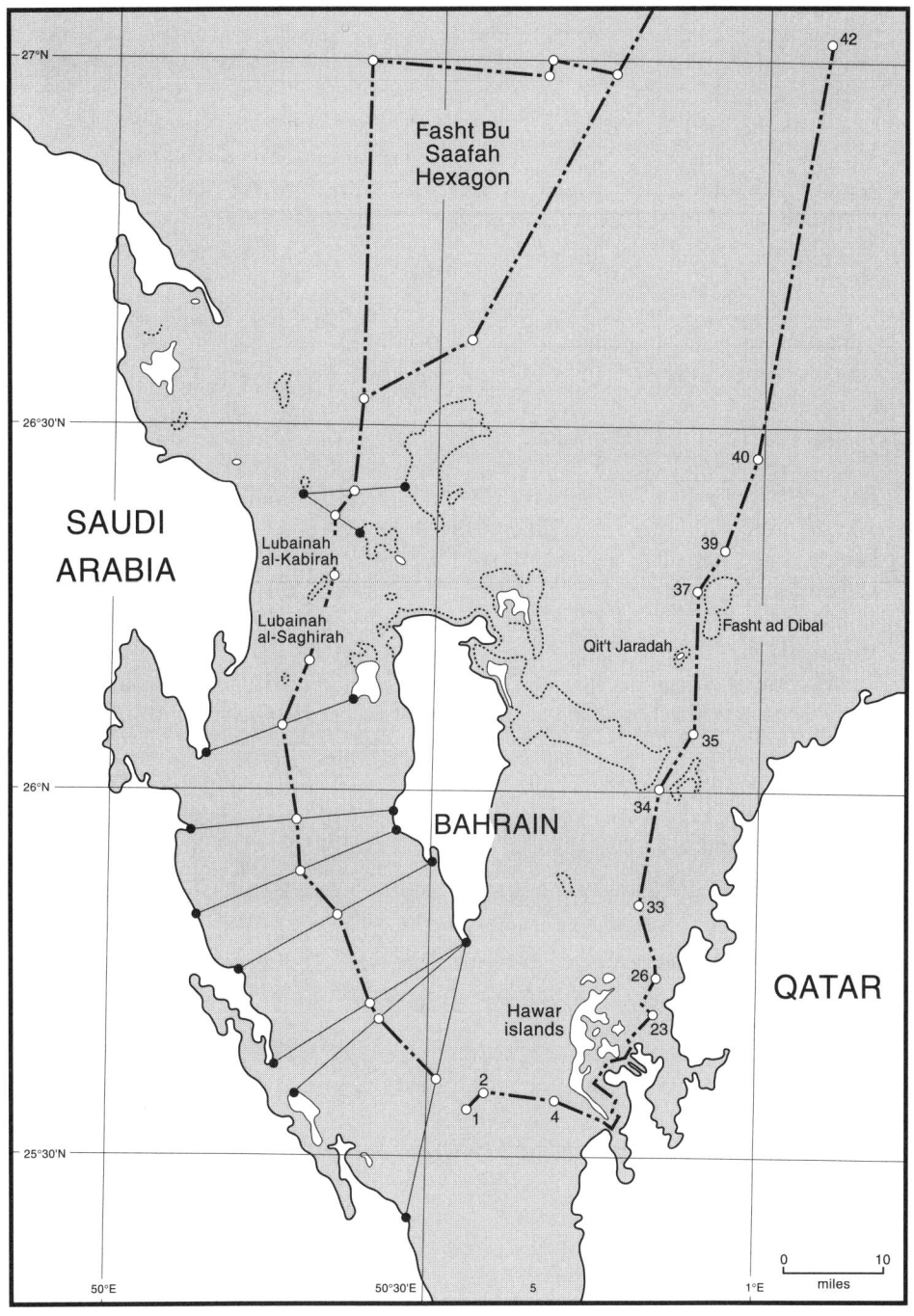

upon the course of what until then had been Arabia's last indeterminate land boundary.[33] Then, in July, the same, decisive momentum that Heir Apparent Abdallah of Saudi Arabia had brought to bear in boundary negotiations with Yemen seemingly also broke the long stalemate in the Kingdom's negotiations with Kuwait over a lateral maritime boundary delimitation in the Persian Gulf. The two sides signed such an agreement on July 2, 2000. The final resolution of Kuwaiti-Saudi maritime disputes also opened the door to the onset during September 2000 of formal negotiations between Iran and Kuwait over an opposite maritime boundary delimitation in northern Gulf waters. Last but not least, the ICJ delivered its verdict on Bahrain-Qatar island and maritime disputes as recently as 16 March 2001.

Here, Bahrain emerged largely as the winner since the sovereignty of the Hawar island group—unquestionably, the chief bone of contention in the case—was confirmed as lying with the island state. Effectively, the ICJ has therefore recognized the status quo as far as ownership of the Hawar group is concerned in ratifying Britain's earlier ruling of July 1939. True, Qatari sovereignty over the locality of Zubarah on its north-western shoreline was confirmed though this part of the ruling was every bit as predictable as the court's treatment of the Hawar group. Although including Zubarah in the range of questions to be decided had originally appeared a boon for Bahrain, it is probably more realistic to surmise that by doing so, the ICJ was ensuring that Qatar would at least go home with something when judgement was made. So much for reaffirmation of the status quo in the ICJ judgement.

What about the court's treatment of the disputed shoals and its announcement of a maritime boundary delimitation between the two states? In dealing with these issues, the court arguably had a little more flexibility. Until the judgement of mid-March, both the Dibal and Jaradah shoals have been occupied by Bahrain and had previously been recognized as belonging to the island state (albeit within a seabed area provisionally characterized as Qatari) after a British ruling in 1947. The court has now ruled that the Dibal shoal belongs to Qatar but that Jaradah belongs to Bahrain as an island. Such a distinction is important for Jaradah's newly-recognized island status has projected the maritime boundary between the states further eastward than would otherwise have been the case. Bahrain probably has more reason to be satisfied with ICJ's maritime delimitation than Qatar.

These positive developments notwithstanding, Iraq's unequivocal acceptance during November 1994 of the earlier UNIKBDC verdict—on the course of its land boundary with Kuwait—will continue to be the subject of close scrutiny. Continuing dialogue is thus needed to ensure that the Lower Gulf islands dispute never becomes more than a symbol of Arab-Iranian rivalry, while the same might be said for the future treatment of the Shatt al-Arab dispute, currently dormant rather than finally settled.

In the end, all of these challenges need monitoring and managing. In addition, substantial attention must also be devoted to the maritime political map, a process that has basically stalled since the mid-1970s. Arguably, there needs to be an inclusive regional structure within which the requisite cooperation to broach these territorial challenges can be nurtured and developed. As discussed above, there are significant existing precedents for cooperation in the area, even if it might probably be asking too much to ever seriously entertain any enlargement of the GCC. Recent Yemeni applications for membership have basically been shelved, while Iran and all GCC member states would probably never be able to agree on the vexed issue of nomenclature. Yet perhaps Iran, Yemen, and, in time, Iraq could realistically play a beneficial role in the GCC's Commission for the Settlement of Disputes, initially as observers, presuming the body is eventually activated. This might just provide the forum needed for closer coordination in territorial and resource issues. It might also provide an inclusive structure in which the more destabilizing aspects of the old "usual suspects" can be closely monitored and freely discussed. After all, if you can't solve them, then manage them!

## Notes

1. J. R. V. Prescott, *Political Frontiers and Boundaries,* London: Unwin Hyman, 1987.
2. This possible symbolic worth is obviously not a phenomenon restricted to the Gulf, as can be seen by the way the Senkaku/Diaoyutai and the Tok-Do (Liancourt Rocks) disputes are respectively utilized as an outlet for the expression of nationalistic rivalries between Japan, China, Taiwan, and Korea.
3. Jacques Ancel, *Les frontieres,* Paris: Delagrave, 1938.
4. Stephen B. Jones, *Boundary-making: A Handbook for Statesmen, Treaty-editors and Boundary Commissioners,* Washington, D.C.: Carnegie Endowment for International Peace, 1945.
5. "Bloody clashes reported on Saudi-Yemen border," in *Yemen News,* 28 January 2000.
6. "UAE, Oman ratify partial border agreement, 27 March 2000," Reuters, 29 March 2000.
7. For greater detail, see Richard Schofield, "Boundaries, Territorial Disputes and the GCC States," in David E. Long and Christian Koch (eds.) *Gulf Security in the Twenty-First Century,* Abu Dhabi: Emirates Center for Strategic Studies and Research, 1997, pp. 133–168; see also Richard Schofield, "Finalizing the Arabian Territorial Framework," in *Geopolitics and International Boundary Studies* 2:3, winter 1997, pp. 90–105.
8. Richard Schofield, "Border Disputes in the Gulf: Past, Present and Future," in Gary G. Sick and Lawrence G. Potter (eds.), *The Persian Gulf at the Millennium,* New York: St. Martin's Press, 1997, p. 129.
9. Hand-drawn lines linking geographic coordinates on British admiralty charts have generally been appended to maritime boundary delimitation treaties.
10. John C. Wilkinson, *Arabia's Frontiers: the Story of Britain's Boundary-Drawing in the Desert,* London: I. B. Tauris, 1991, p. xi.
11. Gulf Cooperation Council, "Closing Statement," thirteenth annual GCC summit, Abu Dhabi, UAE, December 1992.
12. Dispatch dated 16 December 1939 from Lacy Baggallay, Foreign Office, to the India Office in the following file held at the Public Record Office, Kew, London: CO 732/86/17.
13. Glen Balfour-Paul, *The End of Empire in the Middle East: Britain's Relinquishment of Power in Her Last Three Arab Dependencies,* Cambridge: Cambridge University Press, 1991, p. 127.
14. Richard Schofield, *Unfinished Business: Abu Musa, the Tunbs, Iran and the UAE,* London: Royal Institute of International Affairs, 2000 (forthcoming), chapter 4.
15. Charles D. Belgrave, *Personal Column,* London: Hutchinson, 1960, p. 156.
16. Foreign Office Research Department, "Frontiers in the Lower Persian Gulf," 16 June 1969, in *PRO file: FCO 8/965* (Persian Gulf—territorial problems and boundaries).
17. Concluding/summarizing remarks made at a conference entitled *Security Flashpoints: Oil, Islands, Sea Access and Military Confrontation,* convened by the University of Virginia's Center for Oceans Law and Policy, UN Plaza–Park Hyatt Hotel, New York, 8 February 1997.
18. For a more detailed exploration of these issues, see Richard Schofield, "Finalizing the Arabian Territorial Framework," in *Geopolitics and International Boundaries* 2:3, winter 1997, pp. 98–103.

19. Richard Schofield, *Kuwait and Iraq: Historical Claims and Territorial Disputes,* London: Royal Institute of International Affairs, 1993, pp. 24–47 (Hereafter Schofield–Kuwait and Iraq).
20. Richard Schofield (ed.), *The Iraq–Kuwait Dispute,* volume 2, Farnham Common: Archive Editions, 1994, pp. 255–358.
21. David H. Finnie, *Shifting Lines in the Sand: Kuwait's Elusive Frontier with Iraq,* Cambridge, Massachusetts: Harvard University Press, 1992, p. 175 (note 2).
22. For greater detail, see Richard Schofield, "The Historical Problem of Iraqi Access to the Persian Gulf: The Inter-relationships of Territorial Disputes with Iran and Kuwait, 1938–1990," in Clive H. Schofield and Richard N. Schofield (eds.), *World Boundaries 2: The Middle East and North Africa,* London: Routledge, 1994, pp. 158–172.
23. Schofield–Kuwait and Iraq, pp. 127–132.
24. Schofield–Kuwait and Iraq, pp. 186–191.
25. Gerd Nonneman, "The (Geo)political Economy of Iraqi-Kuwaiti Relations," in *Geopolitics and International Boundaries* 1:2, autumn 1996, pp. 178–223.
26. Facsimiles of the original text and associated correspondence reproduced in *The Journal of Foreign Policy,* the Institute for Political and International Studies, Tajrish, Teheran, volume 6, 1993, pp. 193–208.
27. Richard Schofield, "The Last Missing Fence in the Desert: The Saudi-Yemeni Boundary," in *Geopolitics and International Boundaries* 1:3, winter 1996, pp. 247–299. For a shorter revised and updated summary of its content, see Richard Schofield, "The International Boundary between Yemen and Saudi Arabia," in Renaud Detalle (ed.), *Tensions in Arabia: The Saudi-Yemeni Faultline,* Baden-Baden, Germany: Nomos Verlagsgesellschaft, 2000, pp. 15–51.
28. Gerald Blake, "Shared Zones as a Solution to Problems of Territorial Sovereignty in the Gulf States," in Richard Schofield (ed.), *Territorial Foundations of the Gulf States,* London: UCL Press, 1994, pp. 200–210 (hereafter Schofield–Territorial Foundations).
29. For further details, see Richard Schofield, "Borders and Territoriality in the Gulf and Arabian Peninsula during the Twentieth Century," in Schofield–Territorial Foundations, pp. 1–77.
30. Ibid., pp. 55–56.
31. Ibid., p. 52.
32. Rodman Bundy, "Maritime Delimitation in the Gulf," in Schofield–Territorial Foundations, pp. 182–183.
33. The Saudi-Yemeni boundary settlement was certainly hailed as a victory for Yemen by its President, Ali Abdallah Saleh. For a map of the delimitation, the text of the agreement, and various upbeat commentaries see *Al Thawrah* (Sanaa), 22 June 2000. As for the delimitation itself, in the east, it was not incredibly dissimilar to Britain's old claims for the northern boundary of the Aden Protectorate. This made sense for any delimitation decided upon was always likely to reflect the degree to which territory had been effectively occupied. It was also noticeable that the locality of Wadia in the central borderlands (the scene of a violent border incident in 1969) was confirmed as belonging to Saudi Arabia, while the Red Sea island of Duwaima (the scene of a much more recent but equally serious clash) was defined as belonging to Yemen. Maybe there was some sort of trade-off in this respect. As for the agreement between the two states, it was notably short in detail when specifying turning points for the delimitation of which—considering the length of the borderlands—there were surprisingly few. Perhaps the window of political opportunity had come before the technical teams were strictly ready to announce the finer detail of any agreement. Here one recalls Yemeni President Saleh's pragmatic assessment of the Saudi-Yemeni border negotiations back in 1996. He had noted that the territorial dispute would probably only ever be settled by a political decision made at the highest level.

CHAPTER 14

# The Kuwait-Iraq Border Problem

Hussein Hassouna

This chapter deals essentially with the legal aspects of the Kuwait-Iraq border problem, though it also raises other related regional and worldwide issues of current importance. Reference is first made to the history of the Kuwait-Iraq boundary problem in the light of the 1913, 1923, 1932, and 1963 agreements concerning that boundary. In that context, Iraq's sovereignty claim over Kuwait, which provoked both the 1961 and 1990 crises, is examined in some detail. A description then follows of how the international boundary between Iraq and Kuwait was demarcated in 1993, by the United Nations Boundary Demarcation Commission, established pursuant to Security Council Resolution 687 of 1991.[1] A special effort is also made to assess the impact of such demarcation on Kuwaiti-Iraqi ties and the restoration of peace and security in the area. Finally, the remaining contentious issues between the two countries are analyzed, including the consequence of Iraqi weapons of mass destruction, the imposition of sanctions on Baghdad, and the topic of Kuwaiti prisoners and missing individuals. The position of both the United Nations and of the League of Arab States on these matters is highlighted.

The chapter concludes with a general appraisal the situation in the region in light of these developments.

## Historical Background of the Border Problem

The Shaykhdom of Kuwait, situated at the head of the Gulf and encircled by Iraq and Saudi Arabia, was under the suzerainty of Ottoman rulers during the nineteenth century. Faced with a growing threat by Russia to their "position" in the Gulf, British authorities secured a general engagement from the ruler of Kuwait, which greatly enhanced their posture in the area. The 1899 agreement—which spelled out London's conditions—required the ruler of Kuwait to obtain British consent prior to ceding, selling, leasing, or giving for occupation any portion of territory to the government or subjects of another power.[2]

Under the Anglo-Turkish Convention of 29 July 1913, the British and

Ottoman governments reached agreement on their respective spheres of influence in the Gulf. As part of the accord, Turkey recognized the 1899 Anglo-Kuwaiti agreement and pledged not to try to change the Kuwaiti "status quo," whose northern and western boundaries were formally defined in that Convention for the first time.[3] Thus, Kuwait was separated from the adjacent province of Basra within the Ottoman Empire to the north and west by two lines: a *Green Line* running from the coast at the mouth of the Khawr Al-Zubair in a northwesterly direction, passing immediately south of Umm Qasr, Safwan, and Jabal Sanam to the Batin, and then southwest down the Batin; as well as a *Red Line* down the Khawr Abdallah. Both lines depicted the limits of Kuwaiti authority and territorial powers. While the Convention envisaged the creation of a delimitation commission, ostensibly to demarcate the ground boundaries thus defined, such a commission was never set up.[4] In the event, the Convention was never ratified, only to be relegated into oblivion by the outbreak of World War I. Therefore, its boundary definitions were never legally binding on either Britain or Turkey (and, consequently, neither on Kuwait nor Iraq), although they became the basis of future boundary "agreements."

With the declaration of World War I between Britain and Turkey in November 1914, the Shaykhdom of Kuwait was accorded recognition as "an independent government under British protection."[5] At the end of the war, the Ottoman Empire was dismembered and a mandate system instituted under Article 22 of the League of Nations Covenant. The three districts of Mosul, Basra, and Baghdad, which formed a part of Mesopotamia, were merged together to constitute the Kingdom of Iraq. The mandate over this "Kingdom" was conferred on Britain. Importantly, in its administration of the mandate, London sought to define Iraq's boundaries, and, to that end, Sir Percy Cox, then British high commissioner for Iraq, suggested that the Green Line—of the Anglo-Turkish Convention of 1913—be confirmed as the boundary between the two "countries." This was achieved in 1923 through an exchange of letters between the ruler of Kuwait, the British political agent in Kuwait, and the British high commissioner for Iraq, which described the frontier as identical with the frontier indicated by the Green Line in the 1913 Convention.[6]

Just before its admission into the League of Nations in October 1932, Iraq's mandate was "terminated." At the same time, British authorities opted to "reaffirm" the existing frontier between Iraq and Kuwait and, to that end, prodded both Iraqi and Kuwaiti officials to exchange letters. The frontier was "reaffirmed" on the basis of the 1923 definition, through an exchange of letters in July and August 1932 between the Iraqi prime minister and the ruler of Kuwait.[7]

On 19 June 1961, Kuwait's official accession to independence was marked by yet another exchange of letters between the ruler of Kuwait and the British political resident in the Arabian Gulf, Sir William Luce. By virtue of that exchange, Britain conceded the abrogation of the 1899 Anglo-Kuwaiti agreement, which had become "obsolete and inappropriate" and "inconsistent with the sovereignty and independence of Kuwait."[8] The agreement was replaced by a new accord of friendship and assistance.

On 25 June 1961, six days after the signing of this latest compact, the Iraqi prime minister, General Abdul Karim Qasim, announced his claim to Iraqi sovereignty over Kuwait.[9] He declared that Baghdad refused to recognize the 1899 agreement, on the ground that it was imposed by Britain on Kuwait. Iraq further claimed all of the territory belonging to the district of Kuwait, ostensibly associated with the province of Basra, which should therefore come under its authority. Faced with this situation, the ruler of Kuwait requested British assistance, under the provisions of the 1961 Anglo-Kuwaiti accord. A similar request was made to Saudi Arabia. In response thereto, British and Saudi military forces were dispatched to Kuwait, to defend it from an "imminent assault."[10] When Kuwait subsequently requested support from the League of Arab States (LAS) in defense of its independence, a League force was constituted and sent to Kuwait to replace British troops.[11]

While the presence of the League's force contributed to preserving Kuwaiti independence, the root of the problem, namely Iraq's territorial claims, was only dealt with through a change of government in Baghdad. Starting with the February 1963 change of regime, the Iraqi government adopted—ever so gradually—a new policy toward the Shaykhdom. As a result of improved relations between the two countries, an agreement was concluded between them on 4 October 1963, under which Iraq recognized the independence and sovereignty of Kuwait—and its boundaries—as specified in the 1932 exchange of letters between the then prime minister of Iraq and the ruler of Kuwait.[12]

Although Iraq has occasionally questioned the legal validity of the various international agreements defining its boundary with Kuwait, this issue was squarely addressed by Security Council Resolution 687, on 3 April 1991. To be sure, the resolution was adopted in the aftermath of the Gulf War—that is, after the restoration of Kuwait's sovereignty and independence, which were clearly violated by the 1 August 1990 Iraqi invasion and occupation. Yet, the Security Council noted in its resolution that Iraq and Kuwait had signed specific "Minutes" on 4 October 1963 formally recognizing the boundary between the two countries, and allocating certain islands to each party. Resolution 687 further acknowledged that Iraq had accepted the independence and sovereignty of Kuwait within defined borders as specified in the 1932 exchange of letters between the then prime minister of Iraq and the ruler of Kuwait.[13] Consequently, the Security Council demanded that Iraq and Kuwait respect the inviolability of the international boundary—and the allocation of islands set out in the 1963 Agreed Minutes—and decided to guarantee the inviolability of that boundary. In his subsequent report to the Council, the United Nations secretary-general reported that Resolution 687 had been accepted by the parties, signifying Iraq's formal acceptance of its international boundary with Kuwait based on the 1963 agreement. Nevertheless, and despite the Security Council's pronouncement—that the 1963 agreement was binding—the affirmation was somewhat unprecedented, which led to the assertion that a legal tribunal such as the International Court of Justice should have more appropriately determined the validity of such an agreement.[14] Only such an attestation would avoid potential legal or political controversies between the parties.

## Demarcation Of The Iraq-Kuwait Boundary

The Iraq-Kuwait Boundary Demarcation Commission was established pursuant to Security Council Resolution 687 of 3 April 1991, which called on the secretary-general of the United Nations to lend his assistance to and make arrangements with both protagonists to demarcate their mutual boundary. As already noted, that boundary had formally been agreed upon, but had never been demarcated.

After consultations with the governments of Iraq and Kuwait, the secretary-general did in fact establish the Demarcation Commission, composed of five members—three independent experts appointed by the secretary-general, and one representative each of Iraq and Kuwait—to carry out the necessary technical tasks. The Commission held its first session in New York on 23 May 1991. It presented its *Final Report,* dated 20 May 1993, to the secretary-general with a list of geographic coordinates demarcating the boundary, along with an "authoritative" map of the area (see Map 14.1).

A preliminary assessment of this United Nations–appointed body reveals that the Commission performed a technical rather than a political task. It has not reallocated territory between Kuwait and Iraq but has carried out the technical task necessary to demarcate—for the first time ever—the precise coordinates of the international boundary, as reaffirmed in the 1963 Agreed Minutes. Thus, the Commission demarcated, in geographic coordinates, the latitude and longitude of the boundary described in the 1963 Agreed Minutes. It also made arrangements for the physical representation of the boundary through the emplacement of a number of boundary pillars or monuments. Finally, it provided for the arrangement, as well as the continued maintenance and accurate location, of surface markers.

The Commission therefore successfully completed its task of final demarcation of the international boundary between Iraq and Kuwait, the inviolability of which both countries are committed to respect, and which the United Nations Security Council has pledged to guarantee. Indeed, this particular demarcation has allowed the realignment of the demilitarized zone established along that border, precisely within the newly demarcated international border. Without a doubt, such a demarcation will significantly enhance—in the long term—the stability of the border, thereby contributing to the maintenance of international peace and security in the region.[15]

Not surprisingly, Kuwait was the first to welcome the Commission's report, maintaining that the end results represented an important achievement for the United Nations. Kuwait perceived the results as a contribution to the promotion of international peace and justice. Iraq, for its part, expressed initial reservations, describing the Commission's decisions as purely political. Baghdad emphasized that the results were incompatible with international law and justice.[16] Subsequently, the Iraqi government formally confirmed Baghdad's "recognition" of Kuwait and of the international boundary between the two countries, as demarcated by the Commission.[17] The Security Council in turn welcomed this development.

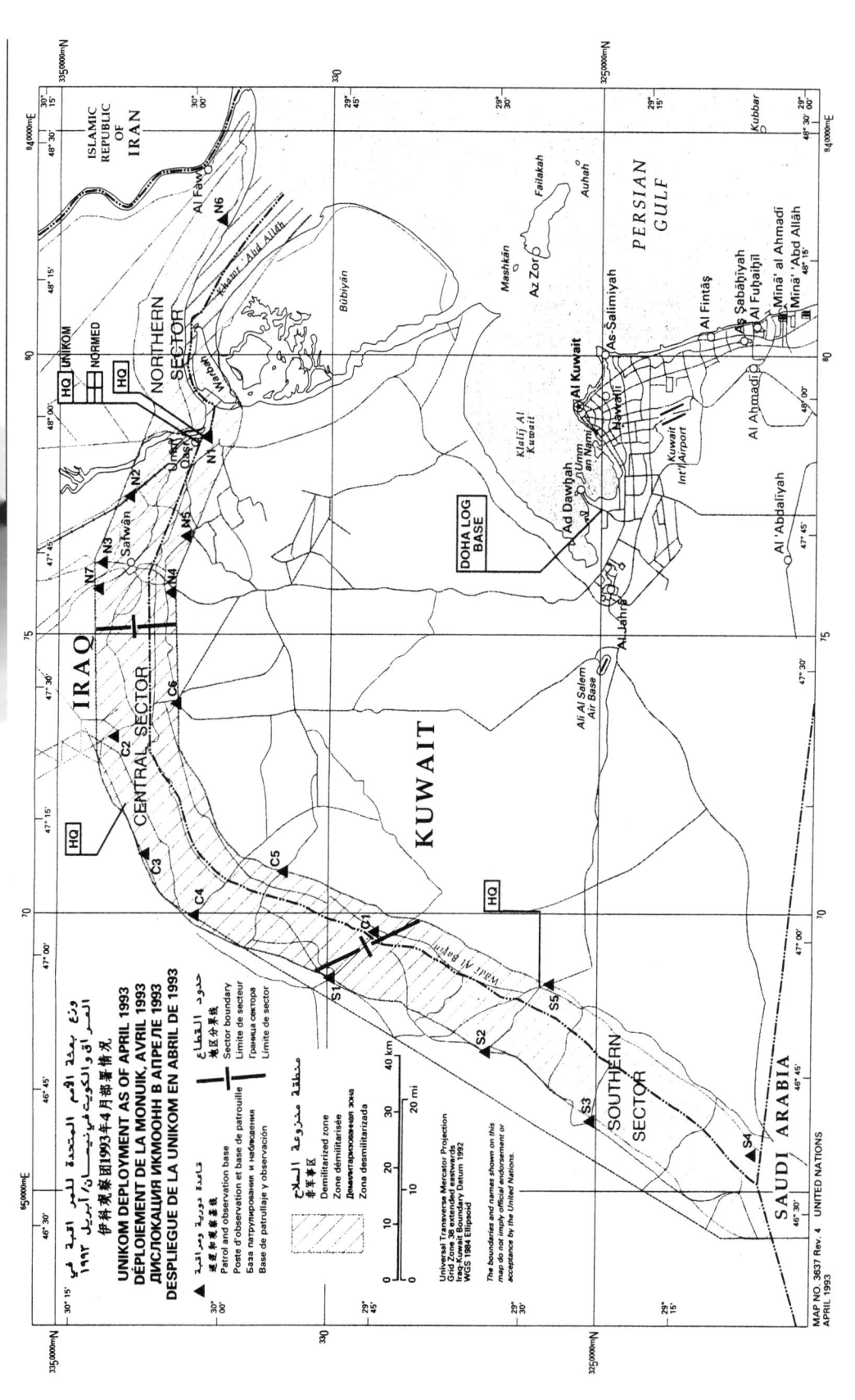

## Remaining Contentions

Despite this successful outcome of the search for a final settlement of the border contest between Iraq and Kuwait, several important questions—arising out of the 1990 crisis—remain as sources of contention not only between Kuwait and Iraq, but also between the latter and the international community. These controversial issues include Iraq's weapons of mass destruction, the festering implications of the United Nations–imposed sanctions against Baghdad, and the troubling consequences of Kuwaiti citizens either taken as prisoners or missing since 1990.

### *Iraqi Weapons of Mass Destruction*

The Security Council first addressed this thorny problem in 1991, under Resolution 687, when it "imposed" strict conditions. Indeed, Iraq was ordered to destroy any such weapons—under international supervision—and not acquire, or develop, new systems. Toward that end, significant progress has been achieved to comply with the provisions of that resolution, although that headway has been deemed as being insufficient. In its Resolution 1284 (17 December 1999), the Security Council concluded that Baghdad failed to meet those conditions that would lift relevant prohibitions imposed against it. In the opinion of the Security Council, Iraq has failed to implement the United Nations resolutions in full.

The League of Arab States, for its part, has continuously called upon Iraq to carry out its obligations under relevant Security Council resolutions, including those pertaining to the issue of weapons of mass destruction. Still, the LAS advanced that the removal of all weapons of mass destruction from the Middle East region, and above all the Israeli nuclear arsenal, was indispensable for maintaining peace throughout the region.[18] To be sure, this position was similar to the declared intention of the Security Council, as underlined in Resolution 687. In fact, this critical resolution specified that the "actions" requested from Iraq represented steps toward the goal of establishing a zone free from weapons of mass destruction in the entire Middle East.

Yet, and while it has formally denied possessing weapons of mass destruction after its arsenal was destroyed, Iraq has refused to accept the Security Council's 17 December 1999 resolution 1284. The latter established a new reinforced system of monitoring, verification, and inspection. Ironically, Kuwait perceived—as declared before the Security Council in December 1999—that Baghdad still possessed weapons of mass destruction and that this remained a source of great concern to the Shaykhdom. Naturally, Kuwait did not trust Iraqi intentions, and believed that such weapons posed a threat to its security and the stability of the Gulf region.[19]

### *Sanctions Imposed against Iraq*

Equally important, and since 1991, Iraq has been subjected to widespread sanctions that, in turn, have drawn the ire of the international community. Senior leaders in a number of countries have publicly expressed their concerns about the deterioration of the economic and humanitarian conditions of the Iraqi population. Such concerns have led the Security Council to adopt new measures aimed at improving the system established under the so-called oil for food program, to meet the humanitarian needs of the Iraqi people (Resolution 1284). The Council further expressed its intention, once satisfied of Iraq's full cooperation with the reinforced system of ongoing monitoring and verification, to suspend for a period of 120 days—renewable by the Council—prohibitions against the export of civilian commodities and products to Iraq.

Baghdad has so far rejected this overture. In fact, Iraq has refused to accept a mere suspension of sanctions, insisting that they should be lifted in their totality because Baghdad allegedly fulfilled previous obligations in toto. In addition to key Western powers, including the United States and Britain—which rejected Baghdad's claims—Kuwait has also expressed certain reservations. Although Kuwait has supported the Security Council's calls for an improvement of the humanitarian situation in Iraq, it has laid full responsibility for the continuation of that suffering on the government of Iraq.

The plight of the Iraqi people, and the urgent need to alleviate their suffering, has been a source of particular concern to the League of Arab States. For the past decade or so, the issue has received constant attention by the League's secretary-general, who reports to the LAS Council of Ministers on whatever developments or progress may be observed. For their part, Arab foreign ministers expressed their full solidarity with the suffering Iraqi people, stressing the urgent need to lift sanctions as soon as possible. To that end, the ministers decided at their specially convened meeting of 24 January 1999 to exert collective efforts, in cooperation with the United Nations and especially with the members of the Security Council, to lift economic sanctions imposed on Iraq. LAS foreign ministers proposed a timetable that would rescind sanctions concurrently with a comprehensive review of sanctions, and in accordance with the international obligations, referred to in Security Council resolutions on Iraq. A follow-up committee was established to take concrete action in that regard, but partly due to Iraq's boycott of the process, limited common action has been achieved to date.

## *Kuwaiti Prisoners and Missing Persons*

A third contention has been the fate of several hundred Kuwaitis missing in the aftermath of the 1991 Gulf War. The Security Council first raised this question of "humanitarian" concerns when it affirmed, under Resolution 687, Iraq's commitment to facilitate the repatriation of all Kuwaiti and third-country nationals. The specific language of the resolution called on Baghdad to extend all necessary cooperation to the International Committee of the Red Cross in carrying out its mission. Nine years later, no significant progress having been achieved on that score, the Council reaffirmed in Resolution 1284 Iraq's obligations regarding the repatriation of all Kuwaiti and third-country nationals—or their remains. The firm language of the Security Council reiterated Baghdad's obligation to return all Kuwaiti property including archives seized during the 1990–1991 occupation. Finally, the Security Council requested the secretary-general to report thereon periodically, and to appoint a high-level coordinator for these issues.[20]

The League of Arab States attached similar importance to this thorny contention. In March 1999, the League's Council of Ministers requested Secretary-General Esmat Abdul Magid to establish a specific mechanism—within the framework of the Security Council resolutions—to help settle the Arab humanitarian problems between Iraq and Kuwait on the one hand, and those between Iraq and Saudi Arabia on the other. The goal of that mechanism was to better support the International Committee of the Red Cross and best assist the latter's efforts in settling remaining matters.[21]

Various consultations were held under that League mechanism with all parties concerned, but no progress has so far been achieved. To date, Iraq has denied the existence of any remaining Kuwaiti prisoners, and has refrained from providing information about known missing individuals. This has led Kuwait to assert—before the Security Council—that Baghdad was not serious about resolving this humanitarian contention. It called on the Council to pursue the issue with vigor.[22]

## General Appraisal

Clearly, the Kuwait-Iraq border problem—like other border disputes in the Gulf region—not only draws its distant roots from the colonial history of the Middle East but is also laden with serious political rivalries. Most of the Gulf states' borders have never been accurately demarcated. Not surprisingly, several have turned into sources of conflict between neighboring countries that, at the dawn of the twenty-first century, remain unresolved. Noticeably, the preservation of borders drawn or imposed by colonial powers—on the basis of the principle of *uti possidetis*—has often failed to ensure regional stability.

Inasmuch as the demarcation of the Kuwait-Iraq border was successfully concluded by the United Nations—after the 1991 Gulf War—a critical new precedent has been set to diffuse a major source of conflict. Still, several controversial contentions remained, and on their resolution will largely depend the restoration of good-neighborly relations between the two protagonists. This remains a precondition for recovering Arab solidarity among LAS member states. Indeed, few crises have undermined the LAS as severely as has the 1990 Iraqi invasion of Kuwait. No matter how controversial their differences, or how expedient United Nations–imposed solutions, the reality of the Arab world surely necessitated a fundamental political reappraisal of ties between the warring parties.

Among those pending issues, a solution to the problem of Kuwaiti prisoners and missing persons would open the door for restoring better Kuwaiti-Iraqi relations, and improving the general atmosphere in the Gulf region.

On the other hand, a final resolution of the issue of Iraq's weapons of mass destruction—in accordance with relevant Security Council resolutions—would certainly increase pressure on Israel to adhere to the 1968 Treaty on the Non-Proliferation of Nuclear Weapons. Such an action would greatly facilitate the creation of a zone free from all weapons of mass destruction throughout the

Middle East, a goal constantly reaffirmed by the United Nations. It might be added that a fair settlement of the "weapons" and "prisoners" problems would undoubtedly lead to the long overdue lifting of United Nations sanctions against Iraq, which in turn would greatly alleviate the serious economic conditions of the Iraqi population.

Finally, the Kuwait-Iraq border problem underscores once more the need to create new regional legal mechanisms for settling legal issues of such nature. Current efforts by the League of Arab States to create an Arab Court of Justice, for example, and its March 2000 approval to establish a new mechanism for conflict prevention, management, and resolution constitute important steps in that direction.

## Appendix 1

United Nations Security Council
RESOLUTION 687 (91)
S/RES/687 (1991)

Adopted by the Security Council at its 2981st meeting, on 3 April 1991.

The Security Council,

Recalling its resolutions 660 (1990) of 2 August 1990, 661 (1990) of 6 August 1990, 662 (1990) of 9 August 1990, 664 (1990) of 18 August 1990, 665 (1990) of 25 August 1990, 666 (1990) of 13 September 1990, 667 (1990) of 16 September 1990, 669 (1990) of 24 September 1990, 670 (1990) of 25 September 1990, 674 (1990) of 29 October 1990, 677 (1990) of 28 November 1990, 678 (1990) of 29 November 1990 and 686 (1991) of 2 March 1991,

Welcoming the restoration to Kuwait of its sovereignty, independence and territorial integrity and the return of its legitimate Government,

Affirming the commitment of all Member States to the sovereignty, territorial integrity and political independence of Kuwait and Iraq, and noting the intention expressed by the Member States cooperating with Kuwait under paragraph 2 of resolution 678 (1990) to bring their military presence in Iraq to an end as soon as possible consistent with paragraph 8 of resolution 686 (1991),

Reaffirming the need to be assured of Iraq's peaceful intentions in the light of its unlawful invasion and occupation of Kuwait,

Taking note of the letter sent by the Minister for Foreign Affairs of Iraq on 27 February 1991 and those sent pursuant to resolution 686 (1991),

Noting that Iraq and Kuwait, as independent sovereign States, signed at Baghdad on 4 October 1963 "Agreed Minutes Between the State of Kuwait and the Republic of Iraq Regarding the Restoration of Friendly Relations, Recognition and Related Matters," thereby recognizing formally the boundary between Iraq and Kuwait and the allocation of islands, which were registered with the United Nations in accordance with Article 102 of the Charter of the United Nations and in which Iraq recognized the independence and complete sovereignty of the

State of Kuwait within its borders as specified and accepted in the letter of the Prime Minister of Iraq dated 21 July 1932, and as accepted by the Ruler of Kuwait in his letter dated 10 August 1932,

Conscious of the need for demarcation of the said boundary,

Conscious also of the statements by Iraq threatening to use weapons in violation of its obligations under the Geneva Protocol for the Prohibition of the Use in War of Asphyxiating, Poisonous or Other Gases, and of Bacteriological Methods of Warfare, signed at Geneva on 17 June 1925, and of its prior use of chemical weapons and affirming that grave consequences would follow any further use by Iraq of such weapons,

Recalling that Iraq has subscribed to the Declaration adopted by all States participating in the Conference of States Parties to the 1925 Geneva Protocol and Other Interested States, held in Paris from 7 to 11 January 1989, establishing the objective of universal elimination of chemical and biological weapons,

Recalling also that Iraq has signed the Convention on the Prohibition of the Development, Production and Stockpiling of Bacteriological (Biological) and Toxin Weapons and on Their Destruction, of 10 April 1972,

Noting the importance of Iraq ratifying this Convention,

Noting also the importance of all States adhering to this Convention and encouraging its forthcoming Review Conference to reinforce the authority, efficiency and universal scope of the convention,

Stressing the importance of an early conclusion by the Conference on Disarmament of its work on a Convention on the Universal Prohibition of Chemical Weapons and of universal adherence thereto,

Aware of the use by Iraq of ballistic missiles in unprovoked attacks and therefore of the need to take specific measures in regard to such missiles located in Iraq,

Concerned by the reports in the hands of Member States that Iraq has attempted to acquire materials for a nuclear-weapons program contrary to its obligations under the Treaty on the Non-Proliferation of Nuclear Weapons of 1 July 1968,

Recalling the objective of the establishment of a nuclear-weapons-free zone in the region of the Middle East,

Conscious of the threat that all weapons of mass destruction pose to peace and security in the area and of the need to work towards the establishment in the Middle East of a zone free of such weapons,

Conscious also of the objective of achieving balanced and comprehensive control of armaments in the region,

Conscious further of the importance of achieving the objectives noted above using all available means, including a dialogue among the States of the region,

Noting that resolution 686 (1991) marked the lifting of the measures imposed by resolution 661 (1990) in so far as they applied to Kuwait,

Noting also that despite the progress being made in fulfilling the obligations of resolution 686 (1991), many Kuwaiti and third country nationals are still not accounted for and property remains unreturned,

Recalling the International Convention against the Taking of Hostages, opened for signature at New York on 18 December 1979, which categorizes all acts of taking hostages as manifestations of international terrorism,

Deploring threats made by Iraq during the recent conflict to make use of terrorism against targets outside Iraq and the taking of hostages by Iraq,

Taking note with grave concern of the reports of the Secretary-General of 20 March 1991 and 28 March 1991, and conscious of the necessity to meet urgently the humanitarian needs in Kuwait and Iraq,

Bearing in mind its objective of restoring international peace and security in the area as set out in recent resolutions of the Security Council,

Conscious of the need to take the following measures acting under Chapter VII of the Charter,

1. Affirms all thirteen resolutions noted above, except as expressly changed below to achieve the goals of this resolution, including a formal cease-fire;
2. Demands that Iraq and Kuwait respect the inviolability of the international boundary and the allocation of islands set out in the "Agreed Minutes Between the State of Kuwait and the Republic of Iraq Regarding the Restoration of Friendly Relations, Recognition and Related Matters," signed by them in the exercise of their sovereignty at Baghdad on 4 October 1963 and registered with the United Nations and published by the United Nations in document 7063, United Nations, Treaty Series, 1964;
3. Calls upon the Secretary-General to lend his assistance to make arrangements with Iraq and Kuwait to demarcate the boundary between Iraq and Kuwait, drawing on appropriate material, including the map transmitted by Security Council document S/22412 and to report back to the Security Council within one month;
4. Decides to guarantee the inviolability of the above-mentioned international boundary and to take as appropriate all necessary measures to that end in accordance with the Charter of the United Nations;
5. Requests the Secretary-General, after consulting with Iraq and Kuwait, to submit within three days to the Security Council for its approval a plan for the immediate deployment of a United Nations observer unit to monitor the [Khwar] Abd[a]llah and a demilitarized zone, which is hereby established, extending ten kilometers into Iraq and five kilometers into Kuwait from the boundary referred to in the "Agreed Minutes Between the State of Kuwait and the Republic of Iraq Regarding the Restoration of Friendly Relations, Recognition and Related Matters" of 4 October 1963; to deter violations of the boundary through its presence in and surveillance of the demilitarized zone; to observe any hostile or potentially hostile action mounted from the territory of one State to the other; and for the Secretary-General to report regularly to the Security Council on the operations of the unit, and immediately if there are serious violations of the zone or potential threats to peace;
6. Notes that as soon as the Secretary-General notifies the Security Council of the completion of the deployment of the United Nations observer unit, the conditions will be established for the Member States cooperating

with Kuwait in accordance with resolution 678 (1990) to bring their military presence in Iraq to an end consistent with resolution 686 (1991);

7. Invites Iraq to reaffirm unconditionally its obligations under the Geneva Protocol for the Prohibition of the Use in War of Asphyxiating, Poisonous or Other Gases, and of Bacteriological Methods of Warfare, signed at Geneva on 17 June 1925, and to ratify the Convention on the Prohibition of the Development, Production and Stockpiling of Bacteriological (Biological) and Toxin Weapons and on Their Destruction, of 10 April 1972;

8. Decides that Iraq shall unconditionally accept the destruction, removal, or rendering harmless, under international supervision, of:
   (a) All chemical and biological weapons and all stocks of agents and all related subsystems and components and all research, development, support and manufacturing facilities;
   (b) All ballistic missiles with a range greater than 150 kilometers and related major parts, and repair and production facilities;

9. Decides also for the implementation of paragraph 8 above, the following:
   (a) Iraq shall submit to the Secretary-General, within fifteen days of the adoption of the present resolution, a declaration of the locations, amounts and types of all items specified in paragraph 8 and agree to urgent, on-site inspection as specified below;
   (b) The Secretary-General, in consultation with the appropriate Governments and, where appropriate, with the Director-General of the World Health Organization, within forty-five days of the passage of the present resolution, shall develop, and submit to the Council for approval, a plan calling for the completion of the following acts within forty-five days of such approval:
      (i) The forming of a Special Commission, which shall carry out immediate on-site inspection of Iraq's biological, chemical and missile capabilities, based on Iraq's declarations and the designation of any additional locations by the Special Commission itself;
      (ii) The yielding by Iraq of possession to the Special Commission for destruction, removal or rendering harmless, taking into account the requirements of public safety, of all items specified under paragraph 8 (a) above, including items at the additional locations designated by the Special Commission under paragraph 9 (b) (i) above and the destruction by Iraq, under the supervision of the Special Commission, of all its missile capabilities, including launchers, as specified under paragraph 8 (b) above;
      (iii) The provision by the Special Commission of the assistance and cooperation to the Director-General of the International Atomic Energy Agency required in paragraphs 12 and 13 below;

10. Decides further that Iraq shall unconditionally undertake not to use, develop, construct or acquire any of the items specified in paragraphs 8 and 9 above and requests the Secretary-General, in consultation with the Special Commission, to develop a plan for the future ongoing monitoring and verification of Iraq's compliance with this paragraph, to be submitted to the Security Council for approval within one hundred and twenty days of the passage of this resolution;
11. Invites Iraq to reaffirm unconditionally its obligations under the Treaty on the Non-Proliferation of Nuclear Weapons of 1 July 1968;
12. Decides that Iraq shall unconditionally agree not to acquire or develop nuclear weapons or nuclear-weapons-usable material or any subsystems or components or any research, development, support or manufacturing facilities related to the above; to submit to the Secretary-General and the Director-General of the International Atomic Energy Agency within fifteen days of the adoption of the present resolution a declaration of the locations, amounts, and types of all items specified above; to place all of its nuclear-weapons-usable materials under the exclusive control, for custody and removal, of the International Atomic Energy Agency, with the assistance and cooperation of the Special Commission as provided for in the plan of the Secretary-General discussed in paragraph 9 (b) above; to accept, in accordance with the arrangements provided for in paragraph 13 below, urgent on-site inspection and the destruction, removal or rendering harmless as appropriate of all items specified above; and to accept the plan discussed in paragraph 13 below for the future ongoing monitoring and verification of its compliance with these undertakings;
13. Requests the Director-General of the International Atomic Energy Agency, through the Secretary-General, with the assistance and cooperation of the Special Commission as provided for in the plan of the Secretary-General in paragraph 9 (b) above, to carry out immediate on-site inspection of Iraq's nuclear capabilities based on Iraq's declarations and the designation of any additional locations by the Special Commission; to develop a plan for submission to the Security Council within forty-five days calling for the destruction, removal, or rendering harmless as appropriate of all items listed in paragraph 12 above; to carry out the plan within forty-five days following approval by the Security Council; and to develop a plan, taking into account the rights and obligations of Iraq under the Treaty on the Non-Proliferation of Nuclear Weapons of 1 July 1968, for the future ongoing monitoring and verification of Iraq's compliance with paragraph 12 above, including an inventory of all nuclear material in Iraq subject to the Agency's verification and inspections to confirm that Agency safeguards cover all relevant nuclear activities in Iraq, to be submitted to the Security Council for approval within one hundred and twenty days of the passage of the present resolution;

14. Notes that the actions to be taken by Iraq in paragraphs 8, 9, 10, 11, 12 and 13 of the present resolution represent steps towards the goal of establishing in the Middle East a zone free from weapons of mass destruction and all missiles for their delivery and the objective of a global ban on chemical weapons;
15. Requests the Secretary-General to report to the Security Council on the steps taken to facilitate the return of all Kuwaiti property seized by Iraq, including a list of any property that Kuwait claims has not been returned or which has not been returned intact;
16. Reaffirms that Iraq, without prejudice to the debts and obligations of Iraq arising prior to 2 August 1990, which will be addressed through the normal mechanisms, is liable under international law for any direct loss, damage, including environmental damage and the depletion of natural resources, or injury to foreign Governments, nationals and corporations, as a result of Iraq's unlawful invasion and occupation of Kuwait;
17. Decides that all Iraqi statements made since 2 August 1990 repudiating its foreign debt are null and void, and demands that Iraq adhere scrupulously to all of its obligations concerning servicing and repayment of its foreign debt;
18. Decides also to create a fund to pay compensation for claims that fall within paragraph 16 above and to establish a Commission that will administer the fund;
19. Directs the Secretary-General to develop and present to the Security Council for decision, no later than thirty days following the adoption of the present resolution, recommendations for the fund to meet the requirement for the payment of claims established in accordance with paragraph 18 above and for a program to implement the decisions in paragraphs 16, 17 and 18 above, including: administration of the fund; mechanisms for determining the appropriate level of Iraq's contribution to the fund based on a percentage of the value of the exports of petroleum and petroleum products from Iraq not to exceed a figure to be suggested to the Council by the Secretary-General, taking into account the requirements of the people of Iraq, Iraq's payment capacity as assessed in conjunction with the international financial institutions taking into consideration external debt service, and the needs of the Iraqi economy; arrangements for ensuring that payments are made to the fund; the process by which funds will be allocated and claims paid; appropriate procedures for evaluating losses, listing claims and verifying their validity and resolving disputed claims in respect of Iraq's liability as specified in paragraph 16 above; and the composition of the Commission designated above;
20. Decides, effective immediately, that the prohibitions against the sale or supply to Iraq of commodities or products, other than medicine and health supplies, and prohibitions against financial transactions related thereto contained in resolution 661 (1990) shall not apply to foodstuffs notified to the Security Council Committee established by resolution

661 (1990) concerning the situation between Iraq and Kuwait or, with the approval of that Committee, under the simplified and accelerated "no-objection" procedure, to materials and supplies for essential civilian needs as identified in the report of the Secretary-General dated 20 March 1991, and in any further findings of humanitarian need by the Committee;

21. Decides that the Security Council shall review the provisions of paragraph 20 above every sixty days in the light of the policies and practices of the Government of Iraq, including the implementation of all relevant resolutions of the Security Council, for the purpose of determining whether to reduce or lift the prohibitions referred to therein;

22. Decides also that upon the approval by the Security Council of the program called for in paragraph 19 above and upon Council agreement that Iraq has completed all actions contemplated in paragraphs 8, 9, 10, 11, 12 and 13 above, the prohibitions against the import of commodities and products originating in Iraq and the prohibitions against financial transactions related thereto contained in resolution 661 (1990) shall have no further force or effect;

23. Decides further that, pending action by the Security Council under paragraph 22 above, the Security Council Committee established by resolution 661 (1990) shall be empowered to approve, when required to assure adequate financial resources on the part of Iraq to carry out the activities under paragraph 20 above, exceptions to the prohibition against the import of commodities and products originating in Iraq;

24. Decides that, in accordance with resolution 661 (1990) and subsequent related resolutions and until a further decision is taken by the Security Council, all States shall continue to prevent the sale or supply, or the promotion or facilitation of such sale or supply, to Iraq by their nationals, or from their territories or using their flag vessels or aircraft, of:
    (a) Arms and related materiel of all types, specifically including the sale or transfer through other means of all forms of conventional military equipment, including for paramilitary forces, and spare parts and components and their means of production, for such equipment;
    (b) Items specified and defined in paragraphs 8 and 12 above not otherwise covered above;
    (c) Technology under licensing or other transfer arrangements used in the production, utilization or stockpiling of items specified in subparagraphs (a) and (b) above;
    (d) Personnel or materials for training or technical support services relating to the design, development, manufacture, use, maintenance or support of items specified in subparagraphs (a) and (b) above;

25. Calls upon all States and international organizations to act strictly in accordance with paragraph 24 above, notwithstanding the existence of any contracts, agreements, licenses or any other arrangements;

26. Requests the Secretary-General, in consultation with appropriate Governments, to develop within sixty days, for the approval of the Security

Council, guidelines to facilitate full international implementation of paragraphs 24 and 25 above and paragraph 27 below, and to make them available to all States and to establish a procedure for updating these guidelines periodically;

27. Calls upon all States to maintain such national controls and procedures and to take such other actions consistent with the guidelines to be established by the Security Council under paragraph 26 above as may be necessary to ensure compliance with the terms of paragraph 24 above, and calls upon international organizations to take all appropriate steps to assist in ensuring such full compliance;

28. Agrees to review its decisions in paragraphs 22, 23, 24 and 25 above, except for the items specified and defined in paragraphs 8 and 12 above, on a regular basis and in any case one hundred and twenty days following passage of the present resolution, taking into account Iraq's compliance with the resolution and general progress towards the control of armaments in the region;

29. Decides that all States, including Iraq, shall take the necessary measures to ensure that no claim shall lie at the instance of the Government of Iraq, or of any person or body in Iraq, or of any person claiming through or for the benefit of any such person or body, in connection with any contract or other transaction where its performance was affected by reason of the measures taken by the Security Council in resolution 661 (1990) and related resolutions;

30. Decides that, in furtherance of its commitment to facilitate the repatriation of all Kuwaiti and third country nationals, Iraq shall extend all necessary cooperation to the International Committee of the Red Cross, providing lists of such persons, facilitating the access of the International Committee of the Red Cross to all such persons wherever located or detained and facilitating the search by the International Committee of the Red Cross for those Kuwaiti and third country nationals still unaccounted for;

31. Invites the International Committee of the Red Cross to keep the Secretary-General apprised as appropriate of all activities undertaken in connection with facilitating the repatriation or return of all Kuwaiti and third country nationals or their remains present in Iraq on or after 2 August 1990;

32. Requires Iraq to inform the Security Council that it will not commit or support any act of international terrorism or allow any organization directed towards commission of such acts to operate within its territory and to condemn unequivocally and renounce all acts, methods and practices of terrorism;

33. Declares that, upon official notification by Iraq to the Secretary-General and to the Security Council of its acceptance of the provisions above, a formal cease-fire is effective between Iraq and Kuwait and the Member States cooperating with Kuwait in accordance with resolution 678 (1990);

34. Decides to remain seized of the matter and to take such further steps as may be required for the implementation of the present resolution and to secure peace and security in the area.

## Appendix 2

United Nations Security Council
RESOLUTION 1284 (99)
S/RES/1284 (1999)

Adopted by the Security Council at its 4084th meeting, on 17 December 1999.

The Security Council,
Recalling its previous relevant resolutions, including its resolutions 661 (1990) of 6 August 1990, 687 (1991) of 3 April 1991, 699 (1991) of 17 June 1991, 707 (1991) of 15 August 1991, 715 (1991) of 11 October 1991, 986 (1995) of 14 April 1995, 1051 (1996) of 27 March 1996, 1153 (1998) of 20 February 1998, 1175 (1998) of 19 June 1998, 1242 (1999) of 21 May 1999 and 1266 (1999) of 4 October 1999,
Recalling the approval by the Council in its resolution 715 (1991) of the plans for future ongoing monitoring and verification submitted by the Secretary General and the Director General of the International Atomic Energy Agency (IAEA) in pursuance of paragraphs 10 and 13 of resolution 687 (1991),
Welcoming the reports of the three panels on Iraq (S/1999/356) and having held a comprehensive consideration of them-and the recommendations contained in them,
Stressing the importance of a comprehensive approach to the full implementation of all relevant Security Council resolutions regarding Iraq and the need for Iraqi compliance with these resolutions,
Recalling the goal of establishing in the Middle East a zone free from weapons of mass destruction and all missiles for their delivery and the objective of a global ban on chemical weapons as referred to in paragraph 14 of resolution 687 (1991),
Concerned at the humanitarian situation in Iraq, and determined to improve that situation,
Recalling with concern that the repatriation and return of all Kuwaiti and third country nationals or their remains, present in Iraq on or after 2 August 1990, pursuant to paragraph 2 (c) of resolution 686 (1991) of 2 March 1991 and paragraph 30 of resolution 687 (1991), have not yet been fully carried out by Iraq,
Recalling that in its resolutions 686 (1991) and 687 (1991) the Council demanded that Iraq return in the shortest possible time all Kuwaiti property it had seized, and noting with regret that Iraq has still not complied fully with this demand,
Acknowledging the progress made by Iraq towards compliance with the provisions of resolution 687 (1991), but noting that, as a result of its failure to imple-

ment the relevant Council resolutions fully, the conditions do not exist which would enable the Council to take a decision pursuant to resolution 687 (1991) to lift the prohibitions referred to in that resolution,

Reiterating the commitment of all Member States to the sovereignty, territorial integrity and political independence of Kuwait, Iraq and the neighboring States,

Acting under Chapter VII of the Charter of the United Nations, and taking into account that operative provisions of this resolution relate to previous resolutions adopted under Chapter VII of the Charter,

1. Decides to establish, as a subsidiary body of the Council, the United Nations Monitoring, Verification and Inspection Commission (UNMOVIC) which replaces the Special Commission established pursuant to paragraph 9 (b) of resolution 687 (1991);
2. Decides also that UNMOVIC will undertake the responsibilities mandated to the special Commission by the Council, with regard to the verification of compliance by Iraq with its obligations under paragraphs 8, 9 and 10 of resolution 687 (1991) and other related resolutions, that UNMOVIC will establish and operate, as was recommended by the panel on disarmament and current and future ongoing monitoring and verification issues, a reinforced system of ongoing monitoring and verification, which will implement the plan approved by the Council in resolution 715 (1991) and address unresolved disarmament issues, and that UNMOVIC will identify, as necessary in accordance with its mandate, additional sites in Iraq to be covered by the reinforced system of ongoing monitoring and verification;
3. Reaffirms the provisions of the relevant resolutions with regard to the role of the IAEA in addressing compliance by Iraq with paragraphs 12 and 13 of resolution 687 (1991) and other related resolutions, and requests the Director General of the IAEA to maintain this role with the assistance and cooperation of UNMOVIC;
4. Reaffirms its resolutions 687 (1991), 699 (1991), 707 (1991), 715 (1991), 1051 (1996), 1154 (1998) and all other relevant resolutions and statements of its President, which establish the criteria for Iraqi compliance, affirms that the obligations of Iraq referred to in those resolutions and statements with regard to cooperation with the Special Commission, unrestricted access and provision of information will apply in respect of UNMOVIC, and decides in particular that Iraq shall allow UNMOVIC teams immediate, unconditional and unrestricted access to any and all areas, facilities, equipment, records and means of transport which they wish to inspect in accordance with the mandate of UNMOVIC, as well as to all officials and other persons under the authority of the Iraqi Government whom UNMOVIC wishes to interview so that UNMOVIC may fully discharge its mandate;
5. Requests the Secretary-General, within 30 days of the adoption of this resolution, to appoint, after consultation with and subject to the approval

of the Council, an Executive Chairman of UNMOVIC who will take up his mandated tasks as soon as possible, and, in consultation with the Executive Chairman and the Council members, to appoint suitably qualified experts as a College of Commissioners for UNMOVIC which will meet regularly to review the implementation of this and other relevant resolutions and provide professional advice and guidance to the Executive Chairman, including on significant policy decisions and on written reports to be submitted to the Council through the Secretary-General;

6. Requests the Executive Chairman of UNMOVIC, within 45 days of his appointment, to submit to the Council, in consultation with and through the Secretary-General, for its approval an organizational plan for UNMOVIC, including its structure, staffing requirements, management guidelines, recruitment and training procedures, incorporating as appropriate the recommendations of the panel on disarmament and current and future ongoing monitoring and verification issues, and recognizing in particular the need for an effective, cooperative management structure for the new organization, for staffing with suitably qualified and experienced personnel, who would be regarded as international civil servants subject to Article 100 of the Charter of the United Nations, drawn from the broadest possible geographical base, including as he deems necessary from international arms control organizations, and for the provision of high quality technical and cultural training;

7. Decides that UNMOVIC and the IAEA, not later than 60 days after they have both started work in Iraq, will each draw up, for approval by the Council, a work program for the discharge of their mandates, which will include both the implementation of the reinforced system of ongoing monitoring and verification, and the key remaining disarmament tasks to be completed by Iraq pursuant to its obligations to comply with the disarmament requirements of resolution 687 (1991) and other related resolutions, which constitute the governing standard of Iraqi compliance, and further decides that what is required of Iraq for the implementation of each task shall be clearly defined and precise;

8. Requests the Executive Chairman of UNMOVIC and the Director General of the IAEA, drawing on the expertise of other international organizations as appropriate, to establish a unit which will have the responsibilities of the joint unit constituted by the Special Commission and the Director General of the IAEA under paragraph 16 of the export/import mechanism approved by resolution 1051 (1996), and also requests the Executive Chairman of UNMOVIC, in consultation with the Director General of the IAEA, to resume the revision and updating of the lists of items and technology to which the mechanism applies;

9. Decides that the Government of Iraq shall he liable for the full costs of UNMOVIC and the IAEA in relation to their work under this and other related resolutions on Iraq;

10. Requests Member States to give full cooperation to UNMOVIC and the IAEA in the discharge of their mandates;

11. Decides that UNMOVIC shall take over all assets, liabilities and archives of the Special Commission, and that it shall assume the Special Commission's part in agreements existing between the Special Commission and Iraq and between the United Nations and Iraq, and affirms that the Executive Chairman, the Commissioners and the personnel serving with UNMOVIC shall have the rights, privileges, facilities and immunities of the Special Commission;
12. Requests the Executive Chairman of UNMOVIC to report, through the Secretary-General, to the Council, following consultation with the Commissioners, every three months on the work of UNMOVIC, pending submission of the first reports referred to in paragraph 33 below, and to report immediately when the reinforced system of ongoing monitoring and verification is fully operational in Iraq;
13. Reiterates the obligation of Iraq, in furtherance of its commitment to facilitate the repatriation of all Kuwaiti and third country nationals referred to in paragraph 30 of resolution 687 (1991), to extend all necessary cooperation to the International Committee of the Red Cross, and calls upon the Government of Iraq to resume cooperation with the Tripartite Commission and Technical Subcommittee established to facilitate work on this issue;
14. Requests the Secretary-General to report to the Council every four months on compliance by Iraq with its obligations regarding the repatriation or return of all Kuwaiti and third country nationals or their remains, to report every six months on the return of all Kuwaiti property, including archives, seized by Iraq, and to appoint a high-level coordinator for these issues;
15. Authorizes States, notwithstanding the provisions of paragraphs 3 (a), 3 (b) and 4 of resolution 661 (1990) and subsequent relevant resolutions, to permit the import of any volume of petroleum and petroleum products originating in Iraq, including financial and other essential transactions directly relating thereto, as required for the purposes and on the conditions set out in paragraph 1 (a) and (b) and subsequent provisions of resolution 986 (1995) and related resolutions;
16. Underlines, in this context, its intention to take further action, including permitting the use of additional export routes for petroleum and petroleum products, under appropriate conditions otherwise consistent with the purpose and provisions of resolution 986 (1995) and related resolutions;
17. Directs the Committee established by resolution 661 (1990) to approve, on the basis of proposals from the Secretary-General, lists of humanitarian items, including foodstuffs, pharmaceutical and medical supplies, as well as basic or standard medical and agricultural equipment and basic or standard educational items, decides, notwithstanding paragraph 3 of resolution 661 (1990) and paragraph 20 of resolution 687 (1991), that supplies of these items will not be submitted for approval of that Committee, except for items subject to the provisions of resolution

1051 (1996), and will be notified to the Secretary-General and financed in accordance with the provisions of paragraph 8 (a) and 8 (b) of resolution 986 (1995), and requests the Secretary-General to inform the Committee in a timely manner of all such notifications received and actions taken;

18. Requests the Committee established by resolution 661 (1990) to appoint, in accordance with resolutions 1175 (1998) and 1210 (1998), a group of experts, including independent inspection agents appointed by the Secretary-General in accordance with paragraph 6 of resolution 986 (1995), decides that this group will be mandated to approve speedily contracts for the parts and the equipment necessary to enable Iraq to increase its exports of petroleum and petroleum products, according to lists of parts and equipment approved by that Committee for each individual project, and requests the Secretary-General to continue to provide for the monitoring of these parts and equipment inside Iraq;

19. Encourages Member States and international organizations to provide supplementary humanitarian assistance to Iraq and published material of an educational character to Iraq;

20. Decides to suspend, for an initial period of six months from the date of the adoption of this resolution and subject to review, the implementation of paragraph 8 (9) of resolution 986 (1995);

21. Requests the Secretary-General to take steps to maximize, drawing as necessary on the advice of specialists, including representatives of international humanitarian organizations, the effectiveness of the arrangements set out in resolution 986 (1995) and related resolutions including the humanitarian benefit to the Iraqi population in all areas of the country, and further requests the Secretary-General to continue to enhance as necessary the United Nations observation process in Iraq, ensuring that all supplies under the humanitarian program are utilized as authorized, to bring to the attention of the Council any circumstances preventing or impeding effective and equitable distribution and to keep the Council informed of the steps taken towards the implementation of this paragraph;

22. Requests also the Secretary-General to minimize the cost of the United Nations activities associated with the implementation of resolution 986 (1995) as well as the cost of the independent inspection agents and the certified public by him, in accordance with paragraphs 6 and 7 of resolution 986 (1995);

23. Requests further the Secretary-General to provide Iraq and the committee established by resolution 661 (1990) with a daily statement of the status of the escrow account established by paragraph 7 of resolution 986 (1995);

24. Requests the Secretary-General to make the necessary arrangements, subject to Security Council approval, to allow funds deposited in the escrow account established by resolution 986 (1995) to he used for the purchase of locally produced goods and to meet the local cost for

essential civilian needs which have been funded in accordance with the provisions of resolution 986 (1995) and related resolutions, including, where appropriate, the cost of installation and training services;
25. Directs the Committee established by resolution 661 (1990) to take a decision on all applications in respect of humanitarian and essential civilian needs within a target of two working days of receipt of these applications from the Secretary-General, and to ensure that all approval and notification letters issued by the Committee stipulate delivery within a specified time, according to the nature of the items to be supplied, and requests the Secretary-General to notify the Committee of all applications for humanitarian items which are included in the list to which the export/import mechanism approved by resolution 1051 (1996) applies;
26. Decides that Hajj pilgrimage flights which do not transport cargo into or out of Iraq are exempt from the provisions of paragraph 3 of resolution 661 (1990) and resolution 670 (1990), provided timely notification of each flight is made to the Committee established by resolution 661 (1990), and requests the Secretary-General to make the necessary arrangements, for approval by the Security Council, to provide for reasonable expenses related to the Hajj pilgrimage to be met by funds in the escrow account established by resolution 986 (1995);
27. Calls upon the Government of Iraq:
    (i) to take all steps to ensure the timely and equitable distribution of all humanitarian goods, in particular medical supplies, and to remove and avoid delays at its warehouses;
    (ii) to address effectively the needs of vulnerable groups, including children, pregnant women, the disabled, the elderly and the mentally ill among others, and to allow freer access, without any discrimination, including on the basis of religion or nationality, by United Nations agencies and humanitarian organizations to all areas and sections of the population for evaluation of their nutritional and humanitarian condition;
    (iii) to prioritize applications for humanitarian goods under the arrangements set out in resolution 986 (1995) and related resolutions;
    (iv) to ensure that those involuntarily displaced receive humanitarian assistance without the need to demonstrate that they have resided for six months in their places of temporary residence;
    (v) to extend full cooperation to the United Nations Office for Project Services mine-clearance program in the three northern Governorates of Iraq and to consider the initiation of the de-mining efforts in other Governorates;
28. Requests the Secretary-General to report on the progress made in meeting the humanitarian needs of the Iraqi people and on the revenues necessary to meet those needs, including recommendations on necessary additions to the current allocation for oil spare parts and equipment, on

the basis of a comprehensive survey of the condition of the Iraqi oil production sector, not later than 60 days from the date of the adoption of this resolution and updated thereafter as necessary;

29. Expresses its readiness to authorize additions to the current allocation for oil spare parts and equipment, on the basis of the report and recommendations requested in paragraph 28 above, in order to meet the humanitarian purposes set out in resolution 986 (1995) and related resolutions;

30. Requests the Secretary-General to establish a group of experts, including oil industry experts, to report within 100 days of the date of adoption of this resolution on Iraq's existing petroleum production and export capacity and to make recommendations, to be updated as necessary, on alternatives for increasing Iraq's petroleum production and export capacity in a manner consistent with the purposes of relevant resolutions, and on the options for involving foreign oil companies in Iraq's oil sector, including investments, subject to appropriate monitoring and controls;

31. Notes that in the event of the Council acting as provided for in paragraph 33 of this resolution to suspend the prohibitions referred to in that paragraph, appropriate arrangements and procedures will need, subject to paragraph 35 below, to be agreed by the Council in good time beforehand, including suspension of provisions of resolution 986 (1995) and related resolutions;

32. Requests the Secretary-General to report to the Council on the implementation of paragraphs 15 to 30 of this resolution within 30 days of the adoption of this resolution;

33. Expresses its intention, upon receipt of reports from the Executive Chairman of UNMOVIC and from the Director General of the IAEA that Iraq has cooperated in all respects with UNMOVIC and the IAEA in particular in fulfilling the work programs in all the aspects referred to in paragraph 7 above, for a period of 120 days after the date on which the Council is in receipt of reports from both UNMOVIC and the IAEA that the reinforced system of ongoing monitoring and verification is fully operational, to suspend with the fundamental objective of improving the humanitarian situation in Iraq and securing the implementation of the Council's resolutions, for a period of 120 days renewable by the Council, and subject to the elaboration of effective financial and other operational measures to ensure that Iraq does not acquire prohibited items, prohibitions against the import of commodities and products originating in Iraq, and prohibitions against the sale, supply and delivery to Iraq of civilian commodities and products other than those referred to in paragraph 24 of resolution 687 (1991) or those to which the mechanism established by resolution 1051 (1996) applies;

34. Decides that in reporting to the Council for the purposes of paragraph 33 above, the Executive Chairman of UNMOVIC will include as a basis for his assessment the progress made in completing the tasks referred to in paragraph 7 above;

35. Decides that if at any time the Executive Chairman of UNMOVIC or the Director General of the IAEA reports that Iraq is not cooperating in all respects with UNMOVIC or the IAEA or if Iraq is in the process of acquiring any prohibited items, the suspension of the prohibitions referred to in paragraph 33 above shall terminate on the fifth working day following the report, unless the Council decides to the contrary;

36. Expresses its intention to approve arrangements for effective financial and other operational measures, including on the delivery of and payment for authorized civilian commodities and products to be sold or supplied to Iraq, in order to ensure that Iraq does not acquire prohibited items in the event of suspension of the prohibitions referred to in paragraph 33 above, to begin the elaboration of such measures not later than the date of the receipt of the initial reports referred to in paragraph 33 above, and to approve such arrangements before the Council decision in accordance with that paragraph;

37. Further expresses its intention to take steps, based on the report and recommendations requested in paragraph 30 above, and consistent with the purpose of resolution 986 (1995) and related resolutions, to enable Iraq to increase its petroleum production and export capacity, upon receipt of the reports relating to the cooperation in all respects with UNMOVIC and the IAEA referred to in paragraph 33 above;

38. Reaffirms its intention to act in accordance with the relevant provisions of resolution 687 (1991) on the termination of prohibitions referred to in that resolution;

39. Decides to remain actively seized of the matter and expresses its intention to consider action in accordance with paragraph 33 above no later than 12 months from the date of the adoption of this resolution provided the conditions set out in paragraph 33 above have been satisfied by Iraq.

## Notes

This paper was prepared by its author in his private capacity.

1. United Nations, Security Council, *Resolution 687 (1991)*, New York, 1991. The resolution is reproduced as Appendix 1.
2. Jill Crystal, *Kuwait: The Transformation of an Oil State*, Boulder, Colorado: Westview Press, 1992, pp. 11–13.
3. J. B. Kelly, *Arabia, the Gulf and the West*, New York: Basic Books, Inc., 1980, pp. 168–72.
4. Frederick F. Anscombe, *The Ottoman Gulf: The Creation of Kuwait, Saudi Arabia and Qatar*, New York: Columbia University Press, 1997, pp. 113–42.
5. Husain M. Albaharna, *The Arabian Gulf States: Their Legal and Political Status and Their International Problems*, Beirut: Librairie du Liban, 1978, p. 254.
6. Ibid., pp. 254–57.
7. Ibid., p. 256.
8. David H. Finnie, *Shifting Lines in the Sand: Kuwait's Elusive Frontier with Iraq*, London: I. B. Tauris and Company, Ltd., 1992, pp. 126–32.
9. Ibid., pp. 132–34.
10. Charles W. Koburger, Jr., "The Kuwait Confrontation of 1961," *United States Naval Institute Proceedings* 100:1, January 1974, pp. 42–9.

11. Hussein A. Hassouna, *The League of Arab States and Regional Disputes: A Study of Middle East Conflicts,* Dobbs Ferry, New York: Oceana, 1975, pp. 98–107.
12. Finnie, *op. cit.,* pp. 149–51.
13. Resolution 687, *op. cit.*
14. M. H. Mendelson and S. C. Hulton, "The Iraq-Kuwait Boundary: Legal Aspects," *Revue Belge de Droit International* 2, 1990, p. 294.
15. United Nations, Security Council, "Final Report on the Demarcation of the International Boundary Between the Republic of Iraq and the State of Kuwait by the United Nations Iraq-Kuwait Boundary Demarcation Commission," S/25811 (20 May 1993), New York, 21 May 1993.
16. United Nations, Security Council, "Letter dated 21 May 1992 from the Minister for Foreign Affairs of the Republic of Iraq addressed to the Secretary General of the United Nations," S/24044 (1999), New York: 17 December 1999.
17. "Letter dated 12 November 1994 from the Minister for Foreign Affairs of the Republic of Iraq addressed to the Secretary General of the United Nations," S/19994/1288, New York: 14 November 1994. The content of this letter may explain the reason why Iraq changed its position on the issue. As stated, it proceeded from the premise that the Security Council would follow up in the implementation of its resolutions, based on the principles of justice and fairness, principally through the lifting of the comprehensive embargo.
18. League of Arab States, "Statement adopted by the Arab Ministers for Foreign Affairs," Cairo, Egypt: 24 January 1999.
19. United Nations, Security Council, "Statement by the Representative of Kuwait before the Security Council," S/4084, New York: 17 December 1999.
20. United Nations, Security Council, S/RES/1284 (1999), New York: 17 December 1999 (see Appendix 2). Ambassador Yuri Vorontsov was appointed for that purpose, and the first report on his activities was submitted to the Security Council on 26 April 2000. See United Nations, Security Council, S/2000/347, New York: 2000.
21. League of Arab States, "Council Resolution Number 5837," 3rd Ordinary Session, Cairo, Egypt: 18 March 1999. Pursuant to this resolution, the League's secretary-general has conducted high-level consultations on that issue with the United Nations secretary-general, the special United Nations coordinator Ambassador Vorontsov, the president of the International Committee of the Red Cross, and Kuwaiti, Saudi, and Iraqi officials.
22. "Statement by the Representative of Kuwait," S/4084, *op. cit.*

# BORDER DISPUTES

## CHAPTER 15

## *Yemeni-Saudi Relations Gone Awry*

### Mohammed A. Zabarah

The Yemeni-Saudi relationship has been a major topic to scholars, policy decision makers, and legalists for several reasons: first, because of the enormous amount of oil on the Arabian Peninsula (nearly 57 percent of the world's oil originates from the littoral states of the Arabian Gulf) and the intense world interest in maintaining security and stability in the region; second, because of the need to see that the "new world order," which calls for the normalization of relations between states, progresses; and third, because Yemeni-Saudi relations have been kept a hostage to the border dispute between them for the past six decades. This has occurred despite the fact that both Arab states have attempted to downplay their contentiousness by emphasizing their intrinsic cultural bonds and their Islamic roots.

It is within this context that the Yemeni-Saudi border dispute is best analyzed. This chapter does not purport to examine the legal aspects of the dispute. Rather, it evaluates its implications in the formulation and conduct of the two states' policies toward each other. Toward this objective, the study analyzes the relationship between the two states by identifying the perceptions each state has of the other, and how those perceptions influence the course of their relationship. The hypothesis contends that the perceptions of the Yemeni governments of Saudi Arabia—which evolved after the Yemeni revolution of 26 September 1962—have been less coherent and more antagonistic.

Following a brief background of the Yemeni-Saudi relationship immediately after the two states became independent, the study will focus on the 1934 Taif Agreement, and how it impacted the relationship between the two neighbors. It will then devote its attention to the ramifications of the political changes that evolved in Yemen, and their impact on the Yemeni/Saudi relationship. Finally, it will examine the consequences of the Yemeni policy during the second Gulf Crisis and the subsequent Gulf War (1991), and how that policy affected the border issues between the two.

## The 1934 Taif Agreement

The 1934 Taif Agreement between Yemen and Saudi Arabia officially ended the brief war between the two states. It is considered the benchmark that has defined their relationship since then. In fact, the war was the culmination of initial confrontational contacts, which began as soon as the Ottoman rule of the Arabian Peninsula ended in 1918. Importantly, the agreement was the first *treaty* between two Arab states, and it impelled both to curtail their differences to ensure their security and independence.

Inasmuch as the confrontational aspect of Yemeni/Saudi ties was directly related to mutual claims on Asir, the province situated south of the Hejaz in the southwestern part of the Arabian Peninsula and bordering on the Red Sea, all subsequent contacts may be understood through the value attached to that strategic territory. The area is larger than Jordan and Lebanon put together. In 1828, Asir fell to Ottoman occupation, and was treated as a semi-autonomous region. When Ottoman rule ended in 1918, Muhammed al-Idrisi, then ruler over the territory, became titular head of the province. Encouraged by both Italy and Britain, which provided him with arms and money, al-Idrisi adopted a policy aimed at establishing Asir as an independent, sovereign state. Britain went so far as to hand al-Idrisi the port city of Hodeidah after bombarding and occupying it in 1918. As a result of al-Idrisi's policies, an open conflict ensued with Imam Yahyah of Yemen, who ruled over the Mutawakilite Kingdom of Yemen.[1]

Imam Yahyah quickly sent his armies to recapture Hudaydah, and began his march into Asir. Ali al-Idrisi, who succeeded his father in 1922, was unable to forestall the advances of the Imam's forces. He, thereupon, proposed an agreement to the Imam recognizing the latter's interests in Asir. Al-Idrisi was willing to pay homage to the Imam and defer to him the rights to be an arbitrator on all issues other than political questions. Still, his proposal fell short of accepting the Imam's outright political control over Asir Province.[2] In the event, and when the Imam rejected this proposal, al-Idrisi entered into negotiations with King Abdul Aziz bin Abdul Rahman Al Saud in Saudi Arabia. King Abdul Aziz, like Imam Yahyah, had been preoccupied with the pacification of the Hejaz. He had marched westward from Riyadh, his capital, to recapture the entire Hejaz, including Makkah and Madinah, the two holiest cities in Islam. In doing so, he established himself as a major power player on the Arabian Peninsula.

These "negotiations" between al-Idrisi and King Abdul Aziz resulted in the 1926 Makkah Treaty that transformed Asir into a "Protectorate."[3] Al-Idrisi waived an independent foreign policy, but retained autonomy in internal affairs. Although Imam Yahyah eventually rejected the Makkah Treaty, he was careful not to provoke King Abdul Aziz. In fact, the Yemeni leader was involved in border clashes with British forces stationed in Aden and the Protectorates. These clashes persuaded the Imam that the British presence in Aden was far more dangerous to his independence than King Abdul Aziz. To his credit, nevertheless, Imam Yahyah was cognizant of the close relationship between the Saudi leader and London, and fearful that the Saudi-British connection could possibly target his rule in Yemen.

The Yemeni-Saudi relationship took a turn for the worst in 1930, when al-Idrisi began to renege on his commitments to the Makkah Treaty. He also began to move closer to Imam Yahyah. In response, King Abdul Aziz was impelled to abrogate the treaty, and al-Idrisi sought political asylum from Imam Yahyah. The latter granted this request and, thus, became al-Idrisi's protector. Encouraged by this new development, Imam Yahyah seized the opportunity to help the Yam tribe in Asir, an offshoot of the Yemeni Hamdan tribe, and sent his troops into the province to occupy the city of Najran. Attempts by both sides to resolve this dispute continued through 1933. Both the Imam and King Abdul Aziz exchanged letters and sent delegations to each other's capitals. All attempts ended in failure. By the end of 1933, tensions between the two countries intensified, largely because al-Idrisi raised the banner of revolt against King Abdul Aziz and, not unexpectedly, Saudi forces in Asir were reinforced. In early 1934, a Saudi ultimatum was sent to the Imam. It demanded the immediate evacuation of all Yemeni forces from Asir, the restoration of the earlier "borders" (implying Yemeni evacuation from Najran), and the extradition of al-Idrisi to Saudi Arabia.

Imam Yahyah ignored the ultimatum as clashes erupted between the two protagonists. The brief war led to the defeat of Yemeni forces and induced the Imam to accept the Taif Agreement, which was mediated by several Arab states. The agreement itself comprised 23 articles and included the three points contained in the Saudi ultimatum. Al-Idrisi was extradited to Saudi Arabia, Yemeni forces were evacuated from Asir, and Najran was relinquished to the Kingdom. Article 22 specifically stated that the agreement was binding for 20 years, subject to renewal.[4]

During these early contacts between Imam Yahyah and King Abdul Aziz, the two men exchanged several communications concerning the border disputes. All exchanges reiterated the Muslim character of both states and emphasized the need for an amicable resolution of existing differences. Still, each ruler perceived the other as too closely associated with an outside power, as Yemen was uneasy over the close Saudi ties to Britain. The Yemeni leadership believed that King Abdul Aziz would not have defeated Sharif Hussein of the Hejaz had it not been for British military and political support. Indeed, the Yemeni government further believed that King Abdul Aziz relied upon British support to "deal with al-Idrisi." According to the Imam, London welcomed the Makkah Treaty, because it absolved the British from honoring their commitments to al-Idrisi.[5] Moreover, the border clashes between Yemen and British forces in Aden and the Protectorates helped King Abdul Aziz consolidate his control in Asir. At the same time, it augmented the Saudi's military capabilities, vis-à-vis Yemen. According to the Yemeni leadership, the tone of the ultimatum, and the quick Saudi military victory over Yemen, indicated close Saudi-British cooperation.[6]

Saudi Arabia was similarly convinced that there was close cooperation between the Yemeni government and Italy. Riyadh considered Italian-Yemeni relations as a threat to the interests of Saudi Arabia and a destabilizing factor in the region. Specifically, King Abdul Aziz was troubled by the Italian assistance to the Imam, in the form of arms and money.[7] He was convinced that Rome was eager to supplement its colonial possessions on the other side of the Red Sea (in

Eritrea), by enhancing its putative influence in Yemen. The King was politically astute enough to place blame—for the differences between him and the Imam—on the Italians. He insisted, for example, that Italian influence on the Imam's government was hindering attempts by the two neighboring governments to formulate a border agreement.[8]

Consequently, the Taif Agreement settled Saudi-Yemeni differences in Asir, and occasioned a relationship based on mutual recognition of their interests. From 1934 until 1962, Yemen and Saudi Arabia cooperated in formulating joint Arab policies and maintained healthy ties. The exception occurred in 1958 when Yemen joined the United Arab Republic in a confederation. The alignment between Yemen and revolutionary Egypt made Saudi Arabia somewhat uneasy, but it did not negatively affect their relationship. This can be attributed to the fact that both political systems were traditional and monarchical. As a leading Saudi scholar observed,

> The political system of a country is undoubtedly a major determinant in its foreign policy behavior. Accordingly, the more closely one country's political system resembles that of another, the greater the degree of mutual understanding which can be expected between them. Conversely, as the differences between the political systems widen, so do their chances for misunderstanding.[9]

Indeed, neither Saudi Arabia nor Yemen viewed each other with hostility, or with misgivings. On the contrary, King Abdul Aziz felt that the Yemenis were "brothers" to the Saudis, and deserving of his support. He maintained that attitude throughout the remainder of his life. When Imam Yahyah was killed in the abortive 1948 coup d'état, King Abdul Aziz was furious. Shortly thereafter, he formulated a policy that was antagonistic to the insurrectionists, and favorable to Imam Yahyah's successor, Imam Ahmed.[10] The 1934 Taif Agreement was renewed in 1954, further illustrating the strong ties between the two countries. Throughout this period, Riyadh represented Sanaa's diplomatic interests where Yemen had no established missions.

### Political Changes in Yemen

The Yemeni revolution of 26 September 1962 profoundly changed the political landscape on the Arabian Peninsula. It ushered into the region a new form of government, the Yemen Arab Republic (YAR), and a new era of configurations and new concepts that wreaked havoc with regional security. In short, it made the area susceptible to incoherence, initially introduced by the revolution itself, and shortly thereafter by the introduction of Egyptian troops into Yemen on behalf of the revolutionaries. The relationship between republican Yemen and Saudi Arabia became strained and antagonistic. The YAR was now an ally of the "progressive" revolutionary Arab movement. Led by Gamal Abdel Nasser of Egypt, the Arab movement called for pan-Arabism and the overthrow of the monarchical systems throughout the Arab world, which were defined as reactionary, anachronistic, and not representative of Arab masses. Republican Yemen was, like Egypt, calling for the overthrow of the Saudi establishment.

During the Yemeni civil war, which lasted from 1962 to 1970, the YAR and Saudi Arabia were at loggerheads. Although both states viewed each other with suspicion and misgivings, Yemeni perceptions of Saudi Arabia proved to be more volatile and highly emotional. Yemeni revolutionary leaders lambasted Saudi Arabia with vehemence, portraying it as anachronistic, reactionary, and a puppet of the United States. They even threatened Riyadh with a massive air strike. Saudi leaders, on the other hand, were far more concerned with the estimated 80,000 Egyptian troops in Yemen. By 1965, the Egyptian presence in the YAR represented the greater threat to the security and interests of the Kingdom. According to a well-placed Saudi analyst,

> The presence of Egyptian forces in Yemen was perceived by Saudi Arabia as an act of aggression aimed at more than merely controlling Yemen or even driving the British from Aden and the Protectorates. The troops, especially in view of Nasser's verbal attacks on monarchical systems in the Arab world, and his threat to attack Saudi Arabia, represented a clear danger to Saudi Arabia.[11]

Saudi fears of whatever intentions Egypt and republican Yemen represented were heightened when President Abdallah Sallal of the YAR "publicly announced his intention to extend a republican form of government to the entire Arabian Peninsula."[12] Saudi policy, as formulated by Riyadh two years after the Yemeni revolution, was to contain the conflict to Yemen proper, thereby avoiding a spillover into Saudi Arabia.

Following the 1967 Six-Day War, Egyptian troops were withdrawn from Yemen, and in accordance with the 1968 Khartoum Agreement between Egypt and Saudi Arabia, Riyadh focused greater attention on events occurring in Aden. Earlier, Britain had agreed to withdraw from Aden and the Protectorates by 1968, which, not surprisingly, led to a struggle between two rivals for power in South Yemen. Starting in 1964, the Front for the Liberation of South Yemen (FLOSY) and the National Liberation Front (NLF) gained in popularity and influence. The contest culminated in the defeat of FLOSY, whose members fled to North Yemen. The NLF was quick to form a new government, which was Marxist in orientation and antagonistic to all the states in the region. Aden then called for the spread of socialism throughout the Arabian Peninsula, a development that clearly implied the region would be unstable. To Saudi Arabia this was a foreboding trend that threatened intrinsic regional interests. Indeed, Riyadh drew clear lessons from the Egyptian intervention in Yemen, and was persuaded that its "security and that of the Red Sea would be threatened if Sanaa were controlled by an unfriendly regime."[13] There was a perceptible recognition by the Kingdom to adopt a conciliatory stand vis-à-vis the YAR. Sanaa had also viewed events in South Yemen with alarm. Both states' apprehensions were further intensified when the radical wing of the South Yemeni Communist Party, led by Salem Rubai Ali and Abdul Fattah Ismail, took power in 1969. Ali and

Ismail formed a radical political organization, the National Democratic Front (NDF), composed of North Yemeni leftists, to undertake subversive activities against the YAR. On the heels of epoch-making developments in South Yemen, Riyadh and Sanaa adopted a policy of rapprochement. Eventually, this led to diplomatic recognition of the YAR by Saudi Arabia, in 1970.

In the end, the conflict between the YAR and the People's Democratic Republic of Yemen (PDRY) was essentially a political and ideological rivalry. Both regimes emerged from similar roots and both shared a nation. In fact, both regimes had attempted to unite in one form or another ever since the British withdrawal from Aden. Nonetheless, the complexity in their rivalry stemmed from the fact that the PDRY became a Marxist-Leninist system closely associated with the Soviet Union and antagonistic to both the YAR and Saudi Arabia.[14] The YAR, on the other hand, had become less revolutionary and less radical, and far more cooperative with Saudi Arabia.

To counter the PDRY's enmity to both Sanaa and Riyadh, both states agreed to form a counter-insurgency movement in South Yemen, composed of former members of FLOSY. Before long, South Yemeni dissidents spread havoc in Marxist PDRY. The situation deteriorated rapidly and developed into an open war between the two Yemens in September 1972.[15]

This latest confrontation was short-lived and was fought to a military standstill. Both parties had overtaxed themselves with continuous military challenges and were, to put it mildly, unwilling to pursue such a path. Under the auspices of the League of Arab States (LAS), both Yemens signed the Tripoli Agreement on 28 October 1972, whereby both Sanaa and Aden agreed to a cease-fire. A proviso calling for unity between the two states within one year of signing was also initialed. The agreement, however, failed to achieve stated objectives because of: "(1), the ideological chasm separating the PDRY and the YAR, (2), the clash of personal rivalries between their leaderships for dominant political influence in any settlement, and, (3), opposition within each state to the unification in any settlement."[16] More importantly, the Soviet Union stood against such a union. In the event, the Kremlin believed that unity between Sanaa and Aden could conceivably lead to the termination of Soviet influence and prestige on the Arabian Peninsula. It became, therefore, a fundamental Soviet policy to oppose any unification movements between the two Yemens. Yemeni leftists and Baathists in prominent government position were encouraged by Moscow to place the onus of the failure to unite on Saudi opposition. Leading Arabist writers fueled this contention further by insisting that Saudi Arabia was opposed to unity. They also projected Riyadh as being "insensitive," "heavy-handed," and "indifferent" to Yemen.[17] Not surprisingly, such views influenced Yemeni perceptions of Saudi Arabia, especially when the border issue was raised.

In compliance with Article 22 of the Taif Agreement, Riyadh raised the renewal issue with Sanaa in 1974. Since Saudi Arabia and the YAR were on excellent terms at the time, the renewal question was not seen as being a problem. Prime Minister Abdallah al-Hajri, who was on good terms with leading Saudi officials, did not hesitate to agree to renew the Taif Agreement. Al-Hajri went so far as to accept that the Saudi-Yemeni border dispute was over and that the frontier between the two states was permanent. This point was made explicitly clear in a joint communiqué issued on 17 March 1974.[18] Moreover, al-Hajri and his Saudi counterpart were in complete agreement regarding the threat emanating from Yemeni leftists and communists. They collaborated in curtailing the latter's advances and nascent influence in the YAR.

Still, the YAR Consultative Assembly rejected the renewal agreement as well as the communiqué. Shortly thereafter, agents of the PDRY, while visiting London, assassinated al-Hajri. These two events magnified Saudi perceptions of Yemen as a volatile nation, prone to radical changes. Indeed, Saudi perceptions were further reinforced when, within one year, President Ibrahim al-Hamdi and President Ahmed al-Ghashmi of the YAR were assassinated.[19] Al-Ghashmi was known as a staunch anti-communist. Like Saudi leaders, he viewed communism as a threat to the security and stability of the Arabian Peninsula. His assassination brought to an abrupt end the close cooperation between the YAR and Saudi Arabia, especially on political matters, including the encroachment of communist ideas throughout the region. Without a doubt, his untimely death left an impact on the Sanaa-Aden relationship.[20] Al-Ghashmi's successor, Colonel Ali Abdallah Saleh, had no previous experience in government. He came to power during a most tenuous time, and his initial inability to calm differences between Sanaa and Aden led in February 1979 to open conflict between the two Yemens. This intra-Yemeni border war was "a mirror image" of the 1972 conflict.[21] It was short-lived but far more favorable to the PDRY, which, along with the National Democratic Front, was able to capture large stretches of North Yemeni territory. Under the auspices of the LAS, a cease-fire was arranged, which was followed by a commitment by both protagonists to work toward unity.

Like the 1972 Tripoli Agreement, this latest LAS mediation, known as the Kuwait Agreement, failed to achieve stated objectives for roughly the same reasons. Evidently, the insistence of the PDRY to have its protégés within the NDF included in the Sanaa government did not help assuage the painful experience of the North Yemeni government. President Saleh showed a resilience that belied his age (he was 34 at the time) and experience. Saleh had overcome, in his first year in office, a Nasserite coup plot, assassination attempts, domestic disturbances, and war with the PDRY. In August 1979, he concluded an arms arrangement with the Soviet Union worth an estimated $700 million, which angered and dismayed Saudi Arabia. To be sure, Riyadh's ire was not without justification, as it had just underwritten a $390 million YAR purchase of American arms. More important, Saudi Arabia had invested substantial capital with the Carter administration to satisfy congressional opposition to the purchase. President Jimmy Carter went so far as to invoke the waiver provision of the Arms Export Control Act to expedite urgently needed deliveries. When Sanaa, however, agreed to the cease-fire, Saudi Arabia held up delivery of the arms earmarked for Yemen. To the Saudis, Yemen's purchase of Soviet weapons was contrary to the "trustworthy" Yemeni-Saudi ties. The motive behind Saleh's move was to illustrate genuine Yemeni independence. For Sanaa, improved relations with Moscow, at the expense of Saudi-Yemeni good relations, was worth the effort. Consequently, Saudi Arabia threatened to withhold all of its financial and economic assistance to the YAR, which obliged President Saleh to quickly send diplomatic envoys to Riyadh. Saleh became engaged in a concerted effort to convince the Saudis that the nascent Yemeni-Soviet connection would never be allowed to become a threat to any state in the region. Once Riyadh was mollified, Yemeni-Saudi relations improved.

Despite this significant effort, regional trends affected the rapprochement between Riyadh and Sanaa. In 1981, the conservative Arab Gulf monarchies formed the Gulf Cooperation Council (GCC), in response to the Iranian revolution and the Iran-Iraq War. Soviet expansionism in Somalia, Ethiopia, and Afghanistan further threatened to change the geopolitical equation throughout the region. World concerns over these dynamic developments concretely manifested themselves in the attitudes of Muslim states as well. On January 1980, the Organization of Islamic Conference (OIC) summit, meeting in Islamabad, Pakistan, condemned the Soviet invasion of Afghanistan, and strongly criticized Moscow's presence in the Horn of Africa.[22] Arab participants, with the exception of the PDRY, condemned Moscow's actions in Afghanistan in even stronger terms.[23] GCC leaders were particularly perturbed by the Kremlin's incursions into the region and believed it to be a menace to their security.

To be sure, the Arab Gulf monarchies' decision to form the GCC reflected their shared concern over their inability to protect themselves from both external as well as internal threats. The formation of the GCC, a military, economic, political, and cultural association, was viewed as a necessary mechanism to defend the region from all forms of threats. It was also formed to protect member states from Iran and Iraq. Most feared that once the Iran-Iraq War was over, the two warring states would attempt to re-establish their predominance over the region.[24] Indeed, "the distinguishing features of the GCC were that it was composed of monarchical political systems, traditionally conservative, rich in oil, weak in military strength, relatively unpopulated, and allied to the West."[25] In other words, the GCC was endowed with unique features that naturally excluded Yemen.

Sanaa was angered by its exclusion from the Riyadh-based regional organization. The YAR accused GCC states of forming a regional grouping that was contrary to the solidarity of Arab states.[26] Inasmuch as the exclusion of the YAR was a political decision, it was equally applied to the PDRY. In fact, GCC rulers recognized that both Yemeni regimes chose "the course of political development through revolutionary coups—a method unacceptable to the six members of the Arab Gulf Cooperation Council."[27] Nevertheless, Riyadh rapidly pacified the YAR's injured perceptions, as it increased Saudi economic and financial assistance through the joint Saudi-Yemeni Cooperation Council (formed in 1976). Sanaa was mollified, and its opposition to the GCC was terminated, even if it felt slighted. This perception festered in the mind of President Saleh and his government, and by 1984 their views of the Kingdom became far more negative.

It is important to emphasize that while overall contacts improved ever so slightly, they in fact deteriorated throughout the rest of the 1980's for two specific reasons: first, because the 1984 discovery of oil enhanced Sanaa's negotiating posture, thereby altering the existing levels of dependency; second, because

Sanaa established closer ties with Baghdad, which in turn further tilted the balance of power on the Arabian Peninsula.

When oil was discovered in the YAR, many believed the economic plight of the country would improve. Still, the amounts were relatively minute, compared to the vast reserves in Saudi Arabia. But, they proved enough to catapult the border dispute between Riyadh and Sanaa to the forefront. With these discoveries, the border dispute was no longer related just to the clauses contained in the 1934 Taif Agreement. It now included more than 1,000 miles of undefined frontier, stretching from the demarcated line with Asir, eastward along the Rub al-Khali to the boundary with Oman. Significant oil led Sanaa to assume that it would no longer be financially dependent on Saudi economic assistance, and that it could now conduct its foreign and domestic policies independent of Saudi pressures.[28] This thinking was linked to attempts by Sanaa to promote relations with Baghdad. Having been excluded from the GCC, Sanaa opted to improve ties with Saddam Hussein, in an attempt to improve and foster its regional significance. There is no doubt that the Baathist members of the Saleh government, who viewed Iraq as a viable alternative ally to Saudi Arabia, motivated this policy. Saddam Hussein was quick to respond in kind. Iraq provided Yemen with financial and economic assistance, in addition to technical assistance to the military. It also helped train Yemeni Republican Guard units and helped in the formation and training of the national security apparatus. Both the Republican Guard and the national security apparatus were modeled after Saddam Hussein's. Naturally, this new Iraqi-Yemeni cooperation was of deep concern to the Saudi government. When Yemen became a member of the Arab Cooperation Council, formed in 1988 by Egypt, Jordan, Iraq, and Yemen, Saudi apprehensions were intensified. Saudi alarm was pervasive and salient, especially since Ali Abdallah Saleh and Saddam Hussein had developed a close personal relationship. To Riyadh's dismay, the official mass media of the Saleh government inferred that Saudi Arabia was against Yemeni national interests.[29] One observer concluded that "having to contend with restive Iraq and Iran in the north, Riyadh has compelling reasons to contain its enemies and obviate the specter of being pressured on two sides."[30] Baghdad's increasing influence on the Arabian Peninsula was clearly evident as Saddam Hussein nudged both the YAR and the PDRY toward unity.

### Consequences of the 1991 Gulf War

The decade of the 1990s began on a high note for North and South Yemen. On 22 May 1990 the two states united to form the Yemen Republic. It was an accomplishment of historic proportion in contemporary Yemeni history. Unity was accompanied by the adoption of constitutional democracy as the basis of its political framework. Political parties, which had been outlawed in both North and South, were allowed to function freely within the parameters of the new political ethos. Liberal laws calling for respect for freedom of thought and expression were enacted. A proliferated mass media came into existence. Remarkably, the exultation and euphoria over unity was exhibited not only in

Yemen, but also throughout the Arab world. Leading Arab scholars were persuaded that Yemeni unity was a prelude to Arab unity.

Although Yemeni unity was regionally and internationally encouraged and accepted, incoherence in Yemeni decision making—vis-à-vis Saudi Arabia—was evident in two specific events. Indeed, the incohesive policies left the impression that Sanaa was muddling through, unable or inept to adjust its decisions. Consequently, the country's economy, regional standing, and ever so fragile ties with Riyadh all suffered. They also intensified the negative perceptions each state had of the other, which frustrated any attempts to resolve the festering border dispute.

## *The 1990 Iraqi Invasion of Kuwait*

Less than three months after the two Yemens united, Iraq invaded Kuwait and, subsequently, incorporated the Shaykhdom as its nineteenth province. The invasion was traumatic to all Arab Gulf states and a rude awakening to the world. It directly threatened Western national interests and portended ill for the sovereignty of the conservative Arab Gulf monarchies. The Bush administration quickly initiated a bold policy aimed at rolling back the Iraqi army from Kuwait, restoring the independence of the Shaykhdom, and re-establishing the status quo ante in the region. Washington considered these objectives as prerequisites to regional security. It was, therefore, essential to enlist Arab as well as non-Arab states in forming the international coalition against Baghdad. Enlisting Yemen in the nascent coalition was determined to be important. The American secretary of state, James Baker, visited Sanaa to seek Yemeni support and participation in the coalition. Sanaa rejected the overture, insisting that the crisis, as an Arab problem, required an Arab solution. Yemen emphatically asserted that the League of Arab States possessed the wherewithal to deal with the crisis. This Yemeni opinion was not shared by most Arab Gulf states or by key Western powers. In the event, Saudi Arabia was incensed by Sanaa's position, since it believed that collective Arab action was not sufficient to dislodge Saddam Hussein from Kuwait.[31] Moreover, the Yemeni position was regarded by several Arab states, including Saudi Arabia, Egypt, and Syria, as well as by major Western powers, as a clear indication that the Saleh regime endorsed Saddam Hussein and his regional policies.

Regardless of what conclusions many drew, Saudi Arabia did not forgive the Saleh regime, especially since the latter benefited from Riyadh's financial largesse. An estimated $100–350 million in financial aid was annually transferred from Saudi Arabia to the YAR at the time. Such amounts were disbursed to ease Sanaa's balance of payments deficits.[32] Equally important, Riyadh had vastly assisted Yemen by granting more than a million Yemenis the right to work freely in Saudi Arabia, and repatriate hard-currency earnings. The privileges given to Yemeni workers in Saudi Arabia were many. They were allowed to travel freely around the country and to own businesses. They were not required to be sponsored by Saudis nor were they forced to carry their residency papers with them. Indeed, Yemeni remittances "fueled growth in all levels of the private sector"[33] and, together with aid, "permitted the government to relax all kinds of economic regulation."[34]

Given this legacy, Saudi Arabia had assumed that Yemen would support it in its hour of need. When Sanaa sided with Baghdad, however, Riyadh and the Gulf Arab states concluded they had been "stabbed in the back." In response to Yemen's position, the Kingdom, Kuwait, and the United Arab Emirates evicted all Yemeni workers from their respective countries. Over one million Yemenis were forced to return to Yemen. The economic hardships on Yemen doubled as the Yemeni riyal began a steady decline in its value vis-à-vis the dollar. Inflation and unemployment rates increased dramatically, further compounded by the fact that practically all aid from Western states was terminated.

What ensued was not surprising. A steady stream of acrimonious exchanges became the trademark between the Yemeni and Saudi governments. Each accused the other of undermining its national interests, and each seethed with anger over the other. Yemen's position was, however, more antagonistic to Riyadh. The discord was illustrated by massive demonstrations against Saudi Arabia, which were clearly staged by Sanaa. Students from the military academy, government employees, and members of national security were encouraged to demonstrate in front of the Saudi embassy in the capital. Government employees were provided transportation to rally the masses in a timely fashion. Some of the demonstrations became vociferous and ugly. Stones, shoes, and sandals were catapulted onto the embassy grounds. King Fahd's pictures were thrown on the ground and trampled upon. Saddam Hussein's photographs, on the other hand, were raised above the crowd. Adding insult to injury, the demonstrations were publicly aired on Yemeni television, even though counter-demonstrations—in support of Saudi Arabia—were not televised or mentioned by the government mass media. Saudi Arabia's wrath intensified when Sanaa denied that the government staged anti-Saudi demonstrations. Riyadh became convinced that the Saleh government could no longer be trusted, and squarely placed the blame for the deterioration in relations on Saleh himself as well as his foreign minister, Dr. Abdul Karim al-Iryani. According to reliable sources, al-Iryani had formulated Yemen's policy during the Gulf Crisis, and may have orchestrated the idea that Saudi Arabia strongly opposed Yemeni unity. It was widely rumored that Saudi Arabia had offered Aden a billion dollars to terminate unity discussions with Sanaa in 1990.[35] Whether these reports were true or not, they reinforced Yemeni perceptions of Saudi Arabia as being opposed to unification.

Against this thorny background, the border issue was shelved, essentially from 1990 until after the Yemeni civil war in 1994. Routine ministerial meetings convened, but far more serious concerns dominated the moribund dialogue.

First, Sanaa and Riyadh engaged in a pervasive antagonism. Their relationship during this period was similar to ties after the Yemeni revolution and the subsequent Egyptian involvement in 1962.[36] In such an atmosphere, the border issue became more of a point of contention between the two sides, made more salient by the fact that 1,000 miles of borderline had not been demarcated. The area stretched along the desolate Empty Quarter to the boundary with the Sultanate of Oman. It was in this vicinity that oil companies were prospecting for oil. Saudi sensitivities further motivated Riyadh to send a warning letter in April 1992 to oil companies warning them not to infringe on its territories.[37]

Second, both Yemen and Saudi Arabia failed to agree on what criteria should be applied to resolve the dispute, as "the principle of self-determination was not applicable in unpopulated areas, and in most parts neither side had a history of local administration, which might reinforce a claim."[38] The two states based their claims on several lines on maps that were drawn as far back as 1914: the so-called Violet Line, drawn in 1914 by the British government and the Ottoman Empire, to separate their areas of influence; the Riyadh Line, drawn by Saudi Arabia in 1935 to separate areas under British control in South Yemen from Saudi Arabia; the 1934 Taif Agreement, which delineated the border line between Yemen and Asir; and the 1938 Philby Line, which marked the line east of Asir, stretching in a southeasterly-northern direction toward Shabwa Province.

Third, Abdul Karim al-Iryani, in the latter part of the 1980s, postulated a theory—later adopted by members of the Yemeni government—that asserted that Saudi Arabia was susceptible to the same contradictions that afflicted the Kingdom of Yemen. As these intrinsic contradictions had led to the demise of Imamate political institutions, the postulate assumed, so would they affect the Kingdom of Saudi Arabia.[39] Yemen, according to this perspective, should not attempt to resolve its border dispute with Saudi Arabia in haste, because there was a likelihood that violent political changes would bring forth a more amicable political system in Riyadh, one that may be willing to be far more flexible in its strategic regional ambitions. Still, this perspective did not imply that the Yemeni government would cease publicizing its readiness to negotiate in good faith with the Kingdom. Rather, it had to improve relations with all Arab Gulf states—and dispel the notion that it had supported Iraq's invasion of Kuwait— even if Yemeni leaders were not ready to pay the price to achieve this aim. GCC states demanded Sanaa admit its policy was a mistake, and that it stop cooperating with Saddam Hussein, whereas Ali Abdallah Saleh's government was not willing to meet such demands. On the contrary, Yemeni leaders invited Iraq's deputy prime minister, Tariq Aziz, in August 1992 to visit Sanaa. In an official policy statement, President Saleh strongly denounced the international sanctions on Iraq, maintaining that they represented violations of Baghdad's sovereignty.[40] Moreover, Ali Abdallah Saleh's close cooperation and friendship with Saddam Hussein did not endear him to Arab Gulf rulers. The Al Saud feared that Saleh, backed by Saddam Hussein, would attempt "to subvert Saudi Arabia in the Asir border area, the target of possible irredentist ambitions by Yemen dating back to the occupation of the region by Saudi Arabia in 1934."[41] To be sure, "there are Saudis who not only still fret over Yemen's ambivalent stance towards Saddam Hussein but who regard the country's republican, multi-party political system (with all its flaws) as subversive in a peninsula dominated by traditional monarchies."[42]

### The 1994 Yemeni Civil War

The civil war erupted in the first week of May 1994 and lasted for 70 days. It was short but devastating. It was a natural outcome of the rivalry for power between the country's two leading political parties, the Yemen Socialist Party

(YSP) and the General People's Congress (GPC). To be sure, the war unleashed regional involvement, specifically from Saudi Arabia. Two reasons account for the Saudi involvement in support of the YSP.

First, Riyadh had come to believe that President Saleh was the man most responsible for the Yemeni policy adopted during the Gulf Crisis.[43] Indeed, Saudi leaders were convinced that it was Saleh and his foreign minister, Dr. Abdul Karim al-Iryani, who insisted on its execution. When war broke out between government forces in Sanaa and the YSP, the Yemeni leadership believed that Riyadh physically, and financially, supported southerners. In fact, the Saudi effort to achieve a cease-fire was also viewed by Sanaa as sustaining the south.[44] To some extent, these perceptions were easy to formulate, especially after Saudi Arabia intensified its attempts to have other Arab governments recognize the so-called Democratic Republic of Yemen (DRY). Sanaa perceived this Saudi policy as clear evidence that Riyadh was against Yemeni unity. Whether Saudi Arabia had encouraged the south to proclaim its independence to make it "possible for Saudi leaders to refer the Yemeni war to the United Nations" is difficult to determine.[45] Nevertheless, the argument presented to substantiate this view rested on the premise that Saudi Arabia would—ostensibly—campaign for international support for the south far more vigorously if Sanaa invaded a neighboring "independent state."[46] In the event, this was the argument presented by Riyadh to Washington, although the latter insisted that "no political party such as the YSP had the right unilaterally to declare secession."[47] There is no doubt that the secretary-general of the YSP, who was then the vice president of the Yemen Republic, believed that declaring secession would relieve the south from Sanaa's military advances. Yet, the declaration—made reluctantly— was primarily "for external reasons, when it became clear that his forces were losing the war and he badly needed international support." "The timing of the announcement," almost three weeks after hostilities had broken out, "was linked to diplomatic activity and was aimed at securing international recognition, so that sympathetic states could provide arms openly rather than secretly."[48]

Ironically, the same Yemeni perceptions of Saudi Arabia—which emerged during the Yemeni civil war—appeared again during the Yemeni-Eritrean discord over the island of Greater Hanish, a Yemeni island on the Red Sea that Eritrea invaded and occupied in December 1995. Eritrea later invaded and occupied the island of Small Hanish. To be sure, Sanaa had not taken any precautionary measures to protect the islands, even though Eritrea had expressed its "intentions" as early as August 1995. Caught by surprise, the Yemeni leadership quickly placed "the blame for its failure to protect the sovereignty of its territories on Saudi Arabia and Israel. Sanaa accused Saudi Arabia and Israel of arming the Eritreans, thus giving Eritrea the wherewithal to attack and occupy Hanish."[49] No matter how convoluted, these perceptions were widely rejected by the Yemeni citizenry, as opposition parties accused Sanaa of dereliction in protecting the sovereignty of the state. They also portrayed the Yemeni leadership as being too preoccupied with enhancing its self-interests, rather than protecting and promoting the national interest.

The second reason for the Saudi involvement in support of the YSP was Riyadh's "imperative" need to have a land corridor south to the Arabian Sea, to ensure that its oil exports would not be subject to a blockade. Saudi Arabia may have access to blue waters but only through three narrow waterways: the Suez Canal, Bab al-Mandeb—both on the Red Sea—and the Straits of Hormuz in the Persian Gulf. More important, Riyadh had no control over either of the three narrow waterways. To alleviate this shortcoming, Saudi Arabia approached both Oman and the PDRY, to solicit their approval for a corridor plan. Both refused, because Riyadh insisted on having the corridor declared as Saudi sovereign territory. When the Yemeni civil war erupted, many observers viewed Saudi support of the secessionists as strategically significant. If the south became an internationally recognized independent entity, a grateful South Yemen could have accepted the Saudi corridor plan.[50]

Against this background, and from 1990 until early 1995, the Yemeni-Saudi relationship was acrimonious and belligerent. It experienced a temporary thaw when both states agreed to resolve their border dispute after an American mediation session, which resulted in a memorandum of understanding signed at the home of Prince Sultan bin Abdul Aziz in Makkah. The 11–point document reaffirmed the commitments of both states to the 1934 Taif Agreement. Both promised not to allow their territories to be used as centers of aggression—against each other—or for carrying out any political, military, or information activities.[51] Committees were also established and charged with determining land and sea frontiers, developing economic cooperation, and preventing troop movements near disputed areas.

Although Yemeni opposition parties criticized this latest accord, the agreement did not specifically renew the Taif Agreement, nor did Sanaa make any major concessions. On 23 June 1995, President Ali Abdallah Saleh visited Jeddah, raising hopes that the bruised relationship would—once again—be beneficial to both sides. Saleh went so far as to state that the 1934 Taif Agreement would be renewed without amendment. Unfortunately, the relationship soured once again in December 1995, when Sanaa accused Riyadh of encouraging Eritrea to invade and occupy Greater Hanish. From that point on, the Yemeni-Saudi relationship reverted to being belligerent, as Yemeni officials initiated a concerted effort to portray Saudi Arabia as the cause of all of Yemen's problems, ranging from limited economic development to kidnappings to corruption.[52] No doubt Yemen appears to be winning the public relations battle, by portraying itself as the victim of Saudi aggression and meddlesome interventions, as it was able to convince Washington to mediate. In turn, the United States responded positively, irrespective of the fact that the State Department was warning American citizens to reconsider traveling to Yemen to avoid "kidnappings" and other assaults on foreigners. The American administration seemed to disregard the views of scholars who contended that the Saleh regime lacked the competence necessary to enforce law and order in the country. Lastly, Washington seemed to have ignored the statement made by Prince Naif bin Abdul Aziz, Saudi Arabia's interior minister, when he declared that "Saudi Arabia is convinced that the dispute with Yemen is in no need of international arbitration."[53]

Washington's readiness to mediate stemmed from its resolve to achieve normal relations between various Arab states and Israel. Given that Saudi Arabia is considered pivotal in the eventual success of this policy objective, it became essential to employ Yemen as a pressure point against the Kingdom. Sanaa seized on this American initiative by adopting a more flexible policy toward Israel. In fact, the Yemeni government's quick response had two primary objectives: to reinforce the view held by many Westerners that Riyadh was strongly resisting the policy of "normalization" (between the Arab states and Israel), and to portray Saudi Arabia as being opposed to resolving festering border disputes. Sanaa hoped that such a policy would gain Western economic and political assistance. To achieve these two objectives, Yemeni officials met secretly with prominent Israeli government officials and initiated a dialogue. Israeli "tourists" were granted Yemeni visas, coincidentally as President Ali Abdallah Saleh was visiting Washington, in April 2000. During Saleh's tour in the United States, he visited the Middle East Center for Peace and Economic Cooperation, a well-known Jewish organization promoting Israeli interests. On the heels of this latest development, the Jordanian newspaper *Al-Majd,* in its 25 April 2000 issue, quoted Western reports and several foreign sources that a military and security pact was indeed signed between Yemen, Israel, and the United States.[54] The newspaper asserted that "actual implementation of the deal began three weeks ago." Without a doubt, such cooperation would affect the security of Saudi Arabia and the Arabian Peninsula, given that it may well allow Israel a non-negligible role in Red Sea.

## Conclusion

The Yemeni-Saudi relationship began on a sour note in the 1920s because the two sides perceived each other as expansionist and a threat to their newly created states. Their antagonisms stemmed from their inability to resolve a border dispute and counter-claims over Asir. Once that issue was resolved, albeit through a war, the discord between the two states evaporated. For nearly 30 years, Yemen and Saudi Arabia experienced an admirable relationship that was based on cooperation and trust. Saudi Arabia became the most reliable ally of Yemen during this period. Naturally, the fact that both countries were monarchies helped them to coexist in relative harmony.

This period was followed by a turbulent era in Yemeni political history born out of the 1962 revolution. The subsequent Egyptian intervention and the introduction of Egyptian troops into Yemen were causes for concern to Saudi Arabia. Facing an aggressive Yemeni government, allied to a similarly aggressive Egypt, Saudi Arabia sought and received American assurances of its sovereignty and independence. Once Egyptian troops withdrew, Saudi Arabia and Yemen forged closer links largely because of the threat emanating from the newly established communist political system in the PDRY. This cooperation lasted throughout the 1970s and early 1980s. When Aden's putative threat diminished, and when Sanaa became an oil producer, the YAR began developing and enhancing its relationship with Iraq. A reinvigorated Yemeni leadership no longer perceived the Al Saud as essential to its regional significance and economic development. Saudi Arabia, in turn, perceived the close Yemeni-Iraqi connection as a threat to its national security. The border dispute between Yemen and Saudi Arabia thus stood out as a sore point. On its own merits, it did not affect negatively the long-established contacts between the two states. However, in conjunction with the improved and personalized relations between Saddam Hussein and Ali Abdallah Saleh, it preoccupied Saudi Arabia. During this period, Sanaa perceived Riyadh as opposing Yemeni unity. That perception increased in intensity in the latter part of the 1980s.

The final period witnessed further impairment in the Yemeni-Saudi relationship, caused by the Yemeni decision to side with Saddam Hussein during the 1990–1991 Gulf crisis. GCC states, especially Saudi Arabia and Kuwait, which had generously supported Yemen's economic development, felt betrayed by Sanaa. In turn, Yemen was shunned and isolated for almost three years, as its refusal to recognize and admit that it had made a policy mistake only reinforced Saudi misgivings of the Saleh regime. The fact that the Yemeni government's negative perceptions of Saudi Arabia were widely publicized in the official media troubled Riyadh further. To the Saudis, Ali Abdallah Saleh and Dr. Abdul Karim al-Iryani were the two political leaders most responsible for the deterioration of relations between Riyadh and Sanaa. Although a memorandum of understanding was signed by both parties in early 1995, both sides remained belligerent toward each other simply because the Yemeni leadership was no longer seen by Riyadh as trustworthy. Irrespective of that, the two nations signed a border and maritime agreement in Jeddah, Saudi Arabia, on 12 June 2000. Although the text and the details of the border agreement have not been made public, both nations expressed their optimism that their relationship has taken a turn for the best.[55] It is, however, too early to conjecture as to whether the incoherence of the Yemeni political decision-making body will be able to chart a more rational policy vis-à-vis Saudi Arabia. Improved Yemeni-Saudi relations depend on the ability of the Yemeni political leadership to persuade the Gulf Arab states, especially Riyadh, that it can be trusted.

## Notes

1. Al-Sayyed Mustafa Salem, *Takwin al-Yaman al-Hadith: Imam Yahyah Bayna 1904–1948* [The Formation of Contemporary Yemen], Cairo, Egypt: The League of States, Center for Arabic Studies, 1963.
2. Issam Dhia al-Din al-Sayyed, *Asir fil-'Ilakat al-Siyassiyah al-Saudiyyah al-Yamaniyyah: 1919–1934* [Asir in the Saudi-Yemeni Relationship], Cairo: Dar al-Zahrah lil-Nashr, 1989, p. 107.
3. Turkey Muhammad al-Madhi, *Al-'Ilakat al-Saudiyyah al-Yamaniyyah: 1904–1954* [Saudi-Yemeni Relations], Riyadh: Dar al-Shail lil-Nashr, 1997, pp. 44–47.
4. Ibid., pp. 227–42.
5. Muhammad al-Shahari, *Al-Matami' al-Saudiyyah al-Tawasuiyyah fil-Yaman* [Saudi Ambitious Expansionism into Yemen], Beirut: Dar ibn Khaldun, 1996, pp. 144–158.
6. Al-Sayyed, *op. cit.*, p. 160.
7. Ibid., pp. 174–75.
8. Ibid., p. 174.
9. Saeed M. Badeeb, *The Saudi-Egyptian Conflict over North Yemen: 1962–1970*, Boulder, Colorado: Westview Press, 1986, p. 92.
10. Mohammed A. Zabarah, *Yemen: Traditionalism vs. Modernity*, New York: Praeger, 1982, pp. 27–29.

11. Saeed M. Badeeb, *op. cit.*, pp. 49–50.
12. Manfred Wenner, *Modern Yemen: 1918–1966*, Baltimore: Johns Hopkins University Press, 1967, p. 195. See also J. E. Peterson, *Yemen: The Search for a Modern State*, Baltimore: Johns Hopkins University Press, 1982; and F. Gregory Gause III, *Saudi-Yemeni Relations: Domestic Structures and Foreign Policy*, New York: Columbia University Press, 1990.
13. M. S. El Azhary, "Aspects of North Yemen's Relations with Saudi Arabia," in B. R. Pridham (ed.), *Contemporary Yemen: Politics and Historical Background*, London: Croom Helm, 1984, p. 197.
14. Abdallah al-Sultan, *Al-Bahr al-Ahmar wa Assira'a al-Arabi al-Israili* [The Red Sea and the Arab-Israeli Conflict], Beirut: Markaz al-Dirassat al-Arabiyyah, 1984, p. 156.
15. El Azhary, *op. cit.*, p. 197.
16. Robert Litwak, *Security in the Persian Gulf: Sources of Inter-State Conflict*, number 2, London: International Institute for Strategic Studies, 1981, pp. 81–82.
17. Leading Arabists considered the Saudi monarchical system as being outdated. They assumed that such a system did not represent the aspirations of the Arab masses.
18. Gause, *op. cit.*, pp. 105–106.
19. "Anonymous" individuals assassinated al-Hamdi along with his brother, Abdallah. Al-Ghashmi was assassinated by an explosive device in a briefcase carried to him by a messenger sent by Salem Rubai Ali of the PDRY. When the briefcase was opened, both al-Ghashmi and the messenger were killed. See Manfred Wenner, "South Yemen since Independence," in Pridham (ed.), *op. cit.*, p. 126.
20. Although al-Ghashmi was a strong ally of Saudi Arabia, he was believed to be cruel and oppressive. He had the misfortune of succeeding al-Hamdi, who was respected as an avowed supporter of Arab nationalism and a political leader of exceptional intelligence.
21. Gause, *op. cit.*, p. 40.
22. Al-Sultan, *op. cit.*, p. 146.
23. Ibid., p. 148.
24. Hamid al-Moufi, "Majlis al-Ta'awun al-Khaliji" [The Gulf Cooperation Council], *Majalat al-Siyasah al-Dawaliyyah*, number 65, October 1981, p. 127.
25. Mohammed A. Zabarah, "Yemen and Regional Security," *Al-Masar*, 1:1, winter 2000, p. 6. See also Abdu H. Sharif, "Yemen and Arabian Peninsula Security: Quest for Inclusion, Consequences of Exclusion," paper presented at the 1994 annual meeting of the American Political Science Association, New York, 1–4 September 1994, pp. 4–5; and J. E. Peterson, *The Arab Gulf States: Steps Toward Political Participation*, Washington D.C.: Praeger, published with the Center for Strategic and International Studies, 1988.
26. Al-Moufi, *op. cit.*, p. 131.
27. This conclusion, by Majid Khadduri, is indeed all-encompassing. See Peterson, *op. cit.*, p. viii.
28. For more details, see Joseph Kostiner, *Yemen: The Torturous Quest for Unity, 1990–1994*, London: Royal Institute of International Affairs, 1996. See also Petroleum Finance, Ltd., "Al-Yaman: al-Kilaf al-Hududi wal-'Ilakat ma'a al-Saudiyyah," [Yemen: The Border Dispute and Relations with Saudi Arabia], paper presented to the Seminar on the Border Dispute between Yemen and Saudi Arabia, Sanaa, Yemen, 7 August 1997.
29. *Al-Thawrah* and *26 September*, various issues from 1988 and 1989.
30. Jamal S. al-Suwaidi (ed.), *The Yemeni War of 1994: Causes and Consequences*, Abu Dhabi: The Emirate Center for Strategic Studies and Research, 1995, p. 98.
31. Mark Katz, "External Powers and the Yemeni Civil War," in ibid., p. 83. See also Zabarah, *Al-Masar*, *op. cit.*, pp. 4–5.
32. Under the National Reconciliation Agreement signed by the YAR and the royalists in 1970, Saudi Arabia agreed to pay Sanaa $100 million annually in budgetary support. See also Caroline Drees, "Saudi Says Acted in 'Self-Defense' in Yemen Clash," Infoseek News Channel, 20 July 1998. More concretely, Saudi economic assistance to Yemen was also apparent in the construction of mosques, schools, and roads.
33. Kiren Aziz Chaudhry, *The Price of Wealth: Economies and Institutions in the Middle East*, Ithaca and London: Cornell University Press, 1997, p. 196.
34. Ibid., p. 206.
35. Yemeni newspapers spread the idea that Saudi Arabia was working against Yemeni unity. It used Foreign Minister Prince Saud bin Faysal's visit to Aden and his alleged offer as such an example.
36. Ahmad Nu'man al-Mathhaji, "Ta'dudiat Marakiz al-Quwa al-Yamaniyyah wa Atharaha alal-Ilaqat al-Yamaniyyah al-Saudiyyah fi Asr al-Dimukratiyyah" [Multi-political Forces in Yemen

and Their Influence on the Yemeni-Saudi Relationship in the Era of Democratization], paper presented at the Conference of the North American Association for Middle East Studies, Washington, D.C., 8 December 1995, p. 12.
37. Ibid. p. 12.
38. Brian Whitaker, "The International Dimension," *Yemen Gateway*, 18 February 2000, p. 3.
39. Colleagues at Sanaa University reiterated that they heard Dr. al-Iryani state his theory at "Qat" sessions in Sanaa before and after the Gulf crisis of 1990–1991.
40. Kostiner, *op. cit.*, p. 54.
41. Ibid., p. 52.
42. Brian Whitaker, "Crisis over the Border," *Middle East International*, number 492, 20 January 1995, p. 11.
43. Zabarah, "Yemen and Regional Security," p. 11.
44. Katz, *op. cit.*, p. 82.
45. Kostiner, *op. cit.*, p. 95.
46. Ibid., p. 95.
47. Michael Hudson, "The Evolution of US Policy Toward Yemen: Seeking Stability in Arabia," paper presented to the Conference on the Future of Yemen, School of Oriental and African Studies, University of London, London, 25–26 November 1995, p. 10.
48. Brian Whitaker, "National Unity and Democracy in Yemen: A Marriage of Inconvenience," *Yemen Times*, 27 November 1995, p. 11.
49. Mohammed A. Zabarah, "The Role of Yemeni Policymakers," Focus Yemen, commentary delivered at the Center for Contemporary Arab Studies, Georgetown University, 1999, p. 20.
50. Whitaker, "Crisis over the Border," p. 11.
51. The memorandum of understanding can be found in *Al-Hayat*, 27 February 1995, p. 5.
52. *Al-Quds al-Arabi*, *Al-Sharq al-Awsat*, *Shu'un Arabiyyah*, various issues, 1998–1999.
53. Ain al-Yaqeen, "Detailing Yemeni Aggressions and Border Movements," 22 July 1998, p. 4.
54. As reported in *Yemen Times*, volume 10, 1–6 March 2000, p. 1.
55. *Yemen Times,* volume 10, 19–25 June 2000, pp. 1–2.

# RELATIONS BETWEEN GCC STATES

CHAPTER 16

## Unity on the Arabian Peninsula

Joseph A. Kechichian

When the six conservative Arab Gulf monarchies (Bahrain, Kuwait, Oman, Qatar, Saudi Arabia, and the United Arab Emirates [UAE]) established the Gulf Cooperation Council in 1981, they specifically identified their "common characteristics and similar systems founded on the creed of Islam" as the defining reasons for their effort.[1] The foreign ministers of the six member states provided even clearer justification for their endeavor at their first pre-summit meeting in Taif, Saudi Arabia. The 4 February 1981 communiqué read, in part, that the conservative monarchies wished to unite "out of consideration of their special relations and joint characteristics stemming from their joint creed, similarity of regimes, unity of heritage, similarity of their political, social and demographic structure, and their cultural and historical affiliation."[2]

Similar statements followed but what they all purported to declare was that unity *on* the Arabian Peninsula was widespread and, more important, that potentially negative underlying currents—including ethnic and religious differences—were the figment of "Orientalist" imaginations. Still, the reality of the GCC in 1981 was evident: The six countries embarked on a helter-skelter unity bandwagon because of perceived threats—especially from the Islamic Revolution in Iran. Nevertheless, and although unity was brought on the Peninsula, it was not *in* it.

Without a doubt, the creation of the GCC represented a momentous step toward unity on the Arabian Peninsula, as was the 1990 effort in Yemen. To be sure, the Yemen Arab Republic (YAR) and the People's Democratic Republic of Yemen (PDRY) united by necessity—perhaps to "correct" the 1962 division that separated them—but the end result was substantial.[3] Undeniably, both the GCC and unified Yemen achieved much, but, as events since 1981 in every Gulf state amply illustrated, major differences among Gulf states remained. Some of these differences were grave, especially in Bahrain, Kuwait, and Saudi Arabia, where dormant ethnic and religious divisions awakened. In Yemen, internal tensions threatened to unravel the meager achievements of unification. Little of what ailed these societies was well understood. Even less was known about the long-term repercussions of domestic conflicts.

## The Political Arena on the Peninsula

Except for Saudi Arabia, an independent country for over 50 years, GCC states were very young sovereign actors in the international political arena. Kuwait gained its independence in 1961, and Bahrain, Qatar, and the UAE in 1971. Although Oman's sovereignty was exercised for several centuries, the Sultanate did not enjoy autonomy before 1970, when Sultan Qaboos acceded to the throne and literally opened his country to the outside world.

In the 1980s and 1990s, several GCC rulers attempted to enlarge popular participation in their political systems, recognizing that internal stability strengthened regional security. Indeed, the absence of effective political participation presented a catalyst for potential upheavals and instability, and the demise of the Shah of Iran in 1979 reminded GCC rulers that no regime, no matter how strong, could remain in power if a population rejected its ruler's legitimacy. While the impact of the Iranian revolution could not be overemphasized, GCC states' political systems amply indicated that authority and legitimacy were institutionalized quite differently than in Iran. Ruling families in the Lower Gulf consolidated power and authority over their subjects through historical tribal allegiances. Moreover, economic and social changes experienced since the discovery of petroleum, as well as the resulting rapid pace of modernization, accelerated the demand for political participation. The pivotal question, as one observer concluded, was "whether change in Arab Gulf societies would be gradual and peaceful, or whether it would produce instability and violence."[4]

Change, of course, meant that the stability of GCC regimes was far from guaranteed. Since political stability required that a system, or sub-system, in the international arena maintain equilibrium among its members, GCC states' search for stability necessitated political cooperation among the six regimes. This was especially significant because the Arabian Peninsula and the Persian Gulf were at the center of international and regional conflicts that threatened both GCC rulers and their subjects. Thus, how conservative regimes absorbed and processed change, while continuing to function normally by stressing their religious and ideological values, remained the key "stability" question. In the absence of mass political participation, stability in GCC states also required that the rulers satisfy certain popular requirements. Among these were the political and socioeconomic needs of their populations, both indigenous and expatriate, and the safeguarding of their citizens from external and internal sources of threat, as well as supporting basic freedoms for all.

Yet, the legitimacy of GCC rulers rested on norms adopted in different times, when the world was not preoccupied with the Persian Gulf. In fact, their relative political successes were largely accomplished through the use of coercion, in a relatively isolated environment.[5] In the post–oil boom era, however, when all six states were endowed with small intelligentsias and when education levels were rapidly rising, political coercion was no longer the most effective tool to achieve stability. Therefore, GCC rulers were faced with new challenges calling for further tolerance of peaceful internal dissension, to strengthen their legitimacy and sources of authority. This was certainly the case with the Shias, whose grievances surfaced with a vengeance after 1979, in large part inspired by the Islamic Revolution in Iran. How Shias were treated in GCC societies illustrated the dilemma of unity on the Arabian Peninsula.

## Shia Communities in the GCC States

To fill its divinely inspired mandate, the Khomeini regime attempted to export its "revolution" within the boundaries of Shia legal thought. Admittedly, it would have been inconsistent for Ayatollah Ruhollah Khomeini to advocate belligerent policies, when Shia religious and legal interpretations prohibited offensive wars. An armed attempt by Muslims to subjugate unbelievers, according to Shia jurisprudence, may only be declared by the imam or his immediate deputy *after* obtaining permission from the Prophet. Such a conflict would be an offensive jihad. A defensive jihad, on the other hand, did not require the imam to ask for the Prophet's or, for that matter, anyone else's permission.[6]

Significantly, all four types of defensive jihads applied to Khomeini's views in exporting the revolution and influencing Arab Gulf societies.[7] Furthermore, since in Shia doctrine it was essential that all Muslims (particularly Sunni Muslims) eventually become true believers, and join the Dar-al-Imam, it was logical to assume that Khomeini considered Gulf Sunni Muslims as apostates even though they were born Muslims (*murtadd fitri*).[8] Indeed, these religious and legal interpretations shed light on Khomeini's understanding of defensive jihad, and, beyond Iran's territorial entity, defensive jihad encompassed the entire Muslim world. Such fundamental assumptions justified Teheran's foreign policies, including Iran's response to the war with neighboring Baathist, but nonetheless Muslim, Iraq.[9] Of course, after 1982, the war with Iraq was no longer a territorial dispute, but a clear attempt to export the nascent revolution to Baghdad.

Thus, except for the war with Iraq, Iran did not attempt to export its revolution through coercive methods. Rather, it endeavored, with limited successes, to invite sympathetic Shias and Iranian nationals in GCC states (and elsewhere) to become true Muslims by simply joining the Dar al-Imam. Toward the fulfillment of this goal, economically and politically deprived Shias were also called to rebel against conservative Sunni GCC governments by demanding that the influence of "Westernization" be curbed. A return to true religious fundamentalism was the order of the day.

Shias across the Gulf formed an integral part of the settled populations and worked their way up the social ladder, enjoying economic prosperity. Yet, despite these gains, Shias throughout the lower Gulf region were always perceived as a distinct group both socially and politically. An additional source of tension was their overwhelming numeric advantage among nationals in Bahrain, Qatar, and, to some extent, the UAE.

Beyond the numbers, however, serious sociopolitical cleavages scarred Sunni-Shia relations in every GCC state. For example, with a large Shia middle-class population, which comprised 70 percent of the island's citizens, Bahrain was a fertile ground for dissent. Since 1978, revolutionary leaders in Teheran frequently called on Bahraini Shias to revolt against Manama, which in turn angered the Sunni-led government. Although an effort was made, at least after the early 1970s, to bring elements of the Shia middle class into the government, tensions did not subside. Nevertheless, Shia officials filled a number of cabinet positions, and in December 1972, 14 out of the 22 elected members of the National Assembly were Shias. Bahrain's experiment with parliamentary life highlighted underlying tensions between reform-minded Shia deputies and more conservative Sunnis, leading the ruler to dissolve the chamber in 1975.[10]

What worked elsewhere in the Gulf could not be applied in Bahrain. Indeed, the dynamic island-state was different because the serious sociopolitical cleavage between the two Muslim communities could not be resolved by mere "deportations," as in the case of expatriate laborers. Most Bahraini Shias were *citizens* and enjoyed full privileges under the laws of the state, which protected them from summary deportations. The challenge facing Manama, therefore, was how to meet the rising expectations of Shia Bahrainis. Moreover, Manama's task was complicated given that Bahraini Shias enjoyed freedom of worship, and the commemoration of Ashura (celebrating al-Husain Ibn Ali's martyrdom—a political as well as a religious phenomenon) was a national holiday. The government, while lenient to religious freedoms, objected to Shia political manifestations, particularly during Ashura, dealing harshly with demonstrators. Noticeably, this trend continued into the mid-1990s, with heavy casualties.[11]

The Kuwaiti Shia population was estimated to hover around 25 percent of the total indigenous population in 1995 (perhaps 250,000 out of an estimated 1 million citizens). In addition, an estimated 80,000 Iranians lived and worked in Kuwait, where few residents were granted citizenship even after decades of successive habitation.[12] A number of pro-Iranian demonstrations were staged beginning in 1979, although the Al Sabah regime did not hesitate to put them down rapidly and severely. Ironically, the conservative Sunni government in Kuwait had an especially difficult task in monitoring the activities of its politically motivated Shia citizens and Iranian residents. Since religious and political meetings occurred in mosques that were under the supervision of the Ministry of Religious Endowments and Islamic Affairs, it was especially significant that in the early 1980s, 9 out of the 25 Shia mosques in Kuwait did not fall under this category and, therefore, lacked governmental oversight. Furthermore, it was assumed that political meetings and paramilitary activities occurred in some of the 60 Shia centers of religious education and propagation (*Husayniyahs*).[13] Recent events in the Shaykhdom, including the devastating Iraqi invasion and subsequent liberation, did not fundamentally alter perceptions of inequality between Shias and Sunnis. By the mid-1990s, Kuwait's Shia population—both Arab and Persian—had gained little additional influence, either in parliament or in the government. In October 1996, several Sunni Islamist groups, led by the Salafiyah Movement, won National Assembly seats that left Shias—once again—out of the political arena.[14]

In Oman, where the majority of the population were Ibadhis, an offshoot sect of Shia Islam, less than 7 percent of the indigenous population was Shia, most of whom were concentrated in the capital city of Muscat. Although the Sultanate did not experience many violent clashes or opposition from its Shia population in the 1980s and 1990s, Muscat was understandably concerned with rapid developments across the strategic Straits of Hormuz and, more important, about the spillover effects of the Iranian revolution. In mid-1994, Omani authorities arrested several hundred "Islamists" who, according to official sources, "had external connections, both financial and organizational." Although the majority of those arrested—and eventually released—were Sunnis, several Shia and Ibadhi Omanis were among those that intended to "overthrow the regime."[15]

In Qatar, the only other state in addition to Saudi Arabia that accepted the call to the Doctrine of the Oneness of God (*al-Daawah ila al-Tawhid*), the number of Shias hovered between 15 and 80 percent of the citizen population, depending on sources.[16] Despite this major discrepancy in statistical estimates, few Qatari Shias were politically active, although it would be a mistake to conclude that the Al Thani did not have to take them into account.

Finally, in the UAE, the native Shia population was estimated to be as high as 41 percent among the Federation's citizens. In this instance, as well, statistical discrepancies abounded.[17] Interestingly, in Dubai 30 to 40 percent of the population were of Iranian origin, most of whom had settled in the Shaykhdom around the turn of the century. Other large Shia populations in Sharjah and Abu Dhabi made the UAE the truly cosmopolitan country it was. Much as in other Gulf states, pro-Iranian demonstrations were staged periodically after 1979, which prompted UAE internal security forces to keep close surveillance of Shias and deport—on a regular basis—convicted violators of UAE laws.

Despite clear gains in certain economic fields, Shias remained essentially outsiders in the sociopolitical arenas of GCC states. The fact that most Shia citizens provided needed assistance in the oil industry was largely and conveniently overlooked because ruling Sunni governments would not absorb them as full participants in GCC states' political life. With the notable exception of a few wealthy merchant families in Oman and Bahrain (by no means representing the large Shia populations in the region), Shias in the Gulf were mostly on the lower social and economic strata. Conversely, almost two decades after the Iranian revolution, Shias failed to develop strong bonds of allegiance to their respective states, and many continued to draw inspiration from the Iranian revolution in their efforts to assert undeniable self-identities.

While the overall number of Shias in the six GCC states hovered around one million, GCC rulers feared a potential alliance between Shias and disenfranchised Sunni groups—presumably with the express support of the revolutionary regime in Teheran—to threaten internal stability. This certainly was the contention of senior Bahraini officials who maintained that disturbances on the island after 1995 were fully supported by Iran.[18] Throughout the 1980s, the Arabian Peninsula experienced the successive jolts of Iran's revolutionary shocks, including the 1981 Bahrain coup attempt, the 1983–1985 multiple bombings in Kuwait, the 1987 Makkah bloodshed (repeated on and off since then), and, of course, the severe jolts of the 1990 Iraqi invasion of Kuwait. These events intensified GCC states' fear of the Iranian and Iraqi regimes, leading to routine expulsions of expatriate workers (mostly Iranians) believed to have been involved in anti-regime disturbances. In turn, Teheran perceived these actions as pro-Western, unjust, and, in the revolutionary jargon, un-Islamic.

Saudi-Iranian relations went from bad to worse throughout the 1980s but, miraculously, improved in the aftermath of the Iraqi invasion of Kuwait. Riyadh re-established its broken ties with Teheran in March 1991 and encouraged its GCC partners to improve ties as well. The Kuwaitis hired several Iranian oil-well capping enterprises, for example, to help Western corporations extinguish some of the 600+ fires set by retreating Iraqi troops. Heir Apparent Abdallah bin Abdul Aziz Al Saud attended the 1997 Organization of Islamic Conference summit meeting in Teheran, where he received special attention. For its part, Riyadh welcomed former President Rafsanjani and sent Foreign Minister Saud al-Faysal for high-level discussions in 1998 with Ayatollah Khatami.[19] Of course, Oman and the UAE, which had nurtured their contacts with Iran even during the most difficult period, were instrumental in the rapprochement under way. GCC states even contemplated security discussions with Iran as a balancing factor vis-à-vis Iraq.

Despite these noticeable changes, the rapprochement between the GCC states and Iran was only an antidote for a serious and, perhaps, permanent disagreement. Relations between Sunni Arab rulers and Shia Persian revolutionaries were too divergent to ensure an enduring truce. GCC states were literally caught in the Saudi-Iranian legitimizing vortex and were, as a result, almost always prey to political and religious pressures from either side. In the past, the small shaykhdoms had looked to Baghdad as a third alternative pole, but in the wake of recent events, it would be extremely difficult, if not impossible, for GCC states to rely on that source in toto—as long as Saddam Hussein remained in power. Still, GCC rulers and populations alike opposed the various embargoes that hurt helpless Iraqis and, to address their concerns, provided material assistance. Nevertheless, and because GCC states knew that Teheran—especially if it formed close ties with its brethren in Iraq—could easily resort to its "Shia" card to influence internal political developments in the shaykhdoms, they looked to Baghdad as a perpetual balancer. This proposition was valid as long as Shias remained disenfranchised, which, subsequently, perpetuated the lack of unity on the Peninsula.

### Evolution of Class Structure in the GCC States

Although any scheme of social stratification on the Arabian Peninsula blurred the lines between social, economic, and political elites and groups, the end result was not always unity. It was important to note that poverty and marginal political power, for example, sometimes accompanied the social status enjoyed by badu tribes. Similarly, the ulama in Saudi Arabia or in Qatar—who enjoyed considerable political influence—did not always enjoy high economic standing. Still, the ruling families remained at the top of the Gulf paradigms because they were the only elites into which members were born. Moreover, due to their high social positions, wealthy Gulf ruling families experienced unprecedented enhancements of their political and social clout. Many members exploited their standings by allocating to themselves a portion of the state oil income, involving themselves in their country's commercial enterprises, and using their spending powers to exercise direct influence on the state.

Yet, even within groups of high standing elites, there was disenchantment. In the post–oil boom era, younger, more educated princes demanded greater participation in the running of their country's internal and foreign affairs. Likewise, Westernized elites in search of an effective voice were increasingly dissatisfied with the established consensus-reaching approaches designed and supported by their elders. Naturally, some senior officials were aware of these subtle changes, and several among them understood that their societies could experience serious upheavals if dissenting calls were not heeded. Still, although key officials were aware of changes within their own ranks, few knew how to address them. If Gulf ruling families could satisfy the genuine needs of younger princes—that is, without jeopardizing the established cohesion at senior levels—then chances were good that the disenchantment within their ranks would be limited.[20]

## Political Participation in the GCC States

Neither the situation of Shias nor the evolution of class structure in GCC societies affected unity on the Arabian Peninsula to the same degree that the call for genuine political participation did. Despite the many accomplishments of the 1970s through the 1990s, GCC citizens demanded even more, insisting that their voices be heard loud and clear. Such calls illustrated GCC citizens' aspirations for genuine unity, and several Gulf rulers responded.

Even before the War for Kuwait, the small northern Shaykhdom was engaged in a political participation experiment, in the form of an elected parliament. Similarly, Bahrain was also a "parliamentary" government, although the institution was suspended in 1975. For its part, the UAE's National Assembly aimed—for many years—to ratify a "provisional" constitution. Oman and Qatar experimented with consultative councils, each with concrete accomplishments to its credit. The winds of change were indeed blowing across the Arabian Peninsula, and by osmosis, war, or both, the trend was for more political participation. Although the conservative Arab Gulf monarchies were perceived as "anachronistic absolute monarchies," in reality they were confronting sociopolitical challenges and, in many respects, growing stronger.

Despite their many shortcomings, Gulf rulers were keenly aware of social developments requiring their attention, ranging from the evolution of class structure to the impact of modernization. In the oil-boom era, GCC rulers assumed that providing the highest possible incomes for their citizens would keep the lid on social problems. In reality, direct and indirect aid taxed services, increased manpower imports, and eroded the value of work. The search for "instant wealth became an end in itself."[21] But when the novelty faded, people turned to the more fundamental questions affecting their lives.

The 1970s—the oil decade—synthesized a new class structure in which the ruling families "enhanced their status as a social and economic elite while retaining political monopoly."[22] This phenomenon was paralleled by the emergence of a secondary elite—akin to a middle class—that benefited from the economic boom and, not surprisingly, became much more differentiated. With better education levels, middle-class members were ideally suited to exploit opportunities as they arose. But the economic recession of the 1980s limited government capabilities to satisfy heightened expectations. And, rather than pursue painful economic policies, Gulf rulers continued to provide free services to maintain the social balance.[23] By failing to swallow the painful economic pill of the past decade, GCC states literally created a post–oil boom generation, whose objective was to maintain its high standard of living at all costs.

The post–oil boom generation gave the rulers legitimacy as long as the latter provided them with material possessions. At some point, it may well be next to impossible to provide everyone with everything, and the middle class will grow and expand its influence in ways that might not be welcomed by the ruling families. It is indeed conceivable that an eventual alliance between middle and lower classes may emerge "to break the oligarchic social and political power of the elites."[24] Signs of this alliance were visible in GCC states' national assemblies and consultative councils, where middle-class members were increasingly popular.[25] Moreover, calls for genuine political participation were emanating from all directions, including from within the ruling families, where younger members, especially from cadet branches, were marginalized with little or no influence on political issues. Although difficult to anticipate with certainty, it may be accurate to conclude that ruling families that failed to heed these calls for political participation could indeed face the ire of their "subjects" in the not too distant future.

### Trends in Arab Gulf Unity

Assuming that the Iranian revolution was the catalyst—and the Iran-Iraq War the excuse—for the six conservative Arab Gulf states to set up a regional security organization without the participation of the two northern Gulf states, what was the nature of Arab Gulf unity? Moreover, whereas prior to November 1980 most Gulf rulers acknowledged that the Gulf region represented the strategic depth for the Arab world facing Israel, developments in both Iran and Iraq—amply demonstrated by the Iran-Iraq War and the War for Kuwait—transformed the confrontation states into the strategic depth of the Gulf countries, vis-à-vis Iran and Iraq. Political and military changes in the Gulf strengthened Arab Gulf rulers' perceptions that the Islamic Revolution was as tangible a threat to their political survival as the Israeli threat was to their physical well-being. Of course, the 1990 Iraqi invasion of Kuwait was even more pronounced, since it affected each and every conservative Arab Gulf state. Consequently, and out of necessity, Gulf rulers were forced to come out of their shells and shoulder the responsibility of providing—collectively—security in the Persian Gulf region. As one observer noted:

To understand the tremendous change that has swept through the Gulf countries, one must realize that a clearer comprehension of the fundamentals of international power plays has become fixed in the minds of Gulf rulers. In consequence of their efforts and commitments towards the non-oil Arab countries, the Gulf producers' intentions must be given very serious weight.[26]

Still, the War for Kuwait altered the balance of power in the region, and further narrowed the parameters of unity on the Peninsula. Once again, necessity was the primary reason for all regional attempts that boxed—as best as possible—those that were in the unity scheme (the so-called GCC+2 [Egypt and Syria]) versus those that were excluded from it, namely Iran and Iraq.[27]

What prompted Gulf rulers to feel secure enough to take a plunge into the GCC+2 scheme varied. First, it was clear that politically they were better entrenched than most other Arab states. Second, their achievements in enhancing the quality of life in their countries, and the desire to develop their societies' potential, permitted them to count on deeds and results. Third, the availability of vast resources obviously allowed Gulf rulers to invest in the future and shed their shyness cloak. Finally, their regional strengths emerged, without ignoring deeply felt commitments to the Arab world, from a sharpened appreciation of what the Iranian revolution and the Baathist regime in Baghdad potentially represented to their way of life. This appreciation coalesced divergent views and, under Saudi leadership, galvanized GCC states to form a genuine alliance against Iran and Iraq. It was not the Yemen but the Iran-Iraq War that motivated GCC rulers into action. Moreover, after the Iraqi invasion of Kuwait, GCC states were further motivated to enter into new alliances with Western powers. In short, both Iran and Iraq helped GCC states to seek a unity of necessity on the Arabian Peninsula. All of their defensive cooperation efforts focused on the two major hegemonic powers. Indeed, Gulf rulers recognized that "Iraq had been a threat before the Iranian revolution and that Iran has been a danger since."[28] They feared these two powers most and knew what the risks were. When Iraq invaded Kuwait, one of the GCC rulers' worst fears materialized. With weak military capabilities, the reliance on Western allies was a foregone conclusion. GCC forces responded as well as they could, but in the two-month-long "war," they were not the critical factor. In fact, the return of the Al Sabah to Kuwait raised the fundamental "outside military support" question forcefully for the GCC alliance. Under the circumstances, it would indeed be quite difficult to shake it off for some time to come. Simply stated, conservative Arab Gulf rulers shed all pretenses and opted for survival when their regimes were at stake. The trend was for more of the same.

Because GCC societies opted to focus on regional and international threats, their quest for unity on the Arabian Peninsula was only partially achieved. Festering internal tensions have meant that every Gulf state has experienced significant social upheavals during the past few years. At least four main sources of instability (or relative stability—depending on how governments responded) can be identified as future indicators of dramatic change:

1. disenchantment with the ruling family,
2. demands made by the intelligentsia,
3. pressures imposed by an increasingly professional military, and
4. competition for power by religious extremists.

Although social upheavals were not intrinsic to the Gulf region, the oil boom of the 1970s disrupted the nature of personal and family relationships, introduced consumerism, subordinated the Islamic principle of egalitarianism to more formal authority structures, and created an economic dependency on the government.[29] Moreover, the oil-boom era literally tore at the fabric of the most traditional societies on earth, where values were measured and implemented by entirely different social yardsticks than the ones practiced in the West. Ironically, most GCC citizens perceived the turbulent decades of the 1980s and 1990s as a reprieve from the chaos of the 1970s. Many compared the 1970s to an age of drunkenness and the period afterwards to a recovery from it. The return, of course, was to the more traditional values one could find in religion, society, and family, even if the more evident signs of modernization were readily espoused. Thus, seemingly contradictory forces in GCC societies coexisted, and the debate was over the level of comfort that these powerful forces—traditions and modernization—imposed on them.

Finally, and although the exploitation of oil produced undeniable economic benefits for a majority of GCC states' populations, a level of disorientation was also apparent because they were thrown into a very complex international arena of politics, economics, and finance, without adequate preparations.[30] Given the speed with which "modernizing" factors were introduced, some of the social changes were clearly instigated by eager governments. Others were unforeseen. A transformation of the economy; the creation of a bureaucracy to allow for new functions; the provision of extensive and mostly free social services; the adoption of all-inclusive development programs; the emphasis on education for manpower development; the shift to and extent of urbanization; the massive influx of close to 5 million expatriate workers; and the considerable defense needs of vulnerable countries all complicated matters for every GCC government.[31]

These social changes left dramatic imprints on GCC societies. Without exception, the badu were partially detribalized as a new national political culture emerged. A more nuclear family arose, leading as well to changes in relations between the sexes. The exposure to alien values and norms meant that a cultural erosion was under way that, in turn, allowed for the evolution of class structure and a greater social stratification. Finally, the changing outlooks of the younger generation raised serious dilemmas for conservative governments. Their response was the adoption of more aggressive policies at the regional level. To be sure, wary rulers addressed internal concerns but only with hesitation and, it seemed, always with a certain level of reluctance. In the long run, GCC internal issues were far more important than any regional hegemonic threats, and it was by addressing intrinsic demands for change that conservative Arab Gulf govern-

## The Political Arena of the Yemen

Unlike GCC states, where unity efforts were the result of necessity, the Yemen Arab Republic (YAR) and the People's Democratic Republic of Yemen (PDRY) coexisted helter skelter, despite serious clashes spanning the period between 1962 and 1990. The fact remained, however, that Yemen was—at one point in history—a united entity, and six decades of wars (civil, regional, and international) notwithstanding, Yemenis craved unity.

### Pre-Unification Efforts

Both the YAR and the PDRY sat at the strategic edge of the world's richest petroleum peninsula for years before the discovery of their own oil reserves. Although poor, the two were not friendly, even though together they formed a buffer zone between the Horn of Africa and Arabia. For years, the Soviet Union backed the PDRY to foster Soviet policy in the whole Middle East, and the last thing Moscow wanted to see was a re-unification with the "capitalist" North. Saudis were also against unification, as they feared that a unified Yemen could end up being dominated by Southern Yemeni communists. Yet, among ordinary people on both sides of the border, pressures for a united Yemen were surprisingly strong.[32] Unification was an emotional issue that transcended economic and global politics. Southerners often spoke of family and friends in the North. Many, including government officials, quietly admitted to a hope that unity would be achieved by political compromise on both sides. In Sanaa, public and private opinions were more guarded (reflecting the area's tribal traditions), but ministers reminded outsiders that the people of Aden were Yemenis just like themselves. In the late 1970s, an economic expert in Sanaa explained a typical personal dilemma by stating:

> My mother and father both came from the North, but I was born in Aden. When the socialists came to power, I came North and stayed ever since. My wife and two children remained in the South and if circumstances changed I would certainly go back. Eighty percent of my business friends come from the South and they would like the opportunity to return.[33]

Periodic outbreaks of violence in both North and South exacerbated these difficulties. But after the February 1979 hostilities, a new government to address intrinsic political and social issues reached a tentative agreement.

President Ali Abdallah Saleh (YAR) was invited by Aden to be the first head of the united nation, and joint committees were created to examine ways of integrating education, currency, and transport. Certainly, the industrialization of the South and the relatively efficient agriculture of the North promised a good economic mix. Moreover, a major stumbling block was removed with the announcement that the socialist PDRY would accept a unity government, which would follow Shariah laws. As the 1970s closed, the political will to unite was present, on both sides. South Yemenis, for example, celebrated the ten-year anniversary of the 1962 coup that had brought the northern regime to power. In 1975, Aden also identified re-unification as a primary goal of the Marxist regime.[34] Although many Northern officials were suspicious of the South's willingness to let President Saleh rule the united country, the latter's personal commitment to unification was strong. In 1978, Saleh overcame two attempted coups by anti-unity groups. The first, in October 1978, resulted in the execution of several army officers, and the second, in May 1979, remained shrouded in secrecy. Shortly thereafter, Lieutenant Colonel Muhammad Yahyah al-Anisi, chief of the Amaliga (an army special forces group), Major Muhammad Sanabani, the commander of the Seventh Armored Brigade, and Major Ali Mahdi Sanabani, the commander of the Reserves, were all removed from their posts, allegedly because of their involvement in the two coup attempts. Such high-level support for coups indicated that the Saleh government was weak. Nevertheless, the president neutralized a large section of the opposition by purging high-ranking officers, which left him fairly free to pursue his own policies.

Over the years, Yemeni leaders' personal commitments to unification changed little. In 1979, for example, Foreign Minister Abdallah al-Asnaq, a prominent opponent of the PDRY government, was downgraded to the position of presidential adviser in the North. Saleh's counterpart in the South, Abdel Fattah Ismail, who came to power in a June 1978 coup when he deposed President Rubai Ali, was by no means a puppet of the USSR, even though Aden accepted considerable aid from Moscow. The PDRY embarked on a five-year plan (1979–1984) that intended to build on an already developing industrial base.

For the leader of a supposedly socialist state, Ismail encouraged several aggressive capitalist schemes. Aden sponsored joint development projects between the public and private sectors; authorized the British Crown Agents firm to continue purchasing for and advising it; maintained telephone links to London, which was Aden's best technical link to the outside world; allowed British Petroleum to fly its flag; and insisted that young men in the civil service and nationalized banks receive Western training. But despite all of these efforts, "unification talks" did not proceed well. Most were held at the informal level, with little progress made on substantive issues.

The underlying external pressures against unification remained and were exacerbated by the February 1979 war in the North.[35] Saudi Arabia's concern over Soviet influence in the region essentially meant that Riyadh remained active in derailing the fledgling talks in the first place. North Yemen was viewed as a buffer state between Saudi Arabia and the PDRY, and every successful unification meeting was looked on with alarm. But, despite the fact that Riyadh provided almost all the cash injected into the YAR, and that Sanaa's armed forces were equipped and trained with Saudi finances, it was difficult to find North Yemenis who spoke favorably of their generous neighbor.[36]

For their part, the Soviets—who provided much of the finances to keep the

PDRY afloat—sought the strategic advantages of a satellite state that provided access to the Arabian Gulf, as well as facilities for a deep-water port at Aden. Despite this close relationship, ties were never cemented between Aden and Moscow. In looking at the Soviet relationship with the PDRY, it is important to examine the former Soviet Union's ties with the YAR as well. Significantly, the USSR was the principal supplier of military and financial aid to republican forces throughout the civil war, even if Soviet relations with the YAR were abruptly broken in 1972. By the end of the 1970s, and although Moscow maintained a very large trade mission in Sanaa, the Soviet influence on the YAR was limited. There were few indications that Moscow understood the Arab world any better in the late seventies than it had prior to the 1972 Egyptian debacle.[37] Slow unification talks made it abundantly clear that the Soviet Union's greatest gain from the February 1979 war was not any direct military successes by the South, but the damaging long-term effects on the Northern economy. Far more important, Arabs who suffered the consequences of economic dislocations were not ready to support, or even tolerate, an outside power bent on regional domination.

No matter how influential outsiders were, or tried to be, and no matter how difficult it was to achieve progress in unification, many North Yemenis claimed that Yemen was one country divided by two governments. What prevented unification, they argued, were the two countries' economic positions and the assiduous work of the Saudis and the Soviets to keep the two sides apart.

If Riyadh and Moscow were too obsessed with Sanaa and Aden, Kuwait was especially interested in fostering reconciliation. Kuwaiti officials helped negotiate a merger agreement in 1979 even if they acknowledged that ideological and other differences between the two countries appeared to be major obstacles to unity. These differences, officials then claimed, were not dealt with by those charged with putting the agreement into effect. Kuwaiti negotiators encouraged the adoption of a Yemeni draft constitution—with 136 articles—expected to be submitted to a referendum after consultations between the two presidents and their legislative bodies. To their credit, the Kuwaitis expected little, as the 1972 agreement stood in stark contrast to the newfound optimism. They certainly favored the union as a means of reducing tension in the Gulf region but also wished to create an alternative source of influence to balance Saudi Arabia's growing pressures on them. Moreover, the Al Sabah hoped that the PDRY, within the framework of a unified state, would feel less threatened by its neighbors and might even loosen its ties to the Soviet Union. Ironically, these ties were substantially strengthened after the 1978 signing of a 20-year friendship treaty between Moscow and Aden.[38] Still, the two Yemens, dominated by socialist and tribal backgrounds, failed once again to heed friendly "pressure," preferring to determine the ideology of their projected unified state themselves. This was a major realization that strengthened both leaderships in ways that few outsiders accepted or understood.

## *Unification*

Unification became a realistic prospect in the late 1980s when oil prices dropped and, more important, when the Soviet Union teetered on the brink of economic collapse. The PDRY lost its principal benefactor, which in turn meant a halt in the country's economic development. Aden's port could not be developed into the world-class facility many hoped for, and lack of cash postponed much-needed repairs to the country's oil fields and assorted infrastructure. A merger, South Yemeni leaders posited, would encourage Western oil companies to return and invest in the nascent Shabwa fields. After the initial step, the reasoning concluded, pre-revolutionary landowners and entrepreneurs who had fled the country years earlier would return and bring back sorely needed capital. Similarly, opportunities derived from a merger appealed to the YAR, after oil exploration in the Maarib area proved to be less promising than originally anticipated. By accepting the merger, Sanaa would double its reserves and acquire of one the best natural ports on the Arabian Peninsula. An accord was reached on 30 November 1989—in Aden—and the two states formally united on 22 May 1990, six months ahead of schedule, into the Republic of Yemen.[39]

Within two months of this dramatic development, Iraq invaded Kuwait, an event that plunged the entire region into a crisis situation. Except for Iraq, no other country suffered more from the War for Kuwait than Yemen. Sanaa opposed the Iraqi invasion but vociferously objected to the U.S.-led foreign intervention. As a result, Yemen received the ire of regional and international actors, led by Saudi Arabia, from where an estimated one million Yemeni workers were hurriedly expelled.[40] Yemen lost its much-needed remittances. It also lost concessionary oil supplies from Iraq, its Arab Cooperation Council (ACC) partner, which forced Sanaa to divert production for internal use. Foreign exchange revenues were halved overnight. GCC states, along with the United States, cut their own financial assistance programs. A relatively poor country sank even lower, which, not surprisingly, added to the strain on internal stability.[41]

### *Post-Unification Efforts*

Several years after unification, disenchantment was still greater in the south than in the north. The Sanaa government edged out Aden, and many southerners regretted the "de-socialization" of the southern part of Yemen. The last of the countless red stars that used to adorn Aden's official buildings vanished, and the slogans of the Yemen Socialist Party (YSP) were carefully washed off city walls. Most portraits of the four "historical" leaders, including Abdel Fattah Ismail, whose assassination on 13 January 1986 had triggered a bloody internal civil war, were also removed.

On the hills that overlooked the harbor, an imposing peace dove replaced the huge color picture of Abdel Fattah Ismail, the martyr ideologist of the YSP. The Abdel Fattah Ismail and Ali Antar Museums, and the museum where the assassination of the four leaders was reconstituted—in the former headquarters of the political bureau—were in a state of neglect for lack of funds and visitors. A recent report claimed that a single building devoted to South Yemeni history would be created to preserve Aden's rich traditions. The monumental complexes housing the YSP and the Institute for Scientific Socialism—gifts from East European countries built in the purest Soviet style—looked like ships adrift abandoned by their crews and passengers. Before leaving for Sanaa, YSP leaders kept their promise and did all they could to clean Aden of anything that might remind Yemenis that it once was a center of socialist influence. Most Yemenis who believed that a new era of prosperity was about to begin enthusiastically welcomed this "de-socialization."

Disenchantment soon set in, however, as southerners discovered that interventionist socialism was gradually replaced by the wild capitalism of the north. "Before, our socialist leaders would exploit us," a worker complained. "Now, the northerners are systematically bleeding the country," he asserted.[42] Northerners traveled to the south loaded with riyals exchanged on the black market, never intending to invest in their country. Engaged in speculation and buying anything that might someday increase in value, they brought with them all of the vices of the north. After 1990, Aden market stalls, which used to be hopelessly bare, overflowed with vegetables, fruits, and other essentials. But prices were prohibitive since subsidies had been abolished immediately after unification, and few could afford them. The market where "qat" (the local euphoric drug) was sold, which did not exist in 1989, looked exactly like its counterparts in Sanaa working-class neighborhoods. It drained a considerable part of the meager wages of southern Yemenis, who were now free to use the substance even if it became a burden on the family budget. "The former South Yemen," an academic opined, "has become the East Germany of re-unified Yemen."[43]

What followed for several years was a price explosion that affected southerners more than northerners, because the latter found ways to double or even triple their salaries, by moonlighting or engaging fiercely in the black market and smuggling. An attempt to introduce an unofficial foreign-currency marketeering in the south was thwarted by the police, now headed by a northerner. There was every indication that officials in Sanaa wanted Aden to become a provincial town. Even government employees' salaries were paid late—in extreme cases up to seven months late—all of which led southerners to lose confidence in unity, and especially in their new leaders in Sanaa. Thus, invectives against YSP officials were a common occurrence, and former PDRY leaders betrayed Yemenis by abandoning them: "We are disappointed and were better off before unification," a disgruntled southerner acknowledged. The high cost of living affected everyone, especially after the subsidization policy was scrapped. Others compared the YSP to "a figurehead on a shelf," without any real control over what was happening in Sanaa.[44]

Southerners, who rejected the YSP in the hope that President Saleh's General Congress Party (GCP) would improve their lot, were clearly "worse off," and totally adrift. They did not know where to turn, especially when they saw corruption setting in—slowly but surely—through northerners working at customs, port, and airport facilities. A new "northern" customs director imposed arbitrary duties on Somali women carrying parcels of clothing for the local markets, which enraged all those who heard about the incident. Diplomatic missions were not immune to such arbitrary decisions. The majority accepted these unofficial rules if they wanted to get their diplomatic bags quickly. Outraged by such occurrences, many Yemenis remained faithful to socialism, which the people of Aden saw disintegrating among the widespread laxness of the re-unified Yemeni society.

The general breakdown of law and order continued unabated as an intense arms smuggling campaign from Saudi Arabia to the Shabwa and Hadhramaut Governorates intensified. Gangs spread havoc on Aden beaches at night, and the number of break-ins increased markedly. Car owners who never bothered to lock their vehicles were taking additional precautions. In order not to be bothered, women increasingly wore a veil. Many dreaded the promulgation of the law allowing polygamy and divorce, both of which had been banned in the south since the 1960s. But some South Yemenis no longer waited; they traveled one hour to Taiz in the north, where a legal second marriage, or a quick divorce from a religious judge, was easily arranged. "The impression was that [northerners] [we]re systematically destroying anything that was good in the South," and many believed that this was Sanaa's doing, to keep the former PDRY in a state of permanent underdevelopment. A United Nations Development Program (UNDP) employee confided how UNDP officials refused to allocate to the south credits that were not used in the north.

Sanaa's oft-repeated promise to turn Aden, which at the time of unification was called "Yemen's commercial and economic capital," into a free port capable of competing with Dubai or Hong Kong remained unfulfilled. After it was postponed several times, the law turning Aden into a free port was scheduled to be promulgated on 22 May 1991. Several years later, the project was still at its initial stages, with an official stating, half-jokingly and half seriously, that it was as difficult to turn Aden into a free port as it was to "turn a church into a nightclub."[45]

Ironically, the committee in charge of studying the project was named the Committee for the Development of Free Ports in Yemen, which hinted that Aden might not necessarily be chosen as the site of the future free zone. There was increasing talk that Hodeidah, in the north, was best located to play that role. The very active "Hodeidah lobby" praised its advantages, arguing that it was already equipped with modern facilities, effective communications means, and a skilled labor force, all of which allegedly was lacking in Aden.

Other concessions were made to Islamists, who proved their strengths in the north at the time of the referendum and remained faithful in opposing the secularism that was rooted in the south.[46] Nevertheless, the Islah, the union grouping the religious and the tribal leaders, achieved a breakthrough in the south after unification, with the help of the League of the Sons of Yemen (LSY).[47] The LSY constituency, repressed under the socialist regime, reorganized with the help of the Islah, creating a formidable alliance between tribes and Islamists. Whether this alliance could impose itself in Aden, where secular traditions were stronger, was difficult to determine. What was clear, however, was that northern Islamists lost a substantial part of their influence after a year of campaigning against the Aden beer brewery, which they called "a center of communism." This battle was lost in part because many of these fierce enemies of the diabolical brew spent weekends in Aden to enjoy such forbidden pleasures. Still, the struggle against the tribal–Islamist alliance was a trump card in the hands of southern leaders, as it enabled them to boost popularity among traditional constituents who were in a state of utter confusion.

### *Political Stability in Yemen*

After 1990, a series of convulsive bloodbaths preoccupied the Yemeni body politic.[48] At the same time, the legacy of this history mobilized Yemeni leaders in their quest for effective government, and despite clashes, real progress was achieved. Yemeni leaders applied what they preached by holding elections and, equally important, by tolerating opposition forces.[49] A new level of political stability was attained as Sanaa struggled to uphold minimum human rights standards and raised the level of tolerance for open political discourse.

The London-based human rights organization Amnesty International confirmed that all known political detainees and prisoners were released prior to unification. In its 1991 report, Amnesty claimed that one prisoner of conscience in North Yemen was released in January 1990, but it was not possible to confirm the release or continued detention of another 26 suspected political opponents. Released detainees from both former states alleged torture and ill treatment. Amnesty maintained that the cases of 50 people who "disappeared" in Yemen before unification remained unresolved. Since unification, however, no death sentences were known to have been ratified by the presidential council (although an estimated 300 Yemenis were detained after the 1994 civil war), which commuted eight such sentences in November 1990.[50]

For all the progress that such developments introduced into the political system, Sanaa faced considerable difficulties as challenges emerged from both left and right following several assassinations. For example, a group of political parties, trade union leaders, and prominent personalities called on the government to launch a full investigation into the killing of Hassan Huraybi, director-general of the Central Highlands rural development project, on 10 September 1991.[51] In a statement issued within hours after the assassination, the group insisted that the authorities were responsible for this incident and demanded that the criminal(s) be apprehended and brought before a court of law. They also warned that lack of government cooperation would open the floodgates of political unrest throughout the country.[52]

When no progress was made in identifying Huraybi's murderer(s), riots swept the capital in late 1991. Violence raged in Sanaa on 19 October 1991 after an army colonel shot dead a traffic policeman who had pulled him over for failing to stop at a red light. The incident took place in the center of the capital, outside the central bank building, in an area where large numbers of unemployed men sat in cafes. Observers said the shooting acted as a catalyst for rising frustrations at the level of joblessness and price increases. Cars and military vehicles were set on fire, and a building in front of parliament was burned. Police used tear gas to quell the demonstrations, and one report from a Western observer claimed that as many as nine people were killed. The government denied this, although demonstrations continued the following day as political parties called for a march to commemorate the fortieth day since the killing of Hassan Huraybi.

A number of political parties, including the League of the Sons of Yemen and the Nasserites as well as the government Yemen Socialist Party (YSP) and General People's Congress, called on citizens not to take part in view of the previous days' events. Nevertheless, the demonstration went ahead with the Tajammu (Yemeni Unionist Alliance) at its head. Other protesters returned to the central bank area, where they held a rival demonstration. A number of arrests were reported, but the government also announced that it would put the colonel on trial for the incident that had sparked the riots. Since the colonel was from President Saleh's own tribe, the latter was under pressure not to show any signs of favoritism.

It also emerged that Sadiq Abdallah bin Husain, a Republican Party representative and the son of the influential Shaykh Abdallah bin Husain al-Ahmar, escaped an assassination attempt outside Sanaa on 18 October 1991. His car was ambushed and three of his companions were injured. Shaykh Abdallah was head of the Hashid tribe and a leading national figure. Shaykh Naji Abdel-Aziz al-Shayef, head of the neighboring Baqil tribe, condemned the incident, and Internal Affairs Minister Mujahid Abu Shawarib called for the issue to be sorted out in a neighborly way. Others maintained that the incident was the latest in a series of attempted political assassinations, with the League of the Sons of Yemen blaming the YSP for failing to maintain law and order.[53]

Acts of violence were not limited to major cities. Two groups of heavily armed saboteurs were arrested in Hadhramaut, the official Sanaa weekly *26 September* revealed in late 1991, asserting that the groups were discovered with machine guns, land mines, rocket-propelled grenade launchers, and communications equipment.[54] In December 1991, two YSP members were assassinated while attending the opening session of a national conference in Ibb. Naaman Qasim Hassan, a member of the local party secretariat, and Nabil Ghaleb were the latest victims of the ongoing spate of violence in the country. *Al-Thawrah*, the YSP official magazine, published a report of their killing, which further increased tensions in the country.[55] In fact, between 1990 and 1994, an estimated 150 YSP members were killed in and around Sanaa.[56]

What these disturbances indicated was that unification did not alleviate Yemen's chronic tribal disputes. They also stood as a stark warning to President Saleh and his successors to assume control over internal stability if outside powers, in particular Saudi Arabia, were not to use this excuse to increase their involvement in internal Yemeni affairs. Consequently, and unless Sanaa gained the upper hand in domestic matters, it faced clear threats to its political stability.

Because President Saleh and Vice President al-Baid could not settle their differences, a growing political rift emerged by 1993, when the latter moved back to Aden. Al-Baid asked for specific reforms, and on 20 February 1994—in Amman, Jordan—a "Document of Bond and Agreement" was signed to bury the hatchet. On 3 April, Sultan Qaboos of Oman welcomed the two Yemeni leaders to Salalah, in yet another effort at reconciliation. Little did the Omani know that within a day of that fateful meeting, military confrontation between northerners and southerners would re-start in earnest.[57] Simply stated, the power game was too well entrenched for any document, or handshake, to carry the day.

The 1994 "civil war" that followed caused serious harm to unity but, in a convoluted way, addressed two perennial problems: outside meddling in internal Yemeni affairs and the legitimacy of state institutions. On both scores, unified Yemen's President Saleh won the day, by holding his ground against Saudi support to the YSP and by staking his rule on "total victory."[58] When, on 21 May 1994, Ali Salem al-Baid announced the establishment of the Democratic Republic of Yemen (DRY)—in effect seceding from the union that was barely four years old—Saleh launched his troops against the "traitors."[59] The move proved to be a last-stand effort that failed, and on 4 July 1994, northern forces occupied Aden and Mukallah. Separatists fled either to Djibouti or Oman, from where they retrenched to other safe havens.

To his credit, President Saleh consolidated his position by proposing several constitutional amendments that strengthened the country's fledgling institutions. Few expected him to challenge the single most powerful organization—the military—reasoning that he could not weaken his own power base. In the event, Saleh de-politicized the armed forces—forcing army officers to resign their party memberships—because he realized that not "uniting" the military after 1990 had been a grave error. Shortly thereafter, the ill-fated Presidential Council was abolished and replaced with an upper house of parliament composed largely of shaykhs and other dignitaries.

Ali Abdallah Saleh managed to reconcile with many southern ex-socialists, who, for one reason or another, accepted to join his successive cabinets after mid-1995. Even Riyadh retrenched and sought to reach an agreement over the long-festering border dispute between the two countries. Although no final accord was signed by mid-1998, Sanaa was confident that one would indeed come about, in the not too distant future. More important, Saleh gained support from various groups that, for a variety of reasons, accepted the inevitability of pluralism. For the first time in several decades, Yemeni leaders accepted to live by democratic rules, opting to gain the consent of the governed.[60]

In the end, unity was ensured, even if the reliance on violence revealed that the union was far from being absolute. Assassinations and an outright civil war underscored Sanaa's inability to impose permanent stability and security without resorting to force. What they indicated was that over six decades of warfare did not diminish the Yemeni appetite for unity. By upholding the rule of law, Saleh surprised many—including himself—by demonstrating that unity could indeed function, even if it were not perfect.

## Notes

1. "Charter of the Cooperation Council for the Arab States of the Gulf," in John A. Sandwick, *The Gulf Cooperation Council: Moderation and Stability in an Interdependent World,* Boulder and Washington, D.C.: Westview Press and American-Arab Affairs Council, 1987, p. 217.
2. "Foreign Ministers' Statement on the Founding of the Gulf Cooperation Council," *Al-Hadaf* (Kuwait), 5 February 1981, p. 5.
3. It is not the purpose of this essay to assess the relative successes of the GCC and the post-1990 Yemeni unification but to infer from both whether they increased—or decreased—unity on the Peninsula. Much has been written on the GCC and Yemen in recent years. For a sampling, see: R. K. Ramazani, *The Gulf Cooperation Council: Record and Analysis,* Charlottesville: University

Press of Virginia, 1988; Sandwick, *op. cit.;* Erik R. Peterson, *The Gulf Cooperation Council: Search for Unity in a Dynamic Region,* Boulder and London: Westview Press, 1988; Emile A. Nakhleh, *The Gulf Cooperation Council: Policies, Problems and Prospects,* New York: Praeger, 1986; Robert D. Burrowes, *The Yemen Arab Republic: The Politics of Development, 1962–1986,* Boulder: Westview Press, 1987; idem, "Prelude to Unification: The Yemen Arab Republic, 1962–90," *International Journal of Middle East Studies* 23:4, November 1991, pp. 483–506; idem, "The Yemen Arab Republic's Legacy and Yemeni Unification," *Arab Studies Quarterly* 14:4, fall 1992, pp. 41–68; Charles Dunbar, "The Unification of Yemen: Process, Politics, and Prospects," *The Middle East Journal* 46:3, summer 1992, pp. 456–76; and Eric Watkins and Patrick Makin, "Yemen's Crisis Threatens the Country's Unity," *Middle East International,* number 463, 19 November 1993, pp. 18–19.

4. Emile A. Nakhleh, *The Persian Gulf and American Policy,* New York: Praeger, 1982, p. 22.
5. For a brilliant essay on this key issue in the conservative Arab Gulf states, see Frank Stoakes, "Social and Political Change in the Third World: Some Peculiarities of Oil-Producing Principalities of the Persian Gulf," in Derek Hopwood, *The Arabian Peninsula: Society and Politics,* London: George Allen and Unwin, Ltd., 1972, pp. 189–215.
6. W. R. Campbell and Djamchid Darvich, "Global Implications of the Islamic Revolution for the Status Quo in the Persian Gulf," *Journal of South Asian and Middle Eastern Studies* 5:1, fall 1981, pp. 31–51.
7. The four kinds of defensive jihads are: (1) jihad to preserve the territory and community of Islam during an attack by unbelievers; (2) jihad to prevent unbelievers from gaining control over the persons of Muslims; (3) jihad to repel a particular group of unbelievers when it is feared that they might gain ascendancy over a particular group of Muslims; and (4) jihad to evict unbelievers where they had succeeded in conquering Muslim territories. For a full discussion, see ibid., p. 33. See also E. Kohlberg, "The Development of the Imami Shii Doctrine of Jihad," *Deutsche Morgen Landischen Gesellschaft Zeitschrift* 126, 1976, pp. 64–86.
8. Manoucher Parvin and Maurie Sommer, "Dar al-Islam: The Evolution of Muslim Territoriality and Its Implications for Conflict Resolution in the Middle East," *International Journal of Middle East Studies* 11:1, February 1980, pp. 1–21.
9. Iranian sources referred to the 1980–1988 Iran-Iraq War as "imposed," not only to buttress Iranian innocence but, more important, to solidify the fledgling revolution. In other words, the war allowed clerics to rally public support by combining revolutionary rhetoric with nationalist tendencies. See Dilip Hiro, *The Longest War: The Iran-Iraq Military Conflict,* New York: Routledge, 1991, pp. 7–39.
10. Nakhleh, The Persian Gulf and American Policy, *op. cit.*, pp. 26–40.
11. For a thorough analysis of internal developments in Bahrain, see Joe Stork, *Routine Abuse, Routine Denial: Civil Rights and the Political Crisis in Bahrain,* New York: Human Rights Watch, 1997; see also Bahrain Freedom Movement, *Facts About Bahrain,* London: BFM, 1997.
12. Ramazani, *op. cit.*, pp. 38–42, 200.
13. Abdallah Muhammad Gharib, *Wajaa Dawr al-Majus: Al-Ibad al-Tarikhiyah wal-Aqaidiyah wal-Siyasiyah lil-Thawra al-Iraniyah* [The Iranian Revolution's Impact on the Historic, Religious and Political Tensions between Sunnis and Shias], Cairo: Dar al-Jil lil-Tabaat, 1981, pp. 320, 323–28.
14. Faris Glubb, "Kuwait: New Parliament," *Middle East International,* number 536, 25 October 1996, p. 14; see also "Fears of Sectarianism Lead to Protest," *Country Report—Kuwait 4: 1996,* London: The Economist Intelligence Unit, p. 14; and Shafeeq N. Ghabra, "Balancing State and Society: The Islamic Movement in Kuwait," *Middle East Policy* 5:2, May 1997, pp. 58–72.
15. Abdullah Juma Al-Haj, "The Politics of Participation in the Gulf Cooperation Council States: The Omani Consultative Council," *The Middle East Journal* 50:4, autumn 1996, pp. 566–68; see also Salem Abdullah, *Omani Islamism: An Unexpected Confrontation with the Government,* Occasional Papers, number 8, Annandale, Virginia: UASR, September 1995.
16. One source advanced the 80 percent figure for 1980. See R. K. Ramazani, *Revolutionary Iran: Challenge and Response in the Middle East,* Baltimore and London: Johns Hopkins University Press, 1986, p. 259. Elsewhere, we have a figure as low as 16 percent. See James A. Bill, "Islam, Politics, and Shi'ism in the Gulf," *Middle East Insight* 3:3, January/February 1984, p. 6. Since all demographic figures on the Gulf region are suspect, caution must be exercised in evaluating them.
17. In Ramazani, the figure is 41 percent, whereas in Bill it stands at 18 percent: see ibid., pp. 259 and 6, respectively.
18. Graham E. Fuller, "Storm Clouds in the Gulf," *The Los Angeles Times,* 3 May 1996, p. B13.

19. Jubin Goodarzi, "Iran's Arab Policy: A Thaw in the Spring," *Middle East International,* number 577, 19 June 1998, pp. 18–20. See also R. K. Ramazani, "The Emerging Arab-Iranian Rapprochement: Towards an Integrated U.S. Policy in the Middle East?" *Middle East Policy* 6:1, June 1998, pp. 45–62.
20. Peter Ford, "In Saudi Arabia, Political Ferment Bubbles Quietly," *The Christian Science Monitor,* 5 June 1991, p. 3. See also Peter W. Wilson and Douglas F. Graham, *Saudi Arabia: The Coming Storm,* Armonk, New York: M. E. Sharpe, 1994, pp. 60–82; and F. Gregory Gause III, *Oil Monarchies: Domestic and Security Challenges in the Arab Gulf States,* New York: Council on Foreign Relations Press, 1994, pp. 78–118.
21. J. E. Peterson, "Social Change in the Arab Gulf States and Political Implications," in J. E. Peterson (ed.), *Saudi Arabia and the Gulf States,* Washington, D.C.: Defense Academic Research Support Program and The Middle East Institute, 1988, p. 54.
22. Ibid., p. 55.
23. Mohammad Rumaihi, *Beyond Oil: Unity and Development in the Gulf,* London: Al-Saqi Books, 1986, pp. 42–43; see also Gause, *op. cit.,* pp. 58–62 and 70–75.
24. J. E. Peterson, *op. cit.,* p. 56.
25. J. E. Peterson, *The Arab Gulf States: Steps Toward Political Participation,* New York: Praeger and the Center for Strategic and International Studies, 1988, pp. 12–26; see also Al-Haj, *op. cit.,* pp. 559–71.
26. Marwan Iskandar, "A New Approach to Gulf Security," *An-Nahar Arab Report and MEMO* 5:7, 16 February 1981, p. 1; see also Joseph A. Kechichian, "The Polarization of the Arab World: The Emergence of a New Regional Order," *Middle East Insight* 7:5, fall 1991, pp. 20–23.
27. For two of the better think-pieces on this key issue, see Tim Niblock, "Arab Losses, First World Gains," and Youssef Choueiri, "Syria and Egypt and the Spoils of War," both in John Gittings (ed.), *Beyond the Gulf War: The Middle East and the New World Order,* London: Catholic Institute for International Relations, 1991, pp. 77–85 and 92–94, respectively.
28. Joseph Wright Twinam, "The Gulf Cooperation Council: The Smaller Gulf States and Interstate Relations," in Charles F. Doran and Stephen W. Buck, *The Gulf, Energy, and Global Security: Political and Economic Issues,* Boulder and London: Lynne Rienner Publishers, 1991, p. 115.
29. Levon Melikian, "Arab Socio-Political Impact on Gulf Life-Styles," in B. R. Pridham (ed.), *The Arab Gulf and the Arab World,* London: Croom Helm, 1988, p. 115.
30. Levon Melikian, "Gulf Reactions to Western Cultural Pressures," in B. R. Pridham (ed.), *The Arab Gulf and the West,* London: Croom Helm, 1985, p. 205.
31. J. E. Peterson, Social Change in the Arab Gulf States and Political Implications, *op. cit.,* p. 48.
32. For a thorough analysis, see J. E. Peterson, *Yemen: The Search for a Modern State,* Baltimore and London: Johns Hopkins University Press, 1982. For a broad analysis of Yemeni society, covering historical, social, religious, political, linguistic, economic, and ethno-musical features, see "Le Yemen, Passé et Présent de l'Unité," *Revue du Monde Musulman et de la Méditerranée,* number 67, 1993.
33. "A Country Divided: Yemen Unity Talks Falter," *8 Days,* 8 September 1979, pp. 6–9.
34. Robert W. Stookey, *South Yemen: A Marxist Republic in Arabia,* Boulder and London: Westview Press and Croom Helm, 1982, p. 68.
35. Robin Bidwell, *The Two Yemens,* Harlow, Essex, and Boulder: Longman and Westview Press, 1983, pp. 294–306.
36. Abd al-Rahman Al-Baydani, *Azmat al-Umma al-Arabiyyah wa Thawrat al-Yaman* [The Arab Union Question and the Yemeni Revolution], Cairo: n.p., 1984, especially pp. 787–816.
37. Norman Cigar, "South Yemen and the USSR: Prospects for the Relationship," *The Middle East Journal* 39:4, autumn 1985, pp. 787–92.
38. "Ideology Blocks Yemens' Merger," *New York Times,* 28 January 1982, p. A17.
39. Abu Bakr al-Saqqaf, "Problèmes de l'Unité Yéménite," in *Revue du Monde Musulman et de la Méditerranée,* number 67, 1993, pp. 95–108.
40. Gause, *op. cit.,* pp. 161–62.
41. Simon Edge, *Yemen: Arabian Enigma,* MEED Profile Number 7, London: EMAP Business Information Limited, 1992, especially pp. 5–14.
42. Jean Gueyras, "Yemen: Fragile Unité," *Le Monde,* 10 July 1991, p. 7.
43. Ibid.
44. "Official Reports 35 Percent of Workers Unemployed," *Joint Publications Research Service Near East and South Asia* 91–063, 13 September 1991, pp. 81–83.

45. Gueyras, op. cit., p. 7.
46. Abd al Aziz Ibn Qa'id al Masudi, "The Islamic Movement in Yemens," *Middle East Affairs Journal* 2:2–3, winter/spring 1995, pp. 26–55.
47. Renaud Detalle, "Les Islamistes Yéménites et l'Etat: Vers l'Emancipation," in Bassma Kodmani-Darwish and May Chartouni-Dubarry, *Les Etats Arabes Face à la Contestation Islamiste,* Paris: Armand Colin and Institut Francais des Relations Internationales, 1997, pp. 271–310.
48. Robert D. Burrowes, "The Other Side of the Red Sea and a Little More: The Horn of Africa and the Two Yemens," in David A. Korn (ed.), *The Horn of Africa and Arabia,* Washington, D.C.: Defense Academic Research Support Program and The Middle East Institute, 1990, pp. 63–74; see also Charles F. Dunbar, "Internal Politics in Yemen: Recovery or Regression?" in Jamal S. al-Suwaidi (ed.), *The Yemeni War of 1994: Causes and Consequences,* London: Saqi Books for the Emirates Center for Strategic Studies and Research, 1995, pp. 57–70.
49. Matthew Gray, "Electoral Politics and the 1997 Elections in Yemens," *Journal of South Asian and Middle Eastern Studies* 21:3, spring 1998, pp. 31–47.
50. *Middle East Economic Digest* (hereafter *MEED*) 35:28, 19 July 1991, p. 32.
51. "Government Reacts to Sanaa Assassination," *Foreign Broadcast Information Service–Near East and South Asia* (hereafter *FBIS-NES*), 91–177, 12 September 1991, pp. 19–20.
52. Fadyah al-Zu'bi, "Al-Jawi Says: We Have Entered Period of Political Assassinations," *Sawt Al-Kuwayt Al-Duwali,* 15 September 1991, pp. 1, 6, in "Spate of Political Assassinations Predicted," *FBIS-NES-91–184,* 23 September 1991, p. 31. Huraybi was shot dead in an ambush in a Sanaa suburb on 10 September 1991. Officials believed that the real target of the killers was Omar al-Jawi, leader of the Yemeni Unionist Alliance, with whom Huraybi was traveling at the time of the attack. Al-Jawi was wounded. Huraybi's son believed that his father was targeted in a tribal dispute, however, and the killing caused widespread shock in the capital. There were immediate calls for a ban on firearms in Sanaa even though it was considered impractical, since it is common practice throughout the country to carry guns. But it was likely that the government would consider some form of weapons control legislation to address this growing problem. The strong statement by political leaders—including the representatives of both pre-merger ruling parties—reflected the widespread anxiety about the vulnerability of the country's fledgling democracy. Al-Jawi's party was sharply critical of Iraq, and took a more explicit stance against the invasion of Kuwait than the government. Although President Saleh instructed the interior ministry to undertake a full inquiry into the murder, no culprits were arrested. See "Killing Shocks Political Leaders," *MEED* 35:38, 27 September 1991, pp. 32–33.
53. "Riots Hit Sanaa as Tensions Mount," *MEED* 35:43, 1 November 1991, p. 24.
54. *MEED* 35:48, 6 December 1991, p. 39.
55. "Two Members of the YSP Assassinated," *MEED* 35:50, 20 December 1991, p. 30.
56. Patrick Makin, "Yemen: Unlikely Panacea," *Middle East International,* number 469, 18 February 1994, pp. 15–16.
57. Patrick Makin, "Yemen: Regressive Road to Divisions," *Middle East International,* number 473, 15 April 1994, p. 12.
58. Mark N. Katz, "External Powers and the Yemeni Civil War," in al-Suwaidi, *op. cit.,* pp. 81–93.
59. Alfred Hermida, "Yemen: The South Secedes," *Middle East International,* number 476, 27 May 1994, pp. 8–9. Four years after these developments, President Saleh continued to use the "traitor" epithet when referring to al-Baid. Interview with President Ali Abdallah Saleh, Sanaa, Yemen, 31 May 1998.
60. Ian Williams, "Yemen Comes in from the Cold," *Middle East International,* number 538, 22 November 1996, pp. 17–18.

CHAPTER 17

*Forging Institutions in the Gulf Arab States*

R. Hrair Dekmejian

The quest for legitimacy, in order to provide a moral basis for the retention and exercise of power, is an ongoing process in the evolution of political systems. In today's milieu of increasing globalization, the need for political legitimization has assumed a new urgency, particularly in the modernizing states of the developing world. In its Weberian formulation, legitimization involves the transformation of rule based on power into authority, where rulership is made popularly acceptable through a combination of charismatic, traditional, and legal rational modalities of legitimacy. Such transformation becomes necessary because rulership based on power alone is manifestly inefficient, costly, and undependable in assuring political longevity and stability.[1] Thus, the central problem of rulership becomes how to find the right legitimacy mix—in the words of Mosca and Lasswell—a "political formula" of "stable governance."[2]

In the newly independent developing states, the usual modalities of legitimization consist of reliance on the charisma of revolutionary leaders and movements and/or appeals to traditional norms and practices, especially in deeply conservative societies, where tribal and religious cultures are prevalent. In the Arab world, Abdul Aziz bin Abdul Rahman Al Saud's legitimacy formula was embedded in the Saudi Arabian traditional nexus of tribalism and Wahhabi Islam, reinforced by his heroic charisma as a victorious prince. A somewhat modified formula obtained in Egypt's non-tribal setting, where Nasser's rule rested on his personal charisma and the pharaonic tradition of omnipotent authority.[3] A host of other developing world leaders, with lesser degrees of success, including Nkrumah (Ghana), Sukarno (Indonesia), Castro (Cuba), Qadhafi (Libya), Mobutu (Zaire), and Numayri (Sudan), used similar formulae. Yet with the passing of the charismatic era, the challenges of modernization have had a withering effect on the old mechanisms of legitimacy, especially because of the reluctance and/or failure of many leaders in building institutions of governance. Such reluctance or failure, to fill the legitimacy vacuum left by the erosion of charisma and tradition, combined with the declining capabilities of ruling elites to provide for the basic needs of rapidly growing populations, has had a destabilizing effect on many emerging societies.

In the Arab context, the building of political institutions has been a tortuous process, often featuring one-party rule backed by the military, or monarchies based on traditional consensual institutions. Thus, political institutionalization based on conciliar bodies and parliaments have been an incremental and cyclical process in most Arab countries.[4] According to Baaklini, Denoeux, and Springborg, however, the situation began to change in the 1990s with a general resurgence of legislative bodies in several key Arab states, which appears to have had a diffusive influence in the Arab orbit.[5] This chapter is an attempt to comparatively assess the emergence and institutional role of assemblies in Kuwait, Oman, Saudi Arabia, and Qatar.

## Common Factors

Despite their obvious commonalities as Arab states, which share cultural bonds and membership in the Gulf Cooperation Council, the four monarchies possess significant differences in wealth, size, and political system. Each constitutes a unique polity formed under particular historical circumstances. Kuwait developed under British tutelage, and soon after independence in 1961, adopted a constitution with an elected parliament. Oman's modernization was begun after the accession of Sultan Qaboos, who set the stage for experimentation with several advisory institutions, culminating in 1991 with the adoption of a quasi-electoral process for a Consultative Council (Majlis al-Shura). In Saudi Arabia, from its founding by Abdul Aziz bin Abdul Rahman Al Saud, several deliberative mechanisms were used until 1993, when King Fahd bin Abdul Aziz decreed the appointment of a Consultative Council as an integral part of his Basic Law of Governance. Qatar has been engaged in a liberalization program in recent years. These countries represent four distinct gradations along the "institutionalization spectrum," phases of a process in institutional development corresponding to the changing political and social environment of each country, and its modernization tempo.

Yet, a unique feature of the Arab Gulf monarchies is that traditional institutions continue to have considerable social vibrancy and political utility, despite the impact of modernization. Therefore, it would be incorrect to posit that the new legislative/consultative organs are meant to radically replace traditional institutions such as tribal councils, religious organizations, or royal conclaves. Rather, the new institutions should be viewed as functioning in tandem with existing institutions or in a supplementary capacity.

Another politically salient feature in the four polities is their internal social complexity. Although culturally united under dual overarching identities as Arabs and Muslims, these societies are highly heterogeneous along tribal, sectarian, and ideological lines.

## Kuwait

The political system of modern Kuwait harks back to the mid-eighteenth century, when the oligarchy of notable families chose the Al Sabah family as rulers. Based on the practice of tribal consensus and consultation (*ijma al-qabaili*), this system broke down in the late nineteenth century. The growth of Arab nationalism and the rise of a new merchant class prompted Al Sabah Amirs to set up an ineffectual council in 1920. In response to renewed demands, Shaykh Ahmad, the Amir in 1938, consented to the formation of a 14–member National Council elected from 150 families, which drafted an interim constitution to limit the ruler's power. Shaykh Ahmad rebuffed these efforts and replaced the National Council with an advisory body, which he soon dissolved for its attempts to limit monarchical power. In 1950, the new Amir set up a new assembly of 20 elected and 11 appointed members, to draft a permanent constitution. The document, which provided for a hereditary monarchy (amirate) based on popular sovereignty and certain restrictions on the ruler's power, was formally adopted in 1962, a year after Britain pulled its military forces out of the northern Gulf. Importantly, the constitution is defined as a "contract" between the ruler and the people, who are represented by the National Assembly; it guarantees personal liberties, the right to social and economic welfare, and freedoms of press, residence, and communication. The National Assembly consists of 50 members, elected for a four-year term, in addition to the cabinet members, who are appointed by the Amir. Members of parliament may question any minister and votes of no-confidence are taken, although only the Amir has the right to call for the prime minister or cabinet to resign. Moreover, the Amir has the power to suspend or dissolve the National Assembly in times of crisis, a prerogative exercised twice since independence. The National Assembly may override the Amir's veto by a two-third majority.[6]

Despite its small size, Kuwaiti society is segmented along tribal, confessional, and ideological dimensions.[7] The Kuwaiti polity consists of eight tribes, two religious sects, two branches of the ruling family, and several ideological factions and interests, with considerable crosscutting cleavages and overlapping loyalties among them. Since independence in 1961, and the adoption of a constitution in 1962, vigorously competing subgroups and interests within the National Assembly have marked Kuwaiti politics. The 50 members of the National Assembly and the 16 members of the cabinet, 4 of which are elected National Assembly members, constitute a power coalition—which brings together the representatives of virtually all the segments of the Kuwaiti electorate, except women. A detailed breakdown of the affiliations of the 1996 National Assembly members would reflect the diversity of groups, constituencies, and interests that are represented.

### *The Tribal Factors*

Tribal representation is one of the most salient dimensions of Kuwaiti politics. In the modern context, tribal membership still constitutes a primary source of identity and pride for a large percentage of Kuwaitis. No less than 28 (56 percent) Assembly members came from various tribal backgrounds. Of the 25 electoral constituencies, tribal majorities populate 13. In 5 of these constituencies, both Assembly members belonged to the same tribe: Awazim (#12, #25), Mutayr (#17), Rawashid (#16), and Ajman (#21). Seven tribal constituencies had split representation, reflecting cohabitation by two dormant tribes: Utaybah/Mutayr (#14), Rawashid/Mutayr (#15), Anaza/Awazim (#18), Mutayr/Anaza (#19), Ajman/Mutayr (#22), Mutayr/Awazim (#23), and Hawajir/Dawasir (#24); one tribal constituency elected two non-tribal deputies. In aggregate tribal representation, the Mutayr controlled 7 seats, followed by the Awazim (6), Rawashid (3), Ajman (3), Anaza (2), Utaybah (1), Hawajir (1), and Dawasir (1), although four additional tribal members were elected from the non-tribal constituencies. The number of those elected from each of the eight tribes roughly reflected their respective numerical strengths in each constituency because of the tradition of tribal solidarity (*asabiyyah*), whereby members are expected to vote for their tribal kinsmen.

### Non-Tribal Factors
The non-tribal population, commonly referred to as *hadar*, includes the traditionally urban merchant class, early immigrants from neighboring countries, and families lacking strong tribal attachments. In all, 12 constituencies were in the hadar category, where diverse tribal individuals constituted a minority population. While non-tribal elements lack the inner solidarity of the tribes, they participate in the political process through membership in a plethora of ideological, religious, and socioeconomic groupings.

### The Sunni vs. Shia Factor
An equally important, and politically significant, factor was the sectarian divide between the Sunni majority (75 percent) and the Shia minority (25 percent). The Sunni majority includes all of the major tribes as well as some of the non-tribal population. The Shia population was mostly concentrated in non-tribal constituencies, with a total of 5 Assembly members: 2 members from the mostly Shia constituency (#13), and 3 from the Sunni/Shia split constituencies (#1, #4, #8).

### Ideological Groups and Interests
To the right of the ideological spectrum are two Sunni Islamist groups that favor conservative lifestyles and full implementation of Islamic law. Of the two groups, the Salafi Movement is the more conservative, representing the puritanical Wahhabi Hanbali creed associated with the teachings of Shaykh Abdul Aziz bin Abdul Wahhab of Saudi Arabia. A less conservative faction, the Islamic Constitutional Movement (ICM) is the political arm of the Muslim Brotherhood. The combined strength of the Salafi and the Islamic Constitutional Movements, along with a half-dozen pro-Islamists, was about 36 percent of the Assembly's membership, representing a cohesive opposition bloc to the government and the advocates of liberalization, particularly those pressing for women's right to vote.

The non-Islamist segment of the Assembly's ideological spectrum consists of "independents" and supporters of the government, as well as the Kuwait Democratic Forum, which advocates liberalization and government accountability.

About half of the non-Islamic members could be considered government loyalists, the rest being independents and liberals.

Class interests also found representation in the Assembly. While Sunni Islamists provided a representation for less affluent Bedouins, the affluent non-tribal districts and the wealthy business families were represented in the Assembly by about a half-dozen deputies.

### Oman

In contrast to the long-term development of Kuwait's parliamentary system, Sultan Qaboos Al Bu Said promulgated Oman's Consultative Council (Majlis al-Shura) only a decade ago. Indeed, the accession of the youthful Sultan to the throne in 1970 marked the onset of unprecedented political and socioeconomic change for one of the world's most traditional monarchies. The British-educated Sultan decreed a far-reaching modernization program that included the progressive institution of a Majlis system, designed to endow what had been an absolutist monarchy with a degree of popular legitimacy.

The first step in opening up the political process was the Sultan's appointment, in 1981, of a 45–member State Consultative Council (SCC). The SCC consisted of 17 government officials, 11 businessmen, and 17 tribal leaders. In 1983, the SCC's membership was increased to 55, with the aim of broadening its dual roles as a consultative and a representational mechanism.[8] In their consultative role, the members would provide the Sultan with expert advice on the country's development programs. Equally significant was the Council's representational role in bringing together three of Oman's major constituencies—senior officials, the urban-based business interests, and the tribal elite from small-town/rural areas. Thus, in his choice of Council members, the Sultan had implicitly acknowledged the segmented nature of Omani society and sought to accord representation to each of the three parts.

In December 1991, the Sultan initiated a new "experiment" by establishing a Consultative Council (Majlis al-Shura), the members of which were chosen through a two-phase electoral-appointive mechanism based on "the proportion of members necessary for striking the required nationwide representational balance."[9] The Majlis was constituted as an independent legal and financial entity, with administrative independence from the rest of the government. Each of its 59 members was chosen by the Sultan from a list of three candidates selected by conclaves of provincial notables. The Majlis membership was raised to 79 for its second term in 1994, in which constituencies of 30,000 or more received two seats, in keeping with the fall 1993 national census.[10] For the first time, women were allowed to stand as candidates from the Muscat area, two of whom were eventually elected as Majlis members.

In preparing for the selection of members for the third Majlis, the government sought to build upon the experience of the previous two terms, by instituting measures that ensured "free and fair" voting. In this instance, nevertheless, suggestions for holding direct elections were rejected. In the words of the interior minister, "We have not yet reached that stage in our step by step approach."[11] On 16 October 1997, about 51,000 voters went to the polls to vote by secret ballot for 736 candidates, including 27 women, who were allowed to run in all the provinces for the first time. The nomination of candidates in the 59 provinces was limited to individuals of "social standing" such as tribal leaders, intellectuals, and businessmen, whose names would be submitted to the interior ministry for final approval.[12] Voters could select four candidates from among the participants in each of 23 provinces with over 30,000 people, two of whom would be eventually selected by the Sultan as Majlis members. The 36 less populous provinces would choose two candidates each, one of whom would be tapped for Majlis membership. The final result of this rigorously controlled system of election and selection was an 82–member Majlis representing different segments of Omani society.

A social background analysis of Majlis members reveals the representational sweep of this institution and the great diversity of constituencies represented therein. These include representation based on Oman's regions, tribes, and sects, as well as gender.

### The Regional and Tribal Factors

All 59 of Oman's wilayas were represented by one or two members, depending on the size of the population. In view of the geographical comprehensiveness of the representational structure, both urban and rural populations were included, particularly the rich variety of Oman's tribes.

Tribal representation in the Majlis al-Shura is significantly large, including individuals belonging to both the Ghafiri and Hinawi tribal confederations. Among the 82 Majlis members, at least 75 have tribal identities such as Wahaibi, Hinai, Hikmani, Kaabi, Harthi, Junaybi, Shuhi, Riyami, Rahbi, Kalbani, Ghaythi, and Ibri. A comparison of the tribal names of Majlis members and a tribal map of Oman reveals a high degree of representation from the country's tribal roots. In fact even some urban constituencies are represented by members with tribal identities due to the ongoing urbanization of tribal populations in recent decades. In view of the role played by tribal alignments in the history of Oman, a high degree of tribal representation should be considered an essential element to promote national unity and political legitimacy.

### The Religious and Gender Factors

Closely related to tribal representation is the sectarian breakdown of Majlis members. Oman's indigenous population consists of an Ibadhi majority, a large Sunni minority, and a small Shia community. Considering that the ruling Al Bu Said family is Ibadhi, balanced sectarian representation becomes a key factor in maintaining national unity and, hence, political legitimacy. There were a total of 48 Ibadhis, 33 Sunnis, and 1 Shia in the 1997 Majlis. These numbers may roughly approximate the sectarian breakdown of Oman's population. It should also be noted that the Majlis Speaker, Shaykh Abdullah Al-Qatabi, is Sunni.

Unlike its GCC neighbors, Oman has been a pioneer in introducing female roles into its political system. In the 1997 Majlis, two women made their mark, in keeping with Sultan Qaboos' repeated efforts to increase female involvement in the political process.[13]

## Saudi Arabia

In the Saudi context, the consultative process developed in an uneven fashion, beginning with the eight-member Shura Council of Hejaz in 1927 under King Abdul Aziz bin Abdul Rahman Al Saud.[14] In 1956, King Saud bin Abdul Aziz (1953–64) decreed an expanded Council of 25, but its functions were soon transferred to the cabinet.[15] Nevertheless, traditional forms of consultation, based on tribal consensus, were followed at different levels of Saudi governance.

In August 1993, King Fahd bin Abdul Aziz appointed 60 members to a new Majlis al-Shura, expanded to 90 members in July 1997. The establishment of the Majlis represented an important step toward institutionalizing a consultative process in the Kingdom, at a time of mounting challenges triggered by the 1991 Gulf War, a sharp economic decline, and pressures from Islamist and nationalist critics for reform and political participation. As prescribed by royal decree, the main purpose of the Majlis is to provide advice (*nasiha*) to the King and otherwise contribute to the development of the Kingdom. The Majlis meets bi-monthly, and its deliberations and advice are held in confidence. There is some evidence that the Majlis has had a considerable impact in shaping the King's decisions.[16] Beyond its general advisory role, the Majlis is permitted to assume a potentially important mediation role between the authorities and the Saudi citizenry. It receives petitions, complaints, and suggestions from the general populace, through its Committee of Petitions (*Lajnat al-Araid*), formed in 1995.[17]

In addition to its consultative/legislative and mediative roles, the Saudi Majlis also serves an important representational function, which can be gleaned from a social background analysis of its members. Indeed, King Fahd's decree identifies certain categories of citizens as participants in the consultative process—the ulama (Islamic scholars and clergymen), Ahl al 'Ilm (people of learning), Ahl al-Ra'i (shapers of opinion), and Ahl al-Khibra (experts).[18] These categories are well represented in the Majlis, although a closer scrutiny of the King's appointments reveals a strategy of wider inclusion aimed at strengthening Saudi legitimacy.

### *The Conservative and Liberal Factors*
The Majlis membership reveals the King's intent to seek a balance to accommodate both the religious and liberal constituencies of the Kingdom of Saudi Arabia. About 17 percent of 1997 Majlis members are religious conservatives, most of the rest being liberals or politically colorless.[19] Among conservatives, several Salafis stand out, even if some had protested the Kingdom's foreign and domestic policies in the early 1990s. Clearly, the King's intention was to co-opt key Islamist critics, along with some liberal nationalists.

### The Religion Factor

The 1993 Majlis included one Shia member, whereas in the 1997 Majlis, there are two. Although this is not representative of the size of the Shia minority, it demonstrates an important element in the Saudi political process. The two Shia appointees are from the top ranks of academia and the bureaucracy, with doctorates from Western universities. They represent the moderate wing of the Saudi Shia community, and their appointment signals the state's ongoing policy of accommodating its Shia population—a policy that was initiated in 1993 to satisfy their aspirations for equality and to neutralize the appeal of pro-Iranian revolutionary groups.

### The Regional Factor

An important aspect of the 1997 Majlis is the large group that hails from Najd (44 percent), in view of the political centrality of Riyadh, and the importance of Najd as the ruling family's home base. The Hejaz claims the second largest group of members (29 percent), most of whom are from the holy urban centers of Makkah and Madinah. The Eastern Province is home to about 9 percent of the members, followed by Asir with 3 percent, and the rest coming from Hail, Jizan, Tabuk, and Al-Baha.[20]

### The Tribal and Class Factors

Although tribal leaders are not by themselves present in the Majlis, about 35 percent of the members come from such major tribes as Anaza, Mutayr, Utaybah, Shammar, Ghamid, Harb, Zahran, and Dawasir. To some extent, the tribal and rural origins of Majlis members indicate that many hail from relatively modest socioeconomic backgrounds, even if most of them may now be considered from the upper middle class. Importantly, the Majlis includes members of notable families and wealthy businessmen, as well as less affluent bureaucrats and academics.[21] No member of the ruling family has been appointed to the Majlis.

## Qatar

Under its new Amir, Shaykh Hamad bin Khalifah Al Thani, the State of Qatar has made unprecedented strides toward democratization through the liberalization of its media, the municipality elections of 1998, and the planned parliamentary elections in the year 2003. Meanwhile, the Qatari Majlis al-Shura has functioned since 1995, as an appointive body.

The Qatari Majlis consists of 35 members who are appointed by the Amir and enjoy parliamentary immunity. It brings together prominent individuals, tribal leaders, businessmen, and senior bureaucrats.[22]

A social background analysis of Majlis members reflects a very large tribal presence—over 80 percent. In addition, several ranking government officials, as well as representatives of some of Qatar's large families and kinship networks, are also represented. Also included are several well-known businessmen. It is notable that one Majlis member is Shia, representing Qatar's minority population.

## Conclusion

Political institutionalization centering on legislative/conciliar assemblies is part of the new wave in the Gulf Arab monarchies. Bahrain and UAE appear to be preparing to follow the pattern set by their neighbors in forming such conciliar bodies. Although the ruler suspended an earlier "experiment" in Manama, and the UAE's federal requirements complicate the appointment of Majalis by individual Emirates, the trend is for more representation. Still, by all accounts, this process of institutionalization is irreversible, even if it is unclear how far it will be permitted to proceed in each country.

Clearly, the Shura Councils of Oman, Qatar, and Saudi Arabia are not as far advanced as the Kuwaiti parliament; and indeed, may develop along different directions. Yet, aside from blatant differences and peculiarities in each case, it is possible to reach a preliminary assessment.

It is clear that beyond their advisory and legislative functions, these "conciliar" bodies play a mediative function between the rulers and the ruled. Moreover, they also play an honorific function to bestow importance upon prominent citizens, and a symbolic function—both domestically and internationally—to "show off" each country's advancement toward modernity. Nevertheless, two further functions emerge from the data presented above that appear in all four of the case studies. These are the representational and co-optative functions, reflecting the consociational nature of these conciliar bodies, which directly contribute to the social stability and political legitimacy of the Gulf Arab monarchies.

## Notes

1. H. H. Gerth and C. Wright Mills, *From Max Weber: Essays in Sociology,* New York: Oxford University Press, 1946, pp. 78–79. See also Robert A. Dahl, *Modern Political Analysis,* Englewood Cliffs, New Jersey: Prentice-Hall, 1963, p. 19.
2. Harold D. Lasswell, Nathan Leites & Associates, *Language of Politics,* Cambridge: MIT Press, 1965, p. 12.
3. R. Hrair Dekmejian, *Egypt Under Nasser,* Albany, New York: State University of New York Press, 1971, pp. 37–47.
4. On Egypt, see R. Hrair Dekmejian, "The U.A.R. National Assembly," *Middle Eastern Studies* 4:4, July 1968, pp. 361–75. See also Abdo Baaklini, Guilain Denoeux, and Robert Springborg, *Legislative Politics in the Arab World,* Boulder: Westview, 1999, pp. 1–3.
5. Baaklini et al., ibid., pp. 1–2.
6. On the history of Kuwait's legislative experience, see Abdo I. Baaklini, "Legislatures in the Gulf Area: The Experience of Kuwait, 1961–1976," *International Journal of Middle East Studies* 14:3, 1982, pp. 362–68.
7. On the divisions within Kuwaiti society, see Jill Crystal, *Kuwait: The Transformation of an Oil State,* Boulder: Westview, 1992, pp. 71–78.
8. On these developments, see Dale F. Eickelman, "Kings and People: Oman's State Consultative Council, *The Middle East Journal* 38:1, winter 1984, pp. 68–71. See also Abdullah Juma Al-Haj, "The Politics of Participation in the Gulf Cooperation Council States: The Omani Consultative Council," *The Middle East Journal* 50:4, autumn 1996, pp. 559–71.
9. *Oman: Political Development and the Majlis Ash-Shura,* Washington, D.C.: Independent Republican Institute, July 1999, pp. 17–18.
10. Ibid., p. 23.
11. Press conference by Sayyed Ali bin Hamad Al Busaidi, Washington, D.C.: National Press Club, 14 October 1997.

12. Ibid., p. 23.
13. See Embassy of the Sultanate of Oman, "News From Oman: Special Basic Statute Issue," Washington, D.C.: 1998, p. 4.
14. *Al-Jazirah,* 7 July 1997, p. 10.
15. *Al-Riyadh,* 8 July 1997, p. 16.
16. *Al-Sharq al-Awsat,* 15 July 1997, p. 5.
17. *Al-Riyadh,* 7 July 1997, p. 15.
18. Madawi al-Rasheed, "God, the King and the Nation: Political Rhetoric in Saudi Arabia in the 1990s," *The Middle East Journal* 50:3, summer 1996, p. 371.
19. R. Hrair Dekmejian, "Saudi Arabia's Consultative Council," *The Middle East Journal* 52:2, spring 1998, p. 211.
20. Ibid., pp. 213–15.
21. Ibid., p. 214.
22. Dawlat Qatar, *Majlis Al-Shura,* Doha, Qatar, December 1998, pp. 27–29.

# RELATIONS BETWEEN GCC STATES

CHAPTER 18

## The GCC States: Internal Dynamics and Foreign Policies
### Muhammed Saleh Al-Musfir

Throughout history, the Arabian Gulf region has been an area of contention among various aggressive international powers, which have sought to control this strategic location to safeguard their own vital interests. Alexander the Great was the first to realize the strategic value of the Gulf for the preservation of his vast empire. After conquering Egypt, he reportedly declared: "I shall never be certain of my army's security in Egypt and the Mediterranean basin as long as the Persians have extended their domination to the Gulf region."[1] The Macedonian emperor's pronouncement marked the beginning of the international struggle for the Gulf area, which continues at the dawn of the twenty-first century.

The purpose of this chapter is to analyze the political evolution of the GCC, and the multiple relationships among its six member states, to assess whether Council members are capable of preserving and shaping their own destinies. An effort is also made to assess the GCC's effectiveness and future viability. The analysis that follows is not intended to be comprehensive but to highlight, from an indigenous perspective, various contentions among the six conservative Arab Gulf monarchies. Intrinsic sociopolitical issues are also discussed to identify regional trends that may further shape GCC states' policies toward each other. How the six rulers responded to underlying currents, and how they factored in changing social pressures in their respective societies, mattered far more than many assumed.

### Historical Overview

Because of fundamental changes in the post-1973 period—when substantial increases in the price of oil created significant financial windfalls in the Gulf—Iran, Iraq, and the conservative Arab Gulf monarchies assumed great economic and strategic importance both in regional and international affairs. With the great wealth from oil came increased feelings of insecurity, as several hegemonic powers threatened the stability of the area. Even earlier, especially after the 1968 British announcement that London would leave the Gulf by late 1971, the smaller Gulf states began to seriously examine mutual cooperation and collective self-defense schemes. During the late 1970s and early 1980s, seven major regional and international developments pushed the Arab Gulf states further to accelerate their search for regional cooperation. In May 1981, the Gulf Cooperation Council (GCC)—Majlis al-Taawun li-Duwal al-Khalij al-Arabiyyah—was established, at the GCC states' first summit meeting, in Abu Dhabi. The significant developments that persuaded Gulf rulers to accelerate their search and settle on specific steps included:

1. the insecurity generated by the world energy crisis,
2. the anxiety resulting from the new wealth of the Gulf countries,
3. the epoch-making 1979 Iranian revolution,
4. the December 1979 Soviet invasion and occupation of Afghanistan,
5. the rise of "Islamic militancy" in several countries,
6. the start of the Iran-Iraq War in September 1980, and
7. the ongoing Arab-Israeli conflict, especially the repercussions of Israeli power throughout the Middle East, painfully displayed in Lebanon.[2]

In response to these significant developments, the six GCC countries—Saudi Arabia, Kuwait, Bahrain, Qatar, Oman, and the United Arab Emirates (UAE)— embarked on their boldest initiative yet. While the actual and minute accomplishments of the GCC since May 1981—ranging from common postal accords to increased investment laws for GCC citizens—are too numerous to cite, the most important exploit has been the mere fact of joining six competitors into a regional alliance. Given the legacy of the region, especially after centuries of foreign control, GCC rulers made conscious efforts to slowly trust their counterparts. In time, and non-negligible shortcomings notwithstanding, they certainly displayed a willingness to cooperate in many important areas. During the last two decades of the twentieth century, the GCC's numerous steps strongly influenced—in some cases, directly affected—both internal and external politics in all six member states and, in doing so, created an entirely new environment for their successors. Inevitably, their emerging outlooks affected all GCC states' foreign policies, security affairs (both internal as well as external), and economic methods.

It is important to emphasize that while GCC states did not always adopt identical policies, they were more structurally immersed in formulating closer steps than heretofore experienced. In other words, while each member state exercised a degree of independence in formulating a specific policy, over time far more coordination occurred among all six than anyone anticipated or believed possible.

Among the more important foreign policy accomplishments, for example, GCC rulers coordinated their opposition to the Israeli presence in Lebanon, the West Bank, and Gaza; rejected the Soviet presence in Afghanistan and South Yemen in toto; backed the Fahd peace plan (also known as the Fez Plan) to settle the Arab-Israeli dispute; and adopted joint policies vis-à-vis the Iran-Iraq

War. All four were laden with controversy, but, at least on this score, GCC rulers found common ground as they formulated appropriate responses. In fact, the nexus that emerged—on these four issue areas—stood out within the larger Arab world, further illustrating GCC states' political advances.

Still, GCC states were far less successful in defense cooperation, an area that touched upon their very survival.[3] What was agreed upon were vague notions calling for defense cooperation to deny the area to "foreign" powers. To be sure, there were sharp disagreements among members on GCC states' relations with the great powers. While some called for non-alignment in defense matters, others were pressing for specific accords with Western powers, including the United States.

Another important area of limited GCC accomplishments was internal security. By all accounts, GCC states were unable to agree on full cooperation in internal security matters, as a draft internal security agreement (ISA)—prepared in 1982—could not be implemented. In the event, the ISA could not be adopted because several states, including Kuwait, found it to be too restrictive on their individual freedom. ISA rules called for cross-border pursuits that were frowned upon for potential violations of sovereignty and territorial integrity. Because all six could not adopt the ISA, member states entered into watered-down bilateral accords, with mixed results.

Somewhat more successful were the GCC's efforts to promote economic cooperation.[4] In late 1982, an economic agreement was approved, which provided for joint planning and development in several sectors—petroleum, investments, and housing. Even more successful were the GCC's efforts in social cooperation. As tribally based Arab countries, the GCC states enjoyed the advantages of common culture, language, and religion. On these scores, at least, progress could be—and was—forthcoming in the development of mutually beneficial social, cultural, and educational programs. Conferences, festivals, and regular scientific exchanges became the norm rather than the exception. Given the substantial progress in these areas, one may indeed anticipate that continued social and cultural integration could increase opportunities for more successful efforts in establishing political and economic unity.

## The GCC Structure

The expressed structural aim of the GCC is to achieve a "confederal" union through coordination, integration, and amalgamation in different fields of human endeavor. As such, the organization is hierarchical in nature, presided over by a Supreme Council, itself composed of the heads of states, who rotate as president on an annual basis. At the second level, where most of the organization's joint decisions are reached, is the Ministerial Council, consisting of the foreign ministers, who meet periodically throughout the year. A secretary-general appointed to renewable three-year terms and six directors supervising 23 departments lead a Secretariat, headquartered in Riyadh. Because of the requirement of unanimity in the GCC's charter, all substantive matters discussed in the Supreme Council and the Ministerial Council are subject to mutual veto. Hence, GCC operations are usually carried out through consensus, and rely on incrementalism.[5]

## Relations among GCC States

If the organization is somewhat handicapped by internal decision-making requirements, member states are free to conduct bilateral relations unhindered. There are, nevertheless, several factors that shape those ties that, in turn, affect both bilateral as well as multilateral contacts. These include the key interdynastic ties that pepper the Arabian Peninsula, long-standing tribal relations, festering boundary disputes that prevent coordination and cooperation, narrow foreign policy orientations that may be temporary in nature (but that affect one or more members directly), wider Arab policy obligations, sectarian limitations that handicap both rulers and subjects, economic ties and oil policies, and, finally, strategic and arms procurement policies.[6] These contentions direct how GCC states behave with each other and, in turn, how such contacts affect the region as a whole. Some of these major bilateral issues—in no specific order—are highlighted, to better identify specific trends on the Arabian Peninsula.

### *Saudi Arabia–Kuwait*

This relationship is cemented by the common Anazi tribal roots of the Al Saud and Al Sabah ruling families, as well as their shared apprehensions of non-GCC powers. Despite common characteristics, differences remain, including Kuwait's refusal to sign the GCC's internal security agreement, and Saudi Arabia's consternation with the Shaykhdom's somewhat liberal social and political outlook. Moreover, Kuwait is opposed to accepting the Saudi predisposition to ignore past inter-Arab tensions, particularly the enmities generated by Iraq's 1990 takeover of Kuwait. Although the Kingdom supported the 1991 war against Iraq, the Al Sabah remain apprehensive of their hegemonic neighbor. The unsettled status of two islands—Umm al-Maradim and Qaru—that may hold substantial oil deposits is a further potential source of conflict between the two.[7]

### *Saudi Arabia–UAE*

Although the disputes over the Buraimi Oasis and the Khawr al-Udayd inlet were resolved in the mid-1980s, additional boundary problems remain to be settled between the two countries. The UAE's leading ruling families—Al Nahyan, Al Makhtoum, and Al Qawasim—are non-Najdi an, thus not tribally linked to the Al Saud. Among the various contentions between the Kingdom and the UAE, none were as problematic as the 1999 discord, over the Saudi-Iranian rapprochement. Because of Iran's continued occupation of three strategic UAE islands (Abu Musa and Greater and Lesser Tunbs, which were first occupied in 1971), Abu Dhabi vociferously protested Riyadh's "friendly" discourse with Teheran. Indeed, the Emirates demanded that a settlement of the Islands issue be a precondition for establishing closer ties with Iran by any of its GCC partners. Faced with the continued normalization of Saudi (and other

GCC states') relations with Iran, the UAE responded by accelerating its decision to reopen its "suspended" diplomatic mission in Baghdad, in April 2000.

*Saudi Arabia–Bahrain*
The historical ties between the Al Khalifah and the Al Saud ruling families is based on their common membership in the Utub branch of the Anaza. Over the years, and primarily because of Manama's security concerns—about revolutionary Iran and the domestic turbulence of the mid-1990s—Bahrain has come to rely on Saudi Arabia for protection. Equally important, Riyadh provided substantial economic assistance, in the form of crude oil and significant trade. In turn, Manama, which was physically attached to the mainland through a bridge in the mid-1980s, provided the Saudi Eastern Province population additional trade outlets. A point of friction remains between the two sides, over the status of Abu Saafah island, claimed by both.[8] Although Bahrain's recent liberalization policies may arouse some concerns in the more conservative Kingdom, Saudi Arabia's rapprochement with Iran over Gulf security has had a calming influence on Shia opposition groups in both countries.

*Saudi Arabia–Qatar*
By all outward indications, Saudi-Qatari relations appear to be amicable. Yet, there remain a cluster of border disputes that are unresolved. One potentially troublesome issue is that of the Khawr al-Udayd inlet—providing the Kingdom access to the Gulf—which was ceded to Saudi Arabia by the UAE, without Qatari consent. As to the disputed Khafus area on the land boundary, the treaty negotiated in the mid-1990s has not been made public, a fact pointing to remaining disagreements. Equally important, several foreign policy differences exist, as Qatar maintains normal ties with Iraq and has developed trade contacts with Israel, both unwelcome in Riyadh. In addition, and surprisingly, Doha sided with the Yemeni president Ali Abdallah Saleh in the 1994 civil war in that country. Senior Saudi officials perceived that development in negative terms. When Qatar took a leading role in hosting the 1997 Middle East Economic Summit, Saudi Arabia led a concerted boycott. Moreover, Qatar's decision to take its border dispute with Bahrain to the International Court of Justice was also opposed by Saudi religious authorities, indicating Riyadh's disapproval.[9] Since 1996, Qatar's liberalization efforts have also met with Saudi displeasure, particularly the epoch-making Al-Jazeera television broadcasts that have galvanized public opinion throughout the Arab and Muslim worlds. Adding insult to injury, "elections" to the municipal council, as well as suffrage for women—even important appointments to positions of leadership by several women—were met by Saudi officials with some apprehension. In a surprise move, in March 2001, Doha and Riyadh signed a pact to end various border disputes even if no details were made public.[10]

*Saudi Arabia–Oman*
In its relations with the Kingdom and other GCC states, Oman has been considered as the *sharik al-mukhalif* (the contrarian partner), particularly in

foreign policy. Oman's ties to Israel, Iraq, and Iran have been at odds with the general direction of Saudi foreign policy. On the matter of Gulf security, the Kingdom opposed the 1994 Omani proposal for an integrated GCC force of 100,000 troops, fearing that a majority would be volunteers from the Sultanate.[11] Similarly, Oman expressed misgivings about Saudi defense minister Prince Sultan's Dara al-Jazirah (Peninsula Shield) scheme as a viable Gulf defense mechanism.[12] Although the two countries demarcated their borders, the Kingdom has expressed concerns about the 1992 Oman-Yemen border treaty, which, allegedly, grants Yemen questionable concessions that, from the Saudi perspective, may be Saudi land. Another potentially troublesome issue is the doctrinal antipathy between Saudi Unitarianism (the Muwahhidun creed within the Sunni Hanbali school of religious doctrine) and Omani Ibadhism, which briefly flared up in the early 1990s.[13]

## Kuwait–UAE

Relations between Kuwait and the UAE have been generally amicable, in part because the two countries do not share borders, and because Kuwait devoted substantial financial resources to the seven Emirates starting in the 1950s. While Abu Dhabi acknowledges the financial assistance provided by Kuwait well after the UAE's 1971 independence, the two countries differ on several foreign policy matters. For example, the recently re-established diplomatic ties between Abu Dhabi and Baghdad were not well received in Kuwait. Furthermore, Al Sabah officials have questioned Shaykh Zayed's repeated calls for a rapprochement with Iraq, notwithstanding any humanitarian motives that the latter may have expressed.

## Kuwait–Oman

Although the Sultanate and Kuwait have had generally amicable relations, several issues divide them, particularly in foreign and security policy. Muscat's uninterrupted diplomatic tie with Iraq, despite the 1990 Iraqi invasion and takeover of Kuwait, has met Kuwaiti disapproval. The Shaykhdom had also opposed Sultan Qaboos' 1994 proposal to establish a GCC defense army of 100,000 troops, because of the likelihood that Omani soldiers would make up a large portion of this force. Even Oman's close relations with Egypt were not looked at with favor, given Kuwait's 1991 objections to an Egyptian military presence in the Gulf—the Egyptian assistance to liberate the Shaykhdom notwithstanding.

## Kuwait–Qatar

Although there are no major contentions between Kuwait and Qatar, their relationship lacks both depth and warmth. Despite the performance of Qatari troops against Iraq during the 1991 war—at the battle of Khafji in particular—Kuwait has tended to downplay the Qatari role, evoking disappointment and even some anger from the Qatari media. In addition, Kuwait has been critical of Qatar's liberalized media policies because of the latter's sympathy with the suffering Iraqi people. In late 2000, Kuwait temporarily suspended the Al-

Jazeera television correspondent's broadcasting privileges from the shaykhdom, further increasing Qatari antipathies. Nor does Kuwait approve of normalized ties between Doha and Baghdad. Finally, Kuwait has traditionally sided with Bahrain on the latter's territorial conflict with Qatar, which, understandably, further muddies diplomatic waters between the two GCC partners.

*Kuwait–Bahrain*
This has been an amicable relationship in recent years, mainly because of the absence of territorial disputes. Kuwait has extended to Bahrain considerable economic aid and appears to favor Manama in its territorial dispute with Doha. Yet their close ties did not prevent Bahrain from re-establishing diplomatic relations with Baghdad in March 2000.

*Oman–Qatar*
Omani-Qatari ties are normal in the absence of border disputes and other fundamental contentions. Qataris admire the Omani administrative system, although the two states are competitors in the rapidly emerging East Asian energy markets, as both states intend to sell substantial quantities of natural gas to India and other developing markets.

*Oman–Bahrain*
Relations between the Sultanate and Bahrain date from the nineteenth century, when Bahrain was under Omani rule. No major issue has divided the two sides in recent years, and normal relations have prevailed between the two ruling families.

*Oman–UAE*
In historical terms, and despite certain interpretations, the UAE constitutes an extension of Oman. To be sure, normal relations have prevailed, especially after the two countries became truly independent after 1971, although several border "disputes" between various Emirates and the Sultanate remain unsettled. Oman's boundary disputes with the Emirates of Ras al-Khaimah, Umm al-Qiwain, Ajman, Sharjah, and Fujairah remain in limbo. Still, Abu Dhabi and Oman did reach a resolution of their overall border concerns in February 2000, with the exception of the Umm al-Zumun enclave, which is claimed by Abu Dhabi, Saudi Arabia, and Oman.[14] In the event, the latest accord was not made public, which may bode ill. Another foreign policy contention is Oman's close relations with Iran, which was formalized into a security treaty in April 2000. Not surprisingly, the treaty is opposed by the UAE, because of the Iranian occupation of Abu Musa and the two Tunb islands. Equally unsettling, at least for Muscat, is Abu Dhabi's acquisition of advanced U.S. weapons systems (especially 80 F-16s) that are perceived by Oman as potentially provocative.

*Qatar–Bahrain*
Relations between these two small states are the most disruptive within the whole GCC structure. At the root of their differences is the eighteenth-century

Al Khalifah family "occupation" of Zubarah, in northern Qatar, and the subsequent British control of the region. What had been a dormant issue under British rule flared up after independence in 1971. Today, a group of 16 islands, including Hawar, Fasht al-Dibal, and Fasht Jaradah, all of which are controlled by Manama on the grounds of historical sovereignty—but claimed by both—stand as concrete evidence of conflict. In both 1978 and 1983, the two countries engaged armed confrontations, after which they requested Saudi mediation. Faced with lack of progress, in 1994 Doha appealed to the International Court of Justice (ICJ), a plea that was rejected by Manama.[15] When the ICJ agreed to take on the case, Bahrain reluctantly accepted to participate, but made a counter-claim citing its historical right to rule Zubarah and its inhabitants, mostly of the Nuaym tribe, most of whose members lived in Saudi Arabia, Bahrain, and the UAE. Signaling its displeasure with the Qatari appeal to the ICJ, the Bahraini chief justice (a religious cleric) expressed his full support of the late Shaykh bin Baz's fatwa (published in Saudi Arabia), on the illegality of a non-Muslim court to decide on a matter between Muslim states.[16] These differences notwithstanding, Qatar and Bahrain have sought reconciliation through mutual visitations and economic and cultural cooperation, especially after the accession of two young rulers in 1996 and 1998, respectively. In early 2000, the ICJ rendered a decision agreeable to both countries, granting the Hawar islands to Bahrain and Zubarah to Qatar. Several reefs will be divided among the two countries.[17] Although some Gulf observers anticipate further difficulties, both rulers have embraced the peaceful resolution of this longstanding dispute, even if the ruling was bittersweet. In Shaykh Hamad's own words:

> Allow me to be frank with you as I have always been: The court award in this respect was not easy upon us. These Islands have a great standing in the hearts of our people, a standing that is deeply rooted in the history of this country and the keenness of its sons to be bound to each grain of its soil. However, despite the pain we feel we think that the court award has, anyway, put an end to the dispute between the two states, and we can now put that dispute, which has become part of history, behind us.[18]

### Qatar–UAE
Most contentions between Qatar and the UAE have been amicably settled. The major exception is the dispute over the Khawr al-Udayd inlet, which was ceded by Abu Dhabi to Riyadh without consultations with, much less approval from, Qatar. In the foreign policy arena, the UAE has had strong reservations about Qatar's ties with Iran, and nascent commercial ties with Israel.

### Bahrain–UAE
Good political and economic ties exist between these two states. Manama is especially close to Abu Dhabi because of the latter's financial assistance and, over the years, encouragement to employ Bahrainis in various UAE government positions.

## Assessments and Conclusions

Any assessment of the GCC's effectiveness, on both the bilateral as well as multilateral levels, must first and foremost analyze the behavior of its members since its founding two decades ago. The regional organization was conceived as an alliance even if it portended to behave as a collective security system, which, in summary, reveals far more than most GCC states' citizens and officials were willing to acknowledge.

### Foreign Policy

In the foreign policy arena, the GCC states declared that they aimed to coordinate and unite their foreign policies, although coordination proved far more difficult than anticipated. With the exception of their united positions to oppose the 1990 Iraqi invasion of Kuwait, the GCC states could not realize pressing issues, including their perspectives on Iran and Iraq. To be sure, member states had major foreign policy differences during their first decade as an alliance—Saudi Arabia, Bahrain, Qatar, and Oman were pro-West, while the UAE and Kuwait tended toward non-alignment. As the Soviet Union collapsed and the Socialist bloc declined in numbers and value, it was not surprising to witness an American victory—by leading a formidable coalition to liberate Kuwait—that, without a doubt, led to the rise of the United States as the sole hegemon in the Gulf region. Ironically, the GCC states have accommodated themselves to the expanded U.S. presence in the region, despite earlier reservations. While the U.S. presence had been limited to Bahrain and Oman until the 1991 war, since then it has expanded as well to include Saudi Arabia, Qatar, and Kuwait. This victory and considerable presence notwithstanding, GCC member states, individually, reassessed their regional ties. In fact, a mere decade after the War for Kuwait, the GCC's united front against Iraq has broken up, with only two sovereign states (Saudi Arabia and Kuwait) without direct diplomatic ties with Iraq.

### Defense Policy

If progress in major foreign policy issues was limited, little has also been achieved in formulating a unified GCC defense policy, especially after the 1991 Kuwait conflict. The pre-war GCC defense project—Dara al-Jazirah (Peninsula Shield)—was too small for an integrated force. Moreover, it was inadequately trained to constitute a viable military organization, especially after GCC heads of state rejected Sultan Qaboos' 1994 recommendation to enlarge it to a 100,000-man army. Instead, Saudi Arabia proposed the expansion and modernization of the Dara al-Jazirah.[19] Because both defense schemes have proven to be stillborn, each GCC government has relied on its bilateral defense ties with key Western powers. At their December 2000 summit in Riyadh, GCC heads of state approved a new defense accord homing on the establishment of an updated rapid deployment force along with coordination of military training and expenditures.[20] It may be too early to determine how fruitful this new cooperative venture might be.

## Economic and Oil Policies

Although a unified economic agreement was accepted and implemented starting in 1982, there has been far more planning and analysis than actual implementation in unifying the GCC states' economic and oil policies. Indeed, it has been difficult to achieve economic cooperation because GCC economies are not complementary, and member states often engage in mutual competition in their industries. The customs union, for example, which was approved by the 1999 summit meeting, is not to be implemented until the year 2005. In setting oil production and pricing policies, GCC states are often in disagreement and, as such, are unable or unwilling to forge a common front to meet constant Western pressure.

## Arab Policies

Finally, in the all too vital Arab political arena, and since the War for Kuwait, GCC member states' ties to the larger Arab sphere have generally declined. Except for the UAE and Qatar, which have called for Arab summit meetings to prevent a full Arab fragmentation, the other GCC states have discouraged attempts at unified Arab action. Since Kuwait's reluctance to adhere to the 1991 Damascus Declaration, for example, no joint Syrian-Egyptian military presence in the Gulf could be exercised. In the alternative, no effort to forge a viable Arab security program emerged, thereby ensuring a Western presence in the region. Support for the Palestinian cause notwithstanding, particularly after the second intifada, the Amman League of Arab States summit meeting in March 2001 unraveled over the adoption of a unified Iraq policy.[21]

## Future Trends

Given present power realities within the GCC framework, it is clear that the member states will be unable to provide for their individual or collective security in the foreseeable future.[22] Thus, the presence of foreign forces is likely to become a permanent feature in most GCC countries. The GCC's security dilemma is further complicated by the looming threat of a full-scale nuclearization of the region, where Israel, India, and Pakistan are already adequately equipped, and Iran aspiring to the same status. Parallel to this measurable development, GCC states' citizens perceive with great apprehension the growing Israeli presence in the Gulf area, as well as the large number of foreigners in the workforce.

Due to the phenomenal growth of educational institutions and universities, coupled with the perceptible impact of the communication revolution, a far better informed citizen pool has now emerged in the Gulf. As a result, public opinion has become a significant factor, impacting on government decisions in various ways. Undeniably, public opinion is being shaped by satellite television stations like Al-Jazeera from Qatar, one consequence of which is a growing desire for greater political participation. Cases in point are the 1998 Qatari decision to grant women full rights to participate in municipal elections, as well as Shaykh Jaber Al Sabah's decree to grant Kuwaiti women the right to participate in National Assembly elections starting in 2003. Oman took similar decisions in the early 1990s.

Under the circumstances, and according to Ibtisam Suhail al-Kutbi, a well-known feminist scholar and commentator, the necessity of constitutional reforms, including women's rights, has emerged as a major factor shaping public opinion in the GCC states, including Saudi Arabia.[23] In turn, a growing public interest in political participation translates into pressure upon GCC regimes to democratize, reduce corruption, achieve a fairer distribution of wealth, and make themselves more accountable to their citizens. With the rapid growth of GCC populations, and the reduction of economic benefits by all six regimes, public demand for political participation and government accountability is expected to increase even further.

In response to changing popular attitudes, several GCC states have taken some tentative steps toward greater openness. Qatar has begun a far-reaching effort to draft a permanent constitution and hold parliamentary elections in 2003. Bahrain, under the leadership of Shaykh Hamad bin Isa, has freed political prisoners as a prelude to a return to constitutionalism. Even in Saudi Arabia, and ever since 1993, the Majlis al-Shura has shown some promise of expanded participation, which may include women members in the near future.[24] Likewise, Oman's liberalizing experiment since the early 1990's and its semi-elected Majlis al-Shura constitute important steps in building a new type of political system. Finally, in the Emirates, there has been a significant liberalization of the press and electronic media, as well as a greater role played by women in the state bureaucracy and the private sector.

Thus, in the context of the contemporary milieu of globalization, the diverse trends—social, political, economic, and cultural—throughout the six conservative Arab Gulf monarchies are bound to transform the GCC states to various degrees. What the full impact of these changes will be is difficult to forecast. Suffice it to say that the GCC, as a regional organization, is probably unlikely to prove its full capabilities. In the end, it will be up to each individual state to accomplish finite objectives, while balancing the needs of the regimes with those of citizens.

## Notes

1. Dawlat al-Imarat al-Arabiyyah al-Muttahidah, *Al-Kitab al-Sanawi* [United Arab Emirates Yearbook], Abu Dhabi, UAE: Ministry of Foreign Affairs, 1972, p. 94.
2. Muhammad al-Sayyid al-Said Idris, *Iqlim al-Khalij* [The Gulf Region], Beirut: Markaz Dirasat al-Wahdah al-Arabiyyah, 1999, p. 162.
3. Abdallah al-Nafisi, *Majlis al-Taawun al-Khaliji* [The Gulf Cooperation Council], London: Ta-Ha Press, 1982, pp. 16–17.
4. Al-Said Idris, *op. cit.*, p. 162.
5. R. Hrair Dekmejian, "Prospects for the Growth and Influence of the Gulf Cooperation Council," Washington, D.C., 1985, pp. 58–77.
6. Ibid., p. 13.
7. Nisrin Murad Taqi, *Al-Ittihad* (Abu Dhabi), 20 February 2000, p. 8.
8. Ibid.
9. Riad Najib El-Rayyes, *Riyah al-Shamal Al-Saudiyyah wal-Khalij wal-Arab fi Alam al-Tisinat* [North Wind: Saudi Arabia, the Gulf and the Arabs in the Nineties], London: Riad El-Rayyes Books Ltd., 1997, p. 60.

10. "Saudi, Qatar end border dispute, sign pact," Reuters, March 21, 2001.
11. El-Rayyes, *op cit.*, p. 60.
12. Ibid.
13. R. Hrair Dekmejian, *Islam in Revolution*, 2nd edition, Syracuse: Syracuse University Press, 1995, p. 159.
14. Nisrin Murad Taqi, *op. cit.*, p. 8.
15. El-Rayyes, *op. cit.*, p. 54.
16. Ibid., p. 62.
17. "Gulf Arabs welcome ruling on Qatar, Bahrain dispute," Reuters, March 17, 2001.
18. *Al-Sharq* (Doha), March 17, 2001, p. 1.
19. El-Rayyes, *op. cit.*, pp. 61–62.
20. Rawhi Abeidoh, "Gulf council states discuss rapid deployment force," Reuters, December 30, 2000.
21. Suleiman Khalidi, "Arab summit, split on Iraq, backs Palestinians," Reuters, March 28, 2001.
22. Muhammad Saleh Al-Musfir, "Security Challenges in the Gulf Cooperation Council," *Majallat Kulliyat al-Idarah wal-Iqtisad,* University of Qatar, 1998, pp. 10–15.
23. Ibtisam al-Kutbi, *Al-Ittihad* (Abu Dhabi) 2 March 2000, p. 16.
24. R. Hrair Dekmejian, "The Saudi Consultative Council," *The Middle East Journal* 52:2, spring 1998, pp. 204–218; see also Amir Talal Al Saud in *Al-Quds al-Arabi,* 27 March 2000, p. 7.

# THE GULF STATES AND WESTERN POWERS

## CHAPTER 19

## Constants and Variations in Gulf-British Relations

### Gerd Nonneman

Past and future trends in British-Gulf relations need to be seen in the context of (1) British foreign policy interests at the global and regional levels and (2) the broader foreign policy interests of the Gulf states. It needs to be recognized that these interests are multiple and varying—both between countries and across time. The context also has to encompass changes in the regional and global systems. While all of this has brought differences and variations in policy output, and therefore in relations, there are nevertheless a number of larger themes that can be identified.

Key categories to be factored in when considering the Gulf side of the equation are (1) the nature of the Gulf regimes and economies, (2) the nature of the regional system in the Gulf, and (3) the changing nature of the global system. Within these categories, two observations stand out. First, there is a clear difference between (i) Iraq, (ii) Iran, and (iii) the other Gulf states. Second, in all three, there has been a shifting balance between external constraints and relative autonomy.

The aims pursued on both sides have been and will continue to be driven by pragmatic calculations of *raison d'état*. In the case of the Gulf states, these center on (1) economic interest, (2) external security, and (3) domestic security. For the Gulf states, in fact, the concern with both external and internal security is key, and indeed arguably encompasses economic matters.

In the case of Britain, the main, inter-related concerns are economic interest and considerations of global politics and security. Three particular contextual features stand out: (1) Britain's historical connection with the Gulf, (2) the increasingly significant European dimension, and (3) the British relationship with the United States—both ally and rival in the Gulf.

### British Foreign Policy and the Gulf

British foreign policy has of course undergone a dramatic shift in the post-1945 era. The loss of empire—starting in India and virtually ending with the withdrawal from the Gulf in 1971—brought with it attempts to find a new role, chiefly to adapt to the country's post-imperial status. In a sense, the entry into the European Community and the withdrawal from the Gulf can be seen as two sides of this coin, along with the construction of the Commonwealth and, probably more importantly, the development of the "special relationship" with the United States. Two key elements underlying policy were, unsurprisingly, the pursuit of economic advantage and the achievement of security. These were accompanied, however, by a third: the maintenance of a semblance of Britain's Great Power status, both because this helped in the achievement of the first two goals and because of a historical sense of Britain's place in the world, which continued to inspire many policymakers. The development of the "special relationship" served the security and status objectives. The belated entry into the EC was recognition that the developing grouping had become a complementary avenue toward securing the status objective as well as that of economic security. A specific, and unquestioned, aim has been maintenance of Britain's status as a permanent member of the United Nations Security Council. There is a mutual (if partial) link between this aim and Britain's retention of its comparatively large military establishment and capability in force projection.

As the post-war era progressed, the economic and security aims became increasingly intertwined in the area of energy supplies, especially from the Gulf. After India's independence, the British presence in the Gulf served both the economic interest and a lingering imperial ambition. From the 1970s, British interests in the Gulf were pursued through maintenance of traditional links with the conservative ruling regimes, and through an increasing reliance on the United States. This latter relationship, however, remained competitive as much as cooperative, especially in the commercial field—London having already largely lost out in oil concessions to Washington and the local states themselves.

In the pre-1945 era (and indeed up to the independence of India), Britain's key reasons for its Gulf presence also included strategic considerations. Indeed, the Gulf was half-way on the routes to the empire's jewel in the crown; this meant it was not only a useful stopover and refueling point, it also brought greater concern over competition for the region from other powers, such as Holland, Russia (later the Soviet Union), and Germany. But in this period too, commerce and, increasingly, access to resources were central to Britain's interests in the Gulf. As has been observed elsewhere,

> it was the British that were most effective at controlling the sea routes and trade to the Indies. As one of the northernmost European countries, Britain paid the highest prices for spices and therefore had major incentives to control the trade. The British ... established workable relationships with local rulers.[1]

In the latter point, one theme of this chapter is already foreshadowed: Britain was successful, in part, because it managed relations with the local rulers successfully. In other words, local actors, even if much the weaker party, did have a certain level of autonomy.

With the shift from coal to oil, which got under way from the First World War, Britain was faced with two countervailing forces. On the one hand, it did not dominate oil sources to the extent it had done for coal and coal trading stations. On the other, oil was becoming crucial to economic activity and military deployment—and Mesopotamia and Persia had shown great promise of reserves. An early decision to try and achieve independence from American oil resulted in a pursuit of exclusive control of these oil fields, and in the link-up with the then small, private Anglo-Persian Oil Company (APOC), which swiftly became a major, government-backed player. Yet Britain never succeeded in controlling the level of oil reserves that could have become the basis for the sort of dominance it had enjoyed in the days of coal. The crucial role of oil was highlighted by Britain's military operations in the Middle East during World War II: These were to a large extent aimed at securing allied oil supplies.[2] The war would also mean economic exhaustion for Europe (including Britain). Just as important, the post-war reconstruction and development needs led to an energy crisis in Europe, "dramatically increasing Europe's dependence on Middle Eastern oil."[3] This is the context in which Britain's opposition to the Iranian nationalist government of Mossadegh and its nationalization of APOC must be understood. At the same time, of course, Middle Eastern oil was now increasingly seen as of strategic importance even for the United States. With the emergence of the Cold War and with Britain a close NATO ally, the security of oil supplies from the Gulf remained a matter of global strategic importance. Even with the development of Britain's own oil resources, this indirect economic and strategic interest, in a global context, remained.

From the second half of the nineteenth century, the effect of British protection, subsidies, and boundary drawing in the Gulf can hardly be overstated. In the shaykhdoms of the Gulf, official dealings with, recognition of, and help for, particular shaykhs and families, through the series of exclusive agreements concluded between 1820 and 1916, transformed the nature of politics, strengthening the position of those so recognized and laying the foundations for the modern states now in existence. In Kuwait, for example, the de facto autonomy of the Shaykhdom was made secure and subsequently given juridical confirmation as a result of Britain's protection from 1899. Several shaykhdoms owe their independent existence to a British decision to recognize a ruling shaykh as partner in an exclusive agreement—thus, for instance, the decision to deal with the Al Thani of Qatar from 1916 (independently from Bahrain). In Oman, the rule of the Al Bu Said dynasty was rescued from the interior's challenge by British assistance between 1955 and 1959. In several cases (most notably the succession of Shaykh Shakhbut by Shaykh Zayed in Abu Dhabi, and that of Sultan Said by Sultan Qaboos in Oman), Britain played a central role in internal transfers of power. Even the construction of the third Saudi state in the first two decades of the twentieth century was assisted by British acceptance and subsidies—assiduously sought by Abdul Aziz Al Saud ("Ibn Saud").

Likewise, a wholly new state was created in Mesopotamia and a monarchy imposed. Boundaries were drawn between these various emerging states. In some cases (such as the later UAE), this process meticulously adhered to local realities on the ground but, nevertheless, thereby "froze" them. In other instances it arguably changed the course of history by stopping Saudi expansion into Kuwait and Iraq (as well as, more indirectly, deterring Ibn Saud from extending his control to the other shaykhdoms). Several British decisions are contested to this day, including the Iraqi-Kuwaiti boundary, placed far enough north to keep the Ottoman Empire or any of its allies or successors from acquiring a secure naval base on the Khor al-Zubair, and the award of the Hawar islands to Bahrain.

In the Arabian Gulf states, this history left Britain enjoying good relations with the ruling regimes and playing a role in domestic and external security issues as well as some other aspects of government. The effect of this link is still visible at the start of the twenty first century. In Saudi Arabia too, Britain retained good links, although here they were soon eclipsed by the United States.

On the other hand, their involvement in the two more populous states of Iraq and Iran in the end helped their demise through the nationalist backlash it created. In these cases too, therefore, the British role had a historic impact on the subsequent nature of politics in the region. In Iraq, this happened swiftly in 1958. In Iran, the Second World War brought British (and Soviet) intervention, and the forced abdication of the nationalist Shah Reza Khan, followed by the accession of his young and inexperienced son, Muhammad Reza. Britain was also instrumental, later, in the overthrow of the nationalist Mossadegh government. All this sowed some of the seeds of the backlash that would, in 1979, overthrow the pro-Western Pahlavi regime altogether.

As one observer has pointed out, the period of British paramountcy and protection

> saw an outside power playing the role of manager, guardian and arbiter of the region. Intervention by outside powers was deterred, piracy and smuggling were suppressed, interstate conflicts were frozen, and coups were either vetoed or encouraged pre-emptively. As a result of the UK's presence, disruptive forces were contained and their manipulation by outside forces prevented. Saudi Arabia was prevented from acquiring the Buraimi oasis; and Iran was denied Bahrain. Iraq's claim to Kuwait (1961) was balked . . . by a British military response . . . Territorial claims between Iran and Arab states were likewise shelved. . . . [A]lso in the thwarting of internal developments, the British exercised a veto. Sheikh Shakhbut in 1966 and Sultan Said in 1970 were ousted to forestall internal discontent. The British role as protector thus guaranteed internal and external security in a region largely insulated from other inter-Arab pressures.[4]

Even if such pressures from Arab politics further afield did begin to make some inroads in the 1960s, this did not lead to any strong domestic demands for British withdrawal. The British decision in 1968, rather, must be seen in the context of a reassessment of the country's overall place in the post-war world by a new Labour government concerned with both resource allocation at home and the worldwide anti-imperialist mood. Indeed, paradoxically the British withdrawal from the Gulf came at a time when growing Western dependence on the region was becoming evident, with projections that it would become acute in the next decade. The financial cost of the UK's presence was negligible (£12 million) and, although the smaller littoral states offered to pay that cost, the UK's imperial era was terminated with a minimum of attention to future policy interests.[5]

Since 1971, Britain has managed to maintain excellent relations with the six monarchical Arab states of the Gulf, and in the case of the five smaller ones, as already indicated, even a significant direct involvement at the security, military, and high official levels. This has been based on the strength of the historical connection perceived by both sides, but also on the British view of how the country's post-imperial interests, as part of the Western economy and the NATO alliance, could be attained. This is best summed up in the words of the late Sir Anthony Parsons, one of Britain's most senior former diplomats, when commenting on the fact that there are "more Britons in the Gulf now than at any time during the heyday of Britain's presence East of Suez":

> To put it bluntly, Britain . . . sees the Gulf in terms of oil, finance and commerce. [Although self-sufficient in oil,] . . . we are a member of the European Community, which is not. . . . We are conscious of the fact that the cumulative importance of the Gulf for the industrialised economies of the Western world as a whole is such that radical changes . . . would, by extension, be seriously damaging to Britain. [Hence, we have a] strong interest in the stability of the Gulf, that is to say in the continued existence of political structures which will ensure an uninterrupted supply of crude oil at stable prices, a rational policy of investment of surplus funds from the Gulf in the West and steady progress in the implementation of social and economic development programmes.[6]

Sir Anthony did not, of course, leave the extensive commercial involvement of British companies in the Gulf unmentioned either. An account of British-Gulf relations in trade, investment, and arms supplies is provided later in this chapter.

### *Key Factors in British Gulf Policy Today*

The concerns underlying Britain's foreign policy in the Gulf today and for the foreseeable future can be summarized as follows: first, direct British economic interests in terms of British exports and possible investments in the Gulf, and the attraction of public or private Gulf funds to the United Kingdom; second, the indirect economic interest that the UK has in maintaining a secure flow of oil at acceptable prices for the world economy as a whole; third, as a consequence, the maintenance of security in the Gulf region, both to deter external interventions and to maintain domestic stability in the friendly states of the Gulf Cooperation Council (GCC).

These concerns are pursued in the context of three particular features of British involvement in the region. The first is the historical link that Britain has retained, especially with the smaller states of the GCC, and with their ruling families in particular. This continues to inform aspirations and expectations both in London and in Gulf capitals. At the same time, it still leaves London with an (albeit diminishing) advantage over competitors, because established patterns of personal relationships, trade, policy advice, and military and security assistance have had a persistent quality. The second feature is that since the 1970s, Britain's foreign policy has increasingly taken into account the European—or rather European Community/European Union—dimension. Although this has developed only very gradually, and often hesitatingly, it has become a recognizable element in British policy. Even when not managing to adopt common positions, there has been an increasingly marked attempt at least to coordinate policy with the rest of the EU. The fledgling Common Foreign and Security Policy (CFSP), and the albeit modest attempts at the construction of a European defense identity, can only further enhance this trend.

In contrast, the third feature is that British policy is also constrained by the "special relationship" with the United States, and the dependence on U.S. power projection capability. The latter can only increase as Britain's own capabilities diminish in line with cutbacks. Washington has been a rival in the Gulf since the 1930s, when American rather than British companies won lucrative Saudi oil concessions. This rivalry continues over arms supplies and trade—a feature that will persist. At the same time, however, in major security issues of global concern, Britain will continue to forge policy in close coordination with Washington. The best recent example is British policy on Iraq, which has been driven at least as much by the American agenda as by Britain's own analysis and interpretation of local political dynamics. Indeed, officials at the Foreign and Commonwealth Office have at times been heard to quip that, on Iraq, Britain "does not have a foreign policy of its own." This does not quite reflect the whole picture, of course. British politicians can on occasion be quite as gung-ho as others.[7] And Britain has, in some areas, pursued policies at variance with American preferences. This should not come as a surprise, given the different interests at stake, to which must be added differing interpretations of Middle East and Gulf political dynamics, as well as the absence in Britain of the sort of pro-Israeli lobbying power associated with the American Israel Public Affairs Committee (AIPAC) and others. In the Middle East at large, this has been apparent in differing approaches to the Arab-Israeli conflict, although London has been cautious to avoid policies that would run directly counter to those pursued by Washington. In the Gulf, the most interesting cases are those of Iran and Iraq. The link between Palestine and the Gulf has also been perceived in different ways on both sides of the Atlantic, which has led to policy differences—not least on weapons supplies to the conservative Gulf states—but this factor has diminished in salience since the 1990–91 Gulf War.

*Iran.* The most obvious clash between British and American policies in the Gulf has been over Iran. London, of course, also had its problems with Teheran, not least over the Salman Rushdie affair. Yet, contrary to the U.S. approach—which attempted to isolate Iran altogether—during the 1990s Britain opted squarely for the European "critical dialogue" solution. It consistently preferred "the overall EU approach to the US boycott for fear of driving the Iranians into a position where they have nothing to lose by being more hostile to the West."[8] There was an appreciation that Iran had itself reason to feel threatened, and that much of its rearmament and rhetoric could be seen in that light. At the same time, at least some foreign "actions" attributed to Iran were seen to be the work of non-governmental organizations, such as a variety of *Bonyads,* as well as of particular elements within the regime's various institutions. Overall, the view was that while this was reprehensible, there was enough evidence of a powerful strand of policy in Teheran aimed at normalizing Iran's international relations. Thus, the decision was made to cultivate this trend rather than undercut it. This view was seen to be validated even on the Rushdie question, when President Rafsanjani tried to disband the *Bonyad-e-15 Khordad,* which had offered a reward on the author's head. When this proved out of reach, the Iranian government eventually "circumvented the obstacle by declaring that no official organ of the state would carry out the sentence."[9]

In other words, the analysis that London, along with the rest of the EU, settled on was similar to that arrived at by many academic analysts of Iranian foreign policy, as well as several former government policymakers in the U.S.[10] Britain and the EU were, of course, in part driven by commercial considerations, but this was no unthinking or unprincipled policy. To quote a 1997 American analysis: "On balance, the evidence does not describe a nation which can best be dealt with as a pariah state. Iran does not seem so rigid and inflexible that political dialogue and economic incentives will have no effect."[11] Along with British policymakers, these analysts concluded that while *military* containment had some value, "dual containment" was ill-advised since it "seems more likely to lock Iran into a pattern of hostility . . . [and] leaves the US with no clear way to respond to any signals from the Iranian leadership." Hence, the authors posited, "a strategy of constructive engagement . . . seems more likely to enhance regional stability. . . . [It would also] offer a greater chance of consensus between the US and its allies while allowing for the fact that Europe and the Gulf states have already adopted many aspects of this policy."[12]

It may be worth recalling that Britain, together with its European partners, branded the American Iran-Libya Sanctions Act (ILSA, expanded to include Cuba) "illegal," in its insistence on extraterritorial legislation to punish foreign companies doing business with these countries. Another, less overt and less acrimonious, difference has existed over the issue of oil pipelines from the Caspian Sea. While Washington has maintained its insistence on a Baku (Azerbaijan)-Ceyhan (Turkey) route, and/or alternative lines that also avoid Iranian territory, there has at least been a willingness in Britain to consider the merits of the proposal of a link through Iran to the Gulf. Arguably, such a direct line makes considerably better economic sense, as well as avoiding the security problems posed by the volatile Caucasus region. In this instance as well, European companies have run up against the risks posed by ILSA.[13]

Since the election of Muhammad Khatami as Iran's president in May 1997, and especially since the parliamentary election victory of the pro-Khatami camp in 1999, this policy was felt to have been vindicated. Full diplomatic relations were restored in September 1998, with an agreement to exchange ambassadors (even if the actual exchange did not occur until May 1999). Generally, a positive tone has predominated since then, both in official and business circles. The visit by Iran's foreign minister Kamal Kharrazi to London in March 2000 was hailed by both sides (and by the British business community) as a success. The following month, it was announced that Foreign Secretary Robin Cook was to return the visit later in the year, the first such visit since the 1979 Iranian revolution.[14]

None of this means that Britain has no reservations about Iran or about aspects of the latter's policies. As a publication of the Royal United Services Institute (RUSI) points out, "an aggressive WMD [weapons of mass destruction] programme for which there is solid evidence would cause the UK to take a much tougher line." Implicitly, however, this recognizes that there is not in fact such evidence. Hence, "in common with other Europeans, Britain sees its role more as a facilitator of enhanced understanding of Teheran's concerns, as well as those on the other side of the Gulf." The piece, written by the head of RUSI's Middle East program, adds: "There is some frustration in European and Gulf quarters with the regular recitation of the 'mantra' of US concerns about Iran, especially with regard to sponsorships of groups actively opposed to the peace process." The author concludes by stating that "without a resumption of Iranian-sponsored terrorism in Europe, or direct threats to the Gulf, there will not be a major adjustment in European policy towards Teheran."[15] It is, perhaps, partly in recognition of this fact that U.S. policymakers since 1999 have embarked on a significant adjustment in their own policy toward Iran.

*Iraq.* By contrast, American and British policy on Iraq has been striking in its coordination. Indeed, Britain has been the only country to stand by the United States in the enforcement of the no-fly zones in Iraq.[16] On sanctions, London has remained close to Washington, notwithstanding increasing criticism from within and outside the Middle East. Indeed, most British military, intelligence, and diplomatic officials are thought to concur with their American colleagues in believing that "while Saddam [Hussein] remains in power, any outside attempts to record and destroy Iraq's still-unaccounted-for hidden stocks of biological and chemical weapons and ballistic missiles will fail."[17] Hence, both British and American officials "insist that although the current situation is far from ideal, the broad aims of the Iraq strategy have been met."[18]

Nevertheless, the countervailing pressures on Britain's policy that were referred to earlier—including the increasingly significant European dimension of foreign policy—along with the different policymaking context, have made themselves felt. Prior to the 1995 defection of Hussein Kamil, British policymakers were already looking for "an orderly way to ease the embargo in due course."[19] This position changed, however, after the revelations that followed the defection. The fact that the "oil-for-food" Security Council resolution was approved that same year took some further pressure off British policymakers on the question of sanctions. Until 1999, Britain along with the United States stood firm against any significant relaxation of the sanctions regime—with the exception, once again, of the expansion of the oil-for-food deal—and the conditions for lifting them. London has also been at the sharp end of accusations over the inflexible position of its representative on the sanctions committee, when it came to clearing Iraqi imports under the oil-for-food program. Yet it remains true that, on the whole, Britain has tried to maintain a common position with the other EU states over Gulf policy.[20]

There is an awareness in British policymaking circles, in part fed by European concerns, of the need to avoid a "Carthaginian peace."[21] In fact, the new Security Council resolution establishing the United Nations Monitoring, Verification and Inspection Commission (UNMOVIC), finally approved in April 2000, was in large measure the result of dogged British diplomacy.[22] The effort was aimed at producing a more realistic option for dealing with Iraq and, at the same time, rebuilding support in the Gulf itself for the international containment of the regime in Baghdad. Indeed, "Britain's patient pursuit of the diplomatic option in drafting and building support for what became Resolution 1284, played well in the Gulf where the return of the initiative of the UN was welcomed." Britain, one analyst has commented, "will take a middle road in . . . [Security Council] deliberations [on Iraq], in contrast both to the French, Russian and Chinese belief that there is little left for the inspectors to do, and the US desire to make the standard of compliance high enough for it to withstand pressure for sanctions to be lifted."[23]

*The Link between Palestine and the Gulf.* The combination of the policymaking context, geographical location, and economic interests, all further reflected in the European dimension of British policy, has produced a different approach to the linkage between the Palestine question and the Gulf.[24] British policy has, to a greater extent than was apparent in the United States, reflected awareness that the concern with a just solution of the Palestinian question that existed among Gulf elites, but especially among the populations of the region, was an issue that could potentially undermine British interests. Hence, Britain's—and Europe's—changing policies on the Arab-Israeli question after 1973. At the same time, this policy also reflected a different perception of Gulf Arab intentions vis-à-vis Israel, and, perhaps most crucially, a much lower identification with the security concerns of Israel and the pro-Israeli lobby in the United States. London and its European partners remained committed to a secure Israel, but did not necessarily swallow all of the Israeli arguments about the threat posed by the Arab states—least of all by the six conservative GCC states.[25]

Together, these features led to a British (and French) ability to supplant the American role as a key supplier of weapons to the Gulf states on several occasions. The most striking example was the conclusion of the so-called Al-Yamamah agreement between Britain and Saudi Arabia in 1985. Concluded after five years of Saudi attempts to buy F-15 fighter-bombers were defeated by effective opposition from the pro-Israeli lobby, this became, at an estimated £20 billion ($30 billion), the largest single defense contract in British history.[26] (Al-Yamamah II, signed in 1993, brought the total value to some £35 billion [$52 billion].) The Al-Yamamah program sustained "an estimated 30,000 jobs in

Britain and a few thousand more in Saudi Arabia" over the next 15 years.[27] The deal, which remains in force at the time of writing, has included the supply of 120 Tornado aircraft and Hawk and PC-9 trainers, as well as naval equipment, construction, and a range of related supply, service, and training contracts. Saudi Arabia pays much of the cost in oil (dealt with by British Petroleum and Royal Dutch-Shell), while the British side pledged to reinvest a portion in the Kingdom under the so-called offset agreement. Under the arrangement, seven joint companies were set up by the end of 1999.[28] This was not the last time that Britain (or France) benefited from the blocking of U.S. arms sales to the Gulf states: further difficulties were created for the U.S. administration by sustained pro-Israeli lobbying in Congress in the years that followed. As a result, Washington was unable to supply Stinger missiles even to friendly Bahrain in the latter stages of the Iran-Iraq War, or indeed to conclude any major arms sales with other GCC states prior to the 1990 Iraqi invasion of Kuwait.[29] Meanwhile, the Al-Yamamah contract had "shifted the entire structure of the Saudi Air Force from dependence on the US to dependence on Britain."[30]

The aftermath of the 1990–91 Gulf War has produced significant change in the dynamic just discussed. This has been driven by a number of factors. Progress in the Arab-Israeli peace process has somewhat reduced the salience of this issue as a spoiler for U.S.-Gulf relations, and consequently Britain lost some of its advantage. Moreover, the importance of U.S. equipment and power projection capability were demonstrated beyond doubt. Finally, the conflict also gave the U.S. administration (*in casu* President Bush) the power to waive the congressional bans and limitations on the transfer of F-15s and Stingers to GCC states.

## The Gulf States' Foreign Policy and Britain

The Gulf states' policy toward and relations with Britain cannot be understood without taking account of the context that has shaped these states' overall foreign policies. In this instance as well, the key categories are the natures of the Gulf regimes, the nature of the regional system in the Gulf, and the changing nature of the global system.

### *Nature and Needs of the Gulf Regimes*
All are rentier states of one sort or another, highly dependent on the revenue generated by the sale of hydrocarbons. Control over these resources has given them a measure of leverage and influence on the world stage, as well as the ability to buy large amounts of weapons. By the same token, especially after the oil boom of the 1970s, which further increased such influence and resources, their *dependence* increased as well: dependence on the revenues themselves, on the consuming markets, and on the suppliers of goods and technology for the spending plans that this wealth made possible. Inevitably this also influenced foreign policy, as none of the Gulf states could opt for autarky, and none—at least since the market effects of the double oil shock in the 1970s became clear—wished to risk endangering continued oil revenue or disrupting industrialized economies.

*The GCC States.* The GCC states consistently aimed for moderate prices in coordination with the main consumer countries. This can be traced to a number of factors, in addition to their historical pro-Western orientation. They are dependent on world markets for the demand and supplies referred to above, and in particular on the West for protection. Approximating ideal-type "rentier state," their regimes are highly dependent on government largesse for political survival. Finally (with the exception of Bahrain, which is in effect subsidized by Saudi Arabia), they are low-population, large-reserves producers, which means they need secure long-term prospects for oil markets but can afford to forgo immediate price maximization.

With specific regard to Britain, the ruling families retained extensive links with their former protector, both practical and personal. Saudi Arabia was never officially a protectorate, and soon veered toward reliance on the United States. But it is worth recalling that the founder of the modern Kingdom actively pursued British protection against both the Ottomans and his rivals, the Al Rasheed, in the first two decades of the twentieth century, and established very close relationships with a number of British figures.[31] Britain, along with the United States, remains a destination of choice for the education of many among the GCC elites. Several members of ruling families—including the rulers of Oman, Qatar, and Bahrain—graduated from Britain's Royal Military Academy at Sandhurst.

There have been areas of tension, too, in particular with Saudi Arabia and Bahrain. In the case of the former, the 1980s episode over the film *Death of a Princess* showed a level of mutual incomprehension.[32] Throughout the 1990s, the presence and activity of the Saudi opposition Committee for the Defence of Legitimate Rights (CDLR), led by Muhammad al-Masaari, brought Saudi demands for its expulsion from Britain. The Conservative John Major government attempted to deport al-Masaari, only to be stopped by legal challenges.[33] Similarly, the Bahraini government, until the political reforms of 2001, objected to the activities of the opposition Bahrain Freedom Movement, and London very diplomatically indicated to its Bahraini equivalents the British concerns over the systematic crackdown on the opposition during the 1990s. Yet these episodes did not undercut the basic positive outlook from the GCC states toward Britain.

For these states, Britain, while not a significant importer of Gulf oil and gas, remains an important source of technical, administrative, and military assistance, as well as of services, high-technology goods and equipment, and arms. It is also an arena offering opportunities for investment and, more generally, recycling of surplus petrodollars—in part through the City of London. Britain is further seen as an important member of the European Union. This link is valuable because the EU represents a crucial market for GCC states' exports, as well as being their main supplier of technology, goods, and services, and offering an arena for investment. Finally, Britain provides a partial alternative to the United States. This is useful for domestic and regional political and commercial reasons, as well as in cases where American policy is constrained by pro-Israeli voices in Congress.

That is not to say that the GCC states have simply adopted British commercial or policy preferences. Rather, Gulf leaders have generally kept their options open, continuing a pattern set in the latter part of the nineteenth century and perfected by figures such as Kuwait's Shaykh Mubarak the Great in 1899, and Abdul Aziz bin Abdul Rahman Al Saud in the first half of the twentieth century. They have themselves used outside powers as much as they have accepted significant elements of dependence on them, and they have preferred, wherever possible, multi-dependence over mono-dependence. This continues to be reflected in Saudi, Qatari, and UAE arms purchases, for instance, and is unlikely to change. Hence, just as London lost out to Washington over Saudi oil concessions, so America lost out to Britain on various occasions in arms deliveries to the Kingdom. Contrary to what dependency theorists used to hold, therefore, these states, considering their basic weakness, have shown a surprising level of relative autonomy.

As one Gulf-based scholar has shown, GCC voting patterns at the United Nations General Assembly provide an interesting illustration of this phenomenon. They reflect, he argues, a foreign policy in which the influence of the relationship with an ally—in this case Britain—is balanced with any other national interest at stake. Voting over the Falkland Islands dispute between Britain and Argentina in the 1980s may serve as a good example: Of the six states, only Oman consistently voted with Britain against the resolution demanding a negotiated settlement; the others abstained—not wishing to take sides—but Kuwait in 1985 switched to voting in favor of the resolution, reflecting the Shaykhdom's then typically independent-minded foreign policy orientation.[34]

*Iran and Iraq.* On the other hand, Iran and Iraq both have nationalist and somewhat anti-Western foreign policy traditions. Their regimes have, especially in the case of Iran, been able to use ideological and non-welfare means, rather than merely relying on oil revenue, to shore up their popularity at home. Moreover, because both have larger population-to-reserves ratios, the dynamic in favor of lower prices does not function quite the way it does for the GCC states. Hence, Iran and to a lesser extent Iraq (which has larger reserves) have shown a tendency to push for relatively higher prices—quite apart from other foreign policy rhetoric critical of the West. Nationalist assertion and suspicion of the West (not least Britain) is an inevitable part of the modern history of both states. Iraq, an artificial British creation, has suffered from insecurity over its borders, its very existence, and the survival of its successive regimes. The phenomenon of Saddam Hussein's dictatorship has merely further illustrated and reinforced these characteristics and their foreign policy implications. Iraq displays some features of a "quasi-state,"[35] with a justifiably paranoid regime relying on both rhetoric and foreign policy action to secure its survival. In Iran, the weakness of the Qajar regime (long "penetrated" by Britain as well as by Russia), gave way to Reza Khan's nationalist search for strength—until Britain and the Soviet Union forced his abdication during the Second World War, for his unwillingness to expel the German presence. The foreign-imposed crowning of his son, followed in 1953 by the British-American-orchestrated coup against the nationalist prime minister Mossadegh, further strengthened underlying nationalist trends, as well as fueling suspicion of Britain in particular. The Islamic Revolution was, in part, a further expression of this trend. Nationalist assertion and wariness of foreign domination remain very much part of Iran's foreign policy culture. Britain, in particular, then, has none of the historical advantages in these two countries that it has enjoyed in its relations with the GCC states.

Yet it has been striking that both Iran and Iraq have been quite restrained in their oil price demands or export conditions, even at the most politically difficult moments. It was, for instance, Washington rather than Teheran that stopped Iranian oil exports to the United States. As for Iraq, in the tense weeks before the 1990 invasion of Kuwait, and even in the immediate aftermath, Baghdad reiterated its willingness to export oil to the U.S. and the West in general, at prices around $22–25/barrel. Additionally, both states have been eager to do business with countries whose policies they have otherwise been critical of. It has in the main been sanctions by *other* states that have curtailed such links. *Political* links have been more problematic in the case of Iran, but here too the evidence since the mid-1980s has shown a trend toward normalization, albeit somewhat constrained by the Khomeini legacy.[36] While this legacy has been most visible in relations with Washington, its most obvious illustration with regard to Britain was the Rushdie case. Even in the case of the United States, however, the improvement in relations has been striking since 1999—Dual Containment notwithstanding. Yet the development of British-Iranian relations since the de facto resolution of the Rushdie affair illustrates that London has realized and exploited the extent of Iranian pragmatism sooner and more fully than has Washington.

*Ideology Takes Second Place.* Clearly, then, the main driving force for Gulf relations with Britain (or, for that matter, with most of the world) has been a pragmatic calculation of national interest, centered around economic and security interests and regime survival—in other words, *raison d'état* and *raison de régime*. Gulf states' previous ties with Britain, and, in the case of Iran and Iraq, the nationalist reflex, remain significant, but do not normally swamp those calculations. Ideology, including its Islamic and Arab themes, has taken and will continue to take a secondary role. The only exceptions are in early revolutionary stages (as in the first decade or less of Iran's Islamic Republic) and as a residual category in nationalist form.

Iraq under Saddam Hussein might seem to contradict this pattern.[37] Yet this is true only for the period since the 1990 invasion of Kuwait. The anomaly is linked to the nature of this particular ruler's regime, in the particular circumstances he found himself after the end of the Iran-Iraq War.[38] Moreover, it should be clear that even in the case of Iraq, much of the ideological rhetoric deployed has been used instrumentally. This is not to deny the relevance of the nationalist reflex, but none of this need obstruct good relations with the West, as Iraqi policy from 1975 to 1989 illustrated. Given a change in the regime, Iraq would doubtless fit back into the pattern.

This analysis does not imply that the "regional" element, especially over values thought of as important in 'Arab' or 'Islamic' terms, has lost its importance altogether. Indeed, both outsiders and local regimes ignore it at their peril—not least precisely because pragmatic calculation of regime interests means these governments cannot afford to be seen blatantly failing to observe such values. Britain's keen appreciation of this fact has at times given it an advantage over the United States, relative to what both states have had to offer in military or economic terms.

### The Regional and Global Systems

There are two regional systemic levels: the Middle East at large, and the Gulf in particular. It is from the wider, Middle East level that the above observation takes its relevance.

*The Middle East System.* In Arab foreign policies generally, the "Arab system" has become gradually less dominant as a determinant since the 1970s. Pan-Arabism as an ideology has virtually vanished from the scene. Arab themes in general no longer have the force they had from the 1940s until the use of the oil weapon in 1973. State and regime interests have become predominant, in a context of interdependence both within the region and with the world beyond it—even if this interdependence is skewed in favor of the industrialized economies. Yet an Arab dimension persists. In part this is true because of residual convictions among ruling elites, but probably more so because many perceive the danger of ignoring what remains a potent, albeit no longer dominant, value among their populations.[39] The Palestine question is still an issue to be reckoned with in this respect. Consequently, close collaboration with the United States retains elements of political risk. This is also true for non-Arab, but Muslim, Iran given that the issue has Islamic as well as ethnic dimensions. In the case of Iran, too, genuine concern with the asymmetrical nature of the Israeli-Palestinian peace process is reflected in its foreign policy stances. Although these perceptions are no longer translated in official support for the eradication of the Jewish State, Iran (and not merely that country's "conservative" factions) still reserves the right to disagree with the nature of the process, outside pressure notwithstanding. This, just like the whole question of outside involvement in the first place, ties in to the nationalist reflex. Teheran also reserved the right to support, for instance, Hizbollah, as a Lebanese movement resisting foreign occupation. Iranians reasonably argue that this is quite different from "sponsoring terrorism." The British position has recognized this distinction. In turn, such recognition facilitates Iranian relations with London, although Britain does retain concerns over actions by radical factions in Iran, and over WMD questions.

The Middle East system also contains straightforward strategic features, quite separate from Arab or Islamic values, which impact on Gulf states' foreign policies. The key elements can be grouped in three categories. First, Israel's regional superpower status and nuclear capability remains a central concern. It is at least part of the reason for feelings of insecurity and attempts to ameliorate this. By the same token, Israeli objections to Gulf states' acquisitions of sophisticated weaponry have long bedeviled U.S.-Gulf relations, hence giving opportunities to Britain and other competitors. Second, the growing influence of non-Gulf powers in the expanding Middle East impacts on the Gulf states themselves. Turkey and Syria present threats and opportunities for Iraq and Iran, while Iran, as already pointed out, faces a range of potential threats along its northern and eastern borders. In turn, such factors inevitably influence perceptions in the Gulf, and beyond. Third are the implications of the rich-poor divide in the region—with the Gulf states, and the GCC in particular, falling into the rich camp. This has long been a source of potential insecurity for the latter, again feeding into their foreign policies both toward the Middle East and potential protectors elsewhere.

*The Gulf Sub-System.* The sub-system of the Gulf has featured several types of clashes. The most obvious have been the ideological ones pitting Arab nationalists, secular republican Iraq, and revolutionary Islamic republican Iran against the neo-traditionalist conservative pro-Western GCC monarchies. It should go without saying that this forms a large part of the explanation for the monarchies' continued desire for outside protection—not least by Britain. It also helps explain the support Britain and others gave Iraq during the 1980s against the perceived threat emanating from Iran's revolution. The nature of the ideological question has been changing, however. By the turn of the millennium, Iran had matured into essentially a status quo power and was increasingly being perceived as such. Instead, a common concern about Iraq united Iran and the GCC states—and arguably helped bring Iran closer to Britain and the West as well.

Ideology, then, was only one factor in Gulf tensions, as plain geostrategic interests were also at stake. Iraq continues to face a problem of access to the Gulf. It has to share the Shatt al-Arab with its main rival Iran, and, since the delimitation of the maritime border by the United Nations in 1993, has lost even most of its navigation channel in the Khor Abdallah to Kuwait.[40] By the same token, Kuwait will always see a threat from its northern neighbor, and all of the GCC states perceive a potential threat from their larger, more populous republican neighbors.

A third type of clash has already been referred to in a different context: that based on differential economic needs. Iran has relatively lower oil reserves and a very large population, and will therefore be relatively less interested in the very-long-term future of the oil market. Moreover, it faces higher immediate needs than Saudi Arabia, Kuwait, and the UAE, where the opposite applies. Iraq falls in between these two ends of the spectrum, although its reconstruction and eventual rearmament needs (or desires) will, for the foreseeable future, nudge it toward a higher-price stance.

*The Changing Global System.* Arguably, the change in the international system represented by the end of the Cold War and the disappearance of the Soviet Union was always likely to increase pragmatic policies toward Britain and the

West, by taking away a key option for playing off East against West. Except for Iraq, that has indeed appeared to be the result. Iran, although not simply for this reason, has moved closer to the United States, having already established strong relations with Britain and the rest of Europe. The GCC states have moved closer to an explicit reliance on Washington and other Western protectors—although this has been mainly the result of the Kuwait crisis. The resolution of that crisis could perhaps also be seen, however, as demonstrating just how unipolar the new world disposition had become.

Yet this is not the whole picture. Among the background causes of Saddam Hussein's Kuwait debacle was precisely his fear that, in the new world order, he and Iraq were being encircled by the United States as the new global hegemon. This had already begun to worsen relations with Britain as well prior to the invasion. In Iran, the foreign policy adjustment has not meant a less critical position on the policies of Israel or her supporters, nor a departure from the country's insistence that Gulf security be left to Gulf states alone. Teheran, moreover, has been moving closer to the GCC states (most strikingly to Saudi Arabia), regardless of the state of its relations with Washington—indeed, quite contrary, at least until 1999, to U.S. desires expressed to those states. This in itself indicated that America's allies in the Gulf still maintained their relative autonomy. It seems plausible that Washington's own mellowing toward Teheran since 1999 was in fact helped along by Riyadh. In addition, although the post–Kuwait War period has seen a resurgence of the U.S. as the largest player in the local arms market, it is striking that the six states have to varying extents maintained the multiplicity of sources for their defense. Kuwait, Qatar, Saudi Arabia, and the UAE all signed defense agreements with London and Paris, as well as with Washington. Saudi Arabia continued with the Al-Yamamah agreement, Qatar with its purchases of French equipment, and the UAE with its own diverse procurement, while Oman's arms imports too continue to be mainly European.[41]

## Trade and Investment

In what follows, a summary overview is offered of Gulf-British economic interaction and, in the subsequent section, of the arms trade in particular, to underpin some of the analysis above.

The UK's trade relationship with the Gulf stands out, when compared to other EU trade partners, by its large surplus, running at between £2–4 billion ($3–6 billion) a year during the 1990s—even without arms and services exports. Given Britain's own oil reserves, its imports from the Gulf consist mainly of petroleum products and re-exports via Dubai. Only a little over 10 percent of its imports from Saudi Arabia—the largest source, followed closely by the UAE—are made up of oil, in the framework of the Al-Yamamah arrangement. Total imports from the Gulf states during the final decade of the twentieth century ran in the region of £1.5–2 billion per year, the vast majority coming from the GCC (see Table 19.1). In 1996, the United Kingdom was the GCC's eleventh largest export destination, accounting for some 1.6 percent, far behind Japan

($27 billion), the United States ($11 billion), South Korea ($11 billion), and Singapore ($8.5 billion).[42]

Detailed available statistics about British exports to the Gulf states only record about one-third of the actual total. Services and arms exports are usually excluded, even if some non-arms but defense-related items do at times feature. Visible non-arms exports from Britain to the Gulf ran at between £4–6 billion per year ($6–9 billion) during the 1990s (see Table 19.2). Figures for 1996 imports into the GCC are representative. They show the United Kingdom in second place with 11 percent, after the United States (16 percent), but ahead of Japan (10 percent), Germany (7 percent), Italy (6 percent), and France (5 percent).[43] The most recent figures that indicate 1999 was the worst year in the decade, with visible exports just topping £4 billion (after a peak of £7.4 billion in 1997). Sir David Wright, the chief executive of British Trade International, a government export-promoting agency, blamed this on the overall "cautious economic and commercial climate" in the region, created in the wake of low oil prices. As he also pointed out, however, exports of services were worth about another £4 billion, leaving the trade surplus at well over £5 billion, "and this in as bad a year as we've had in recent times."[44] The largest single category of non-arms visible exports from Britain to the Gulf was "machinery and transport equipment" (see Table 19.3).

Britain also ranks as the second largest exporter to Saudi Arabia, after the United States. While the Kingdom represents the fourteenth largest market for British goods (1998 figures, not counting arms), it has become the ninth largest market for British services.[45] Arms exports, fluctuating significantly, probably averaged up to £2 billion per year, with over three-quarters going to Saudi Arabia. This means that about half of British visible trade flows to the Kingdom have consisted of defense-related exports, which have to be added to the figures listed in Table 19.2 (roughly doubling them) to obtain a realistic (if no more than indicative) picture.[46] The Saudi arms market has been crucial to Britain's defense indus-

Table 19.1 UK Imports from the Gulf States, 1991–1999 (in £ Million)

|              | 1991  | 1992  | 1993  | 1994  | 1995  | 1996  | 1997  | 1998  | 1999  |
|--------------|-------|-------|-------|-------|-------|-------|-------|-------|-------|
| Saudi Arabia | 964   | 964   | 1,274 | 740   | 721   | 753   | 997   | 892   | 875   |
| Kuwait       | 30    | 127   | 236   | 239   | 151   | 180   | 201   | 186   | 181   |
| Bahrain      | 39    | 50    | 52    | 25    | 26    | 21    | 33    | 67    | 25    |
| Qatar        | 5     | 10    | 20    | 7     | 15    | 11    | 16    | 30    | 40    |
| Oman         | 74    | 83    | 83    | 78    | 74    | 87    | 105   | 92    | 78    |
| UAE          | 232   | 332   | 251   | 231   | 281   | 381   | 516   | 559   | 667   |
| GCC          | 1,344 | 1,566 | 1,917 | 1,321 | 1,269 | 1,432 | 1,868 | 1,826 | 1,866 |
| Iraq         | 3     | ...   | ...   | ...   | ...   | ...   | ...   | 2     | ...   |
| Iran         | 158   | 164   | 245   | 133   | 126   | 119   | 36    | 36    | 37    |
| **Total**    | 1,505 | 1,730 | 2,162 | 1,454 | 1,395 | 1,551 | 1,904 | 1,883 | 1,903 |

Note: ... = less than £0.5 million
Source: COMET (Committee for Middle East Trade, London)

Table 19.2 UK Visible Non-Defense Exports to the Gulf States, 1991–1999, (in £ Million)

|  | 1991 | 1992 | 1993 | 1994 | 1995 | 1996 | 1997 | 1998 | 1999 |
|---|---|---|---|---|---|---|---|---|---|
| Saudi Arabia | 2,229 | 1,968 | 1,826 | 1,516 | 1,644 | 2,483 | 3,800 | 2,690 | 1,529 |
| Kuwait | 178 | 262 | 312 | 312 | 551 | 679 | 504 | 385 | 302 |
| Bahrain | 147 | 167 | 151 | 150 | 151 | 161 | 158 | 144 | 118 |
| Qatar | 109 | 118 | 143 | 128 | 146 | 192 | 584 | 293 | 169 |
| Oman | 238 | 241 | 306 | 362 | 448 | 416 | 370 | 285 | 231 |
| UAE | 760 | 927 | 1,315 | 1,114 | 1,184 | 1,394 | 1,547 | 1,563 | 1,403 |
| GCC | 3,662 | 3,682 | 4,052 | 3,581 | 4,124 | 5,225 | 6,963 | 5,360 | 3,752 |
| Iraq | 4 | 34 | 12 | 10 | 5 | 11 | 6 | 26 | 36 |
| Iran | 512 | 568 | 497 | 289 | 333 | 397 | 396 | 331 | 245 |
| Total | 4,178 | 4,284 | 4,561 | 3,880 | 4,462 | 5,633 | 7,365 | 5,717 | 4,033 |

Note: ... = less than £0.5 million
Source: COMET (Committee for Middle East Trade, London)

try—even though some contracts under the Al-Yamamah deal were rescheduled and experienced payment delays following the 1998 oil price collapse.

Beyond this, British companies in 2000 were also hoping to benefit from the cautious opening to foreign investment in Saudi Arabia.[47] At the time of writing, the Al-Yamamah offset arrangement had already resulted in the creation of seven joint ventures. In addition, there have been cross-investments by British Aerospace and Rolls Royce in two U.S.-sponsored offset investments under the U.S. Peace Shield program. Total British investment in the Kingdom as of 1999 stood at around $3.5 billion, much of it in the Al-Yamamah framework. Nevertheless, as one report noted, "there is still a mountain to climb before the Al-Yamamah offset requirement is met." Outside this framework, much depends on just how open the Saudi economy will in fact become, although there are already an estimated 100 joint ventures.[48] Saudi Arabia's importance in British foreign economic relations is further illustrated by the fact that some 30,000 Britons live and work in the Kingdom.

Elsewhere in the GCC, tentative openings to foreign investment were also being watched closely by British business, in addition to export opportunities.[49] Kuwait's prospective opening of some of its oil sector to outside investment led to the holding of a British Oil and Gas Show there in March 2000. As already mentioned, the UAE is the UK's second largest trade partner in the Gulf. To a large extent this concerns re-export trade through Dubai. In 1998, the UK was the third largest importer of goods from the Emirate. In addition, an estimated 12 percent of the 1,500 companies based in the Jabal Ali Free Zone in 1998 were British.[50]

Outside the GCC, Iran has been a significant market, albeit dwarfed by Saudi Arabia, taking some £500 million in UK exports annually in the early 1990s.

Table 19.3  UK Visible Non-Arms Exports to the Gulf States, by Broad Commodity Group, 1998 (in £ Million)

|   | Saudi Arabia | Kuwait | Bahrain | Qatar | UAE | Oman | GCC | Iran | Iraq | Total |
|---|---|---|---|---|---|---|---|---|---|---|
| 0 | 58.1 | 20.3 | 7.2 | 2.7 | 64.4 | 5.0 | **157.7** | 3.4 | ... | 161.1 |
| 1 | 49.5 | 10.3 | 11.6 | 6.9 | 48.8 | 9.2 | **136.4** | 0.1 | ... | 136.5 |
| 2 | 5.1 | 1.6 | 0.3 | 0.2 | 4.4 | 0.3 | **11.9** | 2.0 | ... | 13.9 |
| 3 | 2.1 | 0.3 | 0.2 | 0.2 | 3.0 | 0.4 | **6.3** | 1.1 | ... | 7.4 |
| 4 | 0.9 | 0.3 | ... | ... | 0.5 | ... | **1.8** | 0.3 | ... | 2.1 |
| 5 | 279.1 | 38.5 | 15.9 | 22.4 | 150.7 | 29.7 | **536.2** | 60.3 | 5.8 | 602.3 |
| 6 | 167.4 | 36.2 | 18.0 | 36.7 | 193.1 | 30.1 | **481.5** | 24.8 | 0.8 | 507.1 |
| 7 | 1,602.3 | 152.2 | 57.2 | 101.0 | 648.1 | 158.1 | **2,718.9** | 206.0 | 15.1 | 2,940.0 |
| 8 | 354.9 | 67.3 | 32.5 | 55.9 | 267.3 | 33.7 | **811.7** | 31.2 | 4.0 | 846.9 |
| 9 | 170.1 | 7.8 | 1.2 | 67.0 | 182.2 | 18.3 | **447.3** | 1.7 | ... | 449.0 |
| 10 | 2,403.7 | 294.2 | 123.6 | 216.2 | 1,259.1 | 251.6 | **4,548.3** | 322.4 | 25.6 | 4,896.3 |
| 11 | **2,690.2** | **294.2** | **123.6** | **216.2** | **1,259.1** | **251.6** | **4,548.3** | 330.9 | 25.6 | 4,904.8 |

*Categories:*
0 Food and live animals
1 Beverages and tobacco
2 Crude materials, except fuels
3 Mineral fuels, lubricants etc.
4 Animal and vegetable oils, fats and wax
5 Chemicals and related products
6 Manufactures classified chiefly by material
7 Machinery and transport equipment
8 Miscellaneous manufactured articles
9 Articles not classified elsewhere
10 5 + 6 + 7 + 8 = Manufactures
11 Total

*Note:* ... = less than £50,000
*Source: UK Overseas Trade Statistics December 1998.*

Notwithstanding improving political relations, however, a sharp drop in 1994 has failed to be reversed: The 1999 figure of £245 million was the lowest of the decade. This appears to have been in part the result of Iran's own economic difficulties. British companies remain keenly aware of the possibilities of the Iranian market, however.[51] Apart from exports, a key area of mutual interest is British investment in the country, both in the oil industry and elsewhere, as the new investment law of 2000 is expected to remove some of the obstacles in the earlier Law 81.[52]

There remains an interest in the potential of Iraq, but this is recognized to be an uncertain prospect as long as sanctions remain. Yet, even though British companies have been "bound by the constraints of British government policy" and were thus long "deterred from conducting exploratory discussions with embargoed Iraq,"[53] by early 2001 it was clear that they too were straining at the leash.

## Arms Trade and Britain in Gulf Security

The key themes and underlying dynamics of Britain's evolving role in arms supplies and Gulf security have already emerged from the foregoing analysis. Apart from its overall influence on developments in the Gulf for the past 150 years, Britain has long had a prominent role in security matters in particular. After the official withdrawal from East of Suez, British personnel remained involved in the Omani armed forces—with several hundred still seconded there in the 1990s—and military and security cooperation remained noteworthy elsewhere in the region too. Omani and British forces continue to exercise together regularly, and, since the Gulf Crisis, joint training has also been undertaken with Kuwait. British advisers were active throughout the 1970s and 1980s in Bahrain and Qatar. Indeed, Bahrain had a former British colonial police officer, Ian Henderson, in charge of its internal security until 1999.

From 1987, U.S. naval forces formed the bulk of the protective shield extended to safeguard shipping in the Gulf from Iranian attack. Nevertheless, British and several other European forces played a significant role too. By the summer of 1988, the United States had 32 warships in the Gulf, compared to the Soviet Union's 8, Britain's 8 (the "Armilla patrol"), France's 7, Italy's 6, and 2 each from Belgium and the Netherlands (in 1987 the European figures were nearly double, including 18 British ships).[54]

This foreign protection changed both its composition and its target between the August 1988 cease-fire in the Iran-Iraq War, and the 1990 invasion of Kuwait. The Iraqi invasion led to a declaration by the European Community of solidarity with the United Nations and the United States in their demands for Iraqi withdrawal. Britain, Italy, and France immediately froze Iraqi assets. This was also one occasion where the Western European Union (WEU) adopted a slightly higher profile than usual, agreeing on 21 August 1990 to step up and coordinate European naval operations in the Gulf. King Fahd of Saudi Arabia accepted the help of American forces on 7 August 1990, and also formally requested forces from Britain, in a conversation with Foreign Secretary Douglas Hurd. On 8 August, London announced that several aircraft would be flown to the Kingdom, and the Armilla patrol was strengthened. On 14 September, Britain decided to send ground troops and tanks (the 7th Armoured Brigade, known as the Desert Rats), plus additional Tornado squadrons.[55] As Operation Desert Shield gradually changed into preparations for Operation Desert Storm, troop levels rose. In the eventual attack against the Iraqi forces, Washington was obviously the dominant partner, but the British Royal Air Force participated extensively in the air war (taking relatively heavy losses), while both British and French troops were engaged in the short land war that followed.[56] It is worth recalling the role Prime Minister Margaret Thatcher appears to have played in firming U.S. President Bush's resolve to react by military means if necessary.

There were three further elements to London's importance for Washington in the Kuwait crisis. First, simply by not being the United States, Britain could add political credibility and acceptability to the undertaking, as well as influence other European powers. Second, it was a permanent member of the Security Council. Third, in military terms, it had useful capabilities and, as a base, a location much closer to the theater of operations than the U.S. itself. These three elements remained significant after the war, when Britain proved a key ally of Washington in the maintenance of sanctions and the no-fly zones over Iraq.[57]

Britain also signed ten-year memorandums of understanding on defense cooperation with Kuwait, Qatar, and the UAE, although decision makers in London were more circumspect than their French colleagues, making these memorandums less explicitly "defense agreements" than was the case with those signed by France. British foot-dragging over UAE preferences in this regard led to French defense suppliers, whose government had acted more swiftly, getting most of the spoils (at least until the decision in March 2000 to purchase 80 F-16s from Lockheed-Martin, worth up to $7 billion).

From a British perspective, such intervention and security cooperation fitted in with the country's European and U.S.-linked interests, as outlined earlier in this chapter. But there was also a direct British economic interest at stake, viz. the gaining and maintaining of a British share in the regional arms market. In this field, Britain will continue to compete vigorously with the U.S. and European suppliers (chiefly France, Italy, and Germany).

In this competition, two main factors have stood out. The first is the constraints imposed on U.S. arms supplies to the region by the pro-Israel voice on Capitol Hill. As outlined above, in the 1970s and 1980s repeated inability to overcome such constraints helped lead to a preeminent position for European suppliers, including Britain. The Al-Yamamah deal, which made British equipment central to the Saudi air force, was a direct result of this dynamic. Only since the 1991 Gulf War has Washington been able to waive such objections from Congress, hence making the U.S. once again a much more formidable competitor. The second factor is evident precisely in the GCC states' reaction to this U.S. constraint. Most have consistently tried to keep their options open, sometimes demonstratively so. Britain, France, and the U.S. have been played off against each other, while other suppliers have also been brought in. Even Oman, which has traditionally bought most of its arms from Britain, has expanded its range of suppliers.[58]

In the course of the 1990s, a further factor took on added importance, although the effect is not yet fully clear. Britain's declining power projection capability, which is recognized by decision makers in the GCC, may mean that British suppliers may encounter greater difficulties in the future.[59] As has been pointed out elsewhere, "recent British force cuts mean that the British Army cannot deploy the kind of armored forces to the Gulf that it deployed in 1990," and U.S. suppliers of main battle tanks and other equipment may therefore have a potential advantage, since buying American would ensure inter-operability with armored forces that are brought in during a crisis."[60]

Saudi Arabia has been, and will continue to be, by far the most important arms market for Britain. Over the period 1976–1994, UK arms exports to the Kingdom totaled some $23 billion, not very far behind the U.S.'s $28 billion. This hides major fluctuations, with the UK taking first place in the periods 1989–1991 (an estimated $8 billion, or 40 percent of the market), and 1992–1994 ($9.4 billion, or 46 percent of the market).[61] Britain, therefore, remains a very important source for Saudi defense imports, even if the first decade of the twenty-first century may well see a reassertion of the U.S.'s preeminent position.

Elsewhere in the GCC, the only buyer looking mainly to Britain has been Oman. Bahrain has bought very little military hardware from the UK, instead sourcing its needs primarily to the United States. Qatar, for its part, has turned to France. Kuwait, with its varied procurement pattern, has been dwarfed by Saudi Arabia as a market for British defense exports. The UAE (with the exception of Hawk training and combat aircraft) has looked more to France and, as of 2000, to the United States. A list of recent British arms supply contracts with the GCC states is given in Table 19.4.[62]

## Conclusion

Relations between Britain and the Gulf states have been driven by pragmatic calculations of *raison d'état,* far more than by ideological considerations. In the case of the Gulf states, this has been focused on economic interest, external security, and regime survival. In the case of Britain, the key concerns have been the opportunities for the economy and, as an indirect but nevertheless crucial interest, the safeguarding of predictable and moderately priced oil supplies to the world economy and to Europe in particular.

British policy has derived both difficulties and opportunities from its historical relations with the region—the difficulties arising mainly with Iran and Iraq, the opportunities with the GCC states. British policy has also been constrained and shaped by its special relationship with the United States and its integration into the European Union. The predominance of pragmatic self-interest over ideological themes, at least since the second half of the 1970s, has been one of the more striking features of the relationships. Another has been the extent to which even the smallest states of the Gulf have continuously striven to balance their dependence on the outside world with the pursuit of a degree of autonomy. This has been clear in the way they played off Britain, even while submitting to varying levels of dependence on it, against other powers—be it the

Table 19.4 Recent and Current Arms Contracts UK-GCC

| Country | Contract/ date | Description | Start Delivery | Completion |
|---|---|---|---|---|
| Saudi Arabia | 1988 | 3 Sandown mine-hunters | 199? | 200? |
| | 1993 | 48 Tornado IDS | 1993 | 1998 |
| | 1993 | 20 Hawk 65 | 1993 | 1997 |
| UAE | 1998 | 18 Hawk fighters | 1998 | 2001 |
| | 1989 | 26 Hawk trainers | 1992 | 1996 |
| Oman | 1992 | 2 Corvette VT-83 | 1996 | 1997 |
| | 1997 | 20 Challenger tanks | 1997 | ? |
| Qatar | 1992 | 2 Barzan fast attack boats | 1997 | 1998 |
| | 1996 | 15 Hawk-100 trainers | 1996 | 1999 |
| | 1996 | Starburst SAMs | 1996 | 1996 |
| Kuwait | 1997 | 60 Sea-Skua SSMs | 1997 | 1998 |
| | 1993 | 254 Warrior AIFVs | 1995 | 1998 |

*Source:* IISS, *The Military Balance 1998/99.*

Ottoman Empire prior to World War I, Iran or Iraq afterwards, or the United States during the 1970s and 1980s. At the same time, other powers were played off against Britain. This began under Abdul Aziz bin Abdul Rahman Al Saud, with Russia, the Ottoman Porte, and later the United States. It continues today, with, for example, Qatar and the UAE consciously aiming at multi-dependence to lessen the asymmetry in their interdependence with the West. It is probable that with the dwindling of Britain's military projection capability relative to the United States, the GCC states will, albeit to varying extents, drift closer to Washington for military supplies. Nevertheless, the drive for relative autonomy, observed thus far in the foreign policies of these states, will undoubtedly persist, thus keeping opportunities for Britain very much alive.

## Notes

1. Geoffrey Kemp and Robert E. Harkavy, *Strategic Geography and the Changing Middle East,* Washington, D.C.: Carnegie Endowment for International Peace in Cooperation with the Brookings Institution Press, 1997, pp. 28, 34.
2. Ibid., p. 41 ff.
3. Ibid., p. 49.
4. Shahram Chubin, *Security in the Persian Gulf 4: The Role of Outside Powers,* London: Gower for the International Institute for Strategic Studies, 1982, p. 111.
5. Ibid., p. 112.
6. Anthony Parsons, "A British Perception of the Gulf," paper presented to the Symposium on *The Gulf and the West,* Centre for Arab Gulf Studies, Exeter University, July 1984, pp. 2–3.
7. Prime Minister Margaret Thatcher's role in firming up President George Bush's resolve to act against the 1990 Iraqi invasion of Kuwait is now well recognized. In 1999, the Blair government is known to have been just as irritated with the American unwillingness to consider the use of ground troops in Kosovo, as U.S. policymakers were annoyed with it.
8. Rosemary Hollis, "Europe and Gulf Security: A Competitive Business," in Christian Koch and David E. Long (eds.), *Gulf Security in the Twenty-First Century,* Abu Dhabi: Emirates Centre for Strategic Studies and Research, 1997, p. 86.
9. Anthony Cordesman and Ahmed Hashim, *Iran: Dilemmas of Dual Containment,* Boulder: Westview, 1997, p. 125. As the authors point out, Iran's strategic environment is anything but

secure. On various sides, the country faces: its former invader Iraq, with whom it shares a vital shipping channel; Turkey; the issue of the Kurds straddling borders with both these powers; the unsettled region of Armenia and Azerbaijan (with the attendant ethnic questions within Iran itself); a nuclear-armed Pakistan; unsettled and unfriendly Afghanistan; and a huge coastline (p. 126).

10. One of the most notable among the latter has been Gary Sick, formerly of the National Security Council.
11. Cordesman and Hashim, op. cit., p. 146.
12. Ibid., pp. 320–1. The authors add: "The key reason for pursuing 'constructive engagement' is that policy must have an endgame. Hostile regimes not only need to be contained; they need to be encouraged to change. 'Dual containment' has no endgame other than a blind hope that the US can persuade its allies to join it in a policy of isolating Iran, and that this will lead to political upheavals that will somehow produce a moderate regime. The West never attempted such a strategy of isolation in dealing with the Soviet Union and the Warsaw Pact" (p. 322).
13. See Kemp and Harkavy, op. cit., p. 151. See also Cordesman and Hashim, op. cit., p. 15; and IRNA dispatches, London, 5 November 1998.
14. "UK and Iran Restore Diplomatic Ties," *The Financial Times*, 25 September 1998. See also "Britain Exchanges Ambassadors with Iran," *The Independent*, 18 May 1999; and "Cook Sees Improvement in Relations with Iran," *The Financial Times*, 22 September 1999; Deutsche Presse Agentur dispatch, 17 April 2000.
15. Neil Partrick, "The United States, Europe and the Security of the Gulf," in *RUSI Journal* 145:2, April 2000, pp. 47–48.
16. France pulled out in 1998.
17. Bryan Bender and Adrian Koch, "Poisoned Cigars, perhaps? Briefing: Iraq," in *Jane's Defence Weekly* 33:15, April 12, 2000, p. 22.
18. Ibid. p. 25.
19. As pointed out by Hollis, "Europe and Gulf Security", p. 86.
20. Ibid., p. 87.
21. An expression used also by Anthony Cordesman and Ahmed Hashim, *Iraq: Sanctions and Beyond*, Boulder: Westview, 1997, pp. 158–160, where they argue, at some length, the need for adjusting the sanctions regime.
22. See *Middle East Economic Survey* (MEES) 43:16, 17 April 2000, for an initial assessment.
23. Partrick, op. cit., pp. 45–46.
24. For a brief examination of the linkage itself, see Gary Sick, "The Ghost at the Table," in *The World Today*, February 1999, pp. 15–17.
25. See also Bichara Khader, "The Gulf, Palestine and the West," paper presented to the Symposium on *The Gulf and the West*, Centre for Arab Gulf Studies, Exeter University, July 1984, pp. 18–19.
26. See Anthony Cordesman, *Saudi Arabia: Guarding the Desert Kingdom*, Boulder: Westview, 1997, pp. 155–58. See also Anthony Cordesman, *The Gulf and the West*, Boulder, Westview, 1988, p. 291.
27. Hollis, "Europe and Gulf Security," p. 83.
28. Cordesman, *Saudi Arabia*, pp. 155–158; and idem, *The Gulf and the West*, p. 291. See also *Gulf Business* 4:6, October 1999.
29. Cordesman, *The Gulf and the West*, pp. 283–295, 361, 419.
30. Ibid., p. 291.
31. The best known of these were perhaps Captain Shakespear, the explorer Philby, and, in a different way, Sir Percy Cox. For an insightful study of the early days of Saudi foreign policy, see Jacob Goldberg, *The Foreign Policy of Saudi Arabia: The Formative Years, 1902–1918*, Cambridge, Massachusetts: Harvard University Press, 1986. See also Gary Troeller, *The Birth of Saudi Arabia*, London: Frank Cass, 1976, which focuses, in particular, on the Saudi-British relationship up to the Saudi conquest of the Hejaz.
32. A British TV dramatization of the events results in the execution of a young Saudi princess and her lover. The screening brought vehement Saudi protest. See Robert Lacey, *The Kingdom: Arabia and the House of Saud*, New York: Avon Books, 1981, p. 458.
33. For a thematic review and analysis of Saudi relations with Britain and the rest of Europe during the twentieth century, see Gerd Nonneman, "Saudi-European Relations 1902–2001: A Pragmatic Quest for Relative Autonomy," *International Affairs*, July 2001, pp., 631–661.

34. Hassan Al-Alkim, *The GCC States in an Unstable World*, London: Saqi Books, 1994, p. 96.
35. The term coined by Robert Jackson, *Quasi-States: Sovereignty, International Relations and the Third World*, Cambridge: Cambridge University Press, 1990. In terms of the implications for regime behavior, Nazih Ayubi's label of "fierce states" is apposite here (even if he coined it with a view mainly to such states' domestic behavior). See Nazih N. Ayubi, *Over-stating the Arab State: Politics and Society in the Middle East*, London: I. B. Tauris, 1995.
36. See Anoushiravan Ehteshami, *After Khomeini: Iran's Second Republic*, London: Routledge, 1995. See also Anoushiravan Ehteshami and Raymond Hinnebusch, *Syria and Iran: Middle Powers in a Penetrated Regional System*, London: Routledge, 1997.
37. For an assessment of Iraq's foreign policy since the 1990–91 Gulf War, see Cordesman and Hashim, *Iraq*, chapter 9.
38. Anoushiravan Ehteshami and Gerd Nonneman, *War and Peace in the Gulf*, Reading: Ithaca Press, 1991, chapter 3.
39. For contrasting views on this question, see Michael Barnett, *Dialogues in Arab Politics*, New York: Columbia University Press, 1998. See also Stephen M. Walt, *The Origin of Alliances*, Ithaca: Cornell University Press, 1987; and the very useful overview article by F. Gregory Gause III, "Systemic Approaches to Middle East International Relations," in *International Studies Review* 1:1, spring 1999, pp. 11–31. See also the forthcoming collective work coordinated by Anoushiravan Ehteshami and Raymond Hinnebusch (eds.), *The Foreign Policies of Middle Eastern States*, Boulder: Lynne Rienner, 2001.
40. Richard Schofield, *Kuwait and Iraq: Historical Claims and Territorial Disputes*, second edition, London: Royal Institute for International Affairs, 1993, pp. 163–198, and p. 206.
41. Anthony Cordesman, *Bahrain, Oman, Qatar and the UAE*, Boulder: Westview, 1997; International Institute for Strategic Studies, *The Military Balance 1998/99*.
42. Bob Edwards, "Balancing Act: The Gulf's Top 10 Trading Partners," *Gulf Business* 3:3, July 1998, pp. 32–37. See also International Monetary Fund, *Direction of Trade Statistics* yearbooks, various issues.
43. Ibid.
44. Speech given by Sir David at the London Gulf Spotlight gathering in London on 17 February 2000; edited version published in COMET's *Opportunity Middle East*, number 28, March 2000.
45. "A Tale of Two Kingdoms," *Gulf Business* 4:6, October 1999, p. 45.
46. Hollis, "Europe and Gulf Security," p. 82.
47. See "Big boost for UK-Saudi business," in *Opportunity Middle East*, number 29, May 2000, pp. 1, 6.
48. "A Tale of Two Kingdoms," p. 45.
49. This is illustrated in a series of UK-GCC mission and roundtable reports, in COMET's third-quarter *Bulletin* for 1999. The Gulf's overall importance within Britain's Middle East trade is further illustrated by the fact that all but one (Egypt) of the events reported concern the Gulf. See COMET *Bulletin*, number 52, September 1999.
50. "A Tale of Two Kingdoms," p. 45.
51. An Iranian-British Trade and Investment Mission took executives of 33 companies to Iran in June 1999. A British delegation attended the Iran Oil and Gas event in Teheran in April 2000, and the Iran Trade and Investment Conference was advertised among British firms for May 2000.
52. Already, the Iranian National Oil Company has offered some 40 buy-back contracts. At the time of writing, Shell and Enterprise Oil were leading bidders. See the report of the June 1999 mission in COMET *Bulletin*, number 52, September 1999.
53. Hollis, "Europe and Gulf Security," p. 81.
54. Nadia El-Sayed El-Shazly, *The Gulf Tanker War*, London: Macmillan, 1998, pp. 239, 256.
55. France followed suit the following day, committing ground troops after its ambassador's residence was assaulted.
56. For an overview of the role of the various WEU states, see Nicole Gnesotto and John Roper, *Western Europe and the Gulf*, Paris: The Institute for Security Studies, Western European Union, 1992. A listing of individual contributions to the campaign up to 6 February 1991 is on pp. 170–180.
57. Britain has contributed 12 Tornado aircraft based in Kuwait, and another 6 in Saudi Arabia, along with an estimated 800 Royal Air Force personnel and hundreds of related non-military personnel.

58. Cordesman, *Bahrain, Oman, Qatar and the UAE*, pp. 171–72.
59. Feisal Al Mazidi, *The Future of the Gulf*, London: I. B. Tauris, 1993. See also Cordesman, *Saudi Arabia*, p. 129.
60. Cordesman, ibid.
61. Arms Control and Disarmament Agency, *World Military Expenditures and Arms Transfers,* issues for 1985–1995, Washington, D.C.: Government Printing Office, 1985–1996. See also *Conventional Arms Transfers to Developing Nations, 1987–94,* Washington, D.C.: Congressional Research Service, 4 August 1994, as quoted in Cordesman, *Saudi Arabia,* pp. 108–111 (Cordesman's own use of the data is, in this case, rather confusing).
62. International Institute for Strategic Studies, *The Military Balance 1998/99,* London: IISS, 1999.

CHAPTER 20

# The Impact of U.S. Policy on the Stability of the Gulf States: A Historian's View

Rosemarie Said Zahlan

Kuwait, Bahrain, Qatar, the United Arab Emirates, and Oman are the product of a special historical process that would be difficult to find in any other modern state.[1] Their political systems, social order, demographics, and economic situations are indeed unique to them.

A mere 50 years ago, the Gulf states enjoyed very loosely defined international standing, and they were poor, isolated, and unknown. British Foreign Office files of the 1940s, and even the 1950s, reveal countless references to Britain's inability to continue protecting them forever. They also reflect a general recognition that Saudi Arabia was Britain's natural successor in the area. As recently as 1961, when the Foreign Office was considering an imminent withdrawal from Qatar, it foresaw its acquisition by Saudi Arabia as a strong possibility.[2]

Such a possibility is no longer valid. During the past 30 to 40 years, the Gulf states have taken enormous steps forward, and have become an essential component of the region. Together, they constitute an economic force arguably equal to those of the other countries of the region. Their population hovers around 8 million (including expatriates) and is forecasted to grow to around 26 million by 2030. Their combined GNPs exceed those of any other Arab state, including Saudi Arabia, making them the largest economic and trading bloc in the modern Arab world. Various institutions have been created and developed at a dramatic pace in each, although generally speaking, most have not received the recognition they justly deserve.

In 1989, for example, on the eve of the Iraqi invasion, scientific output per capita in Kuwait was the highest in the Arab world, and on an absolute level, the University of Kuwait produced more scientific refereed papers than any other Arab university.[3] Moreover, scientific publications from the UAE in refereed journals in 1995 were close to the Korean level, on a per capita basis.[4] Other accomplishments include the creation of the Jabal Ali Free Zone in Dubai, which is one of the largest commercial and industrial establishments in the world, and the maintenance of the offshore banking sector in Bahrain, which plays a substantial regional and international role. The list is long and growing briskly.

This transition from obscurity to prominence was made possible, of course, by the vast wealth that was bestowed on these states as a result of their large oil and gas revenues. It facilitated the swift implementation of new infrastructural, social, educational, and other programs that became the foundations of the modern states. A vital point to bear in mind, however, is that such a striking transformation was achieved without upheavals, and without significant changes in either political structure or geographical boundaries. Equally important has been the influence of the past on the sociopolitical fabric of the Gulf states. Indeed, the historical legacy has been central to their modern development, and will remain essential in any consideration of their long-term stability. Because so much has changed so swiftly, it is easy to lose sight of this reality.[5]

This chapter examines those specific aspects of American policy since 1990 that have left an impact on the stability of the Gulf states. Such an examination requires the benefit of historical analysis, without which no understanding of the dynamics of these unique states would be complete.

## The British Legacy: Maintenance of the Status Quo

A striking feature of the contemporary map of the Gulf region is the wide variety of countries that lie around it: Iran and Iraq, two ancient and densely populated countries with substantial human and natural resources; Saudi Arabia, a vast country covering most of the Arabian Peninsula, with a low-density population and strong dependence on one natural resource; and the five smaller Gulf states precariously located between them, more limited in population but exceptionally well endowed with the same natural resource.

Another notable characteristic is the level of stability that pervaded the region for the first 80 years of the twentieth century and that has been steadily eroded since. During the former period, the three regional powers of Saudi Arabia, Iraq, and Iran underwent massive internal changes, whereas—by contrast—the five smaller states lived in quiet isolation until the production of oil began around the second half of the century. This stability was the product of deliberate British policy that resulted in a geopolitical balance between these eight countries of such different size, power, and political culture.

At its core was Britain's maritime control of the Gulf, including the maintenance of the status quo. This was an integrated twin-track approach that extended to the small British-protected states on the one hand and to the three regional powers on the other.[6] The security system it set up, for example, resulted in the emergence of the Gulf states as separate and independent units. The states themselves evolved from the small tribal groupings of the early nineteenth century into modern contemporary entities in a singular process that acted and interacted with the requirements of British policy.

The most outstanding of these requirements were the treaties that Britain signed with specific tribal leaders whose authority in the coastal areas was recognized by their subjects. The treaties became the mainstay of Britain's power base in the region, ultimately providing it with exclusive rights, and undisputed supremacy. It must be acknowledged that the cumulative effect of the treaties was the sealing off of the small states from the outside world, watched over with great jealousy by Britain. In fact, any hint of possible non-British interest in the area, regardless of how trivial, could provoke a serious crisis. This provided the states and their rulers with external protection and security, while at the same time, it acted as a cocoon that allowed local political systems and social traditions to be preserved.

A peculiar feature of the Gulf states has been the repetition of the same type of events, the same type of protagonists, and the same type of outcome throughout most of the twentieth century. In Bahrain, for example, the major crises and confrontations that occurred at depressingly frequent intervals from the early 1920s continued unabated throughout the 1990s. Another example can be found in the events leading up to the Kuwait-Iraq crises of 1961 and 1990. Many aspects of the first are strikingly similar to those of the second, so much so in fact that 1961 could well have been a rehearsal for 1990, particularly since Iraqi claims to Kuwait had always been contained but never resolved. The periodicity and repetitive nature of behavioral patterns can likewise be found in Al Thani feuds in Qatar that were exacerbated by elderly rulers who invariably became recluses and delegated their own duties to appointed successors. Naturally, this led to power sharing between the two, and resulted in an absence of effective leadership.

To be sure, this repetitive feature was a by-product of the British objective of maintaining the status quo, as illustrated by two specific policies.

### *Triple Containment Policy*

When Saudi Arabia, Iran, and Iraq threatened its supremacy, Britain introduced what in modern parlance could be referred to as a "non-military triple containment policy." The three regional powers had first actively sought to define their international relations, particularly regarding their smaller neighbors, during the 1930s. They manifested their foreign policy objectives in competing with each other for influence in the Gulf. Each made claims to different areas firmly under British protection: Iran to Bahrain as well as the Tunb and Abu Musa islands; Iraq to Kuwait; and Saudi Arabia to parts of Abu Dhabi, Qatar, and Oman. Britain contained these claims in a variety of measures that are in strong contrast with the procedures of contemporary dual containment. Bilateral diplomatic negotiations, the swift admonition of Gulf rulers for having contact with foreigners, and the firm refusal to sanction the establishment of diplomatic relations with any of the Gulf states themselves were some of the measures introduced. Others included a complex set of procedures to balance the conflicts and interests of the three powers and, if necessary, to intervene militarily. This policy achieved two objectives: It protected the Gulf states from the forward policies of the regional powers, and it maintained the balance of power between all three.

### *Micro-Interference in Internal Affairs*

British interference in the internal affairs of the Gulf states was limited to cases in which its own interests were at stake.[7] "Government" was generally left to the rulers, who were personally responsible for fulfilling their treaty obligations, and they alone had dealings with the political agents and residents. In turn, this gave the rulers a generally free hand, and in keeping with tradition, they remained accessible to their subjects at all times. Hearing petitions and grievances on a daily basis was the norm. In principle, the rulers had absolute power, but this was tempered by a process of consultation with senior notables before decisions of any consequence were taken. "Governments" in the Gulf states today have retained many of these features, despite the complex and formal government machinery that has since been set up.

Nevertheless, British interference remained on a micro level, to reinforce its potency and effectiveness. In 1938, for example, reformist movements in Kuwait and Dubai led to elections of quasi-representative assemblies. These were led by men who relegated their respective rulers to positions of nominal authority and then proceeded to embark on ambitious programs for social and economic development.[8] The British political agents regarded the reform movements as internal matters but were primarily concerned with the implementation of British treaty conditions. Thus, they warned rebellious leaders that they would not interfere in their assemblies but would continue to deal and communicate exclusively with the rulers whose sovereignty Britain had acknowledged and recognized. This inevitably weakened the opposition and the possibility of reform, while consolidating the position of the rulers.[9] The reform movements collapsed shortly thereafter. The status quo had been maintained with only minimal British involvement.

## In Britain's Shadow: 1971–1990

When Britain withdrew unilaterally from the Gulf in 1971, there were two immediate consequences that are of relevance to this discussion. First, most of the Gulf states had only just acquired independence and were still in the very early stages of state formation, and second, the United States was poised to replace Britain in the area. Official U.S. interest in the Gulf states had first been expressed during the 1940s,[10] but Britain had consistently prevented Washington from gaining much influence. As late as 1968, for example, Britain persisted in its refusal to sanction the opening of a U.S. consulate in Dubai.[11]

### Stable Dynamics of Change

Notwithstanding such machinations, independence brought feverish activity to the Gulf states, as government departments were set up, infrastructure planned and constructed, laws promulgated, and international relations established. During this time, the Gulf states were subjected to a wide variety of external forces, each of which was potentially capable of destabilizing them. But they remained firm in the face of the surrounding maelstrom. Without a doubt, the strength of their own sociopolitical fabric, supported by the long years of British external protection, had provided them with the ability to withstand the consequences of momentous events. In addition to the sudden and dramatic rise in oil prices, following the 1973 Arab-Israeli War, which brought an avalanche of revenue to tiny entities, the Gulf states were certainly ill-equipped to manage the massive changes that followed. Other developments, including the 1975 Algiers Agreement between Iraq and Iran, which contributed to the end of the war in Dhuffar, the fall of the Shah of Iran and the establishment of the Islamic Republic in 1979, the November 1979 seizure of the Grand Mosque in Makkah, and the Shia riots in the Eastern Province of Saudi Arabia the same year, all contributed to the rulers' rapid political growth.

Equally important, the Gulf states survived the large-scale fighting of the Iran-Iraq War relatively unscathed. Although Kuwait was drawn into the periphery of the conflict, and other states witnessed local reactions to the war, the essential features of the states remained intact. The durability of their social structures, their political systems, and their boundaries were tested and amply reaffirmed. Indeed, their capacity to "cope" with crises of considerable magnitude strengthened their ability to manage externally induced forces to their respective advantages.

### *Twin Pillar Policy*

Even the twin pillar policy, based on a putative alliance between Iran and Saudi Arabia, did not faze them. Adopted by the Nixon administration after the British withdrawal, the policy remained in place until the Shah was overthrown in early 1979. Its primary motivation was the fear of Soviet encroachment on a region of vital importance to industrialized economies.

Iran was regarded as a militarily capable state, able to secure Western interests, and the Shah was seen as a strong and assertive figure, who could play the role of "policeman of the Gulf" in return for substantial American support. Saudi Arabia, for its part, was viewed as the stabilizing influence on the Gulf states, the true successor to Britain in that sense. The support it received as one of the two pillars of U.S. policy enhanced its position locally and throughout the rest of the Arab world. Inasmuch as this policy was a departure from the days of the Raj, when the twin-track approach had maintained the balance of power between the regional powers and safeguarded the small Gulf states, it held great potential for destabilization. First, it de-coupled the regional balance of power from the security of the small states. Second, it placed one of the regional powers in a position of enormous strength and influence. The triple containment policy had sustained the Pax Britannica, but its nascent variations would lead to cleavages in the security framework within a matter of a few years.

Iraq, which was then receiving significant Soviet aid, quietly sought to counteract Iranian influence, by trying to foster some form of regional integration with the smaller Gulf states. Together they established a Gulf University in Bahrain, and implemented a number of economic and social projects. Yet, the American support to Iran was overwhelming, and included covert Central Intelligence Agency assistance to the Kurds in their rebellion against Baghdad. Not unexpectedly, this provided Iran with great leverage over Iraq, enabling it to impose the 1975 Algiers Agreement whereby Baghdad conceded part of the Shatt al-Arab waterway to Teheran.[12] It may therefore be correctly argued that the agreement contributed to the outbreak of the Iran-Iraq War five years later.

## Collapse of the Twin Pillar Policy

Nevertheless, when, in January 1979, the Shah's regime collapsed, so too did a vital component of American policy in the region. The establishment of the Islamic Republic of Iran represented a major shift in the regional power structure. Other events caused Washington to search for an alternative policy: the hostage crisis in Teheran, the seizure of the Grand Mosque in Makkah, and the Soviet invasion of Afghanistan, to name just three.

Within a very short period of time, the Rapid Deployment Force was established—also in 1979—as a major step toward an emerging new policy that was based on direct U.S. intervention in the region. This was underlined by the Carter Doctrine, which warned: Any attempt to gain control of the Gulf region would be regarded as an assault on U.S. interests. The new policy was reconfirmed by the Reagan corollary, which extended the Carter Doctrine to include local destabilization. Indeed, the reliance on American armed forces, rather than those of a regional power, grew as the RDF Joint Task Force was created, and later when it was transformed into the U.S. Central Command.

Noticeably, the outbreak of the Iran-Iraq War in 1980 was the first major conflagration in the region since the days of the Raj. It was also a victim of the twin pillar policy, as one of the many reasons for the conflict was the Iraqi attempt to be rid of binding clauses in the Algiers Accord. Another was a struggle for hegemony in the Gulf. In the event, the conflagration lasted for eight long years, with an estimated million casualties and both belligerents left dramatically impoverished. Within a short period of time, the arena of war extended beyond the borders of Iraq and Iran and began to pose significant threats to the Gulf states themselves. Their initial response was to establish the Gulf Cooperation Council in May 1981. Although this provided some security, it did not protect them entirely, as the 1983 bomb attacks in Kuwait amply demonstrated. Other problems increased tensions, and by 1984 the Iran-Iraq War had entered its "tanker" phase, which included direct assaults on Kuwaiti ships.[13]

It may be worth recalling that several Western and many other states were providing military assistance to both sides, in a cynical attempt to keep them engaged, ostensibly to safeguard the stability of the Gulf states and their markets. Significant U.S. military involvement, however, only began to take shape after a Kuwaiti request to re-flag its tankers. In 1987, a powerful fleet of the U.S. navy, together with the frigates, destroyers, and minesweepers of a variety of other states, began escorting the re-flagged tankers and sweeping the Gulf waters for mines. Within a year, Iran accepted a cease-fire, and the war ended in August 1988.

## Challenges to Stability since 1990

Given this background, when Iraqi forces invaded Kuwait in August 1990, it was not surprising to see Washington lead the international response, thereby establishing its hegemony in a very public and assertive manner. The symbolism with, and differences between, Lord Curzon's imperial visit to the Gulf to establish British hegemony at the beginning of the twentieth century and General Norman Schwarzkopf's reliance on state-of-the-art technologies to project U.S. power at the close of the century are especially poignant.[14] In fact, the high-profile U.S. presence during Desert Storm can be viewed as an affirmation of the state security system that had been so dramatically challenged by the Iraqi invasion, and which U.S.-led forces fought on such a large scale to uphold. It can also be viewed as the first and major step in a new and different direction.[15]

In restoring Kuwait to its former status, Washington underlined its adherence to the state system and political structures that London had put in place earlier. The United States reaffirmed the international boundaries of Kuwait, left its political system intact, and strengthened as well as enhanced the position of the ruler. A corollary of these "achievements" is the cohesiveness of Kuwaiti society. Throughout the Iraqi occupation, all Kuwaitis, including leading members of the opposition, remained loyal to the political system, regardless of their own personal convictions. In one sense, therefore, the U.S. upheld the old order to ensure the external security of the Gulf states. In another sense, it introduced undercurrents of change whose impact on both internal and external stability is potentially negative.

The most obvious of these undercurrents is the introduction of the dual containment policy. Indeed, the dramatic isolation of both Iraq and Iran, coupled with the relentless punitive measures against Iraq, have had disastrous repercussions on the societies, economies, and international relations of both countries. Earlier, the twin pillar policy had provided Iran with considerable leverage over Iraq. Similarly, dual containment proved to be equally divisive. It is earning two potential enemies for the Gulf states and Saudi Arabia. Moreover, it has de-linked the security of the Gulf states from that of the rest of the region, abandoning geopolitical realities and releasing forces that threaten stability. Six major concerns, which stand out as potential irritants, are identified and examined below.

*Unpopular U.S. Policies*
The Gulf states have all entered into bilateral defense agreements with the United States, reviving the old treaty system. As a result, they are very publicly and openly allied with Washington. The recent visit to Sultan Qaboos of Oman by President Clinton—on his return from the Indian subcontinent—reaffirmed the emerging relationships. The American alliance, however, has further exposed the governments of the Gulf states to the inequities of U.S. policy throughout the Arab world. These include, on the one hand, persistently punishing the Iraqi people for the actions of their government, continuing the bombing raids, and sustaining the sanctions. On the other hand, turning a blind eye to Israel's continued violations of international law and United Nations resolutions earned many Gulf rulers the opprobrium of some of their citizens.

Indeed, these inconsistencies are not lost on the people of the Gulf states, as their dissatisfaction with these—and other—aspects of American foreign policy could polarize nascent opposition groups. This possibility has been amplified by high-profile events propagated by the media, which report on events as they occur, bringing home the visual experience of Iraqi civilian casualties, and burgeoning Israeli settlements. Ironically, the proposed Cooperative Defense Initiative would call for even stronger links with the United States, placing Gulf governments in even weaker positions vis-à-vis their citizens.

In the past, unpopular alliances have left their impact on Gulf states' internal affairs. In Kuwait, for example, the frustrations caused by the ruler's open association with Britain during the 1936–1939 intifada in Palestine crystallized into the reform movement two years later. The men who had gathered together to express their anger at the ruler's pro-British attitude toward the Palestinians became the protagonists of the 1938 reform movement.[16] The same situation occurred in Bahrain a decade later, when the United Nations partition plan for Palestine became known and, once again, there was a fusion between the Palestine problem and anti-British sentiments that targeted the ruler and his British adviser.[17]

### Arab Relationships

During their long isolation under British rule, the Gulf states were deprived of strong and free relationships with the rest of the Arab world. Once the barriers were lifted, an extensive and widespread interchange began. On the private level, this took the form of visits, professional meetings, and conferences, as joint ventures and investments flourished. On the governmental level, this included membership of Arab regional organizations, donations, and support for major Arab causes, to name just a few examples.

During the past decade, however, a new separation between the Gulf states and the rest of the Arab world is palpable, echoing many of the features of the old days of isolation. Increasingly, the Gulf states are regarded as supportive of U.S. policies against fellow Arabs that, once again, create unmistakable tensions. Some vocal leaders as well as ordinary citizens are blaming their governments for acquiescing to non-Arab and non-Islamic concerns.

### Dynamics of Decision Making

Because American management systems are quantitatively oriented, and largely based on sophisticated intelligence, they tend to result in rapid decisions. They are in sharp contrast with the procedures that are integral to decision making in traditional societies. The Gulf states are small and slow moving. Management of their affairs is negotiated at an unhurried pace by leaders who value traditional mechanisms. Rulers and governments alike enjoy effective but narrow power bases that have survived through the lengthy processes of discussion, negotiation, and consensus. Each state has its own dynamics and responds in its own way to external pressures. Under the circumstances, the nature of the new relationships with the United States does not allow such discussions and consensus to occur. The result may well translate in undermining internal relationships and time-honored processes.

### Macro-Pressure on Internal Affairs

At least six variables may also be identified to describe the various macro-pressures on Gulf states' internal affairs.

*Arms Sales.* Since the end of Desert Storm, the United States has adopted forward policies to promote the sale of costly weapons systems, civilian aircraft, telecommunications gear, and other civil and military hardware. President Clinton's personal interventions regarding these procurements are well known. In many cases, the Gulf states have made the purchases reluctantly, as their strong financial burdens have been compounded by the ongoing slide in oil prices. These vast expenditures constitute nothing less than macro-pressure. They are draining valuable financial resources and removing a powerful source of socioeconomic stability. As already mentioned, the great wealth of these small societies made the transition from tribal shaykhdoms to modern states a relatively smooth process. Time-tested welfare systems shielded individuals and governments from the uncertainties and vicissitudes of their newfound prominence. An apt example of how government bounty could salvage financial disasters is provided in the 1985 collapse of the Suq al-Manakh in Kuwait. To settle the morass of bad debts and stabilize the badly shaken national economy, the government came up with a wide-ranging package to bail out all individuals and institutions that had been involved in the Suq.[18]

This deus ex machina approach is no longer possible, as dwindling national reserves have inevitably induced reductions in subsidies, benefits, and guaranteed public sector employment. The financial shield that has buttressed the societies of the modern Gulf states, which has been an integral part of their development, cannot be relied on as such in the future. Without it, internal tensions can be expected to rise. Expensive mistakes, such as those made in hitherto subsidized private businesses, will have to be covered by their owners. Competition between nationals in the various economic sectors will increase, as will the rivalries within ruling families.

*Militarization.* When Britain withdrew from the Gulf in 1971, the region was largely demilitarized. Iran was just beginning to expand its land, air, and sea forces, but the remainder of the region was largely free of heavy armaments. This is in strong contrast with the situation today, whereby the smallest Gulf states have sophisticated weapons systems, which they are unlikely to ever use. The origins of this transformation into a heavily fortified camp can be traced directly to the twin pillar policy, which relied substantially on building up Iran's military capabilities. Inevitably, this factor reverberated on Iraq's security requirements, as Baghdad had little choice but to counter the putative Iranian threat. The long Iran-Iraq War further involved the purchase of massive amounts of military hardware by both sides, encouraged by governments and arms suppliers around the world. Saudi Arabia was not left out of this diabolical process at the same time.

Only the Gulf states themselves remained relatively unhampered by this trend until 1990, when events overtook them. Before and since the 1991 war, it seems that American policy has been to market its weapons systems, which consequently resulted in the heavy militarization of all the states of the region—for the first time in history. This is over and above the substantial pre-positioning program of American military need, personnel, and facilities that merely add to the growing military nature of the region. It must be emphasized that this militarization is taking place in societies that are not ready for such sophisticated and highly technical armies. It is engendering a false sense of security and, perhaps inadvertently, making the use of force an available alternative to diplomacy as a problem-solving method.

*Uncertainties of U.S. Policies.* The methods of implementing British policy throughout the twentieth century were generally well known and remained reasonably constant. This enabled rulers to evolve a corresponding pattern for negotiation and response. By contrast, the frequent changes in American policy have been very pronounced, including the shift from twin pillar to the Carter Doctrine to dual containment; more recently, the trend seems to be toward some kind of normalization with Iran—all of which have taken place within a short time span of 30 years. These changes obviously immobilize a sustained pattern of response, and call for constant adaptation, which places considerable pressure on regional governments.

*Increasing Unemployment.* A corollary to the expensive weapons sales, and the consequent decline in national reserves, has been the increasing unemployment among Gulf nationals. Although this process began before the 1990–91 war, it has been exacerbated ever since. The dramatic increase in university enrollment, for example, has resulted in a record number of graduates whose expectations are not being satisfied as the job market has been shrinking. Moreover, the exceptionally high population growth rates (around 3.3 percent and above) have exacerbated the problem by several fold. It has been estimated that the labor force (aged 15–64) has been increasing at rates that vary from country to country between 0.7 percent and 1.6 percent per year.[19] Access to international media and the Internet[20] has also been growing, compounding the frustrations of young graduates.[21] These issues, if not addressed, will ultimately induce calls for transparency and accountability regarding national expenditure, a hitherto taboo subject.

*Residual Internal Tensions.* In each of the Gulf states, there is some residual internal tension, often several decades old. Factionalism within the ruling family (Qatar), uncertainties over succession (Abu Dhabi, Oman), and opposition to the government (Kuwait) are well known examples of this phenomenon. Inter-state border disputes are also several generations old: The Bahrain-Qatar conflict has been ongoing since the 1930s, although the March 2001 ruling by the International Court of Justice on their borders seems to have solved the problem. To be sure, some of these problems have been contained; others have been receiving the attention of the GCC in an effort to solve them quietly and, perhaps, expeditiously. An essential component of these efforts, nevertheless, is the slow and gradual level of social change that has served all five states well and contributed to their survival against some odds. U.S. macro-interference could force the pace and act on these smoldering tensions, possibly resulting in open internal conflict.

*Institutional Interference.* The U.S. relationship with the Gulf states has been formalized in a series of bilateral agreements and joint exercises and through an ongoing flow of visits and consultations between their respective leaders and governments. An integral part of a long-term formal association with Washington is the institutionalization of its concern for, amongst others, the Middle East Peace Process, women's rights issues, the protection of intellectual property, environmental concerns, and many other similar affairs.

These have been extended to the Gulf states and, as such, constitute a form of institutional interference in their internal affairs. The establishment by Oman and Qatar of relations with Israel, for example, can be seen in this light, particularly in the face of non-negligible local opposition. Likewise, the Doha Economic Summit (for the Middle East and North Africa region), which was held in November 1998 despite a noisy Arab boycott—as a protest against Israeli obstruction of the Peace Process—saw six Arab countries in attendance, three of which (Qatar, Oman, and Kuwait) were Gulf states. Another example is the high-profile U.S. support for Kuwait's Amiri decree regarding the enfranchisement of women, to which has been attributed its rejection by the National Assembly.

## Changing Patterns

Among the significant challenges facing Gulf states are those that concern the ruling families themselves. Recent events in Qatar indicate major changes from established patterns. Contrary to tradition, the present Amir deposed his father, which is unique in the history of Qatar (and in most Gulf states), because such behavior does not extend to the father-son relationship. Today, the conservatism of Qatar stands in strong contrast with the avant-garde Al-Jazeera television station, which was established just as the Ministry of Information was abolished. Another break with the past is the relationship with Israel. The recent abduction of an aircraft carrying the Amir's cousin, accused of involvement in an attempted coup, is closer to fantasy than to Qatari tradition. U.S. support for the Amir in these and other innovations, including the much-discussed municipal elections, has been open and public.[22]

All of these initiatives have been taken in an ultra-conservative society, and represent the first manifestation of substantial internal change since Operation Desert Storm. In the past, the periodicity of events had a predictable element to them, but the departure from traditional Qatari patterns of behavior is a move into uncharted territory. Some of the new measures have introduced flexibility, new opportunities, and possibilities, while others hold potentialities for isolation and tension.

## The Special Case of Bahrain

Finally, and while it is outside the scope of this paper—which sets out a broad framework for all of the Gulf states—it is necessary to briefly focus on Bahrain to illustrate the impact of U.S. policies on the island-state's internal stability.

Of all the Gulf states, Bahrain is the weakest and most vulnerable, and the reasons—many of which are unique—are well known. Manama's ruling family did not emerge from within the society, as in the other states, where a social contract with the rulers has maintained stability. The country has a strong confessional (Shia-Sunni) divide, as well as a strong rural-urban divide. It is densely populated and has a white- and a blue-collar labor force. Most importantly, it is not oil rich.

Less well known, perhaps, is the high level of British interference in its internal affairs, particularly during the twentieth century. This contributed in large measure to the pattern of unrest that has plagued the country for decades and that is still ongoing. In 1923, Britain imposed a number of political, legal, and administrative changes that resulted in the enforced abdication of the ruler.[23] In 1938, there were additional impositions, this time regarding employment opportunities, and again in 1954, 1956, and 1965, for different reasons. Opposition leaders were invariably arrested; some were deported, usually to an island in the Indian Ocean.[24] The government made few serious attempts to reach an accommodation with the opposition. London's policy of supporting the rulers strengthened their position vis-à-vis their people.

The election by male suffrage of the first (and only) national assembly, in 1973, looked set to reverse past trends of tension and confrontation with the government. Yet, the Jufair agreement, giving the United States access to naval facilities on the island, became a major stumbling block when the nascent Assembly rejected it. By 1975, it had become such a contentious issue that the Amir suspended the Assembly altogether. Thus, it may be safe to argue that the close U.S. alliance, particularly since Operation Desert Storm, has perpetuated the old patterns of tension. In fact, the movement calling for greater participation, as well as the restoration of the Assembly starting in 1994, has led to a long period of renewed confrontation. Manama's heavy-handed response and the widespread arrests and ill-treatment of prisoners (some of whom have been deported) have attracted regional and international attention, including calls by many human rights organizations for the cessation of repression and torture.

Sadly, the late Amir, Isa bin Salman (1961–99), was unresponsive to the mounting unrest and international criticism of his rule. He was so in the firm knowledge that official and public American support sustained him.[25] This affirmation strengthened the Amir, allowing him to pursue his repressive policies amid local and international clamor for political reform.[26] His son, Shaykh Hamad bin Isa, who succeeded him in 1999, looks set to reverse his predecessors' uncompromising attitudes: the most striking indication has been his repeal in February 2001 of emergency laws, the release of all political prisoners, the sanctioning of a referendum, and other measures that promise to introduce the rule of law to the country.

## Conclusion

Britain's triple containment policy preserved the status quo in the Gulf region, but left many problems frozen and unresolved. Although it imposed stability, it left behind a large number of grievances, which were not overcome. These included territorial claims and border disputes. Indeed, Britain missed a number of opportunities to solve the Tunbs and Abu Musa dispute[27] before it became a stumbling block in Arab-Iranian relations.

Almost as soon as Washington sought to replace London in the Gulf, it initiated a process of militarization with Iran, and to a lesser extent, with Saudi Arabia. During the 1980s, it extended this policy to include Iraq. Until then, the Gulf states had had only limited military means, but since Operation Desert Storm, their burgeoning arsenals are in striking contrast to their earlier levels.

It is safe to argue that many aspects of superpower rivalry have been transplanted to the Gulf. Rather than being shielded from the Cold War, the region gradually absorbed some of its traits, even after the collapse of the Soviet Union. In 1948, the U.S. Joint Chiefs of Staff secretly considered the destruction of Middle Eastern oil fields if it became impossible to defend them against Moscow.[28] Cold War policies were manifested once again in Iran with the infamous 1953 CIA plot to overthrow the Mossadeq government.

Current American policies are driven by a preponderance of military considerations as well. Finding solutions to the intrinsic problems of the region is not a priority. Although the resolution of these problems, through diplomatic channels, would be far more conducive to the security of the region, the current discourses on weapons of mass destruction and inter-ballistic missiles seem to dominate. Under the circumstances, and given their relatively weak positions, the Gulf states remain vulnerable to powerful external forces. Not surprisingly, Washington has succeeded in incorporating them into its own system, which, by all accounts, has severely stressed their economies, labor forces, social structures, and political traditions.

The resulting militarization has been absorbing Gulf states' financial and human resources, as the recruitment of substantial numbers of young men into their military—to manage and maintain the newly acquired sophisticated armaments—is weakening the new generation. It is also weakening its effectiveness to plan and prepare for the post-oil phase. Moreover, the high levels of military procurement will inevitably create new centers of non-productive power. The transformation of these centers into institutional forces, which could polarize the opposition, mostly within the ruling families, could also become significant in future political developments.

In the end, because the Gulf states are young and small, and because they are still undergoing so many dramatic and rapid changes, their futures remain fragile. They have established an enabling environment to manage the process of change, which is demonstrated in their commitment to invest in human resources. The adoption of environmental protection policies, the introduction of quality telecommunication services, and high levels of Internet and computer penetration systems all illustrate Gulf leaders' quest for excellence. Thus, as they enter the new century, the Gulf states bring with them many of the attributes that could propel them into a knowledge-based society, enabling them to become members of the global economy. This would be contingent, however, on the introduction of substantial changes in American policy, whose means do not serve proclaimed objectives. Unless the means are reconciled with objectives, the long-term stability of the Gulf states will, indeed, be imperiled.

## Notes

1. In placing together these five different states for this chapter, there will be inevitable generalizations. Oman, in particular, does not fit entirely into the first part of the paper, since it was technically an "independent" state. But it was bound by other obligations to Britain that resulted in sharing many of the features discussed in this chapter.
2. Public Record Office, London, FO371/156977: FO Minute (Green File), 15 November 1961.
3. A. B. Zahlan, *Al 'Arab wa Tahadiyyat al 'ilm wal Taqanah: Taqaddum min dun Taghayyur* [The Challenge of Science and Technology in the Arab World: Progress without Change], Beirut: Centre for Arab Unity Studies, 1999, pp. 63–9.
4. Ibid.
5. This aspect is discussed at length in Rosemarie Said Zahlan, *The Making of the Modern Gulf States: Kuwait, Bahrain, Qatar, the United Arab Emirates and Oman*, Reading, United Kingdom: Ithaca Press, 1998.
6. To quote a political resident in 1931, British policy in the Gulf was "to maintain the independence of the Arab Shaykhdoms and at the same time to prevent any other foreign power from dominating them or obtaining special privileges in the Gulf." British Library, India Office Collection, L/P&S/12/3727, Political Resident to Government of India, 24 November 1931.
7. This is best illustrated by the fact that there were only four British officers stationed in the entire Gulf region until World War II. Rosemarie Said Zahlan, *The Origins of the United Arab Emirates: A Political and Social History of the Trucial States*, London: Macmillan Press, Ltd., 1978, p. 162.
8. For an account of the events leading up to and following the establishment of the Dubai Majlis, see Rosemarie J. Said, "The 1938 Reform Movement in Dubai," *Al-Abhath* 23:1–4, December 1970, pp. 247–318. There are a number of studies that compare the Kuwait movement with those of Dubai and Bahrain, which also took place at the same time. One of the earliest was Muhammad al-Rumaihi, "Harakat 1938 al-Islahiyyah fil Kuwayt wal Bahrayn wa Dubayy" [The 1938 Reform Movements in Kuwait, Bahrain and Dubai], *Journal of the Gulf and Arab Peninsula Studies* 1:4, October 1975, pp. 29–68.
9. By the same token, Britain could also remove rulers when it found it expedient to do so. The enforced abdication of the ruler of Bahrain (1923) and the British-backed palace coups in Sharjah (1965), Abu Dhabi (1966), and Oman (1970) are apt examples.
10. For an account of the early years of U.S. interest in the region, see Rosemarie Said Zahlan, "Anglo-American Rivalry in Bahrain, 1918–1947," in Shaykh Abdullah bin Khalid Al-Khalifah and Michael Rice (eds.), *Bahrain through the Ages: The History*, London: Kegan Paul International, 1993, pp. 567–87.
11. Public Record Office, London FCO8/37, "US Interest in Persian Gulf Political Affairs." The document advanced the same excuse it had given a U.S. request in the 1940s to establish a consulate in Bahrain, namely, that it would set a precedent that other countries would seize on as an excuse to enter the region.
12. Shortly afterwards, Iraq discontinued aid to the Dhuffar revolution in Oman, a major step toward the collapse of that movement.
13. Nadia El-Sayyed El-Shazly, *The Gulf Tanker War: Iran and Iraq's Maritime Swordplay*, London: Macmillan Press Ltd., 1997.
14. Zahlan, *The Making of the Modern Gulf States*, p. 191.
15. There are of course many well-known studies and publications on the current security situation in the Gulf. See Muhammad Al-Said Idris, *Al-Nizam al-Iqlimi lil Khalij al-Arabi* [The Regional Security System of the Arab Gulf], Beirut: Centre for Arab Unity Studies, 2000.
16. For the details of the leaders of the anti-British movement and how they later formed the nucleus of the 1938 opposition, see Rosemarie Said Zahlan, "The Gulf States and the Palestine Problem, 1936–48," *Arab Studies Quarterly* 3:1, winter 1981, pp. 1–21.
17. Ibid.
18. This included paying off small investors, including those with losses of up to $7 million, partially guaranteeing bank losses, providing ten-year interest-free promissory notes, writing off debts that could not be repaid, and buying shares in the stock market to bring up prices.
19. Nadia Sayyed Ali, "Demography and Development in Three Gulf States," unpublished doctoral thesis, Oxford University, 1998, p. 180. For an examination of the problems of localization and restructuring of the labor force, see Andrzej Kapiszewski, *Native Arab Population and Foreign Workers in the Gulf States: Social, Economic and Security Issues*, Krakow: Taiwpn Universitas, 1999.

20. The Gulf states have the highest number of computers per capita in the Arab world. Moreover, preparations under way—such as those for establishing an Internet City in Dubai—are expected to transform the economies of the different states even further.
21. The remarkably high enrollment figures in all the states reflect the fact that education, particularly higher education, is of relatively recent vintage. In 1970, there were only 30 graduates in the UAE; by 1975, they had increased to 589, a 19-fold increase in just five years. Today, it is estimated that the annual number of graduating engineers alone doubles every four years.
22. After the 1996 attempted coup against the Amir, the U.S. State Department publicly supported the sovereignty and independence of Qatar. A spokesman claimed that the coup could not be likened to the Amir's overthrow of his father, since the Amir had had legitimate concerns.
23. Interference by Major Daly, the political agent, was on such a high level that it is still recalled today in the vernacular as "Daly's rules," an expression of severity in some Gulf states.
24. There are a number of relevant studies on Bahrain. See M. G. Rumaihi, *Bahrain: Social and Political Change since the First World War*, London: Bowker, 1967; and Mahdi Abdalla Al-Tajir, *Bahrain 1920–1945: Britain, the Shaikh and the Administration*, London: Croom Helm, 1987. The harsh treatment of political prisoners became an embarrassment to the British government during the 1960s, when a press campaign in London highlighted their plight. The British government had no choice but to release them. For an overall account of Bahraini unrest up to and including 1995, see Munira A. Fakhro, "The Uprising in Bahrain: An Assessment," in Gary Sick and Lawrence G. Potter (eds.), *The Persian Gulf at the Millennium*, New York: St. Martin's Press, 1997, pp. 167–188.
25. In May 1996, the chairman of the U.S. Joint Chiefs of Staff stated that the United States was "most supportive of Bahrain's efforts to ensure its stability." Reuters, 29 May 1996. This theme was reiterated by President Clinton, who assured the Amir that Washington supported his government and sovereignty.
26. In March 1996, despite the anti-government rallies and street riots, the Clinton administration once again praised Bahrain, this time for its support and attendance at the anti-terrorism summit in Egypt.
27. Rosemarie Said Zahlan, "Al-Niza'a Hawl al-Juzur al-Arabiyyah fil Khalij 1928–1971: Dirasat lil 'Alaqat al-Arabiyyah al-Iraniyyah wa Dawr Britaniya Fiha" [The Role of Britain in the Conflict over the Tunb Islands, 1928–1971], *Journal of the Gulf and Arabian Peninsula Studies* 2:6, April 1976, pp. 9–32.
28. After some debate, they decided to limit the destruction to refining, loading, and transportation systems. There were no plans to consult any of the governments involved. U.S. National Archives, General Records of the Department of State, box 4, "Preparation for Demolition of Oil Facilities in the Middle East," 25 May 1948.

# THE GULF STATES AND WESTERN POWERS

CHAPTER 21

*Gulf States' Links with their Post-Soviet Northern Neighbors*

Theodore Karasik

The late-1989 collapse of the Soviet Union has left a noticeable impact upon and within the Persian Gulf region that deserves special attention. A decade after significant changes in the global balance of power, the legacy of the Soviet system in creating new national leaders is still visible, as a new leadership emerges in Moscow. How these new leaders behave in the Gulf and how they conduct meaningful decision making toward the region are of critical importance because north-south security and trade relations are in full swing. Whether the Gulf States can rely on stable political, economic, and security relationships with Central Asia—while countering the still influential Russian Federation—deserves attention. In recent years, the relationship between Gulf states and several New Independent States (NIS) of the former Soviet Union has shaped slowly evolving security and commercial ties.

Even if Soviet educated, the vast majority of the governing elites in the Caucasus and Central Asia are clan based, which inevitably alters their independent approaches. Under the old Soviet system, local party bosses reigned over their respective republics largely unchallenged, as long as they held to Moscow's guidelines dutifully enforced by Russian first secretaries. After the Soviet breakup, the Russian deputies went home, but left the local Communist hierarchies and the privileges associated with power, complete with their leaderships, intact and in place. The underlying political structures, and the way in which elections were run, retained their previous blueprints in the decade after the area entered its post-Soviet period. Even if these methods gave NIS officials a Western orientation, most local leaders behaved in typically non-Soviet modes, perceiving their independent republics as far closer to traditional entities. Indeed, discarded concepts, ranging from clan fiefdoms to khanates and emirates, were once again in vogue. Several leaders perceived themselves as custodians over substantial mineral resources, which, noticeably, underscores the dormant similarities between them and the Gulf states. At least on this score, the two regions shared much in common, which further endeared leaders to each other.

In addition to this fundamental characteristic, two other salient concerns shaped the overall impact between Gulf states and leading post-Soviet republics: security and commerce.

The newly engaged Central Asian leaders shared similar perceptions of internal and external threats.[1] In some ways, inexperienced leaders—at least by international standards—saw foreign interference through political violence, proxies, assassination, rival governments, and introduction of radical ideologies as potential warnings. In this respect, their views mirrored those shared by several Gulf leaders. Not surprisingly, many developed counter-strategies relying on strong security services. Like their Gulf counterparts, they quickly learned to co-opt dissent, practice divide-and-rule strategies, allow ideological flexibility, and permit, when feasible, pseudo-participation in the political systems.

Equally important is the impact that the emerging north-south commercial nexus has had in a very short decade. Early in the 1990s, leading Gulf states sought to invest heavily in the former Soviet Union to secure lucrative commercial returns, advance cultural and religious coalitions, and develop joint strategies to market raw materials in mutually beneficial ways. Outside the Soviet orbit, few realized that these objectives would be difficult to accomplish, because the overall physical conditions in the north were comparable to those found in developing countries. The region lacked a proper infrastructure, which severely prevented trade. In fact, the area in general lacked long-distance highways, a situation that has changed little in the decade since independence. Existing roads remained in poor condition, railroads were underdeveloped, and airports were sub-standard. These transportation settings made it difficult to move goods both north and south. Moreover, and because they shared similar types of economies, in that leading countries in both areas produced a limited range of commodities—such as cotton, minerals, oil, and gas—their narrow export bases meant that Central Asian and Gulf states competed.[2] Indeed, the direction of trade in the decade since 1990 has recorded substantial advances, as many anticipated, but progress has been slow, leading to substantial reassessments of future trends.

## Gulf States' Impact on Central Asia

The idea of the Central Asian states being pulled away by either Moscow or Teheran seems far-fetched. To be sure, Russia continues to exercise substantial influence in Central Asia, but the latter is loath to sustain umbilical cords when so little benefits come their way. Likewise, many realize that their religious ties run through Makkah, not Qom. Consequently, neither Russia nor Iran has recorded significant advances in Central Asia. The so-called Islamic threat proved to be vastly exaggerated given that few Central Asians were inspired or mobilized to political action. Opposition figures in Central Asia could not rely on religion to catapult themselves to power given the overwhelming secularization process introduced during the Soviet era. Contrary to widespread assumptions, the common Islamic identity in Central Asia remained too vague and too abstract to challenge nationally defined state authority, and boundaries.

Assuming an Islamic challenge, however, has been used as an excuse to justify authoritarian tendencies throughout the region.

Instead, the region was dominated by an entrenched clan structure, which proved critical throughout the 1990s. Importantly, the intricate clan patterns and associations—so necessary to establishing a realistic blueprint of power structure in Central Asia—proved difficult to decipher. As the establishment of Soviet power corrupted most Central Asian societies, and all social structures were preserved by collective forms, little evidence—save for occasional anecdotal vignettes—was available. Still, the Communists altered Central Asia by working within the framework of traditional hierarchies inadvertently failed to dismantle existing clan structures. An alien ideology could not dismantle in 70 years what took centuries to assemble. Central Asia was clan based before 1917 and, despite Communist authoritarianism, would revert to it in 1990.[3]

Of course, the impact of Communist authoritarianism was substantial, as Central Asia experienced undeniable hardships. Remarkably, and despite the extreme political fluidity that marked their recent behavior, several republics successfully re-drafted their own cultural identities, formed new alliances and associations, identified new friends, and forged important ties with their southern neighbors in the Gulf. Regardless of the kind of arrangements that emerged among the Central Asian states, fresh identities, concrete interests, and long-term objectives were all far more likely than generally assumed.

To some extent, the reasons for these positive developments were directly related to strong tribal and clan alliances in Central Asia. The tendency to remain loyal at the local, rather than the national, level dominated. Tribal, ethnic, and clannish associations were favored because they sought to attach loyalty to dominate the economic, political, and security landscape. In such instances, not a single institution, whether it governed economics, politics, or security affairs, was immune from tribal and clan influences.

Given this background, how have local leaders behaved in the decade since independence? Have they altered the ways through which most controlled the region's economic assets—especially within their fiefdoms? To be sure, clan politics, combined with entrenched Russian norms, dominated the political landscape. In fact, a distinctive Russian background among Central Asian societies influenced foreign policy formulation and articulation toward the Gulf states. Moreover, the unique mix found among the Central Asian leadership structure also affected the growth and management of Islamic linkages, economic connections, and regional cooperation. Noticeably, Central Asian leaders approached their Gulf counterparts with both delight and apprehension; they were free to conduct international diplomacy to boost links outside Central Asia, while being limited in their abilities to become part of the greater Middle East. The Russian-trained, clannish leaderships still perceived Moscow—despite the trauma and anxiety of the Soviet collapse—as a patron that, in the long run, ensured continuity.

In the end, Central Asia's Soviet-style patrimony included daunting problems that made Gulf policy objectives difficult to manage. Political elites in each new republic, which had grown accustomed to single-party, winner-take-all systems, wrestled with the myriad problems that came with independence. Like their Gulf counterparts, most preferred central control, thereby limiting political competition and creating opposition groups seeking external support. Rivalries revolved around regional or clan contests, rather than institutions that purported to represent class interests or other ideologies. In similar fashion to their Gulf counterparts, Central Asian leaders resorted to lengthy quotations that emphasized the obligations of the leader, portraying the chief executive as the sole decision maker. Most regarded their citizens as subjects, or passive objects of authority, rather than as sources of legitimacy.[4]

### Iran, Russia, and Saudi Arabia in Central Asia

Within the Gulf, Iran wrestled with the notion that it ought to be the single most important country to Central Asia, if for no other reason than geography and history. Yet, Iran emphasized its religious credentials and attempted to redirect the Central Asian republics away from Russia and the West, by encouraging mutually beneficial trade contacts. In fact, Teheran re-launched the moribund regional Economic Cooperation Organization (ECO) and signed several lucrative oil accords.[5] Inasmuch as developing competing oil producers would affect the entire region, Iran's role in forging safe and secure oil lifelines from this critical region to industrialized countries became critical. Nevertheless, Teheran's various activities—in encouraging Central Asian republics to behave in specific ways—meant that revolutionary leaders were keenly aware of how lucrative the area was. Even if the ECO effort failed to produce desired effects in a timely fashion, Iran was still interested in forging close ties with leading Central Asian states, especially over the long term.[6]

Throughout the 1990s, Iran reasserted its historic and cultural influence in Central Asia, even if Ayatollah Khomeini's teachings and interpretations were not popular among northern-tier leaders. Likewise, Saudis relied on their religious credentials to influence Central Asian masses, if not the leaders themselves. Independent elements within the Gulf were also interested in enlisting Central Asian support against Western—including Russian—interests. But activity alone did not ensure influence. Indeed, Iran, Saudi Arabia, and others failed to exert real authority in Central Asia, because they themselves were weak and divided.[7] More important, the republics, long viewed as falling within the Russian Empire's grip, remained vulnerable in both the Soviet as well as post-Soviet eras. In fact, Communist leaders throughout the region would have probably preferred to delay any breakup of the empire, if only to gain breathing space to resolve some of their problems. Because of the proximity to Moscow, especially in political and economic terms, the Central Asian states have had no breathing room of their own.

Therefore, Russia remained powerful because Iran and Saudi Arabia suffered certain foreign policy limitations. Neither Teheran nor Riyadh could compete with Moscow in terms of military, or even economic, means to carve out a sphere of influence. In addition, each state had its own special shortcomings. Although Iran's location could—in time—mean commercial and transportation links to the southern tier, the country's international isolation reduced its attraction for states just emerging from three generations of colonialism and political quarantine. Moreover, Teheran's severe religious order intimidated those accustomed to secularism. Saudi Arabia competed, but its limited population, remote location, and conservative religious traditions made it less than a formidable contender.[8] As important, the northern tier remained a cauldron of real and potential tribulations. Afghanistan's civil war, which started in the aftermath of the 1979 Soviet invasion, continued, and Tajikistan's civil war, which began in 1992, was in abeyance. Border problems retained their embarrassing values as well, further compounded by ongoing religious, ethnic, and ideological problems that afflicted the region throughout the decade.[9]

In short, the Muslim populations of the northern tier were unlikely to leave Russia's orbit and rejoin the Middle East anytime soon. The experience of such former colonies, as well as the history of Muslim-Christian relations in this part of the world, supported this conclusion. The hyperbole aside, for 70 years the Muslim republics were Moscow's colonies, and it may prove difficult for them to move away from the imperial center. Moreover, Russia differed in important ways from other European colonizers, having demonstrated a greater willingness to use force to cement closer ties. It should come as no surprise if these intense ties with the former colonies continue for the foreseeable future.

## Why the Two Systems are Different

As the Middle East witnessed the creation of a modern state system starting immediately after World War I, Central Asia was forcibly integrated into the newly created centralized authoritarian state of the Soviet Union. Therefore, by the time newly independent state actors had begun to emerge in the Middle East, Central Asia was already off-limits.[10] Not surprisingly, political elites in most Central Asian republics were subdued faster than their Slavic counterparts, whereas Middle Eastern elites quickly became preoccupied with the superpower status of the USSR. Under the circumstances, there was little attempt to develop genuine bilateral relations between Central Asia and the Middle East.

Thus, the actual development of the "state" in the Middle East and in Central Asia was quite dissimilar. If the Gulf states consolidated their power and developed competing claims on the loyalty of the population, such was not the case in Central Asia. In many ways, the way Britain and France "re-invented" the political map of the Middle East stood in sharp contrast to the "creation" of Soviet Central Asia. The vulnerability that almost inevitably accompanies the creation of states with small populations and little sense of territorial unity proved especially egregious in the USSR. Smaller Central Asian republics, many with re-drawn internal borders that further separated ethnic populations into non-homogeneous entities, became susceptible to sustained interference by larger neighbors. For example, the recent Russian presence in Tajikistan stood in sharp contrast to the 1990 Iraqi invasion of Kuwait.[11] Some Tajiks perceived Moscow as a genuine asset—whereas Baghdad was perceived as a hegemon determined to re-draw the regional map.

The literature concerning transitology, the study of how governments evolve from Communist dictatorship to democracies, may be helpful in understanding why the two state systems were so different. Transitologists argue that the Central Asian states were able to move from authoritarianism to democracy. Where were these phenomena evident in the Persian Gulf? With a single exception—Saudi Arabia—all were former colonies, and, while similar in that sense, many more dissimilarities existed. For example, ethnic diversity stood out as a case in point, a phenomenon that was quelled in Central Asia. The sheer magnitude of diversity in the Gulf region and its correlation with religious, political, socioeconomic, and spatial markers stood in sharp contrast to Central Asian states. Similarly, powerful historical meanings attached to ethnicity, nation, religion, and state (all negative under the Soviet system), as well as the role played by socialist regimes in developing a new national consciousness, further separated Central Asia's unique characteristics. To this list of fundamentals, it is also important to add the development of "Sovietized" elites—institutions and proto-states within the "independent republics"—to appreciate how difficult the proposition facing Central Asia at the dawn of the twenty-first century appears to be.[12]

## Consequences of Regional Isolation on the Northern Tier

To be sure, the Central Asian republics may be somewhat isolated from the Gulf states, even if the consequences of that indifference—especially for elites—are non-negligible.

### *Impact on Islam*
Although external influences from the Persian Gulf could play a crucial role, internal political dynamics among individual Central Asian republics were far more significant. Large-scale Islamic fundamentalist movements, which harbored anti-Western sentiments and sought to achieve political power in lieu of the current nomenclatura, were unlikely. Importantly, the Hannafi school of Islamic jurisprudence dominated throughout Central Asia, which translated into a way of life rather than any ideological creed.[13]

What few of Central Asia's leaders were willing to acknowledge was that Islam did not stand as an agent of instability. In fact, religion per se did not offer competition, but stood as an alternative to their inability to rule. How Central Asian leaders managed their economies and governed mattered far more than the populations' religious beliefs. As a consequence, in all of Central Asia, the relationship between Islam and the state remained tense, just as it was during Soviet rule. Noticeably, Central Asian leaders and elites remained far more concerned with the task of restricting the potential spread of "radical Islam" than ruling. Just as some Westerners equated "political Islam" with "fundamentalist" behavior, so did Central Asian elites, and unlike the unique Iraqi case—where religion has been used as an adjunct of extreme nationalism—Central Asian officials did not profess similar beliefs.¹⁴ Islam, in Central Asian mainstream society, became a symbol of cultural freedom, not a movement to reject leadership policies.

*Economics and Trade*

Much of Central Asia has still not fully recovered from the collapse of the Soviet Union and the emergence of Russia. For over a decade, few became aware of the importance of markets, and many experienced firsthand the negative consequences of centralized systems. In fact, prior to the 1998 Russian economic crisis, relaxed border security allowed merchants who wanted to buy and sell goods to move across the borders of the new Central Asian states without much hindrance. Since 1998, Uzbekistan has intensified border controls, particularly in the most militantly Muslim and economically despondent region in all of Central Asia, the Ferghana Valley.¹⁵ The greater its restrictions on cross-border interactions, the more steeply regional trade seemed to decrease, which, in the process, subverted the economic development of the region. Yet, the Russian economy was closely tied to the Central Asian cotton economy, which further illustrated existing links between Central Asia and Russia.¹⁶ Undoubtedly, the Soviet legacy lived on.¹⁷

In the event, at least five agreements existed within Central Asia and the Caucasus to facilitate trade—with each other and Russia—and avoid confusion. Likewise, approximately six international conventions have been developed by the United Nations to ease transit through the landlocked countries of Central Asia. If these agreements were fully implemented, trade might run much more smoothly, as virtually every Central Asian republic prefers to trade with the West. Ironically, most have found little interest in the West, opting to fall back upon their hitherto tested and reliable Eastern partners. In the case of Kazakhstan, for example, trade with China increased substantially. Indeed, Shanghai may be said to have become Kazakhstan's major port.¹⁸

Because of this Eastern outlook, trade between Central Asia and several Gulf states increased. The United Arab Emirates' Ras al-Khaimah airport, for example, expanded facilities to accommodate a large number of tourists specifically from the region, who stocked up on electrical appliances and other "white goods," which they flew back on chartered aircraft.¹⁹ Iran, for its part, exported more than $30 million in natural gas, vehicles, textiles, and foodstuffs to Central Asian republics in 1993, triple the figure for the preceding calendar year.²⁰ Still, these figures were nowhere as impressive as they portended, given the "abundance of resources."

Saudi Arabia continued to push for economic ties with Kazakhstan—even as modest as they seemed—after several failed attempts. In October 1999, over 40 prominent Saudi business leaders visited Astana to discuss bilateral projects.²¹ In July 1997, joint meetings between Saudi and Iranian officials occurred in Almaty, then the Kazakh capital, when the two ambassadors stressed progress in economic relations.²² It was a symbolic passing of the torch to Saudi Arabia. Several months later, Riyadh promised to finance the construction of a diplomatic village in Astana, to host nearly all foreign embassies.²³

It is also important to note that personal interests often motivated Central Asian leaders. Many preferred the confusion of multiple agreements—to further their own economic and political agendas—which did not necessarily advance the interests of the area's populations. Clearly, with the vast majority of that population tied to agriculture and the trading of goods, the implications of declining Central Asian integration, and away from Iran or the Gulf, were ominous.

*Petroleum*
In the second half of the 1990s, international interest in the exploration and production of oil in the Caspian Sea region brought great attention to the oil-rich republics of Kazakhstan, Turkmenistan, and Uzbekistan. In turn, this activity increased the assertiveness of officials in all three republics to move out of Russia's shadow. At the same time, Washington's efforts to diminish the historical influence enjoyed by Moscow over the area—by supporting the construction of the Baku-Ceyhan pipeline, an export oil pipeline that would run through the Caucasus to Turkey, for example—met with approval throughout the area.

Yet, the whole affair remained a doubtful proposition, because the Caspian Sea bonanza may not have been as credible as initially thought.[24] Consequently, the rivalry between Turkey, Russia, and Iran over Caspian Sea mineral resources, and oil and gas export pipelines, weakened the ability of the southern Gulf states to become involved in petroleum economy.[25] Gulf investments in Central Asia could, potentially, produce competition, a proposition that was certainly considered carefully by savvy Gulf merchants. Moreover, both Russia and Iran increased pressure, positing that they must be accommodated in some fashion, for effective and secure regional participation. Under the circumstances, the southern Persian Gulf countries may be left out,[26] especially as several Central Asian states are far more interested in self-sufficiency than exporting crude.[27]

*Transportation Problems*
Starting in June 1996, Iran voiced certain complaints that its abilities to operate fully functional rail operations to and from Central Asia had encountered specific problems. These included travel through a number of former republics, emerging customs restrictions, mountainous terrain, and areas of instability—including the Ferghana Valley. Moreover, Teheran confirmed that the area's overall infrastructure was in poor condition, and that there was a lack of new investment for repair and maintenance. In fact, the Soviet network could not be used with the Iranian rail system, because of gage differences. Geography played a major role as well, since traffic was routed through desert, steppes, and mountainous regions, all of which required security. In the event, internal conflicts greatly disrupted the Iranian mission.[28] Still, in May 1998, Iran completed the Mashad-Sarakhs-Tedzhen railway, a development that supported claims that the Islamic government could facilitate all transportation requirements between the Persian Gulf and Central Asia.[29] Encouraged by this significant advance, Iran opened discussions on building a canal from the Caspian to the Persian Gulf.[30]

## Leadership Traits: The Turkmenistan Example

Turkmenistan represented the ideal case that supported cooperation between Central Asia and the Gulf states. Starting in 1990, Turkmen leaders embarked on a concerted policy to reduce dependence on any one country for the transportation of oil and gas resources. Ashkhabad advocated building multiple pipelines, running in different directions—to the north, south, east, and west. Turkmenistan, as one of the most repressive of the successor states of the Soviet Union, and one of the poorest, was not hesitant in this outlook.[31] Yet, Turkmenistan was rich in natural resources, as its known reserves of natural gas placed it fourth in the world—behind Russia, the United States, and Iran—with an estimated six- to eight-billion-ton oil reserve. Still, geography and politics dictated how it conducted its foreign affairs, and the type of inducements it sought to present to international investors.

Bordering on the Caspian Sea, Kazakhstan, Uzbekistan, Afghanistan, and Iran, Turkmenistan occupies an important strategic position. That very position, however, makes it vulnerable. With a population of fewer than five million, and a very limited pool of educated individuals, Turkmenistan has been unable to make much economic or social progress since 1991. Its governmental practices and attitudes have remained largely Soviet in substance and style, particularly in urban renewal projects.[32]

Under the circumstances, and because Turkmenistan has never been a genuine nation, the nomadic tribes that inhabited the area east of the Caspian have not rejected Ashkhabad's rule. There is no tradition of government and no legal institutions, except what has been inherited from an alien colonial power. It was, therefore, not surprising that Turkmenistan was ruled by a president whose authority was not limited by laws. As under the Soviet Union, Turkmen elections and referenda were nothing but public endorsements of the ruler's decrees. Finally, the government perceived any religious organization as a potential threat to the stability of the state. It should be noted that the Turkmen Muslim population in its vast majority was tolerant and showed no signs of wishing to establish a theocratic state on the Afghan or Iranian models. This archetype of state-Islamic relations serves as a model for other Central Asian states that suffer from militant Islamic insurgencies from abroad.

## Conclusion

The Central Asian region represented a vast potential political, cultural, religious, and economic gain for the Gulf states. Yet, the political and religious turmoil often associated with the region was sometimes considered a serious impediment to the expansion of economic or cultural ties. Three specific factors that rejected Persian Gulf interests were especially noteworthy: the clan system, age-old ethnic conflicts, and religious revivalism or political Islam derived from old cultural links. For the Gulf, these factors complicated or even endangered potential business contacts, sometimes creating protracted conflicts and deteriorating standards of bilateral development and lost opportunities for legal financial gain.

Russia's ability to prevent the emergence of an Islamic country in Central Asia is an important geopolitical concept. Tsarist Russia, the Soviet Union, and its successor have succeeded in suppressing this objective through diplomacy and force. The Russian Ministry of Foreign Affairs and the Russian Ministry of Defense succeeded by building a new security system in the northern band of the Islamic crescent and expanding Kremlin defense policy in the Persian Gulf. It is only natural for the political Islam represented by non-state actors such as Usama bin Laden to replace official Iranian or Saudi cultural religious links in Central Asia.

Moreover, cultural Islam failed, because of Russia's age-old impact on Central Asia, to absorb the teachings and lessons of the 1979 Islamic Revolution and the more potent late 1990s–early 2000 Afghan Taleban or Wahhabi influence, with its overt challenge to Russian imperial authority for political and spiritual control. Russia was astute enough to recognize that when anti–Central Asian subversive activities in the Gulf countries occurred, including the establishment of international networks of clerics against Russian interests and anti–Gulf policy statements and interpretations among the Central Asian elites, an unpleasant side effect was occurring. The driving force behind these feelings of cultural and religious linkages was that clans, ethnic groups, and religious communities involved in challenging state systems were unique in Central Asia, and alien to Persian Gulf religious and political forces. If some believed that the Soviet Union was the continuation of imperial rule, then Russia in the early twenty-first century behaved like its predecessors without question.

For Iran and Saudi Arabia, Central Asia remains impenetrable on the state level because of Russia's strong pull. Unstable conditions faced by the post-Soviet rulers in the Central Asian republics converged with the crisis conditions encountered by the post-Khomeini leadership in Iran and the internal and external threat perception problems in Saudi Arabia. These circumstances led to a growing number of contacts that allowed for the development of an increasingly complex set of economic relationships between Iran and Russia, and not Teheran's northern neighbors. For the most part, Iran's efforts to engage the Central Asian states continued to be a good showing, even if Teheran could not play a major role because of internal pressures. Clearly, Teheran denied the possibility that its involvement with northern neighbors could be anything more than predatory or destabilizing simply because Iran faced huge obstacles in Central Asia.

Likewise, although Saudi Arabia had a good start in Central Asia in both religious and economic affairs throughout the early 1990s, it lost steam because of its own economic problems and its ability to maintain domestic stability.[33] Instead, non-state Saudi actors took advantage of Riyadh's weaknesses. Usama bin Laden and the Arab commander Kattab in Chechnya did not help Central Asian leaders accelerate their ties with the Gulf states. Non-state actors in Chechnya, Afghanistan, and the Gulf began to replace official Saudi ability to export Islamic influence, economic assistance, and diplomatic support.

Finally, in the 1990s, Russia and the Central Asian states were more concerned with their respective policies toward each other then toward Iran. In

1997, Moscow began to pursue military coordination in Central Asia, best illustrated by its substantial involvement in Tajikistan. Later, Russia expressed special interest, and provided substantial assistance to Uzbekistan and Kyrgyzstan to fight non-state Islamic actors.[34] Russia was using its intelligence capabilities and new security agreements, similar to the Soviet period, to prevent a full disintegration of its security and intelligence influence.[35] Vis-à-vis the pro-Western GCC states, Russia was keen to ensure that its rapprochement with Iran was not gained at the expense of its political and economic interests in the Arab Gulf states, or offended southern Gulf states' relations with their northern neighbors. Central Asian republics, despite a strong effort to build new linkages with several neighbors, still find their past, present, and future tied to Moscow.

## Notes

1. Russian arms sales of both conventional and nuclear-biological-chemical (NBC) technologies played—and continue to play—important roles in the evolving relationships between the Gulf states and their northern neighbors, but the focus here is solely on the Central Asian–Gulf states, with a minimal focus on Russian arms sales behavior.
2. Carol Henderson, "Grass Roots Aspects of Agricultural Privatization in Kyrgyzstan," *Central Asia Monitor*, number 5, 1993, pp. 29–35. See also Don Van Atta, "The Current State of Agrarian Reform in Uzbekistan," *Post-Soviet Geography* 34:9, 1993, pp. 598–606.
3. Kadir Alimov, "Are Central Asian Clans Still Playing a Political Role?" *Central Asia Monitor*, number 4, 1994, pp. 14–15.
4. Edward Allworth, "The Cultural Identity of Central Asian Leaders: The Problem of Affinity with Followers," *Central Asia Monitor*, number 6, 1993, pp. 29–30.
5. Eric Hooglund, "Iran and Central Asia," in Anoushiravan Ehteshami (ed.), *From the Gulf to Central Asia: Players in the New Great Game*, Exeter, United Kingdom: University of Exeter Press, 1994, pp. 114–28.
6. Mahrdad Haghayeghi, "Economic Cooperation Organization: A Preliminary Assessment," *Central Asia Monitor*, number 1, 1995, pp. 14–19. The conclusion reached by ECO announced that the discussion and thinking about advantageous oil and gas routes was "a matter for the future." ECO officials did not specify whether they meant the distant or near future, but existing projects still needed technological feasibility studies, and "additional consultations." The main subject of the consultations, understandably, was the lack of financial resources. See *Izvestiya*, 27 February 1998, p. 2, in "Central Asia Put Off Pipeline Route Decisions," *FBIS-NES, FTS19980227001047*, 27 February 1998.
7. Daniel Pipes, "The Event of Our Era: Former Soviet Muslim Republics Change the Middle East," in Michael Mandelbaum (ed.), *Central Asia and the World*, New York: Council on Foreign Relations, 1994, pp. 48–49.
8. Ibid. See also Mark Katz, "Emerging Patterns in the International Relations of Central Asia," *Central Asia Monitor*, number 2, 1994, pp. 23–27.
9. Pipes, *op. cit.*
10. Philip Robins, "The Middle East and Central Asia," in Peter Ferdinand (ed.), *The New States of Central Asia and Their Neighbors*, New York: Council on Foreign Relations Press, 1994, p. 55.
11. The putative Iraqi influence in Central Asia has been largely neutralized since the end of the War for Kuwait. In fact, the War for Kuwait shaped conservative Arab Gulf states' attitudes toward the Central Asian republics because Iraq no longer represented a regional threat. Iran, on the other hand, was perceived as a "destabilizer," a threat to Gulf security but a necessary regional power to act as a local counter-balance to the northern Gulf. Under the circumstances, turning to Russia presented far better odds, especially if Central Asian leaders did not wish to be dragged into Persian Gulf conflicts.
12. Valerie Bunce, "Should Transitologists Be Grounded?" *Slavic Review* 54:1, spring 1995, pp. 125–126. See also Edward W. Said's *Orientalism*. The book explores the problems of relying on European historical traditions (including the growth of a Western-based culture, religion, etc.) for

understanding the Middle East. Said traced its origins from Hellenistic roots, including the perennial European fear of Islam by the seventh century, the emergence of the "us versus them" ideal through the late eighteenth and nineteenth centuries, and the subsequent growth of a discourse in Europe and, later, the United States that placed "the Arab" or "the Muslim" in a second-rate position versus a "much-superior" Westerner. Simultaneously, Said argued that Middle Eastern intellectuals adopted Orientalism, which further solidified the notion of the "evil Arab." *Orientalism*, published in 1978, perceived Middle Eastern studies in need of a fundamental overhaul. See Edward W. Said, *Orientalism*, New York, Random House, 1979.

13. Richard B. Dobson, "Islam in Central Asia: Findings from National Surveys," *Central Asia Monitor*, number 2, 1994, pp. 17–22. See also Mahrdad Haghayeghi, "Islamic Revival in the Central Asian Republics," *Central Asian Survey* 13:2, 1994, pp. 249–266.
14. Shirin Akiner, "On Its Own: Islam in Post-Soviet Central Asia," *Harvard International Review*, spring 1993, p. 21.
15. The Ferghana Valley has been in chaos since before the Soviet implosion. Gulf influence seems to be wholly lacking in addressing the decade-old disorder. The events in Ferghana today seem completely outside the Gulf's orbit of foreign relations. For the evolution of events since 1990, see Theodore Karasik, *Azerbaijan, Central Asia and Future Persian Gulf Security*, Santa Monica: RAND, 1993. Most of the disputes in the Ferghana Valley focus on land distribution for economic development. See "Unrest In Kyrgyzia," *Central Asia and Caucasus Chronicle* 9:3, June 1990, p. 1.
16. Igor Lipovsky, "The Central Asian Cotton Epic," *Central Asian Survey* 14:4, 1995, pp. 529–542; S. Zhukov and O. Reznikova, "Tsentralnaia aziia v mirovoi politike i ekonomike," *Mirovaia ekonomika i mezhdunarodnye otnosheniia (MEMO)*, December 1994, pp. 26–39.
17. Nazif Shahrani, "Central Asia and the Challenge of the Soviet Legacy," *Central Asian Survey* 12:2, 1993, pp. 123–135.
18. Robin Wright, "Beliefs Take a Back Seat to Business as Iran Raises Its Regional Profile," *Los Angeles Times*, 1 January 1995, p. 14.
19. "Those Russians Are Everywhere," *Foreign Report*, 1 June 1995, p. 7.
20. Wright, *op. cit.*, p. 14.
21. SPA, 13 October 1999, as cited in "Nazarbayev Receives Visiting Saudi Industry Minister," *FBIS-NES, FTS19991013001965*, 13 October 1999.
22. IRNA, 29 July 1997, as cited in "Saudi, Iranian Officials Hold Cooperation Talks in Almaty," *FBIS-NES, FTS19970729000880*, 29 July 1997.
23. Interfax, 9 December 1998, as cited in "Saudi Arabia Ready to Finance Building of Kazakh Capital," *FBIS-NES, FTS19981210000463*, 10 December 1998.
24. For the optimistic view, see Judith Robinson, "Caspian Export Markets Grow," Washington D.C.: U.S. Department of Commerce, *BISNIS Bulletin*, June 1998, p. 1. For the pessimistic perspective, see Martha Brill Olcott, "The Caspian's False Promise," *Foreign Policy*, summer 1998, pp. 95–113; and Amy Myers Jaffe and Robert A. Manning, "The Myth of the Caspian Great Game: The Real Geopolitics of Energy," *Survival* 40:4, winter 1998–1999, pp. 112–129.
25. Suha Bolukbasi, "The Controversy over the Caspian Sea Mineral Resources: Conflicting Perception, Clashing Interests," *Europe-Asia Studies* 50:3, 1998, pp. 397–414.
26. Elshan Alekberov, "Despite Political Obstacles, Energy Work Progresses around Caspian Sea," *Oil & Gas Journal Special*, 15 June 1998, pp. 47.
27. James P. Dorian, Tojiev Utkur Abbasovich, Mikhail S. Tonkopy, Obozov Alaibek Jumabekovich, Qiu Daziong, "Energy Investment and Trade Opportunities Emerging in Central Asia, Northwest China," *Oil & Gas Journal*, 15 June 1998, pp. 48–60.
28. *Eqtesad-e Khorasan Economic Weekly*, 15 June 1996, in "Pros, Cons of Central Asian Rail Noted," *FBIS-NES, FTS199615000010*, 15 June 1996.
29. IRNA, 20 May 1998, in "Iran Offers Transport, Trade Link to Central Asian States," *FBIS-NES, FTS19980521000275*, 21 May 1998. India was one of the first to support such a route. See *The Hindu*, 21 May 1996, as cited in "Opening of Ancient Links With Central Asian States Viewed," *FBIS-NES, FTS19960521000401*, 21 May 1996.
30. Aleksei Baliyev, "Volga Flows into Indian Ocean? Large-Scale Geopolitics—In Our Hands," *Rossiiskaya gazeta*, 3 April 1998, p. 11; Aleksei Chichkin, Tatyana Smolyakov, and Aleksandr Shinkin, "Sensation! Sensation? Will the Volga Flow into the Persian Gulf?" 5 August 1996, as cited in "Officials Said Ignorant of Caspian-Gulf Canal Scheme," *FBIS-NES, FTS19960805000535*, 5 August 1996.

31. John Anderson, "Authoritarian Political Development in Central Asia: The Case of Turkmenistan," *Central Asian Survey* 14:4, 1995, pp. 509–527. See also Shahram Akbarzadeh, "National Identity and Political Legitimacy in Turkmenistan," *Nationalities Papers* 27:2, 1999, pp. 271–290. Tribalism was given serious consideration as a destabilizing factor in this case. See especially pp. 282–283.
32. The political and economic impact of the Russian legacy on Turkmen water supplies and distribution illustrated the types of problems Central Asian countries suffered from. See Sarah L. O'Hara and Tim Hannan, "Irrigation and Water Management in Turkmenistan: Past Systems, Present Problems and Future Scenarios," *Europe-Asia Studies* 51:1, 1999, pp. 21–41.
33. Shireen T. Hunter, "Central Asia and the Middle East: Patterns of Interaction and Influence," *Central Asia Monitor*, number 6, 1992, p. 14.
34. *Nezavisimaya gazeta*, 20 December 1997, p. 3, in "Closer Military Integration in C. Asia Eyed," *FBIS-NES, FTS19971224000203*, 24 December 1997.
35. Theodore Karasik, "Rising Russian Security and Intelligence Objectives in Central Asia," *Central Asia-Caucasus Monitor*, 15 April 2000 via www.cacianalyst.org.

# PART III

*Trends for the Future*

… CHAPTER 22

## The UAE Vision for Gulf Security
### Sultan bin Zayed bin Sultan Al Nahyan

Although the United Arab Emirates (UAE) is a medium-size power with several regional contentions, it has a keen sense of history and, more importantly, fully understands its anticipated role in the Gulf region. Much is expected from Abu Dhabi as a "State"—especially from Emiratis who look to their leaders to fulfill the legacy that Shaykh Zayed bin Sultan and his fellow rulers set some 30 years ago. Our responsibilities to our citizens are clear and must be satisfied in toto if we are to meet our regional role. That purpose, to foster positive ties with our neighbors and play a moderating leadership role in the international arena, is not easy to accomplish. But we do not choose to follow the easy path. On the contrary, we choose the difficult course because that gives us the motivation to excel. At times, our intentions and capabilities may seem disjointed, but our vision for Gulf security is certain. Because the Gulf is our home, and allies and neighbors surround us, our ultimate goal is to strengthen existing bonds, and establish closer associations in the few cases where past differences separated us from each other. Abu Dhabi looks at the region with hope, not fear. We intend to increase confidence-building measures to further narrow sociopolitical gaps, all to better serve Emiratis. We owe it to the next generation to set new markers of friendship and cooperation, not just in words but also in deeds.

What Abu Dhabi hopes in its relations with Iran, Iraq, and the other states on the Arabian Peninsula are measured and reciprocal ties, which support mutually beneficial policies. We do not crave territory nor seek to acquire material goods or resources. On the contrary, as Shaykh Zayed has amply demonstrated, we are prepared to share our wealth and resources to achieve regional stability. Still, we are also firmly determined to defend ourselves and our interests—which, hopefully, are identical to those of our allies and neighbors—at all costs, because it is through self-reliance and confidence that we can be good neighbors. Of course, we rely on our allies—both regional and international—to preserve our freedoms, but those associations are defensive in nature and spirit. There is no denying that our region has, unfortunately, experienced two recent bloody confrontations whose legacies will mark all of our societies for years to come.

The Iran-Iraq War and the War for Kuwait are stark reminders of how elusive the search for regional security might be. Nevertheless, we are determined to pursue our objectives no matter how difficult these challenges may be. We are equally determined to find positive language with both Iran and Iraq, the two northern Gulf powers with regional hegemonic aspirations. Our long-term success, or failure, will surely be determined by our abilities to persuade Iran and Iraq to abandon these elusive hegemonic ambitions and to join us in building for the future.

Still, we are under no illusions. Iran is reeling under the unfolding repercussions of the 1979 Islamic Revolution that changed the ideological nature of the area's most populous country. Although President Mohammed Khatami continues to espouse moderate policies that are encouraging and engaging, Teheran's rhetoric outpaces its actions. Naturally, we in the UAE are impressed by President Khatami's desire to extend bridges of cooperation and, toward that end, want to work closely with his administration to help resolve—once and for all—our territorial dispute. Similarly, we intend to establish bridges of friendship with Iraq, especially the beleaguered Iraqi people, who are victims of mistaken policies—both by Baghdad as well as major Western powers who seek to influence President Saddam Hussein by punishing a hapless population—because Iraq is our neighbor and because the Iraqi people are part and parcel of our societies. We must forgive past errors, open new pages, and eradicate the scourge of war from our area. To accomplish those objectives, it is essential that we look at Iraq with a human face rather than the cold and calculating real-politik perspectives that seek to reward the strong and punish the weak.

Finally, the UAE must also concentrate on the Arabian Peninsula by forging even ties with Bahrain, Kuwait, Oman, Qatar, Saudi Arabia, and Yemen. As the UAE considers the Arabian Peninsula its natural cocoon, our alliances with fellow Gulf Cooperation Council members are "partnerships-in-peace." Likewise, Abu Dhabi looks to Sanaa with a clear perspective, to include Yemen in the Peninsula's sociopolitical life, even as it has been in it all along.

The UAE can indeed achieve all of these objectives by remaining true to its character and by pursuing the wise policies established by Shaykh Zayed bin Sultan. Our vision is that of peacemakers who are committed to freedom, the pursuit of cooperative ventures, and the establishment of permanent foundations for the next generations of Emiratis.

### Key Strategic Aims

The paramount strategic objective of the UAE in the Gulf region is to preserve and protect the country's independence and territorial integrity from regional foes. Toward that end, and while Abu Dhabi looks at its neighbors with respect, it has no illusions about intentions that run contrary to neighborly connections. In addition to Iran and Iraq, the UAE aims to improve ties with Yemen, and within the GCC. Our recognition that relations can and must be improved implies that they are not ideally suited. In fact, and despite gargantuan efforts made by Shaykh Zayed, problems linger. Some of these deserve careful assessments, and it is up to us to strengthen existing intra-GCC closeness, to better accomplish our objectives.

## *UAE Intentions*

Since its inception in 1971, the UAE has fostered two fundamental principles, namely the development of the country's human capital and the wise use of its limited natural resources. Our history defines us and we are aware of the tremendous opportunity that the discovery and exploitation of oil has given us. Yet, as Shaykh Zayed and his fellow rulers understood, without intrinsic human capital, all of that wealth might just as well be left underground. We are duty-bound to equip our citizens with the best know-how that we can muster at all costs. Indeed, that is what we are doing, and are committed to for the foreseeable future.

Because the country lacked the human capital to best exploit its resources and build from the ground up, the UAE welcomed a huge number of hard-working expatriates from around the world. Their sacrifices and contributions are undeniable and Emiratis are grateful that so many did so much. While most were financially compensated, what is far more important and must be acknowledged, is that the vast majority were separated both from their families and from their countries. These tremendous sacrifices helped the UAE, and every expatriate resident of the UAE has his or her name etched in our honor rolls. Equally important, and because we welcomed individuals from so many countries, this international presence influenced our foreign and defense policies.

To be sure, the UAE has pursued an Arab foreign policy agenda because it is an Arab country with established social, cultural, and religious ties with the rest of the Arab world. We never doubted or questioned our intrinsic credentials. Even if we fell on the periphery of the Arab world, almost on the edge of the Arabian Peninsula, our Arab credentials were impeccable. Starting in 1971, we stood by our brethren in the Levant and, after the 1973 October War between Israel and several Arab states, Shaykh Zayed initiated the selected oil embargo against the United States and the Netherlands. At the time, our aim was to instill a sense of urgency and, in no uncertain terms, to help persuade major Western powers that Arab views deserved consideration. Even if our successes in this respect were limited, long-held attitudes—ranging from the Orientalist perspective to the "missionary" variety—began to change, and for the better. We played a modest role in shaping Arab policies that added value to the Emirates while it enhanced the overall Arab position. The hundreds of thousands of Arab expatriates, who resided in the UAE, certainly played significant roles in our direction, even if we were in total agreement with their perspectives.

Within the larger Gulf region as well, the UAE's established linkages with Omanis, Pakistanis, Indians, Baluchis, Iranians, and many other nationalities before 1971 certainly guided Emirati leaders' foreign policies after independence. Our tribal inclinations for tolerance and mutual respect were further enhanced by the many contacts that we have had with our neighbors. Long before the Arab Gulf countries joined into an alliance, Emiratis appreciated the tremendous sacrifices that so many of its residents made in fostering closer associations with their respective states.

### The GCC Alliance
Given this legacy, it was natural that the six Arab Gulf countries would join ranks in the Gulf Cooperation Council in 1981. Although the GCC was constituted to meet the challenges created by the 1979 Iranian revolution, the Soviet invasion of Afghanistan, and the 1980 Iran-Iraq War, it was also a natural progression. Going back centuries, Gulf populations shared far more in common than generally assumed. Tribal ties and migrations did not recognize artificial boundaries. Contacts between various communities were ongoing irrespective of what tribal or colonial leaders wished. No matter how determined outsiders were to divide and rule, their reach did not go beyond the surface. Deep-seated bonds that united—and separated—the populations of the Lower Gulf could not be erased.

Still, political necessity brought the six Arab Gulf states together. Prodded by some, and encouraged by others, they embarked on a unique alliance in modern Arab affairs. The GCC states faced clear and specific threats and were determined to address them without hesitation. Much was expected from each member state and even more from GCC leaders. Against some odds, the GCC accomplished a great deal, even if the progress was not always properly measured. The type of political coordination that occurred for the better part of the last two decades was also unique in Arab annals. Because Arab leaders have not publicly revealed their approaches and strategies, the general assumption has been that the GCC was nothing more than a paper tiger, whereas, in reality, the GCC became a stream of political consciousness. Undeniably, the member states held on to their cherished policies and only supported the GCC when it suited them, but on major foreign policy questions, GCC states agreed to preserve the alliance at all costs. GCC leaders learned to trust and, over time, rely on expert opinion as they formulated foreign policy initiatives. In that sense alone, the GCC's accomplishments must rank very high indeed. As far as the UAE is concerned, the GCC proved to be a valuable forum for debate, and while major differences remained, Abu Dhabi perceived the organization as a useful alliance.

If in recent years the UAE failed to gain the GCC's undivided support—regarding its territorial dispute with Iran—Abu Dhabi ascertained that the primary reason for that deterioration was directly related to the Saudi-Iranian rapprochement. Although the UAE supported an overall harmonization with Iran, it preferred a more comprehensive approach, one that would focus on the territorial integrity of every member state. In the event, different interpretations emerged that contradicted previous GCC declarations. Still, the UAE relied on its internal strengths to help resolve its dispute with Iran, without abandoning the GCC mechanism.

### Iranian Cooperation
Short of the GCC mechanism, the UAE has three basic options to settle its dispute over the Iranian occupation of Abu Musa and the two—Greater and

Lesser—Tunb islands, namely reliance on the International Court of Justice (ICJ), reliance on third party mediation, and direct negotiations. Because direct negotiations and third party mediation proved to be elusive, Shaykh Zayed has repeatedly called on Iranian leaders to seek the ICJ's intervention, to permanently solve this festering problem. Naturally, the ideal would be for the UAE and Iran to negotiate in full, and reach a mutually satisfactory solution. The UAE is prepared to embark on such negotiations as well as eager to welcome genuine third party mediation efforts. Yet, because Teheran remains adamant and refuses to engage the UAE on an equal footing, it has become next to impossible to decipher a way out. Shaykh Zayed's consensus-driven policy, which is the unanimous policy of the UAE, has emphasized the need for a peaceful settlement and, short of a mutually agreed solution, to rely on the expertise and justice of the ICJ. The UAE will remain optimistic that such a conclusion may indeed be possible and will continuously urge Teheran to reciprocate.

Lest one conclude that the UAE-Iran islands dispute is the only concern between the GCC states and their northern neighbor, it is important to emphasize that the GCC was created, first and foremost, to meet the challenges posed by the 1979 Islamic Revolution and its potential spillover effects on the Arabian Peninsula. Over the years, the UAE, along with several other Gulf states, played a vital role in limiting the spillover effects of the revolution. At a time when Iran was isolated from the rest of the world, and under an economic and military embargo—at least for most of the 1980s and early 1990s—the UAE played the vital role of retaining certain channels open. We encouraged trade—limited as it was—because it was not in the interests of the Gulf states to strangulate Iran. To be sure, the UAE paid a heavy price for that policy, including assorted smuggling activities that drew the ire of the international community, but we did not punish the suffocating Iranian people. As neighbors and fellow Muslims, we simply could not turn a blind eye on their pain, and did whatever we could to help alleviate it. It is, therefore, doubly stressing to find ourselves at different ends of the spectrum.

Still, the UAE hopes that President Mohammed Khatami will welcome Shaykh Zayed's overtures for peace and the settlement of the islands dispute, either directly or through the ICJ. At the end of the day, what matters is to resolve this festering contest, and establish proper bonds with Iran. We genuinely care about the welfare of the Iranian population and wish to extend our hands in friendship even if we will not surrender one square inch of our national territory. Iran and the UAE have rich historical ties and we must start re-acculturating our respective societies to step away from the xenophobia that allows outsiders to exploit existing differences.

### *Iraqi Cooperation*
Just as we could not turn our backs on the distress of the Iranian populace, we adopted and followed a similar approach with respect to Iraq, even if the UAE stood with Kuwait and the rest of the GCC states against Saddam Hussein. Clearly, the 1990 Iraqi invasion of Kuwait altered the regional balance of power,

which could not be tolerated. It was a foregone conclusion that the UAE would stand with its beleaguered GCC ally. In the event, Kuwait was liberated and Baghdad soundly defeated, even if few Arabs—including Gulf Arabs—rejoiced at the wholesale destruction of Iraqi society, which bore a heavy burden for its leaders' mistakes. After a decade, and at the dawn of the twenty-first century, it is vital that we re-evaluate the current United Nations–imposed policy that is literally choking Iraqis.

Naturally, GCC states' financial assistance to Iraq, which over the years amounted to substantial sums, did not moderate Baathi hegemonic aspirations. Nevertheless, Iraq was and remains of strategic value to the Arab world because it offers geographic depths, provides trained manpower, and controls substantial natural resources, including water and oil. We value Iraq as a determinant factor in Arab affairs. As stated above, the UAE has become a cradle of liberty in the Gulf region, because our varied inhabitants determine the course of its actions. What we clearly object to is stripping any Arabs, including Iraqis, of their religious and political freedoms.

UAE strategic interests require that Iraq be brought out of its current doldrums and be re-integrated in the family of nation-states. While recognizing that the tasks ahead are gargantuan, it is still essential to establish the basis for consultation and cooperation, whenever possible. Every day that Iraq is isolated is a day lost for Arab unity. Every day that Iraq is ostracized is a day that adds to the roster of future opposition forces. Every day that Iraq is cornered is a day that increases the pain of its population. Our objective is to bring Arabs closer to each other. We value the Iraqi populace and wish to cooperate with it to foster mutually beneficial policies, enhance trade opportunities, and intensify our cultural, educational, and scientific links. In addition to these concerns, our openness to Iraq is also a matter of basic human rights, for it is unconscionable to allow Iraqi men, women, and children to wallow in misery, the way they are through no fault of their own. Future generations of Emiratis and Arabs will not look kindly on leaders who turned their backs to the sufferings of the Iraqi population, and this too must change, if long-term Emirati interests are to be preserved.

### *Relations with Major Western Powers*
Because of well-known Iranian and Iraqi hegemonic aspirations in the Gulf region, eminently displayed by various invasions and occupations, the UAE and its GCC partners turned to key Western powers for security assistance. Over the years, that natural turn of events promoted close ties between Abu Dhabi and London, Washington, and Paris. Although the UAE was served well by such security assistance, it must be clearly acknowledged that Western powers did not miss opportunities to advance their own narrow interests either. For most, access to secure sources of petroleum was the paramount reason for whatever human and material sacrifices they made. There was little attention to local needs, especially before 1990, when the Gulf region fell within the Western orbit of the larger East-West divide. After 1990, Western powers could no longer ignore intrinsic Gulf interests, some of which stood out as peculiarly different. For example, the UAE and its regional partners keenly supported the Palestinian and

Lebanese peoples, and opposed Washington's approach in helping settle the Arab-Israeli conflict. Whenever we expressed our views to our interlocutors, chances were excellent that we would be ignored, even if eloquent promises were made. Times have changed and, although our views are still not given the serious attention they deserve, at least they are no longer ignored. In recent years, we have been successful in creating linkages between our security needs and whatever may be on the agenda with major Western powers. Security interests were no longer the purview of an association with a single power, and following in the wise policies of Shaykh Zayed, we adopted a multi-pronged approach to balancing our commitments with the permanent members of the United Nations Security Council.

This is a fundamental principle of UAE foreign policy, that our strategic interests require cooperation with several allies, and that we are beholden to none. Toward that end, Abu Dhabi has established and supports the development of proper ties with Beijing, London, Moscow, Paris, and Washington. We seek enduring associations even if we realize that states have raw interests. We are beholden to our principles of fair play. And we are committed to basic Arab causes with all the baggage that such support carries. Not doing so would betray our commitments to ourselves and to the larger Arab and Muslim worlds of which we are an integral part.

### Vision for Gulf Security

To be sure, our cooperative strategic aims have not always been accomplished and, in the process, our vision for Gulf security has not always been applied. A number of extraneous forces pre-determined the extent to which these aims were implemented, including the presence of major powers in the area, and Gulf states' dependence on foreign forces for security. Nevertheless, and despite many shortcomings, the UAE and its GCC partners pursued independent foreign policies—especially after the establishment of the GCC in May 1981. For small and relatively weak states, these convergences proved far more difficult to implement than generally assumed, because conflicting views shaped emerging perceptions.

For centuries, extraneous forces controlled the destinies of the tribal entities that covered the Arabian Peninsula, because the latter were relatively weak. Long-term occupiers included the Ottomans, Portuguese, French, and the British. More recently, American forces established an over-the-horizon presence, and after the 1991 War for Kuwait, a more direct—though United Nations–sanctioned—presence. It is an undeniable fact that all littoral countries, including Iran and Iraq, share specific navigation and exploitation responsibilities within the Gulf. Simply stated, the waterway is our lifeline, and although the UAE and the Sultanate of Oman have alternative accesses to the Arabian Sea, part of the UAE strategic aim focuses on freedom of navigation through it. Abu Dhabi encourages all littoral states to settle their territorial disputes peacefully and to concentrate on improved trade ties between all concerned.

The UAE and its GCC allies opted to build intrinsic defensive capabilities and deter potential aggressors. Abu Dhabi has no territorial claims on any state and only intends to defend itself from regional hegemons or opportunistic aggressors. It should, therefore, come as no surprise that its first line of defense is the Gulf itself.

### Defense Policy

To deter regional hegemons and opportunistic aggressors, the UAE has devoted a substantial portion of its financial resources to acquire defense-related weapons systems. Moreover, and especially after the 1991 War for Kuwait, Abu Dhabi signed several agreements with key Western allies to help the country defend its territorial integrity. Even if some of these purchases or defense accords seemed exaggerated, the country's overall position required them. Against some odds, when so little existed on the ground at independence, the UAE managed to establish a basic defense infrastructure. Its citizens found merit in defending the Emirates because most concluded that the UAE was truly their nation even if the concept was recent and still "under construction." Without any illusions, Abu Dhabi realized that transforming seven uniquely defined Emirates into a federated state necessitated serious commitments, and it is to its founding leaders' credit that so much was accomplished over so little time.

It is important to emphasize, once again, that UAE defense policies were only unified in recent years, after the strains of early federation were overcome. Confidence-building measures within the federation finally matured to a level that allowed all of its member states to adopt identical policies. In fact, Dubai agreed to integrate its separate units within the UAE Armed Forces in 1998, further illustrating the major advances that were achieved on this front.

Given these policy formulations, the federal government assumed the full gamut of all its member states' many contentions with regional powers, including the Abu Musa and the two Tunb islands altercation with Iran, and the various border variances with Oman, Qatar, and Saudi Arabia. In other words, and although the Abu Musa and the two Tunb islands were issues of concern to Ras al-Khaimah and Sharjah, Abu Dhabi did not forgo its federal responsibilities. Toward that end, it assumed the leadership mantle, as Shaykh Zayed championed various solutions to reach a peaceful settlement with Teheran. Finally, and after several years of constant negotiations, Abu Dhabi reached an understanding with Oman to negotiate on behalf of the six federation members whose territories touched the Omani border.

While these mutually beneficial steps enhanced our relationships with key neighbors, and while Shaykh Zayed has repeatedly called on Iran to settle the islands dispute peacefully, the UAE required defense alliances with major Western powers to deter any force from endangering our independence. Naturally, that pursuit meant that the UAE would depend on these extraneous forces, even if that dependence carried certain consequences on internal UAE affairs. Emiratis reject most Western powers' so-called Middle East policies and fail to understand how local leaders stand by such naïve and shortsighted interpretations. In truth, UAE leaders navigate these waters with the utmost care, to protect their legitimacies while honoring various defense commitments.

*Foreign Policy*

Although we rely on our friends and our allies to provide us with the support and wherewithal required to defend our country, we realize that we must, first and foremost, rely on ourselves. Toward that end, the UAE has forged an independent foreign policy, to better serve its citizens and promote its interests throughout the world. The major principles of that foreign policy are centered around our commitment to freedom, the pursuit of cooperative ventures, and the establishment of mutually beneficial ties, with all.

Naturally, as an Arab country, we strive to coordinate our foreign policy initiatives within a well-defined sphere. Arab concerns are dear to us and we seek to implement what we determine to be in the interests of our nation. Within the Gulf region, more specifically, we are committed to bridging all existing gaps with Iran and Iraq. We do not crave territory and genuinely seek cooperation with our northern neighbors. We adhere to the principles of mutual interest with all, but especially with our neighbors, because what may affect them could have serious repercussions on our society. Foreign policy coordination within the GCC alliance is even more important because we share so much with our friends on the Arabian Peninsula. It is worth repeating that while GCC states may interpret specific concerns from various angles, our views on fundamental issues are identical. We very much hope that joint foreign policy initiatives that serve all member states will be adopted even if narrower matters linger. Our intention is to strengthen the alliance, and even if periodic disagreements or contradictory interpretations arise, we do not let these deter us from the May 1981 march.

As stated above, we also rely on our Western allies and, toward that end, consider their interests carefully. Britain, France, and the United States, in particular, clearly share in the objective to maintain stability throughout the Gulf region. We are amply aware of how major powers, especially the United States, perceive us and devise foreign policy initiatives that serve specific interests. It is for this reason that we constantly sensitize Washington to the many vagaries of the Arab-Israeli conflict. Shaykh Zayed and his fellow rulers trust that the United States, as well as all of our Western allies, will consider these issues more carefully and reciprocate.

## Conclusion

UAE leaders are peacemakers and, as repeatedly demonstrated by Shaykh Zayed, our vision for Gulf security is to preserve every state's interests. Our country harbors no ill will and has no territorial ambitions of any kind. We aim to foster close associations with our neighbors and seek to trade with the rest of the world in an atmosphere of peace and prosperity.

What we strive to accomplish is to provide for the welfare of our people, add value for future generations of Emiratis, defuse regional tensions once and for all, encourage the creation of wealth both at home and throughout the area, and pursue noble objectives for abundant life, increased freedoms, and augmented happiness. These are not easy to attain and we are aware of the many dangers looming over the horizon. Yet, we chose to initiate such objectives because Emiratis deserve nothing less. Our history compels us to overcome hardships no matter how strenuous and, as UAE leaders have illustrated since 1971, assume enormous responsibilities. Relying on our people and ourselves, we hold our heads high, as we forge ahead.

# TRENDS IN GULF AFFAIRS

CHAPTER 23

## *The Gulf Cooperation Council: Future Trends*
Saif bin Hashil Al-Maskery

The Gulf region has been important to world powers—economically, politically, and militarily—long before the discovery and exploration of oil. In fact, the region was a major transit point for trade from Europe to Asia and Africa that, over the centuries, developed into unique patterns. Portugal, Holland, France, and Britain competed for influence by dominating, at one point or another, the entire region. Still, with the discovery of oil, and starting in the 1960s, the Gulf's economic importance increased dramatically. The region gained additional value for key industrial countries—in particular the United States—after 1973, when oil prices rose from $3 a barrel to almost $35. This concrete demonstration highlighted the level of dependence in the clearest terms yet. In turn, industrial countries perceived the region as a "national security" arena, warranting a series of doctrines and assorted policies. As former U.S. president Jimmy Carter declared in 1979, any outside power attempting to gain control of this region would be regarded as a threat to Washington's *vital* interests, facing potential retaliation, with force if necessary.

To fulfill specific doctrines, successive American administrations aimed to partially accomplish their objectives—denying the area to outside forces and benefiting from its natural resources—by providing sophisticated arms to several Gulf states that, presumably, would ensure stability and guarantee the free flow of oil at reasonable prices. Yet, this approach backfired, when the Shah of Iran was overthrown in early 1979. Iran, which was regarded by the West as a major stabilizing force in the Gulf region, became a far greater threat than anyone in Washington or London ever anticipated. Even when the two major Gulf powers, Iran and Iraq, engaged in an eight-year war that stopped in August 1988, few anticipated the economic strangulation that resulted especially for Baghdad. Less than two years later, Iraq invaded Kuwait, which, ironically, ensured a permanent American regional presence. Consequently, Washington, London, and Paris became the arbiters of Gulf security and stability. Together, these two wars provided major powers the justification to adopt specific foreign policy initiatives that did not always coincide with, or best serve, the interests of the Gulf states.

Today, the Gulf states face new challenges to counter not only external threats but, more important, several internal challenges. To their credit, several Gulf leaders have indeed recognized a few notable challenges and have started acting on them, even if the initiatives are slow or sometimes adopted just for cosmetic purposes. How Gulf leaders understand the present situation, and prepare for future challenges, deserves attention if genuine stability is to be secured throughout the region.

### The Vacuous Pre-1971 Period

Given the legacy of British rule that lasted over a century and a half, it is critical to briefly discuss the consequences of this presence, and to highlight key developments before London withdrew its military forces from the area. Prior to 1971, the region was relatively stable, even though the states and shaykhdoms—as well as the sultanate—on the Arabian Peninsula lacked the amenities of modern countries. There were no schools. There were no hospitals. The economy was dependent on narrow trade activities, mostly pearl diving, and some fishing. At that time, the Gulf countries had no independent political activities worthy of any consideration because of various clauses in so-called treaties of amity signed with Britain. Shortly after the 1952 Egyptian revolution, and the rise of pan-Arabism, a few political movements started to flourish in Iraq, Bahrain, and Yemen.

Iraq, at that time, was not a stable country because of military coups and counter-coups. Bahrain faced various labor disturbances, and Yemen was very weak, with unending internal tribal wars. In Iran, Prime Minister Mossadeq organized a sustained shake-up, but was ousted in no time. By 1953, Shah Muhammad Reza, who was assisted by the West to become a watchdog in the Gulf, regained his throne. The other Gulf States had political movements in various stages of development, often trained and backed by East European countries in the name of world socialism.

When Britain declared its intention to withdraw from East of Suez in 1968, the region entered into a frenzied search for adequate security, ostensibly provided in toto by London. The 1968 declaration, made as the Labour government of Prime Minister Harold Wilson faced financial catastrophe, was implemented within three short years. Even if Gulf leaders intended to assume their fair share of responsibilities or enter into arrangements with other Western powers, the 1971 military withdrawal created a political vacuum. The region was literally left vulnerable to outside threats. In the event, Iran took the opportunity to control the Gulf, by occupying the UAE islands of Abu Musa and the Greater and Lesser Tunbs. In fact, and partly as a result of earlier Iranian declarations, several Gulf rulers attempted to persuade Britain to delay its withdrawal, offering to financially compensate London. Although the request was couched in appropriate diplomatic language, the offer was genuine because Gulf rulers appreciated their limitations, and because of existing perceptions of the putative Soviet threat to the area. It may be worth recalling that Moscow's presence in Iraq and South Yemen, themselves revolutionary regimes in their own rights, shaped Gulf rulers' evolving security perceptions.

As these understandings evolved, Gulf rulers also reacted to the Western—especially American—view that considered the Shah of Iran as a "suitable" partner, to maintain regional stability and protect intrinsic Western interests. Inasmuch as the Cold War divided the world into a bipolar system, Gulf rulers reacted to the great divide emerging throughout the area. They knew that the Soviet Union perceived revolutionary Iraq as an ally—and armed that country with sophisticated weapons—even if the West paid lip service to their legitimate needs. Equally important, Gulf rulers were wary of Soviet support of domestic "political" movements that aimed to destabilize their regimes. Finally, Gulf rulers retained their skepticism of Iran—because of the Shah's expansionist ambitions—even if they accepted the Shah as a fellow anti-communist monarch with whom they could do business.

The multiplicity of, at times contradictory, views that Gulf rulers held left most of them "unprotected." What emerged, therefore, were fragile political entities, best exemplified by the 1971 Iranian invasion of the three UAE islands, against which little could be done.

### The Menacing 1971-to-1979 Period

If the pre-1971 period produced fragile political entities that faced the dual challenges of state and nation building, the next decade underscored the almost obsessive approach to Gulf security that Arab Gulf rulers embarked upon.

In 1968, Baghdad entered into its Ahmad Bakr/Saddam Hussein era, which provided stability in Iraq, albeit through brutal means. Supported by the Soviet Union and several Western powers—including the United States, Britain, and France—Iraq built its armed forces, as well its economy. Although key Western countries first opted to isolate Baghdad—thereby leaving the field wide open to the Soviets—most courted Iraq after the Shah's throne started to vacillate. Moscow benefited from its prowess, however, by entering into a valuable strategic alliance with Iraq that certainly served its interests well. Simultaneously, this presence in a major Arab state provided the opportunities to pressure Gulf rulers by organizing, training, and financing so-called opposition political movements. Many flourished in various Gulf countries with support channeled via Baghdad and, in time, Aden in the People's Democratic Republic of Yemen.

The decade's other major development with a clear impact on the Gulf area was the October 1973 Arab-Israeli War. As a direct consequence of this epoch-making confrontation, leading oil producers initiated an embargo against the United States and the Netherlands, specifically to counter the accelerated military transfers approved by Washington to Israel. Within a very short period of time, the price of oil rose from $3 to $35 a barrel, with an immediate transfer of large financial resources to oil-producing countries. In turn, these transfers created a large surplus of funds, which helped Gulf states build modern institutions and sorely lacking infrastructures. In the event, significant expenditures quickly turned the Gulf states into Western "clients," especially for sophisticated—and expensive—weapons systems.

Within less than a decade, the Gulf states' large oil and financial reserves altered their positions in the world economy. Ironically, the added notoriety, as well as enhanced capabilities—as limited as they were—did not dramatically improve regional stability. On the contrary, because the whole international economy was disrupted, Gulf states were perceived as a burden. The entire region became "vital" to the rest of the world.

To ensure their intrinsic interest—a guaranteed free flow of oil at reasonable prices—key Western powers, led by the United States, increased their sales of sophisticated weapons systems: to Iran without much hesitation, and to the Gulf states with some restrictions. The American assistance to Saudi Arabia was a tricky proposition because Washington did not want to upset Israel. This was amply clear during the long and truncated congressional debate over the sale of F-15s and AWACS sentry aircraft, although Riyadh paid for the platforms and committed not to transfer the technologies to third parties. Far more important, Western sales to Iran and Saudi Arabia further isolated Iraq, and encouraged its gradual migration toward the Soviet camp. The 1970s ended with the Soviet invasion of Afghanistan, placing Moscow less than 500 kilometers from the Gulf region. Simultaneously, the Soviet Union built a strong presence in South Yemen, posing a real threat to the Gulf states.

All of these factors ripened the Gulf states for potential conflicts, nestled between two international superpowers on the one hand, and two regional superpowers (Iraq and Iran) on the other.

### The Turbulent 1980-to-1988 Period

Just before the Shah of Iran was overthrown in 1979, his Western allies realized that they would eventually have to deal with a very independent Peacock Throne were he to remain in power. Simply stated, the Pahlavi dynasty's hold on Iran and, indirectly, on the Gulf region was powerful. Although the subject of heated debates, it now seems certain that Western elements, if not governments, encouraged opposition forces. By welcoming Ayatollah Khomeini into France, ostensibly on the grounds of human rights concerns, the West provided the austere cleric with a base of operations and quality media coverage of all of his activities. Even if Western governments believed that the Shah, with further assistance from Washington, would be able to contain the growing uprising, few were actually persuaded that returning him to Teheran—as in 1953—would save the Peacock Throne. In the event, Western hesitancy and miscalculations of the Khomeini fervor ensured the establishment of the Islamic Republic of Iran.

It is important to state without any ambiguity that the 1979 revolution distorted most Western calculations in the Gulf region. In fact, the revolution was perceived as the greatest threat to Western interests in the Gulf, even if later developments would alter this obtuse view. To be sure, the slogans of the new Islamic regime—to export the revolution to the Lower Gulf and, eventually, to the rest of the world—preoccupied many. In time, the revolution was accepted as a genuine domestic Iranian phenomenon, with legitimate aspects.

Still, to placate their miscalculation, Western powers, led by the United States, slowly developed a dual perception of threat by lumping Iran with Iraq in their regional formulations. Given that both countries expressed expansionist ambitions toward the Gulf, starting with the 1980 Iran-Iraq War, the dual approach seemed to function well. Moreover, with significant internal turmoil, it was reasoned that Iraq needed an external foe. As Baghdad did not detect any Western opposition to its choreographed intentions toward Iran—ostensibly to limit the spillover effects of the Islamic Revolution—Saddam Hussein's regime committed one of several major blunders by invading its large and powerful neighbor.

The Iran-Iraq War lasted a full eight years before Teheran accepted a United Nations Security Council–brokered cease-fire resolution. Because so many events were directly tied to the war, a brief discussion of its three distinct phases is warranted.

1. In the first phase of the war, which lasted from 1980 to 1982, Iraq attacked Iran, voraciously destroying many Iranian border cities. Baghdad gained full control over the 30 kilometer Shatt al-Arab waterway, which it had agreed to share with Iran pursuant to the 1975 Algiers Accord, hastily arranged to end Iranian support to Kurdish separatist movements in the north. Between 1980 and 1982, various reports implied that Washington shared advanced satellite-gathered data with Iraq, ostensibly to "better defeat the Iranian foe." In response, Iran threatened to close the strategic Straits of Hormuz, by sinking one or more ships that would have strangulated the oil lifeline.

The Gulf states, for their part, felt threatened by the war. Although they had no trust in the belligerents, they nevertheless were obligated to support Iraq financially—and in some instances, logistically—because Arab Iraq was engaged in a conflict with Persian Iran. If the 1979 Iranian revolution motivated Gulf rulers to act, the 1980 Iran-Iraq War provided them with the excuse to allay whatever mistrusts they may have had, to finally act collectively. Hence, in May 1981, Gulf rulers gathered in Abu Dhabi to formally announce the establishment of the Gulf Cooperation Council (GCC). Importantly, the first heads of state statement—as expressed in the founding charter of the institution—called on all six states to cooperate *in all fields* (eventually leading to a political unity). Not surprisingly, the language of the charter, and the resolutions and communiqués that followed, were intentionally vague. Yet, security matters were the GCC's primary concern, as the organization's "efficacy" depended on fears of external threats. In times of peace, the mistrust and sensitivities among GCC states grew, but disappeared during periods of tension. Unfortunately, and because of evolving perceptions, there were no clear collective agendas, nor a shared vision for regional security among all member states. Each Gulf state looked at the GCC from a different angle. Several perceived the GCC as a tool to legalize their statehood. Others concluded that it was as good a platform as any to realize their political ambitions, while still others found it a useful vehicle for economic prosperity. Still, the Iran-Iraq War helped GCC states bring their concerns to the table, even if all of the many concerns that existed in 1981 were still present two decades later.

2. The next phase in the Iran-Iraq War, from 1983 to 1985, witnessed a relative lull in the fighting. Still, skirmishes continued, fueled by various efforts to

avoid a settlement. Irrespective of motives, the war provided lucrative opportunities to sell arms and, as a strategic bonus, to weaken both antagonists. Under such circumstances, oil prices should have risen, but they tumbled instead. GCC countries, especially Saudi Arabia, increased their oil production to cover Iraqi and Iranian shortfalls. It was then argued that additional sales were required to meet financial obligations for massive weapons purchases, but in reality the increased production came to mollify American pressure. Washington persuaded GCC producers that lower prices would undermine the Iranian economy, further weakening the Iranian revolution and limiting the spillover effects on the Arabian Peninsula.

Throughout this period of time, and having realized its colossal error, Iraq desperately sought to end the war. As a tactical step, and in yet another mistake, Baghdad targeted Iranian oil installations. Teheran retaliated by launching attacks on Iraqi tankers in the north, thereby initiating the so-called tanker war, which in turn rekindled industrial countries' interest in the conflict.

3. Heavy fighting between the belligerents marked the last phase of the war, between 1986 and 1988. Various reports implied that the United States provided some sort of assistance to both countries—to Iraq because Washington still perceived the Islamic Revolution as a threat, and because of lucrative opportunities in a post-war environment; to Iran to wiggle through the murky Iran-Contra machinations, which promised to free Western hostages in Lebanon. In the event, in August 1988, Iran accepted Security Council Resolution 598 and agreed to a cease-fire.

Throughout this period, GCC states provided substantial financial, political, and logistical assistance to Iraq. In return, Iraq successfully portrayed itself as the defender of GCC states—from Iranian expansionist ambitions—even if Gulf rulers were always wary of President Saddam Hussein. Naturally, GCC financial and political support to Iraq antagonized Iran, whose regional ambitions remained intact.

### From One War to Another: The 1988-to-1991 Period

Iraq portrayed itself as a winner in the long and protracted Iran-Iraq War. Millions of Arabs concurred. To be sure, the Iraqi army, straddled with an estimated million-strong population, emerged as a non-negligible force, with more experience than any of its neighbors. As a result of this "legacy," President Saddam Hussein was expected to play a greater role in the region, even if the Iraqi economy was in ruins. Despite GCC states' substantial financial support, Iraq demanded additional compensation for the alleged role played to defend them from Iran.

Simultaneously, Western countries, led by the United States, began to express their growing concerns about the world's "fourth largest army." This "anxiety" gained additional emphasis after Saddam Hussein's April 1990 declaration when the Iraqi strongman threatened to destroy half of Israel by using his super-gun. Iraq further hinted that GCC countries, led by Kuwait and the United Arab Emirates, were pumping additional oil to purposefully keep oil prices low—

thereby undermining the already weak Iraqi economy. Baghdad demanded appropriate financial compensation.

Naturally, this situation was not acceptable to GCC states or leading Western countries, because any control over the lucrative oil reserves of Arabia would mean that almost 60 percent of the world's oil reserves would be under Iraqi control. Hence, a new tactic was pursued by the West to frustrate Iraq and isolate it politically and economically from the Gulf states. Western powers accentuated the fear of a putative Iraqi takeover of the Gulf states. In turn, these steps enhanced existing tensions between Iraq and various GCC countries, as both sides fell into a trap. Accusations and counter-accusations among them ended in the Iraqi invasion of Kuwait in 1990, plunging the whole region into a much greater disaster than the Iran-Iraq War had produced. Once again Baghdad miscalculated, since Iraqi officials believed Western countries would turn a blind eye and allow the invasion to proceed unchecked.

Against this most ominous threat, GCC rulers placed aside differences and united to face the aggression. In the months preceding the 1991 War for Kuwait, Baghdad returned large portions of the Shatt al-Arab waterway to Iran—ostensibly to win Iranian support—but, at very high financial and political costs, Iraq was defeated and ejected from Kuwait in March 1991.

### The Post-1991 Period

The War for Kuwait established certain concrete truths in the Gulf region that must be acknowledged if future similar tragedies are to be avoided:

First, the dangers to regional states come from within the region. Although the Soviet Union and the United States attempted, at one point or another, to interject the Cold War into the area, the two contemporary and devastating wars were initiated by a Gulf state.

Second, GCC states remained vulnerable to outside threats, whether they originated from Iran or Iraq, as corollary, regional antagonisms accelerated foreign deployments on the Arabian Peninsula, further increasing tensions.

Third, GCC countries cannot protect themselves without substantial foreign assistance.

Fourth, all of the weapons systems that were procured by GCC governments—at substantial costs—did not prevent an actual invasion.

Fifth, GCC states were too politically weak to face the challenges posed by the two regional powers without foreign assistance.

Sixth, GCC countries lost confidence in each other, given fundamental differences on how best to tackle domestic and regional threats. In the event, GCC governments could not react positively to emerging situations, falling back on Western policies that were not always in their best interests. The fact that the United Nations sanctioned the War for Kuwait did not diminish the veracity of this variable, as subsequent entanglements between Iraq and United Nations inspectors amply demonstrated. While divisions and mistrust existed throughout the Arab world, what distinguished GCC states was precisely the promise that there was far more among them that existed in common than separated them. A full decade after the end of the War for Kuwait, both Iraq and the GCC countries are still paying a heavy price, given that both are relatively isolated from each other, Baghdad is under severe economic sanctions (with devastating consequences for its population), the adjusted real price of oil is at an all-time low, and GCC states are straddled with considerable financial burdens. Without any regional stability.

### The Elusive Search for Stability

After the War for Kuwait, GCC states entered yet another stage in their elusive search for regional stability. Three specific outlooks may be identified to analyze this investigation.

The first outlook depends primarily on key Western powers to prevent any Iraqi and Iranian expansionist ambitions from materializing. This is the most realistic outlook because of the balance of international and regional powers in favor of the West. Given that the current international system hovers around a unipolar orbit, regional initiatives will not be encouraged or tolerated with ease. Washington's so-called dual containment policies—toward Iran and Iraq—fall within this outlook. As clear evidence of the approach, both Iran and Iraq suffer under strict embargoes. For their part, Gulf states expressed a similar position, albeit in different ways, by accepting "security pacts" and "military exercises" with the United States and other Western powers. To be sure, these recent developments marked a sharp improvement in military equipment and training for GCC countries, but Western powers benefited as well because of rapid deployment opportunities for their air, land, and naval forces.

The second outlook is that the security of the Gulf is part of Arab national security. In the post-1991 period, this approach was articulated through a very limited Arab participation, namely by Syria and Egypt. The so-called GCC+2 approach was to "reward" Damascus and Cairo for their participation in the liberation of Kuwait. Given fundamental differences between the Gulf and the Levant, the "Damascus Declaration" is now almost forgotten, except on rare occasions when a shadowy and inconsequential meeting occurs. The reason for this lapse is due to the fact that most signatories have lost the initiative to search for an Arab solution to what ails Arab states. Moreover, not only was the declaration's timing ill-considered—made at the height of the crisis, when the region was in a state of doubt and insecurity—but it was also shepherded by Americans rather than Arabs. At the time, and since then, both Egypt and Syria pursued their own private agendas, which did not coincide with those of GCC states. Not surprisingly, the GCC+2 outlook caused uneasiness in Iran, which regarded this new Arab alliance as a danger to her putative role in the Gulf region.

The third outlook, though least accepted, is in fact the most realistic because of geographical and historical truths as well as the lessons learned from both wars. This outlook states that the threats come from within the region and that the security of the GCC is the responsibility of the six member states themselves. Oman championed this perspective during His Majesty Sultan Qaboos' chairmanship of the GCC Security Committee (formed in 1990 after the Kuwaiti invasion). The proposal called for a global security concept that would be based on an independent deterrent capability—an army under a professional leadership. More importantly, the proposal called for the creation of a regional cooperation mechanism to include *all Gulf countries*. In the event, the proposal was not accepted because of past failures, especially under Saudi leadership, within the modest Dara al-Jazirah (Peninsula Shield) force that is based in Hafr al-Batin, Saudi Arabia. It must be clearly stated that one of the major reasons that the concept was not seriously considered, despite its merits, was due to Saudi Arabia's keen desire to retain the leadership of the force. There was also the fear of additional financial responsibilities, to be borne mostly by Saudi Arabia, even though the proposal rested on a large Omani constituency.

The dangers of all the above three outlooks are clear. The first tolerates and encourages Western powers to secure their interests in the region without necessarily protecting or serving Gulf states. The danger of dependency on outside forces to provide security does not agree with the fact that the real threat to regional stability comes from within the region. Therefore, the continuous reliance on outside powers actually increases tensions, by jeopardizing the interests of local populations. Clearly, various social and financial implications exist that make such a continuous reliance extremely costly. One example of this phenomenon is the comparison of Gulf financial reserves before and after the 1991 war. Another is the addition of regular invoices submitted by Washington to GCC capitals for various American attacks on Iraq.

## Challenges and the Lack of Stability

Against this background, it is critical to identify the challenges facing Gulf states—as seen by a GCC citizen—to decipher how best to address them and secure effective stability. Two specific types of challenges, internal and external, are identified to better ascertain what needs to be done.

### *Internal Challenges*
Among the more important concerns that face GCC leaders and populations are:

1. Border disputes and differences that have led to mistrust between member states. Lingering disputes, which are periodically resurrected, tend to create a sense of instability that does not endear GCC citizens to each other.
2. Vacillating economic conditions that prevent the development of long-term policies. In the aftermath of the 1974 oil boom period, and the advent of genuine free trade, GCC citizens seek to increase their access to local, regional, and international markets. They aim to eliminate existing restrictions that prevent genuine expansion. The economic structure, which currently depends on only a single source of income—oil—cannot be in GCC citizens' long-term interests.
3. Fast-rising demographic conditions. Increases in GCC populations, with a high percentage of teenagers with minimal job opportunities, will surely

mean severe socioeconomic problems unless such needs are addressed in toto.
4. The quantitative and qualitative demographic differences that should be managed and, over time, addressed honestly. The makeup of populations throughout the region reveals that vast gaps exist between "neighbors." Iran, Iraq, and Yemen enjoy large populations, compared with much smaller figures for GCC states. Equally important are the large percentages of expatriate workers, especially from Asia, who are a potential security risk because of cultural, political, and social implications. Outside forces, ranging from international organizations to human rights movements, are pressuring GCC countries to provide their labor pools with political rights. Such developments may well leave serious political, as well as cultural, legacies that could ultimately change the Arab Islamic culture of the region.
5. Education throughout member states that should encourage modernization, substantial economic knowledge, and versatility to allow each citizen to reach his or her full potential.
6. The need for accelerated economic integration, as well as a collective strategy and vision among GCC states, to eliminate narrow and obtuse individual country initiatives.

**External Challenges**

Equally important are the external challenges, which are complex in nature compared with internal ones:

1. The need to recognize that globalization, with its various and evolving conditions, will provide international enterprises far better opportunities than any single GCC entity might be capable of. Therefore, it is vital that GCC states enter the global environment united, to better serve their citizens.
2. Human rights concerns. As alluded to above, leading industrialized countries, especially in the West, are constantly coercing GCC governments to address these matters in haste. While human rights issues are critical, GCC governments and populations cannot be expected to shepherd any policies with the speed or emphasis not of their choosing. It is important to nurture—through education—a sustained effort to have real and effective human rights initiatives.
3. Middle East peace activities, and what they imply as a new map of the region emerges, giving Israel a major role to play in regional affairs. The Gulf states are part and parcel of the Arab world and have a real stake in a just and lasting peace settlement that will not infringe on Palestinian rights.

**A Future Stability Outlook**

Undoubtedly, the lack of a clear collective vision is one of the main reasons why GCC efforts—to achieve regional stability—have not been successful, to date. A successful effort to achieve a fair regional security system necessitates a clear vision, to differentiate between static and dynamic factors and to balance regional and international responsibilities.

Clearly, the chief regional static factor is geography. Despite changing political systems, economic conditions, and the formation of alliances, regional geographic units remain the same. For example, while the political system in Iran changed, the country remained intact. Even if its putative alliance with the West was dropped by the Islamic regime, Teheran sought to trade with its neighbors, and beyond. Thus, regional political units require that stability be made in relation to, and in cooperation with, all states. Short of that, any long-term regional stability system will be impossible to achieve.

Moreover, it is also necessary to recognize the ability of GCC countries to play a regional role to achieve such stability, which would not be possible without their full participation. In other words, and while GCC governments face various internal challenges, nothing prevents them from active participation in genuine and effective regional initiatives to include Iran, Iraq, and Yemen. Naturally, the more GCC countries have confidence in themselves, the more they can contribute to regional stability. Still, it is important to translate this confidence to a clear and collective vision on the basis that every party in the region, irrespective of its political system and the consequences of previous conflicts, carries its responsibility toward achieving peace and security.

The idea of direct and open discussions—with full transparency—between regional countries is of paramount importance in achieving regional harmony and stability. GCC states should not wait for outside powers to come and act as mediators for solving local issues, including critical border disputes, demographic challenges, and joint economic policies. Conflicts between regional countries, such as the islands dispute between the UAE and Iran, or the conflict between Iran and Iraq, can indeed be resolved with direct diplomatic discussions. What are simply required are firm commitments to rapidly translate agreements into tangible realities.

## Conclusion

Although what follows are not intended to be final positions, an effort is made to raise certain ideas for discussion, to further gel the stability and security concerns identified above. Without a doubt, effective and long-term solutions will necessitate the participation of all Gulf citizens in frank discussions. As discussed above, three specific areas require Gulf states' attention, to bring prosperity and peace in the region.

1. *Internal actions within individual states.* All Gulf countries are vulnerable to international pressure, as their economies depend on one source of income. Clearly, each GCC state should put far more effort into diversifying its economy. Toward that end, it has to be realized that the private sector has reached a certain stage of maturity, and its leaders recognize their responsibilities. To date, private sector leaders have not been involved in decision making, which affects their performances. In some cases, the public sector acts as a competitor to the private

sector, a situation that is prevalent in several GCC countries. Such practices should stop, to let captains of industry assume their fair share of responsibility for their economies. In turn, private sector leaders should take an active role in whatever negotiation may be under way, including the various applications to the World Trade Organization. In short, the public sector should no longer be a sole player in shaping GCC states' economies, a role that may have been justified three decades ago but is no longer sustainable. By unleashing the private sector to perform at its optimum rate, GCC governments would greatly alleviate the existing burden of "guaranteeing" a job for every citizen. Rather, the onus should be on the individual to take part in the economy, add value, and preserve the state's resources.

Equally important in every GCC country are the critical demographic imbalances due to percentage of expatriate workers in the labor pool. It is a fundamental requirement that measures must be taken to encourage citizen participation in the labor pool, while every effort must also be made to guarantee the social rights of expatriate workers. Moreover, specific policies must be adopted to secure their safety while in the Gulf, and to further encourage spending a greater percentage of what they earn locally rather than transferring huge financial resources out of GCC economies. Parallel to these effects, GCC governments must encourage the flow of human resources among GCC states, and provide equal rights to all GCC citizens. This would encourage the movement of local manpower among GCC countries, thus reducing the reliance on expatriate workforces.

On the political side, a lot needs to be done as well, led by institution building. Parliaments must be elected to exercise a fair share of responsibilities. Existing Shura Councils must be strengthened and their jurisdictions expanded, to allow these nascent institutions a larger and more active role in governing the affairs of GCC states' citizens. Freedom of expression and a free press should not only be guaranteed but also encouraged. These tools in the hands of responsible citizens will ensure that decision makers are performing at their optimum, especially within the bureaucracy, where auditing initiatives must be introduced to eliminate corruption. As important, GCC officials and citizens must welcome the creation of research centers to harvest the intellectual capital to better serve their respective societies. GCC intellectuals should be encouraged to voice their opinion freely to better serve their societies and leaders.

All of these actions would help to build a strong state where every citizen would feel that he/she is part of the decision-making process.

2. *Intra-GCC actions.* Similarly, action would be required among GCC states to encourage collective initiatives, because the six member states share far more in common than almost any other regional grouping. Toward that end, there should be concerted efforts to diversify GCC sources of income, by encouraging private institutions to amalgamate. Competition between GCC industries should be lifted. Instead, GCC industries should complement each other, led by petrochemical conglomerates that would coordinate and cooperate to compete internationally. The transport service, including airlines, should also be

coordinated and possibly amalgamated to form stronger competition on a worldwide scale. Telecommunication is yet another field in which cooperation and coordination would bring greater benefit to all GCC countries.

On the social side, the free flow of population among GCC countries should be allowed to flourish, with equal rights guaranteed to all GCC citizens. This would truly create equilibrium in the labor force.

As discussed earlier, and despite the wealth they derive from petroleum sales, GCC countries are weak and must cooperate to thrive. Measures need to be taken to bring about confidence and trust among states by eliminating "sensitivities." These include solving border disputes irrespective of their historical legacies, given that lingering disputes prevent genuine cooperation in so many vital areas.

In short, there should be real transparency among GCC states in all sectors, including the military. It is necessary to have a real defense strategy to defend the region, based on genuine needs, not only on high spending programs. Coordination on such levels is indeed possible, as GCC military programs, though modest, have demonstrated.

3. *Intra-regional.* Finally, to ensure genuine regional stability, GCC leaders and populations must recognize both their specific strengths and weaknesses.

Three important neighbors with varying interests in the Arabian Peninsula must be recognized. Iran, the largest in terms of size and population, with its undeniable economic capabilities, has its own ambitions in the Gulf. Iraq, the second largest country, also with its economic strengths, may be currently strangulated but cannot be denied a long-term role—despite a very narrow access to the sea. It has been proven throughout history that every Iraqi government has treated this issue as a strategically vital one. Yemen, though economically weak, has the largest population of any Arabian Peninsula state; its instability would directly affect every Gulf state.

To attain any semblance of prosperity and peace, it is necessary for the GCC to have a common policy to deal with the many challenges it faces. This policy should originate from within the Gulf states themselves, without any third party involvement. All three neighbors—Iran, Iraq, and Yemen—should be greeted and entrusted with a role in regional affairs. Ideally, there should be transparency among the GCC states and the three neighbors, especially in the military sector. The purpose of such open dialogue would be to eliminate any apprehensions that one party might harbor against another. Such open dialogue would encourage the resolution of all border disputes among the eight countries.

To achieve harmony with and the confidence of their neighbors, GCC states must therefore create a new regional entity consisting of Iraq, Iran, Yemen, and the six Arab Gulf states. The emerging entity should first concentrate on economic activities, similar to ASEAN or even the Common Market in its earlier periods. The new regional bloc would dispose of significant financial resources, population, and economic potential and would represent a great market for industrialized economies. In turn, major industrialized powers will take local needs into special consideration, as they do with the Southeast Asian consortium.

In general, there should be concerted efforts in closing the gaps among the nine regional states, to establish prosperity and stability throughout the region. This task mainly lies in the hands of intellectuals, who will need to have frank and direct discussions to influence decision makers in their respective countries. Delays in starting such debates will further postpone the time when the interests of all nine countries—without the need for external mediators—may be best served. In the end, such an effort will prove to be far less expensive, not only in financial terms but also in terms of human lives.

CHAPTER 24

# The Arabian Gulf at the New Millennium: Security Challenges

Hassan Hamdan Al-Alkim

Gulf security has been a major concern for the Gulf Cooperation Council (GCC) states, Iran, Iraq, and the West, especially the United States. Perspectives on Gulf security, however, have always differed, and while analysts argue that there are three general categories of threat that could disrupt Arabian Gulf oil supplies, the dangers that loom over the horizon are far more serious than generally assumed. To be sure, "the overt use of force by regional hegemons armed with WMD [weapons of mass destruction]; domestic instability and terrorism within the Gulf states themselves; and conflict between regional and outside powers over control and access to the Caspian Basin" are all potential instigators of instability.[1] Yet, the GCC countries themselves, until the 1990–1991 Gulf crisis, were never united in their perceptions of threats to regional security. Earlier, that is, prior to the 1979 Iranian revolution, they accepted the American perception, and relied on the U.S. security doctrine. Nevertheless, the collapse of the Shah's regime and the outbreak of the Iran-Iraq War, as well as the 1990 Iraqi invasion of Kuwait, brought the security dilemma to the surface.

### Regional Security

A specific apprehension of the Iranian revolution inspired greater cooperation between Iraq and the Arab Gulf states, compelling the latter to accept the Saudi perceptions of both external and internal threats. Indeed, the formation of the GCC, as an umbrella for cooperation and coordination of defense and security policies among member states, was seen as the ideal vehicle to fill the power vacuum and maintain the status quo. Yet, the Kuwaiti predicament has presented the GCC states with a new security conundrum. On the one hand, it exposed the unreliability of the Baathist government, while it offset the balance of power in the sub-region, presenting Iran as the most powerful country in the area.

On the sub-regional level, therefore, GCC states faced a triple security dilemma: Iran, Iraq, and Yemen. To be sure, maintaining warm bilateral relations with the three sub-regional states would be the appropriate option, but in fact, relations between the GCC states and both Iran and Iraq have never been stable. Iran's perception of Gulf security is based on the idea that it is the sole responsibility of littoral states. Iranian officials believe that there are three states of importance for any Gulf security arrangement, namely Iran, Iraq, and Saudi Arabia. Thus, any arrangement that does not coincide with this perspective would not be acceptable to Teheran, and this, in turn, explains Iran's opposition to the Damascus Accord (or the GCC+2 scheme that purported to invite Egypt and Syria to help defend the conservative Arab Gulf monarchies), as well as all U.S. regional security doctrines.[2]

In the event, a basic element in a post-war security structure was likely to be an improved and expanded GCC force, probably incorporating contingents from Egypt and Syria, to serve as a partial deterrent or trip-wire against future aggression from Iraq or conceivably Iran. Simultaneously, and directly due to the 1991 war, U.S. foreign policy has shifted from paying lip service, to the notion of genuine collective security. As a result, "the Pentagon pays out between $30 billion and $60 billion a year to defend the Gulf, a formidable sum for protecting the import into the U.S. of some $30 billion worth of oil."[3] Importantly, North American and western Europe respectively import a mere 20 percent and 29 percent of their oil needs from the Gulf, whereas Asia imports a whopping 74 percent. World demand for oil is projected to increase from 71.6 million barrels per day (mbpd), in 1997, to over 115 mbpd by the year 2020. While the Gulf region can meet much of the industrial world's growing demand for energy, such unfettered access requires a modicum of regional stability.[4] Toward that end, Washington proposed several steps to promote stability in the Gulf, including

- improving GCC states' overall defensive capabilities and accelerating the integration of their plans and programs for territorial defense;
- strengthening U.S. military ties with the GCC states;
- maintaining a limited military presence on the Peninsula;
- working with the GCC states to develop a greater role for regional and extra-regional powers such as Egypt, Syria, Britain, and France.

For its part, the Clinton administration proposed a new regional security policy, dual containment, which could just as well be labeled the Clinton Doctrine. Dual containment, ostensibly of both Iran and Iraq, was followed by former New York senator Alphonse D'Amato's congressional resolution that further tightened the economic noose around Iran's neck. As a result of these policies, hardliners in Teheran shrugged off economic stagnation, blaming Washington for all their ills.[5] Ironically, dual containment focuses on both Iraq and Iran, as the main sources of the threat to Gulf security—while nothing is mentioned of Israel—even if the 1991 War for Kuwait militarily neutralized Iraq.[6] Strangely, during his visit to the UAE in October 1999, Secretary of Defense William Cohen stated that Israel posed no threat to the states of the region.[7] Yet several GCC states do not share this American perception.[8] The UAE deputy prime minister, for example, argues that both Iraq and Iran must be engaged. In Shaykh Sultan bin Zayed's own words, "At the end of the day, GCC states are faced with the simple fact that both Teheran and Baghdad are neighbors, even if several of their current policies pose serious challenges."[9]

Still, and despite these measured assessments, Iran continues to pursue a policy of military intimidation toward the GCC countries, all to achieve specific economic objectives. This argument is further substantiated by the fact that Iran's proven reserves amount to about 9 percent of world oil reserves, and 15 percent of world proven gas reserves."[10] By announcing a 12-mile nautical zone, Iran claimed sovereignty over the oil fields on and around various islands that pepper the territorial waters of several Arab Gulf states.[11] It also initiated a $1.7 billion development program on the Iranian side of an oil and gas field that is predominantly under Qatari territorial waters.

These developments notwithstanding, the end of the Iran-Iraq War and Iraq's encroachment on Kuwait provided specific incentives for Teheran to reassess its foreign policy initiatives. In fact, both conflicts played a significant role in Iran's rapprochement with the Arab Gulf states, further accelerated by the May 1997 election of Mohammed Khatami as president. Khatami succeeded in restoring Iran's ties with several Arab neighbors, especially Saudi Arabia, where he paid a state visit in 1999. The UAE, though maintaining diplomatic ties with Iran at the ambassadorial level, is the only GCC member state to be left with political differences, due to the latter's 1971 occupation of three disputed islands, namely Abu Musa and the Greater and Lesser Tunbs.[12] Despite this new thinking, Khatami's initiatives did not clear existing ambiguities in Iran's foreign policy.[13] Abu Dhabi holds the view that "Iran poses a significant and growing military challenge to Gulf security. By holding regular military maneuvers in Gulf waters, most of which test Teheran's offensive capabilities, Iran sends the wrong message."[14]

Given these recent developments, and the existing gap between the parties, foreign powers, including the United States, found it easier to act as supplementary forces to enhance GCC states' intrinsic capabilities. An "over-the-horizon" American presence, and access to local bases, has been agreed to on a bilateral basis between Washington and several GCC countries. In the aftermath of the 1991 War for Kuwait, leading commentators have argued that a more prominent role by Arab states such as Yemen, Jordan, Egypt, Syria, and a rehabilitated Iraq, would be an alternative to total dependence on the West. Moreover, the absence of a stable balance of power in the Arab Gulf region has also necessitated the integration of Yemen within the sub-regional system, to further enhance GCC states' ability to maneuver. Although Sanaa could not be seen as a supplementary power, it could be part of future arrangements for sub-regional security set-ups. Other alternatives may well include a fourfold security arrangement, to maintain the status quo. Rather than concentrate on a GCC+2 scheme, this arrangement may require a six plus three (6+3) equation that would include the GCC states as well as Iran, Iraq, and Yemen.[15] Under such an arrangement, a genuine equilibrium of power in sub-regional politics may well emerge in the Arab Gulf region. Such a scheme is certainly intended to offset Iran's numerical superiority over individual Arab Gulf states, by creating an Arab axis, but it would also deter Yemen from cooperating with Iraq, or vice versa, if either decided to advance its national interests at the expense of any GCC member state. The proposal here is not to minimize the Arab role in Gulf security arrangements, or to call for isolationism. Rather, because Gulf security and Arab unity are interdependent, a GCC+3 arrangement would meet the needs of all three concentric circles, namely the Gulf circle, the Arab circle, and the international circle.

### Harmony and Conflict

Gulf states' relations with each other have never been stable. In fact, political interactions have gone through different phases, as the rivalry for hegemony among sub-regional powers—Iran, Iraq, and Saudi Arabia—proved to be a constant irritant to the smaller shaykhdoms.[16] For most, the absence of a regional balance of power inspired policies toward each other, and the outside world. Furthermore, Iran's relations with the Arab states of the Gulf demonstrate the complexity and multidimensional aspects of Arab-Persian interregional relationships. On the one hand, "the connection includes cultural and social ties as well as active and substantial trading links. On the other hand, the relationship faces mutual distrust and misperception."[17]

Among the major determinants that affected the area's harmony was the American "twin pillar" policy that purported to bring Saudi Arabia and Iran into an alliance that would secure the region from outside threats. Nevertheless, the 1979 revolution shifted this balance of power to a Saudi-Iraqi association that was devised to frustrate the objectives of revolutionary Iran. Saudi Arabia and the states of the Lower Gulf, with the exception of Oman, took sides and supported the Iraqi war efforts against Iran. Most supported Iraq's war efforts both politically and financially. In fact, the GCC states contributed an estimated $200 billion to Iraq, with Saudi Arabia alone assuming the lion's share—a whopping $25 billion.[18] In addition, Kuwait and Saudi Arabia allocated 300,000 barrels of oil per day for Iraq, to compensate for the decline in the latter's exports. Riyadh even permitted the construction of an Iraqi pipeline across the Kingdom to carry 1.5 million barrels a day to the Red Sea to avoid the Iranian blockade.[19]

Although leading Gulf officials maintained that Iraq presented intrinsic value, the GCC-Iraq relationship was valuable but perplexing. As the UAE deputy prime minister, Shaykh Sultan bin Zayed, argued, "GCC states' objectives were clear: support Baghdad because of its intrinsic strategic value and foster ties between Arab Gulf societies and the Iraqi people."[20] In the event, the nascent GCC-Iraq alliance was short-lived, due to the latter's invasion of Kuwait.

Another key determinant was the Iran-Iraq War, which led Saudi Arabia and its neighboring Arab Gulf states to increase cooperation not only for mutual defense and security, but also on a broad spectrum of political and economic issues through the formative years of the GCC. The Iran-Iraq War provided the Arab Gulf states with an opportunity to check the new Iranian "threat" and, simultaneously, exclude Iraq on account of its confrontation. By agreeing to form the GCC at the time they did, member states removed the potential fear of domination that either Iran or Iraq could have exercised on the regional security body. Indeed, GCC states addressed on 21 May 1984 a collective letter to the president of the United Nations Security Council, calling on the latter to shoulder its responsibilities envisaged under the UN Charter, further illustrating the value of their arrangement without either Iran or Iraq.[21] They condemned Iran's provocative acts of aggression and warned against its recurrence. It is interesting to note, however, that the 1 June 1984 resolution condemned the attacks—and demanded that they should cease forthwith—without mentioning Iran by name.[22] On the other hand, the GCC states, out of their desire to keep open channels with Teheran, pursued a dual policy toward Iran. As one observer concluded, "GCC states did not want to abandon all means of contact with Iran, a long-term insurance policy with their larger neighbor."[23] In fact, the Saudi fear of potential Iranian retaliation against GCC states' oil installations may have even encouraged Riyadh to export refined products to Iran to make up for the shortage of petrochemicals.[24]

It must also be added that Baghdad's preoccupation with the war helped Riyadh nudge the Gulf security organization under its protective umbrella, even if Saudi Arabia had concluded an important "bilateral" agreement with the Iraqi government. In 1989, King Fahd and president Saddam Hussein agreed in Baghdad to delineate the territorial boundaries between the two countries and coordinate various security ties. At the time, this accord was heralded as an epoch-making event, given the paucity of such harmony between the two largest Arab Gulf states. Baghdad, however, unilaterally nullified the agreement after the eruption of the second Gulf Crisis.

Today, territorial problems present the most important contentious issues hindering the development of stronger relations among Gulf states. In part, the region witnessed two devastating wars in the last decade, as testified to by how short-lived the "coalition" between Iraq and the GCC countries was. Kuwait's production of $2.5 billion worth of oil from the disputed al-Rumailah oil field, for example, proved to be one of the major Iraqi grievances in the recent crisis. This concrete illustration further revealed the extent to which ostensibly minor disputes took on gigantic proportions, with devastating consequences. To be sure, the Iraqi-Kuwaiti territorial dispute is a long-standing one, and successive Iraqi governments—ever since the 1920s—have laid claim on the Shaykhdom. Though the Iraqis have consistently laid their claim on historical grounds, the geographical location of both countries played paramount roles in shaping both states' foreign policies toward each other. For all practical purposes, without Kuwaiti territorial concessions, Iraq is a landlocked country. Its outlet to the Gulf is a 26–mile narrow corridor, mostly made of shallow waters that are unsuited for port construction or navigation except for small vessels.[25]

This unsettled border dispute, coupled with the 1989–1990 increased oil production by several Arab Gulf oil-producing countries, prompted the Iraqi government to adopt a hostile posture toward the GCC states. In his 17 July 1990 Revolution Day speech, the Iraqi president blasted Kuwait and the UAE as American stooges, allegedly for pumping additional crude to keep prices low.[26] Even if this bombastic statement was rhetorical in nature, Iraq's invasion of Kuwait on 2 August 1990 forced GCC countries to shift their foreign policy orientations from an "alliance" with Iraq to an "alliance" against it. Saudi Arabia was determined not to let Saddam Hussein dictate war or peace in the future. King Fahd, for one, was adamant during the GCC 1990 Doha summit conference, stressing that there could be no "compromise[s] with Baghdad on the territorial integrity of Kuwait or on political concessions that could be seen as a reward for the aggressor."[27] It must be emphasized that the outcome of the 1991 Gulf War, as well as the UN-orchestrated territorial agreement delineating the Iraqi-Kuwaiti border, does not put an end to this festering territorial dispute. The fact that the agreement was imposed on Iraq carries within itself a proven recipe for failure.

It may also be useful to state that the Iraq-Iran, Iraq-Kuwait, and Iraq–Saudi Arabia border disputes are by no means the only territorial problems in the area. The UAE, for example, has territorial disputes with Saudi Arabia, Oman, and Iran, even if the latter's occupation of Abu Musa and the Greater and Lesser Tunb is the most serious. Ironically, and by failing to reach an arrangement with the UAE over the three disputed islands, Teheran delays the normalization of its relations with Abu Dhabi. Noticeably, Iranian intentions were clarified with the August 1992 Abu Musa encroachment, when Teheran took several unilateral actions. By engaging in such acts, the Islamic government showed continuity with its monarchical predecessor in its claim to be the region's paramount power.

Finally the Bahrain-Qatar territorial dispute was brought to an end. Fortunately, both countries accepted the International Court of Justice (ICJ) ruling in April 2001. The penultimate chapter of this territorial dispute reflects the new spirit brought about by the new leaders in both Bahrain and Qatar and marks the beginning of a new era in the two countries' bilateral relations. The two Amirs expressed their desires for closer cooperation, exchanged state visits, and established a joint committee—under the leadership of the Heir Apparents—to delineate their borders accordingly. Other positive developments include the settlements of the Saudi-Qatari and Saudi-Yemeni territorial disputes through bilateral negotiations. Oman and the UAE, for their part, are in the process of finalizing pending territorial differences. Nevertheless, despite recent developments, territorial problems continue to be the major obstacle facing regional integration and security.

Perhaps the most striking illustration of how these unsettled border disputes create an environment of continued political tension is the ongoing regional arms race. Increased defense budgets in every Gulf state provide ample evidence for this trend. Throughout the 1990s, Gulf states imported advanced weaponry, at extremely high costs.[28] Importantly, the United States—despite earlier commitments to freeze military shipments to the Middle East as a whole—ranked ahead of France, Russia, and China in terms of its military contracts.[29] By encouraging these sales, Washington benefits far more than the Gulf states, given the myriad problems in absorbing such sophisticated systems. It is worth underscoring that the direct result of this approach contradicts solemn American commitments to de-militarize the region, and encourages the use of force in foreign policy, which, in turn prompts greater regional instability.

## The Iranian Challenge

As analyzed above, revolutionary Iran displayed continuity with its monarchical predecessor in its claim to be the region's paramount power.[30] According to one observer, and despite the great shift from a monarchical to a revolutionary republican system, Iran's goals in the region have neither shifted nor changed.[31] Moreover, the new Iranian government posed a threat of a different nature to the Arab Gulf states, as it emphasized its commitments to various Shia communities sprinkled throughout the region. It is alleged that several Shia "disturbances" may have been orchestrated from Teheran.[32]

To be sure, Iran's foreign policies are not minimalist, and continue to be bellicose, "animated by general and diffuse ambition, and . . . reactive and opportunistic."[33] Undoubtedly, the advent of the revolution confronted the Arab Gulf states with new problems: It transformed Iran from a strategic shield to a potential threat and placed the smaller states between two mutually hostile regimes. Other equally distressing activities and policies included:[34]

- Iran's continued occupation of the islands of Abu Musa and the Greater and Lesser Tunbs;
- Ongoing Iranian programs to develop a conventional military arsenal and to acquire weapons of mass destruction, including the ambition to acquire nuclear weapons;
- Iranian sponsorship of extremist groups and covert operations around the world;
- Iran's active role in attempting to destabilize Arab Gulf governments;
- Iran's attempt to dominate the Gulf region as the sole hegemonic power.

To be sure, "the very size and weight of Iran will keep alive fears of a constant ambition to exercise Iranian hegemony in the Gulf,"[35] and in light of Iraq's uncertain future, Iran's potential role in Gulf politics cannot be neglected.[36] In the aftermath of the Iraqi defeat, Gulf states in general and the UAE in particular concluded that Teheran was trying to see how far it could push its luck as the emerging dominant regional power. The fear is that Iran, in a bid to establish its dominance over the region, may install Silkworm missile batteries on Abu Musa with which it could control the entrance of the strategic Straits of Hormuz.[37] On 16 November 1996, the former Iranian navy commander Ali Shamkhani acknowledged that Iran had placed missile batteries on the disputed islands.[38] It was also alleged that Iran would use Abu Musa as a base for the three submarines obtained from Russia, to command the entrance of the Gulf. Satellite images of the three disputed islands, however, refuted U.S. allegations that they were militarily fortified.[39] Still, the Iranian military build-up enhances such apprehensions.

Despite GCC states' accelerated military purchases of sophisticated weapons systems, the Iranian military build-up—and its oft-declared and discussed policy to acquire a nuclear capability—increases overall suspicion on the Arabian Peninsula. Iran's defense budget for 2000, for example, stood at $7.5 billion, up from $5.7 billion in 1999—a nominal increase of some 25 percent. Official figures indicate that Iran's defense spending has almost tripled since 1993.[40] Although Iran may well be engaged in a re-building policy in the aftermath of its losses during the Iran-Iraq War—when it allegedly lost an estimated 40–60 percent of its military arsenal—Teheran has opted to pursue a 15-year military build-up program with an emphasis on air defenses.[41] The Iranian armed forces personnel in 2000 was around 513,000. An additional 125,000 troops were available within Revolutionary Guards units, with reserves estimated at 350,000.[42] It may be useful to underscore in this respect that both Russia and China, in part responding to the U.S. so-called dual containment policy toward Iran, have made a strong bid to restore and expand their involvement in the Gulf sub-region by opening up to Iran.[43] In recent years, Iran thus became capable of producing Russian-designed T-72 main battle tanks (MBTs) and BMP-derivative Boragh armored personnel carriers (APCs), under Russian license based on a 1988–89 agreement.[44] The arms-package deal with Russia, signed in 1989, included 200 aircraft, 500 tanks, 3 submarines—carrying sophisticated sonar systems and specialized mine-laying equipment and up to 24 mines, each with 1,000 pounds of explosive—and patrol boats armed with torpedoes.[45] In a further step, Iran and China concluded, in September 1992, a nuclear energy cooperation agreement under which Beijing undertook to provide a Qinshan-1–type 300 megawatt pressurized water reactor.[46] Moreover, the Pentagon believes that Iran is receiving radar testing devices, navigation and avionics equipment, oscilloscopes, logic analyzers, fiber optic cables, digital switches, high-speed computers, remote sensors, and jet engines, all of which have dual military uses.[47] Some observers have further concluded that Iran obtained missiles of different types.[48] What is important in this respect is that the overall significance of the Iranian rearmament initiatives lies in the fact that Teheran ordered equipment designed to take control of the waterway. Clearly, such a projection of power could enable the Islamic Republic to secure its position as the sub-regional superpower of the Gulf.

The Iranian nuclear program constitutes another controversial issue between Iran and the GCC countries. While some analysts argue that Iran is not in a position to finance a large nuclear project,[49] because of the difficulty in acquiring the necessary technology—and because allegedly it does not have a sufficient number of scientists—Teheran surely reached the conclusion that it must acquire such weapons at all costs. This conclusion was made even more urgent after the Iraqi defeat at the hands of the UN-sanctioned U.S. led coalition.[50] One can argue that the American policy toward Iran is unworkable. A clear parallel may be drawn with the American containment policy applied over half a century against the former Soviet Union. In the event, the success of that containment policy was due to Soviet domestic factors rather than any other initiatives. While it could be argued that the Soviets were forced to reallocate their resources and heavily invest in the military establishment—at the expense of political, economic, and social development—many other forces were at play as well. Likewise, one could posit that a world economic recession, coupled with increasing demand for oil, the desire for hard currency by the newly independent former Soviet republics, the absence of an effective world government, and the post-war situation in both Iran and Iraq, will also ensure that dual containment will not be effective either.

The hesitation and the lack of leadership demonstrated by the Clinton administration enhance the argument that American policy toward Iran proved to be inappropriate. Leading American analysts have labeled dual containment more of a slogan than a strategy,[51] while others concluded that the policy was a geopolitical gimmick.[52] In fact, dual containment has had a minor effect on Iran's foreign relations, because the American identification of Iran as one of the chief threats to global security has not prevented leading world powers from developing close ties with Teheran.[53] In 1999, Iran succeeded in normalizing ties with several Arab Gulf states, European countries and Japan, most of which are U.S. allies that opted to pursue independent approaches. Another reason why U.S. foreign policy has not been successful in addressing its outstanding conflict with Iran—let alone to make a breakthrough toward it—can be attributed to the duality in Washington's perception of how to properly handle relations with Teheran. While the Clinton administration sent cooperative signals to the Iranian government, official American statements about Iran were, nonetheless, more frequently tainted with negative attitudinal connotations. While hawkish congressional stances compounded the difficulty with which Washington was contriving a coherent policy toward Teheran, Secretary of State Madeleine Albright seemed to be bridging the gap with Iran. To be sure, the State Department could not ignore the missive that 28 congressmen sent, when they emphasized that "American policy toward Iran should make significant steps in the direction of supporting democracy and human rights in Iran. In addition, increased potential for instability in Iran should lead us to encourage Iranian opposition forces that are conducive to consolidating stability in the long-run."[54] On the other hand, Madeleine Albright expressed her dovish attitude in a March 2000 address to the American-Iranian Council. She expressed the U.S. administration's intention to relax the unilateral American economic restrictions imposed against Iran on importing certain products, including Persian carpets, caviar, and cashew nuts. Albright further expressed regret that past U.S. policies had been designed to side with Iraq during the latter's war with Iran, and for the U.S.-engineered coup d'état against Dr. Mohammed Mossadeq to reinstate the Shah in 1953.[55] These were significant admissions that revealed far more than was generally acknowledged.

### *Winds of Change*
Democratization and human rights issues acquired significant importance in the post-1990 "new world order." In fact, they came to be the main source of political legitimacy, at least as perceived by the United States. The Gulf states, as part of the global village, could not afford to remain indifferent to the political changes influencing world politics even if democratization presented a further challenge to the regime's security. With the exception of Iran, none of the other Gulf states could be viewed as being "democratic." Whereas Iraq is ruled by a totalitarian regime, Iran seems to be on the road to democracy. Though political parties continue to be controlled, and candidates for official posts are carefully

scrutinized in the Islamic Republic, Iranians have the right to elect their representatives and president. The degree of freedom enjoyed in Iran was amply revealed in the aftermath of the 1997 presidential election that catapulted Mohammed Khatami to the highest non-religious post. The choice of Khatami, against the will of the Faqih and the religious establishment—who lent their support to Parliament Speaker Ali Akhbar Nateq Nouri—enhanced the argument that Iran was on the road to democracy. In the words of one observer, "Iran's savvy population is taking stands, making demands, and even defying the ruling theocrats."[56] As if it were the icing on the democratization cake, the Iranian parliament approved, in August 1999, a bill limiting the power of the Council of Guardians to exclude candidates for future parliamentary elections.[57] The results of the February 2000 parliamentary elections, which ushered in a slew of reform-minded candidates, further strengthened this phenomenon.

In contrast, GCC political systems are closed and based on hereditary rule, and while the winds of change seem to have affected the people of the Gulf, they have yet to influence their governments. Since the second Gulf Crisis, Gulf citizens have started to question the "wisdom of their far-sighted leaders,"[58] raise the necessity of political reforms, and encourage more political liberalization. The governments' responses to such public demands have differed from one country to the other, with some embarking on parliamentary experiences (Kuwait) and other adopting less radical initiatives by setting up consultative bodies (Oman, Saudi Arabia, and the UAE).[59]

Under the circumstances, the prospects for democracy in the GCC states, at least within the coming decade, are not promising. Measures adopted by some governments do not meet the aspirations of the masses. Gulf citizens are not optimistic about a gradual and peaceful transition to a power-sharing form of government because regimes "think only of how to maintain power."[60] Yet, the decline in oil revenues, as a result of oil market instability and the fluctuation of the price, coupled with the financial and social costs of the second Gulf Crisis, convinced several GCC states to address serious budget deficits. Others assumed debts that, at least in recent memory, were not common. Only the UAE seems to have emerged unscathed by these economic pressures. In this case, the country's position as the financial power center flows from massive holdings of liquid unofficial overseas assets, rather than from income exclusively generated from oil products. The precise size of these sources of income are not made public, but Western sources estimate that in 1999 the figure hovered around $350 billion, with a return income in the same year around $15 billion.[61] Except for the UAE, therefore, and to cope with mounting deficits, GCC states must either increase taxation, or look for the private sector to assume a greater burden. In both instances, governments would have to concede some of their prerogatives to the private sector, following the well-known adage that there can be "no taxation without representation." Hence, the source of income that enabled ruling families to deny their subjects basic political rights is slowly "persuading" them to concede to future public demands for political participation. Consequently, it should come as no surprise when major political and social changes occur that, by definition, may be destabilizing.[62]

Examples of first changes are numerous. Qatar recently experienced an election at the local government level when, for the first time, Qataris were given the right to choose their representatives to the Municipality Council. As a follow-up, the Amir set up a committee to enact a constitution for the country, which would include a freely elected council with legislative powers. The Qatari ruler spoke privately of no other alternative but democratization as the only viable option for future security. Similarly, Bahrain is experiencing a period of transition toward democratization. Likewise, the new Emir of Bahrain, Shaykh Hamad bin Isa, promised to start a new mode of governance based on the principles of democratization and mutual respect for human rights. He pardoned most political dissidents, freed all political prisoners, and called for the creation of elected local councils. The composition of the Bahraini appointed National Council included for the first time a Christian, a Jew, an Indian dissident, and women. In April 2001, a national referendum on the proposed charter was held, marking the beginning of a new era in Bahraini political life. In the event, Bahrainis voted overwhelmingly—by a whopping 98 percent—in favor of these proposed reforms. Consequently, Heir Apparent Shaykh Salman bin Hamad, presided over a 12 member committee to finalize the application of the National Charter by 2003. These epoch-making developments notwithstanding, Bahrain is also experiencing genuine freedom of speech and associations, long denied for various reasons. In the spring of 2001, a human rights committee was also officially "licensed" to operate freely in the shaykhdom. Despite these positive steps on the road to democratization in both Bahrain and Qatar, much remains to be accomplished, with Saudi Arabia carefully assessing and—to date—tolerating the level of liberalization in the smaller Gulf states.

Ironically, and although the Kuwaiti parliament denied women the right to vote, Bahrain and Qatar decided to grant women equal political rights.[63] The UAE, though continuing with its appointed Federal National Council (FNC), recently tolerated for a while a certain degree of media freedom. The new trend rattled a few ministerial cages in the process by allowing the media to "criticize freely."[64] Still, the move was short lived as more than 18 members of the educated elite were denied access to contribute to local newspapers. Indeed, the democratization process in the UAE is slow, and the government—perhaps because of the country's demographic composition—is reluctant to follow the Bahraini and Qatari approaches. Nevertheless, discussions on the necessity to open up the political system are gaining momentum. Ras al-Khaimah Heir Apparent Shaykh Khaled bin Saqr Al Qasimi called in January 2000 for an elected FNC. It must be pointed out that women in the UAE enjoy almost equal rights and opportunities with men, although there is still room for progress. In the event, the U.S. annual congressional report on human rights praised the way women were treated in the UAE, certainly in comparison to neighboring countries.[65]

Although democracy must find its roots internally, the role played by the United States in the Gulf region easily lends itself to accusations of a double standard on the issue of democracy. Undeniably, the U.S. presence in the area is perceived as a protective shield for GCC political systems. In the past, Gulf regimes relied on the British to secure their survival, whereas today Washington is the guarantor of their destinies. Intentionally or not, the United States is providing these regimes with a security umbrella, rather than helping an evolutionary change toward democratization. Indeed, as several analysts have argued, Washington may well have an extremely limited ability to shape or respond to internal developments affecting Gulf regimes.[66] Yet, the hesitation to encourage democratization may well be designed to prevent Islamist forces from coming to power, on the assumption that they will be against U.S. vital interests in the region. Still, as the only U.S. vital interest in the area is oil, it may be worth repeating that any and all who rule will have little choice but to export the commodity if for no other reason than national survival. This truism notwithstanding, both Americans and Gulf Arabs are victims of false analogies made by the pro-Israel lobby in Washington. It would be unforgivable if America's commitment to democratic principles in the region were in vain. Although leading analysts posit that Washington should adhere to its democratic principles and encourage the development of democratic institutions and practices in the area, the American policy—defending regimes in the Arabian Gulf—is placing American prestige and credibility on the line.[67] Lest one overlook certain basic principles, the lack of accountability, checks and balances, the rule of law, political freedom, and respect for human rights would all inevitably cause domestic instability. One may accurately argue that many of the crises experienced in the region arose because authoritarian regimes did not encourage the steady development of political rights and privileges.[68]

In the end, "constitutional democracy" based on the principles of Shariah (Islamic law) could be seen as detrimental for security and stability for countries in the Gulf sub-region. A real and effective democracy in the GCC states requires the fulfillment of three concentric conditions:

- the redefinition of ties between rulers and the ruled;
- the separation of private and public wealth; and,
- the institutionalization of the democratic process.

The achievement of these goals is not feasible unless these countries undergo a social and political transformation of their governing values. Nevertheless, a reading of current political developments reveals that although democracy may not be realized within the coming decade, it is acquiring a significant importance in GCC states' political lives, further adding challenges to each regime.

### U.S. Gulf Policy

The linkage between vital U.S. interests and Arabian Gulf security construed greater American involvement in the Gulf sub-region.[69] The American policy toward the Arabian Gulf is driven by two factors: securing the free flow of oil and ensuring Israeli security. Gulf countries have perceived the American presence in the area differently. While Iran and Iraq view the American presence in the Gulf as a destabilizing factor, GCC states perceived Iranian and Iraqi regional policies as the catalysts that brought American forces into the region to act as their security shield. Following the collapse of the Shah's regime in 1979, Washington initiated and refined a set of new policies, to further secure its national interests in the Arab Gulf.

To be sure, the 1990 Iraqi invasion of Kuwait prompted greater U.S. involvement in the Gulf sub-region when, for the first time, American-GCC security linkages were publicly acknowledged. On 7 August 1990, President George Bush ordered the deployment of U.S. military aircraft and troops into Saudi Arabia, ostensibly to defend it against potential Iraqi incursions. On 19 August, Bahrain and the UAE permitted the deployment of Arab and "friendly" forces on their soil.[70] Within a few weeks, U.S. allies pledged $54 billion to offset deployment costs, led by Saudi Arabia, Kuwait, and the UAE, which, together contributed $36.9 billion.[71] Undeniably, the crisis provided the U.S. president with the justification to send American troops to the Gulf and waive the congressionally imposed cap on deliveries of F-15 aircraft to Saudi Arabia.

Since 1991, Washington has become the first arms supplier to GCC states, particularly Saudi Arabia and Kuwait. The U.S. adopted a comprehensive approach to strengthening their capabilities as the Bush administration argued that a comprehensive program of well-conceived arms sales would contribute to their stability. The emphasis was on collective action to promote standardization and inter-operability.[72] The U.S. commitment to enhance GCC states' defensive capabilities is a presumptive indication of the concern for GCC-U.S. political and military ties. In March 2000, Washington further agreed to the sale of 80 F-16 fighters to the UAE, worth an estimated $6.3 billion.[73] Continuing U.S. arms transfers to the GCC states, however, could well undermine Washington's credibility as it calls for restraint on the part of other arms suppliers to the Middle East.[74] Ironically, the infusion of arms deliveries to Iran, by a variety of exporters, will almost certainly ensure greater instability.

There is no doubt that successive American presidents have reiterated the U.S. commitment to defending Gulf allies. By January 1999, U.S. forces in the Gulf included the U.S. Fifth Fleet, various amphibious vessels with an estimated 27,000 American military personnel, and 126 combat aircraft. In addition, Washington was capable of calling on its naval assets deployed in the Mediterranean and at Incirlik Air Base in Turkey.

This overt U.S. involvement in the Gulf presents another challenge for future regional security and stability. While the U.S. military presence invigorated tensions between the GCC states and their larger neighbors, Gulf analysts have warned that the military deployments could shift into a permanent residence.[75] The strong U.S. military presence and the subsidies incurred by local governments, coupled with unstable oil prices and the arms race, limit local resources, affect development, and threaten legitimacy. They also instigate power struggles within ruling families on the assumption that the U.S. will side with those who support U.S. Gulf policy. Following the second Gulf Crisis, Washington became more committed to maintaining the status quo than to promoting democracy in the area. In fact, the U.S. concluded bilateral security and defense agreements with individual GCC states, creating greater dependency on the U.S. for each regime's security. Consequently, GCC ruling families became more reluctant to accept concessions and introduce democratic measures.

On the global level, the American hegemony over the Gulf area produced wide-range international criticism. The European Union (EU) deplored U.S. Gulf policies and concluded that the "dual containment" policy was dangerous and self-defeating.[76] For their part, the Chinese regarded "dual containment" as a unilateral initiative, and they, jointly with Russia, disapproved of the American military presence in the Gulf.[77] Given the area's resources, and the increasing dependence of leading world economies on Gulf oil, this may well lead to a renewed competition among the main international actors, ensuring further instability.

### The Israeli Connection

As stated above, the pro-Israel lobby in Washington, aiming at securing greater U.S. commitments for Israeli security, is exaggerating the linkages between the latter's security and American vital interests in the Gulf. As a result, Washington is devoting more resources and time than is required. In fact, the U.S. is taking Israel's side in the Arab-Israeli conflict, and is accused of a double standard. Although the United States is free to pursue its desired policies, its commitments to the Middle East peace process are distorted, precisely because of the influence of a very strong pro-Israel lobby.[78] Notwithstanding this truism, leading analysts have cautioned that "Israeli security, however important, does not represent an extra dimension of U.S. Gulf policy."[79] According to another astute observer, "Europeans blame the U.S. for making Israel its primary interest in the Middle East, raising serious Arab concerns about U.S. even-handedness."[80]

Given these interpretations, and based on the overwhelming sentiments throughout the Arab and Muslim worlds, few should be surprised that the scenario anticipated in the case of failure (of the peace process) would be a radicalization of Arab politics. An Islamist tendency is currently sweeping the region and will surely gain in strength. Although it may be possible to contemplate a "geometric progression," through a unity scheme between the Islamists and residual pan-Arab nationalists against their political regimes, such a union is not required for serious if not cataclysmic changes. For millions of Arabs and Muslims, regional stability in the Gulf is tightly connected to the progress achieved in the Middle East peace process. The GCC states could not be immune from such political turmoil if such a scenario were to manifest inflicting serious instability throughout the area.

The 1990–91 Gulf crisis caused a change in GCC countries' attitudes toward the Arab-Israeli conflict. Both the stance of the Palestinian Liberation Organization (PLO) and the American role in restoring Kuwait sovereignty inspired permanent changes. These changes were best manifested in their acceptance of the American Middle East peace initiative. They attended the October 1991 Madrid Peace Conference and participated in the various multilateral peace talks. When relations with the PLO became strained, GCC states decided to freeze their annual financial assistance, following the American advice to enlist

PLO support. In the event, the ninth round of bilateral peace talks, held in Washington in April 1993, promised to resume financial assistance to the PLO, further illustrating the close cooperation between GCC states and the United States. The Palestinians were wooed back to the peace table.[81] Shortly thereafter, GCC states—except for Saudi Arabia and the UAE—began to relax their boycott laws imposed against Israel. Oman was the first GCC country to start formal contacts with Israel dating back to 1985. Since 1991, relations between the two countries have been promoted to a commercial level. Likewise, Qatar decided to exchange formal commercial ties with Israel, and it was reported that Doha would sell natural gas to Tel Aviv. In fact, and despite regional pressure on Qatar, the latter kept its official contacts with Israel. The Qatari Foreign Minister Shaykh Hamad bin Jaber Al Thani met, in May 2001, with his Israeli counter part Shimon Peres in Washington, D.C. and offered to host a meeting in Doha between Arafat and Peres to discuss the peace process. Kuwait, for its part, decided to lift the names of American companies from the boycott list. According to well-placed sources, most of the minesweepers operating after the Kuwait liberation were brought from Israel through Germany. In February 2000, Shaykh Salman bin Hamad Al Khalifah, the Bahrain Heir Apparent, spoke of a possible opening of ties with Israel.

Despite the peace agreements concluded between some Arab countries and Israel, and the ongoing negotiations between Syria and Israel, the Arab-Israeli conflict continues to be a further challenge to Gulf security. The linkage between Gulf security and the Palestinian question has multiple dimensions. On the one hand, there is the Israeli threat to the vital installations of the Gulf states. On the other hand, there is the fear that a deadlock on the Palestinian issue could cause Palestinian movements to take subversive action against the Gulf countries.[82] To be sure, Israel includes Saudi Arabia in its strategic attention, as it fears that the Saudi arms build-up could end in unfriendly hands.[83] A well-argued study has concluded that such military wherewithal may well have encouraged Israeli forces "to frequently over-fly the area, occasionally going to such lengths as dropping empty fuel tanks on [Saudi military air fields to demonstrate their capabilities."[84] In fact, Israel threatened on 26 March 1988 to launch a pre-emptive air strike against the Saudi Silkworm missiles.[85] In turn, the Saudi monarch declared on 8 April that "the missiles do not carry nuclear warheads and they will not be used against Israel."[86] Riyadh, upon American advice, decided on 26 April 1988 to join the Nuclear Non-Proliferation Treaty, largely to ease Israeli anger.[87]

As these brief illustrations indicate, the outcome of the Middle East peace process would inevitably affect GCC states' foreign policy orientations. The success of the peace talks would mean that, at least for GCC governments, the conflict is essentially over.[88] On the other hand, the success of the peace talks does not mean simply reaching a peace accord. Rather, it requires normalization of relations in all fields, including the political, economic, and cultural spectrums. In other words, accepting Israel as part of the Middle East region will not be an easy task. This would require changes in both the Arab and Jewish perceptions of each other. Such changes would further require a review of "information" about each other as well as dramatic alterations in textbooks that are replete with erroneous data and analysis. In short, the requirements are a "peace of cultures" as well as the settlement of festering but manageable disputes.

Simultaneously, normalization might stipulate political discontent among social forces, especially among Islamists and residual pan-Arab nationalists. It would ultimately lead to a radicalization of Arab politics and probably the demise of existing political regimes. In turn, such dramatic developments could bring the peace agreement to a standstill and possibly revoke it. Clearly, the Israeli refusal to concede to Palestinian calls for self-determination ignited the intifada twice, in 1987–1994 and again starting in September 2000. Under the circumstances, Gulf states had few options and, to buttress the Arab position, supported the Palestinian resistance. Saudi Arabia, Kuwait, and the UAE transferred more than 200 billion dollars to the Al-Aqsa Fund. It is now amply clear that Prime minister Ariel Sharon's policy of escalation—and Washington's unequivocal support to Israel—will ultimately affect GCC-U.S. relations. On May 18, 2001, Heir Apparent Prince Abdallah bin Abdulaziz Al Saud turned down an invitation from President George W. Bush to visit Washington. Likewise, GCC governments are increasingly under pressure to adopt specific measures against the U.S., for siding with Israel. Arab media sources are, once again, discussing how oil may be used as a strategic weapon.

These developments notwithstanding, and despite the possibility of an eventual peaceful settlement, a taboo would continue to exist, namely the Israeli nuclear capability. It could be argued, however, that the Israeli nuclear capability would act as a deterrent force to preserve Israeli security and territorial integrity. On the other hand, maintaining an Israeli military superiority would fuel further arms races in the region, justifying radical forces to oppose the putative peace accord.

## Conclusion

The different challenges facing Gulf security reveal that democratization presents the most important challenge facing Gulf states at the turn of the millennium. Changes in Gulf states' political systems seem to be inevitable. In fact, it is amply clear that long-term regional security and stability cannot be fostered through a dependence on foreign powers. Stability is invariably connected to democratization and political legitimacy. Ideas of political participation, democratization, the necessity to reform, and social justice are spreading among Arab Gulf elites. At present, citizen demands for the reduction of ruling-family privileges meet deep resistance, but it is in the interests of the U.S. to encourage an evolutionary political development throughout the Gulf region. While the Islamist threat to the free flow of oil is a myth—it is an Israeli invention supported by the pro-Israel lobby in Washington—the fact remains that popular demands are based on genuine needs. Future leaders—who come to power as a result of democratization or who evolve and introduce genuine reforms—would still have to sell their oil since there are no alternatives. Thus, a constructive engagement of moderate Islamist forces may well be an alternative option to prevent extremism. At the same time, the U.S. is required to review its Middle East policy and pressure Israel to fulfill its obligations, as well as accept the right of the Palestinians for self-determination to limit growing tensions within allied Gulf societies. By pursuing such policies, Washington will ensure its access to the Gulf's petroleum resources while remaining true to its cherished principles, and at a smaller financial burden.

## Notes

1. Geoffrey Kemp, "The Persian Gulf Remains the Strategic Prize," *Survival* 40:4, winter 1998/99, p. 137.
2. *Al–Arab*, 10 December 1992.
3. Graham E. Fuller and Ian D. Lesser, "Persian Gulf Myths," *Foreign Affairs* 76:3, May/June 1997, pp. 42–52.
4. Kemp, *op. cit.*, pp. 136–38.
5. Shahram Chubin and Jerold D. Green, "Engaging Iran: US Strategy," *Survival* 40:3, autumn 1998, p. 153.
6. Ali Ahmed Al-Ghafli, "Al-Illaqat Al-Khalijiyyah Al-Amirikiyyah" [Gulf-U.S. Relations], in *Al-Taqrir Al-Istratiji Al-Khaliji*, Sharjah, UAE: Al-Khalij, 2000, p. 213.
7. *Al-Ittihad*, 16 October 1999.
8. Zbigniew Brzezinski, Brent Scowcroft, and Richard Murphy, "Differentiated Containment," *Foreign Affairs* 76:3, May/June 1997, p. 21.
9. Sultan bin Zayed bin Sultan Al Nahyan, "Gulf Security: The View from Abu Dhabi," in Joseph A. Kechichian (ed.), *A Century in Thirty Years: Shaykh Zayed and the United Arab Emirates*, Washington, D.C.: Middle East Policy Council, 2000, p. 275.
10. Simon Serfaty, "Bridging the Gulf across the Atlantic: Europe and the United States in the Persian Gulf," *The Middle East Journal* 52:3, summer 1998, p. 341.
11. Shamlan al Essa, "Al Khilafat al Hududiyyah wal-Iqlimiyyah bayna al-'Arab wal-Iraniyyn," *Al Illaqat al Arabiyyah al Iraniyyah* (Arab Iranian Relations], Beirut: Center for Arab Unity Studies, 1996, p. 444.
12. Hassan H. al-Alkim, "The Islands Question: An Arabian Perspective," in Gary Sick and Lawrence G. Potter (eds.), *Security in The Persian Gulf: Origins, Obstacles and the Search for Consensus*, New York: Palgrave, (forthcoming).
13. Shamlan al-Essa, *op. cit.*, p. 69.
14. Sultan bin Zayed bin Sultan Al Nahyan, *op. cit.*, p. 275.
15. For more details, see Hassan H. al-Alkim, *The GCC States in an Unstable World*, London: Al-Saqi Books, 1994, pp. 145–148.
16. David Long, "Saudi Arabia and its Neighbors: Preoccupied Paternalism," in Richard Sindelar and J. E. Peterson (eds.), *Crosscurrents in the Gulf*, New York: Routledge, 1988, p. 190.
17. Anwar Gargash, "Iran, the GCC States, and the UAE: Prospects and Challenges in the Coming Decade," in Jamal S. al-Suwaidi (ed.), *Iran and the Gulf: A Search for Stability*, Abu Dhabi: The Emirates Center For Strategic Studies and Research, 1996, p. 136.
18. *Al-Ittihad*, 17 January 1991.
19. Hassan H. al-Alkim, "al-'Illaqat al-Arabiyyah al-Khalijiyyah ma' Iran: Ru'yiah Mustaqbaliyyah" [Arabian Gulf Relations with Iran: A Future Perspective], Arab *Journal for International Studies* 3:1, winter 1990, p. 24.
20. Sultan bin Zayed bin Sultan Al Nahyan, *op. cit.*, p. 276.
21. United Nations, Document 5/16574, New York, UN, 21 May 1984.
22. United Nations, Document S/RES/552 (1984), New York, UN, 21 May 1984.
23. Abdul Ridha Assiri, *Kuwait's Foreign Policy: City-State in World Politics*, Boulder: Westview Press, 1990, p. 102.
24. *Middle East Economic Digest* (MEED), 29 November 1986, pp. 4–5.
25. Hassan H. al-Alkim, "al-Illaqat al-Arabiyyah al-Khalijiyyah ma' Iran: Ru'yiah Mustaqbaliyyah", *op. cit.*, p. 6.
26. *The Washington Post*, 15 January 1991.

27. *The Soviet Union and the Middle East* 6:12, 1990, p. 25.
28. *The Military Balance 1998/99,* London: IISS, 1998, p. 118.
29. Simon Serfaty, *op. cit.,* p. 347.
30. Shahram Chubin, *op. cit.,* p. 65.
31. Anwar Gargash, *op. cit.,* p. 138.
32. Shahram Chubin, "Iran and Regional Security," *Survival* 34:3, autumn 1992, pp. 64–66
33. Ibid, p. 68.
34. Jamal S. al-Suwaidi, "Gulf Security and the Iranian Challenge," *Security Dialogue* 27:3, 1996, p. 277.
35. Charles Tripp, "The Gulf States and Iraq," *Survival* 34:3, autumn 1992, pp. 52–53.
36. Shahram Chubin, "Iran and Regional Security," p.62.
37. *The Sunday Telegraph,* 27 September 1992.
38. *Al-Ittihad,* 17 November 1996.
39. *Al-Khalij,* 11 March 2000.
40. *The Military Balance 1998/99,* p. 117.
41. Anthony Cordesman, *Dirasat 'Alamiah: al-Qudrat al-'Askariyyah al-Iraniyyah* [Iran's Military Capabilities], Abu Dhabi: The Emirates Center for Strategic Studies and Research, 1996, p. 18.
42. *The Military Balance 1999–2000,* p. 131.
43. John Calabrese, "China and the Persian Gulf," *The Middle East Journal* 52:3, summer 1998, p. 354.
44. *The Military Balance 1998/99,* p. 117.
45. *The Sunday Telegraph,* 27 September 1992.
46. *The Military Balance 1999/2000,* p. 131.
47. Ibid.
48. Anthony Cordesman, *op. cit.,* pp. 70, 88, and 104.
49. Ibid, pp. 122–124.
50. Hassan H. al-Alkim, "The United Arab Emirates and Subregional Powers," in Joseph A. Kechichian (ed.), *A Century in Thirty Years: Shaykh Zayed and the United Arab Emirates,* Washington, D.C.: Middle East Policy Council, 2000, pp. 185–186.
51. Zbigniew Brzezinski, Brent Scowcroft, and Richard Murphy, *op. cit.,* p. 20.
52. Fuller and Lesser, *op. cit.,* p. 47.
53. Ali Ahmed Al-Ghafli, *op. cit.,* p. 210.
54. *New York Times,* 18 March 2000.
55. *Al-Ittihad,* 16 October 1999.
56. Robin Wright, "Iran's New Revolution," *Foreign Affairs* 79:1, January-February 2000, p. 136.
57. Medhat Ahmed Hamad, "Iran 1999–2000," in *Al-Taqrir Al-Istratiji Al-Khaliji,* op. cit., p. 177.
58. *The Financial Times,* 21 December 1999.
59. For more details on the Omani experiences, see Abdullah Juma Al-Haj, "The Politics of Participation in the Gulf Cooperation Council States: The Omani Consultative Council," *The Middle East Journal* 53:4, autumn 1996, pp. 560–571.
60. *Los Angeles Times,* 14 April 1991.
61. *The Financial Times,* 21 December 1999.
62. Fuller and Lesser, *op. cit.,* p. 44.
63. Mohamed Al-Said Idris, "Majlis al-Ta'awun Al-Khaliji 1999–2000," in *Al-Taqrir Al-Istratiji Al-Khaliji,* Sharjah, UAE, 2000, p. 131.
64. *The Financial Times,* 21 December 1999.
65. *Al-Ittihad,* 20 February 2000.
66. Fuller and Lesser, *op. cit.,* p. 44.
67. Madeleine Albright, "The Testing of American Foreign Policy," *Foreign Affairs* 77:6, November-December 1998, pp. 63–64.
68. Abdul Khaliq Abdallah, *al-Nizam al-Iqlimi al-Khaliji* [The Gulf Regional System], Beirut: al-Mu'asasah al-Jama'iyyah Li-dirasat wal-Nashr, 1998, p. 29.
69. Hassan H. al-Alkim, "The Gulf Subregion in the Twenty-First Century: US Involvement and Sources of Instability," *American Studies International Journal,* vol. 38:1, February 2000. George Washington University.
70. *The Washington Post,* 15 January 1991.
71. Congressional Research Service, *Document on Persian Gulf War: US Costs and Allied Financial Contributions,* Washington D.C.: CRS, lB 91019, 21 September 1992.

72. Congressional Research Service, *Document on Arms Sales to Saudi Arabia: Current Status,* Washington, D.C.: CRS, IB 91007, 25 February 1993.
73. *Al-Ittihad,* 5 March 2000.
74. Congressional Research Service, *Document on Middle East Arms Supply: Recent Control Initiatives,* Washington, D.C.: CRS, IB 91113, 22 March 1993.
75. Ali Ahmed Al-Ghafli, *op. cit.,* pp. 216–17.
76. Simon Serfaty, *op. cit.,* pp. 344–45.
77. John Calabrese, *op. cit.,* pp. 354–61.
78. William Wallace and Jan Zielonka, "Misunderstanding Europe," *Foreign Affairs* 77:6, November-December 1998, p. 74.
79. Fuller and Lesser, *op. cit.,* p. 45.
80. Simon Serfaty, *op. cit.,* p. 339.
81. *Washington Post,* 20 April 1993.
82. Hassan al-Alkim, *The Foreign Policy of the United Arab Emirates,* London: Al-Saqi Books, 1989, p. 175.
83. William Quandt, *Saudi Arabia in the 1980s: Foreign Policy, Security and Oil,* Washington D.C.: The Brookings Institution, 1981, p. 61.
84. *Al-Khalij,* 27 March 1988.
85. *Al-Khalij,* 9 April 1988.
86. Hassan H. al-Alkim, "Bi'at Sun'a al-Qarar al-Khaliji al-Saudi" [The Environment of Saudi Foreign Policy], *Arab Journal of Political Science,* number 7, November 1992, p. 66.
87. For more details, see al-Alkim, *The GCC States in an Unstable World,* p. 120.
88. Interview with Dr. Adnan Abu 'Udah, the Jordanian permanent representative to the UN, New York, 29 April 1993, as cited in ibid.

CHAPTER 25

## Outlook for Iranian-Gulf Relations: Greater Cooperation or Renewed Risk of Conflict?

Shireen T. Hunter

Since President Muhammad Khatami came to power in Iran in August 1997, there has been a noticeable improvement in the character of Iran's relations with the Gulf Arab states, after nearly two decades of intense mutual animosity and acrimony caused by the 1979 Islamic Revolution and its fall-out. The only exception to this general trend has been the United Arab Emirates (UAE), which, because of sharp disagreements over the disputed islands of Abu Musa and the Greater and Lesser Tunbs, still has tense relations with Iran. However, this is not an unusual circumstance. Historically, while certain common factors have affected Iranian-Gulf relations, the character of Iran's ties with individual Gulf states has had its own special characteristics. Iran's ties with Iraq are also very tense. Iranian-Iraqi relations have their special dynamics, whose discussion is beyond the scope of this chapter. Nevertheless, it is impossible to analyze the future of Arab-Iranian relations in the Persian Gulf without accounting for the Iraqi factor.

Notwithstanding tensions with Iraq and the UAE, amelioration in Iran-Gulf relations, and especially Iranian-Saudi links, has been particularly impressive. In view of the legacy of Ayatollah Khomeini's deep aversion toward Saudi Arabia and its leaders, improvement of Saudi-Iranian relations has been a significant development, especially since this policy has had the support of all of Iran's major political factions, including the supreme leader, Ayatollah Ali Khamenei.[1] This means that the improvement in Saudi-Iranian relations need not be contingent on the absolute ascendancy of reformist elements. The first important manifestation of improved Iranian-Gulf relations—and Iranian-Arab relations—was the December 1997 summit of the Organization of the Islamic Conference (OIC), in Teheran during Iran's presidency of OIC. A large number of Arab and Islamic heads of state and prime and foreign ministers took part in the conference. Most significant was the presence of Saudi Arabia's Heir Apparent, Prince Abdallah bin Abdul Aziz, because it signaled Saudi Arabia's seriousness to respond positively to President Khatami's declared policy of "tension reduction" (*tashanoj-zadai*) and the replacement of a posture of confrontation with that of dialogue, both regionally and internationally.[2]

The next important step was the visit of former president Ali Akbar Hashemi Rafsanjani to Saudi Arabia in February 1998, during which he met with key Saudi leaders. The only discordant note throughout the trip were some anti-Shia comments made by a Saudi cleric. Rafsanjani also made a side trip to Bahrain. Given the strained Iranian-Bahraini ties since the advent of the Islamic Revolution, this visit was quite significant. Between 1994 and 1996, Bahrain experienced difficult social and political developments, notably agitation by its Shia population. Iran was accused of encouraging and helping these disruptive elements and, according to some, instigating them. Rafsanjani's visit was intended to indicate that Iran was willing to open a new chapter in the two countries' relationship. By agreeing to receive Rafsanjani, the Bahrainis showed their willingness to put ties on a new footing. In view of significant Saudi influence over Bahraini policies, the trip also indicated Riyadh's tacit approval of better Iran-Bahrain ties.

Rafsanjani's trip was the culmination of a decade of slow but consistent efforts by Teheran to improve relations with the Gulf states. These efforts were the outcome of a process, of questioning the wisdom of past policies that Iran underwent, following its defeat by Iraq and the signing of the humiliating cease-fire agreement of August 1988. As a result of this process Iran realized that its ideologically driven regional policies, and its provocative actions and rhetoric against its Gulf Arab neighbors, had calamitous consequences, notably the extensive financial, political, and military support that the Gulf Arabs extended to Iraq during its eight-year-long war, even though Iraq was the aggressor.

After the end of the Iran-Iraq War, Ayatollah Rafsanjani admitted that Teheran had created unnecessary enemies—more by its rhetoric than by its actions, since, as Professor R. K. Ramazani has pointed out, often Iran's bark was worse than its bite. During the 1990s Iran pursued less ideological policies in general toward its Gulf Arab neighbors. For most of the 1990s, however, neither Iran's domestic politics nor regional and international conditions permitted any major breakthrough in Iranian-Gulf relations. Rather, relations were marred by the slow pace of the de-ideologization of Iranian foreign policy and continued disagreements within the Iranian leadership. Other constraints included sharpening dissension about post–Gulf War security arrangements in the region, especially the role of extra-regional powers, and most notably that of the United States; the continuation of certain Iranian actions, such as the holding of anti-American political rallies during Hajj ceremonies, which were jarring to Saudi sensitivities; the revival of the dispute with the UAE over the three Persian Gulf islands; and growing tensions with Bahrain because of allegations that Iran was involved in anti-government disturbances. The victory of the anti–Saddam Hussein coalition in the 1990–91 Gulf War—by drastically weakening Iraq—followed by the collapse of the Soviet Union, reduced the necessity of placating Iran. Between 1991 and 1994, with progress on the Arab-Israeli peace, prospects for regional cooperation in the Middle East and North Africa (MENA) also improved, thus further diminishing the urgency for the Gulf and other Arab states to improve relations with Iran.

## Shifting Political Landscape

By 1996 three major developments had altered the strategic landscape and had caused the Arab states to reassess their policy options, including their approach toward détente with Iran. First, the assassination of the Israeli prime minister, Itzhak Rabin, and the rise to power of Likud Party leader Benjamin Netanyahu set back progress on the Arab-Israeli front because Likud historically has had a less flexible approach toward peace with the Arabs. The slowing of the peace process undermined the credibility of ideas regarding region-wide economic cooperation schemes.

The second development was the growing economic, political, and military cooperation between Israel and Turkey, which has developed into a strategic partnership.[3] This development is potentially threatening both to Iran and to the Arab states. This partnership initially caused serious alarm in Egypt and several other Arab countries. But, Egyptian anxieties later subsided following President Mubarak's meeting with Turkish president Suleiman Demirel.[4] Jordan is a de facto member of the Turkish-Israeli partnership, and Turkish-Jordanian relations were further cemented by the visit of Jordan's King Abdallah II to Ankara on 7 March 2000.[5] Whatever the long-term ramifications of the Turkish-Israeli alliance for Iran and the Arab states, its immediate impact was to enhance their desire for improved relations.

The third development was the coming to power of President Khatami, whose new policy of "tension reduction" provided a more auspicious atmosphere for improved ties with Arab states. The relative thaw in U.S.-Iranian bonds following Khatami's victory meant that Washington would not oppose better Iran-Arab ties. The assumption of a more significant role in managing Saudi policies by Heir Apparent Prince Abdallah, who is more interested in improving intra-Muslim cooperation, was also a contributing factor.

*Acceleration of the Pace of Improvement*
The second important milestone on the road to better Iranian-Gulf relations was President Khatami's visit to Saudi Arabia and Qatar in May 1999. Following these visits, the Iranian side was initially eager and optimistic about the speed with which it wanted to ameliorate relations, including in such controversial areas as defense. The Arab side, however, was more cautious. Thus, Saudi authorities, although characterizing Khatami's visit as very positive, cautioned that time and effort were needed to restore confidence in the relationship. However, by July 2000, Saudi Arabia and Iran were reportedly close to signing an agreement on security cooperation. But Prince Naif, Saudi Arabia's minister of interior, emphasized that this agreement was aimed at fighting crime, terrorism, and drug trafficking, and should not be viewed as a regional defense pact.[6]

President Khatami's visit was followed by return visits to Iran by senior Saudi and other Gulf officials. Defense Minister Sultan bin Abdul Aziz—who, according to some reports, was initially lukewarm toward establishing better ties with Iran—visited Teheran in May. Other Gulf dignitaries who visited Iran in

1998–99 included Kuwait's Heir Apparent and prime minister, Shaykh Saad Abdallah Salim Al Sabah. In the event, Shaykh Al Sabah cut his formal state visit short, because of the death of the ruler of Bahrain. Thus, he made a brief stopover at Teheran airport on 6 March 1999, but the gesture clarified Kuwait's willingness to further explore the Iranian reconciliation strategy. Bahrain's foreign minister visited Teheran in May 1999, when the two countries agreed to exchange ambassadors. There have also been reports that Omani and Qatari leaders intended to visit Iran. In fact, the Emir of Qatar visited Iran in July.[7] The process of Iranian-Gulf reconciliation, however, has not extended to all countries. An especially sour note was the continuation of the frigid and acrimonious relationship between Iran and the UAE, which disapproved of Iranian-Gulf relations before the issue of the three disputed islands was resolved. The UAE clearly expressed its displeasure to its GCC partners. Reportedly, the UAE foreign minister said that Iranian-Gulf reconciliation would come at his country's expense; this view was rejected by the Saudi defense minister.[8] In order to prove that what Arab countries view as the UAE's sovereign rights over the disputed islands would not be sacrificed for the sake of better relations with Iran, the GCC and the League of Arab States (LAS) reaffirmed their support for the UAE's claim to the islands in various communiqués. The victory of Iranian reformists in the February 1999 parliamentary elections was positively received by the Gulf states, on the grounds that this would strengthen President Khatami and would enable him to continue his reconciliation policy. Still, several Gulf states, notably the UAE, have unreasonable expectations about the effects of the reformists' victory. Even the most liberal parliament would not be capable of relinquishing what Iran considers to be its sovereign rights over the two Tunbs and part of Abu Musa.[9] Yet UAE newspapers, such as *Al-Khaleej,* opined that for the reformists, "the key test will be whether Iran revises its policy toward the three UAE islands and accepts a political dialogue on the issue."[10] However, not all channels of communication between Iran and the UAE are closed.[11]

## *A Still Fragile Reconciliation*

Recent improvement in the atmospherics of Iranian-Gulf relations, although a considerable achievement after two decades of intense animosity, is still fragile. A return to the high tensions of the first decade of the revolution and the misgivings of the 1990s is unlikely, but the establishment of full trust and the setting up of a solid framework for cooperation between Iran and the Gulf states will take time and effort. Especially important will be the evolution of Iran's domestic politics, notably whether reformists will be able to translate their popular support into institutional power, thus enabling them to pursue their conciliatory policy toward their neighbors. In view of the Persian Gulf's special strategic situation, which attracts intense interest by extra-regional powers, the future of Iranian-Gulf relations will also depend on the impact of exogenous forces, which historically have determined the character of Iranian-Gulf relations more than the indigenous dynamics of the Persian Gulf region. Given the U.S. preponderance in the Gulf, the state of U.S.-Iranian relations and the American approach toward Iran's regional role will be decisive.

In view of the foregoing, it is necessary to analyze those underlying forces before sketching potential courses that Iranian-Gulf relations may follow in the foreseeable future and assessing prospects for cooperation or risk of renewed discord. These underlying forces can be divided into the following categories: (1) factors indigenous to the Persian Gulf region; (2) factors related to the broader Middle East region and its eastern and western peripheries, including the dynamics of Arab-Iranian interaction and the character of intra-Arab relations; and (3) factors related to the characteristics of the international political system and the policies and interests of its principal actors.

## Indigenous Dynamics of the Persian Gulf Region

Certain specific characteristics of the Persian Gulf region have historically exacerbated the conflictual dimensions of Gulf-Iran relations. In general, they have constituted an undercurrent of suspicion that has made cooperation problematic and, whenever achieved, limited and short-lived. The following are the most significant of these characteristics:

### *Physical Disparities*

The Persian Gulf littoral states vary greatly in their size, their population, the magnitude and diversity of their natural resources, and their diverging economic needs. Tables 25.1 and 25.2 illustrate the extent of these disparities. Three countries—Iran, Iraq, and Saudi Arabia—dominate the northern and southern littorals of the Gulf in terms of size and population. The high percentage of non-indigenous population in some Gulf states is a source of discomfort and a potential security concern as illustrated in Table 25.3. With the reduction in the number of non-Gulf Arabs, this security dimension of non-indigenous populations has somewhat lost its importance. In some of the Gulf states, such as Kuwait, Qatar, the UAE, and Bahrain, Iranians form part of this non-indigenous population.[12]

Since the movement of peoples and cultures across the Persian Gulf has historically been a two-way traffic, there are also Arab elements on the Iranian side of the Gulf, with the highest concentration in Khuzistan Province. People from the southern coasts could freely travel to Iran and live there without any limits as late as 1945. It was only in the 1950s that Iran introduced border controls in the Persian Gulf.[13] The disparities have had significant implications for Gulf states' security concerns and perceptions of potential threats, and their views regarding the most appropriate national and regional policies. The two largest Gulf states, Iran and Iraq, have favored the development of strong national defense capabilities and have opposed the presence of extra-regional forces. Smaller Gulf states, which, because of indigenous manpower problems, are not capable of creating sufficiently strong national defense forces, have welcomed the presence of friendly extra-regional forces as counterweights to the power of larger regional states.

With the increase in its indigenous population, Saudi Arabia has gradually come to favor a stronger national defense, despite some lingering ambivalence.

Table 25.1  Size of Countries

| Country | Size in Sq. Kilometers |
|---|---|
| Bahrain | 620 |
| Iran | 1,648,000 |
| Iraq | 437,162 |
| Kuwait | 17,820 |
| Oman | 212,460 |
| Qatar | 11,437 |
| Saudi Arabia | 1,960,582 |
| United Arab Emirates | 82,880 |

Source: *CIA World Fact Book*

Table 25.2  Population of Countries

| Country | Population Nationals | Population Non-Nationals |
|---|---|---|
| Bahrain | 629,090 | 227,801 |
| Iran | 65,179,752 | |
| Iraq | 22,427,150 | |
| Kuwait | 1,991,115 | 1,220,935 |
| Oman | 2,446,645 | n.a. |
| Qatar | 18,885 | 542,657 |
| Saudi Arabia | 21,504,613 | 5,321,938 |
| United Arab Emirates | 2,344,402 | 1,576,589 |

Source: *CIA World Fact Book*

Following the 1991 Gulf War, King Fahd stated: "We in the Kingdom of Saudi Arabia have made a decisive decision to immediately embark on expanding and strengthening our armed forces, and providing them with the most effective and most advanced land, sea, and air weapons the world has produced."[14] Nevertheless, even in Saudi Arabia's case, close defense cooperation with major powers remain an important component of national defense strategy.[15]

This fact became quite clear during the Iran-Iraq War, when Iran's reliance on its larger manpower potential proved no match for Iraq's more plentiful and modern weaponry. Currently, GCC countries possess more sophisticated weapons and spend more on defense than does Iran. Nevertheless, it is still a fact of international life that smaller and less populous countries feel wary of their larger neighbors. As a large country, Iran has often suffered from this basic characteristic of international relations, when its legitimate defensive actions have generated equally legitimate and understandable concerns among its southern neighbors. In the past the existence of Iranian communities in the Gulf Arab states has caused concern that they might act as a fifth column for Iran, or, as some radical Arab states claimed, try to undermine their Arab character. In the 1960s, Egypt's Nasser claimed that Iran wanted to create another Palestine in the Gulf. Indeed, as pointed out by two keen observers, "the theme constantly emphasized by Cairo was the similarity (explicitly stated) of the Iranian and

**Table 25.3 Ethnic Composition of Non-Nationals in Percentages**

|  | Bahrain | Kuwait | Oman | Qatar | Saudi Arabia | UAE |
|---|---|---|---|---|---|---|
| South Asian | 13 | 9 | n.a.* | 36 | 20 | 60 |
| Iranian | 8† | 4‡ | 1 | 10 | — | 11§ |
| Other Arab | 10 | 35 | — | — | 6 | 12 |
| Other | 1 | 17 | 27 | 28 | 2 | 3 |

Sources: *CIA World Fact Book* and from Anthony Cordesman's calculations.

\* = Cordesman does not cite South Asians for Oman, but according to the *CIA World Fact Book*, there are Indians, Pakistanis, Sri Lankans, and Bangladeshis in Oman.

† = If it is considered that a good portion of native Bahrainis are of Iranian origin (David Holden, *Farewell to Arabia*), the percentage of Iranians in Bahrain increases.

‡ = In Kuwait, too, some Kuwaiti nationals are of Iranian origin.

§ = Cordesman does not mention any Iranians in the UAE, but according to the *CIA World Fact Book*, 23 percent of the UAE population is other Arab and Iranian. Since Cordesman puts the other Arabs at 12 percent, this means that 11 percent are Iranians, which is a conservative estimate. According to the *CIA World Fact Book*, Persian is the second (after Arabic) most widely spoken language in the UAE.

Israeli states, their alleged collusion, and the analogies between Iranian immigration to the Gulf States and the Zionists' earlier immigration to Palestine. This posed, it was alleged, a threat to the Arabism of the Gulf."[16]

After the Islamic Revolution, Iranian communities were viewed as a source of subversion. Iran's efforts to export its revolution, and some Iranian involvement in subversive activities in Kuwait, Bahrain, and Saudi Arabia, strengthened these feelings. Thus, during the 1980s, a number of Iranians residing in Kuwait were expelled. The significant Arab population in Khuzistan created the misinterpretation in Baghdad that, in case of conflict with Iran, it would enjoy the support of Khuzistani Arabs. Iraq, however, was sorely disappointed in this expectation. The vast majority of the long-established Iranian communities on the southern shores of the Persian Gulf, too, have either supported the established order or been politically quiescent. They did not respond to the Iranian revolutionaries' calls for the overthrow of the Gulf Arab governments.

Therefore, it could be argued that under the right circumstances and with the elimination of other sources of tension, these communities could contribute to Iranian-Gulf reconciliation and cooperation.

### *Disparity in Energy Resources and Economic Needs*

Currently, the principal source of wealth in Iran and in the Gulf Arab countries is their energy resources. However, there are vast disparities among them in terms of the ratio of reserves to population and economic needs. Iran's position stands in sharp contrast to that of other Gulf states, including Iraq, as Table 25.4 illustrates. Iran's oil resources are not insubstantial, variously estimated at between 90 and 100 billion barrels, but they are minuscule in terms of size of population, which is still growing, albeit at a slower pace. Therefore, unless Iran reduces domestic oil consumption and revitalizes its fields, it will run out of

Table 25.4  Persian Gulf: Proven Oil Reserves. (As of the End of 1997)

| Country | Reserves in Billion Barrels |
|---|---|
| Iran | 89.7 |
| Iraq | 112.0 |
| Kuwait | 96.5 |
| Oman | 5.1 |
| Qatar | 3.7 |
| Saudi Arabia | 261.5 |
| UAE | 97.8 |
| **Total** | **666.3** |

Source: *BP/Amoco Statistical Review 1999*

petroleum resources in two or three decades.[17] Consequently, since the late 1960s, Iran's preference has been for an oil pricing policy that would maximize revenues and provide it with sufficient investment funds, reducing dependence on oil through industrialization, while Gulf Arabs have tended to favor lower oil prices.[18]

Countries like Saudi Arabia, with much larger resources and smaller populations, have favored relatively lower oil prices. Saudi Arabia has used this advantage as a means of putting political pressure on Iran. This was the case during 1985–86, when Riyadh used its "oil weapon" as a means to weaken Iran. The impact of these basic differences was quite evident during the latest meeting of the Organization of Petroleum Exporting Countries (OPEC) in March 2000, to decide on the timing and extent of changes in production, ostensibly to lower oil prices further. Thus, Saudi Arabia was more willing to increase production sooner, while Iran favored a more limited increase at a later date.

### Sectarian Differences

The Persian Gulf is also a cultural and religious frontier, with Shia/Iranian elements dominating the northern shores and Sunni/Arabs the southern parts. Two factors complicate the sectarian picture in the Gulf and accentuate its potential for creating discord between Iran and the Gulf Arabs. First, in some Gulf states, notably Saudi Arabia, the dominant creed is the strict Wahhabi school of Sunni Islam, after its founder Muhammad bin Abdul Wahhab, which views Shias not merely as misguided Muslims, but as apostates. The politically disruptive potential of such sentiments became clear during Iran's then–President Hashemi Rafsanjani's trip to Saudi Arabia in February 1998, when, during his visit to the Prophet's Mosque in Madinah, the Saudi shaykh called Shias worse than infidels. Rafsanjani left the mosque, but continued his visit—a move that was criticized by conservative newspapers in Iran. They argued that Rafsanjani should have immediately returned home. Some even alleged that powerful circles in Saudi Arabia opposed to the rapprochement with Iran had instigated the shaykh's comments.[19] In return, Ayatollah Khomeini had accused the Saudis of not practicing real Islam, but what he labeled "American

Islam." By applying such labels, he and other Iranian revolutionaries have wanted to delegitimize the Saudi leadership, and to question its pretensions to lead the Muslim world and to act as guardians of Islam's holy sites at Makkah and Madinah. Such statements, together with anti-American political rallies during the Hajj, exacerbated sectarian tensions.

Second, most of the Gulf Arab countries have substantial Shia minorities (close to 40 percent in Kuwait); and, in the case of Bahrain and Iraq, Shias constitute a majority. In Saudi Arabia the Shia minority, although relatively small, is concentrated in the oil-rich and economically important Eastern Province. Elements within these minorities harbor social, economic, and political grievances against the ruling elites, a situation that arouses the authorities' mistrust and leads them to view Shias as potentially vulnerable to Iranian manipulation. Indeed, whenever there have been disturbances by Gulf Shias, all the blame has been laid on Teheran's doorstep, and there has been little willingness to admit that Shias in several countries have real grievances. For example, during 1994–96, when Bahrain was faced with widespread political turmoil, despite the involvement of both Shia and Sunni groups in these troubles, Shias were mainly blamed for them. Bahrain's leadership also accused Iran of complicity in these difficulties and alerted U.S. officials. However, many observers have noted that "no proof existed that Tehran supported Hizbollah Bahrain or any other organization trying to overthrow the Al-Khalifas [sic]."[20] It is possible that Iran had a hand in these disturbances, but it could hardly have created them if local conditions had not been propitious. Several foreign observers and diplomats tended to believe that Bahrain's problems had more home-grown roots, and even some Bahraini Sunnis shared demands for political liberalization, the resumption of parliamentary politics, and the need to address grievances regarding their difficult economic and social conditions.[21]

Even in Kuwait, where the Shias are in a relatively better position, many suffer from discrimination.[22] The Iraqi Baathist regime's anti-Shia policies had begun long before the Iranian revolution. Yet, during the Iran-Iraq War, especially the decisive battle for Basra, Iraqi Shias demonstrated that they were loyal Iraqi citizens.[23] However, it must be stressed that sectarian differences have never by themselves been sufficient to prevent amicable coexistence and even cooperation, when other conditions have been favorable.

## *Arab-Iranian Cultural Rivalry*

Cultural competition between Arabs and Iranians has deep and complicated historical roots, although there has also been much mutually beneficial interaction between the two peoples that few are willing to acknowledge. Indeed, during a January 2000 conference in Teheran on the Persian Gulf, one of the Omani participants admitted that "from the historical point of view, rivalry between Arabs and Persians goes back many centuries."[24] Culture and politics are never totally separate, but with the rise of nationalism, they became particularly intertwined in the second half of the twentieth century. Both Iran and the Arab states experienced a period of intense cultural and political nationalism between the 1930s and the 1970s. The rise of pan-Arabism as a political and cultural ideology aimed at uniting the Arab world, but also with irredentist dimensions, adversely affected Iranian-Gulf relations.

The Persian Gulf, with its unique strategic position and its vast oil reserves, became a special focus of interest for Arab nationalists in Egypt, Syria, and Iraq. The result was a growing linkage between the Persian Gulf region and the rest of the Arab world, ultimately leading to the full integration of the Gulf Arab states into the Arab political system. This development had serious security implications for Iran, and wide-ranging, and at times contradictory, ramifications for the nature and pattern of Iranian-Gulf relations.

At one level, anti-Iran activities in certain countries caused tensions in Iran's relations with key Gulf states, such as Kuwait, where the large Palestinian community was highly receptive to Egyptian president Nasser's pan-Arab and anti-Iran propaganda. At another level, the common threat that radical Arab states in the 1960s and 1970s posed both to Iran and to the Gulf Arab monarchies enabled the latter to put aside their other differences and reach a degree of cooperation on security matters that they might not have otherwise achieved. The best example of such cooperation was that between the Shah of Iran and King Faysal of Saudi Arabia against the common "threat" of Arab socialism and ultra-nationalism aligned with the Soviet Union.[25]

The growing intrusion of other Arab states into the Persian Gulf region made Iran realize that it did not face merely the regional countries but a much wider Arab world. This fact became clear during the Iran-Iraq War, when all Arab countries—Syria and Libya being the only exceptions—lent their financial and military support to Baghdad. Two consequences have flowed from this reality. First, given the close connection between the Gulf region and the rest of the Arab world, the physical and power disparities between Gulf Arabs and Iran became less significant. Second, Iranian-Gulf relations became more vulnerable to the dynamics of intra-Arab politics, and subject to the requirements of Arab nationalism and Arab solidarity. A recent example of this situation was the 25 March 1998 resolution of the LAS, regarding the three disputed islands of Abu Musa and the Greater and Lesser Tunbs. According to the LAS resolution, "the Arab Foreign Ministers underlined the sovereignty of [the] United Arab Emirates over its three islands." The Council also denounced Iran's occupation of these islands and determined to keep the issue on the agenda of the United Nations Security Council until "Iran ends its occupation and the UAE restores full sovereignty over them."[26]

## *Territorial Disputes*
A number of territorial disputes and conflicting claims over various Persian Gulf islands have for a long time been a principal source of discord in Iranian-Gulf relations. The roots of many of these disputes lie in the very long history of Iran, with its many dramatic ups and downs, alternating periods of grandeur and decline, the intrusion of European powers—Dutch, Portuguese—into the region in the sixteenth and seventeenth centuries, and, most importantly, British colonial policies over a period of nearly 150 years.

A detailed analysis of the historic and other causes of these disputes is beyond the scope of this chapter. Suffice it to say that, at least from Iran's perspective, since the late eighteenth century, the dominant trend has been a steady reduction of Iranian cultural and political presence in the Persian Gulf. Still, it should be noted that the British policy of a "systematic de-Persianization" of the region has played an important role in this retrenchment.[27] Indeed, this was reflected in such actions as closing Persian-language schools in Bahrain, importing teachers from Iraq and Egypt, and preventing the Iranian consulate in Baghdad from issuing identity cards to the large Iranian community residing in Iraq, especially in the holy cities of Karbala and Najaf.[28]

Nothing illustrates Iranian retrenchment in the Gulf better than the challenge posed to the historic name of this body of water. Yet Iran's sensitivity regarding the name of the Persian Gulf is often viewed as proof of its aggressive and hegemonic intentions toward its neighbors, rather than the natural reaction of a country that sees the delegitimation of its presence in a region with which it has interacted for nearly 3,000 years.[29] The de-Persianization effort did not start with the Iranian revolution, or even during the later years of the Shah's rule, when Iran assumed a more assertive posture in the region. While concern over the name of the Gulf may be an irritant, the following territorial disputes have had a more serious adverse effect on Iranian-Gulf relations.

*Khuzistan/Arabistan.* In the nationalist Arab mythology, after Palestine, two parts of what it sees as the Arab homeland have been usurped from Arabs because of foreign intrigues. One of them is the so-called Arabistan. The following statement made by Iraq's deputy premier and interior minister Salih Mahdi Ammash in 1969 illustrates this line of thinking. According to Ammash, "Iraq has never seriously differed with Iran over the Shatt al-Arab: *it is Iraqi territory* [emphasis added]. The difference should have been over Arabistan which is Iraqi territory annexed to Iran during the foreign mandate and which is called Ahvaz against the will of the Iraqi people."[30] Throughout the 1970s, Iraq sponsored a number of so-called liberation fronts, including the Ahvaz Liberation Front and the Arabistan Liberation Front. Baghdad Radio continued to push this theme through its reports from "occupied Arabistan."[31]

Nor was this perception limited to Iraq. Indeed, even close Arab allies of Iran such as Jordan subscribed to this view. Thus, while the Shah of Iran and the late King Hussein maintained friendly ties, Jordanian schoolbooks showed Khuzistan as part of the Arab world, thus showing that Iran's relations with the Gulf region cannot be separated from its broader interactions with the Arab world.

Several factors prompted Iraq to invade Iran in September 1980—including the fear of a spillover of the Islamic Revolution—but the belief in the "Arabness" of Khuzistan and the notion that a wrong was done to Iraq by not incorporating it into the new state that came out of the collapse of the Ottoman Empire, along with the desire to remedy this perceived injustice, played a significant role in Baghdad's decision. This belief led Iraq to wrongly assume that Khuzistani Arabs would join Iraqi soldiers against their "Persian oppressors."

Although the Khuzistan issue is not an immediate problem, it could become one once again, as long as there is no peace treaty between Iran and Iraq. Baghdad has not unequivocally renounced its claim to Khuzistan, and the Arab view is that the region remains a usurped part of the Arab homeland.

*Bahrain.* Next to Khuzistan, conflicting Arab and Iranian claims toward Bahrain were a major source of discord in their relations until 1971, when Iran abandoned its claim to the island under British pressure, and because it lacked the means either of enforcing its claim by force or of changing the British view.

As a face-saving device, Teheran accepted a referendum carried out under the auspices of the United Nations to determine the will of the Bahraini people. In reality, however, Iran was not consulted on the arrangements for the island's future. This was in sharp contrast to the activities under way between Bahrain and other Arab states. Even before the announcement of the British decision to withdraw its military presence, visits were exchanged between Bahraini leaders and other Gulf officials, all of whom, especially Saudi Arabia, pledged their support to Manama. Still, Iran contributed to the failure of various Arab schemes to create a more robust federation in the Lower Gulf. In addition to the shaykhdoms that finally formed the UAE, and left on their own, chances were good that the federation would have also included Qatar and Bahrain. By opposing the latter's incorporation in such a scheme, the federation of nine was reduced to a federation of seven. Nevertheless, the impact of Iranian opposition should not be exaggerated. Rather, differences among the Gulf shaykhdoms, notably Bahrain and Qatar, and the ambivalence, and perhaps even opposition, of Britain and Saudi Arabia to the emergence of a potentially more powerful Arab grouping were the primary reasons for the failure of the more ambitious federal scheme.

In the event, the political and emotional cost of "abandoning" Bahrain has never been fully appreciated by outsiders, since they considered Iran's pretensions for calling Bahrain its fourteenth province something of a sad joke or a sign of the Shah's growing megalomania. Yet, the costs have been heavy, especially in light of events that followed Iran's relinquishing of its claim to the island-state, most notably the physical and political linking of Bahrain to Saudi Arabia. From the Iranian perspective, the building of a causeway linking Manama to Dammam has made it a Saudi appendage. Indeed, at the time, Iran's news media characterized the building of the causeway as "the annexation of Bahrain by Saudi Arabia."[32] Such developments, coupled with the absence of any significant Iranian presence in Manama, intensified the feeling that this loss was another stage in the long process in the Iranian political and cultural retrenchment on all its frontiers, including the Persian Gulf. Meanwhile, on the other side, there is a feeling that Iran is still hankering after Bahrain, and would like to increase its influence there. After the Islamic Revolution, some unfortunate statements were made by a minor religious figure, Ayatollah Sadegh Rouhani, to the effect that he would lead a movement to annex Bahrain unless its rulers adopted an Islamic form of government. Although these comments were immediately repudiated by the Mehdi Bazargan government, they intensified misgivings about Iranian aspirations.[33]

Yet, for Iran, the Bahrain problem as a territorial question is settled, and any effort by Iran to reverse Manama's independence would not only end any hope of Iranian-Gulf reconciliation, but would also subject Iran to severe international pressures, especially from the United States, given Bahrain's importance as the home of the U.S. Fifth Fleet. It would also justify the worst fears of Iran's neighbors about its expansionist nature. Nevertheless, within an atmosphere of reconciliation, and in conjunction with confidence-building measures, it would not be unreasonable for Iran to expect to have a more substantial and legitimate economic and cultural presence in the country.

*Troublesome Islands.* With the Bahrain issue settled and Iraq incapable of launching another attack on Iran in the foreseeable future to take over Khuzistan, the only remaining territorial conflict that has the potential of delaying, and perhaps even stopping, the process of Iranian-Gulf reconciliation is the Iran-UAE dispute over the three islands of Abu Musa and the Greater and Lesser Tunbs. The roots of this dispute also lie in British imperial policies and their efforts at controlling as many of the Persian Gulf islands as possible, as well as expanding British control in southern Iran. This British policy was prompted by two aspirations: 1) to gain total control of sea approaches to India; and 2) to prevent any risk that Russia might gain a foothold in this region.[34] The Anglo-Iranian crisis over the Tunbs and Abu Musa began in 1903, when the government of India ordered the occupation of Greater Tunb and Abu Musa by and in the name of the Shaykh of Sharjah. According to British Foreign Office documents, the occupation took place in late June and early July in the form of instructions to the Shaykh of Sharjah to hoist his flag there.[35] This British action was clearly taken out of concern for imperial purposes and not out of a belief in the sovereignty of the Shaykh of Sharjah over the islands. Indeed, it is ironic that the action should have taken place under the orders of Lord Curzon, Viceroy of India, who in 1892 had produced a map that clearly showed the islands as belonging to Iran. Later, of course, the British tried their hand at historical revisionism.[36]

At any rate, this action created a dispute between Iran and Britain that lasted until 1971. Weak as Iran was, it never abandoned its claim to these three islands. As one Iranian scholar has pointed out, "Britain wanted the islands to belong to the Shaykhdoms more than the Shaykhdoms themselves. For example, in 1939, the Shaykh of Ras al-Khaimah decided to surrender the possession of the Tunbs to Iran, as he thought that they were legitimate Iranian territory. The British intervened to disallow the move, forcing the Shaykhdom to keep its flag on the island."[37] The need for a solution became more urgent in the late 1960s, when Britain decided to withdraw from East of Suez.

Iranian diplomacy in handling the Bahrain and three islands questions was not particularly skillful. At a minimum, Teheran should have insisted on clear and legally binding agreements with Britain on the islands, rather than accepting informal or semi-formal compromises, before settling the Bahrain question and the whole issue of creating a federation out of several shaykhdoms. Iran surrendered its leverage by giving up its claim to Bahrain and by recognizing Qatar's independence. In exchange, it only "repossessed" the Tunbs with tacit British approval. By agreeing to vague arrangements and taking possession of the

Tunbs, Iran thus made itself vulnerable to charges of unlawfully occupying Arab lands. In the case of Abu Musa, by contrast, there is at least a memorandum of understanding.[38] This is in total contrast to the resolution of the Abu Dhabi–Saudi Arabia dispute. The British convinced Abu Dhabi to give up its claim to areas coveted by Riyadh so that it could have access to the Persian Gulf. Indeed, Saudi Arabia had made it clear that it would not agree to the formation of the UAE federation without the satisfaction of its demands.[39]

The dangers inherent in the ambiguous Anglo-Iranian arrangements have become clear in the last eight years, as the UAE has launched an all-out campaign against Iran. The event that triggered the latest crisis was the decision of the Iranian authorities in Abu Musa to expel 100 foreigners working for the UAE in April 1992. Iran justified this action on the grounds that the foreigners were involved in espionage and, moreover, that they did not have Iranian visas in their passports. In August 1992, Iranian authorities refused to allow foreigners without Iranian visas to enter the island, thus forcing a UAE vessel to turn back.[40]

The Iranian foreign minister, Ali Akbar Velayati, tried to soothe the UAE's concerns and attributed the Iranian actions to junior officials. Teheran also offered to engage in bilateral negotiations to untangle any differences and to clarify procedures to prevent the recurrence of such incidents.[41] Still, Iran was adamant about its sovereign rights over the islands. In the event, the UAE seized on these incidents to reopen the whole issue of the islands, and brought the question to the United Nations.[42] Some Arab countries, including Egypt, became involved in the controversy as well. Radio Cairo compared Iran's actions to the 1990 Iraqi invasion of Kuwait. Western media outlets adopted a similar line, as demonstrated by the *New York Times,* which maintained that "Abu Musa is the largest of the three islands belonging to the Emirates occupied by Iranian troops in 1971," thus implying that Iran should give them up.[43] Several Iranian scholars have maintained that the Bush administration supported the UAE's claim.[44] This would not be surprising, because it fits well within the overall hardening of the U.S. position toward Iran, which began under the Bush administration. Although the worst fears of a possible military confrontation have not materialized, the UAE has maintained its stand. Currently, it claims that all of Abu Musa's inhabitants are Arab and, moreover, that Iran is building underground military fortifications on the island.[45]

Given the strength of feelings of both sides, the risk of military conflict should not be dismissed. At the very least, serious Iran-UAE tensions would put severe limits on the extent of Iranian-Gulf reconciliation and the stabilization of the region. Already the UAE has begun to improve its ties with Iraq in order to counter Iran's reconciliation with the Gulf states.[46] Moreover, this issue could be manipulated as justification for a more severe punitive policy toward Iran, such as military strikes against key installations.

## Forces Related to the Broader Middle East Region and Its Periphery

The foregoing has illustrated that, historically, forces and dynamics exogenous to the region have affected Iranian-Gulf relations. In particular, these ties were affected by the dynamics of intra-Arab politics and the Arab-Israeli conflict, including, since 1991, improved prospects for Arab-Israeli peace. Gulf Arab states' energy resources had since the 1950s made them a focus of attention and a target of envy for more powerful, but economically less endowed, Arab countries. The dominant Arab nationalist view in the period from the 1950s to the 1970s was that the oil resources of the Persian Gulf Arabs belonged to the whole of the Arab nation and should be equally shared among it.[47] Gamal Abdel Nasser's efforts to destabilize the Saudi monarchy and his forays into Yemen were, in part, prompted by a desire to gain access to the Gulf region's oil resources. Other revolutionary regimes, including that of Abdul Karim Qasim in Iraq, intimidated Kuwait and extorted large amounts of financial assistance.[48] During the 1990–91 Gulf crisis, Saddam Hussein exploited the theme of rich versus poor to garner additional sympathy for Iraq and increase resentment for Kuwait and the conservative Gulf monarchies among Arabs and Muslims.

Iran was not immune to the animosity, negative propaganda, and even active subversion of radical Arab states, most notably Nasser's Egypt, as well as Iraq, Syria, Libya, and the Palestinian movement. One aspect of this propaganda was to portray Iran as a threat to the Gulf Arab states, a danger to the Arab character of the Persian Gulf region, and, in general, an enemy of Arabs because of its close ties with Israel. Yet, the argument is not convincing because Turkey has had closer relations with Israel and, indeed, had recognized it, while Iran had not done so. Yet, Turkey was never the subject of intense Arab animosity, as was Iran. Even today, close Israeli-Turkish relations, the massing of Turkish troops on the Syrian border over the Ocalan affair, and Turkish threats to curtail water supplies to Syria and Iraq have not ignited similar Arab passions. Nor do many Arabs worry about the fate of Iskanderun Province and its Arab inhabitants (an estimated 3 million), in sharp contrast to the case of Khuzistan or the uninhabited Tunbs. The main reason for such diametrically opposing perceptions of Iran and Turkey lies in the geopolitical and economic characteristics of the Persian Gulf—hence the eagerness of major Arab countries, notably Egypt and Syria, to establish their presence in the region and to acquire influence over Gulf Arab states. This desire became quite clear following the end of the 1991 Gulf War, when various schemes were considered for the post-war security structure of the Persian Gulf. One suggestion included the stationing of Egyptian and Syrian troops in some Gulf states.

The GCC+2 scheme did not materialize, but both Syria and Egypt have become involved in Gulf security affairs in the context of the March 1992 Damascus Declaration. By contrast, there has been no structured process of dialogue between Iran and the Gulf states on Gulf security. What this attitude amounts to is the denial of a legitimate role for Iran in the Gulf and the contention that the Persian Gulf is an integral part of a purely Arab geographic sphere in which Iran has no place.

Ironically, since the end of the 1991 Gulf War, and improving Arab-Israeli relations, Iran's excessive zeal to support the Palestinian cause has become a source of irritation in the latter's relations with some Arab countries. This may be one reason why Cairo has been at best ambivalent about better Iranian-Gulf relations. Surely cordial Iranian-Gulf relations—should they be achieved—would reduce Egypt's overall regional importance and its influence in the Gulf.[49] Syria has parlayed its good relations with Iran into greater influence throughout the region, by playing the role of mediator and conciliator. Yet even Syria has not favored very close Iranian-Gulf relations, since this would reduce its own regional weight, and, despite its so-called strategic alliance with Iran, it has also supported UAE claims to the three islands.

There is another way in which intra-Arab politics affect Iranian-Gulf relations, and that is related to intra-Arab political and economic institutions, notably the League of Arab States. These institutions' main goal has been the greater integration and eventual unification of the Arab states in the framework of something akin to the European Union. Therefore, they are not open to non-Arab countries. These are regional Arab organizations, such as the Gulf Cooperation Council (GCC) and the Arab Maghreb Union (AMU), which have their own specific dynamics, although they are considered as building blocks of this broader intra-Arab network.

This situation makes Iran's inclusion in regional schemes of economic and security cooperation quite difficult for the Gulf Arab states, even if Teheran's policies were to radically change. Iraq, an Arab state, does not suffer from this handicap, and would be a natural candidate for inclusion in the GCC under a different regime. The obstacles for such a union would be intra-Arab rivalry and/or opposition from Western powers, which might conclude that a GCC that included Iraq would be too strong and, hence, undesirable even if friendly toward them. Nor are these merely theoretical issues. In the last few months, there have been reports in the Iranian press that Qatar has expressed the opinion that Iran should be invited to join the GCC.[50] The accuracy of such reports is doubtful. But they reflect the reality that such notions are not beyond the realm of the possible, although because of intra-Arab politics and international systemic factors, quite unlikely even in the long term. Problems, disagreements, and diverging interests in the close periphery of the Gulf region, such as South Asia, between Iran and some key Gulf Arab states, including Saudi Arabia and the UAE, have in the past added to tensions between them and could hamper the future reconciliation.

### *Impact of International Factors: Great-Power Policies*
Because of the high degree of outside interest in strategically important regions such as the Persian Gulf, the great powers exert a determining influence in shaping the dynamics of regional politics, choices, and options available for local actors. The foregoing has illustrated how, during the past 150 years, outside interests and great-power rivalries have shaped the political geography of the Persian Gulf. But the most intense period of great-power rivalry in the Persian Gulf region was the Cold War era.

The dynamics of the Cold War, especially the balance of terror between East and West, affected the strategies of the two competing camps toward the region. Unwilling to risk a direct confrontation, both camps tried to establish their own special partners. The series of alliances that the Soviet Union developed in the Arab world with Egypt, Syria, Iraq, Libya, Algeria, and the Democratic Republic of South Yemen were balanced by the U.S. policy of creating "regional pillars"—especially in the Persian Gulf—stark examples of competition by proxy. Since the Soviet Union championed the cause of Arab nationalism, Cold War rivalries had a deleterious effect on Iran's relations with a number of Gulf states, notably Kuwait. Western promotion of Iran as a principal pillar of Gulf security in the late 1960s and early 1970s had adverse consequences for both its internal stability, as demonstrated by the 1979 revolution, and its relations with the Gulf Arab states. Ultimately, it even created tensions in Iran's ties with its main allies, notably Britain and the United States, because it gave the impression that Teheran was becoming too ambitious, eager to be treated as an ally and not a surrogate.

This perception was inevitably brought to the fore by the conflict that exists between the interests of a great power with global interests and those of a regional power—actual or potential—because secondary powers tend to limit great powers' freedom of action. The Shah's insistence that the security of the Persian Gulf should be the responsibility of "riparian states" was a good example of a policy favored by a potential regional power but objectionable to great powers because as a rule they are averse to regional collective security and defense systems in which they have no role, or only play the role of primus inter pares. For example, when Malaysia hinted at the idea of creating a collective security system for the ASEAN countries in the early 1990s, Washington opposed the concept. Similarly, the U.S. is ambivalent about an independent European Security and Defense Identity (ESDI), if it were to develop in a way that would dilute the role of NATO and hence U.S. influence on the Continent.

Therefore, Iran's pretension to play the role of ally rather than surrogate led radical Arab countries to intensify their subversive activities against Teheran. Moreover, although several Western and Arab commentators maintained that the Gulf states perceived pre-revolutionary Iran as a "shield" against radicalism, at the time they did not express this opinion openly. Rather, they interpreted Iran's new role as an indication of the reawakening of its expansionist impulses. When Iranian troops assisted Oman in combating Dhuffari rebels, the Gulf states did not react with appreciation but, like radical Arabs, interpreted the actions as further signs of its imperial ambitions.

### *Post-Soviet System*
The bipolar international system of the post-war world and the existential and global East-West competition had many negative effects for Iran, which was a focus of the East-West rivalry because of its unique position as a formidable buffer between the Soviet Union and the Persian Gulf, and a viable counterweight to Iraq, then a close Soviet ally. Yet the intense great-power rivalry offered Iran room to maneuver, and limited the major powers' ability to pressure it beyond a certain point. This logic was apparent in the U.S. reaction, at least from 1979 to 1986, when Washington treated Teheran with a good deal of forbearance, and even tried a rapprochement, which ended in the Iran-Contra debacle.

It was not until 1987, when East-West relations had already begun to thaw, that the U.S. position decidedly shifted in favor of Iraq—in the Iran-Iraq War—since Washington no longer feared potential Soviet inroads in Iran. The Gulf states were conscious of this fact, despite all the difficulties that the revolutionary regime created for them. The existence of the Soviet counterweight also placed limits on the ability of Western powers to project force, or to pre-position weapons, to areas located in the proximity of the Soviet Union—the only exception being the main Central European theater.

In the context of the Persian Gulf, and because of the Soviet–radical Arab forces connection, the Gulf Arab states did not desire a direct Western presence. Rather, they pushed for an "over the horizon" strategy. It is worth noting that the first major foray of U.S. naval forces into the Persian Gulf—to escort Kuwaiti tankers—began in 1987, when East-West relations began to improve. The East-West progress of the 1980s and the early 1990s certainly facilitated military operations during Desert Shield and Desert Storm. In short, even before the collapse of the Soviet Union, sharp improvements in East-West ties had vastly improved the geostrategic position of the West and its regional allies.

The Soviet Union's collapse in December 1991, coupled with the steady erosion of Russia's military and economic powers, further enhanced Western advantages. In the Middle East/Persian Gulf regions, this dramatic systemic shift weakened the position and influence of radical pro-Soviet countries and those hostile to the West such as Iran, while enhancing the positions of pro-Western states such as those of the Gulf Arabs.

First, the elimination of the Soviet counterweight enabled Washington to establish its military presence in the Persian Gulf, in the form of the Fifth Fleet and the pre-positioning of military hardware and personnel in Saudi Arabia, Kuwait, and Bahrain. Second, it enabled Washington to pursue a severe punitive policy toward Teheran, despite the fact that there had been some moderation in Iran's external behavior. Third, and despite Iranian neutrality during the 1991 Gulf War—as well as its unqualified support for Kuwaiti independence and territorial integrity—the U.S. position toward Iran hardened almost immediately after the allied victory, when President George Bush did not follow up on his promise that "good will begets good will." Thus, the foundation of what came to be known as the policy of "dual containment" in the Clinton presidency was laid during the Republican administration.

Iran's Gulf neighbors benefited from these systemic shifts in several ways. First, they no longer needed to worry about the reaction of Arab radical forces in charting their regional and international policies. Second, they could openly enter into military and security arrangements with Western powers. Third, the U.S. military presence became a deterrent against Iran and Iraq. Fourth, Washington's containment policy meant that Iran could not effectively rebuild its military forces.

All these factors contributed to the cool response that the Gulf States offered to Iranian overtures, despite the fact that Iranian neutrality had contributed to the allied victory. These changed circumstances also contributed to the UAE's decision to reopen the islands issue and pursue it as far as necessary, short of military confrontation, at least in the immediate future. Indeed, according to one observer,

> His [Shaykh Zayed's] choice of 1992 to make an issue out of Abu Musa *was dictated more by the circumstances in the region than by Iranian actions* [emphasis added]. The Iranians had been militarizing the islands throughout the eighties, during the Iran-Iraq War, and he did not make an issue out of it. He did not even make an issue out of it during the Kuwait crisis of 1990–91. He waited until all that was over, and in 1992, when he had the support of the international community, he made an issue of Abu Musa and the Tunbs.[51]

Systemic factors, especially the policies and attitudes of the current dominant international actor—the United States—will play a crucial role in either encouraging or hampering better relations between Iran and the Gulf Arabs. At present, the American attitude seems to be ambivalent. On the one hand, a more positive and friendly Iranian attitude toward the Gulf states would ease their security concerns and enhance their stability, something that Washington would favor. A sharp improvement in such relations, on the other hand, could reduce the need for a large-scale U.S. presence in the region and erode its ability to pressure Gulf Arab governments on issues such as levels of oil production, prices, and purchases of U.S. military hardware. It is perhaps with these concerns in mind that the U.S. secretary of defense, William Cohen, on a visit to the Persian Gulf in April 2000, warned Gulf Arab leaders about the continued security threat that Iran posed to them and, therefore, the need for better defense technology in the region. Cohen's visit and his statements came at a time when Iran, Saudi Arabia, and Oman were beginning a dialogue on security and defense issues.[52]

## Conclusions and Outlook

The character of relations between Iran and the Gulf Arab states, since they began to interact regularly starting in the late 1950s, has been determined by the interaction of a complex set of factors—ethnic, cultural, religious. Other factors, including ideological and political consequences of the process of development and modernization such as the revolutions that swept the Arab world in the 1950s and 1960s and the Iranian Islamic Revolution of 1979, also left their impact. Since the Arab part of the Gulf is organically linked with the rest of the Arab world at various levels, these relations have also been subject to the dynamics of intra-Arab politics. Most important, however, in the last two centuries the nature of the international political system and the policies and practices of its principal actors have affected the character not only of Iranian-Gulf relations but also of the basic political patterns of the region. In coming years, systemic factors will surely continue to impact Iranian-Gulf relations. The key factor will be whether current U.S. supremacy will continue or whether counterweights—or at least serious competitors—will emerge to balance the sole remaining superpower. Equally important, policies pursued toward Iran and the Gulf states, at least for the foreseeable future, are not likely to change, because no such counterweights are on the horizon. Therefore, U.S. policies toward the region, the role of Iran, and the state of U.S.-Iranian relations will play key roles in determining the extent and pace of improvement in Iranian-Gulf relations. Should there again be a crisis in U.S.-Iranian relations, in all likelihood the process of improving Iranian-Gulf ties would be halted. Such a development might even involve a risk of conflict. A crisis over the three islands could provide the spark for such a contest.

Because the state of U.S.-Iranian politics will be affected to a great extent by the state of Iranian internal politics, the evolution of the latter in the direction of reform and liberalization would have a crucial impact in determining the course of Iranian-Gulf ties. Developments in the broader Middle East region, especially the fate of the Arab-Israeli peace process and the prospects for Arab-Israeli economic cooperation, will also affect the course of Iranian-Gulf relations. Brighter prospects on this front might dampen enthusiasm for better ties with Iran. Finally, the fate of the Iraqi regime is another factor with considerable implications for Iranian-Gulf relations. The displacement of Saddam Hussein and the installation of a moderate, pro-Western regime in Baghdad could reduce the impetus for the Gulf states to improve ties with Iran.

In short, the future of Iranian-Gulf relations is contingent on many imponderables. What is certain is that the establishment of mutual trust and the development of an appropriate framework for cooperation will be a lengthy and uneven process. It is highly unlikely that Teheran will be incorporated into some kind of new security structure in the Gulf. Yet, under a positive scenario, mechanisms for consultation and cooperation on security matters and conflict prevention and resolution of disputes could certainly be envisaged. Yet even if the pace of Iranian political reforms were to remain slow, a return to the tension-ridden period of the 1980s and 1990s is very unlikely. Still, real and lasting reconciliation, and the creation of a true Arab-Iranian cultural, economic, and political zone of cooperation, will be a lengthy process. Nevertheless, the continued trend toward reconciliation during 1999–2001, exemplified by the signing of a security agreement between Iran and Saudi Arabia—as well as the visit of Prince Naif to Teheran in the spring of 2001—coupled with expressions of regret by Kuwait for having supported Iraq during the Iran-Iraq War, justify a degree of optimism about the future.

## Notes

1. In his last testament, Ayatollah Khomeini stated that Iran might one day even make peace with Saddam Hussein, but never with Saudi Arabia.
2. For an excellent analysis of the ideological foundations of President Khatami's foreign policy, see R. K. Ramazani, "The Shifting Premise of Iran's Foreign Policy: Towards a Democratic Peace," *The Middle East Journal* 52:2, spring 1998, pp. 177–87.

# OUTLOOK FOR IRANIAN–GULF RELATIONS   447

3. On Israeli-Turkish cooperation and its ramifications, see Daniel Pipes, "A New Axis: The Emerging Turkish-Israeli Entente," *The National Interest,* number 50, winter 1997–98, pp. 31–36.
4. On the evolution of Egypt's views on closer Turkish-Israeli ties, see "Egyptian Foreign Minister on Peace Process, Other Issues," *Foreign Broadcast Information Service (FBIS)–NESA, 98–093,* 4 June 1998. On this occasion, Foreign Minister Amr Musa said that "Turkey knocked on the wrong door when it wanted to return to the Middle East and committed a strategic error with the Arabs when it concluded its strategic alliance." The League of Arab States (LAS) also expressed hope that "Turkey will reconsider the relations of military cooperation with Israel, particularly at a time when the Middle East Peace Process is clearly facing a log jam because of Israel's policy," *FBIS-NESA 98–084,* 27 March 1998. According to the leading Egyptian analyst, Dr. Abdel Monem Said, while speaking on 24 March 2000 in Washington: "Initially there was a big alarm in Egypt about the so-called alliance between Israel and Turkey. After studying it, Egypt realized that it is simply a normal level of military cooperation between states that does not threaten any third party. *That helped smooth problems in the relationship between Egypt and Turkey* [emphasis added]," Washington Institute for Near East Studies, *PolicyWatch,* number 442, 24 March 2000. Other meetings included that between Turkish foreign minister Ismael Cem and President Husni Mubarak, as well as several exchanges between Turkish and Egyptian military officers.
5. On King Abdallah's visit to Turkey and the wide-ranging discussions that took place between him and President Demirel, covering a wide spectrum from water to joint investment and security cooperation, see "Demirel, Jordanian King Address Business Council," *FBIS-NESA 2000–0208,* 8 March 2000.
6. "Iran's Shamkhani: No Limits to Ties with Saudi Arabia," *FBIS-NESA 1999–050,* 1 May 1999. And on Prince Naif's statement, see "Saudi Interior Minister on Yemeni Treaty, Security Pact with Iran," *FBIS-NESA,* 11 June 2000.
7. "Iran: Upcoming Visits by Qatar, Oman Leaders Eyed," *FBIS-NESA 2000–0127,* 27 January 2000. According to the English-language daily *Teheran Times,* "Omani Sultan Qaboos and Qatari Emir Shaykh Hamad bin Khalifa Al Thani have expressed their intention to visit Iran." On the Amir's visit, see various *FBIS/NESA* reports on 17 and 18 July 2000.
8. Douglas Jehl, "Overtures from Iran Ignite a Bitter Debate among Arab States," *New York Times,* 9 June 1999.
9. Since the 18 February 1999 "reformist" victory, the conservative-dominated Council of Guardians has been canceling the results of many elections. These actions have caused popular protest throughout the country. See "Guardians Council Defends Vote Cancellation," *Radio Free Europe/Radio Liberty Iran Report* 3:15, 17 April 2000, p. 2.
10. "Islands Dispute Will Prove Acid Test for Iran's Reformers: UAE Paper," Agence France-Presse (AFP), 22 February 2000.
11. On Iran-UAE contacts, see "Iranian Official Meets UAE Defense Minister in Dubai," BBC Worldwide Monitoring/Middle East, 3 February 2000. The Kuwaiti paper *al-Qabas* reported that according to the UAE defense minister, Shaykh Muhammad bin Rashid Al Makhtoum, the Iranian-UAE relation "was and still is very good." Xinhua News Agency, 18 January 2000.
12. The exact number of Iranians among those who have kept their distinct characteristics and those who have become "Arabized" is not known. What is known from Arab and other sources is that Iranian communities have existed in the Lower Gulf for a thousand years. For more details, see Pirouz Mojtahed-Zadeh, "Perspectives on the Territorial History of the Tunb and Abu-Musa Islands," Hooshang Amirahmadi (ed.), *Small Islands, Big Politics,* New York: St. Martin's Press, 1996, p. 36. Exact current figures for Iranian communities in the Lower Gulf are not available. Moreover, there is a general tendency in recent Arab and Western assessments to give a low estimate of the number of people of Iranian origin. But the pre–late 1960s literature indicates the existence of large Iranian communities. According to David Holden, "a strong strain of Persian blood among Bahrain's people and a majority of Shiites over Sunni Muslims both derive from the Persian years." See David Holden, *Farewell to Arabia,* London: Faber & Faber, 1966. In Kuwait, an Iranian community had existed since 1776. According to H. R. P. Dixon, in 1953, the Persian community numbered 30,000. There have also been substantial numbers of Iranians in Dubai and Qatar.
13. Rupert Hay, *The Persian Gulf States,* Washington, D.C.: The Middle East Institute, 1959, p. 148.
14. "King Fahd Speaks on War Outcome, Government," *FBIS-NESA 91–073,* 16 April 1991.

15. For an excellent discussion on Saudi Arabia's evolving national security strategy, see Joseph A. Kechichian, "Trends In Saudi National Security," *The Middle East Journal* 53:2, spring 1999, pp. 232–53.
16. Shahram Chubin and Sepehr Zabih, *The Foreign Relations of Iran: A Developing State in a Zone of Great Power Rivalry,* Berkeley/Los Angeles: University of California Press, 1974, p. 148.
17. See the interview with Iran's deputy oil minister, "Iran News Say Domestic Oil Consumption Too High," *FBIS-NESA 98–070,* 25 March 1998.
18. William Drozdiak, "Bowing to US, OPEC Agrees to Hike Output; Saudi Arabia, Iran Divided," *Washington Post,* 29 March 2000.
19. On the Iranian reaction to anti-Shia comments, see Seyyed Mohammad Safizadeh, "Diplomacy with a Smile," *Abrar,* as reproduced in *FBIS-NESA,* 13 March 1998. The author argues that since the Wahhabi shaykh called Shias worse than infidels, Rafsanjani should have cut his visit short. See also "Iranian Clerics Sanei, Lankarani Respond to Saudi Shaykh," *FBIS-NESA 98–071,* 13 March 1998.
20. Mark J. O'Reilly, "Oil Monarchies without Oil: Omani and Bahraini Security in a Post-Oil Era," *Middle East Policy* 6:3, February 1999, p. 78.
21. David Gardner, "A Raise of the Stakes: Neighbors and Allies are Watching Closely as Bahrain's Rulers Resist Demand from Shia Moslems for Democratic Reforms," *The Financial Times,* 12 April 1996. According to the London-based paper, "the gap is growing between the rulers and the people of this island, and not only the Shias, says one Sunni businessman."
22. Shafeeq Ghabra, "Kuwait and the Dynamics of Socio-Economic Change," *The Middle East Journal* 51:3, summer 1997, pp. 367–68.
23. On Saddam Hussein's anti-Shia policies, see Hanna Batatu, "Iraq's Underground Shia Movements: Characteristics, Courses and Prospects," *The Middle East Journal* 35:4, autumn 1981, pp. 578–94.
24. "Omani Air Force Official on Iran, Gulf States' Ties," *FBIS-NESA 2000–0205,* 5 February 2000.
25. Judith Perera, "Together Against the Red Peril: Iran and Saudi Arabia, Rivals for Super-power Role," *The Middle East Magazine,* number 43, May 1978, pp. 16–25.
26. On the LAS resolution, see "Egypt: Arab League Resolutions, Recommendations," *FBIS-NESA 98–084,* 25 March 1998.
27. Davond H. Bavand, "Bar-rosie-Mabani Tarikhi va Hoquqi-e-Jazayer-e-Irani-e-Tonb va Abu Musa" [The Investigation of the Historical and Legal Foundations of the Iranian Islands of Tunb and Abu Musa], *Jmeh-e-Salem* 11:7, December 1992–January 1993, pp. 6–19.
28. Fereydoun Adamiyat, *Bahrain Islands: A Legal and Diplomatic Study of British-Iranian Controversy,* New York: Praeger, 1955.
29. "An Egyptian official yesterday criticized statements made recently by President Khatami that the [Arabian] Gulf will remain 'Persian.'" See "Egypt: Official Critiques Khatami over 'Persian' Gulf," *FBIS-NESA 2000–0121.*
30. Quoted in Chubin and Zabih, *op .cit.,* p. 183.
31. Ibid.
32. *FBIS-MEA,* 28 January 1982.
33. R. K. Ramazani, *Revolutionary Iran: Challenge and Response in the Middle East,* Baltimore: Johns Hopkins University Press, 1986, p. 49.
34. Pirouz Mojtahed-Zadeh, *op. cit.,* p. 46.
35. Ibid.
36. The following is an example of such an endeavor. "In the second half of the XVIIIth century, the Arabs of the Pirate (later called the Trucial) Coast of Arabia occupied the islands of Tonb (also called Tunb, Tamb, and Tomb) [and] its dependency, Nabiyu Tanb Abu Musa and Sirri; it seems probably they did so in the very confused period subsequent to the death of Nadir Shah." Quoted in ibid., from the Confidential Document (17188) of H.B.M. Government "Persian Frontiers," 1947, par. 72.
37. Ibid., pp. 48–51.
38. Mohammad Reza Dabiri, "Abu-Musa Island: A Binding Understanding or a Misunderstanding," *The Iranian Journal of International Affairs* 5:3 and 4, fall/winter 1993/94, pp. 575–83.
39. Bruce R. Kuniholm, "Great Power Rivalry and the Persian Gulf," in Robert F. Helms II and Robert H. Dorff (eds.), *The Persian Gulf Crisis: Power in the Post-Cold War World,* Westport, Connecticut: Praeger, 1993, p. 50.

40. "Iran Silent on Expulsions," *New York Times,* 16 April 1992. See also Youssef M. Ibrahim, "Iran Is Said to Expel Arabs from Gulf Island," *New York Times,* 16 April 1992.
41. *Iran Focus,* November 1992.
42. General Assembly Document A/47/316, *Resolution 5223/98/3,* New York: United Nations, 13 September 1992.
43. "Iran Silent on Expulsions," *New York Times,* 16 April 1992.
44. Hooshang Amirahmadi, "The Colonial-Political Dimension of the Iran-UAE Dispute," in Amirahmadi (ed.), *Small Islands, Big Politics,* p. 14.
45. The UAE foreign minister Rashid bin Abdallah Al Nuaymi "urged *Al-Sharq al-Awsat* not just to publish the pictures of the surface of the Abu Musa (as it did in its issue last Tuesday 9th March) but to show the military fortifications underneath the surface of the island. *He asserted that there is not a single Iranian on the three islands, whose inhabitants are one hundred per cent Arab*" [emphasis added]. This statement is astonishing after 30 years of joint Iranian-Sharjah administration of the islands. See "UAE to Accept Iran's Offer of Island Talks If Put to Tripartite Commission," BBC Worldwide Monitoring/Middle East, quoting *Al-Sharq al-Awsat,* 12 March 2000.
46. "Paper Views Gulf States Move Toward Closer Ties with Iraq," *FBIS/NESA,* 27 April 2000: "The ceaseless efforts by the Emirates to get closer to and elevate ties with Iraq are in a way looking for new allies among Middle Eastern countries hostile to Iran."
47. On the Arab nationalist view on oil, see Emile Bustani, *Marche Arabesque,* London: Robert Hale Ltd., 1961. See also David Hirst, *Oil and Public Opinion in the Arab World,* London: Faber & Faber, 1966.
48. According to David Holden, the Kuwait Fund loans were "unofficially but with perfect clarity understood from Casablanca to Baghdad to have been the first installment in Kuwait's protection money." See *Farewell to Arabia,* p. 169. For more details on the use of financial assistance to enhance security, see Shireen T. Hunter, *OPEC and the Third World: The Politics of Aid,* Bloomington: Indiana University Press, 1984.
49. On Egypt's aversion to better U.S.-Iranian relations that would positively impact on Iranian-Gulf ties, see Eric Hoagland, "US Perspectives on Persian Gulf Security," *The Iranian Journal of International Affairs* 5:3 and 4, fall/winter 1993/94, p. 664.
50. "Iranian Official on Iran-Gulf Cooperation," *FBIS-NESA 2000,* 7 February 2000.
51. William A. Rugh, "Past, Present, and Future Leadership," in "Symposium: A Century in Thirty Years: Shaykh Zayed and the United Arab Emirates," *Middle East Policy* 6:4, June 1999, p. 31.
52. Howard Schneider, "Cohen Warns Gulf States on Dealing with Teheran," *Washington Post,* 10 April 2000.

# TRENDS IN GULF AFFAIRS

CHAPTER 26

## *What Makes the Gulf States Endure?*

J. E. Peterson

What has been—and, for that matter, will continue to be—the path followed by the Gulf monarchies, and why has it been so successful? That is the key question that drives any consideration of the strength and durability of the six states that make up the Gulf Cooperation Council (GCC): Saudi Arabia, Kuwait, Bahrain, Qatar, the United Arab Emirates (UAE), and Oman. Ironically, many observers have long regarded the Gulf states as anachronisms, propped up only by oil money and overdue to disappear into the dustbin of history at any time. Yet, the Gulf states not only have survived, they have endured and prospered. Why is this the case?

The central question of this essay is not easy to answer. A simple answer might be that the Gulf states have endured because they are sound regimes based on durable political construction. When compared to their neighbors in the Gulf, the Middle East, Africa, and Asia, there is more than a modicum of truth in this response. Yet, it simply restates the obvious. At the risk of sounding tautological, the Gulf states are likely to endure because they have endured already. Over a few short decades, they have faced down successive challenges of modernization, radical pan-Arab nationalism, and Islamic revivalism. They have demonstrated that they possess the qualifications necessary for survival.

Still, they are monarchies in a world that has rejected monarchies. Granted, there is much about these states that does seem anachronistic and part of a bygone era. For example, the conservative and largely traditional societies, the uncertain criteria for succession, the favored—and resented—status of the ruling families, and the combination of rule by and benefits to what is essentially an oligarchy of political and economic elites. Still, it is also true that these states have seen unprecedented political and social change. The newly built cities of the Gulf, with their expansive boulevards, modern buildings, and crowded shopping malls, vividly illustrate the types of changes that have occurred. At the same time, however, conclusions drawn from these more superficial transformations may give a misleading impression of the persistent continuity in Gulf society.

From another angle, the region's media emphasis on the daily "court report" and the outwardly unaltered structure of the regimes undoubtedly obscures the great extent of change that has occurred already. The first step in properly answering the question of what makes the Gulf states endure must, therefore, be to examine the intrinsic nature of these regimes and the characteristics that set them off from other countries.

## The Fate of Monarchies in the Gulf, 1900–2000

It is worth restating the obvious in a slightly different context. The Gulf states are both Arab and Muslim states, which has endowed them with a profound legacy of political and social norms. Significant among these are Arab and Islamic concepts of legitimacy being invested in rulers who are strong and capable, who govern according to the precepts of Islam (i.e., they permit that which Islam allows and prohibit that which Islam forbids). In this sense, contemporary Arab monarchies can be seen as the heirs to the Umayyads and the Abbasids. The test of legitimacy therefore lay as much in the power and capability of the regime as in its inherent right to rule. When regimes became weak or ineffective, rulers who were stronger and more capable replaced them, as happened in this century across the Gulf with the replacement of the Qajar regime by Reza Shah and the creation of his own Pahlavi dynasty. The emergence of the Gulf states in the last century or more owes much to the appearance of strong leaders, who were able to forge durable tribal coalitions and establish dynastic rule over the proto-states they had formed.

Britain encouraged the existing inclination toward hereditary rule, in imitation of its own monarchy. At the end of the First World War, Britain attempted to replace weak Ottoman authority in the areas under its control with local monarchies—such as the Hashemites in the Hejaz, and subsequently in Transjordan and Iraq, the Sanusis in Libya, and the descendants of Muhammad Ali in Egypt. These particular experiments were not very successful, as illustrated by the disappearance of four of the five monarchies. In Arabia, the Hashemite Kingdom of the Hejaz failed because of the emergence of a stronger regime, the resurgent Al Saud under the redoubtable Abdul Aziz bin Abd al-Rahman (more commonly known in the West as Ibn Saud). In Oman, Britain encouraged the evolution of a hereditary monarchy out of the historical tradition of a sectarian imamate. Elsewhere along the Arab littoral, Britain fashioned treaty relationships with the shaykhly families of the predominant tribes, and these gradually metamorphosed into monarchical forms of government, particularly after rulers became the direct recipients of oil revenues.

Until just a few decades ago, all the littoral states of the Gulf were monarchical. But in 1958, a military coup produced an Arab nationalist, socialist regime in Iraq, and in 1979 political and social upheaval forged an Islamic revolution in Iran. Nevertheless, and despite the divergent ideological threats posed by these changes to the north, aided at various times by active intrigues of new regimes in Baghdad and Teheran, the Gulf states survived, prospered, and endured. Predictions that they would disappear have been ubiquitous over the past decades—particularly from the time of British withdrawal through the Iranian revolution. Luck may, in part, be responsible for their persistence, but a more fundamental reason lies in the deep differences between the Gulf states, on the one hand, and Iran and Iraq on the other.

## What Makes the Gulf States Different?

There are many fundamental reasons why the Gulf states are different from their northern Gulf neighbors. Inherent differences overlaid with variant historical experiences—even when just the twentieth century is considered—have determined evolutionary divergences in social and political organization. Both Iran and Iraq evince complex societies with many different sectarian, linguistic, ethnic, and occupational communities—in contrast to the relatively uniform societies in the Gulf states. Even more obviously, the Gulf states tend to be much smaller in both geographical size and population. As a consequence, societies have been more homogenous, cohesive, and, in a sense, more controllable. Smaller populations also meant that the impact of oil wealth was felt more strongly and positively throughout the population.

Furthermore, Iran and Iraq long enjoyed, at least in relative terms, a measure of economic diversity and development, enabled by such factors as natural resources and education. On the other hand, a principal distinguishing characteristic of the Gulf states before oil was extreme poverty, which retarded economic development and severely restricted education. The Gulf states remain poor in natural resources—with the notable exception of crude oil and in some cases natural gas—and this factor restricts both the direction and the scope of their post-oil development.

Consequently, delayed development in the Gulf states allowed little scope for ideological ferment and discontent. It is no accident that Bahrain is the only country in which serious discontent has occurred. Bahrain was the first country among the Gulf states to enjoy the oil income that prompted significant socioeconomic change. At the same time, however, Bahrain's oil bonanza has been modest and so the distribution of oil wealth has been the slightest there.

Until recently, only Iran and Iraq could be classified as nation-states because of their size, sophistication, experience, interaction with the outside world, and so on. This not only meant that ideologies found fertile ground but that the simultaneous suppression of social complexity and political participation resulted in the revolutionary experience in Iran and in the emergence of a repressive dictatorship in Iraq. The Gulf states, on the other hand, retain many aspects of the traditional nature of their societies, accompanied by an attendant patrimonial form of politics. Rulers are essentially regarded as legitimate, and protests by intellectuals and others discontented with the political systems generally focus on the elimination of imperfection and injustice in the existing systems. Most are not demanding a change of systems.

## How Did the Gulf States Change?

Despite their outwardly traditional character, the regimes in the Gulf states have undergone considerable change in the last half-century. While less altered in appearance than other Middle Eastern entities, Gulf regimes are far from the traditional forms of government that existed before oil. All have undergone roughly similar phases in the transformation from minimalist polities to full-fledged national governments.

The first of these steps was the pre-oil conversion of tribally based systems into quasi-state entities. Broadly speaking, the process was similar in all six states, although the path followed in each country was unique. For Saudi Arabia, the transformation came about through the pivotal role of King Abdul Aziz bin Abdul Rahman. Basing his claim to leadership—and legitimacy—on the historical role of his family, the Al Saud, and in spreading the message of reformist Wahhabi Islam, young Abdul Aziz recaptured the family's capital of Riyadh from his enemies and set about constructing a new state. Within a few decades, his new state had spread from its Najdi center to the shores of the Gulf in the east, and to the Red Sea in the west. Further expansion to the north, east, and south was prevented by the British presence, direct or otherwise, on these land frontiers, as well as by Yemen's mountain fastness (even though Abdul Aziz incorporated much territory along the border).

Oman too underwent transformation. Although comprising a unique national identity and effectively independent for more than a thousand years, the country's political system evolved from the more traditional Ibadhi imamate to a more purely secular-based sultanate, nurtured at first by its overseas interests and then kept alive largely because of British support. Even though Oman retained its independence, tenaciously at times, Britain played an important role in forging a new expression of statehood through its financial and military support during two civil wars on the threshold of the oil era. Like Saudi Arabia, Oman had its own strong ruler in Said bin Taymur, who held the country together during trying times by force of personality as much as anything else.

The smaller states, the emirates, grew in the eighteenth and nineteenth centuries, more directly out of tribal politics. The emergence of dominant tribal clans and their supremacy was solidified through British recognition of Trucial shaykhs in the nineteenth century. New territorial states coalesced around these shaykhs, their clans, tribal allies, and small but pivotal settlements with significant merchant communities. By the dawn of the oil era, a clear-cut system of small states, under British protection but responsible for their own internal affairs, had put down roots.

Although the basic political outlines remained set, with hereditary rulers drawn from fixed families, the introduction of oil income dramatically enlarged the role of the sovereigns, set ruling families apart from the rest of the population, and consolidated power in their hands. Payments made to rulers, first as concession fees and then as royalties on oil production, reinforced the shaykhs' traditional role as benevolent fathers of their communities, responsible for members' material needs. It affirmed the rulers' position as the paramount political authorities, stronger than ever before. It consolidated the primacy of the ruling families—officially in the government and unofficially in their economic prosperity and social elite status.

Oil income provided the opportunity for established merchant families and then for new entrepreneurs to expand their businesses and acquire unheard-of wealth, but always in cooperation with ruling families. It also had the side effect of cementing ties between ruling families and merchants whose origins lay outside the tribal community—such as the Shia in Kuwait, the Hawala in Bahrain, and Iranian and Indian merchants throughout the Gulf. Thus, the ruling families provided the protection that these groups needed to conduct their business, and in return, rulers and ruling families often exploited them for loans. Importantly, many rulers conducted their own commercial interests through these merchants.

Not least of course, oil income to the Gulf states percolated throughout the small populations and raised standards of living immeasurably. This, in turn, strengthened the loyalty of populations to rulers who seemingly had fulfilled their part of the "social contract" by distributing oil benefits and maintaining an atmosphere conducive to the pursuit of material ends within a traditional framework.

Another profound effect of oil revenues was the creation of modern governments. The traditional situation whereby individual rulers were able to oversee the behavior and welfare of all their constituents, and to respond with financial assistance or punitive measures whenever required, soon disappeared. The initial rush to create infrastructure improvements—including roads, harbors, schools, dispensaries, bridges, and airports—created a demand for qualified individuals, beginning with expatriates, to supervise foreign contractors. As projects grew in number and in scope, government departments were created and training and educational programs for Gulf citizens initiated. Where rulers were unable to bridge the chasm between minimalist forms of governing and the delegation of authority to formally constituted and specialized bodies, they were deposed, as in the cases of Shaykh Shakhbut bin Sultan of Abu Dhabi and Sultan Said bin Taymur of Oman.

## Why Have the Gulf States Endured?

Given the unique and legitimate origins of the Gulf states, and their adaptability, the next obvious question is how have they managed to endure throughout the dual pressures of external ideological challenges and internal socioeconomic changes? Perhaps the first relevant factor is that, above all, the Gulf regimes have been competent. They have been responsive—or at least have sought to be responsive—to the needs and demands of their constituents. Just as the shaykh of the tribe assumed the function of, and was regarded as, a father for the members of the tribe, the rulers of the Gulf states have assumed the role of fathers of their national communities. Continued legitimacy depended on protecting the position of the community vis-à-vis the outside world as well as providing protection and justice for members of the community. Just as the head of a family, the shaykh/ruler was responsible for the material well-being of his constituents, which meant sharing his prosperity when appropriate. In the oil era, this responsibility translated into the construction of universal social welfare systems.

At the same time that rulers and regimes sought to preserve the traditional basis of legitimacy, they also endeavored to create a newer, more modern basis by satisfying new demands and criteria on the part of their constituents. Regimes were not shy about impressing their virtues in the minds of their people. Citizens were buffered from the chaos surrounding the Gulf. Within limits, regimes generally permitted their people to conduct their lives and business in relative freedom. The alternative to their benign paternalism, they suggested, was the oppression and uncertainty found in neighboring countries.

Although ultimate decision making in all these states was restricted to the rulers and their immediate families, the small population base and emphasis on education combined to allow talented individuals from many different backgrounds to participate in all levels of government. On many issues, these individuals shaped the debate, and lent their weight to the selection of optimal choices. Above all, the regimes benefited from an emerging culture of materialism and the resultant popular perceptions that the existing systems were responsible for the comfortable standards of living created in the 1970s. The failure of some groups to participate equally in the new prosperity and then the decline of benefits relative to expectations in the 1980s and 1990s have typically resulted in the criticism of certain abuses within the existing systems, not for their wholesale replacements.

The banding together of these six states into the Gulf Cooperation Council in 1981 also has played a supporting role. Despite the early protestations that the GCC was formed to address a multitude of economic, social, and political concerns, it is clear that the primary motivation was to create a defensive alliance in the face of worrisome events in Iran and Iraq. Regional security issues continued to predominate in GCC agendas, especially during and after the Iraqi occupation of Kuwait, even though effective security integration still eludes the Riyadh-based organization. Although GCC security arrangements play only a minor strategic role in the defense of the region, they have imparted a strong psychological impact that, arguably, has carried over into other spheres.

A generation or more of Gulf citizens has grown up with the GCC and the idea that the group of six Gulf states comprises a common identity nearly as profound as the underlying Arab and Islamic identities. Individuals visit and mix with their neighbors in the GCC far more than in the past. People are more inclined to travel within the Gulf for business, shopping, entertainment, and sightseeing, thus adding local destinations to the older ones of Cairo, Beirut, and London. Ties between social and public entities such as professional organizations, universities, and athletic teams have become the norm.

In the economic sphere, the drive toward integration has been long and rocky, and even the interim goals of common tariffs and a common market have yet to be achieved. Nevertheless, barriers are falling and the rights of travel, residence, employment, and ownership between GCC states have taken strong root. Intra-GCC investment and joint business opportunities are on the rise, stimulated perhaps equally by government encouragement and commercial promise. Government reluctance to end protection and subsidization of internal industries appears to be the single most restricting factor in further economic cooperation, but even this is under pressure. In this respect, such an attitude perhaps reflects a more fundamental concern over the submergence of national sovereignty, so recently attained, in an uncertain GCC entity that must inevitably be dominated by Saudi Arabia at the expense of the interests of the other, smaller five.

It must also be said that the durability of the Gulf states has been enhanced by their strategic alliances with the West. This should not be allowed to obscure the deep and profound interaction between the Gulf states and the rest of the Arab world, nor the position of the Gulf states in the Islamic world. After all, much of the wisdom and sweat expended on creating the recent appearance of the Gulf states belongs to expatriate Arabs and Muslims. Yet, the relationship of the Gulf states with these spheres has been troubled, and frequently marked by mutual suspicion. While grateful for the assistance provided, the Gulf states remain wary of adverse political trends emanating from the region. The persistent divisions between the Gulf states and the northern Arab world were vividly illustrated in 1990 by the affirmative reaction of many Arabs to the Iraqi invasion of Kuwait.

On the other hand, the Gulf states have continued to develop and strengthen relations with western Europe and the United States. The interlocking occurs on many levels. While the uninterrupted supply of oil is the West's most obvious interest in the Gulf, the region depends on that same oil for the lion's share of its income and prosperity. For decades, a pattern has been established for the recycling of oil income into infrastructural development, consumer goods, and arms that in turn benefits Western economies. Even before the Kuwait War, the Gulf states' purchase of Western arms and military equipment strengthened the perceived guarantee that the West would intervene to defend the Gulf states against all threats. In fact, payment of top price for materiel, the purchase of more arms and especially equipment than can be used profitably by indigenous forces, and agreements for American and other Western uses of local facilities are all aspects of the formal and/or implicit contract between protectors and protectees.

Thus, it can be said that the military or security connections drive the political relationships, particularly at the top levels. But it should not be forgotten that many of the political, military, and commercial elites of the Gulf received their education or training in the West and retain strong cultural affinities with it. There exists considerable cause for disagreements; still, there is little doubt that Gulf states' populations often regard the West in positive terms.

The price regimes have paid for their reliance on Western governments has been relatively mild—so far. They have suffered some abuse for being American lackeys and must fight off both external and domestic criticisms of continued close alliance with Israel's biggest supporter at a time when Middle Eastern peace prospects appear to flounder. Most have steadily distanced themselves from the UN sanctions regime on Iraq. Indeed, Western criticisms on concerns such as human rights, the lack of formal democracy, and poor treatment of expatriate workers has been largely muted and has not affected government-to-government relations between the GCC and the West.

## What Must the Gulf Monarchies Do to Survive in the Future?

Success in the past of course is no guarantee of survival in the future. To retain an approximation of their present form and function, Gulf monarchies must continue to adapt and change. Regime responses must include the recognition that their populations are changing. The rapid growth of population, with annual rates approaching 4 percent in all the Gulf states, means that emphasis on the personal touch—so important in relations between ruler and ruled, as well as between any two Gulf citizens—will no longer suffice. Growing numbers of people and divergent patterns of education mean that younger generations no longer know all their counterparts. The physical spread of Gulf cities, sprouting ever farther flung housing areas and choked by automobiles, means that traditional daily visits between family members are observed less. Even the personal contact between citizen and his or her government weakens, as busy bureaucrats end up dealing with streams of visitors they do not know. Thus, the growing complexity of government and of public issues means that rulers and senior officials become increasingly over-worked and that rulers and their families grow more distant and aloof as monarchical trappings put down roots.

But Gulf populations are changing in more ways than just sheer size. The expansion and encouragement of education inevitably changes perception of government-constituent relations. Increasing numbers of educated, middle-class, and politically aware citizens are no longer content with the father-child model, and demand greater say in the increasingly difficult choices their countries must make. Throughout the Gulf, one universal source of friction is the privileged status of ruling families, which number in the thousands in some Gulf states. The need to curb the excesses of some family members, and to restrict their many privileges, is not only demanded by political sensitivities but also required by changing economic circumstances.

Ruling families, elites, and general populations alike must deal with the fact that the rush of wealth of the 1970s was an aberration, and sounder policies must apply on a permanent basis. It is understandable that societies suddenly exposed to immense wealth after long periods of poverty should embrace materialism so fiercely. But it is also clear that the existing emphasis on materialism must be tempered with more spiritual, intellectual, and artistic aspirations. Furthermore, insofar as oil is a depreciating asset, Gulf societies must evolve from rentier societies to productive ones. The example of how Japan developed with few natural resources often has been invoked in the Gulf but rarely examined seriously, let alone acted upon. Instead, all too often, Gulf societies betray an extreme dependence on the state, the result of the government being the source of almost all income and the orchestrator of the social welfare system.

Given these key factors, what productive role can the GCC play in this process? Can the GCC be a tool of integration, allowing countries to achieve a sort of social "economy of scale"? Can the opening of borders result in healthier competition and the emergence of the fittest and best qualified? Or will the Saudi big brother crush independent initiative and resolve? So much of what has preoccupied the GCC has remained unfulfilled rhetoric, and the actual accomplishments have been so far achieved through the time-consuming and costly process of consensus building.

Looking farther afield, while there apparently is no other choice than to maintain the strategic alliance with the West, and especially the United States, it is also important to ask whether such a dependent relationship is healthy in the long run. It can only be noted with uneasiness that the United States, as the world's lone superpower, has begun to act more like the global bully. A fundamental emphasis on preserving the status quo has discouraged Gulf rulers from initiating significant reform, while U.S. politicians, seeking to maintain an undisturbed strategic relationship, look at the short-term advantages of dealing with the status quo and avoid the long-term quandaries of pressing for change no matter how necessary.

The 1990 Iraqi invasion of Kuwait illustrated how little had changed in Gulf/Arab relations in half a century. The same battle lines were drawn, the same divisions between "haves" and "have-nots" came to the fore, and the same slogans were shouted. While the bonds between Gulf Arabs and northern Arabs are indisputably fundamental, the relationship in practical terms is fraught with suspicion and often disdain. As an integral part of the Arab world, the relationship between Gulf Arabs and northern Arabs must be propelled to a more harmonious and mutually beneficial level.

Finally, the essential relationship between the Gulf states and the rest of Asia needs re-examination. For the most part, relations with Asia remain minimal or circumscribed. East Asia is a trading partner and only occasionally enters into strategic calculations, such as the Saudi purchase of Chinese missiles as a counter to dependence on the West. South Asia is the source of labor—professional, skilled and unskilled—without which the citizens of the Gulf states would find it difficult to maintain their lifestyles. But Gulf societies have developed a deep prejudice against South Asians, and the only strategic relationship, shaky as it is, is with Pakistan. That, however, is a relationship without much hope for concrete benefits, given the history of chronic political turmoil in Pakistan and its embroilment in crises closer to home.

Furthermore, economic factors—the trade of crude oil and LNG exports for consumer goods, technology, and industrial involvement—necessitate a closer, permanent relationship with Asia. Already, Dubai looks to the example of Hong Kong and Singapore as a model for its development. Political considerations apply as well, ranging from concern over developments in Muslim areas such as Chechnya, Afghanistan, and Kashmir, to emerging perceptions of an Indian Ocean Rim identity.

Not surprisingly, the Gulf states must look to their own devices when assaying their future. Dire predictions of doom, collapse, and revolution have swirled around the Gulf states since before British withdrawal from the region in 1971.

Without a doubt, they will continue into the future. What the Gulf states must therefore do is continue building on the traditions of the past to transform themselves into entirely new entities in the future.

Undoubtedly the grip of rulers and ruling families on their countries will loosen, just as it has occurred already with the rocky but entrenched institution of the Kuwaiti National Assembly, the introduction of new consultative councils in Oman and Saudi Arabia, the reforms of cabinet composition in Saudi Arabia and Qatar, and the emergence of the first wave of a new generation of rulers in Bahrain and Qatar. Even the paternalistic role of ministries of information will continue to be eroded by the effects of increased travel and greater penetration of societies by satellite television and the Internet. Old-fashioned bureaucrats are gradually being supplanted and younger scions of family firms are branching out into new and uncharted commercial waters. The Gulf states will change, but chances are that the change will be gradual, consensual, and peaceful.

# BIBLIOGRAPHY

[Editor's Note—John E. Peterson was kind enough to suggest several titles in this partial bibliography, which assembles recent publications on the Persian Gulf region. Additional materials are included in each chapter.]

Abir, Mordechai. *Oil, Power and Politics*. London: Frank Cass, 1974.
———. *Saudi Arabia: Government, Society and the Gulf Crises*. London: Routledge, 1993.
———. *Saudi Arabia in the Oil Era: Regime and Elites; Conflict and Collaboration*. Boulder, Colorado: Westview Press, 1988.
Aburish, Said K. *The Rise, Corruption and Coming Fall of the House of Saud*. London: Bloomsbury, 1994.
Al-Alkim, Hassan Hamdan. *The Foreign Policy of the United Arab Emirates*. London: Saqi Books, 1989.
———. *The GCC States in an Unstable World: Foreign-Policy Dilemmas of Small States*. London: Saqi Books, 1994.
Amuzegar, Jahangir. *Managing the Oil Wealth: OPEC's Windfalls and Pitfalls*. London: I. B. Tauris, 1999.
Anderson, Irvine H. *ARAMCO, the United States, and Saudi Arabia: A Study of the Dynamics of Foreign Oil Policy, 1933–1950*. Princeton, New Jersey: Princeton University Press, 1981.
Assiri, Abdul-Reda. *Kuwait's Foreign Policy: City-State in World Politics*. Boulder, Colorado: Westview Press, 1990.
Badeeb, Saeed M. *The Saudi-Egyptian Conflict Over North Yemen, 1962–1970*. Boulder, Colorado: Westview Press, 1986.
Bligh, Alexander. *From Prince to King: Royal Succession in the House of Saud in the Twentieth Century*. New York: New York University Press, 1984.
Bulloch, John. *Reforms of the Saudi Arabian Constitution*. London: Gulf Centre for Strategic Studies, April 1992.
Chaudhry, Kiren Aziz. *The Price of Wealth: Economies and Institutions in the Middle East*. Ithaca: Cornell University Press, 1997.
Cave Brown, Anthony. *Oil, God, and Gold: The Story of Aramco and the Saudi Kings*. Boston: Houghton Mifflin Company, 1999.
Anthony H. Cordesman, *The Gulf and the Search for Strategic Stability*. Boulder: Westview Press, 1984.
———. *Saudi Arabia: Guarding the Desert Kingdom*. Boulder, Colorado: Westview Press, 1997.
Crystal, Jill. *Oil and Politics in the Gulf: Rulers and Merchants in Kuwait and Qatar*. Cambridge: Cambridge University Press, 1990.
Darwish, Adel, and Gregory Alexander. *Unholy Babylon: The Secret History of Saddam's War*. New York: St. Martin's Press, 1991.

Dekmejian, R. Hrair. *Islam in Revolution: Fundamentalism in the Arab World*. Syracuse, New York: Syracuse University Press, 1985, 1989.

Ehteshami, Anoushiravan and Gerd Nonneman with Charles Tripp. *War and Peace in the Gulf: Domestic Politics and Regional Relations into the 1990s*. Reading, England: Ithaca Press, 1991.

Fandy, Mamoun. *Saudi Arabia and the Politics of Dissent*. New York: St. Martin's Press, 1999.

Farsy, Fouad al-. *Modernity and Tradition: The Saudi Equation*. London: Kegan Paul International, 1991.

Freedman, Lawrence, and Efraim Karsh. *The Gulf Conflict, 1990–91*. Princeton: Princeton University Press, 1993.

Gause, F. Gregory, III. *Oil Monarchies: Domestic and Security Challenges in the Arab Gulf States*. New York: Council on Foreign Relations Press, 1994.

———. *Saudi-Yemeni Relations: Domestic Structures and Foreign Influence*. New York: Columbia University Press, 1990.

Heard-Bey, Frauke. *From Trucial States to the United Arab Emirates: A Society in Transition*. 2nd edition. London: Longman, 1996.

Hart, Parker T. *Saudi Arabia and the United States: Birth of a Security Partnership*. Bloomington and Indianapolis: Indiana University Press, 1998.

Heller, Mark, and Nadav Safran. *The New Middle Class and Regime Stability in Saudi Arabia*. Cambridge, Massachusetts: Harvard University, Center for Middle Eastern Studies, 1985.

Helms, Christine Moss. *The Cohesion of Saudi Arabia: Evolution of Political Identity*. Baltimore and London: The Johns Hopkins University Press, 1981.

Henderson, Simon. *After King Fahd: Succession in Saudi Arabia*. Washington, D.C.: Washington Institute for Near East Policy, 1994.

Herb, Michael Frederick. *All in the Family: Ruling Dynasties, Regime Resilience and Democratic Prospects in the Middle Eastern Monarchies*. Albany: State University of New York Press, 1999.

Hiro, Dilip. *Desert Shield to Desert Storm: The Second Gulf War*. New York: Routledge, 1992.

Holden, David and Richard Johns. *The House of Saud: The Rise and Rule of the Most Powerful Dynasty in the Arab World*. New York: Holt, Rinehart and Winston, 1981.

Huyette, Summer Scott. *Political Adaptation in Saudi Arabia: A Study of the Council of Ministers*. Boulder, Colorado: Westview Press, 1985.

Katz, Mark N. *Russia and Arabia: Soviet Foreign Policy toward the Arabian Peninsula*. Baltimore, Maryland: The Johns Hopkins University Press, 1986.

Kechichian, Joseph A. (ed.). *A Century in Thirty Years: Shaykh Zayed and the United Arab Emirates*. Washington, D.C.: The Middle East Policy Council, 2000.

———. *Oman and the World: The Emergence of an Independent Foreign Policy*. MR 680-RC. Santa Monica, California: RAND, 1995.

———. *Succession in Saudi Arabia*. New York: Palgrave, 2001.

Kelly, J. B. *Arabia, the Gulf and the West: A Critical View of the Arabs and Their Oil Policy*. London: Weilden & Nicolson, 1980.

Khoury, Philip S., and Joseph Kostiner (eds.). *Tribes and State Formation in the Middle East*, Berkeley and Los Angeles: University of California Press, 1990.

Kostiner, Joseph. *The Making of Saudi Arabia 1916–1936: From Chieftaincy to Monarchical State*. New York and Oxford: Oxford University Press, 1993.

Lawson, Fred H. *Opposition Movements and U.S. Policy toward the Arab Gulf States*. New York: Council on Foreign Relations Press, 1992.

Long, David E. *The Kingdom of Saudi Arabia*. Gainesville, Florida: University Press of Florida, 1997.

———. *The United States and Saudi Arabia: Ambivalent Allies*. Boulder and London: Westview Press, 1985.

Munif, Abdelrahman. *Cities of Salt*. New York: Vintage International, 1989.

———. *The Trench*. New York: Pantheon Books, 1991.

———. *Variations on Night and Day*. New York: Pantheon Books, 1993.

# BIBLIOGRAPHY

Naqeeb, Khaldoun Hasan al-. *Society and State in the Gulf and Arab Peninsula.* London: Routledge; Beirut: Centre for Arab Unity Studies, 1990. Tr. by L. M. Kenny.

Niblock, Tim (ed.). *Iraq: The Contemporary State.* London: Croom Helm, 1982.

―――. *Social and Economic Development in the Arab Gulf.* London: Croom Helm, for the University of Exeter Centre for Arab Gulf Studies, 1980.

―――. *State, Society and Economy in Saudi Arabia.* London: Croom Helm, for the University of Exeter Centre for Arab Gulf Studies, 1982.

Nonneman, Gerd. *Iraq, the Gulf States and the War: A Changing Relationship—1980–1986 and Beyond.* London and Atlantic Highlands: Ithaca Press, 1986.

Peck, Malcolm C. *The United Arab Emirates: A Venture in Unity.* Boulder and London: Westview Press and Croom Helm, 1986.

Plascov, Avi. *Security in the Persian Gulf: Modernization, Political Development and Stability.* Totowa, New Jersey: Allanheld, Osmun & Company, 1982.

Peterson, J. E. *The Arab Gulf States: Steps toward Political Participation.* New York: Praeger, 1988. Published with the Center for Strategic and International Studies. Washington Papers, number 131.

Pridham, B. R. (ed.). *Oman: Economic, Social and Strategic Developments.* London: Croom Helm, for the University of Exeter Centre for Arab Gulf Studies, 1987.

Al-Qasimi, Sultan Muhammad. *The Myth of Arab Piracy in the Gulf.* London: Croom Helm, 1986.

Ramazani, R. K. *The Gulf Cooperation Council: Records and Analysis.* Charlottesville, Virginia: University Press of Virginia, 1988.

―――. *Revolutionary Iran: Challenge and Response in the Middle East.* Baltimore: The Johns Hopkins University Press, 1988.

Al Rasheed, Madawi. *Politics in an Arabian Oasis: The Rashidi Tribal Dynasty,* London and New York: I. B. Tauris & Co. Limited, 1991.

Rumaihi, Muhammed. *Beyond Oil: Unity and Development in the Gulf.* London: Al Saqi Books, 1986.

Al Saud, Khaled bin Sultan (with Patrick Seale). *Desert Warrior: A Personal View of the Gulf War by the Joint Forces Commander,* New York: HarperCollins Publishers, Inc., 1995.

John Sandwick (ed.). *The Gulf Cooperation Council: Moderation and Stability in an Interdependent World.* Boulder, Colorado: Westview Press, 1987.

Shaw, John A., and David E. Long. *Saudi Arabian Modernization: The Impact of Change on Stability.* New York: Praeger, with the Georgetown University Center for Strategic and International Studies, 1982. The Washington Papers, number 89.

Sick, Gary G., and Lawrence G. Potter (eds.). *The Persian Gulf at the Millennium: Essays in Politics, Economy, Security, and Religion.* New York: St. Martin's Press, 1997.

Simons, Geoff. *Saudi Arabia: The Shape of a Client Feudalism.* New York: St. Martin's Press, 1998.

Skeet, Ian. *Oman: Politics and Development.* London: Macmillan, 1992.

Wilkinson, John C. *Arabia's Frontiers: The Story of Britain's Boundary-Drawing in the Desert.* London: I. B. Tauris, 1991.

Yamani, Mai. *Changed Identities: The Challenges of the New Generation in Saudi Arabia.* London: Royal Institute of International Affairs, 1999.

Yassini, Ayman Al-. *Religion and State in the Kingdom of Saudi Arabia.* Boulder, Colorado: Westview Press, 1985.

Zahlan, Rosemarie Said. *The Making of the Modern Gulf States: Kuwait, Bahrain, Qatar, the United Arab Emirates and Oman.* London: Unwin Hyman, 1989. Rev. ed. Reading: Ithaca Press, 1998.

―――. *The Origins of the United Arab Emirates: A Political and Social History of the Trucial States.* London: The Macmillan Press Ltd., 1978.

# INDEX

*Abaya* 116, 123, 124, 126
Abdallah II, King of Jordan 429
Abdul Aziz, Mullah Uthman 59, 61
Abrahamian, Ervand 104
Abu Dhabi 162, 164, 232, 285, 360, 383, passim
Abu Dhabi Investment Authority (ADIA) 167
Abu Musa Island (UAE) 216, 225, 231, 316, 319, 353, 363, 387, 394, 409, 427, 439, 440, 445, passim
Adelkhah, Fariba 194
Al-Din, Ayatollah 'Ala' 59
Al-Jazeera (television network in Qatar) 195, 197–198, 319, 322
Afghanistan 47, 71, 101, 126, 270, 314, 356, 370, 396, 459
Ahvaz Liberation Front 437
Al-Ahmar, Abdallah bin Husain 298
Ajman 163, 166, 319
Albanians (Kosovar) 100
Albright, Madeleine 415
Algeria 83, 101
Algiers (1975) Agreement 89, 90, 226, 355, 356
Ali, Rashid 84, 85
Ali, Salem Rubai 267, 292
Almaty 373
Alwani, Taja Jaber 61
Amara (Iraq) 59
American Iran-Libya Sanctions Act (ILSA) 331
American Israel Public Affairs Committee (AIPAC) 330, 333, 345
Amini, Ebrahim 25
Ammash, Salih Mahdi 437
Amnesty International 297
Amoli, Javadi 9
Ancel, Jacques 214
Anderson, Benedict 201
*Anfal* campaign (Iraq) 92
Anglo-Persian Oil Company (APOC) 327
Al-Anisi, Muhammad Yahyah 292
Antar, Ali 294
Arab Court of Justice 245
Arab Cooperation Council 271, 294
Arab League. *See* League of Arab States
Arab Maghreb Union (AMU) 442
Arabian Peninsula
and bilateral boundary agreements 220–221
and border disputes 213–235
and internal political affairs 282–283

Arabistan Liberation Front 437
Arak 23, 49
Araki, Ayatollah 7
Aramco 118, 119
Ardebili, Abdol Karim Musavi 10
Aref, Abdul Salam 86, 87
Argentina 89, 336
Armenians (in Iraq) 67
Armilla patrol 344, 345
Aron, Raymond 90
*Asabiyah* (in Kuwaiti politics) 306
Association of South East Asian Nations (ASEAN) 405, 443
Ashura 284
Asir Province, Asiris 100, 114, 116, 119, 214, 230, 277
Al-Asnaq, Abdallah 292
Association of Combatant Clerics of Teheran 16, 18
Association of the Seminary Teachers of Qom 25
Assyrians 67, 79, 84–86, 91
Astana 373
Axelgard, Frederick W. 90
Ayubi, Nazih 99
Al-Azhar University (Cairo) 61
Azerbaijan 331
Azeri-Qomi, Ayatollah 8
Azeris 38
Aziz, Tariq 71, 72, 90, 274
Al-'Azm, Sadeq 199

Baath Party (Iraq) 39, 56, 59, 60–61, 62, 65–66, 68, 71, 73–74, 84, 86, 87, 88, 90 and policies towards Shia clergy 58–60, 80
Bab al-Mandeb 3
Baghdad 66, 70
Bahjat, Mohammed Taqi 8
Bahonar, Reza 17, 21
Bahrain 95, 139, 163, 281, 417, 428, passim
and 1981 coup attempt 285
and consultative council (majlis) 189, 284, 323
and economic dependence 179
and Hawala 455
and integration in global economies 181–182
and internal constraints 177–190
and nationalist consciousness 180–181
and political crises 184
and political reforms 187–189

and Qatar border dispute 218–219
and relations with UAE 320
Bahrain Freedom Movement (BFM) 335
Al-Baid, Ali Salem 299
Bakhtiar, Shahpour 36–37
Baker, James 272
Al-Bakr, Ahmed Hassan 86, 395
Balfour-Paul, Sir Glen 225
Baluchis 181
Bani Sadr, Abol Hassan 38–39
Bank for International Settlements (BIS) 146
Baqi, Emad ad-Din 20, 21, 23
Barazani 71, 74, 75
*Basij* [Mobilization of the Oppressed/paramilitary force] 14, 25, 39, 43–45
Basra 59, 73, 238, 435
Batatu, Hanna 86, 88
Bazaar, Bazaaris 104
Bazargan, Mehdi 438
BBC 199
Beduns 181
 in Bahrain 188
Belgrave, Sir Charles Dalrymple 225
Bengio, Ofra 88
Bin Baz, Abdul Aziz (theologian) 200, 202–203, 306, 320
Bin Laden, Usama 105, 376
Boll, Heinrich [Institute in Berlin] 22
*Bonyad-e Mosta'azafin* [Foundation of the Oppressed, or *Bonyads*] 18, 19, 26, 27, 331
Border and territorial disputes in the Arabian Peninsula 213–235
Al-Borujerdi, Murtada 59
Brinton, Crane 105
Bubiyan island (Kuwait) 227, 228
Buraimi 168, 328
Burqa 124
Bush, George H.W. 345, 419, 444
Bush, George W. 422

Caldeans (in Iraq) 67
Camp David agreements 54–55, 164
 and Al Saud reactions to 54
Carter Administration/Doctrine 269, 356, 360, 393
Caspian Basin/Sea 98, 331, 374, 407
Caucasus 213, 374
Central Asia
 and economic and trade ties with Gulf states 373–374
 and Islam 372–373
 and petroleum 374
 and transportation problems
Chechnya, Chechens 100, 101, 376, 459
Chile 104
China 373, 412, 414
CNN [Cable News Network] 14, 178, 199
Cohen, William 408, 445
Co-integration error-correction (of Saudi economy) 139–140
Committee for the Defence of Legitimate Rights (CDLR) 335
Commonwealth 326
Cook, Robin 332
Cossack Brigade 34, 50
Cox, Sir Percy 238
Cuba 104
Curzon, Lord 356, 439

Dahuk (Iraq) 75
Damascus Declaration 222, 322
D'Amato, Alphonse 408

Dara al-Jazirah (Peninsula Shield) 318, 321, 401
*Al-Da'wa* Party 57, 58, 71, 80
Democratic Republic of Yemen (DRY) 275, 299
Desert Shield, Operation 345, 444
Desert Storm, Operation 345, 357, 444
Dhahran 118, 119, 122–23
Diri'yah 127
*Diwaniyas* 184
Dual containment 331, 337, 357, 360, 400, 408, 415, 420, 444
Dubai 113, 162, 163, 164, 285, 342, 354, 459, passim
 and Internet City 166
Duwaima Island 216

Economic Cooperation Organization (ECO) 370
Egypt 85, 106, 112, 113, 114, 177, 195, 266, 313, 400, 408, 429, passim
 and 1960s presence in Yemen 266–268
Ebadi, Shirin 22, 23
Ebrahimi, Farshad 22, 23
Emami, said 15
Empty Quarter (Rub al-Khali-Saudi Arabia) 114, 220, 223, 273
Eritrea 266, 275
European Community 326, 329, 344, 420
Eshkevari, Hassan Yusuf 5–6, 9, 22

Fadlallah, Muhammad Hussein 60
Fatimid dynasty (909–1171) 12
Fallahian, Ali 14, 18
Fandy, Mamoun 99
Fasht al-Dibal 218, 234, 320
Faysal I, King 84
Faysal, Ghazi bin 84, 85
Faysal, Toujan 199
Faw Peninsula 229
Ferghana Valley 373, 374
*Fiqh* (jurisprudence) 8
Firuzabadi, Hasan 46
Firuzkuh 23
Foran, John 107
France 89, 412
Frederick the Great (1712–1786) 196
Front for the Liberation of South Yemen (FLOSY) 267
*Al-Futuwwa* [paramilitary Iraqi youth organization] 84
Fujairah 163, 319

Ganji, Akbar 20, 21, 22, 23
Gachsaran 23
General Congress Party (GCP) 295, 298
Germany 326, 336
Al-Gharawi, Mirza Ali 59
Al-Ghashmi, Ahmed 269
Gibbon, Edward 90
Glaspie, April 227
Goldstone, Jack 97–98, 107
Golpaygani, Ayatollah Mohammed Reza 3
Gorbachev, 25
Greece 101
Gulf Cooperation Council (GCC) 95, 116, 139, 140, 147 213, 216, 270, 281, 335, 356, 397, 407, 432, 442, 451, 456, passim
 and 1971–1979 period 395–396
 and 1980–1988 period 396–398
 and 1988–1991 period 398–399
 and Arab politics 322
 and challenges and the lack of stability 401–403
 and class structure 286–287
 and confederation 315–316

Gulf Cooperation Council (*continued*)
  and economic and oil policy trends 322
  and external challenges 402
  and elusive search for stability 400–401
  and foreign policy trends 321
  and future trends 322–323, 393–406
  and impact of U.S. policies 351–363
  and internal dynamics and foreign policies 313–323
  and internal challenges 401–402
  and internal security agreement (ISA) 315
  and intra-member state ties 316–320
  and outlook 402–403
  and political evolution 313–323
  and political institutions 304
  and political participation 287–288
  and post 1991 period 399–400
  and pre-1971 period 394–395
  and Shia communities 283–286
  and structure 515–316
  and trends in unity 288–291
GCC+2 289, 400, 408, 409, 441
GCC+ 3 410
Gulf Security
  and the UAE vision of 383–392
Gulf States
  and Britain 334–340
  and Commission for the Settlement of Disputes 232, 234
  and democratization 416–418
  and disparity in energy resources and economic needs 433–434
  and endurance 451–460
  and fate of monarchies 452–453
  and internal pressures/arms sales 359
  and institutions 303–311, 361, 404
  and Iranian challenge 413–415
  and Israel 420–422
  and link with Palestine 333–334
  and militarization 359–360
  and political tensions 360–361
  and population figures 177
  and physical disparities 431–433
  and regime competence 455–458
  and regional stability 356–362
  and sectarian differences 434–435
  and security challenges 407–423
  and territorial disputes 436–440
  and ties with Arab World 358
  and ties with Central Asian Republics 367–377
  and ties with Russia 367–377
  and unemployment 360
  and U.S. policies 360, 418–420
  and U.S./U.K. rivalries 330

Habermas, Jürgen 197
Hafr al-Batin 401
Hajj 113, 117, 428, 435
Hajjarian, Said 15, 19, 20
Al-Hajri, Abdallah 268
Halabja (Iraq) 59
Al-Hakim, Sayyid Mahdi 58
Al-Hakim, Sayyid Muhammad Baqir 60
Al-Hakim, Ayatollah Muhsin 57, 58, 60–61, 74
Al-Hamdi, Ibrahim 269
Hanafi (doctrine) 372
Hanbali (doctrine) 306, 318
Hanish islands 275, 276
Hashemi, Faezeh 18
Hashemite (monarchy in Iraq) 56
Hassan II, King of Morocco 206

Al-Hawali, Safar 200
Hawar islands 218, 221, 232, 234, 320, 328
*Hezbollah, Ansar-e* [Helpers of the Party of God] 15, 22, 338, 435
Hejaz Province, Hejazis 100, 125
Henderson, Ian 344
Al-Hilli, Hussein 60
Hormuz, Straits of 276, 285, 397, 413
Al-Humoud, Awad 186
Huraybi, Hassan 297
Hurd, Douglas 344
Husain, Sadiq Abdallah 298
Husain, Tawfiq 84
Hussein, Hujja Muhammad 59
Hussein, King (of Jordan) 437
Hussein, Qussay 72
Hussein, Saddam 55, 62, 67, 68, 71, 72, 73, 76–77, 79, 81, 83, 86, 87, 90, 102, 271, 272, 278, 286, 332, 336, 337, 384, 395, 411, 428, 446, passim
  and expansion of Iraqi military power 88–89
  and the Iranian Revolution 89–91
  and the War for Kuwait 91–92

Ibadhi, Ibadhism 202–203, 285, 308, 454
Al-Idrisi, Ali 264
Al-Idrisi, Muhammad 264
Ikama 125
Image (in Saudi socio-political context) 111
*Imam-e Jome* (Friday preachers) 4
Incirlik, (Air Base-Turkey) 419
India 161–162, 177, 322, 326
Indochina 101–102
International Committee of the Red Cross (ICRC) 243–244
International Court of Justice (ICJ) 218, 220, 221, 232, 239, 317, 320, 360, 387, 412
International law, limitations of 226–229
International Monetary Fund (IMF) 135
Iran 68, 69, 73, 75, 80, 89, 90, 104, 163, 177, 322, passim
  and 1997 presidential elections 194
  and 2000 parliamentary elections 13–27
  and Anglo-Soviet invasion of 1941 35
  and Arab cultural rivalry 435–436
  and Arab Gulf States 14, 427–446
  and armed forces 34
  future outlook 47–50
    and Bahrain 438–439
    and law and order 42–43
    and role of clergy in 38
    and Central Asia 370–371
    and civil-military relations 31–51
  the first republic, 1979–1988, 37–39
  the second republic, 1989–1996, 40–43
  the third republic 1997–2000, 43–47
    and clerical establishment 3–11
    and Council of Guardians 4, 13, 17, 18, 21, 23, 25, 26, 27
    and conservatives in 2000 elections 17–18, 21–26
    and constitutional revolution 34
    and constitutional theocracy 9
    and debate on Islam, *Fiqh* and secularization 9–10
    and democracy 3
    and Executives 6, 17, 18 19
    and Expediency Council 26
    and Majlis 13, 14–15, 16–17, 20, 21, 23, 26, 27, 48
    and military affairs 31–51
    and power of "Guide" 4
    and press under Khatami 14

and putative defense cooperation with Saudi Arabia 126–127
and reformists in 2000 elections 18–19
and (1979) revolution 387
and role of clergy in politics 4–7
and role of press in 2000 elections 19–20
and Servants of Construction 16
and Sharjah Memorandum of Understanding 229–230
and Supreme Council of Armed Forces 37
and (new) theologians 9–10
and treaty of friendship with USSR 89
and UAE islands disputes 216–218, 439–440
Iran Liberation Movement 16
Iran-Iraq War (1980–1988) 31, 38, 41, 59, 71, 91, 226, 232, 397, passim
Iraq 31, 277, 428, 457, passim
 and 1990 invasion of Kuwait 272–274
 and the Assyrian affair 84–86
 and Baath Party role in civil military relations 86–88
 and clergy 55–63
 and domestic politics 65–82
 and France 89
 and General Intelligence Directorate 87
 and ideology in military 83–84
 and Jews 86
 and Kurds 75, 78, 81
 and Kuwait boundary 219–220
 and the military 70, 83–93,
 and ministry of endowments and religious affairs 55
 and non-aggression pact with Saudi Arabia 124
 and "oil-for food" regime 332
 and Royal Military Academy 86
 and security apparatus 70–71
 and Shia clergy 55–56
 political activism of 56–58
 population 78–81
  and Shias of Iranian origin 71
  and Soviet Union 89
  and State relationships with ethnic communities 68–69
  and Sunni elite 66
  and Sunnis 55
  and ulama 55
  and weapons of mass destruction 242–243
  and youth vanguards 87
 as a landlocked country 227–228
Iraq-Kuwait boundary 240–242
Iraqi Communist Party 71, 80, 85, 86, 87
Iraqi Islamic Party 61, 81
Iraqi National Congress (INC) 69, 81
Irbil 75
Al-Iryani, Abdul Karim 273–274, 275, 278
Islam and democracy 194–195
Islamic Unity Movement [Harakat al-Wahda] 61
Islamic Republic News Agency (IRNA) 45
Islamic Revolutionary Guards Corps, *see* Revolutionary Guards
Ismail, Abdul Fattah 267, 292, 294
Israel 86, 89, 99, 112, 275, 322, 338, 395, 408, 429, 457, passim

Jaafar, Ayatollah 59
Jala'ipur, Hamid-Reza 20
Jani, Yacoub 186
Jannati, Ayatollah 21
Jaradeh shoals 218, 234, 320
Jeddah 113, 119, 185, 276

Jones, Stephen 214
Jordan 112, 119, 189, 429, 437

Kadivar, Jamileh 17
Kadivar, Mohsen 4–5, 8, 9, 10, 11, 15, 17
Kamil, Hussein 332
Kant, Immanuel 197
Kar, Mehrangiz 22
Karbala 62, 79, 437
Karbaschi, Gholam Hosain 14, 18
Al-Kassim, Faisal 197, 199
Kashani, Emami 9
Kazakhstan 373, 374
Kazim, Safian 199
Al Khalifah (Bahrain) 188, 225, 317, 320, 435
Al Khalifah, Hamad bin Isa 323, 362
Al Khalifah, Isa bin Salman (1961–1999) 362
Al Khalifah, Salman bin Hamad 421
Khadmiya (Iraq) 79
Khafji 318
Khafus incident 219, 220, 317
Khamenei, Ayatollah Ali Hossein 3–4, 5, 6, 7, 8, 14, 15, 16, 23, 24, 25, 26, 41, 45, 46–47, 427
Al-Khalili, Ahmad bin Hamad 202
Khalkhal, 23
Khalkhali, Mohammed Sadeq 6
Kharazi, Kamal 332
Kashmir, 459
Khatami, Ayatollah Mohammed 4–5, 6, 7, 10, 13, 15, 17, 18, 20, 21, 22, 24, 25, 26, 37, 43, 46–47, 48, 286, 331, 384, 387, 409, 416, 427, passim
 and presidency 13–16
 and revolutionary guards 44–46
 and 1999 visit to Saudi Arabia 429–430
Khatami, Reza 16
Khuzistan (Arabistan) 39, 431, 433, 437–438
Khoeiniha, Mohammed 6
Khoi, Abdul Majid 59
Khoi, Ayatollah Abol-Qazem 4, 20, 58, 59, 60, 74
Khoi Foundation 59, 80
Khomeini, Ayatollah Ruhollah 3, 4, 7, 8, 10, 11, 14, 16, 25, 36, 37, 39, 41, 49, 80, 89, 104, 337, 370, 396, 427, 434, passim
Kirkuk (Iraq) 70, 79
Kirkpatrick, Jeane 103
Korea (North) 126
Kosovo 101–102
Kostiner, Joseph 104
Kurds 57, 59, 61, 66, 69, 71, 72, 92, passim
 and Failis 71
 and insurgencies in Iran 38
 and Johoosh (tribal leaders) 74
Kurdistan Democratic Party 91
Kuwait 84, 91, 95, 101, 102, 106, 139, 173, 195, 281, 354, 360, 409, 417, passim
 and economic dependence 179
 and integration in global economies 181–182
 and internal constraints 177–190
 and Iraq border problem 237–245
 and Islamists 185–186
 and "liberation" cost 179–180
 and nationalist consciousness 180–181
 and parliament (National Assembly) 185, 305–306, 460
 and political crises 184
 and political institutions 304–307
 and political reforms 185–187
 and prisoners/missing persons in 1991 War 243–244
 and relations with Bahrain 319

# Index

Kuwait (continued)
  and relations with Oman 318
  and relations with Qatar 318–319
  and relations with UAE 318
  and tribal factors in political life 305–306

Lankarani, Fazel 6, 8
League of Arab States 237, 242–243, 245, 268, 272, 322, 430, 442, passim
  and military intervention in Kuwait 238–239
Lebanon 71, 314
Libya 104, 164
Lingah 162
Liwa 168
Lomperis, Timothy 102
Loujian, Khalifa 186
Luce, Sir William 225, 238

Maadan (Iraq) 69
Maarib 294
Madinah 113, 117, 121, 126, 264, 434, 435
Magid, Esmat Abdul 244
Maidan Saleh 121, 122
Al-Majid, Ali Hassan 91
Al-Majid, Husayn Kamil 91
Al Makhtoum 163
Al Makhtoum, Rashid bin Said 163
Makkah 113, 117, 121, 264, 355, 356, 368, 435
Malaysia 155
Malek, Reda 199
Marja'e, Marja', Marja1 al-taqlid, Marja'iyya [Imitation, Imitator] 7, 55, 57, 58, 60, 79, 81, passim
Al Masaari, Muhammad 335
Mashad 17, 49, 60
Mat'ams (in Kuwait) 184
MBC (Middle East Broadcast Corporation) 200
Media in the Arab world 193–195
Meshkhani, Ali Akbar 9
Militant Clerics Association 5
Minbar 205
Mohajerani, Ataollah 13, 15
Mohtashemi, Ali Akbar 6
Montazeri, Hossein Ali 6, 7, 8, 20
Morocco 112, 195, 206
Mossadeq, Mohammed 35, 327, 328, 337, 363, 394, 415
Mosul (Iraq) 70, 79, 238
Mottahari, Morteza 11
Movahedi-Kermani, Mohammad Ali 17
Al-Mudarris, Abdul Karim 60
Musavi, Mir Hossein 4
Muscat 195
Muslim Brotherhood 56, 57, 58, 306
Muslim Brotherhood (in Iraq) 61, 62
Muslim World League 137, 163
Mutawwa ("morals" security forces in Saudi Arabia) 122
Muthanna Club 84
Muwahiddun (Wahhabis) 318

Nafisi, Abdallah 200
Al Nahyan 162, 327
Al Nahyan, Shaykha Fatima bint Mubarak 173
Al Nahyan, Sultan bin Zayed bin Sultan 408, 410
Al Nahyan, Zayed bin Sultan 163, 164, 168, 173, 318, 327, 383, 387, 391, 445, passim
Najaf (Iraq) 56, 57, 58, 60, 61, 74, 79, 437
Al-Najafi, Bashir Hussein 59
Najran Province 265
Al-Naqeeb, Khaldoun 178
Nasriyah (Iraq) 59

Nasser, Gamal Abdel 106, 266, 303, 432, 441
Nateq Nouri, Ayatollah 6, 43, 416
Netanyahu, Benjamin 429
Nicaragua 104
Nouri, Abdollah 10, 14, 17, 19, 23
Nouri, Ali Reza 17

Oman, Sultanate of 95, 101, 139, 173, 195, 273, 281, 360, 443, passim
  and consultative council 307–309, 460
  and Dhuffar/Dhuffari rebellion 443
  and gender factors in Shura council 308
  and information and authority 193–207
  and mass higher education, language and community 195–96
  and political authority 205
  and relations with Bahrain 319
  and relations with Israel 361
  and relations with Qatar 319
  and relations with UAE 319
  and religious and political expression 201–204, 308
  and state consultative council 205, 304
  and tribal factors 308
  and UAE border accord 219
*The Opposition Direction* 197, 199, 200
Orbit Communications 199
Organization of African Unity (OAU) 232
Organization of Islamic Conference (OIC) 270
  and 1997 Teheran Summit 14, 427
Organization of Petroleum Exporting Countries (OPEC) 88, 126, 434
Oslo Accords 183
Ottoman Empire 56, 347
  and succession patterns 12–13
  and Iraq 66

Pahlavi, 31, 34, 38, 50
  and Mohammed Reza Shah 33, 37–38, 51, 89, 105, 206, 228, 282, 328, 355, 393, 394, 415, 437, passim
  and role in Iranian military 35–36
  and Reza Shah, 32–33, 34–35, 50, 328, 336
Pakistan 31, 270, 322, 459
Palestine 73, 84, 86, 330, 338, 442
Palestine Liberation Organization 420
Palestinian National Authority 200
Parsons, Sir Anthony 329
Pasdaran, *see* Revolutionary Guards
Pastor, Robert 104
Patriotic Union of Kurdistan 71, 91
People's Democratic Republic of Yemen (PDRY) 268, 269, 270, 281, 295, 395, 443, passim
  and Communist Party 267
Peres, Shimon 421
Persia, Persians 38, 206
Philippines 104, 125
Pickering, Thomas 227
Portsmouth Treaty 85
Prescott, Victor 214

Qaboos, Sultan of Oman 282, 298, 303, 307, 327, 357, 400, passim
Qaboos, Sultan (University) 195, 202
Qajar 34, 224, 336
Qat 295
Al-Qatabi, Abdallah 308
Qatar 95, 163, 173, 281, 360, 409, 430, passim
  and censorship 195
  and consultative council 310–311
  and information and authority 193–207

# INDEX 469

and mass higher education, language and community 195–96
and ministry of information 195
and relations with Bahrain 319–320
and relations with Israel 361
and relations with UAE 320
and satellite television 196–201
Al-Qaradawi, Yusuf 199
Qassem (Qasim), Abdul Karim 86, 239, 441
Al Qasimi, Al Qawasim, 163, 219, 224
Al Qasimi, Khaled bin Saqr 417
Qazvin 42, 49
Qom, 45, 46, 60, 79, 368
Qomi, Ayatollah Mohammed Tabatabai 3–4, 7

Al-Rabi'i, Abdul Razzaq 60
Rabin, Itzhak 429
Rafiqdoust, Mohsen, 46
Rafsanjani, Ali Akbar Hashemi 4, 6, 16, 18, 20, 23, 25, 37, 39, 42–43, 286, 428, 434, passim
Rahami, Mohsen 22, 23
Rahimi, Azizollah Amir 43
Ramadan, Taha Yasin 87
Ramadi (Iraq) 61
Ras al-Khaimah 163, 166, 219, 224, 319, 373, 417, 439, passim
Al Rasheed 335
Red Sea 114, 116, 119
Regression analysis (of Saudi economy) 131–158
Representation (in Saudi socio-political context) 111, 119
Republican Guards (Iraq) 74, 91–92
(Special) Republican Guards (Iraq) 92
Revival Movement [Harakat al-Nahda] 61
Revolutionary Command Council (RCC-Iraq) 87
Revolutionary Guards [Iran], 14, 15, 17, 18, 19, 20, 21, 24, 25, 26, 38, 39, 44–44, 46, 47, 49, passim
and corporate interests 40–42
Rezai, Mohsen 18, 40, 44
Rida, Hujja Muhammad 59
Riyadh 119
Rouhani, Sadegh 438
Royal Military Academy (Sandhurst) 335
Royal Saudi Air Force (RSAF) 105, 149
Royal United Services Institute (RUSI) 332
Rub al-Khali. *See* Empty Quarter
Ruhani, Hasan 17
Al-Rumaihi, Muhammad
Al-Rumailah oil field 411
Rushdie, Salman 6, 14, 330, 337
Russia, Russians 100

Al Sabah (Kuwait) 186, 284, 289, 318, 322, passim
Al Sabah, Saad Abdallah Salim 430
Al Sabah, Sabah al-Ahmad 186
Sabians (in Iraq) 67
Al-Sadr, bint al-Huda 58, 89
Al-Sadr, Muhammad Baqir 57, 58, 74, 79, 89
Al-Sadr, Sadiq 59, 60
Safari, Latif 21
Safavi, Rahim 15, 44
Al-Sahlani, Ali 59
Al Said, Said bin Taymur 454
Al-Said, Nouri 84, 85
Salafiyah Movement 284, 306
Saleh, Ali Abdallah 269, 271, 274, 276, 277, 278, 291–292, 298, 317, passim
Sallal, Abdallah 267
Sanaa 216, 294

Sanabani, Ali Mahdi 292
Sanabani, Muhammad 292
Sana'y, Youssof 6, 10
Al-Saqr, Jasim 186
Al Saud 98, 107, 119, 277
Al Saud, Abdallah bin Abdul Aziz bin Abdul Rahman (Heir Apparent) 14, 115, 234, 286, 422, 427, passim
Al Saud, Abdul Aziz bin Abdul Rahman (King 1932–1954) 98, 119, 126, 264, 303, 304, 309, 327, 336, 347, 452, passim
Al Saud, Bandar bin Khaled 114
Al Saud, Fahd bin Abdul Aziz (King 1982– ) 114, 273, 304, 309, 344, 411, 431, passim
Al Saud, Naif bin Abdul Aziz 276, 429, 446
Al Saud, Saud bin Abdul Aziz (King 1954–1964) 309
Al Saud, Saud bin Faysal bin Abdul Aziz 286
Al Saud, Sultan bin Abdul Aziz (Defense Minister) 116, 276, 429, passim
Al Saud, Sultan bin Salman 116, 120
Saudi Arabia, 193, 199, 203, 234, 269, 275, 277, 281, 292, 396, 409, 434, passim
and agriculture 142–143
and Central Asia 370–371
and clean tourism 114
and construction 144–145
and conservative forces 309
and consultative council 103, 309–310, 460
and consumption 153
and defense expenditures 132–139
and economy 131–158
and electricity, gas, and water 145–146
and expatriate workers 120, 125
and financial sector 146–147
and global capitalism 111–113
and Gulf region (leadership role in) 351
and investments 152–153
and liberal factors 309
and minerals and mining 144
and "muddy edges" of controlled tourism 121–125
and National Guard 106
and national identity 111–113
and national museum 119–120
and non-oil development issues 139–140
and non-oil manufacturing 143–144
and oil boom 131–158
and opposition forces 98–107, 114
and patterns of growth and expenditures 132–139
and photography 122–123
and private expenditures 148–153
and regional factor in Shura 310
and relations with Bahrain 317
and relations with Oman 317–318
and relations with Qatar 317
and relations with UAE 316–317
and relations with Yemen 263–278
and religious factor in Shura 310
and "rentier" state 131–158
and role of military in future uprisings 105–107
and role of women 120, 124–125
and role in 1994 Yemen civil war 275
and security issues 123–124
and service sector 147–148
and State breakdown 96–98
and susceptibility to revolution 95–107
and tourism 111–128
and tourism itineraries 119–121
and tourism monopoly 125–126
and transportation and communications 146
and wholesale and retail trade 145

Saudi Arabia (*continued*)
  and Yemen border dispute 214–216
SAVAK 36
Al-Sawaf, Muhammad Mahmud 57, 58
Schutz, Alfred 201
Schwarzkopf, Norman 356
Serbs 100
Shabestari, Mohsen Mojtahed 5–6, 9, 10
Shamkani, Ali 413
Shariah (Islamic) law 418
Shariat-Madari, Ayatollah Mohammed Qazem 3, 7
Sharjah 163, 164, 166, 219, 224, 319, passim
  and 1971 Memorandum of Understanding with Iran 229
Sharon, Ariel 422
Shatt al-Arab 90, 213, 218, 226, 227, 228–229, 234, 339, 355, 397, 399, 437
Shaybah (UAE-Saudi Arabia border oil fields) 223, 294
Al Shaykh family, 15, 35, 84
Al Shaykh, Saleh bin Abdul Aziz bin Muhammad bin Ibrahim 35
Shawkat, Sami 84
Shia 104, 181, 203, 455, passim
  and clergy (in Iran) 5
  and riots in Saudi Arabia 355
Shiraz 17, 49
Shirazi, Sayyid Hassan 58
Shirazi, Makarem 8
Shura, 55
Sidqi, Bakr 84, 85
Singapore 155, 459
Sirri island 225
Sistani, Ayatollah Ali 55, 60, 79
Society of Militant Clerics 16
Soroush Abdul-Karim 8, 11
Soviet Union 25, 35, 268, 326, 336, 428, passim
  and role in Yemen 268–269
Stockpol, Theda 96–98
Sudan 104
Al-Sudayri, Salman 116
Suhaili, Turki 200
Sulaymaniah 75
Sunni 181, passim
Sunni-Shia factor (in Kuwaiti politics) 306, passim
Sunni clergy 55
Supreme Council of the Islamic Resistance in Iraq (SCIRI) 61, 80
Syria 339, 400, 408

Tabatabai, Sayyid Zia 34
Taif, 1934 Treaty of 214, 229, 230, 264–266, 274
Tajikistan 371
Talabani 74, 75
Taleban 47, 126, 376
Taleqani, Mahmud 8
Tammuz 1 (Osiraq nuclear reactor) 89
Teheran 17, 49
Teheran Militant Clergy 5
Teheran University 19, 23
Thatcher, Margaret 324
Al Thani (Qatar) 196, 285, 327
Al Thani, Hamad bin Khalifah 196, 310, 320, 421, passim
Tikrit 61, 67, 86
Al-Tikriti, Usama 61
Tilly, Charles 99
Treaty on the Non-Proliferation of Nuclear Weapons 244, 421
Tunb Islands (UAE) 216, 225, 316, 319, 353, 363, 387, 394, 409, 427, 439, 440, passim

Al-Turabi, Hassan 200
Turkey, 31, 69, 75, 331, 339, 429, passim
Turkmenistan 374
  and leadership 375
Turkomans (in Iraq) 67, 79

Ulama (plural of 'alim-religious scholar), 55, 58, 200, 202, 286, passim
'Ulum, Bahr al- (family) 59
'Ulum, Bahr al-, Ayatollah Mahdi 61
'Ulum, Bahr al-, Muhammad 61
Umrah (minor pilgrimage) 117
Umm Qasr (Iraq) 227, 228
Umm al-Qiwain 163, 319
United Arab Emirates (UAE) 95, 139, 140, 164, 273, 281, 345, 373, 383, 427, passim
  and birth of 163–164
  and British rule 161–163, 351
  and defense policy 390
  and economic development 164–169
  and education 170
  and Federal National Council (FNC) 165, 173
  and foreign policy 391
  and GCC alliance 386
  and intentions in Gulf region 385–386
  and Iran 386–387
  and Iraq 387–388
  and islands disputes 216–218
  and Jabal Ali Free Zone 166, 167
  and role of women 172–173
  and Palestinian Question 388–389
  and Saadiyat Free Zone 166
  and social development 169–173
  and social and economic policies 161–174
  and strategic aims 384–389
  and territorial disputes 412
  and vision for Gulf security 389–391
  and Western powers 388–389
United Kingdom [Britain] 35, passim
  and arms trade with Gulf states 344–346
  and foreign policy in Gulf 325–334, 329–330
  and legacy in Gulf region 352–354
  and policy differences with U.S. over Iran 330–332
  and policy similarities with U.S. over Iraq 332–333
  and relations with Gulf States 325–347
  and role in Bahrain 361–362
  and role in Gulf boundary disputes 224–229
  and triple containment policy 353
United Nations Development Program (UNDP) 296
United Nations Iraq-Kuwait Boundary Demarcation Commission 220, 228–229, 234, 237
United Nations Monitoring, Verification and Inspection (UNMOVIC) 333
United Nations Security Council 223, 239, 345, 411
  and Resolution 687 240, 243, 245–253 (text)
  and Resolution 1284 242–243, 253–260 (text), 333
United Nations Special Commission (UNSCOM) 92
United States, passim
  and Fifth Fleet 419, 439, 444
  and Gulf policies 418–420
  and policy perceptions in Gulf region 357–358
  and presence in Gulf (1971–1990) 354–356
  and "Twin Pillar" policy 355–356, 360, 410
United States Central Command (USCENTCOM) 356
Uzbekistan 373, 374

Va'ezain, Mashallah Shams ol- 21
*Velayat-e Faqih* (Rule of the Jurisconsult) 3, 6, 7–9
*Velayat-e Motlaq-e Faqih* (Absolute Rule of the Jurist) 8

# Index

Velayati, Ali Akbar 4, 440
Versailles 81
Vietnam 102

Al-Wandawi, Munir 86
War for Kuwait
    and socio-political implications 183
Warbah island (Kuwait) 227, 228
Western European Union (WEU) 344
Wickham-Crowley, Timothy 105
Wilson, Harold 394
World Bank 147
World Trade Organization (WTO) 111, 154, 404
Wright, Sir David 341

Yahyah, Imam of Yemen 264–165
*Al-Yamamah* (arms program) 333, 340–342, 345
Yanbu 116
Yazdi, Misbahi 9, 11

Yazidis 67
Yemen, Republic of 177, 206, passim
    and 1990 unification 271–172, 291–299
    and 1994 civil war 214, 274–277
    and fate of its expatriate workers 272–273
    and impact of oil 271
    and impact of War for Kuwait 271–274
    and relations with Saudi Arabia 263–278
    and ties with Israel 277
Yemen, Arab Republic 106, 266, 270, 281, passim
    and 1962 revolution 266–271
    and political stability 297–299
Yemen Socialist Party (YSP) 294, 298

Zadeh, Mohsen Said 5, 9, 10
Zahedan 49
Zibakalam, Sadeq 20
Zubarah 218, 225, 234, 320